TALIESIN'S MAP

The Comparative Guide to Celtic Mythology

J. Dolan

First published 2022 by J. Dolan

ISBN 9798766418764

Table of Contents

Preface

This book is an exploration working from the basis of one significant development within Indo-Iranic studies which occurred during the 1940s. This development bore the promise of clarifying how archaic certain portions of the mythic corpus could be. The discovery to which I refer was the explication of the deeper theological layer of the characters of the *Mahabharata* laid out by the Swedish Iranist Stig Wikander in his "Pandavasagan och Mahabharata mystika forutsattningar" ("The Legend of the Pandavas and the Mythical Substructure of the Mahabharata") in 1947. Wikander explained that the seemingly human heroes of the great Kurukshetra War, and the Pandavas in particular, were in fact incarnations of the central gods of society, as can be verified by their enacting known elements of these gods' myths.[1] This hypothesis is supported by

---

1 "Probably the most important single contribution was made in 1947 by Stig Wikander, who demonstrated that the gods of the Rig Veda which reflected the three functions— Mitra, Varuna, Indra, and others— were transposed into the heroes of the Mahabharata, and thereby opened up a whole new prospect for the study of Indo-European mythology" (Georges Dumezil, *Gods of the Ancient Northmen, Intro,* xv).
"In 1947 a Swedish scholar, S. Wikander, made a discovery that profoundly modified the perspective of the religious history of India. It had been known for a long time that the great epic the Mahabharata sometimes told, as a digression and in a new guise, legends that the Vedas do not mention, but of which the Iranians or other Indo-European peoples offer other

v

the proclamation of the text of the *Mahabharata* itself which states that these heroes are "partial incarnations" of their divine fathers, who bestow them upon their mothers (*Mahabharata, Sambhava Parva* LXVII*)*. But what Wikander was able further to do was to clarify the degree to which these incarnations held onto truly archaic mythic content and to specify the way in which these god-heroes also made clear a well-ordered, tripartite social and religious structure, so that their actions in the war could be interpreted mythically and religiously in a greater sense. The account of the war in the epic was thus shown to be a deeply religious one, the seemingly human heroes enacting the primordial myths of the gods.

The comparative philologist Georges Dumezil latched onto this explanation, even translating and republishing much of Wikander's investigations on the subject in his *Mythe et Epopee*, and further developing their implications. He was able to show that these Indian epic heroes correspond sometimes imperfectly with the oldest written religious document of India, the *Rig Veda*, but have very close correspondences with the Iranic gods, and thus the god conceptions that the Indian epic heroes bear forth must be something close to consistent with the Indo-Iranic deities from *before* these branches, the Indian and the Iranic, split apart. As this split occurred around 1800 BC and the *Rig Veda* is believed to have been composed in its current form between 1500 and 1200 BC or so (the dating being itself contentious, see Brereton and Jamison *The Rigveda: A Guide,* p. 10-14), this places the god-conceptions buried in the Indian epic heroes almost half a millennium earlier, if not more, than those found in the *Rig Veda*, which text already shows significant differences from the Iranic mythology. In a general sense,

---

versions. For example, the story of the fabrication and destruction of the giant Drunkenness, which has been analyzed in our first chapter. Now we know more: the central heroes of the poem, with their characters and their connections, also continue an Indo-Iranian ideological structure, in a form that in part is more archaic than are the hymns and the whole of Vedic literature. These heroes, five brothers, the Pandava or pseudosons of Pandu, are in reality the sons of five gods who, with and under Varuna, constitute the oldest canonical list of gods of the three functions: Dharma "Law" (obviously a new form of Mitra), Vayu and Indra (two Indo-Iranian varieties of warriors), the two twins Nasatya or Asvin ("third function"). The order of their births conforms to the hierarchy of functions, while the characteristics and behavior of each son conforms to the functional definition of his father. Only Varuna has no representative in this list, but it has been easy to show that he is not absent from the poem. With some of his more specialized traits he has been transposed to the previous generation in the person of Pandu, supposed father of the Pandava. The transposition is not limited to this father and his sons. The authors of the immense poem have explained it systematically at the beginning of the first book and recalled it many times later, that the heroes who oppose one another or cooperate are not men except in appearance. Whether they are sons or incarnations of either gods or demons, they represent in reality cosmic interests. It is the very drama of the mythical Great Times that they present, direct, or play" (Georges Dumezil, *Gods of the Ancient Northmen*, 53).

deities who are found to be combined in the *Rig Veda* (as Dumezil sees it) can
sometimes be seen as distinct and clear individuals in the *Mahabharata* narrative (Vayu
and Indra mostly combined in the Veda, per Dumezil, but their incarnations Arjuna and
Bhima distinct and contrasting in the epic), which fact in itself tantalizingly suggests a
window into a time closer to when the Indo-European religion was unified, organized,
and well-defined. In such an idealized archaic period, deities would presumably have
had important and distinct tasks to fulfill, and gods becoming blended together would
indicate a departure from that period. Dumezil calls the heroes of the epic, the Pandavas,
"the oldest canonical list of gods of the three functions" (*Gods of the Ancient Northmen*,
53). The depiction of course cannot be perfect, as the *Mahabharata* did not come into
written form until between 400 BC and 400 CE (Brockington, J.L., *The Sanskrit Epics,*
1998, p. 26), but the deep impression we are left with from Wikander and Dumezil's
studies on the issue is the incredible conservative nature of the epic tradition, which
apparently, in this case at least, preserved, almost in amber, archaic religious material
that the main strictly religious texts sometimes did not. This is not to say that the epic
poems themselves were not seen as inherently religious, but what we seem to learn is
that, though more explicit religious material (hymns, etc.) can sometimes be quite
conservative, it is also frequently subject to greater change via reforms, trends, socio-
political shifts, and simple daily usage, while religious material contained, almost
hidden, within the figures of epic heroes, is more likely to survive unchanged (as long as
kept carefully by a healthy oral tradition) because of its relatively unassuming, coded
nature and the fact that these heroic and epic traditions are subject to fewer incentives for
change and more for preservation. Religions, though conservative, are fiercely fought
over and do frequently change, but, for the most part, people do not want to hear a story
told wrong, particularly their national epic. This does not mean that the *Rig Veda*
contains no archaic material, as nothing could be further from the truth, but it
emphasizes the fact that the *Rig Veda* and the epic tradition often preserve different parts
of the archaic material, and for different reasons, and suggests that the epic heroes
should be given a special place in terms of envisioning the outlines of the archaic gods.

Hence, the idea naturally occurred to Dumezil that this approach should be applicable
to the great European epic as well – to the *Iliad* of Homer. To this end, he made only a
couple suggestive stabs but did not focus a great amount of time on the project. I have
only picked up this thread, to see how far it would lead, and specifically how it could
illuminate Celtic mythology in turn. Upon investigation, it may be said that Indian epic,
Greek epic, and the most archaic strands of the various Indo-European mythologies form
something of a contemporaneous strata of myth in which we find broad-ranging
agreements across numerous cases. Thus we must go to this level in comparative
analysis when possible: we must take epic, and in particular the *Iliad*, along with other
legendary material, seriously as mythology in order to progress.

Following Dumezil, this present study primarily follows a structural approach, in an attempt to see in what ways these various branches share an overarching "pattern," a purposive theological organization as hinted at by the well-ordered and distinct personae of the *Mahabharata*. We assert that if we are to take the original religious unity of the Proto-Indo-Europeans seriously, and then to take seriously the religion these people and their various descendants practiced, it must necessarily imply the coherence, stability and lucidity of that religion at one time long ago. We either believe that these religions were once relatively united and from the same origin or we do not, and we either believe that in their united form they were fully lived and comprehended by their practitioners or we do not. If they were, then some significant degree of "structure" at one point must have existed.

As the clearest and sometimes most archaic canonical texts, we have occasionally leaned on the Vedic sources in this investigation in order to cast light on the other branches. Sometimes this priority is the due course, and other times it may be more debatable. With respect to the question of textual priority, difficult questions of interpretation arise, such as: if Norse Njordr's Vedic parallel is a god of the moon, Soma, as we will explore, is Njordr then a god of that same celestial body itself, and is the deeper meaning that his myth cycle bears out a lunar one? Or do he and his Vedic parallel merely trace back to a shared deity, perhaps centered on sacred waters, with only the Vedic version of the deity coming to be identified with the moon itself? We expect our readers will come to such questions with their own knowledge and critical sense to be able to weigh the priority of the ancient texts in each case for themselves and to improve on our bare presentation of the details with their own interpretations. Once it has made the comparative framework and most pressing problems clear, our work will have fulfilled its purpose. This can be said for many key points in the text. In the interest of keeping this book to one rather than three or more volumes, citations and scholarly apparatus have been limited to what is necessary to convey the core comparisons at hand, which either stand or fall on their own merits.

Taliesin's Map

Taliesin is a Welsh seer-poet, almost a shaman-like figure, who accidentally tastes the liquid of poetic illumination while it is cooking and goes through a series of magical transformations into various animals to escape a pursuing goddess, finally becoming a seed, being eaten by the goddess who pursues him, and being reborn as a supernaturally inspired poet who tells of his unification with the forces of nature and the cosmos. His tale is told in the *Hanes Taliesin* collected in the *Mabinogion,* and his ecstatic poetry appears in the *Book of Taliesin* (see in particular "The Battle of the Trees"). His birth name being Gwion and his myth matching closely that of the Irish Fionn, who is enlightened by accidentally tasting the Salmon of Knowledge while it is cooking, he may be an iteration of the same underlying god, in Vedic terms a "Rudraic" god (as we will see), also called Gwyn ap Nudd in Welsh folklore. Taliesin's series of transformations can be seen as an initiatic process which dramatizes and exteriorizes his apprehension of the forms of reality from within, as he becomes one with them in their multifarious changings. As such, he gains true knowledge of the forms and plays out their transformations in himself. Considering that the inner transformations of the forms within the soul of the seer esoterically speaking must match those of the forms of the cosmos at large, Taliesin's journey through his various shapes enacts an enlightenment that pierces through all levels of existence. If Taliesin, then, were to have created a map of the esoteric landscape he explored in this journey, it would be a map of the transformations of the cosmic forms themselves. This would be, in brief, a multidimensional diagram of the cosmic Powers and their Metamorphoses. In one sense, the cosmic Powers and their Metamorphoses are also what we are confronted with in Mythology, when we read it as it is meant to be read, as both esoteric and exoteric *theology*. In Mythology, the gods and their actions are the cosmic Powers and their Metamorphoses. As Taliesin is the archetypal bard in the Welsh tradition, it may even be that his journey is in some way a reflection of actual bardic initiations, and these initiations would themselves have been intimately bound up with training in the traditional mythological poetry and the literal or symbolical drinking of the illuminating liquid.

Just as that Roman archetypal poet Ovid's own tracking of the mythological *Metamorphoses* did, or as we envision Taliesin's Map would do, so this book seeks to investigate and cast light on the structure and metamorphoses of the Cosmic Powers, as the ancient Celts once saw them. Taliesin's Map is what we are in search of. As a first map of one particular path through the mythic darkness, this book is necessarily only a preliminary. One thing, however, is vital: the map must be taken as a whole, for, while the terrain is at times dazzling and winding, what begins to reveal itself in the end is a *structure*.

1

The Heroes of the Iliad as Indo-European Gods: A Mythological Rosetta Stone

"Traditional characters are not "made up," or to put it another way they've been shaped for centuries, in this case for millennia" - Gregory Nagy[2]

"…the ancient Greek myths about [Apollo] as well as [Achilles]—and even their names—can be traced back, precisely in the context of their roles in Homeric poetry, to an Indo-European background" - Gregory Nagy, "Comments on Comparative Mythology 2"

---

2   HS Dialogue with Gregory Nagy, "Achilles as cult and epic hero, and initiatory experiences,"
8:57-9:06. https://www.youtube.com/watch?v=ZtfDR3_ghqA. Accessed May 2021.

Introduction

"The authors of the immense poem have explained it systematically at the beginning of the first book and recalled it many times later, that the heroes who oppose one another or cooperate are not men except in appearance. Whether they are sons or incarnations of either gods or demons, they represent in reality cosmic interests. It is the very drama of the mythical Great Times that they present, direct, or play." (Georges Dumezil, discussing the *Mahabharata* in *Gods of the Ancient Northmen*, 56)

Comparing the *Iliad* to another Indo-European epic, the Indian *Mahabharata,* and these to the Irish *Battle of Magh Tuireadh*, as well as the Welsh *Mabinogion* and the related Celtic texts, we can see quickly that the *Iliad* is descended from the same tradition, the same material, but recast in a Greek form. This being plain from a host of examples which will become apparent, and following the established tradition in myth studies (Wikander, *Religion och Bibel*; Dumezil, *Gods of the Ancient Northmen*, etc.) that has shown the heroes of the *Mahabharata* to be specific divine incarnations, it should follow that the active figures of the Trojan War are representatives – *incarnations* – of the most archaic primary gods, and should carry bonafide elements of their myths. Georges Dumezil hints as much when he points out that Achilles and Arjuna come from the same original (Dumézil 1968: 48; 1985: 17, 71). Both are the somewhat sensitive but terrifyingly powerful princes who hold themselves back from the action to brood over some issue, questioning whether they should fight, then coming through in the end to wreak havoc on the opponent's greatest warriors at the key moments. And as Arjuna is the spiritual son of Indra, Achilles and Arjuna then are each in their own way the more chivalrous-type warrior god, Indra in Vedic religion, made flesh. If this really is so, then what stops us from looking further to see if the other main gods appear in Greek guises within the pages of the *Iliad*?

There is nothing to assure that such a venture would be successful. There is no telling how much change the Greek version of the epic had undergone before reaching its final form, how much the characters of the heroes had been warped, merged, or even removed from the story. However, it should be remembered that the *Iliad* is thought to have been composed in its present form around the mid 8th century BCE (Vidal-Naquet, Pierre, *Le monde d'Homère (The World of Homer)*, p. 19), well before the writing down of the

Mahabharata, which itself preserves the characters of the gods so clearly. And when we begin to investigate the question we quickly find that the *Iliad* too has been surprisingly conservative in content, and a significant amount remains within the traits of the main heroes to indicate their specific divine and Indo-European origins.

In the *Mahabharata*, the primary protagonists, the Pandavas and their mortal father Pandu, are spiritual sons and incarnations of the gods of society: Varuna and Mitra, Vayu and Indra, Nasatya and Dasra. This makes three pairs of gods, each pair representing one of the functional levels in the tripartite social division – the Priest-Sovereigns, the Warriors, and the Producers; or, First, Second, and Third functions, as Dumezil calls them. On the opposing side, the Kauravas, are the incarnations of Dyaus Pitr, Surya, one of the Rudras, Bhaga, the demon Kali, and the embodiment of the Dwapara Yuga, among other warriors who may or may not have divine connections. Therefore, these in particular are the gods we should look for in the heroes of the Trojan War. Doing so will help us greatly clarify these archaic Indo-European divine archetypes.

Key Combatants of *the Mahabharata* (see *Sambhava Parva LXVII)*:

The Pandavas

Pandu: incarnation of Varuna, The Terrible Sovereign

Yudhishthira: incarnation of "Dharma" aka Mitra, The Lawful Sovereign*

Bhima: incarnation of Vayu, The Wind God

Arjuna: incarnation of Indra, The Thunderer

Nakula and Sahadeva: incarnations of the Asvins, the Horse Twins

Drishtadyumna: incarnation of Agni, The Fire God

Vidura: incarnation of Aryaman, Lord of Noble Society

* Dumezil simply states that "Dharma 'Law'" is "obviously a new form of Mitra." Though not necessarily as obvious as he implies, this claim is borne out by the fact that Yudhishthira and Vidura mirror the close relationship and characters of Mitra and Aryaman in the hymns, and is further confirmed by the large web of correspondences we find to Yudhishthira when he is understood as the Mitraic hero. It is an error to interpret "Dharma" here as Yama, god of the dead, who also bears this title. We must remember that the epic that Yudhishthira is a part of reaches back to a time when Mitra was a much

more prominent god, and that, by the time of its writing down, Mitra was enormously minimized in Indian religion, while Yama was still relatively prominent, leading to the common misidentification of this "Dharma" as Yama, who also is closely connected to Dharma and ideal kingship. Indeed, it is true that Yama and Mitra overlapped from the beginning in their quality of ideal sovereign, each one being instances of the Dharmaraj, and the two gods likely shared this title. One of the tasks of this book will be to show that Yudhishthira is, with certainty, a Mitraic hero. Mitra and Varuna are the keepers of *Rta* and *Dharman* in the *Rig Veda* (RV 8.25). They are called righteous *Rtavan*, promote righteous rites *Rtavardha*, and are lords of truth and light (*Rtasya jotisaapathi – RV.* 1.2.8; 1.23.5; 1.136.4; 2.27.4; 5.63.1).

The Kauravas

Dhritarashtra: incarnation of Bhaga, Lord of Destiny or Apportionment

Duryodhana: incarnation of Kali, The Demon of the Dark Age

Karna: incarnation of Surya, The Sun God

Bhishma: incarnation of Dyaus Pitr, Father Sky

Ashvatthama: incarnation of one of the Rudras, Storm Attendants

Shakuni: incarnation of Dwapara, Lord of the Second-to-last-Age

Drona: incarnation of Brihaspati, High Priest of the Word

Agamemnon

Agamemnon – Varuna (The Terrible Sovereign)

Agamemnon is the older brother of Menelaus and the reigning king of Mycenae. He is known as a fierce warrior and he is acknowledged commander-in-chief of all the assembled armies, called "wide-ruling" (*Iliad* 1.354) and "the king of men" (1.172). As such he represents the power of kingship. His parallel, King Pandu of the *Mahabharata*, likewise begins the events leading to the war as the king of the Kuru Kingdom. As Dumezil outlines it, the Varuna archetype is always a conqueror who expands the territory of his kingdom in the early days of his power, which is exactly what

4

Agamemnon and Pandu are said to do. Pandu is described as swallowing up kingdoms: "Pandu, that oppressor of foes, like unto a mighty fire whose far-reaching flames were represented by his arrows and splendour by his weapons, began to consume all kings that came in contact with him. These with their forces, vanquished by Pandu at the head of his army, were made the vassals of the Kurus" (*Mahabharata, Adi Parva*, CXIII). Similarly, after regaining his father's lost kingdom, Agamemnon's conquests make him the most powerful king in all of Greece. Agamemnon is not always a peaceable ruler, and he is famous for the conflict with Achilles in which he takes from him what he feels to be his own kingly due, the woman Briseis. This general character recalls the descriptor which has been applied to Varuna: "The Terrible Sovereign." It is Varuna whose sometimes violent but vital power forges kingdoms (as seen in the case of the Varunian Romulus), and it is he whose snares and spies exact justice from all within his domain. Agamemnon is highly destructive on the battlefield, a mirror image in fierceness of Achilles, and is known as one of the best three Greek warriors along with Ajax and Diomedes (when Achilles is not present).

While the loss of a *hand* is a trait associated with the Mitra type by Dumezil (Tyr, Scaevola), the First Kings, Irish Nuada and Greek Agamemnon, both significantly sustain a wound instead to their *arms*, causing each to retire from battle for a period of time. Nuada is the First King of the Irish gods known as the Tuatha de Danann, and he expands their kingdom via the war with the Fir Bolg upon first arriving in Ireland. It seems that the loss of Nuada's *arm* has led to a confusion of Nuada with the Mitraic type, who Dumezil attempted to associate with a motif of one-*handedness*. However, it is crucial to emphasize the fact that Nuada is the First King, and this heavily positions him as a Varunian figure in a structural sense. The confusion of Nuada with Tyr or Mitra, one of the greatest red herrings in Celtic myth, arises in part from the superficial likeness of arm and hand: Agamemnon and Nuada are wounded in the *arm* during *battle* while the Mitraic god Tyr instead loses a *hand* during a questionable *contract*. Understanding this difference unlocks much of the Irish mythology for proper comparison and is a key correction to Dumézil's work, though one that he too seemed to realize later in his life, based on his comments on his work in the 1970s. As Wouter W. Belier explains, commenting on Dumezil's evolving framework, "Finally, in 1977 Nuada is also removed from the list of one-handed figures" (Belier, *Decayed Gods*, 153), Dumezil calling the circumstances of Nuada's disfigurement not clearly 'functional' enough, in Dumezil's specific sense, to warrant the comparison to Tyr. Scholar Garrett Olmsted summarizes, "With little else upon which to build his case, Dumézil himself (1974: 21; 1977: 199) later recanted his suggestion that Lug and Nuada were the Irish correlatives of Vedic Várunaḥ and Mitráḥ" (Olmsted, *Gods of the Celts and the Indo-Europeans*, 90).[3] He concludes in the same vein that we will take up further along, saying, "Dumézil was entirely correct in recanting his earlier suggestion that Lug should be a correlative of Váruṇaḥ and Óðinn. Indeed, here we shall examine evidence that Lug actually corresponds to Mitráḥ and Týr. Although Lug does not lose a hand, he possesses many other traits fundamental to Týr. He is even closer to Mitráḥ, as both Mitráḥ and Lug keep their hands. In being a correlative of Mitráḥ and Týr rather than of Óðinn and Váruṇaḥ, Lug cannot possibly be the 'one-eyed god' sought by Dumézil" (Olmsted, 58).

To bring home this connection of Irish Nuada to Vedic Varuna, rather than to Tyr/Mitra, we will note briefly that several other points connect this Nuada to Varuna, the First King, lord of water and the sovereignty of night sky. As Isolde Carmody explains, Findias, the Island of Nuada, has a meaning related to light, whiteness, holiness, and swiftly running water (as in "white water"), while the druidic teacher from Findias is named Uiscias, which is most likely from the root *uisce*, "water."[4] Nuada's wife Boand is the central river goddess of Irish myth, a parallel of Vedic Saraswati, as will be seen later on. John Carey specifically points out that Nuada and another god of sacred water, Nechtan, were confused only in late sources (where the name Nuada Necht begins appearing), and that "The most satisfactory explanation seems to be that Nechtan was in origin a deity who shared with Nuadu the proprietorship of the waters of knowledge" (Carey, "Nodons in Britain and Ireland," 9). At the temple of Nodens, the Romano-British Nuada, in Lydney, he is shown riding a chariot across the sea. Of this temple, Carey states that "The inscriptions identify Nodons with Mars, and the iconographic evidence at Lydney associates him with water and with dogs" (Carey, 20). "Several images of dogs have been found, as well as bronze plaques depicting water-monsters, fishermen and ichthyocentaurs" (Carey, 4). As Guillaume Oudaer points out, according to Nennius, the waters of Llyn Llywan, located not far from the sanctuary of Lydney Park dedicated to Nodens, would swell if one got too close, and it was in its waters that the Welsh "Primal Salmon" resided. He explains that in this temple, overlooking the Severn and the expanse of the estuary, opposite the tidal bore, there is also a statue of a fisherman harpooning a salmon. Oudaer further points out that Lludd (aka Nudd), a Welsh version of Nuada, is described going into a tub of cold water at one point as well (Oudaer, "Teyrnon Twryf Lliant"). Carey, referring to Nuada/Nodens' possible connection to the waters of the sky, that is, clouds, says, "Only in Wales, by contrast, is a connection with clouds apparent; this is evidently due simply to the survival in Welsh of *nudd* with the meaning "mist, haze" (Carey, 21). Varuna being a

---

3   Also: "Ernst Windisch, A.H.Krappe and Jan de Vries have all suggested that the surviving account of how Nuadu lost his arm in battle represents a relatively late attempt to explain his epithet. Some further evidence might appear to support their contention" (John Carey, Nodons in Britain and Ireland, 12).

4   Isolde Carmody, https://storyarchaeology.com/four-cities-four-teachers-four-treasures/. Accessed May, 2021.

god of both waters and the night sky, Kevin Maclean furthermore connects Nuada to the nocturnal realm by way of his paternity. He points out that, From O'Mulconry's glossary we see that an "Echtach" is called the father of Nuada, and that this is said to be another name for a nocturnal Bacchus whose rites were celebrated at night. Maclean asserts that Echtach may refer to a type of night bird and that Echtach flies through the air at night. Like other Varunian heroes and gods (Agamemon, Odinn), Nuada too is associated with the spear of battle: "O Nuada, (you) will thrust them away by a spear-tip of battle, and battle will be verified and portended" says Figol's prophecy in the *Cath Maige Tuired*. While Nuada abdicates the throne temporarily when he has his arm severed in battle, Pandu, Varuna's incarnation, abdicates the throne when he is cursed to be unable to embrace his wife, which seems to be based on a similar idea of the tainted or maimed king not being fit to rule. In a myth which Pandu's myth perhaps echoes, Varuna becomes impotent and has to be healed by the Gandharvas. There is also a notably similar trait of binding or catching related to this god type. Varuna is known for his fetters or his noose, with which he catches and binds the liar and sinner (RV 1.24.15; 1.25.21; 6.74.4; 10.85.24), while Odinn is also associated with bindings (and nooses), as when he binds the wolf Fenrir, and the name Nodens is believed to derive from *noudont-* or *noudent-*, which J. R. R. Tolkien argued was related to the Germanic root *neut-,* "acquire, have the use of", earlier "to catch, entrap (as a hunter)," and thus he called him "Nodens the Catcher" (Tolkien, "The Name Nodens").

With this Irish comparandum in mind, and returning now to Greek Agamemnon, we see that his life is bookended by motifs very similar to those found in the story of King Pandu in the *Mahabharata*: Agamemnon's family had been cursed by Myrtilus as he died by Agamemnon's hand, resulting in infighting and death to several generations of the Atreides family. Pandu's curse, given to him by the Rishi Kindama as he died by Pandu's hand, was that he could not embrace his wife with intent of love and so could not have children at all. Both curses caused great difficulty to the accomplishing of each king's duties, and to successfully furthering their lines. Indeed, Agamemnon's own son and wife, Orestes and Clytemnestra, were also caught up by the inter-family violence resulting from the curse, while his daughter was sacrificed to the gods. In the end of Pandu's life, he one day is overwhelmed with love and embraces one of his wives, bringing about his death. Agamemnon dies when he returns home to his wife, either at the hands of his wife's lover or her own, depending on the source. Each king arguably dies as a final result of their curse and this occurs at the moment they return to their wives. Agamemnon and Menelaus also are forced into exile (related to the curse) before the events of the Trojan war, as the Pandava brothers similarly must endure exile before returning to fight the Kurukshetra War.

- Terrible Sovereign: (Agamemnon, Varuna/Pandu, Nuada)

- Has a curse that affects his progeny

- Is First King

- Expands territory

- Is exiled before the war

- Is wounded in the arm

- Exacts justice in a harsh manner which leads to conflict with the Thunderer and death of the Thunderer's son/favorite (see part 4)

- Dies when he returns to his wife

Menelaus

Menelaus – Mitra (The Lawful Sovereign)

First we must look at the structural order of the high kings in the Greek epic. Just as Mitrá and Varuṇa form a divine pair who contrast as sovereigns, so we find in the *Iliad* that Menelaus is Agamemnon's closely-tied younger brother, and both are kings in their own right. Agamemnon is older than Menelaus, as Varuna is the older First King, and Mitra the younger Second King[5]. In Dumézil's terms, although Varuna represents a more

---

5   The Mitraic archetype is "Second King" only in relation to his paired sovereign, the Varunian sovereign. In both Irish and Norse myth, as we will explore later on, another god – the Sun god (Bres in Irish or Ollerus in Scandinavian) – is technically the second king who fills an interstitial reign between the Varunian and Mitraic kings. In *Mitra-Varuna,* Dumezil describes how Varunian festivals tend to be in the first part of the year and Mitraic ones in the latter half, reflecting their roles in relation to the beginning and end of the larger cycle: "It is therefore probable that, like Christianity in other times and other places, Mazdaism was simply 'sanctifying' the previous state of affairs when it balanced its year on two great festivals separated by the maximum interval (spring equinox to autumn equinox) and clearly antithetical in their meaning and their myths. And those festivals are placed under two invocations, one of Ahura-Mazdah, the other of Mithra. On the cosmic level, Nauroz, the Persian New Year and feast of Ahura-Mazdah, celebrated 'on the day Ohrmazd' of the first month, commemorates creation. The feast of Mithra {Mithrakana, Mihragan, Mihrjan…}, celebrated on 'the day Mihr' in 'the month Mihr,' prefigures the end of the world. Why is this? Albiruni replies (The Chronology of Ancient Nations, 1879, p. 208): 'Because, at Mihrjan, that which believes attains its perfection and has no more matter left to believe more, and because the animals cease to couple; at Nauroz it is the exact opposite'" (*Mitra-Varuna*, 91). The Irish case maps well

seemingly "youthful," creative and violent power, while Mitra represents a power more august and peace-seeking (Yudhishthira generally portrayed with a character reminiscent of a placid and wise Brahmin), in the epic tradition it is still commonly the Varunian hero who is older (because first) while the Mitra type is younger. In the *Satapatha Brahmana*, Mitra-Varuna is called "the Counsel and the Power," Mitra the priesthood, and Varuna the royal power. In his *Mitra-Varuna*, Dumezil emphasizes that the Varunian principle comes first, to create and expand, and the Mitraic comes second, to consolidate and regulate[6]. The greatest difference between the Indian and Greek versions of the "Mitrá" and "Varuṇa" epic incarnations is the fact that, in the *Mahābhārata*, Pandu (the Varuṇian incarnation, per Dumézil) and Yudhiṣṭhira are father and first son, while in the *Iliad*, Agamemnon and Menelaus are instead older and younger brother, but their pairing as first and second at the top of the sovereign hierarchy remains consistent in both epics.

Like his Vedic counterpart Yudhishthira, Menelaus too is a king, but he is known to be more peaceable than his brother Agamemnon. In William Smith's commentary we find that "Menelaus was a man of an athletic figure; he spoke little, but what he said was always impressive [cf. *Rig Veda* 3.LIX.1: "Mitra speaking stirs men"]; he was brave and courageous, but milder than Agamemnon, intelligent and hospitable" (Smith, *A Classical Dictionary of Biography, Mythology, and Geography,* 1038). Yudhishthira becomes king succeeding Pandu, but his more restrained character is shown in the fact that he does not kill many prominent warriors, until he is called on to uphold dharma. Menelaus kills only 8 men in the war, according to Hyginus, while Ulysses is said to kill 12, Diomedes 18, Agamemnon 16, Telamonian Ajax 28, and Achilles 72.[7] As the ideal Brahmin and embodiment of dharma, Yudhishthira does not desire revenge but undertakes it as a

---

to the seasons and their connections to the Varunian and Mitraic principles: the Varunian Nuada being connected to the early part of the year (creation, generation, the first war), the Sun god Bres characterizing high Summer and reigning between the other two, and the late-coming Mitraic Lugh being connected to Autumn (completion, final victory, regulation of what exists).

6 "In this opposition between immobilized perfection and creative force, there is no difficulty in recognizing the theological adaptation of an old law-magic, conservation-fecundity opposition that we have seen expressed in India by the couple Mitra-Varuna and in Rome – even apart from the opposite and complementary activities of flamines and Luperci – by Numa 'perfecting' the 'creation' of Romulus. There is an even more precise correspondence, however: this division of seasonal roles (the beginning of winter, the beginning of summer) between Ahura-Mazdah and Mithra, in accordance with the 'faculty of growth' and the 'arrest of growth' that they express, clearly rests on the same symbolism as the assimilation of Mitra to the waning moon and Varuna to the waxing moon, which has sometimes been rather overhastily attributed to the 'fancy' of brahman authors" (Dumezil, *Mitra-Varuna*, 91-92).

7 Hyginus, 1960, p. 114.

matter of duty in the key moment. He is calm and difficult to provoke. In the climactic moment of the war he throws his spear, blessed by Shiva, into Shalya. The spear kills Shalya, triggering a full retreat that effectively ends the war. Yudhishthira's relatively more peaceable character is marked: "O royal Yudhishthira, mercy and self control, and truth and universal sympathy, and everything wonderful in this world, are to be found in thee. Thou art mild, munificent, religious, and liberal, and thou regardest virtue as the highest good" (*Mahabharata, Udogya Parva,* VIII).

Despite Menelaus' restrained character, he is still a skilled warrior, and he features in a scene similar to the death of Shalya: the throwing of the spear in an attempt to end the war (Chapter 2 will make a closer investigation of the important differences between these spear-throwing motifs). Menelaus seeks out Paris to take his revenge for the theft of his wife and in order to end the war, and so Hector suggests that Paris should fight him in single combat so that the war can be finished. When they face off, Menelaus throws his spear at Paris. It goes through his shield, but Paris is rescued by Aphrodite before he can be killed. Triangulating this scene further are the Celtic cases: Lugh, who takes the Mitraic role in the Irish epic, comes in late to the action just in time to throw his sling-stone or spear, depending on the version of the tale, into Balor's eye, effectively ending the war. His Welsh counterpart, Lleu Llaw Gyffes, even more identical to Menelaus in several ways, seeks revenge on his adulterous wife Blodeuwedd's lover Gronw Pebr "The Radiant." Lleu throws his spear at Gronw and it goes through the stone slab that he hides behind, just as Menelaus' spear had gone through Paris' shield. However, in this case Gronw is killed rather than rescued. The Vedic Yudhiṣthira specifically trains with the spear[8]. When he kills Shalya, Yudhishthira too is first pierced in the chest by a spear and then Bhima, instead of him, destroys the shield of Shalya, before Yudhishthira pierces Shalya in return with the spear blessed by Shiva. It is said that Shalya "pierced the heroic Yudhishthira of terrible might in the chest with shaft possessed of the splendour of fire or the sun. Deeply pierced, O king, that bull of Kuru's race." And of Bhima: "the illustrious Bhima cut off with ten arrows the unrivaled shield of the advancing hero" (*Mahabharata*, Book 9: *Shalya Parva,* XVII). Menelaus does complete the circuit with a final conclusive kill as well – in the end he kills Helen's second foreign husband Deiphobus after the death of Paris.

---

8   J.P. Mittal, *History of ancient India: a new version,* 477. A kind of rumor exists in secondary material found online claiming that Yudhishthira can throw his spear so hard that it goes through stone as if it were paper, Wikipedia also repeating this claim. This would match exceedingly closely to Lleu's feat of throwing his spear through a stone slab. However, we have not yet been able to substantiate this claim by means of the text of the *Mahabharata* or other primary sources.

In the *Iliad*, Aphrodite and Helen are somewhat shadows of each other (this is not necessarily to say that they are to be identified). Aphrodite is the one who helps set off the war by conspiring to help Paris steal Helen, and it is Aphrodite who is there at the spear-throwing face-off to save Paris. These two roles are somehow combined into one in the Welsh version with the figure Blodeuwedd, who is both adulterous wife stolen from the Lawful Sovereign, and conspiring, deceiving goddess in one. Irish Lugh also has a wife who cuckolds him. Her lover is Cermait, who Lugh kills in revenge ("How the Dagda Got His Magic Staff").[9] This suggests that the theme of the cuckolded king and his revenge was quite well-established and firmly attached to the Lawful Sovereign.

While Menelaus at first desires to kill Helen for her betrayal, the softening of his heart and the mercy he ultimately shows her further demonstrate that he possesses the qualities of the more merciful Lawful Sovereign, in meaningful contrast to Agamemnon. Similarly, Yudhishthira attempts more than once to negotiate peace and avoid war. Menelaus does as well, saying at the duel with Paris, "I propose that the Greeks and Trojans part in peace" (*Iliad*, 3.99). Additionally, the Vedic Mitra is the god who was seen as uniquely in possession of the ability to marshal the people (*yātayati* – **to join, to unite, to cause to fight, to cause to be returned, to requite, to reward or punish, from *yāt* – to keep peace, to marshal, to animate, to impel men to exertion** (Sanskritdictionary.com, *"yāt"*)), the only god with this trait, (MacDonell, Arthur Anthony, *A Vedic Reader*, pp. 78–83, 118–119, 134), just as Menelaus marshals the people by the Oath of Tyndareus in order to pursue his cause of war. This word, *yātayati*, can be said to sum up many of the paradoxically coexistent elements of the Lawful Sovereign's nature. The *Iliad* describes Menelaus marshaling his people and

---

9   The match between Lleu's adulterous wife Blodeuwedd ("Flower Face") and Lugh's adulterous wife Buach is not exact, and a certain splitting up of this myth has occurred which we will explore further along. Blodeuwedd's myth seems to be paralleled in a more specific manner in the legendary layer of Irish literature, where the king of Munster, Cu Roi, takes Blathnat ("Little flower") as spoil of war, despite her love for Cuchulainn, Cu Roi's warrior. Cu Roi and Cuchulainn have a dispute over Blathnat and Cuchulainn is shamed and punished. Blathnat then betrays Cu Roi to Cuchulainn by alerting Cuchulainn of when the king is home, leading to Cuchulainn killing Cu Roi. This seemingly later, legendary form of the myth combines motifs we see separately elsewhere: the king and warrior disputing over a woman who is taken as a spoil is clearly an echo of what we find in the *Iliad* as Agamemnon and Achilles' central dispute over Briseis. This would then once again be the tension between the Sovereign and Warrior, or First and Second functions. Blathnat then betraying Cu Roi to her lover is reminiscent of the flower-named Blodeuwedd betraying Lleu to her lover. However, we must remember that Agamemnon is also betrayed and killed by his own adulterous wife and her lover, and so the legendary form may be seen as consistent if viewed from that angle. Nonetheless, the theme of the flower-named wife betraying her husband to her lover by giving knowledge of how or when to attack may connect Blodeuwedd and Blathnat.

"urging" them to battle using several terms that exactly match the meanings found in the Sanskrit word: "these were led by Agamemnon's brother, even Menelaus, good at the war-cry, with sixty ships; and they were **marshaled** apart. And himself he moved among them, confident in his zeal, **urging his men to battle**; and **above all others** was his heart fain to get him **requital** for his strivings and groanings for Helen's sake" (Homer, *Iliad*, 2.585-90). Of Lugh it is said: "Lug was urging the men of Ireland to fight the battle fiercely" (*Cath Maige Tuired*, 129).

As Yudhishthira is the only Pandava to finish the Himalaya pilgrimage and attain Paradise in the end of the epic, so Menelaus is one of only two of the Greek heroes who were thought to attain divinization (the other being Diomedes, discussed later). It had even been Athena's plan that Menelaus would not die in the war, which she ensures when she directs Pandarus' arrow away from his vitals. According to Proteus' prophecy in the *Odyssey*, the gods ordained that Menelaus would not die in the war and that they would take Menelaus and Helen to Elysium after a happy life together:

> But for thyself, Menelaus, fostered of Zeus, it is not ordained that thou shouldst die and meet thy fate in horse-pasturing Argos, but to the Elysian plain and the bounds of the earth will the immortals convey thee, where dwells fair-haired Rhadamanthus, [565] and where life is easiest for men. No snow is there, nor heavy storm, nor ever rain, but ever does Ocean send up blasts of the shrill-blowing West Wind that they may give cooling to men; for thou hast Helen to wife, and art in their eyes the husband of the daughter of Zeus.[10]

Additionally, Yudhishthira and Lugh are both carefully guarded or held back for a long time by their own men in order to protect them. Yudhishthira, being the king, becomes the target of the Kaurava forces (particularly led by Drona on Day 11), who wish to cut the head off their foes' army. Irish Lugh is said to be kept out of the fight by a guard in order to protect him: "In order to protect him, the men of Ireland had agreed to keep Lug from the battle. His nine foster fathers came to guard him: Tollusdam and Echdam and Eru, Rechtaid Finn and Fosad and Feidlimid, Ibar and Scibar and Minn. They feared an early death for the warrior because of the great number of his arts. For that reason they did not let him go to the battle" (*Cath Maige Tuired*, 95). They guard him until he is able to slip past them, shortly before urging his men to battle and the climactic spear-throwing moment: "the Tuatha De Danann arose and left his nine companions guarding Lug, and went to join the battle. But when the battle ensued, Lug escaped from the guard set over him, as a chariot-fighter, and it was he who was in front

---

10 *Odyssey* 4.561-56; trans. Murray, 1919.

of the battalion of the Tuatha De" (*Cath Maige Tuired*, 129). We can only hypothesize that the guarding of Lugh could have had a similar meaning to that of Yudhishthira.

Just as Yudhishthira is the one who loses the dice game resulting in him losing the wife and the kingdom, which leads to the war, so it is Menelaus who loses his wife which leads to the war. Again there is a larger circuit of correspondences here: Dumezil argues that the Germanic myth of the death of Baldr is a depiction of this same dice game scene in a different permutation (*Gods of the Ancient Northmen*, 63), and again it leads ultimately to the events of war (here Ragnarok). If so, then the Welsh version seems to miraculously tie the Germanic and Greek versions together. Just before the spear-throwing scene in which Lleu kills Gronw, as mentioned we have the adultery of Blodeuwedd with Gronw. This leads to a scene astonishingly similar to the death of Baldr. The substitution of Baldr for Lleu is explained by the fact that Baldr's analogue Aryaman is a god who is intimately tied to Mitra, an extension of his divine power who is almost an aspect of him – this is explored in the chapter "The Case for Tyr = Mitra"). Lleu is under a magical *tynged*, a protection from being killed, so that Blodeuwedd, conspiring with Gronw, decides she must ask him just how his death could ever be accomplished. Lleu guilelessly explains to her that he "can only be killed at dusk, wrapped in a net with one foot on a cauldron and one on a goat and with a spear forged for a year during the hours when everyone is at mass" (*Math fab Mathonwy*). Like Baldr, he is invincible until the malicious one finds out his sole vulnerability. Blodeuwedd passes this information on to Gronw and directs him how to accomplish the murder, which he attempts with a thrown spear. This does not set off a full-scale war exactly, but Lleu does in fact marshal his kingdom's forces to pursue Gronw. The lack of a full-scale war at this point may be because Welsh myth focused more on the war involving Bran and Branwen, in the tale *Branwen, daughter of Llyr*, and compressed Lleu's battle down to a shorter series of events. Yet the Welsh version proves the key to uniting all these branches together and glimpsing the essence of the Lawful Sovereign's story.

Lleu Llaw Gyffes' myth is so identical in nearly every part to the story of Menelaus that it begins at first to seem like it may have been a direct borrowing by the Welsh from the *Iliad*. However, the problem of there being no *Iliad* translations in the common languages of Northwestern Europe until after the writing down of the tales that became the *Mabinogion* at the very least detracts from this possibility. The Latin prose versions which are known to have existed during the medieval period, Dictys and Dares, either leave out the spear duel scene entirely, or leave out a multitude of other important details such as Menelaus' spear going through Paris' shield, as does the Latin verse summary known as the *Ilias Latina*.[11]

---

11 Regarding the story of Bran and Branwen in a separate branch of the Mabinogi, *Branwen, daughter of Llyr,* Cheryl Steets proclaims that "The framework of the story, however, is a

The uncanny correspondences are as follows: Gronw Pebr "The Radiant" comes to Lleu's kingdom while Lleu is visiting his maternal great-uncle (the idea that he is Lleu's grandfather is also not excluded in this) Math fab Mathonwy; Paris of astonishing beauty comes to Menelaus' kingdom while Menelaus is about to leave for the funeral of his maternal grandfather Catreus. Gronw is there on a hunting expedition; Paris is there on a pretended diplomatic expedition. Lleu's wife, Blodeuwedd, commits adultery and conspires with Gronw; Paris conspires with the goddess Aphrodite in order to adulterously steal Menelaus' wife Helen (Blodeuwedd combining both of these female roles in one). Lleu marshals all of his kingdom and crosses the river Cynvael to pursue Gronw and Blodeuwedd ("Then they called together the whole of Gwynedd, and set forth to Ardudwy" (*Math fab Mathonwy*)); Menelaus marshals all of the allied kingdoms and crosses the Aegean Sea to pursue Paris and Helen. Lleu is under a magical protection against death (a *tynged*, which is a kind of spoken fate pronounced over him); Menelaus is under a prophecy that the gods will not allow him to die yet and will take him to Elysium at the end of his life[12], which Athena ensures, as well as a truce. Note: in the *Iliad,* the "duel" and the "wounding" scenes are switched in order compared to the Welsh version. Blodeuwedd guides Gronw in how to throw the spear to kill Lleu; Athena guides Pandarus to shoot the arrow at Menelaus. Lleu is struck in his side by the spear, breaking the magical *tynged*, undergoes a symbolic death, and is revived by his implied father and god of magical illusion and intellect, Gwydion; Menelaus is struck in the abdomen (the belt region) by the arrow, breaking the standing truce, and is aided by his older brother, Agamemnon, and protected from death by a goddess of magical illusion and intellect, Athena. Lleu has to be healed of this wound by physicians ("and there were brought unto him good physicians that were in Gwynedd"); Menelaus is healed of this wound by the physician Machaon. Lleu's great-uncle Math then discusses

---

clear borrowing: O'Brien has pointed out parallels between the language of the Mabinogi concerning the rescue of Branwen and the Homeric account of the Atreidae's pursuit of Helen of Troy" (Steets, "The Sun Maiden's Wedding," 26, citing Stephen O'Brien, *Dioscuric Elements in Celtic and Germanic Mythology*). Besides the fact that linguistic parallels do not necessarily indicate borrowing, as many examples will show, the possible borrowing of Bran and Branwen's story does not tell us much about whether Lleu's story was borrowed. If the *Iliad* narrative was consciously borrowed into the Bran and Branwen tale, it is in fact hard to believe that the same narrative would be borrowed a second time into the much more compressed and unrecognizable tale involving Lleu, which also contains details comparable to details in the *Iliad* which are not present in the medieval summaries of the *Iliad*. Still, we will have overwhelming reason to question the case for borrowing in either tale, considering our present findings.

12 "And one day, when you round the last bend and finish life, you shall be called a god, and with the Dioskouroi you shall share 10 libations, and with us you will have the hospitality of men [...] And for wandering Menelaos it is his destiny by [will of] the gods that he dwell in the Islands of the Blest" (Euripedes, *Helen*, 1666, 1676-77).

revenge with Lleu ("'Truly,' said Math, 'he will never be able to maintain himself in the possession of that which is thy right.'"); Menelaus' older brother Agamemnon then discusses revenge with Menelaus ("the oath-breakers will pay with their lives, and their wives and children too […] holy Troy will be razed in time" (*Iliad*, 4.160-4). When Lleu comes to confront him, Gronw in fear begs his attendants to stand in for him and receive the blow; when Paris and Menelaus arrive at the duel, it is said that Paris first becomes "sick at heart" and then "shrank back in the ranks" (*Iliad*, 3.32). Lleu and Gronw finally face off (in a formal confrontation) in order to put their dispute to rest: Lleu throws his spear through a slab of stone that Gronw hides behind, killing him; Menelaus and Paris finally face off (in a formal duel) in order to put their dispute to rest: Menelaus throws his spear through Paris' shield and Paris has to be rescued by Aphrodite before he is killed. Gwydion is merciful in not killing Blodeuwedd, but curses her with the form of an owl instead; when Menelaus confronts Helen later, he shows her mercy, and kills her second foreign husband Deiphobus, completing the circuit.

During the truce, Athena, disguised as Pandarus' comrade, and with deception and desire to sow conflict in mind, tells Pandarus he should shoot Menelaus and win glory: "Aim a swift arrow at Menelaus, win glory and renown among the Trojans, and please Prince Paris most of all" (*Iliad*, 4.94). In the same way, the Norse Höðr is guided by Loki in the parallel case to cast the dart at Baldr, and Gronw is instructed by Blodeuwedd in throwing the spear at Lleu. Hence Athena here plays both sides for a moment, actually slipping into what would be the Lokian role and then turning around and guiding the "bitter dart" away from its deadly path and more safely into Menelaus' abdomen.

The argument against simple borrowing in all of this (outside of the noted unavailability of complete *Iliad* translations) also involves the question of whether a borrower would have copied so many of these small details, buried in the narrative and sometimes switched in order as they are, while also making the other changes that are evident. The other question would be whether such a borrower would have been able to accurately recognize the relatively unassuming Menelaus and the central god Lleu as the same divine type to begin with, and understand exactly which elements were essential to the myth of his type. The question should be investigated further; yet, when the correspondences to other branches are considered, it appears very likely that we are dealing with a large web of consistent parallels suggesting a deep, ancient, shared tradition.

Menelaus is also most prominently tied to the central oath of the epic narrative, The Oath of Tyndareus (Pseudo-Apollodorus, *Bibliotheca* 3.10.9). All the suitors of Helen make an oath that they will come to the aid of the one who wins her hand, if need be. Thus it is this oath which Menelaus (along with Agamemnon) invokes in order to compel the others to join him in the attack on Troy. Mitra is primarily a god of contracts and oaths and so it would only be fitting for Menelaus to be the beneficiary of the central oath which ignites the epic and brings together the forces into a united war-band. Menelaus also binds a seer named Proteus in Egypt, with a chain. This allows Menelaus to learn that the gods are angry about the fall of Troy and to appease them with an offering. There is a similarity between this tale and the role of Mitra as a god of binding (by contracts), which may also be illustrated, according to Dumezil in *Gods of the Ancient Northmen,* in the account of the binding of Fenrir by the Norse Mitraic god Tyr and the Aesir, a subject which will be discussed in-depth in another chapter.

We can also say that Pandarus attacking Menelaus to break the truce is fitting, since Menelaus, as Mitra, himself symbolizes or *is* the truce oath, and his wounding is symbolically identical to the breaking of a truce. As the Vedic scholars Joel Brereton and Stephanie Jamison explain: "A mitrá was an 'ally' or an 'alliance,' and Mitra is therefore the god of alliances [...] As the god of alliances, Mitra governs peace agreements between different people, ensuring that they will take their proper places (III.59.1, 5; cf. VII.36.2) and remain in them (III.59.6) (*The Rigveda: A Guide*, 88). In the scene of the duel, just as Menelaus enters, the soldiers say, "let solemn oaths bring friendship between us" – "Mitra" having the meaning of both "contract" and, later, "friend or ally" – and then Menelaus gives a speech about the truce oath and anyone who would break it, ending with "let my hand strike him down, so that future generations shall shudder at harming a host who shows them friendship" (*Iliad,* 3.354).

Though peace-seeking and serene, both the Iranic Mithra and Celtic Lugh/Lugh amply enact the role of punishing breakers of contracts or executing harsh justice. Of Menelaus previously it had been said that "above all others was his heart fain to get him requital." After Menelaus' wounding, Agamemnon comments on "the Trojans, who in wounding you have trampled their solemn oaths underfoot [...] Yet an oath over clasped hands, with the blood of lambs, and offerings of pure wine, is a thing not so easily annulled. Though Zeus delays punishment, he will punish fully in the end: the oath-breakers will pay with their lives, and their wives and children too," after which Menelaus, though we know him to be fiercely seeking requital, tells his brother to "be calm" (*Iliad,* 4.155, 184). This is a near-perfect example of the dynamic interaction of the paired sovereigns of Justice, the Varunian and Mitraic, the terrible and the serene, both seeking ultimate justice for the broken contract of friendship though characterized by contrasting natures. As Dumezil puts it: "Mitra is the sovereign under his reasoning aspect, luminous, ordered, calm, benevolent, priestly; Varuna is the sovereign under his attacking aspect, dark, inspired, violent, terrible, warlike" (Dumezil, *Mitra-Varuna,* 71). In the *Taittiriya Samhita*, the merciful Mitra is said to pacify the cruel-minded Varuna, just as Menelaus pacifies Agamemnon: "Mitro hi kruram varunam shantham karoti (Mitra makes peaceful the cruel-minded Varuna" (*TS* 2.1.9.5).

At times we might be tempted to suspect a movement toward combining the Mitra and Varuna aspects into one god in the Celtic Lleu/Lugh, in tales such as the Irish *Fate of the Children of Tuireann,* with Lugh's fearsome justice. Indeed, as we will see, Lugh conflicts with the sons of the presumed Thunderer Tuireann in a similar fashion as Agamemnon (Varuna) conflicts with the Thunderer Achilles. There may be some grain of truth to this perspective, a general inheritance of certain "Varuna" powers by some "Mitra" gods or heroes who have of course succeeded the Varunian sovereign; however, viewing Lugh as actually being both gods is a fairly convoluted approach, and it is not necessary to adopt this view. We must recognize that, though Varuna and Mitra contrast in key ways, Vedic Mitra too has the potentiality of wielding the fearsome power of Justice, and it is well understood, as seen in the Vedic hymns, that Mitra and Varuna are sometimes indistinguishable and freely shared prerogatives, becoming the dual form "Mitra-Varuna" on numerous occasions. As is stated of the Mitraic incarnation Yudhishthira in the *Mahabharata,* "When I think of his wrath, O Sanjaya, and consider how just it is, I am filled with alarm" (*Mahabharata, Udyoga Parva,* XXII). And in the Iranic *Avesta* it is said that Mithra catches the evil or lying man with his long arms, no matter where he goes (*Avesta, Mihr Yasht,* 104), just as Lugh is prominently called *lamhfada,* "of the long arm." The "long arm" of Mithra and Lugh, the Lawful Sovereigns, though it may have other layers of significance as well, is indeed the Long Arm of the Law.

Nor is the significant wounding and temporary retirement (their symbolic death) we see in Lleu and Menelaus absent from Yudhishthira's story. Yudhishthira does, as previously mentioned, receive a spear to the chest just before killing Shalya. However, this particular blow does not actually greatly slow him. It is instead during his direct confrontation with the incarnation of the Sun God, Karna, that he becomes so wounded that he must temporarily remove from battle (*Mahabharata, Karna Parva,* 62), just as the other Mitraic figures are often near-mortally wounded in close connection with a comparable confrontation (Lleu temporarily killed by Gronw "The Radiant," Menelaus wounded by Pandarus, etc.). It is also at this point that Yudhishthira comes into hostile conflict with Indra's incarnation and his own ally, Arjuna. He suggests Arjuna give up his signature bow because he has not succeeded in killing Karna, at which instigation Arjuna almost decides he has to kill Yudhishthira as a matter of honor. This killing is only narrowly avoided by means of a technicality. This conflict of course parallels very nicely the conflict between the Second Function Warrior Hero and the Sovereign of Justice (which role can be performed by either the Terrible or Lawful Sovereign), Achilles in conflict with the Varunian Agamemnon and Tuireann with the Mitraic Lugh.

17

In the Indian case, Pandu (Terrible Sovereign hero) has already died, so the Mitraic sovereign Yudhishthira is the only figure remaining who can fill the Sovereign of Justice role in conflict with the Thunderer at this point in the narrative. Thus, this version has the Lawful Sovereign hero conflicting with the Warrior class ("Thunderer") hero, which again matches best with the Irish version where this mytheme is taken by the Mitraic Lugh, the Lawful Sovereign. Ultimately, Yudhishthira's wounding at the hands of the Sun hero Karna and Welsh Lleu's wounding at the hands of the sun hero Gronw "The Radiant" shows a great amount of direct continuity between the Vedic and Celtic understandings of these myths.

Menelaus' oft-repeated epithets are *xanthos* – a word denoting a range of colors from "strawberry blonde," "auburn" to "honey blonde" – and "beloved of Ares." Although *xanthos* is often used to describe objects that are simply yellow, the 4th-5th Century BCE d-scholia of the *Iliad* substitutes *purros* for *xanthos*, *purros* meaning "red," suggesting that this may have been closer to an ancient understanding of the color. Thus some modern English translations use "blonde" while others call Menelaus simply "red-haired." The early morning, with which Mitra was identified[13], can then be said to resemble this *xanthos* due to the sunrise. A god of the time of sunrise could predictably be *xanthos*-haired, a shining and blazing color whether red or blonde, and indeed this would be the expected hair color of such a god. While other *Iliad* characters' hair colors are also described as *xanthos*, Menelaus has this word attached to him more than any other hero, being called *xanthos* twenty-seven times, making it his particular characteristic. The hair of Achilles, by contrast, is only called *xanthos* twice.

Lastly, the etymologies of Menelaus and Yudhishthira yield surprisingly similar results. Menelaus is believed to derive from *ménō* ("stay, wait for") and *lāós*, ("people.") As Douglas Frame explains: "Menelaus…is usually derived from the verb *ménō*, 'await, withstand'" (Frame, *Hippota Nestor*, 2.94). **Μένω** - (*ménō*) has the primary meaning "I stay, wait (in battle)," with the sub-variations "1. I stand fast," "2. I stay where I am," and "5. (*of things*) I am lasting; I remain, stand." We could then deduce a meaning for Menelaus' name to be something like, "the stay or steadfastness of the people in battle." Frame, emphasizing the usages common to Homer rather than the more speculative archaic root, phrases it as "he who withstands the [his own] warfolk." Yudhishthira's name, on the other hand, derives from युध् - (*yudh*), meaning "1. to fight, battle" and थिर

---

13 The morning *upasthaana* prayer, recited to the risen sun after the Gayatri mantra is chanted at sunrise, is a collection of Vedic verses addressing Mitra. Mitra is associated with sunrise in the *Atharvaveda*, contrasted with Varuna in his association with the evening (Macdonell, Arthur Anthony, *A Vedic Reader,* pp. 78–83, 118–119, 134.) Varuna becomes Agni in the evening, and rising in the morning he becomes Mitra (*AV* 2.28.2). Mitra is also worshiped alongside Surya in the Mitrotsavam festival of Surya.

- (*sthir*) stable, steady," as in a *sthir deś*, or stable nation. As such, Yudhishthira's name is usually summarized to mean "firm in battle," with the word for "firm" also having the general connotation of "stable." So Menelaus is "steadfastness/withstanding [of his own people?] in battle," while Yudhishthira is "firm and stable in battle." It is possible that what we have here is the same preserved original meaning, progressing with only slight variation into these two very distant languages. Frame further argues that Menelaus's name has the meanings of "he who incites the warfolk" as well as "he who withstands the warfolk [as their leader]," saying that both are ultimately valid, as is "he who reminds the warfolk." The role of inciter of the warband, so important and specially characteristic to Vedic Mitra, may then still resonate in Menelaus' meaning-rich name.

Lugh, for his part, could be connected to a similar concept of steadfastness. The names of the *sidhe* dwellings of the gods may to be related to the gods' functions. The dwelling of Lugh is named *rodruban*. According to the Electronic Dictionary of the Irish Language (eDil), *rod* can mean "red," "impetuous," "strong," or "conflict." EDil redirects *ruban* to *ruiben*, which means "stays, abides remains, endures." This dwelling would then be that of "the strong endurer" or "the one who abides in the conflict," remarkably close to the etymologies of Menelaus and Yudhishthira which we have compared above. Lugh's wife, meanwhile, is named N*ás*, which eDil subjoins to *nasad,* meaning "gathering or assembly of festive or commemorative nature or place of assembly," or "death" (consider Lugh*nasadh*, a festival commemorating the death of Tailtiu). *Nasc* meanwhile means "a. a fastening or tie,"and "b. legal term for a bond obligation; a general term for every method of legal binding."[14] For example, "secures (by pledge, *etc.*), makes sure (a bond, contract, promise)" is *atait secht nadmand* **nascar** *la Feineor nasad,* and "binding to a combat" is *Fer rogain fri* **nascad** *niad.* Cf. *Naiscid*, "a. binds, makes fast," and "b. legal term binds, exacts a pledge (promise, obligation, payment)." Even the *dáil n-asdadha*, the "decree of binding," which is chanted by Lugh after the Fomorians are defeated, connects to this root *nasad*, and seems to establish law via a ritual binding. It is interesting to note that while Lugh's wives are Buach and Nas, the phrase *buad nāis* (from the root *nás*), found in the Middle Irish *Aislinge Meic Conglinne* 7.30, means "victory over death." Finally, M, as a war leader, is a bringer of death to his enemies. Any of these related meanings would put this wife, Nas, squarely in the Mitraic semantic field.

Alwyn and Brinley Rees point out that the originator of assemblies was Lug, and that he also instituted horse races, "an important feature of assemblies" (Rees and Rees, *Celtic Heritage*, 143). They note furthermore that "According to the *dindsenchas* it was

---

14 I owe credit to Kevin Maclean for first stating this connection. www.fortressoflugh.com.
   See eDil: http://www.dil.ie/search?q=ruban&search_in=headword.
   http://www.dil.ie/search?q=nasad&search_in=headword. Accessed May 2021.

at a great peace-making assembly held there that the death of Lug was encompassed by the three grandsons of the Dagda" (Rees and Rees, 158), which is reminiscent of Menelaus' wounding (his symbolic death) during the great peace treaty. The *Lebor Gabala Erenn*, discussing Lugh, indeed calls him the bringer of assembly and horse-racing to Ireland: "he is the first who brought chess-play and ball-play and horse-racing and assembling into Ireland [...] Lug son of Ethliu, a cliff without a wrinkle, with him there first came a lofty assembly" (*Lebor Gabala Erenn* §64).

The fact that these two brothers, Agamemnon and Menelaus, so well embody the same contrast of wrathful king and peaceable king (who is still capable of just retribution) that we find in Varuna and Mitra, reinforces the overall case for each parallel. Bernard Sergent has shown, furthermore, in his "La Representation Spartiate de la Royaute," that the Spartan dual kingship had a particular repeating, ideological character. This kingship was divided between two families, the Agiades and the Eurypontides, and the histories of the kings from each family tend to follow two separate patterns. The Agiades almost always are involved in wars, the founding of colonies, military expansion, and rule as war-kings. The Eurypontides kings are depicted as relatively more peaceful and are married to what Sergent calls "bad women" (Sergent, 14) – adulterous wives – or may be diverted from their duties by their wives. Eurypontides kings are prone to becoming corrupted in general. As Sergent puts it [translated]: "This insistence on making Eurypontides kings peaceful or incompletely warlike indicates without question that in Spartan thought the Eurypontides are marked, characterized, by peace, facing the Agiades characterized by war" (Sergent, 17), and calls the Eurypontides "victims" of cuckolding (Sergent, 20). This is a pattern that repeats over and over again in the records of these Spartan kings, indicating, in Sergent's view, that the very education of the sovereign families reinforced these behavior patterns, or that Spartan historians, guided by the inherited ideology, selected and shaped the historical material to fit it, or some combination of both. Oddly (to us), Sergent sees the warlike Agiades as embodying the traits of Menelaus, while he claims the pacific Eurypontides have a connection with Agamemnon. From our foregoing analysis it seems that, on the contrary, the Eurypontides pattern is a facsimile of the career of Menelaus, from his association with peace-making attempts to his cuckolding (which is much more central to the narrative of the *Iliad* than Agamemnon's is), and that of the Agiades is clearly a match to the mythos of the expansionist war-king, Agamemnon. Even the noted corruptibility of the Eurypontides repeats the great sin of the Mitraic Yudhishthira, who participates in one half-lie and loses the symbol of his perfect righteousness (his floating chariot), due in part to his tendency toward passivity, when he passively helps to trick Drona into believing his son is dead. As the paragon of righteousness and peacekeeping, the Mitraic figure is the most vulnerable to corruption, and his corruption also holds the most symbolic weight. What Sergent's remarkable article demonstrates is that this duality was a deeply ingrained pattern in the region, one which Greeks like the Spartans would have immediately understood when hearing the story of Agamemon and Menelaus, and which some Greeks even integrated into their own sovereign structure and cultural ideology well beyond the archaic period.

Lawful Sovereign: (Menelaus, Mitra/Yudhishthira, Lugh/Leu)

- Is Second King

- Is peaceable and merciful though still a skilled warrior

- Loses his wife to another man which starts the war, sometimes while visiting his maternal grandfather

- Marshals the united armies to regain her or the kingdom

- May be held out of the fight for a time for his protection

- Is protected by a divine or magical fate against death

- Is wounded in the abdomen, requiring healing by physicians

- When wounded, is aided by a god of magical illusion and intellect and an older brother or father

- Attempts to take revenge on his wife's lover

- Throws the spear to end the war or to attempt to end it

- Throws the spear through a stone slab or shield

- Kills his wife's lover either with this spear or at a later time

- Shows mercy to his wife by sparing her life

- Survives the war and goes to Paradise as an Immortal

Ajax

Ajax – Vayu (The Lord of Wind)

Telamonian Ajax seems the obvious match for the powerful Lord of Wind, Vayu, and his incarnation, Bhima. The most immediate connection is the size and strength of both

Ajax and Bhima. Ajax is known as the tallest of the Achaean warriors. He is so large that he can be identified by the Trojans from their ramparts. His frame is also said to be colossal and he is the strongest of the Achaeans, called "the bulwark of the Achaeans" (*Iliad*, VI.5). Bhima likewise is both the strongest and largest of the Pandavas. Ajax's name meaning "he who laments" could, in this interpretation, relate to the sound of the wind, poetically compared to lamentation; or we may consider its alternate meaning, "eagle," as a possible symbol of the airborne strength of the wind god.

Beyond this, the main evidence for Ajax's identification with Bhima is Ajax's role as primary one-on-one opponent of Hector, paralleling the battles between Bhima and the incarnation of Kali, Duryodhana, in the *Mahabharata*. Ajax is known to be so powerful and courageous that when it comes time to draw lots to face Hector in single combat, Ajax steps forward and all the Achaeans pray that he will be chosen. Only Diomedes or Agamemnon are thought to suffice if it is not Ajax. He is chosen and greets the news with joy, and thus we get the formalized bout between the two bafflingly powerful heroes in which Ajax fights Hector to a draw and they exchange gifts. Later they fight again when Hector charges the ships and succeeds in burning one of them. In one of their several different face-offs, Ajax nearly kills Hector by smashing him with a large rock, knocking him unconscious. Hector has to be revived by Apollo, and ultimately Ajax saves the ships (except the one) and saves the Greeks from losing the war then and there.

These one-on-one battles mirror those between Bhima and Duryodhana in the *Mahabharata*. Duryodhana is the primary warrior of the Kauravas and childhood sparring partner of Bhima. In the war they famously face off several times as Ajax and Hector do. In their final confrontation, a formalized bout, Bhima smashes Duryodhana's thigh with a mace, and there is no god who comes to revive him to fight on. He dies from the blow. If we take these two formalized bouts to be identical at their root, then it seems possible Hector may have been revived in the Greek version so that this climactic kill could be given to Achilles. However, we should be cautious about assuming a priority for the Indian version.

A couple of other interesting connections require speculation. At one point, Ajax is struck by Poseidon in order to renew his strength. This is reminiscent of the scene where Bhima is dropped down, unconscious, into the underwater kingdom of the Nagas and is given his superhuman strength by the king who reigns there. In each case the Lord of Wind is given strength by a divine underwater king. Ajax dies after the war from dishonor from killing a herd of sheep (that he thought were his comrades); Bhima dies after the war from the sin of gluttony; their Irish parallel, the Dagda, is mocked (but does not die) for eating a giant pit-full of sheep and porridge. Can we posit a hypothetical connection here, of the Lord of Wind dying from gluttonous dishonor or sin over eating a massive amount of sheep?

Finally, just as Agamemnon and Menelaus are paired as brothers and just as the two heroes of the Third Function are paired, Ajax also is paired closely with the other hero of his function. Ajax and his contrasting hero of the second function, Achilles, are said both to be trained together by the centaur Chiron. This connection is reinforced as they are said also to be cousins. Ajax is also strongly marked by his association with Heracles, another demigod who Dumezil identifies as of the Bhima type and a strong symbol of the warrior function in general.

Lord of Wind: (Ajax, Vayu/Bhima, the Dagda)

- Is the largest and strongest warrior

- Scene involving many sheep over which he is mocked or incurs shame

- Fights a closely matched formalized bout with the Demon of the Dark Age, as well as several other one-on-one battles with him. Is the nemesis and primary opponent of the Demon throughout the war

- Smashes the Demon of the Dark Age with a blunt object, killing him or requiring a god to revive him

Achilles

Achilles – Indra (The Thunderer)

The main example Dumezil uses to demonstrate that Arjuna is Indra's incarnation (along with the fact that he is the "spiritual son" of Indra) is that during the mythic battle between Indra and Surya, Surya's chariot loses its wheel, leading to Indra's victory. During Arjuna and Karna's battle during the Kurukshetra War, Karna's chariot wheel gets stuck in the mud, leading to Arjuna's victory. Dumezil has already discussed the parallel between Greek Achilles and Arjuna as well. The most well-known sections of both the *Iliad* and *Mahabharata* feature these two heroes: these are Achilles' withdrawal from the war in protest of Agamemnon's insult to his honor, around which the narrative is structured, and Arjuna's withdrawal from the war due to his internal conflict regarding fighting his cousins, leading to the section known as the *Bhagavad Gita*. Each hero in his own way displays a particular kind of sensitivity, a brooding introversion, specifically over questions of honor and dharma. In addition, each culture seems to have used this episode as a major jumping off point for new movements of moral and political philosophy thereafter. Thus the protest of the Thunderer-hero, the warrior god protesting against the power of the sovereign and priestly-judicial caste, massively influenced the respective cultures, India more in the direction of the dissolving of the ego in impersonal dharma, and Greece toward a more overt conflict of the atomized individual against the collective or sovereign order. After keeping aside from the war for a certain amount of time, each hero returns to be perhaps the most important warrior for their side, slaying key enemy warriors and turning the tide of the war.

As has been mentioned as well, Achilles' pairing with Ajax as trainees of Chiron reproduces the archaic duad of Indo-European warrior gods, the "brutish" and the "chivalrous," the wind and the thunder. When Achilles fights Hector, Athena returns his spears to him continually. This is reminiscent of Thor whose hammer returns to him or Zeus in his Thunderer aspect dealing out his endless stock of lightning bolts. It is said that only Achilles can wield his spear, while a similar trait is attached to Norse Thor[15] – only Thor is strong enough to wield the thunder hammer Mjolnir. Thus both Achilles' spear and Thor's hammer could parallel the *vazra,* the thunder weapon of Indra.

Finally, both Arjuna and Achilles are famous for their mourning over another warrior's death, a warrior who is beloved by and tied closely to them. For Achilles this is Patroclus, Achilles' comrade from youth, but for Arjuna it is instead his son, Abhimanyu. The general parallel has been noted before, but it can actually be seen that this is not merely a vague similarity, but that the same story is being told in both cases. Both Patroclus and Abhimanyu are tasked with a sort of suicide mission, because Achilles or Arjuna are occupied elsewhere – Achilles protesting in his tent and Arjuna being distracted on a distant part of the battlefield. Abhimanyu has to enter the ranks of the enemy's infamously unassailable Chakravyuha formation alone and to fight them singlehandedly. Patroclus, in the Greek epic, is urged by Nestor to lead the Myrmidon's on what becomes a mad assault on Troy's walls. Though fighting valiantly with impressive slaughter, each one is unable to safely leave the enemy ranks and is killed by being attacked by many enemy heroes at once. Patroclus is killed when Apollo himself dazes him from behind, so that Hector can strike, and then Hector threatens to ignobly give his body to the dogs. Abhimanyu is killed by a gang attack of many of the enemy heroes attacking at once from all sides, which Arjuna afterward interprets as unjust. Each death highlights the dishonorable actions of those who do the killing. Upon receiving the news, the lamentation of both Achilles and Arjuna are proverbial. Each then vows revenge on the killers of his comrade or son. As Arjuna says, "Listen now to another

---

15 Credit to Owen Thebes for this connection.

oath of mine! If tomorrow's sun set without my slaying of that wretch, then even here shall I enter the blazing fire!" (*Mahabharata, Drona Parva,* LXXIII), while Achilles exclaims, likewise mentioning the burial fire, "I will not give thee burial till I have brought hither the armour and the head of Hector, the slayer of thee, the great-souled; and of twelve glorious sons of the Trojans will I cut the throats before thy pyre in my wrath at thy slaying" (*Iliad,* 18.334-6).

It is interesting to attempt to draw a parallel between this episode and the Irish version of the Thunderer's myth, as found (in a perhaps more embroidered version) in the relatively late tale *The Fate of the Children of Tuireann*. [This tale could be a late elaboration of a brief mention in *LGE*. We analyze and include it nonetheless as it does build on a germ of possibly traditional material regarding the confrontation of Lugh and the offspring of Tuireann.] Tuireann, like Arjuna, is best known for his heart-rending lamentation at the deaths of his sons. There are three sons this time, but the doubling in the names Iucha and Iucharba and the fact that only Brian speaks, except one time when they speak among themselves, suggests that they may be a triplication of a single figure, or simply that Brian is a more important figure than the others. In addition, these deaths and the ensuing lamentation happen as a result of, and repeat, the conflict between the Thunderer and the Sovereign of Justice, which we see in Agamemnon and Achilles' conflict. In both the Irish and Greek stories, justice is being exercised by the god of justice in what is arguably an overzealous manner. Agamemnon exacts Briseis from Achilles because Chryseis is taken from him, and as king and commander-in-chief he feels he is owed and is able to take compensation. This kingly justice, of course, is unjust and insulting from the perspective of Achilles, and it ultimately causes Achilles to be absent when Patroclus has to undertake his mission, thus leading to Patroclus' death. Lugh exacts a series of difficult-to-obtain objects in repayment from the sons of Tuireann because Lugh's father has been taken from him, killed at their hands, and as king and as son he feels he is owed, and is able to take, compensation. His demanded recompense is extravagant, but is still within the realm of reason, as he easily could have simply killed the sons of Tuireann for their crime. The fact that the final task leads to their mortal wounding walks the line between justice and excessive punishment. Lugh must have known they would be seriously wounded from this task and when they ask him to be healed by one of the magical items they had obtained, he refuses it to them, and they perish. His justice is not absurdly unfair, but it is terrible in its absoluteness, a drawn out execution where mercy is refused, despite the fact that Lugh had told them they could live if they retrieved these items, giving them false hope that a non-fatal recompense was possible. Theirs is indeed a suicide mission too.

Both Agamemnon and Lugh's actions can be said to follow a logic of compensatory justice, and yet they also have a dimension of questionable harshness. This harshness of applied power leads ultimately to the death of the Thunderer's son(s) or close friend. Tuireann then weeps and laments, and dies of grief. The form this death takes may be, as in some other Celtic tales, due to this tale having been, very slightly, separated from the context of the Great War. Whereas Arjuna says he will throw himself on the fire if he does not kill his son's killers by the end of the next day, Tuireann figuratively does just this by perishing from his grief, unable to take revenge. As both the Vedic and Irish cases involve the sons of the Thunderer, it is plausible that Patroclus being only a close comrade and not a son may have been a Greek alteration of the myth. It has also been suggested that the close friendship of Duryodhana and Karna on the other side of the war, and the lamentation of Duryodhana at the death of Karna is more of a match to that of Achilles and Patroclus, that the two similar parallel relationships and deaths were combined into one in the Greek epic.

So who is Abhimanyu/Patroclus/The Sons of Tuireann? Abhimanyu is the reincarnation of the moon god Chandra's son. His central epithets are "son of Subhadra," "son/successor of Arjuna," and "son of Chandra." Patroclus' name means "glory of the father," and his father's name Menoetius is believed to mean "defying fate" or "ruined strength," deriving from *ménos*, "strength, force, might," and *oîtos*, "fate." As we will see in a later section, the Greek concept of the Fates derived from a word related to the moon, and the moon, as the great Measurer, was seen as being directly related to the operation of fate. While the moon may be connected to fate, it defies it as well, as it is seen to die only to revive again, as it wanes (ruined strength) and waxes again. Meanwhile, the stem "ménos" always holds the possibility of a lunar double meaning with the stem "mḗn," related to the word for month. As Abhimanyu is the reincarnation of the Moon God's son, given to Arjuna to raise as a son, so Patroclus is also given to Achilles by his father Menoetius as a mentor and friend (this is because Patroclus had committed the sin of killing another youth. Murder is Patroclus' sin, just as murder is the sin of Tuireann's sons). Both Abhimanyu and Patroclus are manifestations of the duty of a son (this much is true of the Sons of Tuireann as well), and they are the sons of potentially moon-related figures.

The name *Akhilleus* means "he who has the people distressed," which relates him to the frightening storm and its swift killing power, but also to the concept of distress generally which manifests in his stormy brooding. The fact that he is known as the swiftest Greek could be an expression of his connection to the lightning.

The Thunderer: (Achilles, Indra/Arjuna, Tuireann, Taran

- Is the central and most skilled warrior

- Retires from battle for a period of time due to sensitivity regarding an issue of honor/dharma

- Has justice harshly exacted on him by the Terrible Sovereign, leading to the death of his favorite or son

- Laments over the death of his favorite or son and may die in the resulting events

Odysseus and Diomedes

Odysseus – Nasatya

Diomedes – Dasra (The Horse Twins)

This pairing of heroes may seem surprising at first as their horse associations are not blatantly obvious and they do not seem to be depicted as blood relatives. This is trivial, however, when the greater pattern is considered. Many a wrong identification of the Horse Twins has been made by thinking that "horse association" plus "twinning motif" equals Horse Twins, without understanding what these gods really were about. The Horse Twins were always known as warriors, but the Greeks and Romans emphasized the warrior aspect of the Dioskouroi perhaps even more than other branches. The Spartan army carried the *dókana,* symbol of the Twins, before them during war, and the Dioscuri were known to them as inventors of war dances. Their standard oath was "by the two gods," referring to the Dioscuri. The Twins also aided the Romans in battle and were especially beloved by the cavalry. They were seen as generals and ideal warriors while still having a closeness with the "human" level of normal people, gods of the "third function" as they are. They were said to have led the legions of the commonwealth in the battle of Lake Regillus and to have carried them to victory. A Horse Twin god like Aengus Og in Irish myth (as wee will see) is more well-known for his association with love and wooing and youthfulness, but in more obscure epithets he is still called "of the battle squadrons" (*Dindshenchas, Ailech III*) and "red armed" (*Dindshenchas, Brefne*). The incarnations of the Vedic Horse Twins the Asvins in the *Mahabharata*, that is Nakula and Sahadeva, were known as highly skilled warriors as well. Hence Diomedes being one of the fiercest and bravest of the Greek warriors should come as no surprise. The fact that he is called the most feared warrior among the Achaeans shows just how high in reverence the Greeks held the Horse Twins and particularly how highly they rated their martial aspect. Nakula, paralleling the famous prowess of Diomedes, is called "skillful in all forms of war" (*sarvayuddhaviśārada*, 7.165.7364), "fighting in a wondrous manner" (*citrayodhin*), but also "the most beautiful of heroes" (*darśanīyatamo nṛṇām*, 2.75.2555).

However, along with this martial skill, the Horse Twins are known for their intelligence and particularly their cunning or trickery. They are always tricking someone out of something or going on covert missions or cattle raids. Aengus Og tricks the Dagda or Elcmar out of Brugh na Boinne by means of the clever wording of an agreement. This is where Odysseus in particular comes in, and with this framework perhaps we can understand the origin and significance of Odysseus' fabled cunning. Whenever a question of intelligence or stratagem arises, Odysseus is called upon, and he becomes most famed of all for coming up with the Trojan Horse plot. Yet in the *Iliad* there are many other instances of Odysseus, almost always accompanied by Diomedes, performing some kind of covert mission. Diomedes and Odysseus are sent on a night mission to gather Rhesus' horses. Diomedes and Odysseus may also have been sent on a peace mission to try to negotiate terms of truce after Paris was killed. Odysseus and Diomedes are sent on another mission to steal the Palladium statue, Troy being prophesied to be unconquerable while the statue remained within it. Odysseus and Diomedes also kill Palamedes together using trickery. Meanwhile, Sthenelus and Diomedes go on one mission to steal the horses of Aeneas. And Diomedes, in a move highly reminiscent of Aengus tricking the Dagda out of Brugh na Boinne, tricks Glaucus into trading his gold armor for Diomedes' bronze, such a cunning trade thereafter being referred to as a Diomedian swap.

Indeed, Odysseus and Diomedes are constantly together, doing numerous significant things together in the war, and we can consider this to be what is left to us of their "twinning" motif (it is not unusual for the Horse Twins to have separate parentage). As Achilles and Ajax trained together under the same teacher and were both connected to Heracles, so Odysseus and Diomedes were both said to have met and teamed up already on "several adventures" when in Aulis before the war and were the two favorites of their shared patron, Athena. They each share the traits of their patron goddess, each one marked by her wisdom and cunning, her courage and skill in battle, though to different degrees. While Odysseus is known as the craftiest Greek and the go-to strategist, Diomedes is repeatedly praised for his exceeding intelligence especially for his young age. And this combination of intelligence and great youthfulness is often repeated. Nestor commends his intelligence and says that no one of such young age has Diomedes' wise counsel (Sahadeva is similarly known as Yudhishthira's wise private counselor), after which he reiterates, "thou art in sooth but young, thou mightest e'en be *my son, my youngest born*" [italics mine](*Iliad* IX.57). He is known as the youngest of the Achaeans and his youth is brought up repeatedly. This again parallels exactly the Irish Aengus Og, his nickname *mac oc* amounting to "the young son," who was said to be perpetually youthful, a god of youth, love and beauty, but also, as aforementioned, of cunning exchanges and "of the battle squadrons." This is paralleled also in the name of the Welsh Mabon ("young son"), and by the Asvins, who were known as the "sons of God" and associated with youthfulness and the power to regenerate youth: "The Asvins are young (7.67.10), the TS [Taittiriya Samhita] (7.2.7.2) even describing them as the youngest of the gods [...] They are beautiful (6.62.5; 6.63.1)" (Arthur A. Macdonell, *Vedic Mythology*, 49).

While, as mentioned, Odysseus and Diomedes' horse associations are not blatant, they are not absent either. Two of their missions involve the capture of horses, and one of them leaves Diomedes the owner of Aeneas' famed horses, the second fastest after Achilles' divine ones. The name "Horse Twins" for the Asvins meant primarily that they owned horses (*Aśvínā* - "Horse-Possessors"), as when they go into exile Nakula and Sahadeva take on the disguises of a higher class horse owner and a lower class cattle keeper, the lower class brother being the more crafty of the two ("they are opposed to each other as 'warrior horseman' to 'intelligent cattleman'" says the scholar Douglas Frame (*The Myth of Return in Early Greek Epic*, 6.4)), which seems also to parallel the kind of distinction we see between Diomedes, owning the second-finest horses, and Odysseus being the craftiest man of all, though sometimes cowardly (perhaps a symbolic lower-class vice to match the lower-class virtue of cunning), and described as somewhat shorter (shorter by a head than Agamemnon (3.195), who is shorter than the others) and having less nobility in his form and the way he carries himself than Diomedes. At one point Odysseus' surprising speaking ability is described, but is contrasted to his graceless demeanor:

> There was no play nor graceful movement of his sceptre; he kept it straight
> and stiff like a man unpractised in oratory—one might have taken him for a
> mere churl or simpleton," after which his words come pouring out "like
> winter snow before the wind [...] and no man thought further of what he
> looked like. (*Iliad*, 3.215)

Odysseus' most famous stratagem even takes the form of a horse – the Trojan Horse – and he and Diomedes lead this mission from within the wooden representation of their divine form. Diomedes is also said to have had a white horse sacrificed to him in the worship of the Heneti. The horse associations of the incarnations of the Horse Twin incarnations in the *Mahabharata* are not particularly prominent either. As aforementioned, they disguise themselves as a horse keeper and a cattle herder, but in general they too are primarily characterized by a specific pattern of traits: their cunning, youth, beauty, counsel, skill in battle.

Diomedes also fulfills the important Horse Twin role of rescuer in one instance during the war when he bravely saves Nestor from Hector's attack. And as the Horse Twins are associated with sea voyages and sea rescues, Odysseus is closely identified with his own long sea voyage home. Paralleling the Horse Twins' attributes exactly, one of Odysseus' epithets is "master mariner," while one of Diomedes' is "breaker of horses." In the *Iliad*, Castor of the Dioskouroi himself is also called "the horse breaker" (*Iliad*, 3.255). As the Horse Twins are also connected with oaths (particularly the Roman Dioscuri; see also: "Dioscuric Elements in Celtic and Germanic Mythology," *Journal of Indo-European Studies*, Steven O'Brien p. 118), it is fitting that the central Oath of Tyndareus, which Menelaus enforces, is thought up by Odysseus.

The Horse Twins are somewhat of divine climbers – while the Vedic Asvins, for example, were initially excluded from the higher pantheon of gods, they eventually attained recognition and immortality when they were admitted into the *soma* sacrifice. Irish Aengus likewise is said to drink a drink of immortality at Goibniu's Feast and ascends to lordship of the great burial mound Brugh na Boinne when he is of age. This divine climbing aspect may be reflected in Diomedes' well-known clashing with the immortal gods on the battlefield. This bold vying demonstrates both his closeness with the world of mortals, in his antagonism with the higher divinities, but also his ambition to put himself on a level with the highest immortals. Diomedes wounds two immortals in one day, becoming the only human ever to do so. This episode may have a faint echo in the Kurukshetra War of the *Mahabharata*, for Nakula, the horse keeper brother, while being called a child, is at one heated moment during the war warned to fight only his equals in battle: "Do not, O son of Pandu, fight again with those amongst the Kurus that are possessed of greater might. O child, fight with them that are thy equals" (*Karna Parva*, XXIV). Variant tales tell that in the end Diomedes, similar to the immortalization of the Asvins, had a "mysterious apotheosis," (Strabo, *Geography*, 6.9.3) or even was given immortality by the goddess Athena (per Pindar, *Nemean* 10.7) and became worshipped as a god. A scholiast on this poem even has it that Diomedes lives with the Dioskouroi in heaven as an immortal god, suggesting that the tradition retained a deep connection between them (J.B. Bury, Pindar: *Nemean Odes*, 199).

Lastly, just as Aengus Og is said to be accompanied by birds that fly over his head, so Diomedes is said to have birds that follow him and his soldiers, birds which "used to be his companions" (Virgil, *Aeneid* XI.246–247). One of the islands named for him is said to be known for its mysterious birds (Aelian, *On Animals*). Another legend states that the albatross sang for him when he died, and others say that when he died his companions "were changed into birds resembling swans…They are called the birds of Diomedes" (*Bibliotheca Classica*, John Lempriere, "Diomedes"; see Virgil, *Aeneid*, XI.246-247). The Irish Aengus transforms into a swan at the end of his wooing story.

For a counterpoint to this section see Nick Allen's "Why Did Odysseus Become a Horse?" and his argument that Odysseus also shares elements with the hero of the *Mahabharata,* Arjuna, incarnation of Indra. It is of course possible for motifs to be split differently in the different branches, and overall we stand by the evidence we have laid out for Achilles as Arjuna and Odysseus as a Horse Twin. It is true, however, that Odysseus is likely the most mysterious and complex of all the *Iliad* heroes in terms of comparativism. As Gregory Nagy, among others, has suggested, the Odysseus of the *Odyssey* seems almost like a different character from Odysseus of the *Iliad*.[16] Even Nick Allen points out that "If the careers of Odysseus and Arjuna are cognate at one point in their respective epics, it by no means follows that they will be cognate at other points" (Allen, "Why Did Odysseus Become a Horse?"). Thus we would suggest that the Odysseus of the *Odyssey*, newly taking on the central position of the epic narrative, has also taken on mythoi from the other now absent gods or heroes, such as the Thunderer, and that his alignment much more with the Horse Twin Hero Sahadeva in the *Iliad,* and not at all with the Thunderer there, must be grasped.

A final possibility must also be entertained for this complex figure. Odysseus is the great-grandson of the god Hermes. This god's cunning nature and association with thieves was concentrated in his son, Autolycus, who is also Odysseus' grandfather. Thus we can see Odysseus perhaps taking on certain traits from this specific inheritance. This opens the possibility that Odysseus incarnates the god Hermes, who in a later section will be compared to the Vedic Gandharva. From this angle, Odysseus would not incarnate a Horse Twin, unless the cunning Horse Twin and cunning Hermes traits became combined in his mythos. One of the Canaanite youthful divine twins (Arsus or Monimos) is compared to Hermes while his brother (Azizos) is compared to Ares and the Morning Star (as the Horse Twins are) in Dacian inscriptions and Roman sources (Emperor Julian citing Iamblichus), as we will discuss later on. This implies that the identification of a comparable though non-Indo-European divine twin with "Hermes" was an idea current in the region of the Mediterranean during ancient times.

---

16 "I too linger a lot about how Odysseus is developing in many ways into a different kind of character than what we saw in the *Iliad*. I'm not sure I'm ready to say that he is simply different, but certainly the *Odyssey*, and the preoccupations of the *Odyssey*, about the need to make it back safely to Ithaca, that really does affect how we think about this character. It's destabilizing [...] In some cases I think [his epithets] really are [different in *Odyssey* compared to in *Iliad*]. The *Iliad* certainly doesn't emphasize that Odysseus has an epic reputation of traveling many places and suffering a lot. There are some cases, so we can't say that the *Iliad* is completely innocent of the kind of Odysseus that is now developing, but certainly you're so right [...] that there is definitely a difference, we're now seeing more clearly the many-sidedness of Odysseus" (Gregory Nagy, CHS Dialogues, "What's Special About Odysseus," 1:30-3:41). https://www.youtube.com/watch?v=YtTTUB2b1nA. Accessed May 2021.

Another explanation of Odysseus' Hermetic heritage, which incorporates the Horse Twin possibility, is also available: as we will see further on, the Welsh figure Pwyll is also likely the same as Hermes and the Vedic Gandharva, and his son Pryderi is the primary Welsh Horse Twin. In this Welsh case, we would have the Gandharvic god as the recent ancestor of the Horse Twin, one god of cunning giving rise to another, though they remain distinct. As we have seen such a close connection between the Welsh tradition and the *Iliad* tradition, the possibility that Odysseus is a Horse Twin hero descended from a Gandharvic god should not be excluded, and the close twinlike linking in action of Diomedes and Odysseus should be remembered.

The Horse Twins: (Odysseus and Diomedes, Nasatya and Dasra/Nakula and Sahadeva, Aengus, Mabon/Pryderi)

- Skilled warriors and generals

- Cunning strategists, wise counselors

- One or both of them is known for his youth

- Vie to become like the immortal gods

- Birds fly over the head of one of them

- Horse associations, owners and breakers of horses

- One (or both) of them becomes an immortal

- Associated with sea voyages

- Rescuers

- Usually act together

- Associated with transformation into swans or similar birds

Paris

Paris – Surya (The Sun)

It may be surprising to some, but as we have mentioned, the incarnation of the Sun God Surya in the *Mahabharata,* that is Karna, fights on the side of the Kauravas, the force opposing that of the protagonist Pandavas. Karna clearly incarnates the Sun god mythos of his father, Surya, even having his chariot wheel get stuck in the mud during his fight with the incarnation of the Thunderer, Arjuna, while in the *Rig Veda* (1.175.4; 4.30.4; 5.29.10) Surya himself is disabled by Indra when Indra detaches the Sun god's chariot wheel. Karna's face shines with the solar light of the earrings and breastplate given to him by his Sun God father. That this Sun God incarnation, Karna, fights on the side of the opposition may represent the idea of a conflict of the gods of the potentially destructive or impersonal natural forces (Sun, Sky, Destiny, etc), against the gods of "society," those gods who represented the three social classes. For instance, Vayu and Indra, though gods of the fearsome and destructive natural forces of wind and storm, were able to be brought into the social structure as representatives of the ideal warrior nobles, Indra later as the ideal king as well. The Sun God, however, was always seen very ambivalently and this may have put him in an uneasy and antagonistic relationship with ordered society.

Mircea Eliade explains the esoteric layer of the ambivalence and antagonism of the Sun God in his *Patterns in Comparative Mythology*. He states:

> though immortal, the sun descends nightly to the kingdom of the dead; it can, therefore, take men with it and, by setting, put them to death; but it can also, on the other hand, guide souls through the lower regions and bring them back next day with its light. That is its twofold function-as psychopomp to 'murder' and as hierophant to initiate [...] The sun draws things, it 'sucks in' the souls of the living with as much ease as it guides the souls of the dead to whom it acts as psychopomp through the western 'gate of the sun' [...] Clearly, the fate of all the souls who plunge into the setting sun is not the same; not all gain what we may call 'salvation'. That is the point at which the redemptive power of initiation enters, and the part played by the various secret societies in choosing the elect and separating them from the amorphous mass of common men (the separation expressed in the mystique of sovereignty and the 'children of the sun'). (Eliade, 145-146)

Hence, as we find with Karna, Surya's incarnation, and as with Paris, the Sun God in the epics we have analyzed is always conceived of as at best a long lost half-brother of the other gods, his true parentage only revealed later after he has been raised separate from them. Karna is conceived by Kunti (who later becomes mother of the Pandavas) with the Sun God Surya. She is unmarried at the time, so she puts Karna in a basket and sends him down the Ganges river. The baby ends up being adopted by a certain couple, who themselves are of a relatively lower social status, from the charioteer and poet class, and who work for the Kaurava king Dhritarashtra. The fact that Karna is believed to be of low birth is an impediment and thorn to him throughout life. It is later revealed to the Pandavas that he is their half-brother. Paris, repeating much of this story very closely, is conceived by Hecuba, the queen of Troy; however, she has a dream that she will give birth to a flaming torch, and, it being prophesied that the child would lead to Troy's destruction, the king instructs their herdsman to kill him. In the end, however, the herdsman takes and ends up raising Paris away in the countryside. Hence, just like Karna, Paris, the long lost brother, is believed to be of low birth until he returns to court and is finally recognized as the forgotten prince. This theme of the Sun God being the forgotten half-brother of the gods seems to be reflect an idea of the sun originating from out of darkness each day, forgotten during the night until he returns to his rightful place on high and his regality is recognized. Paris, as has been thoroughly discussed in a previous part, also has a direct parallel in the Welsh solar figure Gronw Pebr "The Radiant," who commits adultery with Blodeuwedd and confronts Lleu, in the same way that Paris duels Menelaus after stealing his wife.

The Sun God heroes are always depicted as morally ambivalent, yet highly noble nonetheless. This is due to the way the Indo-European peoples viewed the Sun, as often inhospitable, even abusive, potentially exceedingly destructive, a psychopomp who draws souls down to their fates and then to the land of the dead, and yet as beautiful, life giving, a symbol of intellect and sovereignty, and associated with the elitist esoteric pursuit of immortality. Mircea Eliade explains it thus: "The sun's ambivalence is shown also in its behavior towards men. It is, on the one hand, man's true progenitor [...] On the other hand, the sun is sometimes identified with death, for he devours his children as well as generating them" (Eliade, *Patterns in Comparative Religion*). The sun, so powerful and uncompromising, a god even of devouring Time itself, seems to have been found difficult to bring into the social order and to count on as a benefactor of society. He has a different and necessary role in the cosmic structure. Karna distinguishes himself for his noble character, is an exemplary friend, generous in charity, hard working, piously devoted to the Sun god Surya, compassionate to those in need, and is known for his "glowing" beauty and loyal friendship, yet his hot temper leads him to insult Draupadi and to order that she be assaulted. He is oversensitive and arrogant. He is a skilled speaker, but he fights for the adharmic side of the war, abetting the destructive actions of Duryodhana. He is at times cruel and abusive, as he is toward Draupadi. Paris, in his turn, is noted for his truthfulness and his fairness (which leads to his being chosen to judge the beauty contest of the goddesses), and he is recognized for his astonishing beauty and intelligence. Yet he commits the theft of the foreign queen which starts the war, and in Homer's account he displays significant cowardice[17] (which Homer may

---

17 "But Hector saw him, and chid him with words of shame:"'Evil Paris, most fair to look upon, thou that art mad after women, thou beguiler, [40] would that thou hadst ne'er been

34

have emphasized more than the most archaic tradition had), and is considered as lacking in certain kinds of warrior skill (this aspect also does not appear in the other traditions where the sun hero is generally a highly skilled warrior).

These Homeric exaggerations could come from the fact that Paris is said only to fight well with ranged weapons, specifically bow and arrow. This was a trait which was vulnerable to being targeted for accusations of cowardice in Homeric and later times, if other factors made the questionable virtue of a given archer present to mind, as in Paris' case. Combined with Paris' other dubious actions, the fact that he did not engage in hand to hand combat to the same degree as other heroes did him no favors in terms of his heroic depiction in the world of Homer's epic. This view of ranged weapons was, however, a socially contingent issue and unlikely to have been more than a very recent development, as archaic heroes such as Heracles were lauded for their bow-centric prowess with no hint of skepticism toward the use of such a weapon[18]. This mode of

---

born and hadst died unwed. Aye, of that were I fain, and it had been better far than that thou shouldest thus be a reproach, and that men should look upon thee in scorn. Verily, methinks, will the long-haired Achaeans laugh aloud, deeming that a prince is our champion because a comely [45] form is his, while there is no strength in his heart nor any valour (III.37-45)[…]Wilt thou indeed not abide Menelaus, dear to Ares? Thou wouldest learn what manner of warrior he is whose lovely wife thou hast. Then will thy lyre help thee not, neither the gifts of Aphrodite, [55] thy locks and thy comeliness, when thou shalt lie low in the dust. Nay, verily, the Trojans are utter cowards: else wouldest thou ere this have donned a coat of stone by reason of all the evil thou hast wrought.' And to him did godlike Alexander [Paris] make answer, saying: 'Hector, seeing that thou dost chide me duly, and not beyond what is due (Iliad, III.51-59). When Menelaus arrives at the subsequent duel Paris shrinks back in the ranks, a clear act of cowardice. After Aphrodite has to save Paris from the duel, Helen declares "I'll never go back again. It would be wrong, disgraceful to share that coward's bed once more" (III.474-475).

Shot by Paris' arrow, Diomedes impugns him: "'Bowman, reviler, proud of thy curling locks, thou ogler of girls! O that thou wouldst make trial of me man to man in armour, then would thy bow and thy swift-falling arrows help thee not; whereas now having but grazed the flat of my foot thou boastest vainly. I reck not thereof, any more than if a woman had struck me or a witless child, [390] for blunt is the dart of one that is a weakling and a man of naught. Verily in other wise when sped by my hand, even though it do but touch, does the spear prove its edge, and forthwith layeth low its man; torn then with wailing are the two cheeks of his wife, and his children fatherless, while he, reddening the earth with his blood, [395] rotteth away, more birds than women around him" (XI.385-395).

18 Although even Heracles is targeted by a villainous quip criticizing his supposedly unmanly use of the bow, "that coward's weapon," in the later Euripides' *Herakles* 157-164. A rejoinder to the quip counters the claim of cowardice, calling the bow "trusty," and demonstrating that the status of the bow was not settled but did leave one open to haranguing if it was one's sole focus in battle. Much later, Pausanias would comment with regard to the bow that "the only Greeks whose custom it is to use that weapon are the Cretans" (Pausanias, *Description of Greece*, 1.23.4).

fighting is of course the fitting and natural metaphor for the action of the Sun, who shoots his rays from afar, and bow and arrow are common solar symbols. Furthermore, Paris insults the goddesses Hera and Athena at the contest of beauty, similar to Karna's insulting of Draupadi.

We can see most of this archetype reflected in the Irish god Bres the Beautiful as well. Just as Karna and Paris, a disowned half-Kaurava and disowned Trojan by birth, "go back and forth" in their allegiances, at first allied with and then breaking their allegiance to the gods of society, so Bres, a half-Fomorian half-Tuatha De Danann by birth, originally fights on the side of the Tuatha De Danann against the Fir Bolg. He then takes over the kingship from Nuada temporarily, but proves to be the definition of inhospitable. Under Bres' rule, the gods' "knives were never greased and their breaths never smelled of ale" (*Cath Maige Tuired*), and they are subjected to hard labor under his command (perhaps as we all must labor under the hot sun). He is, however, known as "the Beautiful," "ornament of the host," "with a visage never woeful," "flower of the Tuatha De," and "hot of valour," yet he sparks the war with the Tuatha De Danann due to his own inhospitality, resentment and temper. As Paris becomes the lover and husband of Helen, possibly an incarnation of the Dawn Goddess as we will see, Bres becomes the husband of Brigid, the well-recognized Irish Dawn Goddess. Understanding Bres as a Sun God clarifies why an ambivalent, sometimes quite negatively depicted figure like Bres would be married to the central Irish goddess of all benevolent aspects. Nor would Bres' association with a knowledge of agriculture be amiss for a Sun God, Eliade emphasizing the common role of Sun gods in the agricultural sphere (Eliade, 127). Bres' beauty and noble battle exploits early on contrast with his inhospitable and even adharmic action later on, making him the most ambivalent of the gods. It must be remembered that Karna and Duryodhana in the *Mahabharata* also fight on the same side as the Pandavas before the Kurukshetra war begins, and that Paris was allied to Menelaus before he ignited hostilities, both figures following the same pattern of alliance and betrayal that Bres does. During Bres' inhospitable rule (this being the sun at its height in the noonday sky or the summer at its peak) a satirist makes a satire upon him, the first satire in Ireland, and it causes the sun king to be blighted from then on. It is said that "naught but decay was on him from that hour," and indeed the sun at its peak falls in the sky, as its power also decays after the summer solstice as the days progress toward the dark half of the year. Thus Bres' reign is likely analogized to the summer months, situated between the reign of Nuada, ruling during some part of the first half of the year, and the reign of Lugh, the beginning of which is signified by the time of Lughnasadh around August 1st and leading into the period of autumnal harvest.

Paris, like both Karna and Bres, is one of the two central warriors of the antagonist side of the war. There are generally two central warriors of this oppositional side, between whom a couple of mythoi may combine in different ways. These warriors are Greek Paris and Hector, Indian Karna and Duryodhana, Irish Bres and Balor, Balor being an outlier here. One of these two is always the Sun God, the other is generally the Demon of the Dark Age, but in the case of Balor, it should be noted, he seems to be closer to the incarnation of one of the Rudras (as we will elaborate further along), paralleling the Indian Kaurava called Ashwatthama. As Karna insults Draupadi and abets Duryodhana's taking of Draupadi and the kingdom, helping to spark the war, so Paris steals Helen (the slight difference here will be explained in the next part). This leads the gods of society to seek him out for vengeance in both cases. All three cases of the Sun God hero mentioned die in the war or immediately after. Paris dies from a poisoned arrow while Bres is made to drink poisonous red liquid or sewage (perhaps unrelated, the similarly antagonistic Norse Loki for his part is tortured using venom). We consider that this motif of death by poison, in the cases of the Sun God heroes, could be somehow connected to an allegory for the colorful sunset. The sun was seen to die each day, and thus its death, surrounded by strange reddish hues, could have been seen as a the ingestion of a red poison. Karna too is killed by an arrow, which, though not said to be poisoned, is no ordinary arrow but is said to be a special "anjalika" arrow, "extremely difficult to withstand," "capable of destroying the body," and "capable of penetrating the inner organs," which blazes like the sun and like fire and is compared to Indra's *vajra* weapon (*Mahabharata*, *Karna Parva,* 91).

The Sun God may have gotten a fairly negative treatment in most of the epics and myths due to his innate and necessary antagonism (Karna being perhaps the most balanced version) and, with Paris and Bres, who have taken on a more direct and active role in inciting the war, may even have begun to bleed together with the Demon of the Dark Age figure, perhaps becoming symbolically united with or corrupted by him in some texts. However, this negative treatment masks an esoteric meaning which we will expand on in the conclusion: as Eliade explains, the Sun God was after all the fearsome Lord of devouring Time and even of Death (Eliade, 146), governing and harshly imposing our movement toward death within the realm of Samsara, marking the hours by his burning rays. His movement across the sky indicates with painful precision the steady march toward death. But precisely because of this he was seen as the guardian of the gateway to the esoteric truths lying outside the realm of Time (these, according to Eliade, were often pursued by the royalty or elite priesthood), if one only knew how to overcome him, to thus esoterically unite with him, and then to continue on the path he guarded (Eliade, 135-146).

Without question, some elements of the Sun God type we have just examined consistently overlap other related figures. Paris, for example, is prophesied upon his birth to one day bring destruction to Troy. Meanwhile, it is Duryodhana rather than

37

Karna who is prophesied upon his birth to one day bring destruction to the world. Nonetheless, it is Paris and Karna who are sent away as infants to be raised by families of lower-rank, only to return when grown to be recognized as a prince once more. This "returned prince" motif once again connects to their solar role: it is the sun that is the prince, forgotten in the night, who returns each morning to rule on high and his royalty is recognized once more. For this reason this motif must attach to the solar hero, whereas between the *Iliad* and *Mahabharata*, the precise agent of prophesied destruction shows a certain amount of variability, and indeed more negative traits have been attached to the sun hero in the Greek case.

***

An important mythic parallel between Karna and Bres should put their identification, which we have here theorized, beyond doubt, and thus indirectly support their identification with Paris. This parallel regards the very close similarity of the accounts of their conceptions, similarities which extend, interestingly, to the use of the unadorned word for "intercourse" or "copulation" at the same point in each case. I will reproduce each account in full so the full effect of the comparison can be appreciated.

First is the conception of the Indian hero Karna, found in the *Srimad-Devi Bhagavatam,* Book 2, Chapter 6. The tale is found also in the *Mahabharata* (Vana Parva, Pativrata-mahatmya Parva, CCCIV), but in that version it is said only that Surya "enters" and touches Kunti on the navel, rather than having intercourse with her. This seems to be a clear euphemism of the brash plainspeak of the likely more archaic form of the tale for a more sensitive audience. Kunti is said in some versions to be the incarnation of Siddhi, a name connected to Parvati, Devi, and Shakti. However, this appears to be a late assimilation of an earlier goddess to the primary goddesses of the time in which the text was written down. Kunti's original name Pṛthā is the feminine form of *pṛtha* "flat," closely related to *pṛthvī,* which is the name of the archaic Mother Earth Goddess (Pṛthvī), suggesting that Kunti may originally have been an earth goddess heroine who was later assimilated to Devi-Parvati, who indeed absorbed many earlier goddess conceptions.

"The Sun, then, assuming an excellent human form, came down from the Heavens and appeared before Kunti in the same room. Seeing the Deva Sun, Kunti became greatly surprised and began to shudder and instantly became endowed with the inherent natural quality of passion (had menstruation). The beautiful-eyed Kunti, with folded palm;

spoke to Sûrya Deva [the Sun God] standing before :— 'I am highly pleased to-day seeing Thy form; now go back to Thy sphere.'

Sûrya Deva said :— 'O Kunti! What for you called me, by virtue of the Mantra? Calling me, why do you not worship me, standing before you? O beautiful blue one! Seeing you, I have become passionate; so come to me. By means of the mantra, you have made me your subservient so take me for intercourse.' Hearing this, Kunti said :— 'O Witness of all! O knower of Dharma! You know that I am a virgin girl. O Suvrata! I bow down to you; I am a family daughter; so do not speak ill to me.' Sûrya then said :— 'If I go away in vain, I will be an object of great shame, and, no doubt, will be laughed amongst the gods; So, O Kunti! If you do not satisfy me, I will immediately curse you and the Brâhmin who has given you this mantra. O Beautiful one! If you satisfy me, your virginity will remain; no body will come to know and there will be born a son to you, exactly like me.' Thus saying Sûrya Deva enjoyed the bashful Kunti, with her mind attracted towards him; He granted her the desired boons and went away. The beautiful Kunti became pregnant and began to remain in a house, under great secrecy. Only the dear nurse knew that; her mother or any other person was quite unaware of the fact. In time, a very beautiful son like the second Sun and Kârtikeya, decked with a lovely Kavacha coat of mail and two ear-rings, was born there."

The following is the conception of the Irish god Bres, found in the *Cath Maige Tuiredh*. Eriu is the embodiment of the land of Ireland, as her name tells us. The deeper etymology of the name appears to be "abundant," a description of the fundamental quality of the fertile and sustenance-giving earth.

"Now the conception of Bres came about in this way.

One day one of their women, Ériu the daughter of Delbáeth, was looking at the sea and the land from the house of Máeth Scéni; and she saw the sea as perfectly calm as if it were a level board. After that, while she was there, she saw something: a vessel of silver appeared to her on the sea. Its size seemed great to her, but its shape did not appear clearly to her; and the current of the sea carried it to the land.

Then she saw that it was a man of fairest appearance. He had golden-yellow hair down to his shoulders, and a cloak with bands of gold thread around it. His shirt had embroidery of gold thread. On his breast was a brooch of gold with the lustre of a precious stone in it. Two shining silver spears and in them two smooth riveted shafts of bronze. Five circlets of gold around his neck. A gold-hilted sword with inlayings of silver and studs of gold.

The man said to her, 'Shall I have an hour of lovemaking with you?' 'I certainly have not made a tryst with you,' she said. 'Come without the trysting!' said he.

Then they stretched themselves out together. The woman wept when the man got up again. 'Why are you crying?' he asked. 'I have two things that I should lament,' said the woman, 'separating from you, however we have met. The young men of the Túatha Dé Danann have been entreating me in vain—and you possess me as you do.'

'Your anxiety about those two things will be removed,' he said. He drew his gold ring from his middle finger and put it into her hand, and told her that she should not part with it, either by sale or by gift, except to someone whose finger it would fit.

'Another matter troubles me,' said the woman, 'that I do not know who has come to me.'

'You will not remain ignorant of that,' he said. 'Elatha mac Delbaith, king of the Fomoire, has come to you. You will bear a son as a result of our meeting, and let no name be given to him but Eochu Bres (that is, Eochu the Beautiful), because every beautiful thing that is seen in Ireland—both plain and fortress, ale and candle, woman and man and horse—will be judged in relation to that boy, so that people will then say of it, 'It is a Bres.''

Then the man went back again, and the woman returned to her home, and the famous conception was given to her.

Then she gave birth to the boy, and the name Eochu Bres was given to him as Elatha had said. A week after the woman's lying-in was completed, the boy had two weeks' growth; and he maintained that increase for seven years, until he had reached the growth of fourteen years."

Later in the same text, when Bres has grown:

"Then he went to his mother and asked her where his family was. 'I am certain about that,' she said, and went onto the hill from which she had seen the silver vessel in the sea. She then went onto the shore. His mother gave him the ring which had been left with her, and he put it around his middle finger, and it fitted him. She had not given it up for anyone, either by sale or gift. Until that day, there was none of them whom it would fit."

If it is not patently obvious to the reader just how similar these two passages are, we will enumerate the ways in which they match each other almost line for line, though the order of the events is in a couple places switched and the Irish passage consistently uses oblique allusions where the Indian passage states what it means directly.

1. **The Sun god appears suddenly to the woman in her room.** In the Indian case this is explicitly stated. In the Irish case, the fact that this is the Sun god is only alluded to by the description of his gold circlets, clothes, hair, and jewelry. Despite this allusiveness, Elatha's identity as a sun god has long been guessed, as the scholar T.F. O'Rahilly did in 1946 (On the Origin of the Names Erainn and Eriu, Eriu Vol. 14, p. 26), and it can not be said to be hidden. The correspondence to the Indian myth merely confirms what has long been the leading thought.

2. The woman is possibly an earth goddess. As aforementioned, Kunti's original name Pṛthā is the feminine form of *pṛtha,* closely related to Pṛthvī, goddess of Earth. Eriu, as indicated by her name, is the embodiment of the land of Ireland. Each have been closely related to the concept of sovereignty as well (sovereignty goddesses), which may have helped Kunti's assimilation to Parvati.

3. **The woman is a virgin.** This is stated outright in the Indian case. In the Irish passage, Ériu comments that "the young men of the Túatha Dé Danann have been entreating me in vain," implying that she had been a virgin as well.

4. **She denies him with her first words.** The first thing Kunti says is: "I am highly pleased to-day seeing Thy form; now go back to Thy sphere." The first thing Ériu says is: "I certainly have not made a tryst with you."

5. **He is pushy, and asks specifically for "intercourse" or "copulation."** Surya says, "you have made me your subservient so take me for intercourse." In Elizabeth Gray's translation, Elatha says, "Shall I have an hour of lovemaking with you?" However, this translation and others have euphemized the original language here, which has generally been seen as too brash in its phrasing, in which the word for "copulation" is used at this point just as the word for "intercourse" is used in the Indian case. Morgan Daimler, in a literalist translation, translates it as: "Shall I have an hour of copulation with you?" Thus the similarities of the two texts occur right down to the use of approximately the same explicit terminology at a key moment.

6. **They lie together.**

7. **The woman expresses anxiety over losing her virginity.** Just before they lie together, Kunti says, "O Witness of all! O knower of Dharma! You know that I am a virgin girl. O Suvrata! I bow down to you; I am a family daughter; so do not

speak ill to me." Just after they lie together, Ériu says that one of the things she laments is that "The young men of the Túatha Dé Danann have been entreating me in vain—and you possess me as you do." That is, she is anxious about having given up her virginity.

8.   **He removes her anxiety about this.** Surya says, "If you satisfy me, your virginity will remain." Elatha says, "Your anxiety about those two things will be removed," and gives her a gold ring. Because there is no clear indication of how the gift of the ring will alleviate her anxiety over her lost virginity, the possibility must be considered that Elatha may also restore Ériu's virginity along with this gift, and that this fact is again only being obliquely alluded to, as other details have been. However, it must be said that the restoring of virginity seems like a trope more common in Indian myth than in Irish. Yet, due to all of the other alignment between these parallel passages we must attempt to imagine that these details regarding the alleviation of the virginity-anxiety may have in some way had a unified meaning in some kind of a shared origin.

9.   **The father foretells that a son will be born. A son is born who is exactly like his father.** This is stated explicitly in the Indian case: "there will be born a son to you, exactly like me." The Irish case similarly has: "You will bear a son as a result of our meeting." However, in the Irish case, the fact that the son is just like his father is only alluded to, but it is not exactly hidden either. The ring that Elatha gives to Ériu he takes off of his own finger. He then tells Ériu to give this ring only to the man whom it will fit. The only man whom the ring fits ends up being Elatha's own son, Bres, and it would fit no other. With the context of the Indian version, it becomes clear that this is an illustration, as opposed to an outright statement, of the same fact that we find in the Indian case: that the son is identical to the father. The father's ring fits only his son because his son is just like his father. Their fingers, as every other part, are perfect doubles. Their fingers are being used as synechdoches in this way, one part standing in for the whole. The full meaning of this Irish passage can indeed only be grasped by its comparison with the Indian case: it is not telling us that Bres has only a family resemblance to his father – it is telling us that Bres is his father's double. And as his father Elatha is the golden-haired god wearing the golden circlets and clothing, a blatant solar figure, so Bres is also the Sun God, born again from his Sun God father.

10.   **The son is specifically said to be very beautiful upon his birth.** "In time, a very beautiful son" is born, says the Indian text. So beautiful is Bres said to be upon his birth that he is named "Eochu Bres (that is, Eochu the Beautiful), because every beautiful thing that is seen in Ireland…will be judged in relation to that boy, so that people will then say of it, 'It is a Bres.'"

11.   **A type of ring jewelry is given by the father to the son which marks him as son and double of the Sun god.** Surya's son, Karna, is born wearing earrings that make his face shine, along with a breastplate. It is implied that these come from his Sun God parentage, inborn gifts from his father that manifest his solar quality and show him as the son of the Sun. Elatha gives Ériu the ring upon Bres' conception that Ériu later gives to Bres, which itself is a symbol of Bres' identity with his father the Sun. Thus although Bres receives the ring later, while Karna has the earrings at birth, they carry the same meaning and provenance.

12.   **The father leaves the mother abruptly immediately after the conception, and the son does not know his true father until an event connected to the Great War.** Karna does not find out his true parentage until well into the Kurukshetra War, while Bres finds out who his father is after the First Battle of Maige Tuireadh and right before he sparks the Second Battle of Maige Tuireadh, thus midway through the double war of the Irish myth.

13.   **From one of the two of this parent couple springs many of the other main gods or god-incarnations.** That is, this is an important divine "ancestor" pairing. In the Indian version, Kunti becomes mother of Karna, incarnation of Surya, but then also becomes the mother of the incarnations of Mitra, Vayu, Indra, Nasatya and Dasra — the Pandavas, or the incarnations of the gods of society. In the Irish case it is instead the *male* in this pairing from whom spring many of the main gods: Bres, the Dagda (from whom many more deities spring), Ogma (who likewise engenders key deities), Elloth/Lir (father of Manannan), as well as Delbaeth and Fiacha. Why the male deity in one branch and the female in the other is made the more important ancestor figure within this paring could be investigated further on both theological and anthropological grounds and could come from different views of patrilineal and matrilineal descent.

14.   While Karna is explicitly a manifestation of the Sun deity, Bres is called "Eochaidh," or "Horseman," a not uncommon title for various chiefs, but also fitting for a solar figure, the horse being a common solar symbol. He also is said to grow, from birth, at twice the normal rate, another solar trope possibly mirroring the sun rising rapidly in the sky.

It should be more than evident that these two passages are from the same original myth, connected in both cases to a pair of father and son Sun Gods. The fact that Bres and Elatha are *both* Sun gods, rather than merely one or the other being such, is extremely surprising and likely never could have been predicted or perhaps even believed without comparative analysis making the conclusion undeniable. The motif of a higher god incarnating into his spiritual son repeats numerous times in the *Mahabharata,* but is never otherwise seen in the Irish mythic cycle, indicating just how important this specific god-reincarnation myth must have been. The Sun god, apparently, is the god above perhaps all others who is reborn into a son who is his double, and does so not only on the legendary plane, incarnating into a mortal son such as Karna, but on the divine mythic plane as well, seemingly engendering a son as much a god as himself in the Irish Bres.

The uncanny closeness of these two passages, separated by nearly four millennia (considering when each passage was committed to writing) and yet more similar to each other than some myth variants of a single tale within a single tradition are, represents a shining pearl in the comparative mythology treasure trove, and gives to us the gift of a confident identification of the father and son Irish Sun gods. The fact that these passages can have been preserved so closely for so long is a minor miracle and should inspire any reader with a new respect for the conservative quality of the Irish and Indian traditions in general and the quality of the *Cath Maige Tuired* in particular. This comparison also confirms much of what we have implied about the Fomorians: they are not to be seen as pure evil beings – they include the Sun gods, and could include other sometimes benevolent, if potentially asocial and antagonistic divinities as well, if we could successfully excavate them and see them for who they are. The king allied to the Fomorians, Indech, whose name means "interweaving" or "weaver," reminds us of the fact that the king of the Kauravas, Dhritarashtra, is considered by Dumezil to incarnate the god of apportioned destiny, Bhaga. Thus the possibility that this Indech the Interweaver could likewise be a god of destiny should be an obvious avenue for future investigation.

The comparison of these passages highlights a sometimes distressing issue in the scholarship of *Cath Maige Tuired* and other Irish texts. A trend toward the over-application of historicism has developed, in the name of judiciousness, in the study of the Irish mythological and other medieval texts. John Carey, one of the most respected scholars in Irish studies today, analyzes the *Cath Maige Tuired* in terms of the supposed political struggles of the tale's purported time of composition. This is a valid enterprise in itself, yet when it begins to overstep what can be claimed with actual certainty it can become destructive and can even begin to rob from the people their true national epic. Carey posits, among other things, that the meeting of Elatha and Ériu to conceive Bres is merely a generic liaison story-type, one among many, and has been specifically crafted in this case to villainize the English foreigners who would try to take the sovereignty of Ireland, represented here by the foreign Elatha marrying Ériu, personification of Ireland.

This would be a reasonable, though, given what we see in comparison, not entirely necessary hypothesis to put forward, if it was merely attempting to add a political layer to the mythic layer of meaning. Myth is commonly used in this way by those who mold it, and it is difficult to prove one way or another if such a meaning was part of the intent of the text's composer in this case. But when this purely hypothetical political lens, employed by a respected scholar, is imposed upon and fully overshadows genuine mythic content, which must have been there in nearly the same form for millennia, and which we can see for ourselves, claiming it, mistakenly, to be a recent fabrication, it can obscure this mythic tradition and negatively impact how its legitimacy is assessed. This damage is only sometimes reparable, as the deeper, clarifying truth is not always recoverable. We believe the intentions of such scholars are generally pure and the historical and political readings of myths are often of great use. In this case, however, it is only by a miracle that the parallel Indian text was preserved in order to vindicate the authenticity of the mythic content of the Irish text.

Furthermore, Carey posits that Bres' depiction as harsh and villainous is a product of political tensions of the time. He bases this claim in part on a competing textual tradition that describes Bres nobly, associating him primarily with Brigid and the gods of skill. He concludes that the sovereign order of kings found in *Cath Maige Tuired*, starting with Nuada who is succeeded by the cruel Bres, is a political fabrication of the time that cannot have had deep roots, saying: "There is accordingly a significant body of evidence indicating that the picture of Bres painted in the *CMT* is isolated and anomalous for the early period. In other sources Bres appears not as a matrilineal interloper but as a legitimate member of the Tuatha De, closely associated with the *dramatis personae* of poetic lore: Brigit, Ogmae, 'the three gods of skill' and presumably Elatha. His role in *CMT* is to be understood as a radical adaptation of his original character." Knowing what we do about the Sun God type, however, this type being the most ambivalent of all, and knowing that Bres is such a Sun God, we can see plainly now what Carey had no context to see: the Sun God Bres is *both* things. He is noble and venerated and associated with the good deities of the arts, he is a god of creation, agriculture, and his father and double is a divine ancestor figure, but he is also harsh and cruel in turn, specifically in relation to his noonday or drought sun aspect, or in relation to his role as imposer of doom via Time and as devourer of souls that he draws toward him as he descends to the underworld (based on the Vedic conception), and his cognates are often aligned with the forces who oppose the gods of society in the various traditions we have analyzed.

The vital contribution of Carey's essay lies in his emphasis on this more positive side of Bres that did exist in the Irish tradition. Bres was not some narrow villain[19]. Epithets

---

19 Gael Hily supports Carey's general supposition regarding Bres being not always a
  negative figure, with a similar conclusion arguing for two separate traditions [translated]:
  "This rather gloomy portrait of Bres does not agree with other accounts known of him.
  Indeed, he is generally presented as a full member of the Túatha Dé Danann and his
  actions are positive, as this passage from Cóir anmann shows:

that belong to him in the poem *Carn Hui Neit* in the *Dindshenchas* are "kindly friend,"
"with a visage never woeful," "gifted with excellences," "flower of the Tuatha De
Danann," "ornament of the host" (*host* considered as an army, while Karna is "the
ornament of battle" in Karna Parva, 72), "noble and fortunate," "hot of valour" and
"gifted with love spells." We can read for ourselves in these epithets how positive of a
figure Bres was understood to be despite his cruelty. His association with friendship
reminds us of Karna, perhaps the most loyal friend of the Indian epic in his devotion to
Duryodhana, while "gifted with love spells" reminds us of the Sun god's usual role as
lover of the Dawn goddess, most explicitly depicted in the case of the hero Paris who
apparently has a spell-like power to steal away Helen. The sun is indeed *the* object
whose visage is never woeful, and which is the ornament and flower of the host above
all others. Thus Carey's emphasis on this other, positive side of Bres is exceedingly
important in rehabilitating him from a narrow villain to a multidimensional deity, but we
should not go too far and erase his destructive side or too quickly call his description in
CMT a radical departure or fabrication, even if we can agree on the word "adaptation."
This destructive side may indeed have been played up in a political context, and we
concede this much at least as a possibility to Carey – we have already pointed out that
some roles taken by the Demon of the Dark age in the Indian version are taken by Bres
in the Irish, for instance his directly sparking the Great War due to his greed, though also
by the Sun hero Paris in the *Iliad* – but from our analysis some degree of harshness, as
well as his alignment with the "opposition" forces, seems perfectly mythically legitimate
and correct.

Carey persists in this line, further stating that, "the king list was composed by splicing
together the pedigree of the Ua Neill [...] and that of the Eoganachta; the juxtaposition
of Nuada Finn Fail and Bres Ri is therefore due simply to their positions in their
respective pedigrees," concluding that "The idea of a Nuadu-Bres opposition is the
product of developments in Irish historiography, and can scarcely be dated more than a
century earlier than the composition of *CMT*" (Carey, 57-58). We will see, in our

---

Bres rígh 'king', that is, he was a king by virtue of his royal qualities. His deed, honor
and reign were royal, and he routed the Formorians in many battles, expelling them
from Ireland.
(Bres rígh .i. Ba rígh ar ríghdacht é .i. Roba ríghda a ghnim a enech a fhlathius, dobhris
sé ilchatha for Fomhóire aga ndichur a hÉiriu.)
Here, Bres therefore fights the Fomoire, while in the *Cath Maige Tuired*, he reigns in their
name. The only point in common between the two Breses remains the function of
sovereign. This discrepancy can be explained by the existence in Irish traditions of two
Breses, one benevolent and the other malicious, and the archetype of the bad king would
have been transferred to his person. In relation to our research, the essential point to
remember is that the Bres of *Cath Maige Tuired* was a bad king" (Hily, *Le Dieu Celtique
Lugus*, 132).

chapter "Ullr and Bres," that the solar archer Ullr, who also prominently is known for his ring, rings even being offered to him at his shrines, under the name "Ollerus" is in the very same position as Bres in the succession of kings recorded in Saxo Grammaticus, being the second king who reigns in an interstitial period while the first king, Oðinn, like Nuada, is seen to be unfit to rule, and this Ollerus rules up until that first king returns to rule again, as Nuada returns to take over from Bres. Thus Carey's claim of fabrication again seems at least potentially contradicted by an understanding of the deeper comparative myth structure. The comparison of this sequence of kings may not be considered definitive on its own, but along with all else we have seen it must give pause. In general, all of this should make historicist scholars much more cautious when proclaiming these texts as recent fabrications in one fashion or another and basing such proclamations off of only a small selection of preserved historical data that rarely tells the full story. Indeed, if we have not misunderstood him, Carey seems to at least complicate his own position on the royal succession in his later essay "Nodons in Britain and Ireland" when he discusses "the evident antiquity of tales of rivalry between Nuadu and Bres," saying "the *Dindshenchas* and the expanded version of LG's second recension mention a variant legend of Bres's deposition and Nuadu's reinstatement, the existence of which argues for an early date for whatever source it and the regnal material share with CMT" (Carey, 2009).

Having vindicated portions, at minimum, of the Irish text against the best criticisms of this venerable scholar, we must support the caution of historicists, but urge readers to remain open to mythic interpretations of such texts, and to carefully weigh the historicist hypotheses with the other evidence. Comparative mythology is one of many tests which must be applied to texts such as *Cath Maige Tuired* in order to establish or critique their mythological legitimacy. Thus Carey simply has lacked this test when he sums up in the first of his essays we have discussed, "The evidence adduced above strongly indicates that Eriu's seduction by Elatha, and the depiction of Bres as Nuadu's avaricious successor, reflect the deliberate manipulation of tradition by a ninth-century author. I have argued that the former symbolizes capitulation to foreign influence; I believe that Bres, condemned for his foreign associations and his failure to perform a king's traditional duties, is intended as another example of the erosion of native values" (Carey, 58). We do not say some degree of alteration and political influence could not have occurred, in particular Bres possibly, though not definitively, taking on more of the directly antagonistic roles (but remember that Lleu's only antagonist is the Sun god Gronw, that Paris certainly is central to sparking the war, Karna is a main antagonist as well, and that the Sun god has been interpreted by some as a main opponent of Roman Mithras), but this kind of reading must be much more carefully kept within bounds as it has destructive force. This outcome perhaps is to be expected, however; after all, it is Dr. Carey's stance that "the narratives that presumably formed part of the culture of the pre-

Christian forebears of the medieval Irish: the real 'Celtic mythology,'" despite "however many traces and reflections it may have left in the literatures of the Celtic peoples and their neighbors, is lost to us forever" (Carey, *The Mythological Cycle of Medieval Irish Literature*, ii). It will certainly be lost if it is actively obscured.

This issue of historicism indeed repeats again and again, as the confusion which often reigns in relation to Irish texts leads to understandable skepticism and a desire to use the historical lens as a scalpel. Let us take some care. In spite of rumors the patient still has a beating heart.

Thus established, the Sun gods Bres and Karna point from West and East at their (partially degenerated) Greek counterpart, Paris.

Sun God: (Paris, Surya/Karna, Elatha/Bres, Gronw Pebr)

- Morally ambivalent yet noble

- Hot tempered and inhospitable

- Unknown parentage revealed later to be a lost half-sibling of the other gods, or has some kind of split-allegiance between the two sides, allied with the gods of society at first and then turning against them

- One of the 2 main warriors for the "opposing" side of the war

- Known for his beauty and speaking skill

- May steals or insults the central female goddess or heroine, helping to start the war

- Is associated with speaking skill

- Lover of the Dawn Goddess

- Dies in the war or in the immediate aftermath

- Often an archer, though not in the Irish case where archery is more uncommon

- May die from poison

- may be son and double of the elder Sun god

Hector

Hector – Kali (The Demon of the Dark Age)

This identification will seem the strangest by far, at first, but if the reader agrees that the parallels thus far have revealed a true pattern, they will be rewarded for trusting a bit further. Duryodhana of the *Mahabharata* is considered to be the incarnation of the demon of this dark and last age, Kali, and this is confirmed in the *Mahabharata* as well as by Georges Dumezil (*Gods of the Ancient Northmen,* 56). Duryodhana conspires to trick Yudhishthira into losing his kingdom in the fateful dice game, and is the hell-bent motive force pushing the war forward. He is also the primary warrior on the Kaurava's side, wreaking havoc on the Pandava forces. His skin is said to be made of lightning and his name means "hard to kill."

It is in the structural position of Hector's character: his role as prince, heir to the Trojan throne, primary and fearsome warrior for his side, and one-on-one opponent of the Lord of Wind (Ajax), that he best fits the Demon of the Dark Age archetype. As previously mentioned, the one-on-one battles between Bhima and Duryodhana, including the final formalized bout in which Duryodhana's thigh is crushed by Bhima, form a central part of the war narrative. In the same way, the face-offs between Ajax and Hector, including the formalized bout where they prove evenly matched and exchange gifts, form a central portion of the *Iliad*. Bhima crushes Duryodhana's thigh with a mace as Ajax smashes Hector with a large rock. Hector's "Kali" character may also be seen in the sheer destruction he wreaks on the Greeks: no other warrior on either side kills as many men as Hector, and his body count may have been as high as 31,000. The Greeks describe him as a rabid "maniac," (9.238) and he strikes terror in even their bravest leaders. One of his epithets is "manslaughtering," and this is not accidental.

However, there is an undeniable shift in the Greek epic of the negative traits of the "Kali" archetype onto the more unlikeable character of Paris, who had come to be associated with cowardice and selfish, deceptive wife-stealing. In the dice game that sets the conflict off in the *Mahabharata* and which parallels the theft of Helen as well as the death of Baldr and the temporary death of Lleu (as argued in a previous section), it is Duryodhana rather than Karna the Sun God hero who tricks and defeats Yudhishthira, the Lawful Sovereign hero, and in the winnings takes Yudhishthira's wife as a slave. It is also Duryodhana about whom a terrible prophecy is pronounced at his birth, which tells that Duryodhana (like Kali) would cause the end of the universe. In contrast, it is instead Paris who in the *Iliad* is prophesied, at birth, to one day bring the destruction of Troy, as Paris takes the more active and destructive role of setting off the war via his deceptive wife-taking. As a result, we can see that the Greeks desired to make Hector a more purely noble character, the sins which in the Indian case are the Demons' shifted instead to Paris, leaving a more black and white moral dichotomy between the two. In Hector's opposition to the war he even is reminiscent of the noble figures of Bhishma or Sarpedon (discussed later), which is not at all Duryodhana's stance in the *Mahabharata*. Nick Allen also makes this point of Hector sharing some Bhishma-Sarpedon traits in his article comparing Sarpedon and Bhishma, "Dyaus and Bhisma, Zeus and Sarpedon: Towards a History of the Indo-European Sky God."

However, the other elements we have discussed confirm that Hector is still from the same root as the Duryodhana archetype, just as Sarpedon is the more proper parallel of Bhishma. The death scene of the morally questionable Duryodhana brings to the front all of the noble traits contained within this sometimes demonic figure. Having been mortally wounded by dishonorable means, struck below the belt while Krishna aided Bhima with illusions and advising, Duryodhana indicts all the Pandavas for their trickery and dishonorable actions. The gods shower flowers on him, while the Pandavas weep for their disgraceful behavior and Duryodhana's glory is vindicated. Duryodhana is said to go to heaven before the Pandavas do and is there seated in glory for his bravery, loyalty, and strong rulership. It seems fair to say that from such a germ of nobility the Greeks could have derived the noble character of Hector. As Duryodhana is killed via dishonorable means, due to the illusions and assistance of Krishna, so Athena creates illusions of Hector's brother to mislead him in the battle, and when Achilles throws his spears Athena continually returns them to him, giving Achilles an insurmountable advantage over Hector. As Bhima strikes Duryodhana dishonorably below the belt, and is derided for his dishonorable fighting, Achilles purposely dishonors and attempts to desecrate Hector's body after death (though it is protected by Apollo and Aphrodite). This leads to an outcry from the gods and ultimately paints the Greek hero in a dishonorable light, which is contrasted with Hector's nobility, just as Duryodhana's death highlights his own nobility and the dishonor of the Pandavas. These death scenes are so similar in their structural elements that they even preserve the surprising fact that the great warriors Hector and Duryodhana both are struck by fear and flee their opponent just before the final portion of the confrontation, knowing that the tides and the gods have turned against them.

The Demon of the Dark Age: (Hector, Duryodhana/the Demon Kali)

- The central warrior of the "opposition"

- Son of the king and heir to the kingdom

- Wreaks immense slaughter on the army of the gods of society

50

- Fights Lord of Wind one-on-one in an arranged match which they fight to a draw or nearly a draw

- Fights Lord of Wind several other times and is smashed by a blunt object in one of these face offs

- Dies through the trickery or divine collaboration of his opponent and is seen as noble but mistreated in death

- Flees before the end of the final fight

Helen

Helen – Ushas (The Dawn Goddess)

Helen in the *Iliad* occupies the "central young queen" position comparable to that of Draupadi in the *Mahabharata*. Draupadi's divine affiliation is not clear[20] and so we are left to speculate. However, her epithets such as "maker of garlands," "one who never grows old," and "born from sacrificial fire" (as the Dawn itself was seen as brought on by the morning sacrifice[21]), as well as the accusation that she is "unchaste" (perhaps a reflection of all of the forces that center around her and seem to compete for her each morning; perhaps as well the analogy of Dawn with Spring and its theme as a time of procreation) due to her five husbands, suggest that she could have a Spring or Dawn association. The greatest obstacle to this identification may be Draupadi's epithet *krsna*, meaning "dark." However, this could reasonably refer to the darkness out of which dawn first arises. The dawn is at first a shadowy and shrouded time. Of course, other explanations could be imagined.[22] Dumezil in his analysis connects her instead to the

---

20 That the text says she comes as an incarnation from Shachi/Indrani, the wife of Indra, suggests that, due to Draupadi's marriage to Arjuna, Indra's preeminence has over time influenced a change of the heroine's archaic identity to conform to that of Indra's canonical wife)

21 "The sacrificial fire being regularly kindled at dawn, Agni is naturally often associated with Usas in this connexion, sometimes not without a side-glance at the sun, the manifestation of Agni which appears simultaneously with the kindling of the sacrificial fire (1.124.1-11 &c.) Agni appears with or before the Dawn. Usas causes Agni to be kindled (1.113.9)" (Arthur A. Macdonell, *Vedic Mythology*,48). "By sacrificing before sunset he produces him (the sun), else he would not rise" (*Satapatha Brahmana*, 2.3.1.5, cp. *Taittiriya Samhita*, 4.7.13.3).

22 One of these explanations could be a slippage between the goddess of Night and that of Dawn as the one who proceeds the day. This seems also to have left a trace in Norse

goddesses Saraswati and Lakshmi (both connected to his "trifunctional goddess"), and it may well be that in the Indian and Greek epics a different goddess occupies the same comparable structural position, or that over time different mythic elements were superimposed on this heroine.

Draupadi is the subject of a competition for her hand in marriage, and when Arjuna is selected, all the other Pandava brothers become her husband in common, by the accidental pronunciation of their mother. This marriage competition parallels the competition for Helen's hand and the Oath of Tyndareus in which her suitors all become bound to each other, sworn to come to the aid of whoever wins her. When Yudhishthira loses the dice game he loses not only the kingdom but Draupadi as well, who is taken as a slave by Duryodhana. This causes all the Pandavas, now doubly bound by blood and marriage, to seek together to gain back what has been taken from them. When Helen is taken from Menelaus by Paris, this causes all the kingdoms linked by the Oath of Tyndareus to join the fight to bring her back. In Irish myth, the goddess consort of the Sun God Bres is the Dawn Goddess Brigid[23] (whose name derives from PIE *$b^h\acute{e}r\acute{g}^honts$, "high," cognate with an epithet of the Vedic Dawn Goddess Ushas: *Bṛhatī* (बृहती) "high") repeating the marriages of the sun heroes Paris with Helen and the adulterous union of Gronw with Blodeuwedd. In Welsh, the woman stolen from the Lawful Sovereign by the solar figure Gronw Pebr ("The Radiant") is this Blodeuwedd, who seems at first to be more of a Spring or Love goddess, entirely created out of flowers as she is. Yet the Spring is the time of love-making and was associated with Dawn goddesses (Brigid, Eostre, etc.) and their festivals, and so this "flower face" goddess Blodeuwedd may also have only been another aspect of this same goddess. As previously noted, the specific plot roles of Aphrodite and of Helen, conspirator and stolen wife, combine in the figure of Blodeuwedd, attesting to an overlap in the realms of Love, flowers, Spring, and the glow of new morning. One corroboration of this idea may be the fact that the Greek Dawn Goddess Eos' robe is said by Homer to be woven with flowers, and to have the white wings of a bird, while Blodeuwedd is created

---

myth, with the goddess Nott marrying a god of Dawn, Dellingr, and giving birth to Dagr, god of Day, with no sign of a specific Dawn goddess. Macdonell says of the relation between Night and Dawn goddesses: "[Ushas] is also sister (1.113.2-3; 10.127.3) or the elder sister (1.124.8) of Night; and the names of Dawn and Night are often conjoined as a dual compound (usasa-nakta or naktosasa)" (Macdonell, 48)

23 As for Brigid, the names of the Greek Dawn (Eos) and Hearth (Hestia) goddesses appear to go back to one shared linguistic root, implying that the Dawn goddess and Hearth goddess were originally one being (Gregory Nagy, *Greek Mythology and Poetics*, 148-149). This seems also to be reflected in Brigid, who carries both of these functions in the folk traditions that have come down to us.

entirely from flowers and in the end is changed into an owl, and Draupadi is called "maker of garlands."

Helen herself has been suggested to be the same figure as Vedic Sarama (see Muller, *Lectures on the Science of Language*, 490; Cox, *The Mythology of the Aryan Nations*, 540). This was believed by both Max Muller (*Lectures on the Science of Language*, 481, 487-491) and Sri Aurobindo (*The Secret of the Veda*, 211) to be a name of the Dawn Goddess Ushas, as one of Sarama's two epithets, "the fortunate/beloved one," was shared by Ushas. However, Muller also hypothesized that "Helene" could derive from Selene, goddess of the moon. This would make Paris the Sun God who steals the moon. However, the name of the moon goddess Selene and that of Helene could simply both derive from a word relating to general brightness, Selene seemingly coming from PIE *swelō*, "dazzling light." Otto Skutsch claims Helen's name derives from *Suelena*, also possibly from this PIE *swelō*, and which he relates to Sanskrit *svarana*, "the shining one." Another etymology (Lang, *Helen of Troy*) gives Ελενη, a torch or corposant, which could be simply related to the torch-like brilliance of the dawn.

However, beyond mere etymology, Helen's own family relations greatly strengthen the case that she is nonetheless The Dawn: her father is Zeus and her brothers are said to be the Horse Twins Kastor and Polydeukes, just as the Dawn Goddess is often said to be daughter of the Sky Father (see *Rig Veda* 1.30.22 and 6.64.5, and see Brigid as daughter of the Dagda) and a sister or close relation to the Horse Twins (Brigid as sister of Aengus, Ushas as sister of the Asvins (RV 1.180.2)).

Various other details seem to solidify this case. In Euripides' *Helen*, verse 1495, she is described riding home in the horse-drawn chariot of the Dioskouroi, as the Dawn goddess also rides in the chariot of the Horse Twins. Cheryl Steets notes of Helen that "epithets reflect her solar nature; she is clothed in shining, immortal garments, she uses shining materials, she has shining attendants" and that "Her epithet [*Dios thugatēr*] is cognate with Vedic *diva duhita*, an epithet of Usas." ("The Sun Maiden's Wedding," Steets, 18). Steets further points out how Theokritos' *Idyll 18* directly compares Helen's beauty to the golden and rosy Dawn: "Fair, Lady Night, is the face that rising Dawn discloses, or radiant spring with winter ends; and so amongst us did golden Helen shine. As some tall cypress adorns the fertile field or garden wherein it springs, or Thessalian steed the chariot draws, so rosy Helen adorns Lacedaimon" (A.S.F. Gow, *Theocritus*). Steets comments on how the poem goes on to describe the maidens vowing to hang a garland of flowers on a plane tree for Helen, connecting again to the theme of garlands we have seen, and particularly pointing to similar customs at May Day and related festivals.

Further supporting the case, Arthur Anthony Macdonell explains that in the *Rig Veda* Ushas is "closely associated with the sun. She has opened paths for Surya to travel (1.113); she brings the eye of the gods, and leads on the beautiful white horse (7.77). She shines with the light of the Sun (1.113), with the light of her lover (1.92). Surya follows her as a young man a maiden (1.115): she meets the god who desires her (1.123). She thus comes to be spoken of as the wife of Surya (7.75) and the Dawns as the wife of the Sun (4.5)" (Macdonell, *A Vedic Reader*, ch. 10, "Usas"). This describes quite perfectly the relationship between Helen and Paris. As the Veda says, "She who is rich in spoil, the Spouse of Sūrya, wondrously opulent, rules all wealth and treasures. Consumer of our youth, the seers extol her: lauded by priests rich Dawn shines out refulgent" (7.75.5-6).

Importantly for the deeper meaning of the epic, and as this last verse hints: the Vedic Dawn Goddess Ushas was seen as a bringer of strife and a waster of human life, a bringer indeed of the passage of Time each day ("consumer of our youth"). So also can we describe Helen, for she causes the Great War by her beauty and acquiescence to the Sun God, leading to the wasting of the lives of untold thousands of men. Hers is the face that launches *every* ship, each day, with all that it brings.

Dawn Goddess: (Helen, Draupadi/Ushas, Brigid, Blodeuwedd)

- The most beautiful of women

- Promiscuous, multiple husbands and multiple suitors

- Her marriage to the Lawful Sovereign ends up linking all of the Gods of Society and allies together

- Is taken from her husband the Lawful Sovereign by the Sun God, sparking the war

- Is not killed but may be cursed in punishment

Sarpedon

Sarpedon – Dyaus (Father Sky)

Beginning with perhaps the most important detail of all: while the Vedic Bhishma is the spiritual son of Dyaus, the Greek Sarpedon is said to be the son of Zeus (cognate of

Dyaus, Father Sky), and is the only warrior said to be so. In the *Mahabharata*, this makes Bhishma Dyaus' incarnation, but in the *Iliad* the deeper identity of Sarpedon, the fact that he is an incarnation of Father Sky, is not at all made explicit. Both Bhishma and Sarpedon are generals not directly of the royal Kaurava or Trojan families, but are brought in as allied forces. They are also the foremost of these outside generals. Each one, as well, has reservations about the war or does not want to fight it. Bhishma is uncle to and loves the Pandavas, so his heart is not in the fight and he does not wish to kill his nephews. Sarpedon for his part complains during the war that he has no reason to hate the Greeks and no reason to fight them. Each one is forced to fight by bonds of alliance and loyalty. Sarpedon gives a speech to Glaucus on the duty of kings to honor their subjects by fighting and dying bravely. Bhishma, as he is dying, gives a speech to Yudhishthira about dharma and the duties of a king.

Bhishma and Sarpedon both die in the war, and their deaths bring their divine connections emphatically to the forefront. Both of their death scenes involve divine elements, drawn out ceremony, and the consciously exercised decision of when to die. Bhishma is filled with so many arrows that when he falls back they make a bed for him, holding him off the ground. He does not die yet as he has the power to stay alive until the moment he chooses. Arjuna gives him another "pillow" of three vertical arrows pointing from the ground up to the back of his head, and shoots the ground nearby causing the Ganges water to spring out to slake Bhishma's thirst. His death is drawn out as he gives his speech to Yudhishthira. After 58 nights he gives up his life and attains salvation. In the Greek epic, Sarpedon is mortally struck in battle by Patroclus, and Zeus debates whether to save his son's life, but Hera convinces him this would be unjust. As Bhishma becomes so filled with arrows that he can lie back on them like a bed, it is said of Sarpedon that "A man had need of good eyesight now to know Sarpedon, so covered was he from head to foot with spears" (*Iliad*, XVI.635). After he is mortally wounded, Sarpedon calls on Glaucus to rescue his body and then Patroclus removes the spear from him (his soul does not leave him until this is done, as similarly Bhishma giving up his breath was postponed and made a significant detail). Apollo then takes his body and washes it in the river Xanthus and anoints it. This moment seems to parallel the moment where Arjuna places the arrow under Bhishma's head and provides the water to soothe him from the sacred river Ganges. While Sarpedon does not have the power of choosing when to die himself, the question is still discussed by his father Zeus who exercises this same choice for him. Indeed, in both cases the choice to not die exists, but the decision in the end is made in favor of allowing death to come. Zeus then has Apollo rescue Sarpedon's body. As Bhishma dies with drawn out ceremony, it is also said that Apollo washes and anoints the body of Sarpedon with ambrosia, and then delivers it to Hypnos (Sleep) and Thanatos (Death) to take back to his homeland for funeral ceremonies. This is a unique death scene in the epic, and other warriors' deaths are not treated in this way

– tended to by the gods, anointed, washed in the river and taken to their homeland for burial – which indicates a deep significance in the scene.

The parallel between Sarpedon and Bhishma provides some of the only *definitively* archaic mythic material belonging to the original Father Sky of the Indo-Europeans, and thus we would be wise to speculatively compare both of these episodes to the death of Irish Father Sky the Dagda, and *perhaps* to the Welsh first "human" king, the parallel of Vedic Yama who is thus a sort of repetition of Father Sky on the earthly plane, Bran the Blessed. Welsh Bran is killed in the war in Ireland, mortally wounded in the leg. He then gives a speech telling his men to cut his head off and return it to his homeland of Britain, to the White Hill of London to watch and protect against invasion from France (performing this kingly duty thereafter). Before burying the head there, Bran's men feast together with it for 80 years of joy and mirth, during which Bran is "not more irksome" than before his head was severed. This period is called "The Entertaining of the Noble Head." As Bran's head watches over and protects his kingdom, Bhishma's specific vow had been not to die until the kingdom of Hastinapur had been secured from all directions, and this was part of the reason he took such a length of time before giving up his breath. The Dagda is mortally wounded in the war with a poisoned spear or "dart of gore" (as recorded in the *Lebor Gabala Erenn)*, thrown by a female, Cethlenn. Interestingly, it is Arjuna and Shikhandi – who had been a woman in a previous life and whose well-known femaleness is used to deter Bhishma from attacking them – who kill Bhishma. It takes 120 years until the poison is able to kill the Dagda, during 80 of which he reigns as king. Thus his death, like Bhishma's, is the longest and most drawn out of all, and he maintains his kingly duty in spite of his approaching doom.

The great comparativist Nick J. Allen, using different evidence than we have presented here, has argued for this exact parallel in "Dyaus and Bhisma, Zeus and Sarpedon: Towards a History of the Indo-European Sky God," and reading his article along with our chapter should put the identity of Sarpedon and Bhishma beyond any possible doubt. As of this writing, his article is freely provided online.

Father Sky: (Sarpedon, Dyaus/Bhishma, the Dagda)

- Is against the war but fights for the "opposition" as one of its main commanders

- Has no antipathy toward his enemies in the war

- Gives a speech on the duty of kings

- Dies in the war, his death scene is extended and he is in some way preserved by the gods

- In his death scene he is washed in or slaked by a sacred river thanks to the aid of another figure

- The conscious choice of when he will die is exercised by himself or another

- His body is covered excessively with projectile weapons on his death

- May be taken to his homeland for special burial ceremonies

Conclusion

We thus have the six main heroes of each epic standing in the exact same order: descending by age and social class in *Mahabharata*, and seemingly descending by degree of military authority in the *Iliad*, from the Terrible Sovereign down to the "Young Son" Horse Twin. On the other side we have the three main warriors of the opposition, as well as the central young queen in more or less the same positions in each epic. Are we prepared to say that this pattern is no more than an extremely elaborate mirage? Beyond the central characters thus far mentioned, the divine identities of the less prominent *Iliad* characters become less certain as they are less fleshed out. The King and Queen of the Kauravas, Dhritarashtra (as Dumezil argues, the incarnation of Bhaga) and Ghandari can easily be said to parallel King Priam and Queen Hecuba of Troy. Hecuba bears a son who is prophesied to destroy their kingdom, while Ghandari's son is prophesied to destroy the kingdom and the rest of the universe as well. Cethlenn, wife of Balor in the Irish myth, is a prophetess and warns Balor of his doom, just as Cassandra, sister of Hector does for him. If Norse Loki is also in the Demon of the Dark Age mold, as Dumezil has argued in *Gods of the Ancient Northmen*, has he taken on any elements of the Sun God, an overlap we seem to find in Paris and possibly Bres? Or perhaps the scheming half-blooded illusionist uncle who guides Duryodhana to spark the war, Shakuni, incarnation of the Dwapara Yuga, is closer to the missing element in the Loki question? We can see a direct line through from Krishna to Athena to Gwydion as wise divine helpers in particular scenes, but this brings as many questions as answers, as in another place Athena also plays a quintessential role of Loki's, provoking and directing the attack on Menelaus in a very similar manner as Loki does on Baldr. In the section on the funeral games of Patroclus, does Diomedes win the chariot race precisely because he is a god of horses? The Dioskouroi were after all known to be fervently celebrated and thanked after victory in chariot races, as Cicero records regarding Simonides of Ceos. Their Vedic parallels the Asvins win their bride Savitri in a chariot race against the other gods. It is quite incredible that Odysseus is able to wrestle the strongest warrior,

Telamonian Ajax, to a draw – is this only possible due to the fact that the Horse Twins Castor and Polydeuces were famed for hand to hand combat (more often boxing), hence the strongest warrior and the warrior of specialized hand to hand fighting must reach a draw in a wrestling match? Achilles tells Agamemnon that he automatically wins the spear throwing contest as no one could beat him. Is this because the spear was always associated most with the "Mitra-Varuna," Lawful-Terrible Sovereign duo, whether its wielder was Agamemnon, Yudhishthira, Lugh, or Óðinn?

There are much deeper layers to the story of the epic, but for starters we may attempt to reconstruct a naturalistic meaning of the central plot-line of the *Iliad*, the myth of the Dawn Goddess cuckolding the Lawful Sovereign with the Sun God. Crucially, the Lawful Sovereign Mitra was early on associated with the morning sky and the daylit sky generally[24]. Hence in the morning, perhaps before the Sun itself quite comes into vision, The Lawful Sovereign is united with the Dawn and rules unchallenged as peace-loving lord of all creation. The Sun, moving on its path from the low and unknown darkness, far from its proper home on high, then breaks up this peaceful marriage and takes away the Dawn, who yields to it, as it rises in the sky and becomes the inhospitable lord of noontide, shooting its rays from afar with the golden splendor now all for itself, the Sun finally recognized as the forgotten but returned prince. The Lawful Sovereign, he whose special power is to unite the armies by oath of alliance (which is Society itself), then pursues his wife's captor along with the other Gods of Society: the celestial gods, those of the tumultuous middle atmospheric region, and those of the flourishing earth. The Sun God conspires with the Demon of the Age, of linear time, decay, destruction, to wear away at the Gods of Society and visit them with much death. The seemingly eternal war is also the cycle of the day. The Sun is eventually struck down and goes down to the Underworld, and its kingdom burns up in the Sunset. The Spear of Eternal Law, of the natural law of the cycle, wielded by the Lawful Sovereign, cannot be stopped by any shield or stone, but goes through them like paper. The Dawn is reunited with the Lawful Sovereign for the following morning.

Placed in a highly simplified "initiatic" or generalized esoteric framework, the Soul of the righteous and sovereign one (the Lawful Sovereign), is united with the essence of sovereignty/divine glory which is identified with the golden glow of Dawn, in a golden age of early morning or a primordial unity where peace and justice reign. Through ignorance and foolish overconfidence the Soul is passive and lets his guard down, which is the sin corresponding to his archetype. The forces of Time and Decay represented by the Sun and Demon of the Dark Age cause the dark night of the soul, the wound in the

---

24 Mitra is connected to sunrise in contrast with Varuna who is connected with evening in *Atharvaveda* 13.13.13. AV 9.13.18 describes Mitra as revealing in the morning what night and Varuna have veiled.

abdomen, the fall into matter and decay (as Lleu here begins visibly decaying and dropping putrefying carrion[25]) and the great crucible: the loss of the Divine Sovereign Principle and the breaking down of the material self in the esoteric test. This is a necessary decaying of the ignorant state however, an alchemical dissolution, and aided by the god of Wisdom (Gwydion/Athena) the Soul is healed enough to marshal the other powers available to him. An internal battle ensues to regain the Divine Power/Sovereignty/The Golden Age, with all marshaled forces.

Each of the metaphysical forces corresponding to the gods has a particular strength required for this task as well as a sin or danger they are prone to, and these ruling forces, as they operate in the Soul, must be regulated carefully. This is not to say that each of the other gods do not have their own separate myths, but they can also be seen in their relation to the Lawful Sovereign. The violent nature of the Terrible Sovereign's retribution is prone to destructive harshness, yet the fierce power of this commander-in-chief is required as a force of vitality and creative action. The Lawful Sovereign's calm and wise Righteousness, which creates unities, is required, and yet the Soul must not let its guard down or succumb to too great of detachment, slipping into an avoidance of conflict. The Wind God is also known as the Lord of Life, as the wind is the breath-soul and source of life. Hence he is the embodiment of overflowing vitality and raw power. The Lord of Life then becomes the fitting force to oppose, like a nemesis, the Demon of Decay and Decadence, the Demon of the Dark Age, Decay being that which afflicts all things more and more in the last days of the Yuga and which is responsible for spiritual and material destruction and degradation on an unmatched scale. These two fight one-on-one, to a draw, until the Lord of Life finally overcomes the Demon by possibly underhanded means. The Demon is fated to be vanquished at the end of the age, yet as a force of Fate he too has his necessity, his role, and his honesty as such an impersonal force shows in thought-provoking relief the necessary artifice that Life always uses in service of its continuation. Life is always wedded to Maya (which means illusion but also a magical power) as it exists within Becoming, within the material world of Samsara. Its danger or sin is falling into overindulgences of the material world, of falling too deeply into Maya, of abusing Dharma, becoming too drunken with Life that one brings shame on oneself or becomes weighted down by material desires. On the path to

---

25 See Kennard on the alchemical phase known as Putrefaction: "In alchemy at large, we find it is the arcane substance that undergoes these tortures of transformation—'like the rebirth of the bird, which is burnt to death.' Mahdihassan (1991) notes, 'putrefaction is [submerged] growth, starting with [a] dissolution of previous elements … a destruction leading to a new reconstruction' (p. 31). Putrefaction in alchemy represents the process of histolysis in metamorphosis, which works to break down the old tissues and bonds, in the original structure or psychic state (Jung, 1955/1970)" (*Medieval Haṭha-Yoga and Hindu Alchemy: A Jungian Approach to Tantric Immortality*, James Kennard, 173).

transcendence, even illusion necessary to life must be overcome. The power which is embodied by brooding thought, and by the duality of Skill and the sensitivity that comes with it (as seen in the Thunderer), is perhaps the most essential power in the esoteric battle, though it also has a fragility to it. It is able to perceive and understand the deeper layers of Dharma, of Cosmic Balance, and to perform the skillful operations needed to to wage the Greater Holy War and attain the Divine Glory. Its dangers are overconfidence in its Skill (the reason Arjuna is said to die before reaching Paradise) and its proneness to falling prey to powerful emotions or internal storms that can destroy or paralyze action (as with Achilles). Hence the Soul must master all internal storms as well as personal attachments. Cunning, as belongs to the Horse Twins, for planning and carefully sieging the place where the Divine Glory is kept, is required, as are the Youthfulness of Spirit to give one enough boldness to vie with supernatural powers when one must. The mortal sins of the Horse Twins in the *Mahabharata* are said to be Sahadeva's pride in his wisdom and Nakula's pride in his beauty, thus vanity must be defeated within. Odysseus' famous hubris of announcing his true name after tricking the cyclops Polyphemus in the *Odyssey*, a kind of pride in his own cleverness which leads directly to his catastrophe, seems like a direct echo of this same sin of Sahadeva's. From the *Iliad* there may also be added the occasional cowardice of Odysseus and possibly the overstepping of Diomedes (though this is mainly lauded). Ultimately, the Soul confronts the Sun God (ie the Mitraic figure here confronts the Surya-type hero exactly as Roman Mit*hras* confronts the Sun God in the Mithraic Mysteries), the ultimate double-sided god with one face governing Time and thus the world of Decay, the other pointing to the Absolute and the world of Divine Glory, its keeper and gateway. The Sovereign Soul uses its Spear of Dharma (which represents a power of concentrated asceticism in the *Mahabharata*, prayed over for many years) to at last overcome the Sun God and his generals and recapture the Divine Glory, the Golden Glow.

This is a very rough proposed outline of the esoteric *superstructure* of *the* standard list of events that theoretically existed in the tradition of the epic poets and that formed the underlying framework of the epic as it spread. The theoretical list of events of the broader *Iliadic* epic tradition, as Franco Montinari explains, was "marked by a strong tendency to preserve its content," while "strong deviation from the contents of the story that had been established" was not allowed (Franco Montinari, *Introduction to the Homeric Question Today*). The layers of the epic we have suggested here, as well as others, exist simultaneously. The whole war can be seen as a naturalistic allegory of the cycle of the day or year, an allegory of the pursuit of transcendence (primarily the esoteric path an ideal King must walk), and an allegory of the cycle of the age all at once. It is a case of microcosm equals macrocosm; as above, so below. These all are the same thing on different metaphysical levels. It seems that this epic had a religio-mythic basis to its deep structure, and if it did, while being as central to the cultures that carried it as it clearly was, then all of these levels would have been active in the minds of the poets and audiences at once. This is after all how myth works.

To be certain, there is far more that can be learned by a patient study of the Greek epic. What seems almost incontrovertible from this perspective is the idea that these epics, the Greek and the Indian, as well as the Celtic myths, share a common origin, that they are the same myth with the same characters and events. The idea that all of this is only a case of borrowing also seems far-fetched from this perspective: much of the parallelism here described can only be grasped when one knows the proper pattern of other Indo-European correspondences, so buried in the texts as it is. Whatever influence the Greeks may have taken into their mythology later, the *Iliad* preserves a deeper, more archaic mythological framework carried by these Indo-European people, that perhaps remained relatively untouched by later influences as its ancient meanings were slowly forgotten and the heroes became seen as only mortal. Take this foundational European epic in hand and you will be able to see things in other parts of the mythological web with new eyes. Understand its pattern and you will have equipped yourself with one more Rosetta Stone.

Title	Vedic	Greek (Epic)	Irish	Welsh
Terrible Sovereign	Pandu/Varuna	Agamemnon	Nuada	Lludd Llaw Ereint
Lawful Sovereign	Yudhishthira/Mitra	Menelaus	Lugh	Lleu Llaw Gyffes
Lord of Wind	Bhima/Vayu	Ajax	The Dagda	
Thunderer	Arjuna/Indra	Achilles	Tuireann	Taran
Horse Twins	Nakula and Sahadeva/Nasatya and Dasra	Diomedes and Odysseus	Aengus	Pryderi/Mabon
Sun God	Karna/Surya	Paris	Bres	Gronw Pebr
Demon of the Dark Age	Duryodhana/Kali	Hector		
Dawn Goddess	Draupadi/Ushas	Helen	Brigid	Blodeuwedd
Father Sky	Bhishma/Dyaus	Sarpedon	The Dagda	
Son of the Moon	Abhimanyu/Varchas	Patroclus		

2

The Climactic Spear-Throwing Scenes of Celtic Myth:

Lugh as Yudhishthira-Mitra and Balor as one of the Rudras

The Spear of Lugh

If we look at the Welsh myths, the spear-throwing motif appears in quite a simple and direct form. There is one main spear-throwing sequence, found in *Math fab Mathonwy*, where Gronw Pebr pierces Lleu Llaw Gyffes with a special spear, and then after a space

Lleu returns and kills Gronw with his own thrown spear. This thrown spear of Lleu accomplishes two distinct tasks. Firstly, it ends the conflict, the "mini-war," that has arisen from the adultery of Blodeuwedd and Gronw. We can see indeed that to pursue Gronw, Lleu has to martial the warriors of his kingdom, to cross a body of water, and to confront Gronw who is among his own men, just as if two armies were facing off for battle. We have shown previously how exactly and uncannily this sequence parallels the events of the Trojan War as found in the *Iliad*, so that we feel it is more than fair to call Lleu's killing of Gronw a symbolic ending of a "mini-war," which is at its root precisely the same war myth that has here been compressed to a much more compact version, and this killing therefore brings a cessation of hostilities and peace to the land through Lleu's enactment of justice. The fact that this sequence is drawn from the same war myth is highlighted by the fact that Lleu and his marshaled allies cross a body of water, the river Cynvael, to pursue Blodeuwedd, just as Menelaus and his allies cross the Aegean sea to pursue Helen and Paris. Secondly, this spear-throwing kills the adulterous lover of Lleu's wife, gaining Lleu revenge on a more personal level. That is, in one spear throw, Lleu ends the war *and* gets revenge on his wife's lover, Paris, who we have previously identified as a Sun God.

In the Irish version, things are not so simple at all. Instead, these two events are split apart, and we have two separate tales to accomplish what the Welsh version achieves in one. Yet mostly the same elements are present. Lugh famously casts the final projectile of the Second Battle of Magh Tuireadh (it is said to be a sling stone in *Cath Maige Tuired,* even though Lugh's legendary spear is mentioned at the beginning of that text, and the projectile is a red spear made by Gavidin (aka Goibniu) in "Balor on Tory Island" (Jeremiah Curtin, Michael Curran, "Hero-Tales of Ireland"), and a red-hot iron rod in "A History of Balor" (John O'Donovan, Shane O'Dugan, *Annals of the Kingdom of Ireland by the Four Masters*)), ending the conflict and bringing peace to the land. However, it is not the lover of his wife who is thus killed with this projectile, but simply a king and lead general of the opposing army, Lugh's own grandfather, Balor the Fomorian, "of the Evil Eye." In an entirely separate account, "How the Dagda Got His Magic Staff," we learn that Lugh kills Cermait Milbel, son of the Dagda, for having an affair with his wife, Buach. Indeed, the figure we have called the primary sun god, Bres, and his wife, the Dawn Goddess Brigid, deities who in other branches would be identical to Lleu or Menelaus' wife and her solar lover (Gronw or Paris), are here instead completely separate from Lugh's personal affairs. That is, the solar figure who in other places is only singular (Gronw or Paris) seems to be doubled in the Irish version in the figures of Bres and Cermait. In one account, found in the *Metrical Dindshenchas of Carn Hui Neit,* Lugh does kill Bres as well, getting him to drink a poisonous liquid when the war ends, while in the *Cath Maige Tuired* he spares Bres' life after a negotiation.

63

In the Welsh version, found in *Math fab Mathonwy,* Gronw strikes Lleu first with a spear, causing Lleu to undergo a symbolic temporary death, where he transforms into an eagle and flies up to the top of some kind of otherworldly tree, possibly even the World Tree. Lleu then is healed, returns, and kills Gronw, as we find in the *Metrical Dindshenchas 86, Loch Lugborta.* For Irish Lugh, it is only *after* killing Cermait that Cermait's sons take their turn and kill Lugh. The order of the confrontations in the Irish version is flipped compared to the Welsh, as we saw the order also flipped in a different way in the *Iliad* version. While Welsh Lleu had been speared while standing with one foot on the back of a goat, and one on the edge of a cauldron of water, by the side of a river, Irish Lugh for his part is killed by being speared in the foot and then drowned in Loch Lugborta. The theme of spearing combined with water seems to at least create a possible continuity between these death scenes, with a possible esoteric significance in the combination of these elements. The Welsh version certainly implies the breaking of a magical *tynged* and a temporary death, while the Irish spearing and drowning combination could have a magico-ritual significance as well.

What we find in the Greek version appearing in the *Iliad,* which has proven to be so uncannily close in so many ways to the Welsh version, is that there is a kind of splitting of the scene which occurs here as well. In the duel scene where Menelaus attempts to settle the dispute, end the war, and kill his wife's lover Paris, Menelaus throws his spear through Paris' shield, but in this case Paris is too agile and dodges the dart, being rescued just after by Aphrodite and spirited safely away. It isn't until much later that another warrior, Philoctetes, finishes Paris off with a poisoned arrow (consider here the poisoning of Bres). And finally, according to the *Aeneid,* near the end of the war, when they have infiltrated past Troy's walls, Menelaus slays his wife Helen's second foreign husband, Deiphobus, rather than Paris, her first, concluding the conflict. Thus, similar to how in the Irish version there are the two solar figures Bres and Cermait (not to mention his avenging sons), this motif is also split between the two figures, Paris and Deiphobus, in the Greek version (add also Pandarus, who plays the role of wounding Menelaus), while the Welsh myth uses only one figure who performs all functions in one: adulterous lover of the Dawn Goddess, who "kills" Lleu, and is in turn killed by him, which ends the war.

The killing of Deiphobus by Menelaus may more properly parallel the killing of Balor by Lugh in fact, as the great facial disfigurement Deiphobus receives when he is killed is emphasized, potentially relating him to Balor whose eye is pierced, and his name bears the meaning "hostile panic flight," relating him to the terrifying petrific powers that we will also see connected to Balor and Ashwatthama. The inclusion of Pandarus in the role of wounding Menelaus can then theoretically be accounted for in this way: he is famed as an archer as Paris is also, and thus he may represent one aspect of the solar deity of which Paris represents another. This idea is supported by what we have shown regarding Welsh Gronw performing both the "Pandarus" and "Paris" roles himself. If Pandarus and Paris represent a splitting of the solar role into two, this could again mirror the division we find between Bres and Cermait (or Cermait's sons), acting out in a divided form a role that Gronw performs singly in the Welsh case.

The possible reason that the Irish myth has focused on a deity completely separate from the solar figures of this tale of adultery and revenge mentioned thus far, to receive the final dart of the main war – that is, the Fomorian Balor – is that there in fact exists at least one other "end of war" spear-throwing motif in the Indo-European corpus, as can be seen in the Indian *Mahabharata,* and which may have survived in a similar form in Ireland as well. The confusion perhaps originates from the fact that the Lawful Sovereign or Mitraic deity sometimes performs *both* of these spear killings (as Lugh does, killing both Balor and Cermait, not to mention Bres with the sewage in one version), though they are directed at totally different opponents. In the Indian version, this second type of spear scene occurs right before the end of the war, in the face-off between Yudhishthira (incarnation of Mitra) and the Kaurava general Shalya, which is followed shortly by the destructive outburst of another Kaurava, Ashvatthama. Ashvatthama is the incarnation or spiritual son of "one of the rudras." However, it is also said that Drona prayed to Shiva for a son like Shiva, and thus Shiva gave him Ashvatthama, so Ashvatthama's identity may either be an incarnation of Rudra-Shiva himself or an incarnation of one of Rudra's attendants, the rudras. In the latter case he would be the embodiment of the destructive aspect of one of the rudras, the troop that attended Rudra who were either associated with destruction generally, destructive winds, or were identified with the destructive rain deities the maruts. The overlapping of the rudras and maruts has proven a contentious topic among interpreters and in brief they are clearly interlinked and one seems to be a species of the other. Kris Kershaw passes on one interesting opposition between a Marut-related figure and Mithra: "Wikander gives further examples from Iran, 85ff. Mairyo in Avestan is "meistens auf dem Weg, zu einem rein 'daevischen' Worte zu werden" (32). Mairyo is the enemy par excellence of the Mithra community (33). Mairyo is a "dangerous, hostile being" who robs the followers of Mithra (34f)." Ashvatthama has a gem of power in his forehead which gives him power over lower nonhuman beings, protects him from hunger, thirst, fatigue, snakebite, ghosts, and unnatural death, and contributes to his prowess on the battlefield. As we will see, Balor seems to combine myths that in Vedic are seen attached to at least two separate figures: Ashwatthama and Shalya, who is the last Karuava general of the war and who is killed by the dharmic spear of Yudhishthira.

Now, to begin the battle sequence in question, right during the climactic scene that ends the Kurukshetra war, found in *Shalya Parva* section 17, Yudhishthira (Lugh

65

parallel) throws his spear blessed by Shiva through the final commander of the Kaurava army, Shalya. This climactic spear throw is described thus:

> Yudhishthira the just, took up a dart whose handle was adorned with gold and gems and whose effulgence was as bright as that of gold. Rolling his eyes that were wide open, he cast his glances on the ruler of the Madras, his heart filled with rage […] then hurled with great force at the king of the Madras that blazing dart of beautiful and fierce handle and effulgent with gems and corals. All the Kauravas beheld that blazing dart emitting sparks of fire as it coursed through the welkin after having been hurled with great force, even like a large meteor falling from the skies at the end of the Yuga.

The spear "was incapable of being baffled," and it is said of it that

> That weapon seemed to blaze like Samvartaka-fire […] Unerringly fatal, it was destructive of all haters of Brahma. Having carefully inspired it with many fierce *mantras,* and endued it with terrible velocity by the exercise of great might and great care, king Yudhishthira hurled it along the best of tracks for the destruction of the ruler of the Madras. Saying in a loud voice the words, "Thou art slain, O wretch!" the king hurled it […] stretching forth his strong (right) arm graced with a beautiful hand, and apparently dancing in wrath.

We are reminded that, as the "stretching forth" of Yudhisthira's "strong (right) arm" is emphasized in this climactic throw, one of Lugh's primary epithet sis *Lámhfhada,* "of the long arm." Furthermore, Yudhishthira is said to be "apparently dancing in wrath," while Lugh, for his part, enters the great battle by performing what O'Davoren's Glossary calls as a "crane-slaying magic," *corruginecht*, before his troops, and which can be compared to a "crane dance."

Similarities should also be noted in the description of Yudhishthira's spear and that of Lugh's spear, the Gae Assail (Spear of Assal) or Areadbhair (Slaughterer). Lugh's spear, one of the Four Jewels of the Tuatha De Danann[26], is said to ignite into flame and flash forth fire of its own accord and so must be kept in a pot of water[27]. Isolde Carmody has shown that the island from which the spear originates, Gorias, is linguistically connected to fire, heat and inflammation[28]. Likewise, Yudhishthira's spear emits "sparks of fire"

---

26 *Cath Maige Tuired, 4; trans. Gray, 1982.* "From Gorias was brought the spear which Lug had. No battle was ever sustained against it, or against the man who held it in his hand."

27 *Oidheadh Chlainne Tuireann.* "'[…] its head is kept steeped in a vessel of water, the way it will not burn down the place where it is.'"
"And then they found the spear, and its head in a cauldron of water, the way it would not set fire to the place."

28 Isolde Carmody, "Four Cities, Four Teachers, Four Treasures."

and seems to blaze "like Samvartaka-fire," its appearance being compared to that fire of the sky, the flaming meteor. It should seriously be considered that this comparison of Yudhishthira's spear to a meteor and the fact that Lugh's weapon with which he kills Balor is described variously as either a spear or a sling stone may indicate a shared thematic between the Irish and Indian versions: the sling stone symbolic of the meteoric fire of the sky which is an aspect of the deity's power and which in the Indian version is a feature of the spear, combined into one image of meteor and fire-lightning-spear. Lugh's sling stone, called *liic talma* in Cath Maige Tuired[29], and *cloich tabaill* in the *Lebor Gabála Érenn* from the *Book of Leinster,* is also called a *tathlum* and given a perhaps more detailed description in a poem in Egerton MS. 1782 as noted by Eugene O'Curry[30]. In this poem, the sling-stone or *tathlum* is described as "heavy, fiery, firm." The poem, as translated in this lecture by O'Curry, explains that the *tathlum* stone has been formed of the blood of deadly animals, mixed with sand: "The blood of toads and furious bears,/ And the blood of the noble lion,/ The blood of Vipers, and of Osmuinn's trunks,/ It was of these the *Tathlum* was composed." This *tathlum* seems to be of the same type as the "ball of brains" that Geoffrey Keating describes in his *General History of Ireland.* "Whenever a Champion overcame his Adversary in single Combat, he took out his Brains, and mixing them with Lime, he made a round Ball, which, by drying in the Sun, became exceeding solid and hard [...] a Trophy of experienced Valour, and certain Victory"[31]. Keating describes how this ball of brains is fired from a sling by

---

https://storyarchaeology.com/four-cities-four-teachers-four-treasures/. Online Resource. Accessed September 2021. "*Gor* is an adjective with the root meaning 'warm'. It has two significant specific meanings. The first is the warmth (*goire*) of affection, particularly the affectionate duty of a child toward their parents. This is found throughout the law texts, as a *mac gor*, 'dutiful son', has better standing than a *mac ingor*, 'undutiful son'."

"The second specific meaning of goire, 'warmth', is the heat associated with illness and infection. It is used to signify the 'matter' that seeps from an infected wound, and may be related to the English word 'gore'." See also: eDIL s.v. 1 gor. (a) Med. Inflammation, pus, matter (gore?).

29 "Then Lug cast a sling stone at him which carried the eye through his head [*Fucaird Luch iersin liic talma do, co ndechaid an suil triena cend*], and it was his own host that looked at it. He fell on top of the Fomorian host so that twenty-seven of them died under his side." Gray, 1984, 135.

30 "The ammunition that Lugh used was not just a stone, but a *tathlum*[according to a certain poem in Egerton MS. 1782 (olim W. Monck Mason MS.), the first quatrain of which is as follows:

Táthlum tromm thenntide tenn robūi ag Tūath Dé Danann, hī robriss súil Balair búain tall ar toghail in tromshlúaigh —Meyer (1905) ed.

A tathlum, heavy, fiery, firm, Which the Tuatha Dé Danann had with them, It was that broke the fierce Balor's eye, Of old, in the battle of the great armies. —O'Curry (1873) tr." (O'Curry, Lectures Vol. 1, p. 252).

Ceat.[32] Yudhiṣṭhira's spear, in a description perhaps comparable to the composition of the *tathlum*, is said to be "a consumer of the life-breaths and the bodies of all foes." Yudhishthira's spear is said to be "incapable of being baffled," while of Lugh's it is said that "No battle was won against it or him who held it in his hand." Yudhiṣṭhira is specifically trained in spear skill by Drona, while Welsh Lleu throws his spear through a slab of stone to kill Gronw Pebr, and Menelaus throws his spear through Paris' shield in the analogous duel scene. To emphasize the general comparability of these spear-wielders once more: while Lugh is said to reign for 40 years after the war, which he ends with this spear, Yudhishthira is said to reign for 37 years after the war, which he ends with his.

The Eye of Balor

In the very next sentence after the killing of Shalya, Shalya's son is beheaded and the Kauravas go into a full and final retreat. Likewise, immediately following the killing of Balor, the Fomorians make their final retreat. In the Indian version, as a last gasp effort, Ashvatthama attacks the camp of the Pandavas and kills almost all of the warriors including all the children of the main heroes, the Pandavas. Only the main incarnations of the gods of society, the Pandava brothers themselves, survive. As punishment for this attack, Ashvatthama has the gem of power removed from his forehead. Balor's evil eye is driven out of the back of his head in the Irish conclusion.

Thus, in quick succession to end the war we have: spear blessed by Shiva is thrown by the Lawful Sovereign and kills the commander of the opposing army, a beheading, a final retreat, and the mass slaughter of the protagonist forces by the incarnation of a god of destruction who has a source of great power in a magical object resting in his forehead region. These four climactic events may have been combined in the death of Balor as depicted in *Cath Mag Tuired*: he is killed with the *tathlum* projectile or spear by the Lawful Sovereign, he is beheaded after the battle (only, however, in the early modern version of The Battle of Mag Tuired and the folktale "Balor on Tory Island"[33], and the variance in the depictions of this beheading could accord with the fact that Shalya is not

---

31 Keating, 1723, p. 182.
32 Keating, 1723, p. 185.
33 Curtin, 1894; Ó hÓgáin, 1991, p. 43. The type of weapon used for Balor's death vary in the different sources."Balor on Tory Island": red hot spear, Curtin, 1894, p. 293. *Cath Mag Tuired*: sling stone, Gray, 1982. *Early Modern Cath Mag Tuired*, sling stone, then slain and beheaded (11 1134-1294).

himself the one beheaded in the Indian version, his son is), there is a final retreat, and his magical eye of destruction is unleashed, though on his own army. His eye is removed by Lugh's projectile whereas Aśvatthāmā's gem of power too is removed after his onslaught[34]. In fact, the combining and compressing of this sequence of events is very typical of the Celtic myths, which, compared to the stretched out and detailed style of the *Mahabharata*, are notably concise. We have already seen the Welsh tale of Lleu compress the same narrative found in a large section of the *Iliad* down to a few pages. To further bolster this comparison, we find that Ashvatthama also invokes a celestial weapon of mass slaughter, the Narayanastra, which is said to turn on its user (if used twice). This is similar to what we see of Balor's eye, which turns on his own army when it is driven out of his head. Shalya for his part is the final commander-in-chief of the Kauravas when they are defeated, just as Balor is the commander of the Fomorians upon his death which marks the end of the war.

One possible etymology of Balor's name is "the deadly one," from Common Celtic *Baleros*. This would make it cognate with Old Irish *at-baill*, "to die," and Welsh *ball*, "death, plague." Another perhaps more favored etymology of the name is Common Celtic *Boleros,* "the flashing one," which is attractive due to the connection it can suggest to Balor's piercing eye. "The flashing one" would also describe well the star Sirius, the brightest star in the sky, which appears to flash red and white when near the horizon, and whose name in Greek means "scorcher." In Sanskrit, Sirius is known as *Mrgavyadha* "deer hunter," or *Lubdhaka* "hunter." As Mrgavyadha, the star represents Rudra-Siva, according to Stella Kramrisch (Kramrisch, *The Presence of Siva*, 96-97). These somewhat speculative etymologies are of interest when we look at the comparative evidence related to Vedic Rudra. Based on the earliest Rig Vedic material,

---

34 "If this gem is worn, the wearer ceases to have any fear from weapons or disease or hunger! He ceases to have any fear of gods and *danavas* and *nagas!* His apprehensions from *rakshasas* as also from robbers will cease. Even these are the virtues of this gem of mine. I cannot, by any means, part with it. That, however, O holy one, which thou sayest, should be done by me. Here is this gem. Here is myself. This blade of grass (inspired into a fatal weapon) will, however, fall into the wombs of the Pandava women, for this weapon is high and mighty, and incapable of being frustrated. O regenerate one, I am unable to withdraw it, having once let it off. I will now throw this weapon into the wombs of the Pandava women. As regards thy commands in other respects, O holy one, I shall certainly obey them." Sauptika Parva 15). "Vaishampayana continued, "Drona's son, then, having made over his gem to the high-souled Pandavas, cheerlessly proceeded, before their eyes, to the forest. The Pandavas who had killed and chastised all their foes, placed Govinda and the island-born Krishna and the great ascetic Narada at their head, and taking the gem that was born with Ashvatthama, quickly came back to the intelligent Draupadi who was sitting in observance of the *praya* vow" (*Mahabharata, Sauptika Parva* 16).

Rudra is especially the god of the destructive power of nature and the terror it causes (Chakravarti, *The Concept of Rudra-Siva Through the Ages*, 8), and is a bringer of both disease and death. His attendant gods known as "Rudras" or "Maruts"[35] are destructive divinities of storm, and of wind or rain more specifically. It is important to note how much Rudra and the rudras are depicted as gods of destruction and struck absolute terror into the hearts of people in the earliest evidence: he is "regarded with a kind of cringing fear, as a deity whose wrath is to be deprecated" says Mahadev Chakravarti (8). R.N. Dandekar explains, "Rudra's name is never directly mentioned. According to the *Aitareya Brahmana* 34.7, a particular Rgvedic mantra must be recited to avoid the evil consequences of such a mention" (Dandekar, *Rudra in the Veda*, 95), and he notes that Rudra was referred to as "that god." Kris Kershaw explains, "According to the *Aitareya Brahmana* […] Rudra is the compound of all terrible substances, while the *Satapatha Brahmana* tells us […] that even gods are afraid of him" (Kershaw, 353). Chakravarti holds that Rudra's beneficent, healing aspect became emphasized over time as, due to his immense destructive power, he was propitiated in the belief that he would have the power also to do the opposite of destroying, that he would heal the people or spare them his destruction. The whole basis of the Indo-European mythic war-of-the-gods cycle, as we have described it, boils down to the struggle of the gods of society against the destructive forces of nature, or more exactly against the "impersonal" gods of fate, decay and destruction. Balor can be interpreted in this line as a god of some destructive force of nature or the spirit world. If he is an embodiment of the force of destructive flood waters struck down by the god of light, Lugh, this would put him directly in line with the torrential rain-associated Rudras/Maruts. If he is a more generalized force of destruction and death, then Lugh is the bringer of order and life against chaos, blight and disease.

Kris Kershaw describes the variety and particular natures of the Rudras, noting that "There are 'countless thousands' of rudras (*Satarudriya* 10); like their leader they have bows and arrows and "attack man and beast with disease and death" (*VM* 76)" (Kershaw, 356), saying that "At the end (64-66) the *SR* actually accounts for 150 rudras in three divisions of 5x10" (356). She explains that: "The tenth stanza of the Satarudriya is a litany for warding off every conceivable sort of rudra" (357). She also gives insight into the common confusion between Rudra and rudras that we also have dealt with: "Since Rudra himself is ubiquitous it is not always clear whether one has to do with a rudra or with the god himself. They seem to be pictured thus, spooking singly, but also as a troop, *gana, sardha*" (356). She calls Rudra "leader of the daemonic host, and 'master of the

---

35 "The most important rudras are the Maruts […] 'The Maruts are a subset of the rudras; they are always together as gana, mahagrama, vrata or sardha', They are often called rudras in the RV and sometimes Rudriyas. They are Rudra's sons; Rudra is invoked as 'Father of the Maruts' at the opening of RV 2.33 and 1.114.6&9, and they are invoked with him in 1.114.11 and alone in 2.33.13" (Kershaw, 357-358).

entire demon-world,'" and paraphrases Dandekar saying that because he is "Inherently associated with the demon-world," he "is thereby clearly isolated from other major Vedic gods" (355), which could explain why Balor seems isolated and opposed to many of the other more positive deities.

Kershaw notes a further characteristic that links Rudra with the world of demons and spirits: "A striking difference between the Maruts and their father is that they partake of the Soma-sacrifice, together with Indra or Agni, an honor from which Rudra is excluded. They also, however, receive sacrifices which are appropriate only for demons: when the cow for the MitraVaruna sacrifice is pregnant, for example, the raw foetus is offered to the Maruts. Arbman notes, too, that the Maruts are often pictured as birds, and that otherwise only the Pitaras (manes) or demons are pictured in this form" (360). In the later recensions of the *Lebor Gabala Erenn*[36], as well as material from the *Lebor na nUidre,* the Fomorians, among whom Balor fights, are described as having one arm and one leg each, and in *Sex Aetates Mundi* from the *Lebor na hUidre* they are classed with beings having the heads either of horses or of goats[37], and this combined with Balor's strange eye seems to have lead them to be seen as grotesque and disfigured on average. As for Rudra's host, a similar image emerges. Chakravarti notes that "in the Epics and the Puranas, the Parisadas or associates of Rudra-Siva have become increasingly repugnant and obnoxious and are said to be his manifold forms. They are now dwarfish, pot-bellied, cock-faced, long-necked, big-eared, with deformed organ of sex, fiercely energetic, gigantic in size and outlandishly dressed" (Chakravarti, *The Conception of Rudra-Siva Through the Ages*, 53). The horde of beings who appear from the sacrificial fire when Ashwatthama, incarnation of a rudra, invokes Rudra-Siva before his final assault are described thus:

> And some, O king, had no heads, and some, O Bharata, had faces like those
> of bears. The eyes of some were like fire, and some had fiery complexions.

---

36 R. A. Stewart Macalister (ed. & trans.), *Lebor Gabála Érenn: The Book of the Taking of Ireland Part III,* Irish Texts Society Vol. 39, 1940, pp. 2-15, 72-75, 85.

37 *Lebor na hUidre* (ed. Best and Bergin), p. 2a, *Sex Aetates Mundi,* line 124, "genatar luchrupain & fomóraig & goborchind". See Revue Celtique 1, p. 257, Stokes: "Melanges, Mythological Notes": "of him [Ham, successor of Cain] were born Luchrupain and Fomóraig and Goborchinn (horse- heads?) and every unshapely appearance moreover that is on human beings." There is some uncertainty about the meaning of this *Goborchinn* and "goat-headed" is a possible reading. See John Rhys, Hibbert Lectures p. 593: "It is not quite certain that it should not be rendered 'goat-headed.' Cormac's Glossary (Stokes-O'Donovan ed. p. 83) explains that *gabur* was a goat, while *gobur* meant a horse."
See also John Rhys, *Hibbert Lectures* p. 593: "In the same class must be placed a certain Echaid Echchenn, or Echaid Horse-head, king of the Fomori," and he cites here *The Four Masters*, A.M. 3520.

The hair on the heads and bodies of some were blazing and some had four arms, and some, O king, had faces like those of sheep and goats. The colour of some was like that of conchs, and some had faces that resembled conchs, and the ears of some were like conchs, some wore garlands made of conchs, and the voices of some resembled the blare of conchs. Some had matted locks on their heads, and some had five tufts of hair, and some had heads that were bald. Some had lean stomachs; some had four teeth, some had four tongues, some had ears straight as arrows and some had diadems on their brows. (*Mahabharata, Sauptika Parva*, 7)

Why is Rudra, this terrible and destructive deity, sometimes depicted so negatively, and at other times praised so vehemently in the *Veda*, along with his Rudra or Marut host? Kershaw gives insight here once again: over time, "Rudra's host has been split. The Rudras must originally have been both wild and dangerous and benevolent and bountiful, just like their human counterparts [the sacred, ecstatic war-band of youths], but when these disappeared from the religious and social structure, the Furious Host became goblins, while the kindly weather-spirits were worshiped with affection-despite the traces of their dangerous ancestry" (389). We hypothesize that a division may have occurred between the positive and negative, the beneficent and destructive, sides of this deity type as manifested in the Irish sources. Balor would then be the negative aspect, while, as Kershaw, citing Piggott, suggests[38], and as we will discuss later on, Fionn mac Cumhaill would embody the positive side of the same general deity type. As Kershaw elucidates, Fionn is Rudra because he is the *männerbünd* god, and the life of his Fianna in the woods resembles the pattern found in other known *männerbünde*. To phrase their opposition in another way, Balor is analogous to one of these many rudras, essentially distinguished from Fionn (who could be called the parallel of Rudra-Shiva himself) but related in some sense, ultimately overlapping with the world of demons generally, almost the demon of death itself. We already have seen that although both Rudra and his rudras/maruts are praised in the *Rig Veda*, the incarnation of the Rudraic deity, Ashvatthama, nonetheless fights on the side of the Kauravas and even kills the children of the divine heroes of society. Thus Balor, a terrifying figure, could fight against Lugh and be a Rudraic deity without his necessarily being reducible to pure evil. His opposition to Lugh in battle simply is not enough to brand him as solely evil in an Indo-European context, just as we have seen in the case of the Sun god Bres. Instead, Balor is a force of deadly destruction, aligned with indifferent Nature and the ambivalent spirit

---

38 "The god or gods of the Celtic Mannerbunde are unknown, though Stuart Piggott remarked, back in 1949, on the resemblance between Rudra leading the Maruts and Finn and the Fianna" (Kershaw, 314).

world, and thus he is an obstacle, a force that must be neutralized and put in its place by the gods of society, almost as if they were (temporarily) defeating death itself.

Remarkably, there is a possible trace of this suggested link between Fionn mac Cumhaill and Balor as positive and negative "sides" of one deity type, or stemming from a single family of deities, and this example solidifies the counterintuitive idea that Fionn and Balor are indeed two sides of one divine coin. A figure said to be a member of the Fianna [see: Rudras/Maruts] and a paternal uncle of Fionn, by the name of Goll "one-eyed" mac Morna, kills the father of Fionn and becomes the leader of the Fianna. As Kershaw and Piggot suggest, the Fianna war-band would be the parallel of the Vedic Maruts or Rudras. Goll then becomes an ambivalent ally to Fionn, eventually allowing Fionn to take control of the Fianna when he has grown. Goll even marries Fionn's daughter for an act of bravery (killing the witch Irnan) in which he specifically *takes Fionn's place*. In another tale, Goll betrays Fionn and fights with Cairbre against him ("The Battle of Gabhra"). Goll, then, is in a close but uneasy relation to Fionn. In folk variants of the Battle of Maigh Tuiredh tale (William Copeland Borlase, *The Dolmens of Ireland*, 807) this Goll is said to be the *main* opponent of Lugh or "Lughaidh Lamhfada" in this battle, and is said to be blinded in one eye by him in the fight. This places Goll in the same position as Balor, as if he is a localized folk variant of the same figure which became closely associated with the local Fianna tradition specifically, as scholars have long recognized (Ó hÓgáin, Dáithí. *Fionn Mac Cumhaill: Images of the Gaelic Hero*. Gill & MacMillan, 1988. pp. 10-11). An acknowledged doublet of Balor is one of the main Fianna, the Irish parallels of the Rudras, then, and thus the mythic parallel between Balor and the Indian Ashwatthama (the incarnation of a rudra), which we demonstrated previously, makes complete sense.[39]

Thus while Rudra is "the destroyer" who brings plague and other forms of death, Balor is the flashing or deadly one, and his eye is said in *The Second Battle of Magh Tuiredh* to have "poisonous power" imparted to it by the "venomous power" of a druidic

---

39 Goll mac Morna's original name is Aed, meaning "Fire," but he gains the name Goll due to the loss of his eye, a typical Rudraic symbol. This may indicate an esoteric understanding of the interrelatedness of the Fire and the Rudraic divine essences, Rudra in a sense being the terrible, shining essence in the heart of cosmic Fire. Stella Kramrisch elaborates on this theme: "Of Agni and Rudra, cooperating powers to the point of identity, Agni is the first-born, and their roles are not always reversible. **Agni acts in Rudra** and Rudra exceeds him in intensity. **He is Agni's incandescence**. As such, Rudra is 'king of the sacrifice' (RV.4.3.1), 'priest of both worlds' (TS.1.3.14.1), and 'fulfiller of the sacrifice' (RV.1.114.4). Rudra, for not playing Agni's sacerdotal role, is overcompensated and raised above Agni, the high priest. Paradoxically, Agni is praised as the Rudra of sacrifices (RV.3.2.5)" (Kramrisch, *The Presence of Siva*, 50 [e-book pagination]).

brew (*CMT* 133). In a folktale version of Balor's story recorded by John O'Donovan, the eye is called venomous, and also said to petrify those it looks upon like a basilisk: "by its foul distorted glances, and its beams and dyes of venom, like that of the Basilisk, would strike people dead" (O'Donovan, *Annals of the Kingdom of Ireland*, Volume 1, 18). Another variant, from County Mayo, says he had a "venomous fiery eye" (Daithi O' Hogain, *Myth, Legend & Romance*, 43). The eye is there called "piercing," and it is said that it takes the strength from men: "The host which looked at that eye, even if they were many thousands in number, would offer no resistance to warriors." In a similar vein, Kershaw compares the one-eyed Rudraic god Oðinn's power of taking the strength of men in battle to that of the rudras. As she puts it, Oðinn sometimes "blinds, deafens, or paralyses the enemy troops" (368). In *Ynglingasaga* we read that he even has the power to make his enemies become like stones: "He could make his enemies blind and deaf, or like stones with fear, and their weapons could no more cut than sticks"(*Ynglingasaga*, 6). Though it may simply refer to the sun as one of his eyes, one of Oðinn's names is *Báleygr*, "flaming or shifty eyed" (*Grimnismal* 47).

Meanwhile, Ashvatthama clearly displays a terrifying character reminiscent of Balor. He is described thus:

> The sound of Ashvatthama's bow, inspiring foes with terror, was repeatedly heard by us in that battle, O king, to resemble that of a roaring lion [...] With mouth wide open from rage and with the desire to retaliate, and with red eyes, the mighty Ashvatthama looked formidable **like death himself**, armed with his mace and filled with wrath as at the end of the Yuga. He then shot showers of fierce shafts. With those shafts sped by him, he began to rout the Pandava army. (*Mahabharata, Karna Parva*, 56)

And of Ashvatthama's appearance it is said: "The form of Ashvatthama became such in that battle that men could with difficulty gaze at it," (*Karna Parva*, 56) while Balor has the great piercing, evil eye that destroys or petrifies what it looks on.

Other key connections between Yudhishthira and the other Lawful Sovereign figures, namely Iranic Mithra, Welsh Lleu, Irish Lugh and Greek Menelaus (and consider also Roman Numa Pompilius and Norse Tyr) reinforce the continuity of this archetype. Lugh's very name has been proposed to come from *(h2)lewgh-* meaning "to bind by oath" related to Old Irish *luige* and Welsh *llw*, both meaning "oath, vow, act of swearing" and derived from a suffixed Proto-Celtic form, *lugiyo-*, "oath," while the Vedic god of this archetype, Mitra, is theorized to have originated as the god embodying the contract founded on obligatory gift exchange[40], the oath being one species of

---

40 "It becomes apparent that this word, formed with an instrumental suffix or an agent-suffix on the root *mei-* ('to exchange'), this word to which we find so many others related

contract. Gael Hily explains that the two most common theories regarding the name *Lugus* are * leu-, "light," and "v.irl. luige (<* lugion) "oath" (Hily, *Le Dieu Celtique Lugus,* 105). Garrett Olmsted expands upon the second of these thus: "An alternative and possibly more likely etymology for **Lugus*, favored by Meid and Hamp, is to see an origin from the zero-grade of the apophonic forms **leugh-, *lough-, *lugh-* "oath, vow"(**h₂leugʰ-*) (as suggested by Wagner, 1970, 24). One should note, however, that this root is usually presented as an io-stem and only attested in Celtic (*lugiio-*; DPC: 247) and Germanic (IEW: 687; only the full-grade and the zero-grade are attested). From this view, the deity-name *Lugus* likely meant "God of Vows", giving Lugus a role as a god of contracts like Mitráḥ and Mithrō. Meid would see *Lucus* as simply an orthographic variation of *Lugus*" (Olmsted, *The Gods of the Celts and the Indo-Europeans,* 97). Hily, on the other hand, places slightly less weight on the "oath" etymology (though his reason for doing so is less than clear), and more weight on an etymology relating to "light," while still affirming the importance of the connotation of "oath": "it seems difficult to explain Lugus by the name of the 'oath'. Rather, it is a play on words, a common practice among medieval Irish scribes; it often reflected an association of ideas between the terms used. In other words, the pun between Lugus and the 'oath' must be taken into account in the analysis of this god" (Hily, *Le Dieu Celtique Lugus,* 107). It should be noted that an etymology relating to light also supports a Mitraic reading of Lugh, especially in contrast to Nuada as Varuna, Sovereign of the Night Sky, and indeed a pun between the two meanings of "light" and "oath" is plausible.

All of these figures except perhaps the notably pacified Vedic Mitra, but including his incarnation Yudhishthira, are great warrior figures, and associations with Ares (as Menelaus has) or identifications with Mars (as Lugh and Tyr) are found attached to them repeatedly. Dumezil sums up the paradoxical warlike character of this sometimes peaceful god in the section of his *Mitra-Varuna* titled "Mithra Armed," describing how Iranic Mithra is clearly a warlike god, closely associated with the spirit of offensive victory, Verethragna, and wields the *vazra* lightning weapon, while in India Indra has

---

throughout the Indo-European territory - words with nuances of meaning as diverse as Sanskrit *mayate* ('he exchanges'), Latin *munus* ('gift, service performed, obligation, duty') and *communis*, Old Slavonic *mena* ('change, exchange, contract') and *miru* ('peace, cosmos'), and so on - this word **mitra-* must have originally denoted the means or the agent of operations of the potlatch type - in other words, of 'obligatory exchanges of gifts.' Evolving from customs in general, and doubtless as a result of contact with very early civilizations which possessed codes, the meaning of the word naturally narrowed to the more precise one of 'contract,' as occurred in Iran. On the other hand, however, the state the potlatch inevitably creates between its participants, of peace, of order, of collaboration, with alternating rights and duties, is indeed a beginning of 'friendship'" (Dumezil, *Mitra-Varuna*, p. 68).

absorbed Verethragna, become the primary warrior god and wielder of the *vajra* lightning weapon, Mitra there no longer being seen as a combatant (perhaps due to his peace-loving, "friend" side). Yudhishthira himself embodies this paradox: he is depicted as an ideal Brahmin, a wise, justice-loving ascetic who desires to negotiate peace and avoid conflict, but who is eventually inspired to do battle in the name of justice and in order to avenge the dishonor done to his wife, and who leads his forces to victory while achieving the climactic kill with his terrifyingly unstoppable spear. Dhritarashtra vividly sums up this paradoxical character when he says of Yudhishthira,

> If he were not high-minded, they would in wrath burn the Dhritarashtras. I do not so much dread Arjuna or Bhima or Krishna or the twin brothers as I dread the wrath of the king [Yudhishthira], O Suta, *when his wrath is excited* [italics mine]. His austerities are great; he is devoted to *Brahmacharya* practices. His heart's wishes will certainly be fulfilled. When I think of his wrath, O Sanjaya, and consider how just it is, I am filled with alarm. (*Mahabharata, Udyoga Parva*, XXII)

The key to this is that he is violent and terrifying "when his wrath is excited," and that his wrath is just. He brings peace, but does so through sometimes terrible violence.

What we see most clearly is that some societies chose to emphasize the Mitraic Lawful Sovereign's peaceable, Brahmin aspect, while others emphasized his War God aspect (perhaps none more so than did the Irish, but the Irish and Avestan versions come exceedingly close together in this). Thus also, the association of the Lawful Sovereign archetype with the lightning bolt weapon (*vazra/vajra*), which one of Lugh's weapon may parallel, would find agreement in Iranic Mithra with his *vazra*[41], to the Gallic god Romanized as Mars Loucetios (of the lightning). Dumezil even *speculates* that Zeus could partially be seen in this light, a speculation we will show more evidence for as we further our investigations. As he puts it, it is "possible that the Iranian Mithra, a fighter armed with the vazra, simply developed a power already inherent in the Indo-Iranian *Mitra, one that the Vedic Mitra let fall into disuse" (Dumezil, *Mitra-Varuna*, 117). Roger Woodard agrees that the Roman sovereign god so closely identified with the lightning, Jupiter, is comparable to Mitra-Varuna of the Vedics.[42]

---

41 See also Dumezil's comment on Roman Dius Fidius, who he assumed to be Mitraic: "But when such distinctions become necessary, daytime lightning is called *fulgur dium* and is understood to come from Dius Fidius (alias Semo Sancus) or from Jupiter (when his name is understood according to the strict etymological value expressed by the root *deiw-*)" (Dumézil, 1988, p. 73). Roger Woodard, however, has demonstrated a line connecting Dius Fidius to Heracles and back to Vedic Indra. Woodard, 2006, p. 205.

42 "Varuṇa and Mitra, as we have seen already (§1.3), occupy a position in Vedic India equivalent to that of Jupiter in Rome" (Roger Woodard, *Indo-European Sacred Space*,

What we hope to conclude from this is that, whether the spear throw kills the Sun God lover of the adulterous wife, or instead kills the final commander of the opposition's army who may or may not be a god of destruction, these great spear throws are very often performed by the Lawful Sovereign, also known as the "Mitráic" deity. The exceptions are that the Sun God hero of the Kurukshetra War, Karna, is killed by Arjuna after Karna badly wounds Yudhishthira, but even this killing is done on the Mitraic Yudhishthira's command; and similarly Paris, who after dueling Menelaus, and after Menelaus is wounded by Pandarus, is killed not by Menelaus but by Philoctetes, Menelaus instead killing Helen's other husband Deiphobus (who we will explore as a parallel of Balor). In the Irish version, Lugh in fact performs all of these possible killings: the spear thrown through Balor to end the war, the killing of Cermait in revenge for his affair with Lugh's wife, and the killing of the solar Bres by poisoning in one version. What does not change is that there are two main types of spear-throwing scenes, both types usually accomplished by the Mitraic Lawful Sovereign, the god who can throw spears through stone or can throw them to end wars, always throwing them justly, always winning victory thereby.

As we have noted, the name of Lugh's wife *Nas* has a meaning related either to binding or to assembly and he is the first to establish assemblies in Ireland. Meanwhile, Mithras is the chief of assemblies among chiefs of assembly, who binds the hands of those who lie to him. As victory is a satellite or possession of Mithra, Lugh's other wife is named Bua/Bui/Buach, which could be related to a word for "victory."[43] He of course

---

252).

43 Wiktionary.com gives: "**bua** (*genitive singular* **bua**, *nominative plural* **buanna**) 1. (*sports, competition*) victory, win."

See also eDil: http://www.dil.ie/1655. eDIL s.v. airbúaid.

"n (búaid) **great victory, triumph:** trí hurbhuadhaibh Erenn, **TBC-LL**[1] p. 801 n.9 (tri urbadha, text).

n (búadach): mac ruc dar berna b.¤ (: cass) ` victory ', **Metr. Dinds.** iv 202.6 (buachas, buades, *v.ll.*). buadhchas .i. buadhachas, **O'Cl.** buadhachas m. ` victory , triumph ', **Dinneen** .

u, m. vn. of **búadaigid. act of vanquishing, triumphing (***over***), winning; victory , triumph:** nírbu lour leusom buaduguth dib, **Ml.** 33c13 . ilach iar mbuadugad .i. ilach buaidi[g]the, **Laws** v 358.5 , 360.1 Comm. b.¤ do Grecaib dona Troiandaib *that the Greeks had triumphed over*, **TTr.**[2] 180. ar mbuadugad cacha báire, **MR** 244.21 . mergi buadaigthi ꝛ coscair, **Fen.** 166.4 . ag buadhughadh ar lucht na críche `*prevailing over*', **Keat.** i 204.10 . ná léig don duine búadhughadh, **Psalms** ix 19."

búaid. http://www.dil.ie/7221.

"**(a) victory , triumph:** buaidh ` victory ', **Eg. Gl.** 64. buáid et indocbál domsa, **Wb.** 30d13 . a mbuáid inna mmíled talmande, 11a10 . is óinfer gaibes buáid diib, 11a4 . ní ba unus gebas a mbuáid huáibsi, 11a6 . di buaid inna mbabelóndae, **Ml.** 115d9 . amal runucad buáid diib `*as victory had been won over them*', **Ml.** 104a8 . *Cf.* **IT** i 72.10 (**LMU** 8). aní

wins victory for the Tuatha De, and can be said to be closely associated thus with victory, just as Iranic Mithra "establisheth nations in supreme victory," is "Victory-making" and drives in his chariot accompanied by "the Victory made by Ahura," that is, by the embodiment of Victory known as Verethragna. Lugh may have elements or roles which cause him to seem to overlap with certain Terrible Sovereign gods (Oðinn) or Thunderer gods (Indra, Zeus, Thor), but we must attempt to distinguish role from essence by tracking the core myths and central features of the god. Doing so shows him as a Lawful Sovereign god who has become so central that he sometimes controls adjacent domains. Beneath his many roles, Lugh is the god of the contract or oath, he is the god of light who appears bright as the sun coming over the hill in *The Fate of the Children of Tuireann* but who is not the Sun God himself, and he is the late-coming god, the sovereign of endings rather than beginnings, whose festival of Lughnasadh is in fact a harvest festival bringing on the end of Summer leading into Autumn, and he is the god who brings final victory and rules as Sovereign of Justice after the great war of the gods. This is an exceedingly specific role in the Great Structure and has a specific theological meaning. He is the Mitraic god.[44]

---

atreba b.¤ no molad gl. palmarium, **Sg.** 35a10 . iar ṁb. ⅂ coscur, **Fél.** Ep. 23. b.¤ Maicc Dé dia námait, Feb. 15. **PH** 4900. cach buaid fri hU Neill, **Lat. Lives** 81 .z . do ruc buaidh na coimhlinga, **Feis Tighe Chonáin** 994. seoid ⅂ maine . . . log a mbuada, **TTebe** 24651 . buaidh cogaidh, **Stair Erc.** 2130. buaidh cáigh ar Laighnibh *the Laigin conquered all*, **LBranach** 2427 . Eagluis na mBuadh *Church Triumphant*, **Eochairsg.** 73.12."

Wagner (1981) suggests instead that Lugh's wife Bui is related to Indo-European *bovina* 'cow-like-one,' proposing a connection to the Boyne River.

Recall also that Tyr is cuckolded by Loki, and that Loki's wife is said to be Sigyn, *Sig* also being a word for "victory." If Sigyn were originally the wife of Tyr, god of the victory rune, and was taken from him by Loki, this could then potentially create a parallel between Sigyn and Buach, the wife that cheats on Lugh with Cermait. There lurks in this parallel the uncertain possibility that Cermait could be a partial parallel of Loki, though in some other ways Cermait's double Bres also evidences parallels to roles attached to Loki, such as the instigator of the war. This goes back to the theme of the overlap or confusion of Sun God and Demon of the Last Age.

44 My gratitude to Philip Cunningham and Kevin Maclean for first bringing this possibility to my awareness, as well as to Garrett Olmsted who has written on this connection previously.

3

Fionn, Gwyn, and Taliesin: The Celtic Rudra

The case for the identification of the Irish Fionn, the Welsh Gwyn, and the Welsh Taliesin/Gwion with the Vedic Rudra, which we have noted above, will be summarized here. As Kris Kershaw has demonstrated, Rudra is the *männerbünd* god, the exemplar and leader of the band of ecstatic warrior youths that formed a crucial element of archaic Indo-European society (the *koryos*).[45] This band of warrior youths would be sacrally dedicated to the *männerbünd* god and the spirit host he lead and were thought to *become* the dead ancestors in battle, as Kershaw details. As such, the war-band was the material manifestation of the band of ancestral ghosts and daemons that attended this god. On the spirit plane, this is the Wild Hunt of souls, and the Rudraic god is the Wild Hunter. Fionn leads the warrior band, who are also hunters, while his Welsh linguistic cognate

---

45 See also Brereton and Jamison: "As a social phenomenon, the Maruts [a type of Rudra, per Kershaw] represent the Männerbund, an association of young men, usually at a stage of life without significant other social ties (such as wife and children), who band together for rampageous and warlike pursuits. The violence of the thunderstorm is akin to the violence of these unruly age-mates, raiding and roistering. It is likely that Vedic society contained and licensed such groups among its young men, given the frequent warfare depicted in the Ṛgveda, and the divine Maruts provide the charter for this association and behavior" (Brereton and Jamison, *The Rigveda: A Guide*, 85).

Gwyn is a much more outwardly frightening figure, specifically leading the Wild Hunt of souls, attended by a troop of spirits and ghosts. Thus both the material and spirit plane manifestations of the war-band are connected to hunting and to wolves and dogs, even being identified with wolves and dogs in certain cases (see: the Germanic *Ulfheðnar*). Fionn and his band are hunters, habitually depicted in this activity, and closely affiliated with their hunting dogs Bran and Sceolan. These dogs are actually the nephews of Fionn, who have been turned into dogs by a magic spell, thus repeating the human-canine identification that is noted in connection with this deity type. Rudra for his part is connected to "dog-leaders" and "masters of dogs" in 16.27-28 of the *White Yajur Veda*, while his devotees, the *vratyas,* are known as "dog-priests."

As we have delineated, among the leaders of the Fianna is Fionn's uncle Goll, the one-eyed, who embodies the destructive aspect of the Rudraic deity type and is a double of Balor. Furthermore, the Fianna themselves are sometimes described as supernatural forces of the Otherworld and in one text are even specifically mentioned next to the Fomorians, among whom we of course find Balor. As John Carey summarizes, "Some Middle Irish sources suggest that the *fiana* were themselves supernatural inhabitants of the wilderness: in the *dindshenchas* poem on Slige Dala they are paired with the Fomoire (TLS 10. 280. 49); and in *Cogadh Gaedhel re Gallaibh* (ed.J.H.Todd, London 1867, 114) with the troops of the *sid* [burial mounds]" (Carey, "Nodons in Britain and Ireland," 20). Thus the Fianna have a side that clearly merges with the domain more usually associated with Balor. Fionn is even said to have a shield called *Sgiath Gailbhinn*, the Storm Shield, which, when it "called out," could be heard throughout Ireland. This storming, shouting shield was made from the wood on which Balor's head was placed after the Second Battle. It is very strange indeed that Fionn, a hero who does not even appear in that battle, would be given this specific relic of Balor's, until we realize that the shield is properly Fionn's as he is of an essence with Balor: Fionn and the Storm Shield together symbolize the combined power of the destructive and benevolent Rudraic aspects in one. Finally, as Rudra has healing powers which are the flip-side to his destructive powers, so Fionn is also a healer, able to heal with water, as in *The Pursuit of Diarmuid and Grainne*. Compare also the Gaulish god named Apollo Vindonnus, whose name could come from the same root as Fionn (Proto-Celtic *Windos*), and who is connected with the waters of healing springs and particularly with the healing of eyes, as bronze plaques and votives from his temple at Essarois demonstrate (Carey, John, "Nodons, Lugus, Windos", in *Études Luxembourgeoises d'Histoire & de Science des Religions* 1, 99-126).

Goll is not the only member of the Fianna who embodies their destructive side. Another member of the Fianna, Fionn's nephew Caoilte, goes on a rampage that may reflect an ancient ritual role of the Rudraic deity type: "And when Caoilte heard Finn

80

had been brought away to Teamhair, he went out to avenge him. And the first he killed was Cuireach, a king of Leinster that had a great name, and he brought his head up to the hill that is above Buadhmaic. And after that he made a great rout through Ireland, bringing sorrow into every house for the sake of Finn, killing a man in every place, and killing the calves with the cows. And every door the red wind from the east blew on, he would throw it open, and go in and destroy all before him, setting fire to the fields, and giving the wife of one man to another" (Lady Gregory, *Gods and Fighting Men*, "The Best Men of the Fianna"). Similarly, Kershaw goes as far as to say that Rudra is known as the cow and man-killer: "what stands out in the conception of this many-sided personality is the polarity cow-man-killer = fructifier," noting that in the Siilagava sacrifice, "One night a year, after midnight, a householder would bring the best bull from his herd to a place north of and outside the village, devote it to Rudra, and slaughter it. By this act he purchased health for the rest of his herd and for his family'. Behind this rite, in which the cattleman himself led his own beast to sacrifice, lay an older practice in which vratya bands [the Indian mannerbunde] came storming into the farmsteads in the night, stole cattle, drove them out of the village, slaughtered an animal, and feasted together. When the vratyas disappeared, the householders carried on the ritual to buy Rudra's good will, and thus health and prosperity, for that year" (Kershaw, *The One-Eyed God*, 402). She also notes that in a certain legend "The king is livid because his cattle are dying, because Rudra in the form of Pasupati is killing them. Vaka can put an end to the death of the cattle by an offering to the god" (405). So Caoilte of the Fianna killing the cows and men across the land and bringing destruction is very interesting indeed, right in line with what we would expect from the ancient "Rudraic" role. Caoilte engages in this rampage of destruction just before rescuing Fionn, and both Goll and Caoilte are listed among the "best men of the Fianna," suggesting that the destructive and beneficent sides of the Fianna were fully combined in these figures.

As for the Welsh Gwyn: like the rudras, divinities of storm and rain, Gwyn and his host are closely connected to clouds. In a poem of the medieval poet Dafydd ap Gwilym, clouds are "the family of Gwyn (*tylwyth Gwyri*)" and are "the moor of the headland" of Gwyn and his family. The Wild Hunt is alternately called in Welsh *Own y Wybr*, "Hounds of the Clouds," while Gwyn's dog is said to wander "upon Cloud mountain (*gruidir ar Wibirwinit*)," yielding an image of the Wild Hunt racing through the upper air. He is followed by the *ellyllon*, "bogeys, sprites, elves, phantoms, " and is even said to be one of the lords of Annwn, the Otherworld, where the souls of the dead are taken during his hunt.[46] "God put the vigor of the devils of Annwn into him to prevent the ruin of the present world: he will not be spared thence" says a description of him in *Culhwch*

---

46 *Gwaith Dafydd ap Gwilym* (GDG), ed. Thomas Parry, Caerdydd 1952, 127.29-30, 150, 52; 26.40; 68.32, cf. Line 40;127.32.

and Olwen. Compare this narrative to that of the Norse Wild Hunter, Oðinn, who faces the forces of destruction to stave off the world's ruin, and is not spared in the end. Like Rudra, Gwyn is a god of war generally, called "the hope of armies" and "the hero of hosts" ("The Dialogue of Gwyn ap Nudd and Gwyddno Garanhir"). He declares in this poem, "I come from battle and conflict." Carey notes how he "goes on to describe having been present at so many battles of all periods that Rhys suggested that he is really some kind of war-spirit" (Carey, 14). Balor/Goll fighting Lugh at Magh Tuireadh also has a slight similarity to the arc of Gwyn's own destructive campaign: abducting Creiddylad from her beloved, making Cyledr eat his father's heart, and then climactically fighting Gwythr every May Day for Creiddylad's hand, which can be seen as a battle between seasonal forces, winter and summer, related to the holiday. This career of Gwyn's may also parallel the narrative of another Fionn, Fionnbharr of the Daoine Sidhe, known as a king of the dead and a lord of the fae realm. He is called a commander and is known for kidnapping women. The one-eyed giant Ysbaddaden, who also appears centrally in *Culhwch and Olwen*, the hand of his daughter being sought after as Balor's daughter's is, and who is in general a relatively obvious Balor analog, would then carry the remainder of the destructive side of the Welsh Rudraic mythos[47].

The theme of the waters of ecstatic illumination also seems to be a Rudraic theme common to the Celtic parallels. Kershaw notes that "Rudra is the god from whose cup the kesin, the long-haired ecstatic of RV 10. 136, drinks the drug," and that he is connected with various ecstatic practices, particularly in relation to the Vratyas (outsider warrior-ascetics) and other manifestations of the ecstatic youthful *männerbünd*. She notes that the youths who were members of the sacred war-band were also trained to be poets, and spent half of their year studying this art. Thus, it would make perfect sense if one of the core Rudraic myths involved gaining an ecstatic poetic enlightenment.

Irish Fionn and Welsh Gwion do exactly this. Fionn is minding the cooking of the Salmon of Knowledge, which has eaten the hazelnuts from the waters of the well of wisdom, *Segais,* and which has been caught by his teacher, the poet Finn Eces (another poet Finn, and so possibly the teacher aspect of the Rudraic deity type[48]). Fionn has been

---

47 Kershaw notes that the mannerbund warriors would have to ritually cut their hair as part of their coming-of-age ceremony, possibly marking the fact that they are putting aside the wild war-band lifestyle and entering the tribe as adults. Meanwhile, one of the trials demanded of Culhwch is, strangely, to retrieve special, difficult to obtain, haircutting implements and to cut the hair of Ysbaddaden, who we claim is a rudraic figure. This part of the myth could then have an origin in the ritual cutting of the hair of the members of the rudraic war-band in order to complete an initiation into adulthood.

48 However, Fionn's grandfather (or ancestor of ambiguous distance) Nuada is also occasionally called Finn-Eces, which either shows the overlap of the two deities or the general closeness of Nuada to Fionn. Welsh Gwyn is son of Nudd (parallel of Nuada)

instructed not to taste of the salmon as he cooks it, as Finn Eces intends the wisdom for himself. Testing the fish with his thumb to see if it is done, Fionn burns his finger, and presently places it in his mouth to soothe the pain. He is suddenly imparted all of the knowledge stored up in the salmon, and his eyes now glow with illumination. Thus the poet Finn has imparted the wisdom to the young apprentice via the tasting of a fish that has the waters of wisdom within it.

It has long been recognized that the story of Welsh Gwion Bach, aka Taliesin, matches Fionn's in large part. Gwion is merely another form of the name Gwyn, name of the frightening Wild Hunt specter Gwyn ap Nudd. These names in turn are the Welsh forms of the Irish Fionn, the interchange of *G* for *F* being common between the two languages. Fionn/Gwyn/Gwion mean "white, bright, blessed, holy"[49] and come from Proto-Celtic *Windos,* likely from PIE *weyd- "to know, to see," emphasizing how central the role of seer is to this deity. He is "The Knower." Note as well Eber Fionn, one of the Sons of Mil, from the pseudo-historical layer of the *Lebor Gabala Erenn,* suggesting that this may be a deeply established divine name. John Rhys points out that Finn ua Nuadat and Gwyn fab/ap Nudd are linguistic cognates (Rhys, *Hibbert Lectures on the Origin and Growth of Religion as Illustrated by Celtic Heathendom,* 179). Finn ua Nuadat, the grandson of Nuada (Nuadu mac Achi[50]), is then the parallel of the Wild Hunter Gwyn ap Nudd, the son of Nudd, and in another aspect is parallel of Gwyn's linguistic double Gwion.

As told in the *Hanes Taliesin,* a tale recorded in the 16th century and included by Lady Charlotte Guest in her *Mabinogion,* Gwion, in a similar manner to Fionn, is made to tend the cooking of another special meal, another comestible that grants knowledge. This is a potion of poetic inspiration being prepared by the enchantress or goddess Cerridwen and intended for her son. As such, Gwion has of course been instructed not to taste the potion as it cooks. However, three drops of the potion leap out of the hot cauldron and land on Gwion's finger, burning him. He quickly puts his finger into his mouth to soothe the pain, as had Fionn. He instantly gains all the wisdom and poetic inspiration of the potion, the rest of the cauldron suddenly becoming poisonous and useless. A chase ensues during which Gwion uses his newfound wisdom to change into a series of animals to

---

rather than grandson (or "descendant"). Eces translates as "seer."

49 The Rudras "are shining, brilliant, golden; they are fires, or they are bright like Agni. They wear golden mantles and ornaments of gold, and they travel in war-chariots. In all this they resemble their father in his brighter moments" (Kershaw, 358). Of Rudra: "He shines in splendour like the Sun, refulgent as bright gold is he" (*RV* 1.43.3).

50 Also Nuadu Necht in the poem "Slan seiss a Brigit." Furthermore, Carey notes that "An ancient genealogical poem edited by Meyer traces three paternal lines of Nuadu Necht's descendants, two ending in Finn File and Finn mac Umaul" ("Nodons in Britain and Ireland").

escape the enraged Cerridwen. She mirrors him by transforming into animals well-suited to catch him in each form. He changes into a hare, so she becomes a greyhound; he changes into a fish, so she becomes an otter; he changes into a bird, so she becomes a hawk. Finally, he transforms into a grain of wheat. Cerridwen turns herself into a hen and eats him. Instead of dying, however, he gestates in her womb, and is reborn to her as Taliesin. The name *Taliesin* could be a variation on the theme of shining brightness common to the names of Fionn and Gwion and means "radiant brow," while the shining brow is also a symbol of the power of the mind of the seer. Cerridwen, unable to kill the beautiful child, casts him into the waters. He washes up in the fish-weir of Elffin ap Gwyddno, who raises him to become the most famous of Welsh bards.

Just as Fionn's teacher and cooking master had carried a version of the name Finn, so Gwion is likewise surrounded by figures with variations of this name in their names. Cerrid*wen* has the adjective *wen* in her name, which, if it does not derive instead as a corruption of -*ven*, "woman," usually is derived from *gwyn/gwen*, the same name we have had to deal with so far. Cooking master *Finn* Eces would then make a curious parallel with cooking master Cerrid*wen*. And again, when Taliesin washes up and is discovered, his discoverer is Elf*fin*, which may come from the Irish *ail* "rock" and *fion* "white/bright," the second portion being the same name we have been tracking. Thus the man who raises and presumably teaches Gwion/Taliesin bears a variant of the name Fin(n), as does the teacher of Fionn, Finn Eces. Meanwhile, even the potion of inspiration is in Welsh named *Awen*, appears at first to connect once again to the same word – *wen*, which would emphasize its central role in the seer's vocation – however, the etymology appears instead to be from *-uel*, meaning 'to blow,' with the same connotation as the English verb "inspire," which comes from PIE *(s)peys*- ("to blow, breathe"). The appearance of *wen* in this word could of course be no accident, an instance of esoteric wordplay, both meanings being present and indeed related to one another on a deeper level.

One last *Fin* needs to be mentioned here, and that is the Irish Fintan or Fionntan mac Bocra. With the multiplication of this general name, which we have traced so far, and with the multiplicity of the Rudras and Maruts in Vedic tradition, there is little reason to exclude the possibility that Fintan too may reflect one of the Rudraic/Fenian deities. He is called "the wise," and is known as a seer. He has lived for several millennia and has used his power of transformation to live as a series of different animals. While Taliesin changes into a hare, a fish, and a bird, Fintan changes into a salmon, an eagle, and a hawk. Fionn gains the sum of the world's knowledge from a salmon while Fintan carries in himself the world's knowledge and lives in the form of a salmon, leading to a common confusion between these two salmon. Curiously, The Salmon of Knowledge is also called *Goll Essa Ruiad,* "One-Eyed of the Red Waterfall," while Fintan also is said to be one-eyed when he is a salmon (MacKillop, *An Oxford Dictionary of Celtic Mythology,* 230), repeating the connection between this god-type and one-eyedness. Due to his great age and the wisdom he has gained over so many generations, Fintan becomes known as the storehouse of all Ireland's knowledge. In "The Settling of the Manor of Tara," a narrative reminiscent of Taliesin's display of poetic skill and prophetic knowledge before the king Maelgwn Gwynedd, Fintan appears before king Diarmaid mac Cearrbheoil and answers a series of challenging questions, including why Tara is in the center of Ireland. Fintan even meets up with Fionn at the end of their lives to share their knowledge together, perhaps signaling the deeper connection between the two.

Taliesin comes to be considered The Prime Bard, the Chief of Bards in the Welsh tradition, and his name becomes synonymous with poetry. A similar thing happens in the Irish case, but this role seems to be focused into Fionn's son, Oisin. As Gwion had transformed by a rebirth into Taliesin, Oisin is instead born as son to Fionn, but a similar division or second birth as Prime Poet exists in both branches. We note again a similarity between the last portions of each of these names, *-sin.* Due to the general similarities of these two poets, Louis Herbert Gray suggested that *Oisin* could speculatively be equivalent to *-essin* or *-eisin* in *Taliesin.* In truth, Oisin seems to come from *os,* "deer," and the diminutive suffix *-in,* making the etymologies outwardly incompatible. Still, surface similarities should be duly noted as homophony is important in poetic material as well as religious naming. Oisin then becomes one of the great representative names of the Irish poetic tradition, as Taliesin does for the Welsh, and the tales of the Fianna are attributed to him as their author and narrator.

We see that the Rudraic mythos, so multiple in its manifestation, is divided in different ways even between these two closely situated insular Celtic cultures. Fionn, Goll, Oisin and Fintan reflect different Rudraic roles that are mirrored in Gwyn, Gwion, Ysbaddaden (parallel of Goll/Balor), and Taliesin in Wales. Fionn specifically matches aspects of Gwyn (Wild Hunter), Gwion (waters of illumination), and Fintan (transformations, storehouse of wisdom) while Taliesin matches Fintan in part as well as Oisin (national poet), but all of these figures overlap in more complex ways than such a reduction can sum up. When we compare the Celtic case once more to the Norse case of the Rudraic god Oðinn, the elements are again divided differently. Oðinn has one eye, like the ambivalent and destructive Goll, but he is not fully a god of destruction as we see in the form manifested by Balor, who loses an eye as well, even though he shares some of his specific paralytic powers. Instead, Oðinn brings the dangerous Rudraic element within bounds and directs it toward the project of order and societal benefit. He parallels the myth of the tasting of the liquid (or fish) of inspiration when he drinks of Mimir's well and in this myth his one-eyedness also comes about. There is also an additional tale of Fionn in which he drinks from a well of wisdom and foretelling, recorded in the account of Fionn's boyhood deeds in versions such as "The Coming of Fionn" in *Gods and Fighting Men*. As such, Oðinn combines something of the Goll/Balor element with the Fionn/Gwyn element, as leader of the Wild Hunt and of the warrior bands, ecstatic poet and seer, keeping in reserve the destructive power connected to the frightening spirit world. These deities all overlap because they are all of one type or may even be aspects of one whole, they all share the same general powers and potentialities but directed toward different roles and ends – they are all "Rudras."

Varuna-Rudra and the Oðinnic Question

When Nuada is understood as Varunian (as we have suggested) and the above Celtic figures as Rudraic, we are able to shed some light on the great mystery of how the Norse god Oðinn can seem to "combine" the Rudraic divinity with the Varunian role in himself. The Varunian Nuada being grandfather of Fionn and his cognate Nudd being father of Gwyn may hint at a deeper connection between the two deity types. Carey submits that "Insofar as the meagerness of the Welsh evidence allows us to judge, therefore, Nuadu/Ludd [aka Nudd] and Finn/Gwyn represent different aspects of Nodons [...] The overlapping attributes of Nuadu and Finn, and the identification of Nodons with Mars, suggest that the divine ancestor [Nodons] in fact comprises all of these functions and that his offspring reflect facets of his character" (Carey, 21-22). He then expands upon this theory that the British Nodons may combine in himself both the "Nudd" and the "Gwyn" deities in one figure (though this theory is difficult to prove due to the stated overlap), that is, that Nodons combines the Varunian and the Rudraic, similarly to what we see with Oðinn, concluding: "Nodons thus appears as a god of multifaceted but consistent character: a shining royal warrior presiding over the chaotic in nature, society and the Otherworld (water, war, the devils of Annwn). It is of further interest that such a figure should appear as a dynastic ancestor, and the eventual victim of the forces which he dominated" (Carey, 22). Rudra is lord of thieves and a deceiver, friend of rakshasas (demons) (see: *Yajurveda* XVI.21) and also their destroyer. Not only does Fionn have a back-and-forth rivalry with Goll, who represents the destructive side of his own otherworldly host ("the forces which he dominated"), but he also fights an otherworldly fire deity as does Oðinn. This is Aillen, "the burner," who emerges from the underworld of Mag Mell and burns Tara to the ground every Samhain until Fionn finally defeats him. This feat is connected to Fionn ascending to leadership of the Fianna, but in the context of what we have just discussed, it could also parallel the destructive burning fiend Surtr, who Oðinn's army is forced to contend with at Ragnarok. Though Fionn keeps Goll and Aillen and the Fianna in line for now, the cyclical nature of Aillen's attack makes it tempting to speculate that one day "the burner," in whatever manifestation, might return to overcome Fionn's resistance and burn the world just as Surtr does in the war with Oðinn and the Aesir.

We will see, further along (in the chapter "The High Priest of the Word"), that the Vedic deity Brihaspati is *also* bafflingly intertwined with the Rudraic (the two being fully combined in Greek Apollo, for instance, and having a father-son relationship as the Indian Drona and Ashwatthama). In that chapter we will furthermore identify the Irish parallel of Oðinn hanging on the Windy Tree, which is once more found in a tale of the Rudraic hero Fionn. Brihaspati, on the other hand, likely corresponds to yet another aspect of Oðinn. We will see that the Irish Brihaspati is Dian Cecht, and that *his* son Cian is yet *another* Oðinnic aspect. Meanwhile, Dian Cecht and Balor are the two grandfathers, and Cian the father, of Lugh, who we have shown to parallel Tyr and Baldr, sons of Oðinn according to Snorri. Beginning with this Rudra-Varuna/Fionn-Nuada/Gwyn-Nudd concatenation, a full picture of Oðinnic Celtic-Norse parallelism will be gradually built up through the subsequent chapters, and the underlying interconnection of Oðinn's several "aspects" will be seen with a new clarity.

****

Cerridwen, Boann, and Saraswati

The scholar Gwilym Morus-Baird has argued that the aforementioned Cerridwen could parallel Vedic Saraswati.[51] This is interesting because there is no other goddess in Welsh myth who resembles Saraswati more than she, so his hypothesis could well be accurate, even if it is impossible to say for certain due to how little material there is on Cerridwen. The specific Irish parallel of the primary river goddess of Vedic myth, Saraswati, is certainly the primary river goddess of Irish myth, Boann/Ethniu, as we will see in more detail in a later chapter. So if we look at the parallel myths — Cerridwen guiding Gwion Bach to cook the potion of inspiration in Wales, and, in Ireland, Fionn-Eces guiding Fionn MacCumhaill to cook the Salmon of Knowledge (each with very similar outcomes) — we see that Fionn Eces is sometimes a name of Nuada, as we have discussed above. Who is the consort of Nuada? Boann, the Irish Saraswati. It could then make sense that Cerridwen would be the cognate of Saraswati, if we have Nuada as the

---

51 Web. https://www.youtube.com/watch?v=lhDBCXYUVYU. Accessed June 2021.

cooking instructor of Fionn in Irish, and Cerridwen, the parallel of Nuada's consort, as the cooking instructor of Gwion in the matching Welsh myth. Nuada and Boann/Cerridwen would be co-guardians of the waters of illumination. Moreover, the river in which the Salmon of Knowledge swims in the myth paralleling Cerridwen's is the Boyne, Boann-Saraswati's own river. So it is from those waters that the Irish version draws the same inspiration that is given by Cerridwen's cauldron. The famous well, which is the source of the Boyne, and in which the Salmon eats the Hazelnuts of Wisdom, is known as the *Well of Segais*, Segais being an alternate name of Boann, and the Boyne also being called the *Sruth Segsa*: "Segais was her name in the Sid [ie. Otherworld]/ to be sung by thee in every land:/ *River of Segais* is her name from that point/ to the pool of Mochua the cleric" (*Metrical Dindshenchas, Boand I*).

In his argument, Morus-Baird quotes John Muir's commentary on the *Rig Veda* describing Saraswati as "a goddess that embodies knowledge, arts, music, melody, muse, language, rhetoric, eloquence, creative work and anything whose flow purifies the essence and self of a person," while Cerridwen guards and dispenses the potion of inspiration and is thus the primary female Welsh figure associated with liquid that grants knowledge. Meanwhile Cerridwen means something like "Crooked(?) White," and Boann comes from *Bo Find*, meaning "White Cow." The endings of both names are from the same root word, *find/wen*, from Proto Celtic *vind* or *windos*, meaning "white, fair, sacred." The first part of Cerridwen is uncertain, "crooked" being only one possibility. However, it could plausibly refer to a crooked, winding river. The Vedic goddess Vac (who seems to be a form of Saraswati) is emitted after a performance of tapas and is fashioned into a cow in *Jaiminiya Brahmana* 2.252, and in RV 8.89.11 Vac is called "the Gladdener, yielding food and vigour, the Milch-cow Vak." Saraswati pours for Nahusa "her milk and fatness" in RV 7.95.2.

Sheena McGrath[52] points out a passage from the *Tain bo Fraech* which highlights a clear connection between Boand and Saraswati-Vac with regard to being a "mother" of music, and this points back to Cerridwen again:

> Gentle and melodious were the triad, and they were the Chants of Uaithne (Child-birth). The illustrious triad are three brothers, namely Gol-traiges (Sorrow-strain), and Gen-traiges (Joy-strain), and Suan-traiges (Sleep-strain). Boand from the fairies is the mother of the triad: it is from the music which Uaithne, the Dagda's harp, played that the three are named.

Anthony Murphy notes:

---

52 https://earthandstarryheaven.com/2017/05/03/boand-anahita-saraswati/.

Of huge significance is the fact that the [Boyne] river would appear to have been considered the earthly reflection of the Milky Way, the bright band of our galaxy which runs through the night sky. The river is *Abhann na Bó Finne.* The Milky Way is known in Irish as *Bealach/Bóthar na Bó Finne,* the Way/Road of the White Cow. Newgrange is known in Irish as *Brú na Bóinne,* the mansion or womb of *Bóinn. (Murphy, "Newgrange and the Boyne Valley monuments — advanced lunar calculations and observation of the effects of recession of the equinoxes in Neolithic Ireland — Part 2")*

Thus the Boyne is the earthly manifestation of the celestial, archetypal stream, which statement we can then compare to the central Vedic river, the Saraswati.

4

The Dagda, The Irish Wind Harvester

There is a parable in the *Briharayandaka Upanishad* that tells of the special role of the god Vayu. Vayu and the other gods of the bodily functions made a test to decide the greatest among them. One by one the gods left the body of a man. The man could carry on, in better or worse shape, when each of the various other gods abandoned their posts. However, when it was Vayu's turn to leave the body, not only was it robbed of life, but each of the other gods was overpowered and pulled out along with Vayu. They quickly realized the supremacy of this wind god's power. If this was not enough to illustrate his importance to the Vedic people, the *Chandogya Upanishad* teaches that only by knowing Vayu in the form of the syllable *om* can the spiritual seeker know Brahman.

Dagda and Thor

On the surface, the Irish god the Dagda is somewhat difficult to neatly match to Vedic myth, and in general has proven to be controversial and mysterious to interpreters who would seek to shoehorn him into a typical Indo-European mythological framework. Due to his blunt weapon and great appetite, along with his position as paragon of strength, one would be forgiven for thinking his most obvious match would be the Germanic god Thor, who was written and sung about in such a lively way in Iceland, Ireland's closely connected neighbor to the north, along with the other parts of the Germanic and Scandinavian world.

The scholar John Shaw has written compellingly about this mythological connection, pointing to similarities, in stories such as the Dagda's retrieval of the magic harp, which connect the Dagda to Thor as well as to Zeus. Indeed, the Dagda is said in the *Dindshenchas of Mag Muirthemne* to banish some sort of underwater octopus creature, just as Thor in a similar way was known to do battle with the aquatic Midgard Serpent. In fact, Shaw's essay "The Dagda, Thor and ATU 1148B: Analogues, Parallels, or Correspondences?" brings forward a host of evidence in support of this thesis and is almost entirely convincing in making the Dagda the Irish Thor. It is a valuable essay and the connections it highlights are important to know. However, scholars such as Matthias Egeler have cast these parallels into doubt (*Celtic Influences in Germanic Religion*), and as any such scholar will also be able to tell you, another mystery remains. Thor is linguistically cognate with the continental Celtic god Taranis (and perhaps with the Irish Tuireann) – a god whose descriptively literal name earns him the title "Thunderer." As such, Taran and possibly Tuireann are often seen as represented in the East by the powerful god of thunder and war, Indra. Thus, in linguistic terms at least, it would seem that the Dagda and Thor are simply a mismatch of archetypes, that an Irish "Thunderer" may already exist, a god who is clearly separate from the Dagda, and that the undeniable similarities in the Dagda and Thor mythos are perhaps later developments due to borrowing or incidental overlap. Yet, in spite of all this, there is a lens through which we can justify the core linkage between the Dagda and Thor while recognizing also that another archetype is more fully at play here. This involves understanding the Indo-European Wind God, that deity known to the Vedics as Vayu.

Relation of Thunder and Wind Gods in the Warrior Function

While both Thor and Indra may be, in shorthand, referred to as "the Thunderer," due to their control of thunder and lightning, this does not actually indicate the whole character of the god we see in either the Germanic or Vedic myths. The mythologist Georges Dumezil outlines a crucial feature of the gods of the warrior or "second" function, and it is a key to understanding Indo-European myth as a whole. Just as the first and third functions have two representative deities who form a partnership or duad (Mitra-Varuna, for example), in a similar way the Second Function has for its exemplars the two contrasting warrior gods – in Vedic myth and hymn: Indra and Vayu. Dumezil describes their contrast as the same as that seen between Achilles and Hercules, calling the first "the chivalrous," and the second "the brutal." Arjuna, incarnation of Indra, and Achilles in similar fashion, are depicted as brooding figures, each rather sensitive in their own ways, hanging back from the events of battle for a time in reaction to an internal crisis, and yet in the crucial moments leading the vanguard of military generals and victorious in key one-on-one battles that turn the tide of the war (i.e. Achilles over Hector, Arjuna over Bhishma and Karna). Bhima – incarnation of Vayu – like Hercules, is defined by his brute strength (which is paired with comically massive appetite), and he is in general a loyal and unfazed soldier, performing great military feats with steadfast effectiveness. Alongside the aristocratic Achilles we picture the superhuman strength and brutishness of the Bhima-like Ajax.

Now, those familiar with the relevant myths might object: "Thor and Indra both are famed for their strength, their appetites, and have enough comic brutishness between them to match Hercules, Ajax, or the Dagda!" Dumezil has an answer for this. According to this esteemed scholar's judgment, by the time of the rise to supremacy of Indra to which the *Rig Veda* bears witness, Vayu had greatly receded in importance and had largely been neglected by the prominent *rishis*. There are fewer than ten full hymns to Vayu in the *Rig Veda*, leading many to write him off as an unimportant deity, despite the fact that he is incarnated in one of the five Pandavas in the *Mahabharata,* who represented the archaic primary gods. As Dumezil puts it, "the role of Vayu within the warrior function…is very nearly effaced in the Veda" (*Destiny of the Warrior*, Dumezil, 73). But more than simply receding and vanishing, Vayu's mythos, according to Dumezil, was rather absorbed by the inexorably expanding figure of Indra, so that the Indra of the *Rig Veda* could properly be called Vayu-Indra, with an emphasis of course on the traits of Indra. Dumezil points out that in the *Mahabharata* the incarnations of Vayu and Indra are distinct from one another and form a clear contrast, and that in the Iranic Avestan literature, the "Vayu" we find also attests to this distinct character. The presence of this clear Vayu/Indra contrast in both Vedic and Iranic branches attests to the archaic Indo-Iranic timeframe of the distinction (see *Destiny of the Warrior* for Dumezil's detailed argument on this complex topic). As he summarizes it, we have "the two types of warrior god – represented in the pre-Vedic period, presumably, by Vayu and Indra, combined in the *Rig Veda* under the name of Indra, but attested as distinct in their sons, the heroes Bhima and Arjuna, up to the time of the epic" (90, *Destiny of the Warrior*, Dumezil). Likewise of Thor, Dumezil says he should more accurately be seen as a manifesting traits seen as belonging to both the wind and thunder gods in the Vedic branch: similarly to Vayu-Indra we seem to have in the Thor of Germanic myth a Wind-Thunder god, in Dumezil's estimation, however, this time with a significant shift toward the outward character of (counterintuitively) the Wind God. In fact, Dumezil goes as far as to say "except for his role as the god of thunder and lightning, Thorr owes practically nothing to this aspect [the chivalrous-Indraic aspect], and, in contrast, develops the other [the brutal- Herculean/Vayu aspect]" (90, *Destiny of the Warrior*, Dumezil).

In support of a wind aspect for Thor, Richard Perkins points out that, in sagas and tales such as Rögnvalds þáttr ok Rauðs, among others, Thor is associated with sailing and with the fair or foul winds looked to on sea voyages. There are "numerous written examples of Norse sailors attempting to conjure up wind magic, often through the invocation of the god Thor, who is charged with special responsibility for the weather," as Katrina Burge summarizes Perkins' argument (Katrina Burge, *"Thor the Wind-Raiser and the Eyrarland Image* (review)," 253). Perkins argues that the famous bronze artifact known as the Eyrarland image depicts Thor emitting the wind from his mouth, and that "The argument that Thor was visualized as blowing out the wind, and that he was invoked to influence the wind leads to the conclusion that the Eyrarland image and other similar artifacts can be identified as amulets carried by those, presumably sailors, who most wanted to control the wind" (Burge, 253). Burge concludes: "Perkins relies on a detailed explication of a passage from the little known Icelandic þáttr (tale) to argue that, as with his better-known hammer-wielding influence over thunder, the god's control of the wind is instrumental" (Burge, 253). We also have a direct connection of Thor to control of the air and wind in Adam of Bremen, who says: "Thor, they say, presides over the air, which governs the thunder and lightning, the winds and rains, fair weather and crops" (Adam of Bremen, *Gesta Hammaburgensis* 26)

The "Splitting" of the Warrior Function?

Thus our usual understanding of the "Thunderer" gods is an incomplete one. Among all of the paired duads of gods, and no less with the Wind/Thunder pair, there is an observable flow of characteristics from one to the other over time, often resulting in an amalgamation of the two, or at least in a wind or thunder god who has acquired parts of the mythos or simply conquered roles of the other while the other recedes more or less into the background. It is something like the twin who absorbs his brother in the mother's womb. For the Vedics, Indra rises and absorbs certain "wind" traits, Vayu is reduced and pushed aside. For the Germanics, Thor rises and absorbs, combining elements found in both Indra and Vayu. In Ireland, however, Tuireann, the oft-presumed Thunderer, is brought low and killed off, registering very little in extant Irish myth outside of the tale of he and his sons' deaths. According to the Roman Sulpicius Severus, Gallo-Romans considered Taranis to be *hebetus*, stupid, and in some degree neglected his worship as a result. This cannot be extrapolated to the Irish case with confidence, but it can allow us to speculate one possibility: that the Celts, at least in some areas and probably only in later times (judging by the many Taranis inscriptions nonetheless found in continental Celtic regions), may have gradually lessened their focus on the classic Thunderer deity. Instead, we have in the Irish case a prominent god, the Dagda, who has some mythic similarities to Thor, but who does not bear the typical Thunderer's name (while Tuireann's name at least suggests a possible link) and who has other key differences with the thunder gods Thor and Indra. And we even have another god, Lugh, possibly taking on many of the "princely-chivalrous" roles that in India would have been expected of the Indra type. In fact this theorized splitting up of the "Indra" mythos would actually put Germanic and Irish myth in near alignment with one another on this point. While, as Dumezil argues, Óðinn takes on the princely and chivalrous traits and roles found in Indra, leaving the thunder and lightning to the more Vayu-like Thor, in a similar fashion Lugh could take traits and roles that are connected in the Vedic case to the Indra mythos, and Dagda could take others.

Connections to the wind god have been argued for Óðinn as well, which may suggest that the "First Function" roles connected to the forces of Thunder and Wind were seen as domains of Óðinn, while the "Second Function" traits associated with these divine forces were viewed as belonging to Thor – simply a different theological understanding of the domains of these deities when compare with the Vedic religion. By understanding this event, the differing distribution of the would-be "Indra" element between the god of the Wind and the Sovereign god archetypes, we can begin to understand a set of key

94

theological differences between the Indo-European religions of Northwest Europe and that of Vedic India. In this context, we should press forward our investigation of the various strikingly Vayu-esque traits possessed by the Dagda.

Wind Traits of Dagda

When trying to assess the "Wind God" traits of the Dagda, his magical harp is a first possible connection – it possesses the power to induce sleep and has the name "the 4-angled music." It has been said that this refers to the four seasons and his control of the weather and perhaps the cycles of time (he halts the Sun's movement in another myth). However, it can also be read as having the alternate meaning of the four cardinal directions for which the winds are named. And indeed the changing winds and the changing seasons are intimately intwined. Furthermore, it is a mystery why the seasons would be associated with the concept of angles. It is actually the cardinal directions and their winds and not the seasons that can be more accurately described by the word "angled." Consistent with this famed harp of the Dagda, Vayu was also known as the king of the celestial musicians according to the *Visnu Purana*, wind being the originating force and essence of music. It has been suggested by the commentator Scott A. Martin ("The Names of the Dagda", 2008, 4) that the Dagda's claim when speaking to the daughter of Indech, that his footprint would be on every stone, signifies his connection to lightning and storm. Yet how frequently does lightning hit a given stone? What is more likely to leave its mark on *every* stone, the sporadic and rare lightning, or the pervading and persistent erosion of the wind? Indeed, though storm in a general sense has some relevance to the issue, lightning itself hardly makes sense in this context on closer inspection. Admittedly, the storm rain is a possible interpretation, but so is the erosive wind, and the wind god comes along with the rains even in the *Rig Veda*. More than these points though, an analysis of the Dagda's names appears very capable of supporting a wind interpretation.

Dagda's Names

In Isolde Carmody's translation of the names of Dagda[53], *Dein* translates as "swift" or "mighty." *Dictionary of the Irish Language* (DIL) here gives "swiftness, speed, impetuosity, vehemence," with the alternate meaning of "pure, clean, neat and powerful." These hardly require argument, as the wind and the deity associated with it are universally known as swift and impetuous, as well as powerful. Later the Dagda is called "harsh and stern" as well as "hardy and resolute in moral quality," the wind being famous for its harshness and the wind god for his exemplary resoluteness. *Fer Benn Bruaich*, which the Dagda calls his "lawful" name, Carmody translates as "man of the peaks and shores." What do peaks and shores have in common besides the presence of wind? *Bogail Broumide* Carmody interprets as "large lapped farter," which certainly could be a comic description of the wind, and what other god than the Wind god could it be acceptable to called flatulent? *Cerbaid Ceic* means "cutting mountains," and one could picture a sharp wind cutting once again through the high peaks. But in fact, Vayu also has a prominent myth in which he literally *cuts a mountain.* In the *Bhagavata Purana*, at the request of the sage Narada, Vayu attacks the polar mountain, Meru, breaking off its summit with storm winds and throwing it into the sea. Hanuman, Vayu's son, also once tore up a mountain and took it with him in order to bring a healing herb to his dying ally Lakshman. "Great Lying Bag" (*Rolaig Buile*) I have a hard time seeing as other than something like the fabled bag of wind, as the one kept by the Greek wind god Aeolus, or even the common expression "windbag"; moreover, lies are often poetically compared to the wind, unstable and impossible to pin down or depend upon. *Labair Cercce Di Brig,* "Talkative Hen on the Hill," continues the theme of noisiness on high locations. *Oldathair Boith,* "Great Father of Being," and *Athgen mBethai Brightere,* "Regeneration of the World of Dry Land," both fall in line with the Upanishadic notion of the Wind/Air as the master of life, and further than that we may picture the wind as the primary scatterer of seeds which bring new life to the world each year, fostering cyclical regeneration. In fact, Vayu in the *Rig Veda* is called "Germ of the world" (X.CLXVIII.4), that which makes the world germinate, generate, and grow. Another name of the Dagda's is *Rig Scotbe*, which means "King of Speech," and what is more vital to speech than the breath itself, the wind which we blow forth as spoken words? The wind of Vayu is said to redden the sky (RV 10.168.1), while the Dagda is the red lord, *Ruad.*

As for the title *Rofhessa* – "Lord of Great Knowledge" – within the scope of our interpretation this may be explained in one of a couple possible ways. The title of "all-knowing" generally originated with the great Father Sky (Dyaus), whose position in the all-surrounding firmament, along with the sun and stars which were said to be his eyes and his spies, allowed him to bear witness to and know all things in the world. As we will discuss later on, it was very common for another god to inherit this title from the sky god when the sky god receded from prominence. Alternately, he could have simply

---

53 https://storyarchaeology.com/names-of-the-dagda/. Accessed December 2019.

gained the epithet through the association of the wind with the breath, prana, *om*, and esoteric pursuit.[54] Vayu too was associated with the *soma* sacrifice, which gives enlightenment and immortality, known as the first to reach it and taste its delights due to his unmatched speed. Perhaps connected with this, he was also sometimes said to keep his own store of the nectar of immortality, the *amrita*: "Thou art our Father, Vāta, yea, thou art a Brother and a friend,/So give us strength that we may live./The store of Amṛta laid away yonder, O Vāta, in thine home,—/Give us thereof that we may live" (RV, X.CLXXXVI.2-3). While Vayu has this store of the nectar, the Dagda is famous for his large, never-dry cauldron of plenty. We do not deny that Dagda also has many roles of Father Sky, and so the Wind and Sky motifs relating to knowledge may be overlapping.

Dagda's title *Eochaidh*, commonly translated as "horseman," gives no trouble to our comparison with Vayu. There is ample evidence in the *Rig Veda* that Vayu was strongly linked to horses, often said to be carried by a fleet of a thousand of them, often drawn in a chariot:

> Come with thy team-drawn car, O Vāyu, to the gift, come to the sacrificer's gift. (RV, I.CXXXIV.1)

> Two red steeds Vāyu yokes, Vāyu two purple steeds, swift-footed, to the chariot, to the pole to draw, most able, at the pole, to draw. (RV, I.CXXXIV.3)

> come Vāyu, to our feast, with team of thousands, come, Lord of the harnessed team, with hundreds, Lord of harnessed steeds! (RV, I.CXXXV.1)

> Drive thou thy horses, Vāyu, come to us with love, come well-inclined and loving us. (RV, I.CXXXV. 2)

> Come thou with hundreds, come with thousands in thy team to this our solemn rite, to taste the sacred food, Vāyu, to taste the offerings (RV, I.CXXXV.3)

> Harness, O Vāyu, to thy car a hundred well-fed tawny steeds,

> Yea, or a thousand steeds, and let thy chariot come to us with might. (RV, IV.XLVIII.5)

> To you pure juice, rich in meath, are offered by priest: through longing for the Pair of Heroes. Drive, Vāyu, bring thine harnessed horses hither: drink the pressed Soma till it make thee joyful. Whoso to thee, the Mighty, brings

---

54 For Vayu as *prana* see Gonda, *RI* 51. Kris Kershaw notes: "In his own circles Vayu is the warriors' god as well as ruler of heaven and hell" and cites Wikander, *Vayu* 49; "Konigsgott" 81; associated with ecstatic visions 77.

oblation, pure Soma unto thee, pure- drinking Vāyu, That man thou makest famous among mortals: to him strong sons are born in quick succession. (RV, VII.XC.1-2)

O VĀYU, drinker of the pure, be near us: a thousand teams are thine, Allbounteous Giver.

To thee the rapture-bringing juice is offered, whose first draught, God, thou takest as thy portion. (RV, VII.XCII.1)

Borne on his car with these for his attendants, the God speeds forth, the universe's Monarch. Travelling on the paths of air's mid-region, no single day doth he take rest or slumber. Holy and earliest-born, Friend of the waters, where did he spring and from what region came he? Germ of the world, the Deities' vital spirit, this God moves ever as his will inclines him. (RV, X.CLXVIII.2-4)

The wind is here associated with horses due to its great speed and strength, the team of horses being the natural symbol of this combination. Besides this though, *Eochaidh* or *Eochu* are fairly common titles among the Irish gods and legendary figures, and could be interpreted as meaning something similar to chevalier or denoting a powerful king (a lord owning many horses and characterized by their sovereign symbolism).

Dagda and Bhima

This is all very suggestive, but so far perhaps not conclusive. Mythical associations are commonly stretched and twisted by each new interpreter to fit their desired pattern. Some things that could be interpreted as descriptive of wind could also be interpreted a descriptive of thunder, lightning, rain, or sky. However, looking at Bhima, the wind god Vayu's incarnation in the *Mahabharata*, while clarifying Dumezil's meaning regarding the contrast between Vayu and Indra, will reveal several similarities between him and the Dagda which become increasingly difficult to put aside. The Pandavas, sons of the primary gods and so their mortal stand-ins in the *Mahabharata* (as Dumezil and Stig Wikander before him have pointed out), preserve much of the archaic mythos of their respective god-fathers, provably dating from before the Indo-Iranic split due to shared elements found in Iranic myth and the myths of the European branches (this fact forms a foundational element of Dumezil's analysis of Germanic myth in *Gods of the Ancient Northmen*). So it is the case with the Pandava warrior Bhima, the second born of the Pandavas, born as spiritual son of Vayu when Kunti prayed to him for a son.

Bhima is known as the strongest of all the Pandavas. He is said to have the strength of ten thousand elephants and to singlehandedly defeat all one hundred of the Kauravas in the Kurukshetra War, among other senior warriors, and on one day to slay one hundred thousand soldiers. He is a one-man wrecking crew who is unmatched in raw power on the battlefield. Indra himself is said to not be able to subdue him in battle. He is also described as a figure giant in stature, the largest of the Pandavas. His appetite matches – one epithet names him *Vrikodara,* "wolf-bellied." Half of the food allotted to him, his brothers and their mother was eaten by him alone, the other half split between the remaining five family members. In one tale Bhima is sent into the forest with a great cart of food intended to lure in a menacing monster. The monster approaches and is distraught to see Bhima calmly eating the food. When he has finished his feast, Bhima makes short work of the monster. In the end of the *Mahabharata*, one of the reasons Bhima is said to fall dead before reaching paradise is his excessive appetite.

Likewise, the Dagda is described as a giant with unmatched strength, and his incredible appetite is illustrated in an episode just before the Second Battle of Moytura. The Dagda goes as an envoy to the Fomorians to ask for a truce, in order to buy time for his allies and to spy on the opposing army. (Vayu too was known to take the role of messenger or envoy of the gods due to his unrivaled speed, and his son Hanuman was the one chosen to retrieve the healing herb from the Himalayas for Lakshman because no one else was as fast as him.) The Fomorians pour a mass of food into a pit in the ground – "four score gallons of new milk and the same quantity of meal and fat […] goats and sheep and swine […] porridge" (*Cath Maige Tuired*) — and tell the Dagda he must eat all of it or be killed, which he promptly does with his massive ladle, enjoying well the feast intended to mock him. Afterward he falls asleep. In a tale somewhat reminiscent of this, Bhima's rival and future war enemy Duryodhana poisons his food as revenge for his own failure to defeat Bhima in wrestling. The poison is not able to kill Bhima but knocks him unconscious. Just as the Dagda eats the dirt and gravel with the food served him in the pit, Bhima is said to have "digested the poison with the food," and just like the Dagda this results in him falling asleep or unconscious. After which, Bhima is thrown into the ocean. In one version he has the good luck to sink down to the kingdom of the Nagas, whose king revives him and bestows on him his famed strength. In another, he is said to be bitten by snakes under water but to resurface unscathed: "The wicked son of Dhritarashtra gave poison to Bhima, but Bhima of the stomach of the wolf digested the poison with the food. Then the wretch again tied the sleeping Bhima on the margin of the Ganges and, casting him into the water, went away. But when Bhimasena of strong arms, the son of Kunti woke, he tore the strings with which he had been tied and came up, his pains all gone. And while asleep and in the water black snakes of virulent poison bit him in every part of his body. But that slayer of foes did not still perish" (*Mahabharata*, Adi Parva, LXI). Like Bhima, the Dagda is known for his incredible strength and is a kind of one-man army in battle. Just as Bhima surpasses his brothers with the greatest raw battle prowess, when the various warriors of the Tuatha de Danaan announce one by one what means of war they will use, the Dagda in his turn announces that he will use *all* of the various powers of war mentioned. One description of Bhima describes him similarly as a warrior who wields all weapons and powers of war – sword, bow, dart, steed, elephants, chariot, mace, and strength of arm: "The mighty-armed Bhima of immeasurable energy hath already turned back for the fight. The son of Kunti will certainly slay many of our foremost car-warriors. With sword and bow and dart, with steeds and elephants and men and cars, with his mace made of iron, he will slay crowds of our soldiers." (*Mahabharata*, Drona Parva section 22).

There are further curious parallels between Bhima and Dagda. One of these comes with Bhima's association with cooking. In the Pandavas' period of exile, Bhima becomes a cook. So strongly is he marked by this vocation that he gains the epithet *Ballava*, "cook," and is often depicted in iconography with a cooking bowl or pot of food and a ladle. Dagda, of course, is known for the great cauldron he carries around, from which no one ever comes away unsatisfied, and the ladle he scoops up food with. In iconography this makes the Dagda and Cook Bhima look rather alike. Less well-known is the fact that the Dagda is also recorded as a cook, owner of a stupendous "cooking oven": when his son Bodb Derg inquires what will be his marriage portion, we read that "it is likely the Dagda put up his cooking oven there, that Druimne, son of Luchair made for him at Teamhair. And it is the way it was, the axle and the wheel were of wood, and the body was iron, and there were twice nine wheels in its axle, that it might turn the faster; and it was as quick as the quickness of a stream in turning, and there were three times nine spits from it, and three times nine pots. And it used to lie with the cinders and to rise to the height of the roof with the flame" (Lady Gregory, *Gods and Fighting Men,* 70). Quite a lot of cooking could be done with such an oven.

Of course, to pair with his cauldron, the Dagda also has a massive club, capable of killing with one end and reviving with the other. But Bhima has an almost identical iconic weapon of choice (though without the magical properties), a great mace, huge in size and said to be equivalent to a hundred thousand maces. He is often depicted with this weapon and one of his primary titles is *Gadahara* – "mace wielder." Dagda's club, like Bhima's, is said to be made of iron. Bhima's mace is described as "a mace made entirely of Saikya iron and coated with gold" (*Mahabharata*, Vana Parva, CCLXIX), while in a description of Dagda it is said that "In his hand was a terrible iron staff (*lorg* [...] *iarnaidi*)" ("The Intoxication of the Ulstermen"). As Bhima's mace is said to be equivalent to a hundred thousand maces, Dagda's club is said to be so large it has to be wheeled around on a cart and is "the work of eight men to move, and its track was enough for the boundary ditch of a province" (*Cath Maige Tuired*).

One of Dagda's more cryptic epithets is *Cera*, which is uncertain in translation, but either relates to the word for "jet," which could connect again to a jet of wind, or could alternately mean "creator" (Monaghan, 83). It is not clear if the Dagda has a role in the cosmic creation proper, but he does do plenty of building and assigning of the dwellings of the gods, and in several places is seen to be a great shaper of the landscape, such as his trench-digging in *Cath Maige Tuired*. Bhima likewise carries the title "creator" – *Hanyalaurya* – though again his role in the creation is not entirely clear.

Dagda and Vayu

If we focus specifically on the comparisons between the god Vayu himself and the Dagda, we find that both have a son who is killed for some great transgression and then restored to life after their father grieves powerfully for them. For Dagda this son is Cermait Milbel; for Vayu it is Hanuman. Hanuman is born to a married human woman when she catches some "sacred pudding" dropped by the Wind God. Hanuman later on is killed by Indra for trying to take something that is not his – the sun – and his father Vayu then withdraws dejectedly from the world, causing great suffering to all beings by his absence. Vayu finally returns when Shiva decides to revive Hanuman. The Dagda's son, Cermait Milbel, is killed by Lugh after committing a sin perhaps comparable in gravity to stealing the sun: having an affair with Lugh's wife. The Dagda is said to have cried tears of blood for him and carried his body on his back as he withdrew to the East, where later on he revived him with the healing staff he acquired there. Though Cermait's birth is not described, Dagda's other son Aengus Og is indeed fathered on a married woman. The Dagda does not drop sacred pudding on her, but it amounts to the same thing.

A further very speculative parallel could be attempted, by seeing the dwarves that the Dagda takes his magic club from as stand-ins for the minor gods of bodily function found in the Upanishadic parable described at the beginning of this chapter. Just as Vayu in the parable demonstrates his power over life and death by leaving the body, overpowering the minor gods, and then returning, which restores life, the Dagda touches one end of the magic staff to the dwarves, who are killed, and when he sees fit he simply touches them with the other end, restoring life and demonstrating the supremacy of his power. He draws life away and returns it without effort. In fact we could even choose to see another echo of this general theme in the scene in *Cath Maige Tuired* where the Dagda proclaims that he will wield all the many powers of war. Once again he demonstrates his unmatched power over dealing out life and death while making those around him appear as pawns in comparison, showing that he is the god that cannot be done without.

The Agricultural Role

An agricultural role is also important to The Dagda (see: *Gabail in t-Sida; The Wooing of Etain*). If we briefly consider a broader comparative panorama, there are more than a few reasons to believe that Wind gods are naturally suited to an agricultural role, a role which must have expanded over time for the Indo-European Celts, who had developed from a pastoralist nomad people.

Enlil

As a comparative reference to a Neolithic, agrarian culture, consider a case from Sumerian myth: in the Sumerian religion, the Wind god Enlil was the chief of the pantheon from the 24th Century until the 12th, after inheriting the kingship from the primordial sky god, An. Enlil is known as the inventor of the mattock, a fundamental tool of farming, and as patron of agriculture generally. Enlil was, at this time, the supreme god and the god of kingship as well. He is known as "the Great Mountain," and his temple as "the Mountain House," and he is described as a "wild bull." He is seen as a creator, king, and father, but also as the lord of the universe. He is capable of granting immortality (as he does for Ziusudra, hero of the flood myth), and of decreeing justice and fate. In the Akkadian version, Enlil is the god responsible for causing the great flood that wipes out mankind. Enlil is iconographically represented by a horned cap with seven superimposed sets of ox horns, which was a traditional symbol of general divinity. The Dagda's "lawful name" *Fer Benn*, man of peaks, has been interpreted both as relating to the peaks of mountains and to the points of antlers or horns, suggestive of Dagda theoretically having some kind of antlered headdress or horned form, or of being associated with horned animals (this has sometimes been used to connect him to "Cernunnos"), even if we have focused on the meaning of this name relating to mountains above. In one last intriguing connection, we find that one of Vayu's names is *Anil*, which like the name *Enlil* translates to the word for the wind itself. The name *Anil* is by no means an exact match to his counterpart in Sumer (in relative terms, not so very far from India), *Enlil*, but the strange echo should be noted nonetheless.

This does not tell us anything certain, as the Sumerian culture is distant and separate from the Irish, but the example can help us visualize one possible scenario of how the Dagda, as Wind God, could have reasonably fitted an agricultural role as well, via adaptation to existing agrarian culture patterns as the Celts moved through central Europe. One possible meeting point of Wind God and the agrarian activity may have been the prominent role of the wind in scattering seeds and leading the way for the rains.

Vayu and Agriculture

Like the Dagda, Vedic Vayu is at least sometimes a god related to agrarianism and the produce of cattle. To him the nectar-yielding cow pours out its milk and butter (RV 1.134), and for Vayu, "never shall [the cows] be dry" (RV 1.135), while the Dagda's cauldron is known as the never-dry. More strikingly, Vayu himself is depicted holding a goad (though also with a club), which is a farming tool used to spur oxen or other cattle as they draw a plough or cart in the agrarian activity. He is prayed to for wealth in steeds (RV 7.90.6) and the gods generated him for wealth (RV 7.90.3). One can imagine how a god closely connected with the produce of cows and with the wealth of steeds, who carries the plough goad, could naturally be adopted to a larger agrarian role if the situation called for it, considering also the wind's spreading of seeds and the common association of the wind with the agrarian role in other cultures.

Wind or Sky God?

As Shaw points out and as the Sumerian example demonstrates, when an atmospheric god took over for or usurped the kingship of the Primordial Sky, he might inherit many of the traits and abilities, even myths, from the Sky God. So it is in the case of Sumerian Enlil, and so it also is for Vedic Varuna, who inherits the domain and omniscience of Father Sky or Dyaus Pitr, and is then referred to as though he is the sky itself. Zeus absorbs traits and roles of his predecessors as well, becoming an all-in-all deity, copious and omnipotent, referred to with the celestial name Zeus despite actually being the grandson of the primordial sky, Ouranos. Something similar could the case fore Dagda. Based on the myths and traits we have discussed, Dagda often appears to be *the* most fatherly, *the most* absolute of the gods, or *the* Divine Masculine incarnate. This is all correct enough, and yet, as demonstrated, due to his abundance of additional Vayu-like characteristics, this could be due to an absorption of roles and abilities from Father Sky, in the same general fashion as we see with Enlil just as much as it could derive from his being the original Father Sky. The Dagda is clearly more than simply the great and withdrawn sky. He has the whole set of traits and myths connected with the Indo-European god of the wind on top of whatever he embodies of the primordial "Dyaus." Somewhat like Thor, he partly matches the archetype of the Wind God and cannot be summed up merely as the god of sky. Indeed, to a remarkable degree the Dagda preserves the archetype of the brutish and powerful lord of life and wind, maintaining a broad set of shared elements found in the oldest texts in both India and the Germanic world relating to this deity. The Dagda does have myths that seem to belong to Father Sky as well, as we have illustrated in our *Iliad* analysis. But this simply does not complete the picture. Again and again, considering figures like Zeus, Jupiter, Varuna, Enlil, and perhaps Oðinn, we see deities who have inherited some roles from Father Sky but who seem to have at least one other aspect, their more active face so to speak, or as if a god has taken over the sky kingship, absorbing, or in Zeus' case, explicitly "swallowing" his predecessors. The Celtic Irish are after all a fairly typical Indo-European people. It should be expected for the primary active gods of the Indo-Europeans to be somewhere present in the Irish pantheon until proven otherwise. And as for the god of wind, so important to the Indo-European divine world picture, he has been poorly accounted for in Irish mythological study.

Eliade again has a helpful distinction. There are two perennial lines of development for gods who inherit the sky from Father Sky or who are simply absorbed into him as his active aspect, found across many mythologies, he says. These are roughly the Varuna/Mitra line and the Vayu/Indra/Rudra/Parjanya line of development; that is, the "absolute sovereign (despot), guardian of the law" sky god and the "creator, supremely male, spouse of the great Earth Goddess, giver of rain […] fecundator […] ritual and mythical connection with bulls" sky god (Eliade, *Patterns in Comparative Religion*, 82). Along these lines we can perhaps understand the relationship of Dagda and Lugh (with Nuada) as contrasting sovereigns within the Irish pantheon. Dagda represents the Vayu-Parjanya-Indra-type path of inheritance, and Lugh, with Nuada, represents the complementary or rival Mitra-Varuna path. Each in their way reflect a part of the total sky sovereignty. For further discussion see *Patterns of Comparative Mythology*, "The Sky and Sky Gods":

> The fact that the actual name of the Aryan sky god stresses his shining and serene quality, does not exclude the other sky theophanies (hurricanes and rain and so on) from Dieus' personality. It is true, as we shall see further on

(§ 26), that a great number of these sky gods as it were 'specialized', and became gods of storm or of fertility. But these specializations must be seen as the result of various tendencies often to be found in the history of religion (the tendency towards the concrete; the turning of the notion of 'creation' into that of 'fertility', and so on), and, in any case, they do not prevent meteorological functions from existing alongside the notion of a god of the bright sky. (Eliade, 66-67)

The 'specialization' of sky gods into gods of hurricane and of rain, and also the stress on their fertility powers, is largely explained by the passive nature of sky divinities and their tendency to give place to other hierophanies that are more concrete, more clearly personal, more directly involved in the daily life of man. This fate results largely from the transcendence of the sky and man's ever-increasing 'thirst for the concrete'. (Eliade, 82)

In the end the 'specialization' of sky gods may change their whole form radically; by abandoning their transcendence, by becoming 'accessible', and so indispensable to human life, by changing from *dei otiosi* into *dei pluviosi*, generative gods in the form of bulls, they are constantly taking to themselves functions, attributes and honours foreign to them, and for which they had no concern in their superb celestial transcendence. Like every divine 'form', in their tendency to become the centre of every religious manifestation and to govern every region of the cosmos, the storm gods and the life-giving gods absorb into their personality and into their worship (particularly by their marriages with the Mother Goddess) elements which did not belong to their original celestial make-up. (Eliade, 92)

We also observe the reverse happening: a local god that has become, owing to its 'historical' circumstances, a supreme god, takes to itself the attributes of sky divinity. Assur, the divine protector of the town of the same name, borrowed the attributes of the supreme Creator and Sovereign and thus became one with the sky gods (cf. Knut Tallquist, Der assyrische Gott, Helsinki, 1932, pp. 40 ff.). (Eliade, 92)

This perception of The Dagda as the god of wind can be taken to a more esoteric level as well. Vayu, as the god of wind was, as we have seen, also the god of air itself, the god of breath and so of life force, *prana*. For some in the East of Iran he was "elevated to the rank of supreme deity" as "appears clearly in the fifteenth Yast," – and we should be aware by now from the great similarity of Irish Lugh to Iranic Mithra just how close the Iranic and Irish god-conceptions often are – "Ahura Mazda prays to him [...] He is in fact superior to good and evil, and like the warrior caste of which he is the patron, he manifests himself through force" (Zaehner, 83). These Iranians also came to see him as

105

"the life-giving power" which corresponds to "the 'fiery wind' in the body of man 'which is the breath-soul (Jan)'" (Zaehner, 85). One of Dagda's epithets among the others is *Aed*, or "fire," and he also is the progenitor of "Fire," that is, his son *Aed*. With these Eastern Iranic people described by Zaehner, Vayu came to be identified with both space and time, with the void, with the atmosphere, and with the space between the light realm and the dark realm, and was seen as both life-giver and the demon of death – truly a god of two sides.

There is something about this cosmic side of Vayu that lends him, and the Dagda with him, to comparison with the cosmic Hindu god of destruction and healing Rudra-Shiva, as Phillip Cunningham has pointed out. From the Dagda's own powers of death-dealing and life-giving to his mysterious druidic magic to his name "the Great Father of Being," his association with mountains and his mating with the goddess of destruction the Morrigan, it is a tempting comparison to make. In addition, since he resides at the burial mound Brugh na Boinne it is possible that he also had a role as a god of the underworld. This would of course connect to his ability to kill and revive and would parallel the Iranic Vayu's role of psychopomp and god of the dead. Dagda is sometimes named Dagda *Donn*, Donn being a god of the dead among the Irish, possibly aligning or uniting him with that role.

It must be said that very specific linkages between Dagda and Rudra-Shiva are difficult to establish, and we have chosen to emphasize the Vayu thread here. For one thing, the Hindu Rudra-Shiva over time appears to have absorbed attributes of various related deities, often even being seen as combined or identified with Vayu in numerous Hindu texts. But this does not mean that Rudra and Vayu were necessarily identical in the earliest period (although this is a topic of heated debate), or, more importantly, that the Irish treated their analogues as identical in myth. As we have discussed in relation to Fionn and Balor, Kris Kershaw, in her book *The One-Eyed God: Odin and the (Indo-)Germanic Männerbünde*, has pointed us toward the more likely conclusion that the Rudra mythos rests in the Irish Fionn mac Cumhaill and his band of Fianna and that his Welsh parallels are the wild huntsman Gwyn, son of Nudd, and Gwion/Taliesin. The Wind God was after all so close to and overlapping with Rudra-Shiva that he could have developed similar traits in the same direction, yet for different reasons. As mentioned, some within the Hindu religion choose to see Vayu and Rudra-Shiva as one and the same deity, as is reflected in certain Vedic and Puranic literature. This subject could easily occupy another full article or book of its own and we only mention it here as an acknowledgement of further paths of comparison.[55]

---

55 A further connection between Vedic Vayu and Irish Fionn (Rudra) can be found by aligning the Irish tale "The Hospitality of Cuanna's House," the tale of Norse Thor in the land of Utgarda-Loki found in *Gylfaginning*, and the tale of Bhima encountering his

Whatever the case, what we are left with is a great giant with his club weapon, who it is permissible to call flatulent in a religious context, a god of druidry, of giving and taking life, of overpowering and creative vital force, of the cosmic masculine that unites with and masters the terrible feminine, of strength, speed, battle, resolve, of agriculture and of harvesting with great appetite, and, like his Vedic counterpart, a god of wind, and thus likely of breath and *prana* – in the end, the Dagda is the god that cannot be done without, he is the Germ and Regeneration of the World.

---

brother Hanuman from the *Mahabharata*. This could suggest an overlap of the Wind God and Rudraic god in the Irish branch. See *Celtic Influences in Germanic Religion: A Survey*, Mathias Egeler.

5

The Case for Týr = Mitra

Georges Dumezil, in his *Mitra-Varuna*, makes a case in passing for the identification of the Norse god Týr with the Vedic god Mitra. This case is brief, but is a central pillar of the overall argument of his book. Týr, for Dumezil, makes up the "Mitra" half of the paradigmatic duad of Mitra-Varuna. However, though very influential, the argument is controversial and far from universally accepted, primarily due to the scanty actual evidence we have which depicts or describes Týr in the primary mythological sources and material archaeology. Specifically, there is a common objection that Dumezil has stretched the evidence too much and has invented a character for Týr to fit his structural theory which the evidence does not actually warrant. However, the idea that the case is based on nothing could be classed as uncharitable at best, ignorant of the details at worst. The evidence for Týr's equivalence should be laid out and carefully reassessed. What *is* the whole of the case for Týr = Mitra?

Dumezil's starting point for the comparison should be clearly distinguished from the common idea that Týr's name, meaning "god," would connect him to the theorized Proto-Indo-European god *Dyéws Ph₂tér*, Father Sky, "Týr" appearing to be similar to cognates of Indo-European words for "sky." In fact, Dumezil explicitly questions this oft-repeated supposed etymological connection (which would suppose Týr > *Tiwaz* > *Dyễws*). He connects Týr instead to cognates such as Latin *deus*, meaning "god" rather than Latin *dius*, meaning "heavenly" (from *dyễws,* "sky"), and traces the etymology of Týr back to the Proto-Indo-European *deywós*, "god" or "shining one" instead, closely related to but distinct from the word for the sky itself, and so also distinct from the names of "Sky Father" gods such as Zeus and Iupiter. As such, Týr, meaning "god," is related to Latin *deus*, also meaning "god," even if some question the idea of Týr being cognate with Zeus/Iupiter, or with Sanskrit Dyaus Pitr, "Father Sky."

As William Reaves summarizes Dumezil's stance:

> Georges Dumezil, recognizing the inherent problem with the linguistic argument in the 1950s, embraced DeVries' tripartiate theory, emphasizing the function of gods over their names, thereby equating *Tiwaz* and Oðinn with the Hindu gods Mitra and Varuna, whom, he saw as fulfilling first function roles of lawgiver and king. (Reaves, *Odin's Wife*, 171)

Reaves goes on to quote Dumezil's argument on this score, in which Dumezil points to the fact that "there are reasons for deriving *Týr* and *Zio* rather from *deiwo-*, the generic Indo-European name for the gods" and criticizes the connection of Týr to Father Sky by saying

> these consequences are founded on a simplistic and erroneous interpretation of this equation, and more generally on a false conception of the role and prerogatives of linguistics in such matters," concluding that "The agreeable phonetic conformity of *Zeus, Jupiter,* and *Dyauh,* precious to the linguist, does not carry the mythologist very far. He quickly notices that the first two gods and the third do not in the least do the same things. (Dumezil, *Gods of the Ancient Northmen*, 37)

Despite the fact that all of these words may have originally been in some way related terms, this says nothing at all about Norse *Týr* ever having any *direct* relation to a word meaning "sky," or a sky function of any kind. Lotte Motz summarizes the scholarly opinion on the question in her "The Sky God of the Indo-Europeans," explaining that there are two separate groupings of names, one of them being names meaning "god" (from *deiuo-s*) [such as *Týr*] the other names meaning "sky" or "day" (from *deieu-*) and that even the words for sky and day themselves do not necessarily overlap, the meaning "sky" seeming only to develop in the Indo-Iranian languages. We cannot actually tell how these two groupings were meaningfully connected, and between the roots meaning "god" and those meaning "sky" or "day" Motz says, "There is no community of meaning between the two roots" (Motz, 32). She then concludes that we really cannot say that the gods whose names are derivations of these separate roots with distinct meanings are the same deity, as in the various cases they are also attached to gods of different mythic and cultic roles.

Dumezil's starting point, instead, is the idea that Vedic Mitra arose as the embodiment of the contract itself, and may originally have been considered a god of contracts and oaths (which may also have connected to his association with heavenly light and day). Dumezil details how Antoine Meillet first developed this thesis in 1907 (see *Mitra-Varuna*, p. 67), and explains the connection between the concepts of the "contract" and the "friend" which are often seen to surround Mitra. Dumezil theorizes that this identification of Mitra as god of contracts connects him to the main scene surviving in the Norse mythology which features Týr. This scene is the binding of the wolf Fenrir and the loss of Týr's hand. In order to convince Fenrir to submit to its magical binding, Týr places his right hand into the wolf's mouth as supposed surety of the Aesir's promise not to trap him as they put the fetters on him. Thus we have the enactment of a contract between the parties, an agreement that the wolf will allow himself to be bound, with Týr's hand given as an exchange backing up the promise of the Aesir that they will not act duplicitously toward the wolf. Týr's pledge hand is given, by definition, a strong symbol, as this would be the hand given during a contract or oath, the hand of open dealing, honesty, as well as justice. In *Gylfaginning* 34, this hand is specified by Snorri as his right hand. When the Aesir are revealed to have tricked the wolf, he devours this hand in response. Thus, the loss of the god's pledge hand, as Dumezil implies, symbolizes the hobbling of justice and righteousness in the present age, connected with the tricky legalism of the existing system of justice. If Týr is a god of contracts or of Justice more generally, then his missing pledge hand would symbolize the breakdown of the operation of Justice within the society. Indeed, it is said pointedly of Týr that he does not promote settlements among men. Why would this need to be pointed out of this god specifically, unless this fact had particular negative weight relating to his supposed positive function? The claim is also undercut by the fact that Tyr is the only god that Fenrir initially trusts, having demonstrated a strong ability for peacemaking by befriending this terrible beast in its youth. Furthermore, the statement that Týr does not promote settlements is made in the same sentence in *Gylfaginning* 25 with the mention of his lost hand, linking this claim with Týr's famous engagement in the questionable contract. Dumezil claims that this claim reflects the way the operations of the judiciary system were seen at this point in Germanic society, as by no means creating peace. The wording of contracts (which are the specific domain of Mitra) can easily be seen as prone to generating strife. Loki specifically needles Týr on this point in *Lokasenna*, saying "you can't be the right hand of justice among the people" without his right arm, which would make no sense if Týr hadn't been the right hand of justice among the people to begin with. As is consistent with the poem *Lokasenna*, Loki is providing truthful mythological material, but giving it the most negative interpretation possible, turning it meaningfully on its head, twisting mythic truths into barbs.

Not only does this episode in itself form a strong case that Týr's function had something to do with contracts and the tricky legalism of the judiciary system that generally go along with them, but we can also identify an episode extremely similar to it in content if not in form in an event in the story of the incarnation of Vedic Mitra, Yudhishthira. During the Kurukshetra War, the protagonist heroes the Pandavas need to achieve the death of the opposition's deadly and wise general Drona. In order to do this, Yudhishthira, until this point a paragon of virtue and justice, has to participate in a deceptive half-truth. The Pandavas know that it is impossible to defeat Drona while he is armed, so they hatch a plan to disarm him. Thus they decide to kill an elephant bearing the same name as Drona's son, Ashvatthama. When he hears rumor of "Ashvatthama"'s death, Drona seeks out Yudhishthira specifically, due to the fact that he is known as a paragon of honesty (just as Týr specifically is the one trusted by Fenrir to give him an honest surety) and asks if it is true that Ashvatthama has been killed. To this Yudhishthira responds with a statement true in content, but deceptive in its enactment: "Ashvatthama is dead. But the elephant and not your son," he says, but Krishna instructs loud trumpets to be blown during the second part of the statement, and thus Drona only hears the affirmation and not the clarification, resulting in him believing that his son has perished. Thus he descends from his chariot and lays down his arms in meditation and grieving. The Pandava Dhristadyumna seizes the opportunity to avenge the death of his father, and kills Drona. As a result of this event, it is said that Yudhishthira's chariot, which had ridden at a four-finger height off the ground, symbolic of his absolute truthfulness and justice, dropped to the ground and no longer floated thenceforth. Týr's missing hand of righteousness would then be identical to Yudhishthira's no longer floating chariot of truth in this interpretation, while the deceived and trusting Fenrir would be a functional match to the deceived and trusting Drona. Dumezil failed to make the connection between these two very similar episodes, and we must assume that this was because, in the Indian case, it must be admitted that Yudhishthira's action does not relate in any clear way to a concept of contracts or oaths, and so is not clearly "functional" in the sense Dumezil cared about. However, the connecting thread of the violation of truthfulness via a technicality in order to deceive and disarm a powerful opponent, and the resulting conspicuous visible loss of the very symbol of that truth or righteousness, seems to be a strong enough through-line to say that these episodes are likely to be from the same ultimate original myth, with the contract aspect emphasized in one version and the truthfulness aspect emphasized in the other. A final possible support to this parallel is the fact that it is Menelaus of the Greek *Iliad,* who we have already demonstrated falls fully in line with the Mitraic "Lawful Sovereign" archetype, who is the one who is said to bind the shapeshifting seer god Proteus at one point with chains until he tells Menelaus that the gods are angry and desire sacrifice. The episode is much less fleshed out and morally weighted in the specific ways that the other scenes discussed are; however, the fact that we once again have a Lawful Sovereign archetype binding or incapacitating another supernatural opponent, provides one small piece of evidence that is imagistically striking and consistent.

* * *

The second pillar of Dumezil's argument is Týr's connection to war, the understanding of him as a "war god," and, along with this, the connection of war back again to the judicial. The spearhead of this pillar – so to speak – is the possible identification of Týr with the cryptic figure known as Mars Thingsus/Thincsus. Two inscriptions are known from Roman Britain naming a god as "Mars Thincsus," and the votaries are recorded in these inscriptions as saying that they will "willingly and deservedly fulfill their vow." Hence we have a god who definitively, but in a loose way, is associated with both a war god (Mars) and oaths. The piece of evidence tying this further together is the word "Thincsus," which has been theorized to relate to the great assembly of the Germanic world known as the Thing. The Thing was known as a time of judicial and legislative proceedings, among other important social happenings. If this interpretation of the inscription is correct, it implies that there was a god who was associated with Mars (thus likely but not definitely his war aspect), oaths, and the great assembly which centered around judicial proceedings. It is not hard to imagine that a god named Mars Thincsus could be the presiding god of the Thing itself, which is what Dumezil presumes.

While the equations of names in the days of the week themselves should be questioned and is a subject with its own long and complex history, it is not without significance that Týr was identified with Mars in the Germanization of the Roman weekdays. *Martis* became *Tiwesdæg* (Tuesday) in the Anglo-Saxon world, for example, suggesting that the people of the time indeed saw some important similarity between Mars and Týr/Tiw which they chose to enshrine in their calendar. Even the modern Dutch and German names for Tuesday reflect the day's enduring association with the Thing, called Dinsdag in Dutch and Dienstag in German, meaning either "Day of Thingsus" or "Day of the Thing," probably from *þingsus-dagaz*.

Dumezil extrapolates this further by pointing out that there was a continuity in the Germanic culture between war and judicial proceedings. According to Dumezil, war was seen through a judicial lens, as a kind of trial before the gods, surrounded by legalistic framings and enactments. Thus Dumezil asks us to imagine the Germanic judicial and

112

martial arenas as unified and reigned over, in at least one dimensionality, by a single god. Dumezil does clarify that Óðinn is the primary god of war in the other martial dimension, the magico-religious aspect of war. Furthermore, Dumezil points out that an assembly was known to be held at place named for Týr, Tislund in Zealand. While perhaps a vague and questionable piece of evidence, we should not simply discount the idea that a central place of assembly might bear the name of a god of assemblies.

Complicating this pillar of the argument, however, is the fact that the inscriptions to "Mars Thincsus" are so indeterminate. It is in fact not agreed upon whether Thincsus even refers to the Thing, and other possibilities have been brought forth. Nor is it known what aspect of Mars this Romanization is here drawing a connection to. One would assume it was his war aspect, but Mars has other well-known aspects, including agricultural and lustral ones. And many gods, not only the primary god of contracts, are known to have had oaths given to them. Indeed, each part of the Mars Thincsus case can be taken apart and questioned, as there simply is not enough supporting material to bring it to an absolutely definitive conclusion one way or the other. Even so, most critics will also agree that nothing has truly disproven the identification of Mars Thincsus with Týr, nor has any alternative interpretation dislodged this identification as the most complete or most widely-favored option. Still, we simply cannot say with certainty who Thincsus was.

It cannot be said that there is no reference to Týr as a martial god in a general sense, at least in the younger, *Prose Edda*, the work of Snorri Sturluson. In the *Gylfaginning* of the *Prose Edda* Snorri affirms that Týr is

> most daring, and best in stoutness of heart, and has much authority over
> victory in battle; it is good for men of valor to invoke him. It is a proverb that
> he is Týr-valiant, who surpasses other men and does not waver. He is wise,
> so that it is also said, that he that is wisest is Týr-Prudent. (*Prose Edda,*
> *Gylfaginning*)

For whatever reason, Snorri believed that Týr had not little, but "much" authority over victory in battle, that valiant warriors indeed invoked him, and that it was seen as good and proper for them to do so. Clearly, Snorri viewed Týr as some sort of significant war-related god, for it is not an insignificant god or a god unrelated to the martial that will have any authority over battle victory, let alone "much" authority over it. This further connects to the so-called "Týr rune," also known as the "victory rune," which connects Týr to the concept of victory, especially in the inscriptions that accompany this runic symbol. "Victory-runes you must cut if you want to have victory, and cut them on your sword-hilt; some on the blade-guards, some on the handle, and invoke Týr twice," reads the *Poetic Edda* poem *Sigrdrífumál,* stanza 6. The "Týr rune" appears to be in the shape of a spear, thus also potentially connecting Tyr to the spear of Victory and Dharma wielded by the other Mitraic parallels, as when Yudhishthira defeats the final Kaurava general Shalya with his great spear, leading the way to victory. Furthermore, the other attributes of Týr here mentioned paint a complex picture of the god, one which begins to be reminiscent of the complex and sometimes paradoxical character of Yudhishthira-Mitra. Not only is Týr said to be daring and an authority in battle victory, but he is also wise and prudent, the traits of a good Brahmin (who themselves oversaw judicial proceedings, requiring prudence and wisdom in that sphere as well), just as Yudhishthira balances his wise and prudent character with the decisive actions in battle that bring the war to a close, such as the killing of Shalya with his spear.

Týr's characteristic of not wavering is also not in the least insignificant, as Yudhishthira is known known for his stability and calm bearing. Yudhishthira's very name means "firm/stable in battle" (from युध् - (*yudh*), meaning "1. to fight, battle" and थिर - (*sthir*) stable, steady,"), while Menelaus' means something like "the steadfastness (of the people) in battle" (from *Μένω* - (*ménō*), meaning "I stay, wait (in battle)" (with the sub-variations "1. I stand fast"), and *lāós*, meaning "people"). For a war god, prudence is not the first trait that comes to mind, hence it would be fairly coincidental for Týr and Yudhishthira each to have this same rare signature combination of characteristics.

If we look only at the hymns of the *Rig Veda*, we will be under the impression that Mitra is only a peaceful and minor assistant god to the greater Varuna and Indra, and could never have been a god of war likened to Mars. However, as we have detailed, Dumezil has a simple and clearsighted explanation for this, laid out in the section "Mithra Armed" in his *Mitra-Varuna*. Iranic Mithra is indeed a warlike god, a combatant wielding the *vazra* weapon and is closely tied to the embodiment of offensive victory, Verethregna, while simultaneously being a god of the priestly caste. In the Iranic Avesta, Mithra is called "a chief of assemblies amongst the chiefs of assemblies [recall Thincsus' association with the great assembly]," "a warrior with strong arms," who "establisheth nations in supreme victory," and is "victory-making [remember the victory-deciding quality of Týr]," "the most valiant of all the gods [remember Týr-valiant being an epithet for the most valiant men]," "army-governing," "who sets the battle going, who stands against (armies) in battle," "then he binds the hands of those who have lied to Mithra," and "He is the stoutest of the stoutest [as Týr is best in stoutness of heart], he is the strongest of the strongest, he is the most intelligent of the gods [remember Týr-prudent as an epithet for the wisest men], he is victorious and endowed with Glory," and "a creature of wisdom" (*Avesta, Mihr Yasht*). It is indeed remarkable how closely the description of Mithra in the *Mihr Yasht* matches Snorri's description of Týr in the *Prose Edda*. Mithra, Yudhishthira and Lugh most clearly embody the tension in the Mitra archetype between the war god and the god of contracts, the victory-deciding god and the god of the peace-seeking, justice-determining, *gravitas* of the Brahmin. Thus, if Týr was identified with Mars, this would make no problem with his identification with Mitra, the sometimes-peaceful war god, peace-seeking but armed for victory, victory-*attaining*. In fact this identification would actually be an excellent fit, as combining the peace-bringing and battle-deciding functions is in the essence of the Mitraic Lawful Sovereign.

From our own comparative researches into the Indo-European epic tradition and mythologies we can add certain other supports for the general case of Týr = Mitra. First of all, one of the central myths that one discovers when looking at the various branches of the Indo-European epics, specifically the Celtic, the Greek, and the Vedic, is the fact that the "Mitra" or "Lawful Sovereign" figure is always made a cuckold in some sense, and this usually motivates an important revenge plot and sometimes the Great War itself. This theme is seen most clearly in the figure of Greek Menelaus. In the central plot line of the *Iliad*, Menelaus is cuckolded by Paris, who steals Helen away and takes her to Troy. Menelaus then must duel Paris, and finally concludes, after being wounded in the abdomen and healed, by killing Helen's second foreign husband, Deiphobus, after Philoctetes finishes Paris off. In the Welsh myth the Greek plot is paralleled most closely, with Lleu cuckolded by Gronw Pebr, who plots with Lleu's wife Blodeuwedd to kill Lleu. Lleu receives a mortal wound in the abdomen and then, after being healed, concludes by killing Gronw. Irish Lugh is cuckolded by Cermait with his wife Buach, and then hunts Cermait down and kills him. In revenge, Cermait's sons seek out Lugh and kill him. The Vedic version is less of a clear cuckolding, yet Yudhishthira clearly does lose his wife to set off the war, in close parallel to Menelaus. Specifically, Yudhishthira gambles away his wife Draupadi during his dice match with Yudhishthira, in which he also loses his kingdom. As a result Draupadi becomes the slave of Duryodhana. However, after she endures a lengthy humiliation and series of insults at court, king Dritharashtra, father of Duryodhana, finally allows Draupadi to go free and return to Yudhishthira and the other Pandavas. Thus the loss of the Lawful Sovereign's wife, and its role as one of the chief inciting actions for the war that follows, remains intact in the Indian epic; however, though the Kauravas attempt unsuccessfully to disrobe Draupadi, she never is shown to commit adultery.

Now, it must be said that the consistency we find in the other branches of the Mitraic figure or Lawful Sovereign being cuckolded suggests that the Indian version may simply have been cleaned up, presented in a more conservative fashion by removing the actual adultery, or that the Indian poets simply had developed too much respect for this god or this goddess to depict him as cuckolded by her. In any case, it is by no means a stretch to see Yudhishthira losing Draupadi into slavery and her attempted disrobing as carrying the same meaning as the cuckolding of the other gods of his archetype. What this brings us to is the fact that Týr, too, is significantly singled out by Loki as having been cuckolded, and cuckolded by Loki himself. "Shut up, Týr, my son came from your wife. And you haven't been paid a penny or an ell of cloth as recompense for this, you rat," Loki says in *Lokasenna*. It must be pointed out here that Duryodhana, who wins Draupadi from Yudhishthira in the dice game, is said to be the incarnation of the Demon of the Last Age, also known as Kali. He is the driving demonic force which opposes the heroes of society in the Kurukshetra War. Dumezil points out that Loki, in several places, including the scene of the death of Baldr, fills this "Kali" role in the Norse mythos (*Gods of the Ancient Northmen*). Further, Duryodhana's close partner in war, the incarnation of the sun god, Karna, mocks Draupadi after she has been lost in the dice game, and specifically calls her "unchaste," just as Loki mocks and accuses Freyja for promiscuity in *Lokasenna 30*. We have shown how in other branches this Demon of the Last age and Sun God are often partially blended together, elements switched around between them. In the Greek and Celtic branches, it is typically a Sun God who cuckolds the Lawful Sovereign, while in the Indian epic it is the closely associated Demon who wins her and the Demon and Sun God who together insult and humiliate her. Thus, Loki mocking Freyja and Týr, the one for being promiscuous and the other for being cuckolded, actually matches extremely well the mocking words of Duryodhana and Karna of the *Mahabharata*. Indeed, it may even be possible to understand Loki's cryptic claim that "you haven't been paid a penny or an ell of cloth as recompense" if read in this light. Yudhishthira literally loses Draupadi for nothing in the dice game, and is payed nothing in recompense, as Draupadi becomes Duryodhana's slave. Karna rubs this point in by telling Draupadi to choose another husband from the servants' quarters as they will not gamble her away as Yudhishthira has done. This barb is not far off from Loki's, as both seek to cruelly drive in the point of how foolishly and completely the Mitraic figure has lost his wife outright and with nothing in return.

* * *

A third pillar of Dumezil's argument must be marked as more speculative; however, in the context of comparative study it is perhaps one of Dumezil's most successful and ingenious comparisons, and is not without its catalog of supports. I am referring to Dumezil's identification of the sometimes brothers of Týr (as they are recorded by Snorri in the *Prose Edda),* namely Baldr and Höðr, with the divine attendants of Mitra: Aryaman and Bhaga.

Dumezil shows the way in which Bhaga and Aryaman develop out of the orbit of Mitra-as-god-of-social-cohesion-well-being-and-justice. Bhaga appears as the god of Destiny considered as Apportionment (of boons in particular), while Aryaman, as his name indicates, appears as the god of the flourishing of the "Aryan" people specifically, of the tribe or in-group society. In this constellation of figures, Aryaman takes on the role of the cupbearer of Mitra. In the epic version of this grouping, found in the *Mahabharata*, we have King Dhritarashtra as (per Dumezil) the proposed incarnation of Bhaga, and his brother Vidura as the proposed incarnation of Aryaman, both of whom are uncles to and advisors of the incarnation of Mitra, Yudhishthira. We should make very clear at this point that this means that the versions of these attendant gods that we find in the *Mahabharata* are one generation back, uncles of the proposed Mitra figure rather than his brothers, as compared to what we find in the Norse version (Týr, Höðr and Baldr being a group of three brothers instead of a nephew and two uncles). Yet Dhritarashtra and Vidura remain the two divine incarnations surrounding the orbit of both the Mitraic and the Varunian heroes, Dhritarashtra blind and Vidura "the champion of peace," as Dumezil puts it, just as the blind Höðr and beloved Baldr are the immediate family of Týr (in Snorri) and Óðinn. Thought of from the Norse perspective, the three brothers, Týr, Höðr, and Baldr would then express a constellation of intimately interconnected gods, who are so closely tied as to almost overlap, which would be one explanation of why Snorri has here made them siblings.

In support of his identification of Bhaga-Dhritarashtra with Höðr, Dumezil connects their blindness, but goes further to show how, in the scene which incites the Great War in both cases – the death of Baldr in the Norse and the dice game of Yudhishthira in the Indian – both Höðr and Dhritarashtra are put in the position of being able to stop the "Demon" figure from accomplishing his nefarious purpose, of setting the war in motion, but fail to do so. Höðr and Dhritarashtra, per Dumezil, are akin to a dam which has a chance to hold back the demonic power from breaking forth, yet which gives way at last and becomes a "blind" instrument of that power. His "only weakness [his blindness] was the cause of all their misfortune" (*Gods of the Ancient Northmen*, 55), as Dumezil says of Dhritarashtra, and it is easy to see how this applies to Höðr as well, Loki tricking and guiding the blind god to cast the deadly dart at Baldr. Bhaga being the god of the apportionment of destiny, Dumezil calls Dhritarashtra "an image of fate," saying that "his hesitations, his capitulations, and his decisions laden with misfortune copy the behavior of fate" (57). Dhritarashtra, "for a brief moment…will have the choice in the gravest of circumstances of damming up evil or letting it loose," and, "resists, hesitates for a long time between the wise advice and honest entreaties of Vidura and the violent entreaties of his son Duryodhana. Finally, he yields" (55). Dumezil points out as well that the words habitually used surrounding Dhritarasthra in the poem (*daiva*, *kala*, etc.), along with his actions, repeatedly connect him to Fate and Destiny.

117

Of Vidura, Dumezil points out that "although he is recognized as excellent, his advice is not followed" (56), just as Snorri says that while Baldr passes just judgments, none of them hold or come to fruition. Furthermore, Vidura and Dhritarashtra closely collaborate with Yudhishthira in his peaceful reign after the war, a clear symbol of their close metaphysical alliance, just as Höðr and Baldr return after Ragnarok to rule together along with the mysterious Lord of the endtimes, according to *Voluspa* (stanza 62). And even more remarkably, Vidura is said literally to transfuse himself into Yudhishthira upon death, throwing himself into the being of Dharma (Mitra), as other figures on their deaths in the same section of the *Mahabharata* are said to return to the deity from which they have incarnated. Dumezil points out that Mitra and Aryaman in the Vedic hymns are intimately tied, "sometimes to the point of identity" (56). The epic itself claims that Vidura is a partial incarnation of Mitra (in *Mahabharata* called by the name Dharma or Dharmaraj) just as Yudhishthira is. Vidura is said to die in the arms of Yudhishthira and to give his power to him, explaining that each of them are parts of Dharmaraj.

Indeed, this near-identity of Vidura-Aryaman and Yudhisthira-Mitra is the central key to the whole question of the relationship of Týr and Baldr, from a Dumezilian perspective, as we will see. Speaking of Vidura, Dumezil says that Yudhishthira "is almost himself" (57), i.e., they are almost one being. This opens up the possibility of a continuity between Norse Baldr and Týr, perhaps called brothers for this specific reason, who then are seen by Dumezil as almost aspects of one deity. This allows Dumezil then to point out that Baldr's son, Forseti, is explicitly said to own a hall in which "legal disputes go away reconciled; that is the best court known to gods and men," and to use this fact as another point in favor of Týr's connection to the judicial sphere. From this perspective, Týr, Baldr and Forseti are all theorized in some fashion to have a connection to the operation of justice, and are placed in a continuum which is reasonably argued and supported, this proposed continuum itself in the end supporting the concept of the judicial functioning of Týr, by his indirect but close association with Baldr and Forseti. Dumezil sums up the parallel between the two pivotal scenes – the death of Baldr and the dice game of Yudhishthira – by arguing that in each case there is a game that Baldr or Yudhishthira under normal conditions should be able to win, but in which, in this case, the instrument of the game has been tampered with and the adversary uses supernatural subterfuge: the dice Duryodhana uses are enchanted, and the dart Hothr throws has not sworn the oath to do no harm to Baldr. In both cases this event leads to the great loss and helps to incite the Great War. Dumezil goes as far as to say that Baldr has the main emphasis of the general Mitraic mythos in Norse myth, while Tyr is paradoxically still the Mitraic god proper: "it is Balder who concentrates in himself the essences of Mitra and Aryaman, the roles that the Mahabharata distributes between Yudhisthira and Vidura" (63).

118

From our own comparative research we can add support to this portion of the theory. In the Greek (Iliadic), the Welsh, the Irish and the Indian (Mahabharatic) cases, there is repeated some permutation of the scene in which all is lost by the Mitraic Lawful Sovereign and/or he receives a near-mortal blow (these are sometimes separated into two scenes, as they are in *Mahabharata*). As already mentioned, Yudhishthira loses his kingdom, his wife, all his family and possessions, and is finally forced into exile due to his series of dice game losses, and later in the war receives a near-fatal wounding from Karna, having to retire from battle for a time. But it is the Welsh version of this theme which actually accords in a more obvious and striking way with the Norse death of Baldr, and is one of the most enigmatic concordances in all of mythology, as it raises the question of why the seemingly central Welsh god Lleu undergoes a fate so similar to that of the Norse god Baldr, whose myths are comparably scant, and who is not the proposed Mitraic god as Lleu is.

The Welsh version of this loss/mortal wounding scene appears as follows. Lleu is known to have a *tynged*, a kind of spoken fate, over him, which makes him invulnerable to all attacks, just as Baldr is said to be under the protection of an oath of (nearly) all things in the world, and thus rendered (nearly) invulnerable. However, Lleu's wife Blodeuwedd becomes the adulterous lover of the hunter Gronw Pebr, and the two conspire to find out how to kill Lleu. Blodeuwedd asks Lleu how this might be accomplished, under the guise that she wants to protect him from its occurrence, and he guilelessly tells her that he can be killed, but only by fulfilling the riddling conditions of striking him while he has one foot on a goat, one on the edge of a tub of water, while he is under an eave, with a spear forged for a year only on Sundays when others are at church. He agrees to demonstrate this to his wife a year later, and Gronw, on that day, prepared with such a spear, pierces Lleu's side. Thus the magical *tynged* is broken and Lleu's invulnerability is subverted by the malicious scheme of his adversaries. As a result, Lleu transforms into an eagle and flies to the top of a tall tree, which seems to be a representation of the World Tree or of an otherworld location. Many interpreters here have seen this as a symbolic death, Lleu temporarily disappearing to the otherworld. It is said that "putrid flesh and vermin" fall from Lleu as he rests on that tree, further signifying his deathlike state. Eventually, Gwydion tracks him down and coaxes him down from the top of the tree, transforms him with his magic, and brings him a physician who gradually heals his wounds. Once recovered, Lleu musters all of the forces of his kingdom and pursues Gronw and Blodeuwedd, and we have previously shown how this sequence of events conforms to the narrative of the *Iliad* to the point of nearly seeming like a borrowing, down to the fact that Menelaus and Lleu are both away at their maternal grandfather's or grand-uncle's when their wives commit adultery with Paris and Gronw.

In the Greek case, when the events of the Trojan War resume on the battlefield of Troy, nine years have gone by; however, one of the first sequences we are then given is the duel between Menelaus and Paris (*Iliad*, Book 3). Menelaus throws his spear through Paris' shield, just as Lleu throws his spear through the stone slab behind which Gronw hides when Lleu catches up to him. Paris, however, is rescued by Aphrodite in this case. Nonetheless, due to this duel, a truce-oath is struck between the Trojans and the Achaeans. This truce-oath (much like the truce-oath which the things of the world had sworn regarding Baldr) is then broken by the Trojan archer Pandarus. Athena (taking the Lokian role, if only for a moment), desiring the war to go on, changes her shape to that of Pandarus' comrade, and tells him to shoot Menelaus and win glory, and win the approval of Prince Paris most of all. Beguiled by Athena thus, Pandarus shoots his arrow at Menelaus; however, Athena then intercepts the arrow and guides it away from Menelaus' vitals, and safely to the belt-region of his abdomen, where it strikes a serious but non-fatal blow, allowing Menelaus to recover and return later, like the other Mitraic figures. We find that not only was Menelaus protected by a supposed truce-oath in this scene, which was transgressed through subterfuge of a wily deity, but that he was also under a broader protection of Fate and the gods and had been prophesied to survive the war and to be brought up to Elysium after the completion of his life. Further, he is manifestly protected by Athena in this scene, so that the wound that he sustains does not end up being fatal. Instead, a physician is called in by Agamemnon, just as Gwydion had called a physician for Lleu, and after a time Menelaus is healed and returns to battle, to complete his revenge on Paris and Deiphobus, as Lleu completes his on Gronw, and as Yudhishthira recovers and orders Arjuna to kill Karna and himself slays Shalya.

In the Irish version, things are much vaguer, and Lugh, after killing the lover of his adulterous wife, Cermait, is killed by Cermait's sons. His death also has a magical suggestiveness to it, though, as he is speared through the foot and then drowned in a lake, perhaps similar to how Lleu had been speared while on the edge of a tub of water next to a river. And in Lugh's case, as Kevin Maclean has put it, "the Irish sources are often loath to proclaim Lug's death." For instance, as he argues, in the tale "The Phantom's Frenzy," "Lug" comes to Con saying that, despite his death, he is not a phantom or spectre, and has come to tell Con the length of his reign.

Indeed, while Baldr along with the mysterious "Lord" of the Endtimes are the central survivors in the Norse myth, Baldr coming back from Hel to help lead the new cycle, it is Yudhishthira who is the last Pandava standing in the Indian epic. After the war, it is Yudhishthira who rules for another 37 years, as Lugh rules for 40 in the Irish version. The five Pandava brothers then embark on a pilgrimage in the Himalayas. One by one they are said to die on the journey, each one due to a different sin characteristic to them.

Only Yudhishthira survives the entire pilgrimage and reaches the top of the Holy Mountain, passes the final tests, and is admitted into Paradise.

To recap: both Yudhishthira and Menelaus are admitted to Paradise at the ends of their lives after winning peace in the war and ruling well after it; Lleu dies, goes to an otherworldly tree and revives, and leads his kingdom to peace via the enactment of justice; while Lugh dies and is rumored to return eventually to do similarly for his people; and Baldr dies, goes to the underworld and then returns to be the central survivor and, along with the mysterious Lord of the Endtimes, to lead the next presumed golden age. All of these figures are in the Lawful Sovereign/Mitra archetype, with the notable exception of Baldr (if we maintain the premise that the proper Norse Mitraic god is instead Týr). Readers will generally acknowledge that each of these figures, besides Baldr, are the kings and military leaders in their kingdoms. They are central heroes or central gods, while Baldr sometimes appears evanescent, pushed to the side, and is portrayed as perhaps even too perfect to be effective in this world. He dies before the final Great War and returns after and thus does not participate in it. Thus, if we argued merely from the weight of comparative evidence, we would expect the Mitraic Lawful Sovereign of the Norse myth to be the one to die while under a magical fate or protective oath, go to the underworld, and return to rule their people in a golden age and/or achieve Paradise. However, it is Baldr along with a mysterious unnamed "Lord" who does so in the Norse version. In this interpretation then, the identification of Baldr and Týr as Aryaman and Mitra, and thus as two closely connected aspects of one deific complex, becomes even more paramount. This seeming contradiction between the Norse version and the other branches is resolved if we take Baldr to be *almost* like an aspect of Týr, or the two gods to be so intimately connected that they are nearly identified on a deeper level. If we accept this series of arguments, it becomes easy to imagine how certain myths could have shifted from one to the other between these overlapping deities, whether in one direction or the other, or how the other Indo-European branches could have consolidated these myths in only a slightly different manner. Indeed, in the conclusion we will explore the possibility that Týr could after all be the mysterious Lord who rules with Baldr's assistance in the endtime.

* * *

There is also an important case to be made that the fathers of both Týr and Lugh are parallels, which would further strengthen the argument for the identification of Týr (with Baldr) as a Mitraic deity. The scholar Thor Ewing has shown that the story of Lugh's birth, involving the infiltration of Balor's fortress by Cian and his impregnation of

121

Balor's daughter Ethliu, matches in numerous details the infiltration of Óðinn into the mountain fortress to steal the mead of poetry while also sleeping with Gunnlǫð. Ewing explains in his essay "Óðinn and Loki Among the Celts" the several features shared between the myths of Óðinn and Cian, which are also in part shared by Welsh Gwydion, the likely father of Lleu.

As Óðinn must infiltrate the giant Suttungr's mountain fortress to regain the Mead of Poetry, so Cian must infiltrate the fortress of the giant Balar to regain the cow of the miraculous milk known as Glas Gaibhnenn. Suttungr's daughter Gunnlǫð gives the Mead of Poetry to Óðinn as Balar's daughter Eithne gives the halter to lead the Glas Ghaibhleann to Cian. Óðinn sleeps with Gunnlǫð as Cian sleeps with Eithne. Wages that are promised to the infiltrator (Óðinn), who has disguised himself as a worker, are not paid by Baugi, as wages that are promised to the infiltrator (Cian), who has disguised himself as a worker, are not paid by Balar. Ewing further notes that in the subsequent tales, Cian's son Lleu perches on an otherworldly tree that "grows in upland ground" and has been "drenched by nine score tempests," while Óðinn hangs from the world tree Yggdrasil for nine nights – a mysterious correspondence that may symbolize yet another important mythic element that could have shifted from one deity to another via close association. The fact that both the father of Lugh and the father reported by Snorri of Týr share this central infiltration myth creates the possibility that the son of Cian and one of the sons of Óðinn were then the same or overlapping.

Additionally, per Ewing, while Cian follows a wandering cow, the Welsh Gwydion follows a wandering sow, and each one stands as the protective father figure to Lugh and Lleu respectively, this correspondence suggesting a greater circle of parallels between the three figures of Óðinn, Cian, and Gwydion, which will be explored in its own chapter. Jones' Celtic Encyclopedia, citing Chris Gwyn, suggests *Gwydion* to be the same as Gaulish "Mercury *Uiducus*," meaning Mercury the Woodsman or the Wise. Gwydion is a wily trickster magician figure, using his magic to create a woman out of flowers and to transform her into an owl, among other things; he is a father figure, is seen as a forerunner of Merlin, and is often compared to Óðinn.

We must reiterate that this familial connection between Óðinn and Týr mainly relies on the perhaps less reliable *Prose Edda*, and contradicts parts of the *Poetic Edda* that make Týr instead the son of Hymir. However, the fact that Snorri's *Prose Edda* genealogy aligns so well, and so conveniently, with the *Mahabharata* genealogy, in the way thus far described, reinforcing the closeness of the Mitraic and Aryamanic figures, forces one to question whether Snorri was not basing his genealogy on other unknown primary material or in some other way had a true and archaic understanding of the divine genealogy. If Tyr was instead only foster son of Hymir and true son of Oðinn, as Snorri's account might suggest, this would match Lugh being separated from his father after his birth and fostered by various figures (Tailtiu, Manannan, etc.) while actually being son of Cian, the parallel of Oðinn. If followed to its ultimate conclusion, this parallel would imply that the jotunn's daughter Gunnloð could be Tyr's true mother and that she was impregnated when Oðinn stole back the mead, just as Cian fathered Lugh on Ethniu/Eithne, the daughter of the Fomorian Balor when he stole back the wondrous cow that gave the sacred liquid. For more evidence demonstrating the parallel between Cian and Oðinn, see the chapter "The Celtic Pushan: Gwydion, Cian, Oðinn, Pan."

Another detail in line with such speculation is the association of the Mitraic archetype with canines. Upon Yudhishthira's ascent of the Holy Mountain, he is asked by Indra to abandon the dog which has been accompanying him thus far. Yudhishthira refuses, claiming that it is a sin to abandon an innocent and loyal animal. Upon this refusal, it is revealed that the dog was Yudhishthira's spiritual father, Dharma (Mitra), all along. The placement of this dog-loyalty motif at the end of the epic, along with the importance it is given (we are reminded as well of the companion dog repeatedly depicted alongside Roman Mithras in the widespread reliefs, Irish Lugh's dog Failinis, and the close association of dogs with Cúchulainn, son of Lugh), has to make us think of the dog and wolf affinity associated with Týr in the Norse sources. Týr is said to be the only one courageous enough to feed the wolf Fenrir. He also gains its trust enough for the wolf to accept his hand as good surety. But even more interesting, perhaps, is that Týr also meets his end side by side with a dog. For it is said that Týr and the dog Garmr will do battle at Ragnarok, and that each will kill the other. This dog is said to howl to signal the onset of Ragnarok. Furthermore, a dog which some scholars believe to be this same Garmr is said to be met by Óðinn when he travels to Hel. Thus, Yudhishthira is tested with a dog right before entering the gates of Paradise while another dog, possibly associated with Týr, may be met at the gates of the Norse Hel. Scholars have debated whether any of these three canines — Fenrir, Garmr, and the dog of Hel —are the same or distinct. Regardless, Týr's close association with at least two of them may itself suffice as one more clue to his identity.

From these arguments, one of the first questions that should arise is: if Baldr is the god who dies, revives, and is one of the last survivors and leaders, why then is he not the Mitraic "Lawful Sovereign"? Indeed, this possibility has to be seriously weighed. After all, Baldr is the one said explicitly to have a hall where judgments are passed and peace is sought, and to have a son whose sole function seems to be to undertake legal proceedings and to champion fairness. Much more so than Týr, Baldr and his son Forseti are straightforwardly associated with the judicial sphere in the available myths. It has also been theorized that the variation of Baldr's name, "Baldag," may mean "bright day," while the Mitraic god is the very god of the daylit sky.

Yet the counterarguments to the suggestion that Baldr ought to be the Mitraic god are many as well. Firstly, Baldr's judgments are said not to be effective, they do not hold despite his attempts to champion goodness, peace, and justice. This connects, as aforementioned, to Vidura, incarnation of Aryaman, whose counsels to Dhritarashtra to pursue peace and fair dealing are likewise ultimately ignored so that fate and the dark age can pursue their course unrestrained by ideal goodness. Baldr is also not a military leader, which each of the other Mitraic figures is, and which is one of the central elements of their archetype. Baldr does not even participate in the war of Ragnarok, but only emerges when it is finished, while Týr does battle in it as a Mitraic war god should. In addition, Baldr's description as having a brow so white that the whitest of grasses is compared to it, aligns him with the idea that, like Aryaman, he is specifically the designated god of the society of the noble in-group, the extremely white brow being a common symbol of nobility and purity. One of the layers of meaning of Baldr's name could even relate to a word for the color white, as a comparison to Lithuanian *báltas, * 'white,' suggests (De Vries, *Altnordisches Etymologisches Worterbuch*, 24). Many other parallels already adduced in this chapter also point to Týr being the Mitraic god, most significantly perhaps the parallel of Týr's lost hand and Yudhishthira's no longer floating chariot.

It seems that, if we choose to follow Dumezil, then the simplest explanation of this issue is that Baldr and Týr indeed are connected deities, almost aspects of one another, or esoterically continuous in some way. Dumezil's aforementioned suggestion that both the Mitraic and Aryamanic roles are more concentrated in Baldr in prominent versions of the Norse myths while Tyr nonetheless more directly parallels Vedic Mitra, when the deeper pattern is understood, seems apt. From this perspective we would say that the magical invulnerability, death and resurrection motif, often seen in the Mitraic gods of other branches, was, in the Norse case, attached to Baldr; that the Mitraic "bright sky" association shows itself more clearly in Baldr's name as well; but that the judicial and contract-related roles are shared in some fashion between Baldr and Týr; while Týr would be said to have taken for himself the Mitraic war god role and perhaps the role of god of the Thing as well – "a chief of assembly amongst the chiefs of assemblies" as Iranic Mithra is called in the *Avesta*. The evidence has been presented, and so the question will be decided by each interpreter.

Excerpts from *Mihr Yasht* of the *Avesta* relating to Týr, Lugh, etc.:

Who breaks the skulls of the Devas?, and is most cruel in exacting pains; the **punisher** *of the men who lie unto Mithra, the* **withstander** *of the Parikas; who, when not deceived, establisheth nations in supreme strength; who, when not deceived, establisheth nations in supreme* **victory** *(line 26)*

Victory-making, **army-governing**, endowed with a thousand senses; power-wielding, power-possessing, and all-knowing; Who sets the battle a going, who **stands against armies** in battle, who, standing against armies in battle, breaks asunder the lines arrayed. The wings of the columns gone to battle shake, and he throws terror upon the centre of the havocking host (35-36)

And when Mithra drives along towards the havocking hosts, towards the enemies coming in battle array, in the strife of the conflicting nations, then **he binds the hands** of those who have lied unto Mithra, he confounds their eyesight, he takes the hearing from their ears; they can no longer move their feet; they can no longer withstand those people, those foes, when Mithra, the lord of wide pastures, bears them ill-will (48)

Who takes possession of the beautiful, wide-expanding **law**, greatly and powerfully (64)

a chief of assembly amongst the chiefs of assemblies; sovereignty-giving; a creature of **wisdom** (65)

accompanied by **the wheel of sovereignty, the Glory,** and **the Victory** (67)

He cuts all the limbs to pieces, and mingles, together with the earth, the bones, hair, brains, and blood of the men who have lied unto Mithra (72)

125

the awful, most powerful Mithra, the worshipful and praiseworthy, the glorious lord of nations (78)

He was given the mastership of the world; and [so did they 1] who saw thee amongst all creatures the right lord and master of the world, **the best cleanser of these creatures** (92)

Oh! may we never fall across the rush of Mithra, the lord of wide pastures, when in anger! May Mithra, the lord of wide pastures, never smite us in his anger; he who stands up upon this earth as the strongest of all gods, **the most valiant** of all gods, the most energetic of all gods, the swiftest of all gods, the most **fiend-smiting** of all gods, he, Mithra, the lord of wide pastures (98 and 135)

We sacrifice unto Mithra, the lord of wide pastures, sleepless, and ever awake;

Whose **long arms**, strong with Mithra-strength, encompass what he seizes in the easternmost river and what he beats with the westernmost river, and what is by the boundary of the earth.

And thou, O Mithra! encompassing all this around, do thou reach it, all over, with thy arms.

The man without glory, led astray from the right way, grieves in his heart; the man without glory thinks thus in himself: "That careless Mithra does not see all the evil that is done, nor all the lies that are told (104-105)

He is the strong, heavenly god, who is foremost, **highly merciful**, and peerless; whose house is above 2, a stout and strong warrior (140)

Victorious and armed with a well-fashioned weapon, watchful in darkness and undeceivable. He is the stoutest of the stoutest, he is the strongest of the strongest, he is **the most intelligent** of the gods, he is victorious and endowed with Glory: he, of the ten thousand eyes, of the ten thousand spies, the powerful, all-knowing, undeceivable god (141)

self-shining like the moon, when he makes his own body shine (142)

Whose face is flashing with light like the face of the star Tistrya; whose chariot is embraced by that goddess who is foremost amongst those who have no deceit in them, O Spitama! who is fairer than any creature in the world, and full of light to shine (143)

Truth-speaking (7 and 144)

Tyr and The Mitraic Lord of the Endtimes

In the Buddhist case, a derivative form of Mitra's very name is preserved attached to a figure who is explicitly the bringer of renewed dharma in the endtime. This is *Maitreya*, a boddhisattva to come who will achieve full enlightenment and teach a pure and renewed form of dharma. Maitreya is sometimes depicted riding a white horse, reminiscent of other endtimes figures such as the Hindu Kalki. The Iranic form of this endtimes "savior" myth is seen in the figure known as the Saoshyant. It is the Saoshyant who brings about the final revolution and destroys evil in the *Younger Avesta* (*Frawardin Yasht*, 129). As C.P. Tiele says in his book *The Religion of the Iranian Peoples*, "No one who has studied the Zoroastrian doctrine of the Saoshyants or the coming saviour-prophets can fail to see their resemblance to the future Maitreya" (Tiele, 159). Avestan Mithra himself is called "the best cleanser" of the creatures of Ahura Mazda's creation (*Mihr Yasht*, 92).

Interestingly, the noun *airyaman*, meaning "member of the community" is used as an epithet for the Saoshyants. We have seen that the god Aryaman is an attendant of and even seen as of the same essence with Mitra in the Vedic tradition. The Saoshyant is alternately called *astvat-ərəta* "embodying righteousness," coming from the root *arta* meaning "Truth," terms which would clearly describe the Mitraic god type just as well, the god of truth and justice, Mitra being called a protector of the divine *Rta,* from the same root as *arta*. Verethragna is the weapon of the Saoshyant in Yasna 59.1, just as

127

Verethragna, embodiment of Victory, is the close attendant of Mithra in the Avesta (*Mihr Yasht*, 80). In *Zam Yasht* 88-96, it is stated that the Saoshyant will make the world perfect and immortal, and evil and injustice will disappear. In the *Denkard* 7.10.15 the Saoshyant has the "royal glory" of the *Khvarenah*, which the solar halo of Roman Mithras can also be compared to.

Based on the foregoing, if the Norse case is at all conformable to the other branches we have analyzed and not a great outlier, we must say that the unnamed Lord who arrives at the end of *Voluspa* to rule ("There comes on high, | all power to hold, A mighty lord, | all lands he rules" (Voluspa 65)) would have to be a Mitraic figure[56]. This means that either Tyr himself returns to rule at this point, without his name being mentioned (this implies the audience already knew who this Lord was or that his role was here being downplayed for other reasons), or that some divine or semi-divine figure arrives who is a partial or full reincarnation of Tyr's essence, as the Saoshyant seems to be such an incarnation of the essence of Mithra. It is true that things always could have changed in the Norse case and Norse myth could break the trend we have seen. However, the position of the Mitraic god here at the endtimes is important on a deep level. The Varunian god is the sovereign of beginnings, the Mitraic god is the sovereign of endings, as Dumezil has shown in his *Mitra-Varuna*, and so it is always he who comes in the endtimes to rule and bring justice. If Tyr rules in the endtime aided by the returned Baldr and Hodr, then this would well match the case of Yudhishthira ruling after the great war helped by the returned Vidura and Dritharashtra.

---

56 The word used to describe this Lord, *ǫflugr*, "mighty, strong," connotes in particular an overwhelming or overpowering strength. This adjective can of course be theoretically matched to many gods, but it is not at all amiss in relation to the Mitraic deity type. Mithra in the *Mihr Yasht* is called "overpowering" (verse 5), "all-powerful" (v.23, 63) "power-wielding" and "power-possessing" (v.35), "most powerful" (v.78), and "powerful" 19 times, many more times than even the paradigm of strength, Vayu, is called "powerful" in the Avesta.

6

Ullr and Bres: Identifying The Germanic Sun God

The recognition of Bres as occupying the position of Sun God in the Irish mythology (in the first chapter) opens up a further layer of comparison to the Norse god known as Ullr. In his *Mitra-Varuna*, Georges Dumezil points out that Saxo Grammaticus' *Gesta Danorum* contains an account of a sequence of rulers which matches very closely the pattern we also find in Irish mythology. Despite recognizing this parallel, Dumezil was operating under a false understanding of Irish Nuada as a Mitraic god (an understanding which he recognized later in his career as erroneous) which prevented him from accurately uncovering the significance of this parallel. If we recall the Irish sequence of divine rulers found in the *Battle of Magh Tuireadh* narrative, first is the king Nuada, who rules from the time the Tuatha de Danann arrive to Ireland, during their war with the Fir Bolg, and up until he has his arm severed in that war. Bres then ascends to the kingship, and though he had been a good warrior for the Tuatha de Danann, his rule is marked by despotism and inhospitality. After seven years, Nuada's arm is replaced by Miach with a magical silver arm, making him fit again to rule, and so he is restored to the kingship. Bres is exiled, leading to his incitement of the subsequent war with the Tuatha de Danann. When Nuada is beheaded during the Second Battle of Magh Tuireadh, Lugh

129

takes his place as king, strikes the climactic blow against Balor, and leads the Tuatha de Danann to victory, reigning justly afterward for 40 years. Thus we have Nuada, followed by an interlude of Bres, the return of Nuada, and concluding with Lugh. After Lugh's death, the Dagda reigns for 80 more years before dying of the wound he suffered in the Second Battle. In our identification of these figures in terms of Vedic archetypes they are Varuna, followed by Surya, with the returning Varuna, followed by Mitra, concluding with Dyaus/Vayu.

In Saxo's Norse sequence of successions, the first ruler is Othinus. When Othinus is exiled, Ollerus takes over the kingship, ruling for ten years (compared to Bres' seven) before Othinus returns and is restored to the kingship. Ollerus is ejected. In a subsequent section, Othinus goes this time into voluntary exile, and in his absence a figure named Mithothyn takes over his kingdom and begins to change the religious ordinances. In this episode, Mithothyn is portrayed in a negative light by Saxo, allowing Othinus to return again and take over the kingdom, reasserting himself as the dominant kingly and deific force. Based on his actions as described by Saxo, Dumezil calls Mithothyn "the 'distributor'" and "the judge-leader (mjotudhinn)" (Dumezil, *Mitra-Varuna*, 129). Dumezil considers this figure then to be of the Tyr type[57] (and indeed the similarity between the name Mithothyn and Mithra/Mitra is itself striking, if it is not a coincidence), and suggests that Mithothyn's negative portrayal and the positive portrayal of the "inspired madman" Othinus reflects the ideals of Germanic society at this time. He says of Othinus that his "entire life consists of one vast Lupercalia [a Roman pastoral festival]…" and that for the Germanics it "would have been their ideal to lead such a life, and that they pretended to live it" (Dumezil, *Mitra-Varuna*, 130).

Significant to making the parallel between the Irish and Danish accounts match is the fact that Othinus returns after exile between the reigns of Ollerus and Mithothyn, just as Nuada returns after hiatus between the reigns of Bres and Lugh. That is, both Ollerus and Bres are the second kings in the sequence, ruling in an interstitial period while the first king has left the kingship after becoming unfit, and up until that first king returns. Ollerus rules ten years while Bres rules seven. Thus, we have in the Danish pseudo-history a sequence to parallel the one found in Irish myth, and it runs: Othinus, Ollerus,

---

57 Rudolf Simek states that Mithothyn's name means "the ordering, divine, but mostly impersonal omnipotence" and that in the narrative he represents "an action of an ordering power who considers every individual sphere of human action, whilst Odin embodies a form of governing which takes everything into a single grasp, a totalitarian rule (de Vries). It is not unlikely that an antagonism surfaces here which might well be connected with the story of Odin's exile and the usurpation of the divine rule by other gods" (*Dictionary of Northern Mythology*, 218). This reading tends to support Dumezil's identification of Mithothyn as a Mitraic figure connected to a specific kind of "ordering" and a specific form of governing which is contrasted with the Oðinnic form.

Othinus, Mithothyn, with the final return of Othinus to reassert his preeminence in the Germanic pantheon and his embodiment of their ideal; whereas Father Sky/Wind, the Dagda, completes the cycle for the Irish. Thus if we make the likely parallels between Saxo's sequence and that found in Irish myth, we end up with Othinus = Nuada; Ollerus = Bres; Lugh = Mithothyn; and Othinus also = Dagda. Of course, with our understanding of Lugh as Mitra, his equation with the figure whose name means judge, who Dumezil compares to Tyr, and whose name also bears a striking similarity to the name Mitra/Mithra itself, comes as little surprise. Likewise, if we understand Oðinn as, in part, carrying the Varunian mythos, then Othinus' equation to Nuada, who we have directly equated to Varuna in our *Iliad* analysis, makes perfect sense. And again, if Oðinn also occupies in some measure the role and mythos comparable to Dagda, that is Dyaus-Vayu, Father Sky/Lord Wind, then the fact that he rules at the same points as Nuada and Dagda is to be expected. Indeed, we maintain that both Nuada and the Dagda are gods who each parallel separate aspects of the Norse Oðinn, corresponding to Vedic Varuna and Dyaus (or an aspect of Vayu). The most interesting comparison yielded by this equation then is between Ollerus and Bres. As previously mentioned, because Dumezil believed erroneously that Nuada should equate to Tyr, this led him to believe that the order had been switched around in this sequence on one side or the other. Furthermore, he did not understand that Bres was in the position of the Sun God himself, as we have found in comparison with the other epics. With this understanding we can see that the two sequences may indeed follow the same order: Terrible Sovereign, then Sun God, return of Terrible Sovereign, then Lawful Sovereign, concluding with Father Sky and/or Lord Wind. If so, this seems to suggest that Ollerus may stand for the figure who would have been the central male solar deity of the Germanic pantheon at one time, that indeed Ullr is the Sun God, known by the Vedics as Surya.

Though this sequence is a striking structural piece of evidence and very suggestive, this hypothesis would need to be supported by other specific evidences connected to Ullr the actual deity, and not only his pseudo-historical hypostasis Ollerus. If Ullr can be demonstrated to be a solar figure, then the case for his equation with Bres and then with Surya becomes much more convincing. There are indeed several characteristics pertaining to Ullr which suggest that he was indeed a very solar god. First, Ullr is preeminently known as an archer, indeed as the best of all archers. Snorri calls him "such a good archer and ski-runner that no one can rival him" (*Gylfaginning*, 31). The activity of bowmanship is an exceedingly common symbol of solar activity, standing naturally for the action of the sun which shoots its rays from afar. Both Greek Paris and Vedic Karna, who we have shown to be incarnations of Surya previously, are known primarily as archers. Welsh Gronw is a hunter and is on a hunting expedition when he comes in conflict with Lleu. Ullr too is called "hunting god," *veiðiass*, in *Skaldskaparmal XIV*.

Second, Ullr is said to have been such a great warrior that his name became a byname used to refer to warriors. The aforementioned Karna is one of the greatest warriors in the war and is so terrifying a force for the Kauravas that only the foremost warrior of skill, Arjuna, is at last able to match him. On the other hand, Paris' warrior character evidently degenerated to the point where he was seen as cowardly in war, his estimation seemingly affected by the ambivalent valuation of archers, connected to societal and military developments recent to Homer's time.

Third is Ullr's connection to dueling, as he is said to have been invoked by duelists. We see both Karna and Paris facing off in significant duels in their respective epics, including the one which the whole epic turns upon in which Paris is bested by Menelaus. The equivalent duel forms almost the entire climax of the Lleu Llaw Gyffes myth, as Gronw first temporarily kills Lleu, then is killed in return in the rematch. Karna, however, wins nearly every one of his face-offs during the war, including causing king Yudhishthira to retire from battle for a significant amount of time, until he is finally killed by Arjuna on Yudhishthira's command. Falling to the great Arjuna, the most skilled of the Pandavas, is no shame to a warrior, and indeed it is a fate required by Karna's theological role. There is also the colloquial association existing today of dueling and high-noon, the time when the sun is highest in the sky, as if it were the governing deity of that activity. John Julian Molin claims that Ullr's association with duels can be explained by his role as upholder of law and justice, a role commonly connected to solar gods (Molin, *Ullr: A God on the Edge of Memory*, 110).

Fourth is Ullr's physical description, in which he is called fair-faced or bright, while Bres' nickname is "The Beautiful," Gronw's is "The Radiant," Paris is said to be beautiful, and Karna's personal beauty likewise is central. Karna is known for the earrings and breastplate that he is born with which "make his face shine" and make him invulnerable. In the *Mahabharata* it is said of him that "He is the ornament of a battle. Karna is strong and insolent. He is skilled in weapons and a *maharatha*" (*Karna Parva*, 72), and that "he was as radiant as the morning sun. He had a beautiful face" (*Adi Parva*, 126), and, "He is extremely valiant and handsome" (*Karna Parva*, 72). In the Irish version they say of Bres that "he was so beautiful that everything beautiful was called a Bres" (*Cath Maige Tuired*) and he is called "ornament of the host" (*Carn Hui Neit, Dindshenchas*) compared to Karna's "ornament of battle"; of Ullr it is said, "He is beautiful to look at as well" (*Gylfaginning*, 31).

Fifth, along with the obviously solar description of Ullr as "bright," a further solar indicator may be his association with skiing. We will see in our investigation of the Lunar Cycle that Skaði, also prominently said to be an archer and skier, is likely a solar princess. Hence this motif of combining both archery and skiing may have consistently been attached to solar figures in Norse myth. The sun, then, may have been likened to a

132

skier due to its light gleaming all down the snowy slopes, or due to it appearing at the tops of the mountains each day, or perhaps due to its gliding across the sky. That Ullr both crosses the seas on his magical transport and skis down slopes is also reminiscent of the motion of the sun as its light crosses the faces of the mountains, earth, and sea.

Ullr is known for his ring and/or shield, which could refer to the golden circle of the sun itself. *Skalskaparmal* 61 states: "the shield is also called Ship of Ullr [...] On ancient shields it was customary to paint a circle, which was called the 'ring,' and shields are called in metaphors of that ring." The last and most emphatic oath in a series of three is sworn "by Ullr's ring" in *Atkavida*. 65 amulet rings, dated to between 660 and 780 CE, were found in 2007-8 at an open air shrine to Ullr, called Lilla Ullevi, in Uppland, Sweden. Arrow tips and possible parts of a shield were also found at the site. Meanwhile, Irish Bres is the god whose mother was given a ring by his sun god father at his conception, later passed on to him as a symbol of his solar quality, and Indian Karna is similarly depicted as born wearing earrings with the same significance, gifts traceable to his solar father, which likewise manifest Karna's solar quality by making his face glow. Thus Ullr, Bres, and Karna are all prominently gods of rings or earrings (thank you to Grief, Rubezhal, and Skinfaxi for their help and contributions regarding this point). The association of the Sun with a shield is already attested elsewhere in Norse myth, the Sun being said to have a shield covering named Svalinn, which keeps it from burning the hills and sea (*Grimnismal* 38).

The name Ullr is believed to mean "glory," and the sun is one object whose connection to glory needs no explanation. However, the name *Ullr*'s proposed (though unproven and theoretical) Proto-Germanic root, ***wulþuz**, has also been reconstructed to mean "shine, radiance, glory, splendor" (cf. Gronw "the Radiant"). Intriguingly, the Irish have a sun goddess named Aine, the etymology of whose name is "brightness, glow, joy, radiance; splendour, glory, fame," uniting precisely the same concepts of radiance and glory in her solar nature, and demonstrating that this combination was a common theological conception found in relation to Northwestern European solar figures. Aine, as we will see later on, actually parallels Skaði, and Skaði and Ullr actually share exceedingly similar descriptions in the myths. This similarity has been noted (Reaves, "The Identity of Ull's Father"), the two of them both being snow-shoe gods (she *öndurdis* in *Haustlong* 7 and he *öndurass* in *Skaldskaparmal* 21) and archers who are bright or shining. If Ullr's name means "the glorious one," this could connect to the theme of the Solar Glory or Golden Glow of Sovereignty, which the Mitraic god or hero has to retrieve from the Sun God, as seen in previous chapters.

Molin points out the fact that the theory that Ullr may have been a sun god has gained widespread popularity with scholars in the last three quarters of a century, and sums up this trend thus:

Ullr has been thought by some to have been a Swedish and Norwegian sun god of the Bronze Age, a god who, by the time of the Viking Age and the first Nordic literary sources, had faded only into the distant cultural memories of the descendants of those who had known his former cult. This proposition, taken up most prominently by Ohlmarks (1943, 1947, 1948, 1963a, 1963b, and so on) and most recently by Dronke (2011), has been one of the most frequently espoused theories regarding the god's role in modern scholarship. (Molin, 124)

Molin himself supports this theory, adding that "Swedish rock images bear great witness to the importance of the relationship between shields, ships and the sun" (Molin, 128), and that, regarding the shield as Ullr's ship, "The idea of the sky as an ocean, a reflection of that on earth, on which the sun sails, is common in primitive cultures" (127). To this he adds (among other things) that

It has furthermore been established that the *hringr* [ring] sometimes was considered an allusion to the sun itself, as is evident from both place names and mythological literature. The ship in which mythology tells us Baldr burned, bore the name Hringhorni 'ship with circle [sun?] on the stem', and King Skjöldr's ship in the Beowulf legend likewise bore the epithet hringedstefna (Ohlmarks, 1946, pp. 199-200), a peculiarity also noted by Gelling and Davidson (1969, p. 157). (Molin, 126)

The fact that Ullr has only a known step-father, Thor, and no known biological father, along with the fact that he is described so similarly to Skaði, a jotunn, suggests that his father could have been a jotunn, or at least part-jotunn, as well. This possibility is encouraged by the Irish comparative case: Bres is half-Fomorian (the Irish cognate of the jotnar), his father being a Fomorian who leaves right after his conception. Bres then has to be raised by the Tuatha De, and does not know his father until he grows up, as Ullr is raised by the Aesir while having an absent father. If the Norse case were to match the Irish or Indian, Ullr could even have been the son of a goddess such as Jord or Frigg (an earth or mother goddess, with Sif indeed being a possible candidate as well) and an unknown jotunn. Jord or Frigg could then have placed Ullr on a shield and sent him across the water, as the possible incarnation of the Goddess Earth, Kunti, places her son Karna in a box and sends him down the river in the Indian case. Ullr then would have been found and raised by Sif and Thor. This possibility, though highly speculative, has a support: the legendary figure known as Sceafa is found as a baby floating on a skiff and becomes a great king. His close descendant, Scyld (meaning "shield"), is said to be sent out on a ship into the ocean upon his death, just as he had been found as an infant. A rite recorded in the 13th century *Chronicon de Abingdon* describes how a sheaf (*sceaf*) of wheat was placed on a round shield (*scyld*) and sent down a river to decide a land

134

dispute. This foundling myth-type, similar as it is to the myth of Karna, is thus here associated with a shield, while "ship of Ullr" is the most prominent kenning for a shield in Snorri, giving us an image of Ullr himself floating the waters on a ship that is a shield. We are then left with the possibility that Sceafa/Scyld could be remnants of, or from the same root as, Ullr's own original myth, a myth which would have explained why Ullr's father, and more speculatively still, perhaps even his mother, as in the Indian case, are absent. Rydberg brazenly deduces Hermodr as another name of Odr and as a brother of Ullr, and it is worth noting that a Heremod is prominent in the line of Sceafa/Scef/Strephius, between Scef and Scyld/Sceldwa (these variations found in *Aethelweard's Chronicle; Beowulf; Prose Edda; Gesta Regnum Anglorum*) and specifically as the father of Sceafa in several of these.

Ullr's mythology is so scanty that it has been difficult to get a very clear picture of him. Likewise, it has been remarked countless times that no explicit male Sun God seems to exist in the Norse myth. However, from the scraps of attestation in the myths along with the structural argument, now clarified and made interpretable, we can form a solid case that Ullr may after all have been the male god of the sun for the Germanic people at some early point, and that they too had a male manifestation of this deity, just as did the Vedics (Surya), Romans (Sol), and Greeks (Helios) and that they had both a female and male manifestation just as did the Irish (Grian and Bres). The Ullr we know now from the myths may even, with equal fairness, be called a derivation of the original sun deity, over the centuries become more narrowly specialized in the solar art of archery and retaining the solar glory.

7

The Great Lunar Cycle: The Horse Twins and the Grail

[A glossary of relevant names and charts of parallels appear at the end of this chapter.]

The Aesir-Vanir War and the Holy Grail

The Aesir-Vanir War's place in comparative mythology has perplexed and misled interpreters for a long time now, not least because it is somewhat unclear if there is an exact example of the same motif in any other branches. Some point to the Deva-Asura conflict of the Vedic religion, but this can be shown to have at its root an internecine dispute possibly stemming from the archaic time of Indo-Iranic unity, out of which arose, over time, the demonization of the favorite gods of the Iranics by the Vedics as "asuras" and the demonization of the favorite gods of the Vedics by the Iranics as "devas" (scholars call this event of mutual demonization "The Pandemonium"; see: Jaan

Puhvel, *Analecta Indoeuropaea, 167; Alfred Hillebrandt, Martin Haug, Vedic Mythology, Vol. 2, 264; Jacob Grimm, Deutsche Mythologie, 985).* The division between the Asuras and Devas fails to match the division between the groups of gods who make war in the Norse myth. These are not the same groups of gods coming in conflict. To greatly simplify the matter: in the Deva-Asura war, Indra the Deva and his faction make enemies of Varuna and Mitra and theirs, or alternately their opponents are mere demons and monsters. That is, at bottom we have one of the Second Function warrior caste gods (Indra) set against the gods of the First Function, the priestly-sovereigns (Varuna and Mitra), or simply against the demonic forces if Varuna and Mitra are sometimes excluded.

In the Norse case, on the other hand, we can see right away that the Second Function thunder and warrior god, Thor, is fully united with the celestial gods of the First Function, the gods of magical and juridical rulership (Óðinn, Baldr, Tyr) and does not oppose them. The Aesir-Vanir war, instead, seems to be a conflict between these allied First and Second Function gods with another set – Freyr, Njörðr, etc. – who are repeatedly associated with marriage, generation, wealth, and the fertility of the sea or land. That is, the group that the First and Second Function gods face off with are primarily Third Function gods.

As such, in the course of this series of chapters we will demonstrate, as others have theorized before us, that Freyr is one of the "Horse Twin" gods, those gods who have been called the quintessential gods of the Third Function by the philologist Georges Dumezil[58]. Freyr's father Njörðr, too, who takes part in the war, has sometimes been connected to this twin pair of gods, as Dumezil himself has done. However, due to the fact that Njörðr is Freyr's father rather than his brother, this has been a difficult identification to solidify, to say the least. Others attempting to pin down Njörðr's identity have pointed to the fact that the goddess known as Nerþus may have had a Mother Earth role, and the similarly named Njörðr may have derived from her milieu in some way and thus would be a connected sort of deity. Whatever the case, Njörðr is believed to govern the plentifulness of the sea, and perhaps of the land as well, and thus he, like Freyr, seems to be a quintessential Third Function god, and would himself be tied closely to the Horse Twin mythos as the father of the proposed Horse Twin, Freyr.

If we designate only Freyr as a Horse Twin, then (which will be supported further on), a war between the third function Horse Twin (along with other allied gods) and the first and second function gods, is what we would hope to find a parallel for in the other mythological branches. Third function vs. a coalition of First function and Second function. And yet this exact arrangement is, on first glance, hard to identify in other

---

58 Dumezil, *Gods of the Ancient Northmen, Introduction*, vii.

branches, and it begins to look as though this myth may have been unique to the Germanic branch. The Irish First and Second function gods – Nuada, Lugh, and the Dagda – do indeed engage in war, yet they do not fight against the Horse Twin, Aengus, but against divinities of destruction, of the impersonal forces of nature and fate, while Aengus seems to be on the same side as the chief god Lugh during the great battles. In the *Iliad*, again the Horse Twin heroes Diomedes and Odysseus fight alongside the first and second function gods Agamemnon, Menelaus, Ajax and Achilles, against the Sun God Paris and the slaughterous Demon of the Last Age Hector. In the *Mahabharata*, the first and second function divinely incarnated heroes are brothers to and again fight alongside the Horse Twin incarnations (I refer here to the Pandava brothers). There is no war of the Dioskouroi against Zeus as far as we know in Greek myth, though their fight against their cousins Idas and Lynceus could after all be a distant reflection of some part of the theme if it does not fulfill a different part of their myth.

Indeed nothing *obvious* comes into view in the form of a full-blown *war* with these particular combatants in any of the other branches – except perhaps the Roman. As Georges Dumezil convincingly demonstrates, the Roman pseudo-historical episode from Livy, known as the "Rape of the Sabine Women," with its connected war, is likely the same myth in another form (*Gods of the Ancient Northmen*, 24). Romulus here stands for the higher function gods, the First Function magical sovereign comparable to Oðinn, while the Sabine king Titus Tatius stands for the Third Function gods. The Sabines have the women needed by the Romans for wives, which emblematizes the fact that the Sabines are the Third Function element related to fertility. The two sides do battle, the Sabines almost capture Rome, and the ultimate result is a stalemate and a compromise, in which the Sabines are integrated into Roman society, resulting at last in a fully well-rounded social picture: the First, Second, and Third Functions in harmony; the priestly, warrior, and producer roles filled (See Dumezil, *Archaic Roman Religion* for a full discussion of this comparison). As the Roman example shows, this is a myth of the founding and perfecting of human society as much as it is a myth of the perfecting of divine society.

Beyond these, there is in one branch a single battle, if not a war, with a curious resemblance to the Norse example. This battle, more of a face-off, may after all provide the clue to uncovering the remnants of the "Aesir-Vanir War" motif in other branches, in mutated forms. For there is after all one key confrontation between the Vedic Horse Twins, the Asvins, and the warrior king of the gods, Indra, in the Vedic mythology, though it is easy to overlook in this connection, as the Horse Twins themselves do nott actually take part in the fight. This confrontation proves, as we look into it further, to be the link between the Vedic Asvins and the Norse and Celtic Horse Twins, demonstrating the myth's widespread currency across the various Indo-European nations.

The story that results in this face-off is the story of the meeting of the Asvins and the sage Chyavana, the resulting marriage of Chyavana to the princess Sukanya, and the attempted wooing of Sukanya away from Chyavana by the Asvins. When we have recognized the pattern of this story, we will subsequently come to see how it connects with both the Celtic and Germanic branches via the Irish *The Wooing of Etain*, *The Dream of Oengus*, and the Scandinavian *Skirnismal* (along with the *Prose Edda* and other texts), as well as the Welsh *Mabinogion*. The denouement of this story, in the Indian version, is that the Horse Twins (Asvins) gain access to the *soma* sacrifice and become full immortal gods. Before this point, the higher gods had looked down on the Asvins as mingling too much with humans, debasing themselves, and in general not being godlike enough, and thus the high gods had excluded the Twins from the *soma* sacrifice and thus from immortality. However, the princess Sukanya makes a promise to the Asvins that if they will renew her husband's youth, she and her husband will help the Asvins gain access to the *soma* sacrifice. The Asvins uphold their part of the bargain, and so Sukanya and Chyavana fulfill theirs. With their help, the lowly third function gods are admitted to the society of the higher gods and gain the *soma*.

What is key to connecting these branches, is the fact that, while in one version of the Indian tale, from the *Satapatha Brahmana* (IV.1.5), the Asvins are admitted to the sacrifice only after trading a riddle for an invitation, in another version, that found in the *Mahabharata* (*Vana Parva*, 122-5), in order to win the Asvins their place in the sacrifice, the sage Chyavana takes it upon himself to aggressively confront Indra. He demands justice for the Asvins and that they be treated as full gods. Indra disagrees powerfully, and lists off the faults of the Asvins, pointing out their ignoble closeness to humans, and that they are mere servants. Chyavana ignores Indra's rejection of the Asvins, and instead goes to give them a share of the *soma*, upon which Indra attempts to throw his thunderbolt at Chyavana. Chyavana, however, magically paralyzes Indra and raises a great demon against him. The demon nearly devours Indra before Indra finally remits and agrees to allow the Asvins to be admitted to the sacrifice. The Asvins then join the sacrifice, join the society of the higher gods, gain a sort of equality with them, become immortal, and further, become priests of the sacrifice.[59]

---

59 Dumezil further notes that this demon, *Mada*, has a name meaning "drunkenness" (compare *mead*). As such he seems to parallel Norse *Kvasir*, another being created by the gods in connection with the parallel war, who is a living embodiment of the intoxicating mead.

"This enormous monster's name is Mada 'Drunkenness': he is drunkenness personified. Even Indra gives in, peace is made, the Nasatya definitely join the divine community, and no allusion will ever be made to the distinction among gods or to the initial conflict. But what to do with this character, Drunkenness, whose task is finished and who is now only dangerous? The one who created him, this time with the accord of the gods, cuts him into

If we break this myth down into its essential components, we have 1. Horse Twins, who have been excluded from the high rite due to their low status and mingling with humans 2. a battle against the chief of the higher gods on their behalf (in which magic is used to defeat the high god) 3. resulting in them joining the society of the higher gods 4. gaining access to the high rite for the first time 5. and them becoming priests of the sacrifice.

---

four pieces and his unitary essence is split up into the four things that, literally or figuratively, are indeed intoxicating: drink, women, gaming, and hunting.

Certainly the differences between Germanic and Indie myth are striking, but so is the analogy between their fundamental situations and results. Here are the differences: among the Germanic peoples, the character

'Kvas' is formed after the peace is concluded, as a symbol of that peace, and he is made according to a precise realistic technique, fermentation with spittle, whereas the character 'Drunkenness' is made as a weapon, in order to force the gods into peace, and he is made mystically (we are in India), by the force of ascetism, without reference to a technique of fermentation. Then, when 'Kvas' is killed and his blood divided in thirds, it is not done by the gods who made him, but by two dwarfs, whereas in India, it is his creator who at the order of the gods dismembers "Drunkenness" into four parts. Further, the dismemberment of 'Kvas' is simply quantitative, into three homogeneous parts (three vessels receiving the blood, all of the same value, though one happens to be larger than the others), whereas that of "Drunkenness" is qualitative, into differentiated parts (four sorts of drunkenness). In Germanic legend, it is simply as a lying explanation that the dwarfs afterwards tell the gods of an intolerable force (of a purely intellectual kind), out of proportion with the human world, which would have led to the suffocation of 'Kvas,' whereas in the Indian legend the excess of force (physical, brutal) of Drunkenness is authentically intolerable, incompatible with the life of the world, and as such leads authentically to his being dismembered. Finally the Germanic legend presents 'Kvas' as a benefactor from the beginning, well disposed toward men— a sort of martyr—and his blood, properly treated, produces that most valued thing, the mead of poetry and wisdom, whereas in India "Drunkenness" is a malefactor from the beginning and his four fractions are the scourge of mankind.

All this is true, but it would only prove, if there were need of it, that India is not Iceland and that the two stories were told in civilizations that in content and form had developed in almost diametrically opposite directions. Notably their ideologies of insobriety had become just about inverse. There exists nevertheless a common pattern. It is at the moment when divine society is with difficulty but definitively joined by the adjunction of the representatives of fecundity and prosperity to those of sovereignty and force, it is at the moment when the two hostile groups make their peace, that a character is artificially created incarnating the force of intoxicating drink or of insobriety and is named after it. When this force proves to be excessive for the conditions of this world— for good or for evil— the person thus made is then killed and divided into three or four intoxicating parts that either aid or threaten man.

This pattern is original. It is not met with anywhere in the world but in these two cases"
(Dumezil, *Gods of the Ancient Northmen*, 22-23).

Though the confrontation between Chyavana and Indra is brief and can easily be overlooked, it fulfills functionally the exact role that the Aesir-Vanir war does in the Norse mythology. Again, in the Norse case (*Voluspa* 21-24; *Heimskringla* 4; *Skaldskaparmal*) we have: 1. Horse Twin(s), who are seen as outsiders to the society of the high gods and to the high rite (Ursula Dronke argues the Vanir were seen as "all-too-popular" and that this motivated the Aesir to exclude them from sharing tribute (Dronke, *Poetic Edda*, 134)[60], which matches the accusation against the Asvins that they spent too much time with humans, and indeed the Aesir-Vanir War is said specifically in *Voluspa* 23-24 to involve the question of whether or not worship and tribute should belong to all the gods alike, and that "the wall that girdled the gods was broken," which could indicate a barrier between the higher and lower gods being ruptured) 2. a battle between these lower gods, their allies, and the high gods (in which magic is used to defeat the high gods in both cases) 3. resulting in them joining the society of the higher gods 4. gaining access to the high rite for the first time 5. and they too are said specifically to become the priests of the High Gods' sacrifice (*Heimskringla, Ynglingasaga*, 4). If one accepts the premise that Freyr is a Horse Twin (which will be supported in the following series of sections), the match between these two myths is so perfect it is hard to understand how they have only rarely been compared (credit to Jarich G. Oosten who has separately identified this general connection, in his book *The War of the Gods,* as well as certain comments by Dumezil which pointed out this direction). In fact, to understand simply that the core of the myth is the story of a lower set of gods battling the high gods, joining their society, accessing the highest rite, and then becoming priests of their sacrifice, and that in the Vedic version these lower gods are the Horse Twins, in itself supports the idea that either one or both of Freyr and Njörðr are Horse Twins. While Freyr does seem to be one of the Horse Twins, as we will see, the elder of the two, Njörðr, will be found to be more comparable to the mysterious older figure who fights the battle for the Asvins, Chyavana.

---

60 "hvart - gialda: afrad is a legal term for 'tax', 'dues', but in colloquial idiom afrad gialda has become a proverbial phrase meaning 'to pay excessively, suffer great loss, get the worst of a bargain (see Fritzner s.v. afrad, NGL v s.v afrad). If (as I understand it) the Aesir are faced with surrendering their monopoly of godhead and its revenues and joining with the all-too-popular Vanir, they are contemplating a very great loss in self-esteem and in wealth.

eda - gildi eiga: if they do agree to share with the Vanir, then they must be all gods together, recognized as equally genuine (gild) gods, to whom honour (gildi) is due, partners in the divine 'guild' and its sacred banquets (gildi), equally entitled to tribute (gildi). The poet plays on all the relevant senses of gildi noun, and gildr adj. (see Vigfusson, Fritzner s. vv.). The Aesir's only alternative to this unprofitable and demeaning share-policy is to attack again: which they do" (Dronke, *The Poetic Edda, Vol. II*, 134).

From this point it becomes even more difficult to find cognates in other branches. However, what we can find are possible fragments of the basic theme, and these sometimes in interesting places. We have previously theorized that Diomedes of the *Iliad* is the incarnation of one of the Horse Twins, who is specifically cognate to the "Young Son" Aengus Og and possibly to Freyr as well. In the *Iliad*, we find Diomedes acting out a pattern reminiscent of the one at issue. Diomedes famously is the brazen warrior who fights the immortal gods. At two different points we see Diomedes attacking the gods themselves, first wounding Ares and then Aphrodite. These confrontations of the gods seem wild and foolhardy on the part of the mortal Diomedes, but seen in the light of Diomedes' identification with the Horse Twins they have echoes of the Vanir battling the Aesir and of Chyavana battling Indra. The attacks of Diomedes catch the gods off guard and surprise them with how daring they are, and the ultimate result, besides anger and distress, is that Diomedes wins increased respect from the gods. It is afterward said that no mortal ever wounded more immortals in a day than did Diomedes. To finish the pattern, Diomedes is said (Pindar, *Nemean,* X) to be given immortality by Athena and to become a god at the end of his life. Only Menelaus and Diomedes, of the primary *Iliad* heroes, are said to achieve this immortalization, and we have already shown that Menelaus' divinization is explained by the fact that he is cognate to King Yudhishthira-Mitra (one of the high god incarnations), who is the last hero standing in the Indian epic, achieves the Golden Age internally and externally, and is admitted as an immortal to Paradise on the Holy Mountain.

Thus Diomedes again fulfills the same pattern we have seen thus far. 1. Horse Twin 2. fights a battle with the higher immortal gods 3. gains immortality and divinization and is admitted into the society of the high gods. The one important element missing from this is that he is not specifically mentioned as becoming a priest of the sacrifice, though he is said to marry the daughter of Menelaus, truly becoming integrated into the society of the higher gods and possibly dwelling with the Greek Horse Twins, the Dioskouroi, themselves, as aforementioned, much as the Horse Twin incarnations of the *Mahabharata* are absorbed back into the Asvin gods upon the deaths of these incarnations. Furthermore, the myths of the Dioskouroi themselves may complete the picture. Pollux, son of Zeus is said already to have immortality, but he shares it with his mortal brother upon his brother's death, and the two Twins alternate their dwelling between Olympus and Hades as a result. Thus they both end with a kind of immortality. Most importantly to the pattern we are discussing, as the Vanir and the Asvins are said to become priests of the sacrifice in the end, the Dioskouroi are said also to be initiated into the Eleusinian Mysteries, which could be the Greek version of the Asvins becoming initiated into the *soma* sacrifice as priests. Thus, while Diomedes enacts the first portion of this mythological pattern, the myths of the Dioskouroi complete the picture, with them ending as initiates into the high rites which bring metaphysical elevation and an improved state in the afterlife (Xenophon, *Hellenica*, VI).

The fragments of this myth become even less clear as we look at the mythology of the insular Celts, and yet the mythical implications become all the greater, as they lead us on a path toward the Grail legends. One resonance with the overall pattern is Irish Aengus Og (who we will later explain as the Irish Horse Twin), who famously tricks either the Dagda or Elcmar (Nuada) out of the sacred sídhe Brugh na Boinne. This would have been a main base and site of sacrifice for Elcmar and the Dagda, high gods indeed, and Aengus, a Horse Twin, usurping it, would mark his ascendency as a full divinity. If, as most scholars agree, Elcmar is Nuada by another name (James MacKillop, *A Dictionary of Celtic Mythology*, "Elcmar"), this would put Elcmar in the same position as chief sky god Oðinn in the Norse version or chief god Indra in the Indian, making the whole narrative seem to align with the motif thus far discussed. Elcmar is said to have a fork or wand of white hazel and a cloak with a gold brooch when Aengus comes to him, designating him as druidic and so a First Function figure. Indeed, since both Nuada and Dagda are likely parallels of different aspects of Oðinn, it makes sense that either of them could be the god that Aengus challenges, as seen in the variant versions of the myth. The fact that Aengus is said not to know until just before this confrontation that the Dagda is his true father also would make sense in this pattern: the god of the Third Function becoming re-integrated into the higher divine society from which he was alienated since birth, but for which he is destined. While the Vanir specifically use magic to defeat the Aesir, and Chyavana specifically uses magic to paralyze and subdue Indra, Aengus uses both a military "feint," or diversionary attack, and a verbal trick to finally win the Brugh na Boinne (*The Wooing of Etain*, Part I). This verbal trick can be seen in this context as a kind of magic, like a spoken charm which overpowers the High King. It is no stretch to read this trick as such a kind of magic, considering the magical power the Celts saw invested in poems, satires, and other verbal charms, and this interpretation is confirmed by another version of the same story. In "The Fosterage of the House of the Two Pails," Manannan and Elcmar discuss the magic lay or charm that Aengus is given in order to compel Elcmar out of the Brugh na Boinne. In this case, this magic charm is given by Manannan to Aengus for this purpose, and when it is used Elcmar calls it "a charm and omen by magic and devilry to banish me." Thus it can be said that Aengus indeed uses magic, along with military force, to overcome the High King of the gods and take the *sidhe*. In a separate tale, we hear that Aengus is known to take the food and drink of immortality at Goibniu's Feast, this feast itself and its drink having a clear analogy to the *soma* sacrifice which brings immortality. Thus the basic elements of this mythic pattern are present in the Irish case as well, if in highly fragmented form. However, even more interesting is the Welsh case. As we will see from a thorough analysis of the Welsh Horse Twin myths, they are the basis of the legends of the famous

Grail quester Perceval. That is, following the trail of connections across Europe, it will be shown that the Holy Grail legend and the Aesir-Vanir war are, in fact, one and the same myth.

* * *

Chyavana and the Asvins

The Chyavana story in Vedic myth goes back at least to the hymns of the *Rig Veda*, and is told as well in the *Mahabharata* and the *Brahmanas*, and can only be described as an extremely central myth of the deities known as the Horse Twins. Remarkably, this story actually appears in recognizably similar form in Irish myth as well, and by this comparison we can begin to narrow down a picture of these deities. Comparing, then, the myth of Chyavana as found in the *Rig Veda*, the *Mahabharata* and the *Brahmanas* with the Irish *The Wooing of Etain,* we find that these stories preserve key dramatic beats and remarkable small details, though sometimes in altered forms, across a vast amount of space and time. As such it seems that this myth must date back to a time before the *Rig Veda*, to before the time when these ethnic branches split from one another, in the mists of Indo-European prehistory.

Debatably the earliest recorded mention of the myth occurs in the *Rig Veda* in a hymn addressed to the Asvins: *"That gift, which all may gain, ye gave Cyavana, when he grew old, who offered you oblations, when ye bestowed on him enduring beauty"* (Rig Veda 7.68.6, hymn to *"Asvins"*). This verse contains the general outline of the myth in question.

However, this is not all that is relevant to this connection. Three different "wooing" story groupings, which as we will see have become intertwined, present themselves to us stretching from Ireland to Wales to Scandinavia to India. These groupings are marked by uncanny similarities down to minute details difficult to explain at such a distance of space and time. We must trace these groupings in succession, then, and pay close attention to the ways in which they have begun to overlap and become blended together.

Firstly, we have the aforementioned tale of Chyavana: in its essential structure this is the marriage story of a figure who gets poked in the eye and then demands a fair maiden in recompense, ultimately participating in a "choosing" scene. This very same narrative pattern can be found in the story of Irish Midir. This grouping, then, equates Irish Midir with Indian Chyavana.

Grouping 1: Chyavana = Midir

1. Eye Poking, Maiden in Recompense

- Chyavana gets eyes poked with a branch by the "frolicking" Princess *or* clods of dirt thrown at his eyes by youths while they are playing. He asks the king for the Princess' hand in marriage in recompense. (*Mahabharata, Satapatha Brahmana*)

- Midir gets eye poked out with a "spit" of holly that is thrown at him by a group of quarreling youths while they are playing. He asks Aengus to woo Etain for him in recompense. (*Wooing of Etain*)

2. Encounters Rival Wooers (Named "Horseman")

- Chyavana's wife is approached with attempt to woo by the Asvins (name meaning horsemen). (M)

- Midir's wife is approached with attempt to woo by Eochu (name meaning horseman) Airem (name meaning ploughman). (WoE)

3. Transformation Test

- Chyavana goes into a lake and emerges young and rejuvenated. He now appears similar to the Asvins, and Sukanya has to pick him out from among them in his changed form. She chooses correctly and they live happily. (*M*)

- Midir makes Eochu pick Etain out from among a group of other identical women. Eochu chooses incorrectly and confuses his daughter for his wife. Midir and Etain live happily. (*WoE*)

We can see, then, a direct line between Chyavana and Midir. And yet the identity of each remains mysterious. However, from an analysis of the *Rig Veda* hymns, it becomes apparent that one of the main religious traditions belonging to the Asvins is that they were either the rival wooers or emissary wooers to the Moon God Soma for the hand of the Daughter of the Sun, Suryā. Furthermore, it is said that after their wooing they became bridesmen at the joyous wedding of Soma and Suryā just as the rival Asvins ultimately aid Chyavana and his wife Sukanya. This wedding tale is told in the long and detailed hymn 85 of book 10 of the *Rig Veda*, referred to as "Suryā's Bridal," which becomes key to our further interpretation of the larger puzzle.

The hymn narrates,

> 14 When on your threewheeled-chariot, O Asvins, ye came as wooers unto Suryā's bridal, Then all the Gods agreed to your proposal, Pusan as Son elected you as Fathers.

> 15 O ye Two Lords of lustre, then when ye to Suryā's wooing came [...]

> 18 By their own power these Twain in close succession move;

> They go as playing children round the sacrifice.

> One of the Pair beholdeth all existing things; the other ordereth seasons and is born again.

> 19 He, born afresh, is new and new for ever ensign of days he goes before the Mornings

> Coming, he orders for the Gods their portion. The Moon prolongs the days of our existence.

> 20 Mount this, allshaped-, goldhued-, with strong wheels, fashioned of Kimsuka and Salmali, lightrolling-, Bound for the world of life immortal, Suryā: make for thy lord a happy bridal journey.

> 21 Rise up from hence: this maiden hath a husband, Seek in her father's home another fair one, and find the portion from of old assigned thee. Seek thou another willing maid and with her husband leave the bride. (10.85.14-21)

We see that after the marriage, a pair, perhaps the Asvins, go round the sacrifice like playing children, just as the Asvins gain access to the *soma* sacrifice at the end of the Chyavana myth. We also find that Soma, that is, the Moon God, is said to prolong the days of our existence and to lead his bride to the life immortal, as Chyavana seems in his myth to be in charge of admitting participants to the *soma* rite, which brings immortality. "One of the Pair" is said to be born afresh, which is the power demonstrated by the Asvins in the tale which they use on Chyavana, but also parallels Welsh Pryderi being caught in the Otherworld and then released again (a possible dying and rising motif), or

146

Greek Castor dying and going to the underworld before being recuperated by his brother, and also may suggest the repeated theme of the Horse Twins at last achieving immortality. This "One of the Pair" is also said to order for the gods their portion, exactly as the Asvins in the Chyavana tale become priests and administers of the *soma* sacrifice in the end.

Can it in fact be believed that there is more than one tale of the Asvins as rival wooers, followed by a happy marriage in which they assist, afterward gaining access to the *soma* sacrifice and becoming its priests and administers? It is possible, as mythology is full of repeating and similar patterns, but seems unlikely, that there could be two separate tales with this pattern and outcome, and thus we are forced to conclude that the most likely true identity of Chyavana of the tale is none other than the Moon god, Soma, and that his bride Sukanya is the daughter of the Sun, Suryā. In this context, things become clearer and clearer. Why, in fact, does Chyavana have the power to disarm the King of the Gods, Lord Indra, and to then give access to the *soma* sacrifice to the Asvins? With this power and privilege he cannot be some mere human or semi-divine ascetic. The fact that he so closely parallels other gods (Midir, Njordr, as well as Dionysus, as we will see) means he is certainly a stand-in for a god. Being Soma himself, however, his power over who may attend the *soma* sacrifice becomes clear as crystal, and on reflection seems the only logical thing. His power over Indra when in this domain can only be explained by his being some god on the highest level. His being the lord of the Moon itself and the lord over the central rite would be one of only a couple possible identifications that could explain such power. The reason more scholars have not clearly seen Chyavana as Soma may be the absence of the other figures who appear in the hymn – the other husbands mentioned such as the Gandharva and Agni – from the Chyavana myth. As we will see further on, this absence can be more than explained, and it turns out that the marriages of the Gandharva and Agni to the Daughter of the Sun can be traced in tales separate but related to that of Chyavana, and that this pattern of three separate but connected marriages repeats across several of the other branches as well.

Furthermore, once his lunar identity is understood, the entire theme of an old and withered Chyavana having his eye poked out and then being renewed in youth can be seen as a lunar allegory. The moon, as the hymn alludes, and as ancient sources from many cultures tend to confirm, was seen as the source of immortality due to its eternal cycle of waxing again once it has waned, of being born again, made young again, each monthly cycle. Hence the poking out of the eye may be seen either as an eclipse or as the extinguishment of the old moon, the "Dark Moon" when its face has become fully invisible and it is about to begin a New Moon. Hence it is imaged here as an old man with his eye poked out. The Asvins then renew Chyavana's youth and make him young again. This is the Waxing Crescent as it comes into view and signifies the young, new life of another cycle. The Daughter of the Sun and the New Moon being wed seemingly indicates the sun's rays striking the moon in this waxing phase, illuminating its surface and being united with it there, or it may have symbolized a synchronization/conjunction of the sun and moon during this phase of the cycle in a more specific manner. Another option is the time of dusk or dawn when the moon and sunlight both occupy the sky and the sun can be seen to shine upon the moon.

It is a controversial subject, but there is textual evidence that at least as far back as the Iranic *Avesta*, the Indo-Europeans may have had a concept of the moon being lit by the sun. Hartmut Scharfe argues that because, in one verse, Mithra is described as having self-luminosity *and* being like the moon (see *Mihr Yasht*, 142), that this must mean that the moon was *not* seen as self-luminous itself. He argues that a fact such as the moon's self-luminosity would never need to be pointed out (as the sun is never called "self-luminous" either), and so the description of self-luminosity in this hymn must be a way of distinguishing the self-luminosity of Mithra from the light of the moon, while comparing the splendor of the two ("Rgveda, Avesta, and Beyond – ex occidente lux?", Scharfe). In the Rig Veda, According to Scharfe, Mithra's splendor is being described as like the moon *and* self-luminous. In the *Rig Veda*, Soma is said to shine like or with the sun or to clothe himself in its rays, which are the Daughters of the Sun, thus being called "he who is adorned with Sūrya's arrowy beam" (RV 9.76.4), for, "He hath assumed the rays of Sūrya for his robe" (RV 9.86.32; cp. RV 9.71.9, "he hath assumed the brilliancy of Sūrya"). However, when born, he is called a bright son who causes his parents to shine (RV 9.9.3). In any case, one or other interpretation does not change the underlying symbolism here, primordial and central, which is the marriage of the lunar and the solar, as the marriage of Soma and Surya makes explicit. As Soma clothes himself in the rays of the sun (that is, the Sun's Daughter(s)), it is also said that the Daughter of the Sun purifies him (RV 9.1.6).[61]

James Francis Katherinus Hewitt as early as 1908 also made the connection between Chyavana and Soma. "There is a variant of Chyavana's story in the Rig Veda, X.85, 8-20," he says. "There, the rejuvenated Chyavana is the Moon-god Soma, married to Surya, the Sun-maiden [...] The Aswins (Gemini) assisted at the marriage [...] By this hymn, the Ashwins were summoned to the assembly of the gods" (Hewitt, 310). Thus, while the identity of Chyavana remains contested, we build upon an established notion and add evidence to it.

---

61 See also Erick Dodge: the moon "was seen as a vessel which was filled with soma by the sun. The texts state that it was a soma-spring from which ancestors and deities drank (Gonda 1985)" (Dodge, "Orpheus, Odin, and the Indo-European Underworld," 50-51).

While the power of Soma-Chyavana seems to be to give immortality itself, it appears to be the function of the Asvins within this network of gods to play the instrumental role of giving renewed youth, so that the gods do not merely live forever in an aged and decrepit state. This role relates astrologically to their possible identification as the morning and evening star[62] or with the sky at that time – as the hymn says, going before the morning, apportioning the *soma*, and as the myths show, mystically healing the gods of wounds and agedness. Discussing theories of the Asvins' identities, Brereton and Jamison say: "Of these theories, perhaps the most influential and enduring has been that the gods represent the morning and evening stars (see, for example, Gotō 2009)" (*The Rigveda: A Guide*, 83). Both they and Arthur A. Macdonell (*Vedic Mythology*) find the evidence inconclusive. Chyavana itself means "the slipping one" or "the moving/falling one," supposedly from the idea that he slipped from his mother's womb early. This birth myth may theoretically have a second meaning, the idea of the premature birth perhaps being a way of expressing the fact that the moon is commonly seen to rise in the sky before the sun has set and before night has yet arrived. It is indeed born prematurely each evening, if we take the dark night sky to be its proper domain.

If we suppose then, by our equation, that Irish Midir as well still carries this Moon God identity and mythos, certain passages become more clear.[63] In particular is Midir's

---

62 As Donald Ward details, supported by Mannhardt and Biezais, the Divine Twins are directly identified as the Morning and Evening star in Baltic tradition (*Divine Twins*, Donald Ward 65; 100 Mannhardt, Die lettischen Sonnenmythen, 87; Biezais, Die himmlische Gotterfamilie, 492 and passim.). Cheryl Steets says, based on comparative analysis, that the Horse Twins "apparently represent the morning and evening star (the latter identification, although contested in the case of the Vedic Asvins, is well supported in the remainder of the IE divine twin material)" (Steets, "The Sun Maiden's Wedding", 175).

Steets expounds the issue: "The saules meita [Baltic Daughter of the Sun] is promised in marriage to the Sons of Heaven, but given to the moon, paralleling one Vedic version of Surya's betrothal to her suitors, the Asvins, but subsequent marriage to Soma, who has a lunar identity. In the Latvian dainas, as in the Rg Veda, the identity of the sun maiden's husband changes in certain verses: another daina portrays her as marrying the twins with the moon as a kind of 'best man.' In a third daina the moon abducts the bride from the twins and takes her 'from the Daugava to Germany'" (Steets, 16-17). This last directly parallels the tale of Midir abducting Aengus' beloved, Englec (*Dindshenchas, Cnogba*).

63 Note also, in relation to Midir, the existence of the Gaulish theonym *Toutatis Medurinis* (*Meduris, Medru,* etc.), possibly from **medu-renos*, glossed as "flood of drunkenness or mead," though Garrett Olmstead translates it as "Who Renders Judgment" (compare Midir's name also meaning "judge"). This could mark a double meaning. One inscription (CIL XIII 6017, Brumath, Alsace) bearing the name *Medru* includes a relief of a figure wearing a bull's head, while a bull form, as we will see, is prominent in the myths of Soma and his Greek parallel, Dionysus. See: Helmut Birkhan, *Celts. Attempt at a complete representation of their culture,* 673; Garrett Olmstead, *The Gods of the Celts*

primary physical description that "he was always fair, but on that night he was fairer" (*The Wooing of Etain*). Indeed, he is here being physically described at nighttime, and with a passage that would be more perfectly applied to no other thing than the moon. He is also said to carry "A silvern shield with rim of gold slung over his back, and a silver strap to it and boss of gold thereon" – a silver shield or other circular object of course making a classic lunar symbol. The fact that he is said to have in his hand "a five pronged spear" may connect him to the wealth of the sea, an association we know Njörðr and Soma both to have (as we will see further on). In fact, 5-pronged fishing or eel-hunting spears have been common in Ireland. N.C. Mitchel and Arthur E.J. Went note that the 5-pronged spear was one of the two most common types of fishing or eeling spears in Ireland (Mitchel and Went, "Irish Fishing Spears"). A god with a 5-pronged spear could easily be thought of as a fisher. He is also called the father of Lir, the sea, in the poem "Baile Suthain Sith Eamhain," reflecting the metaphysical conception that waters have their source in the moon, and also matching Njordr's close association with the sea. Additionally, Midir is called a powerful magician, just as Chyavana's magico-ascetic force is feared by both Sukanya's father and Lord Indra himself. And one of the main powers Midir demonstrates is the power to put others to sleep (Chyavana's demonstrated power is to paralyze), as he does to Ailil, again only during nighttime when his trysts with Etain are planned, the power of putting to sleep being an obvious nocturnal and thus lunar power. Midir is also said to have three wondrous cows at his stronghold in the Land of Promise, while, as we will see in a later chapter, the wondrous cow Glas Gaibhnenn is a stand-in for the sacred "*soma*" liquid in another tale. Lastly, Midir is able to transform himself and Etain into swans in the conclusion of their tale, white birds which are exceedingly common lunar symbols (although solar symbols as well in certain contexts), so that they may escape together. As such, this final self-transformation may be merely like a combining of the renewal-transformation of Chyavana and his subsequent marriage into a single concise tableau – the union of moon and ray of sun in the waxing crescent, pictured as two swans embracing in flight.

* * *

and the Indo-Europeans.

The Norse Lunar Cycle

Now that we know the basic elements of this lunar Soma cycle, we can begin to spot them, in an exceedingly fragmentary form, just where we would expect them, in a series of tales about the Third Function gods of the Norse, the Vanir, and the Aesir-Vanir War in which they are combatants. For if the tale of Chyavana and the Asvins fighting Indra, and the Asvins becoming priests of the sacrifice, is the same as the Vanir fighting Óðinn and the Aesir, and becoming priests of their sacrifice, then we should find more or less the same events in the myths of the gods who fight this war in each case.

It first needs explaining that Mani, the generally recognized Moon God of Norse myth, does not seem to figure in this sequence of events which we have named "lunar." However, what basic analysis of the myths has shown is that the Indo-European people often had more than one moon deity or moon-related deity, just as they sometimes had more than one sun deity or sun-related deity. These could of course designate different aspects of the moon or sun. In the Vedic case, one form of the moon god is Chandra, whose name means "shining," who is an ancestor figure of the Lunar Dynasty, which spawns the Kuru kings who fight the Kurukshetra War. The god of the *soma* plant is theorized to have at one point been a separate god and then to have become identified with the moon as well as with associated figures such as Indu ("bright drop"), and Osadhipati ("physician, lord of herbs"). Whether the Soma God was originally only a plant god or was always seen as a lunar deity, there was certainly a period where Soma, Chandra, and the others were associated but had separate myths of their own, until at last they were simply known in Vedic myth as Chandra-Soma or simply Soma. There is, however, no reason to think that the moon and lunar plant/waters gods *necessarily* became one deity in the European branches in the same fashion.

As we have seen, the "Surya's Bridal" hymn involving Chyavana is about the Moon God Soma specifically, rather than Chandra, and it seems to contain themes relating to both his lunar function and his function as god of the *soma* plant and sacrifice. Indeed, the hymn to "Surya's Bridal" was likely composed in its existing form after the *soma* plant god had been identified with the moon, as the opening verses of the hymn clearly suggest Soma's lunar character. The scholars Jamison and Brereton, translators and editors of a current benchmark scholarly edition of the *Rig Veda (2014)*, believe that this was the first hymn in the *Rig Veda* to clearly identify Soma with the moon. However, language relating to "waxing" or "swelling"[64] is used to describe Soma elsewhere in the

---

64 "In the ritual there is a ceremony called *apyayana* or causing the half-pressed Soma stalks to swell by moistening them with water afresh. The beginnings of it are found in the MS

Veda as well, and even if he was only a lord of plants or waters originally these could have been seen as spheres under the domain of the Lunar power from the start, hence why he was eventually syncretized to Chandra (the moon) at all. In the first book of the *Rig Veda* we find: "Soma, wax great. From every side may vigorous powers unite in thee:/Be in the gathering-place of strength./Wax, O most gladdening Soma, great through all thy rays of light, and be/A Friend of most illustrious fame to prosper us" (1.91.16-17). Book 9, usually considered a more archaic book than book 10 or book 1, calls Soma "the drink of heaven" (RV 9.110.8), "in his celestial home of flowing light, above the firmament, in the highest heavens of light" (RV 9. 86.15). How and when Soma was combined with the moon itself, if he was ever *fully* separate, and then with Chandra, then becomes a key subject for further research.

Thus, in keeping with the parallels we have demonstrated thus far, we may consider the myths of the Vanir and the Aesir-Vanir War potentially as a centering on a lunar myth specifically connected to the Norse version of the *soma* as the liquid of immortality given to the gods in sacrifice. The culmination of the war in an exchange of hostages associated with divine drinks or liquids (Kvasir, Mimir and Njorðr in *Ynglinga Saga*, Mimir and Njorðr in other sources) and the accession of the Vanir to priests of the high sacrifice underscores this connection to the *soma*. Mani, on the other hand, not connected to this cycle, may more accurately be seen as either comparable to Chandra or perhaps even as another manifestation of the moon divinity in an aspect unrelated to either Soma or Chandra.

In fact what we find in the sequence of myths connected to the Aesir-Vanir War are nearly all of the elements of the Chyavana tale, however they have been split up and distributed to a few deities rather than attached only to one. Despite this splitting up, it cannot be ignored that the same elements exist here, often linked one to the next and including the confrontation of the lower gods with the higher and their ascendence to priests of the sacrifice. Thus, as we go along in examining these linked motifs, we are tasked with deciding if each of these gods who take roles paralleling the Indian Chyavana-Soma are related directly to the lunar epiphany in some way, as aspects of the moon in some sense, or only as auxiliary performers in a lunar cycle, with separate identities.

The story of Iðunn and the golden apples, found in *Skaldskaparmal*, which begins the events that lead up to the marriage of Njorðr and Skaði, shares the identical main theme

---

(4.5.5). The verb *a-pya* 'to swell', occurs in the RV. in connexion with Soma (1.91.16-8); 10.85.5); but here it seems to refer to Soma as identified with the moon. In one other passage, however, (9.31. 4) it may have a ritual application. Soma is also said in the RV. to swell (*pi, pinu*) like a sea or river (9.64.8 . 107.12) (Macdonell, 107)

of the Chyavana tale: the matter of renewing the youth of the gods when they begin to grow old. For the Norse, this important function is performed by the golden apples, tended by Iðunn. In the Vedic version, this same function is performed by the special herbal paste, one form of which comes to be known as the Chyavanaprash, which the Asvins give to Chyavana when he goes into the water and has his youth renewed. As we can see, these objects are quite different and their keepers are here so dissimilar that they are of opposite genders. So important, however, is their function that we must look past these surface differences to see the way in which each object plays a key role in very similar sequences of events.

Specifically, we see that the abduction of Iðunn causes the identical problem, the identical state that we encounter at the beginning of the Chyavana tale: Chyavana on the one hand and the Norse gods on the other have now grown old and decrepit, and require the herbal paste or the golden apples to renew their youthful state. Furthermore, the killing of Thjazi for stealing these apples, which follows, incites the same situation and outcomes that the poking of Chyavana's eye by Sukanya (or alternately by the playing youths) does: Thjazi's daughter Skaði must be given recompense for this deed, concluding with a marriage involving a "choosing" scene, just as Chyavana must be recompensed, concluding with a marriage, followed by an analogous "choosing" scene. Tellingly, one of the recompenses to Skaði for the killing of Thjazi is the removal of Thjazi's eyes and their placement into the sky as stars. Therefore once again, right where we would expect a key element – the poking out of eyes – we find it, only changed slightly. In the Norse version the eye-removal motif is itself one of the recompenses, while in the Indian version the poking of eyes is one of the *causes* which require recompense. And of course, in the Norse version it is the female deity, Skaði, who is given the husband, Njörðr, as the final recompense, while it is the male Chyavana who is given the female princess Sukanya in the Indian version. The roles have simply been reversed, while the outcome is identical: each pair undergoes the "choosing" scene (Skaði choosing Njörðr (whose feet have been kept young by the waters of his domain) from among the gods by looking only at their feet and Sukanya choosing Chyavana (who has just emerged from the waters of a lake renewed in youth) from among the same-looking Asvins), and the gods acquire or reacquire that which renews their youth, the golden apples or the magical herbal paste.

Above all, what this sequence suggests is an identity between Njörðr and Chyavana-Soma, and between Skaði and Sukanya, while Thjazi then is either embodying a role related in some way to the cause of the decaying of the gods and/or the waning of the moon. The identification of Skaði with Sukanya-Surya would of course imply that Skaði could be a daughter of the Sun, which would not fit the interpretation of Thjazi as part of the lunar hierophany. Thus we would have to suggest that Thjazi could be a destructive aspect of the sun which may have been seen as greedily taking away the youth of the gods or the light of the moon in some manner. We could of course conclude that this exact familial relationship may have been altered in one tradition or the other, just as several other details show the signs of change and difference. Thjazi is a giant also said to be *skaut-giarn,* which has been translated in one case as "eager for shooting" – archery being an extremely common indicator of solar activity in myth, the sun shooting rays from afar, while Skaði is known as "the shining bride of the gods," and is said to use both bow and skis as the solar Ullr also does.

The only manuscript of *Hyndluljod,* found in *Flateyjarbok*, appears to have *skaut-giarn* in this description of Thjazi, which some scholars have emended to *skraut-giarn,* adding a *k* to try to make sense of the word. *Skaut-giarn,* the compound word as it is in the manuscript, has several possible meanings, recorded by the LaFarge-Tucker *Glossary to the Poetic Edda* (1988): "eager for shooting," which interpretation however requires us to read the "au" as a stand-in for u-umlaut *ö,* making the first word *skröt,* said to be an allowable reading but not the simplest one; "fond of disguises (Gerring) or fond of sailing (Finnur-Jonsson)." The reading of "eager for shooting" does not seem to be the one favored by the greatest number of scholars, but remains a possibility if we consider that the mythic context for it may have been lost. We merely note this as an uncertain epithet with several other possible meanings. However, we must also note that the more favored reading, "skraut", requires the addition of a full letter, *r.* We hold that Thjazi very well could be connected to an aspect of the sun, but that this is by no means necessary for our overall argument. This detail could have shifted as the distinct branches developed. In the case of Sukanya, she is the great-granddaughter of Vivasvan, the Sun god himself, and because she is the *incarnation* of the Daughter of the Sun, her own immediate father does not have to incarnate the Sun god as well, her solar lineage already being taken care of via her great-grandfather. A grandfather of Skaði rather than Thjazi could then connect her to the solar mythos in the Norse case and this would conform the closest to the parallel with Sukanya, if this solar parentage was not forgotten altogether in the Norse version.

If we accept Viktor Rydberg's equivalency of Thjazi with the smith Volund, found in his *Investigations*, which argument cannot be fully laid out here, then there is further support for the idea that Thjazi "loves to shoot," and also for the idea that he could be a solar divinity of some sort[65]. In *Volundarkvida,* Volund uses skis in order to hunt bear,

---

65 In fact, Aine, the Sun Princess wife of Irish fire god Mannanan (thus paralleling Skadi when she is transferred in marriage to Odin in his fire aspect, as we will detail further on), this Aine is called the daughter of the smith-king Cuillean or Guillean, who creates magical weapons and armor for kings and is said to be "remembered in horror in the traditions of the peasantry" (**Nicholas O'Kearney,** ***Journal of the Royal Society of***

causing him to appear similar to Skadi and Ullr, the other prominent ski and bow wielding divinities. He is called "sharp-sighted marksman," or, in another translation, "weather-wise bowman" (*Volundarkvida* 8). Whether Thjazi loves to shoot or not, Volund, his posited double, obviously does. Volund also is called an elf king (*Volundarkvida* 10) (even if he appears only to be half elf), the *alfar* having solar associations as we note elsewhere. It is said that at his hall he has 700 rings (*Volundarkvida* 10), while rings are one of the central symbols, as we have seen, of the Sun God Ullr. Thjazi himself, like Volund, is in general closely associated with gold, gold being known as "Thazi's testimony/speech" (*Skaldskaparmal I*, p. 92), which could have a specific mythic meaning while also expressing the fact that gold can be poetically likened to an emanation of the sun. Thjazi's father, Ölvaldi, is said in the same section to be very rich in gold.

Due in part to this name of Thjazi's father, Rydberg argues that Thjazi-Volund is one of the "Sons of Ivaldi," divine artisans of the Norse pantheon who compete in an artistic competition, and compares these figures to the Vedic Rbhus, divine artisans who compete in a very similar competition. The Rbhus seem themselves to have been solar deities. "Initially, Ribhus [singular] was an early Vedic sun deity," says Charles Russel Coulter. He notes that in some passages they are called sons of the goddess of morning light, Saranyu, who is the consort of aforementioned sun god Vivasvat, and in the *Atharvaveda* they are said to be sons of Sudhavan, the "good archer" (Coulter, 1892). Similarly to Adityas, Maruts and Vasus, the Rbhus "appear as stars or rays of the sun" (1893) (remember that Thjazi's eyes become stars). In the *Aitareya Brahmana* (III, 30) they are called the "sun's neighbors or pupils," and are said to periodically dwell in the house of "he who is not to be concealed," *Agohya,* an epithet of the Sun. If this singular figure Ribhus was a "sun deity" in the earliest phase, this could explain why Thjazi appears in such a solar family, as the father of a sun princess, and why he enacts a mythic role related metaphysically to the excessive heat of the sun's rays. We could then either interpret Thjazi as a hypostasis of the sun itself, or as only a family member or descendant of the sun who shares in and passes along its qualities to his solar daughter, as the Sun Princess incarnation Sukanya is herself a great-granddaughter of the sun god.[66]

Antiquaries of Ireland, Volume 2, 1855, 32-33). This Cuillean/Guillean the Smith has been suggested to be a linguistic cognate of Weyland (Volundr) the smith, a result of a lenition (softening) of the initial consonant (or the reverse) ("Völundr, Wayland, Weland and the Irish Cuillean"; "Wayland Revisited: A Pan-European God?", *The Atlantic Religion* blog, https://atlanticreligion.com/. Accessed May, 2021). This would nicely align Aine with Skadi and Cuillean with Thjazi as Volundr.

66 If we follow Rydberg down this path, and accept also Volund's brother Egil (as great an archer as can be found in Norse legend and myth) as the father of Ullr (and thus seemingly an elder Sun god like Irish Elatha), then we have suddenly a fully united

Njörðr and Soma

family of Sun deities: Thjazi, his daughter Skadi, his brother Egil (along with a third brother), Egil's son Ullr, and, if Rydberg is correct in his further equations, a brother of Ullr, Odr, who is the lover or husband or Freyja. Earendel, a form of *Aurvandil*, who Rydberg equates with Egil, is called the "true light of the sun" in the medieval Christian poem *Crist I*, and, in the *Blickling Homilies*, makes way for and announces a younger "Sun" god, here said to be Christ, who perhaps takes the position previously held by the younger Sun god Ullr. *Earandel* is also used in the Old English corpus to translate, among other things, *oriens,* the Latin term indicating that which comes from the East and implying the rising sun. The interpretation of Norse Aurvandil as the Morning Star makes little sense, considering it is his toe that becomes a star, possibly the Morning Star. The toe of the Morning Star would not become the Morning Star, though the toe of a solar god could surely become a star, just as the eyes of Thjazi become stars. The reconstruction of Aurvandil's name as coming from Common-Germanic *Auza-wandilaz,* "wand of Dawn," makes more sense, identifying him with the rising morning light which emanates from the early morning sun. This identification could work with what we have proposed of him being the "rising sun" above.

If the aforementioned Odr, called Ullr's brother by Rydberg, is also a sun deity, like the other members of his theorized family, it would lend credence to the idea, which we will touch on further along, that Freyja stands as a parallel to the Dawn goddess. We would have Odr and Ullr as solar brothers, at least one of whom weds this goddess. This then would seem to be the imperfect parallel of what we find in the case of the *Iliad:* Helen adulterously marries not just one solar figure, but two brothers in succession, the sun incarnation Paris and his brother Diephobus. Ullr does not necessarily need to be a lover of Freyja for this parallel to prove meaningful, as the role of husband of this goddess could have been held only by his solar brother in the Norse case. In counterpoint to this, however, Diephobus of the *Iliad* could instead be a Rudraic figure similar to Balor or Ashwatthama: his name means "causing hostile terror," his face is disfigured and "brutally torn" when he is killed (Virgil, *Aeneid,* Book VI) as Balor's eye is driven out of his head, and he is one of the final opponents killed to end the war, specifically killed by the Mitraic hero, Menelaus, as his final great stroke, slightly similar, then, to the death of Balor by Lugh.

This perspective also makes possible one explanation for why the myth of the Sun God and Dawn Goddess marriage is split from the myth of the cuckolding of the Mitraic god in the Irish case. There we have two potentially solar figures: the Sun God Bres, who marries the Dawn Goddess, and Cermait, "of form all fair," with a tongue of honey, who cuckolds Lugh and is killed in revenge. In this case Bres and Cermait are not brothers, however, but they are still closely related, Bres being the paternal uncle of Cermait. Cermait dies but rises again, revived by his father the Dagda, further opening him up to a solar interpretation.

We would be left then with Njörðr as the primary repository of the Soma-type mythos in Norse mythology, as the presumptive *"soma"* plant (whatever its Norse equivalent was) and moon god, and, if the Norse model matches the Indian, lord of the liquid of immortality, and a lord of the liquid element generally, of the waters. This would connect very well with Njörðr's close association with the sea, the moon seen as the master of the waters of the ocean and of waters generally. Encyclopedia Britannica describes the deity Soma thus:

> The personified deity Soma was the 'master of plants,' the healer of disease, and the bestower of riches […] The pressing of soma was associated with the fertilizing rain, which makes possible all life and growth.

Njörðr is repeatedly associated with wealth as well as the sea, as when he and Skadi go to live at the sea periodically during their marriage. His home by the sea, Noatun, means "ship-enclosure." In *Gylfaginning* 23 he is said to be prayed to for sea voyages, fishing, and wealth: "He is invoked by seafarers and by fishermen. He is so rich and wealthy that he can give broad lands and abundance to those who call on him for them." In the same passage, Snorri says he has the power to still sea and fire. He is called "the giving god" in *Skaldskaparmal,* and in *Heimskringla* is called "wealthy" again and is said to have power over general prosperity and the growth of crops, another perennial lunar power. Similarly, endless associations of the Vedic god Soma to both wealth and waters can be found by a brief perusal of book 9 of the *Rig Veda,* the book of the *Rig Veda* entirely dedicated to Soma (also called here "Pavamana" and "Indu"):

"The mighty waters, yea, the floods accompany thee Mighty One" (9.2.4)

"The lake is brightened in the floods. Soma, our Friend

this God dives into waters, and bestows

Rich gifts upon the worshipper

Away he rushes with his stream, across the regions, into heaven,

And roars as he is flowing on." (9.3.5-7)

"O Indu, bring us wealth in steeds, manifold, quickening all life." (9.4.10)

"Flow on to us and make us rich.

Send down the rain from heaven, a stream of opulence from earth. Give us,

O Soma, victory in war." (9.8.7-8)

"In the stream's wave wise Soma dwells, distilling rapture" (9.12.3)

"O Pavamana, bring us wealth bright with a thousand splendours." (9.12.9)

"May they in flowing give us wealth in thousands, and heroic power,—

These Godlike Soma-drops effused." (9.13.5)

"Comprising all the treasures that are in the heavens and on the earth,

Come, Soma, as our faithful Friend." (9.14.8)

"Becoming Sovran of the streams.

"He, over places rough to pass, bringing rich treasures closely packed.

Descends into the reservoirs.

Men beautify him in the vats, him worthy to be beautified,

Him who brings forth abundant food." (9.15.5-7)

"He who containeth in his hands all treasures much to be desired:

All-bounteous art thou in carouse." (9.18.4)

"O Pavamana, find us wealth." (9.19.6)

"For he, as Pavamana, sends thousandfold treasure in the shape

Of cattle to the singing-men." (9.20.2)

"Pour lofty glory on us, send sure riches to our liberal lords,

Bring food to those who sing thy praise." (9.20.4)

"Thou, Soma, boldest wealth in kine which thou hast seized from niggard churls" (9.22.7)

Perhaps most striking,

"Soma, Lord of wealth:

Fill full the sea that claims our praise." (9.29.3)

"O Indu, as thou flowest on bring us the wealth of earth and heaven,

And splendid vigour, in thy stream." (9.29.6)

"The Soma-drops, benevolent, come forth as they are purified,

Bestowing wealth which all may see." (9.31.1)

"the rivers flow to thee Soma" (9.31.3)

"Like waves of waters, skilled in song the juices of the Soma speed

Onward" (9.33.1)

And:

"From every side, O Soma, for our profit, pour thou forth four seas

Filled **full of riches** thousandfold." (9.33.6)

"Pour forth on us abundant wealth, O Pavamana, with thy stream.

Wherewith thou mayest find us light

O Indu, swayer of the sea, shaker of all things, flow thou on,

Bearer of wealth to us with might." (9.35.1-2)

"May Soma pour all treasures of the heavens, the earth, the firmament

Upon the liberal worshipper." (9.36.5)

"Flow on, O thou of lofty thought

Preparing what is unprepared, and bringing store of food to man,

Make thou the rain descend from heaven." (9.39.1-2)

"O Indu, Soma, send us now great opulence from every side, Pour on us treasures thousandfold.

O Soma Pavamana, bring, Indu, all splendours hitherward:

Find for us food in boundless store.

As thou art cleansed, bring hero strength and riches to thy worshipper,

And prosper thou the singer's hymns.

O Indu, Soma, being cleansed, bring hither riches doublypiled,

Wealth, mighty Indu, meet for lauds." (9.40.3-6)

"Pour out on us abundant food, when thou art pressed, O Indu wealth

In kine and gold and steeds and spoil.

Flow on thy way, Most Active, thou. fill full the mighty heavens and earth,

As Dawn, as Sūrya with his beams.

On every side, O Soma, flow round us with thy protecting stream,

As Rasā flows around the world." (9.41.4-6)

"Soma, while purifying, sends hither all things to be desired

159

Soma, effused, pour on us wealth in kine, in heroes, steeds, and spoil,

Send us abundant store of food." (9.42.5-6)

"O Soma Pavamana, find exceeding glorious wealth for us,

Wealth, Indu, fraught with boundless might." (9.43.4)

"So, to increase our wealth to-day, Inspirer" (9.44.6)

"Unbar for us the doors of wealth." (9.45.3)

"Thus, Soma, Conqueror of wealth! flow, finding furtherance for us,

Giver of ample opulence.

Lord over riches" (9.46.5)

"Wealth-winner, dwelling in the sky" (9.52.1)

"Pourst down the rain upon us, pour a wave of waters from the sky,

And plenteous store of wholesome food." (9.49.1)

"Indu, Wealth-giver" (9.52.5)

"pour forth the food that streams with milk

Increase the sea that merits laud." (9.61.15)

"Soma who rainest gifts, may we win riches with our hero sons" (9.61.23)

As Eliade sums it up, the moon governs the seas and the rains, and all fertility is its gift (Eliade, *Patterns*, §§ 49 ff). "The organic connection between the moon and vegetation is so strong that a very large number of fertility gods are also divinities of the moon," he says, further asserting that "In almost all the gods of vegetation there persist lunar attributes or powers – even when their divine "form" has become completely autonomous"(Eliade, 162). The moon was seen as an agricultural god (by Indo-Europeans as well as other peoples), a source of vegetative powers, rains, and the wealth they bring, just as Njörðr is most prominently known to be god of the sea and of wealth.

Njörðr's unsuccessful marriage to Skaði, where three nights would be spent at sea and nine would be spent on the mountain tops, could then indicate an understanding of the seasons or lunar phases, certain ones ruled by the moon, others more dominated by the ray of sun which rises above the mountain peaks and gleams down their snowy slopes like a skier. Indeed, wolves disturb Njörðr in the mountains by their howling (a striking lunar image), and it is said that he loves rather the placid lunar animal the swan (the animal Midir turns into with his bride). Skaði is awoken each morning by gulls, as could be said of the sunbeam. Their failed marriage then would be seen on the material level either as the waning and vanishing of light from the moon, or as the transition from night to day, where the sunbeam must be wed to other husbands, or as some seasonal or lunisolar change.

It may be objected here that if the son of Njörðr, Freyr, is supposed to be the Horse Twin God, then he ought to be the son of Father Sky, as seen in Vedic, Greek, and Irish myth, or at least the son of the Sun God, as in some versions of the Vedic tradition. After all, the Twins, and indeed Freyr himself, seem to be very solar gods. How then could a Horse Twin have been born of a moon god?

The more specific evidence for Freyr as a Horse Twin will be presented in the subsequent parts. One possibility is that, by the Asvins' important association with Soma as seen in the primary myth we have been discussing, the Horse Twin(s) and Moon God may have become so closely linked to one another as to become considered father and son in the Norse version. Alternately, the moon as father of the Horse Twins could have been the more archaic and original parentage, though this can only be speculated upon. Ultimately, the fact that both the Horse Twins and the Soma God have close associations to plentifulness, wealth, and other such "third function" domains, and that their central myth involves them teaming up against the higher gods in order to win admittance to the sacrifice, makes the pair a natural grouping and gives them a true familial character.

It must be remembered that Njörðr is almost never proposed to be Father Sky or the Sun God in the first place, but is generally supposed simply to be a sea deity or perhaps a god of the plentifulness of both land and sea, pictured as a hypothetical mate to the theorized Earth goddess Nerthus. Thus to claim Njörðr is in fact Soma, the plant and moon god, is no more a problem for Freyr's proposed Horse Twin parentage than the usual interpretations are. And as we can see from the fact that Vedic tradition already shows examples of the Horse Twins' parentage changing from Sky to Sun, it is evident their parentage was not unchangeable. The Moon God, after all, a great celestial deity already closely associated with them in myth, would be a more logical alternate of the Sky Father than a "sea god" would. In fact, the Horse Twins are not purely solar gods, and are more accurately markers of the transitional state between night and day, associated with morning and possibly evening stars as well as sunrise and possibly sunset, known primarily as bringers of light from the darkness.[67] Hence, the Horse Twin

---

[67] "The Asvins may originally have been conceived as finding and restoring or rescuing the vanished light of the sun" (Arthur A. Macdonell, *Vedic Mythology*, 51). The mythically central burial mound Brugh na Boinne/ Newgrange, which Aengus wins from Elcmar or the Dagda is referred to as "Mac an Og's [Aengus'] brugh brilliant to approach." Of Aengus' Brugh, Anthony Murphy tells of its alignment with Venus, the Morning Star: "In 1958, in his book about primitive mythology, Joseph Campbell recounted a folk tale from

Freyr could be seen as son of the Moon in this sense, following his father's setting by rising as the morning star and leading the way for day via his wedding to another of the shining maidens of the house of the sun god.

One very strong support for the Horse Twin-Moon God son-father pairing is the case of the Irish Midir, who we have identified with Chyavana and Njörðr. While the Irish Father Sky god the Dagda is the father of the Horse Twin Aengus, *Midir is said to be Aengus' foster father*. Thus Father Sky and the Soma Moon God share the paternal role in relation to the Horse Twin, the parallel of Freyr, in the Irish version. This may be evidence that the Moon god and Father Sky were originally seen as sharing parentage of the Horse Twin in a certain way. This dual parentage of Aengus by Dagda and Midir proves the key to aligning the Norse case with the other branches, to seeing why Njordr rather than Father Sky is father of Freyr. Furthermore, in the Welsh version, the figure known as Pwyll, father to Pryderi the "Young Son" Horse Twin born on the same night as (as if twinned with) a horse to his horse goddess mother, appears also to be a lunar-associated god, analog of the Soma-associated Gandharva, as we will see. Thus the Welsh version would also break the tradition of Horse Twin as son of Father Sky, instead making him son of a lunar-related deity once again. The Norse, Irish, and Welsh cases all showing moon-related gods as father figures to the Horse Twin(s) would constitute a veritable trend in this direction, indicating that in Northwestern European this lunar heritage of the Horse Twin(s) was well understood

---

the Boyne Valley in which a local had told him the light of the Morning Star, Venus, shone into the chamber of Newgrange at dawn on one day every eight years and cast a beam upon a stone on the floor of the chamber containing two worn sockets. This might seem like an incredible suggestion, except for the fact that it is astronomically accurate. Venus follows an eight-year cycle and on one year out of every eight, it rises in the pre-dawn sky of winter solstice and its light would be able to be seen from within the chamber," and that, additionally, "Christopher Knight and Robert Lomas, authors of *Uriel's Machine*, suggest that a series of eight x-shaped markings on the lintel stone of the aperture above the entrance of Newgrange – the so-called 'roof box' which allows light into the chamber – represent the eight-year cycle of Venus. However, they were not aware when writing their wonderful book of the story that had been told to Joseph Campbell about the Morning Star shining into the chamber. How did local people living in the Boyne Valley in the 1950s come into the possession of knowledge describing an astronomical phenomenon that was likely to have taken place at Newgrange in the ancient past?" (Anthony Murphy, "Newgrange and the Boyne Valley monuments – advanced lunar calculations and observation of the effects of precession of equinoxes in Neolithic Ireland").

Gullveig, Heiðr and Mímir as Lunar Aspects?

The lunar theme surrounding the Vanir does not seem to end with the identification of Njörðr as Soma, and a few of the other figures surrounding the Aesir-Vanir War itself must each be (much more speculatively) looked at from the perspective of this Great Lunar Cycle. For there are others involved in the lead up and aftermath of the Aesir-Vanir conflict who seem to make no appearance in the Indian version and who it would be prudent to attempt to account for in the context of the lunar theme.

First is Gullveig, a mysterious personage who is suggested to have had some unspecified role in the inciting events of the war. She is killed three times for some unstated offense, being born again each time. Dumezil notes her similarity to the Roman Tarpeia, a Sabine woman who betrays the Sabines to the Romans hoping for a payment of gold, but is instead killed. One common position holds that Gullveig is merely a goddess or demon of greed of some kind, her name possibly meaning "gold intoxication." Some interpreters also relate her to the goddess Freyja (see Rudolf Simek). However, knowing that the context in which she appears is a lunar myth cycle, if we instead begin by attempting to read Gullveig in terms of lunar symbolism, we can perhaps better understand her nature and why she is involved with this cycle to begin with.

According to the *Voluspa*, Gullveig tames wolves, as the moon, especially when full, often seems to do; she knows magic arts, which are sometimes associated with the power of the moon, as with the magical powers of the Irish Midir and Indian Chyavana; and she "is the joy of evil people," as night itself certainly is, especially when well lit by a clear moon, the time for shameful hidden crimes and other wicked possibilities. One meaning of *veig* is "alcoholic drink," which itself could ultimately derive from the association of the moon with various special beverages and with derangement of the senses (lunacy) in all forms. Gullveig dies and is reborn three times, just as the moon is a master of repeated resurrection as it wanes and waxes again. The full moon, after all, is generally seen to last three nights, just as Gullveig is killed and reborn three times. Her name, also containing *gull*, meaning "gold," suggests that she could then be a hierophany of the moon at its maximum power, when it is exercising its fullest and most dangerous lunar influence, intoxicating people and enabling evil to be done by its light; that is, the full moon, and more specifically the golden-yellow full moon. What would symbolically match the idea of a "golden alcoholic drink"? The sun? No, it is golden but not intoxicating or as closely associated with liquid. Gold itself? No, it is not associated with liquid. The golden moon, repeatedly connected with waters and beverages, would be a correct symbolic match for this concept.

If this is so, then it is the frightful influence of this golden-yellow full moon that may be part of what causes the gods to have to kill her three times to quell the powerful, destructive force she is able to exert on people and perhaps gods alike. Her power has become too great and must be reduced. She is finally neutralized and transformed, fittingly, into the more benign "Heiðr," meaning "bright, clear" (meaning also "fame"), perhaps a placid, no longer dangerously golden-yellow moon.

Ursula Dronke, in her translation of the *Poetic Edda*, points out that the root of this name, *heið-*, is found as an element in names relating to the sacred mead: *Heiðrun*, the goat that "yields the 'shining mead' of the gods" in *Grimnismal* 25, and *Heiðdraupnir*, the "skull that drips sacred mead" in *Sigrdrifumal* (Dronke, 131)[68]. As such, Dronke, like Robert Hockert before her, suggests that Heiðr may have had an intimate connection to the mead. Hockert himself argues that Gullveig and Heiðr could even be "interpreted as a personification of the mythical mead" itself (Kuusela, "Halls, Gods, and Giants: The Enigma of Gullveig in Óðinn's Hall," 28). The Norwegian word *veigja,* and the Icelandic *veig*, both contain the element *veig* and mean "intoxicating drink." Building on the possibility of Gullveig as directly connected to the mead, and bringing it back to the *soma* sacrifice, around which so much Vedic mythology seems to orbit: could the changing of the color of the moon from gold to white have been seen as a process of purification also of the mead that metaphysically originated there? Was this heavenly process also repeated in the processing of the *soma* or mead that was offered at the archaic sacrifices, the juice of the plant at first being yellow, overly strong, then being mixed and clarified into a final form fit for sacrifice, just as the full moon itself changes from yellow to white?[69] In just such a way, Encyclopedia Britannica describes the process of preparing the Iranic version of this drink, the *haoma*: "The juice, described as yellow, was filtered and mixed with milk, and perhaps with water too, to cut the bitter taste" (Encyclopedia Brittanica, *Encyclopedia of World Religions*, 510). The Vedic *soma* is described as being made "from a dried plant, which was first soaked in water and then pressed to produce a yellowish juice, which was then mixed with water and often also with milk. Unadorned it was apparently quite bitter" (Brereton and Jamison, *The Rigveda: A Guide*). The "purification and mixing" of the *soma* juice is the subject of the

---

68 "Gullveig; (b) *heid-* as an element in the names of *Heidrun* (the goat that yields the 'shining mead' of the gods, *Grim* 25) and *Heidraupnir* (the skull that drips sacred mead, Sigrdr 13-18) could evoke the bright elixir — *veig* — in her old name (cf. *skirar veigar*, BDr 7) ... The most valuable discussion of the term *heid-* signifying 'bright mead' is still that of Hockert" (Dronke, *The Poetic Edda, Vol. II*, 132-33).

69 Bellows also sees an allegory of refinement here, saying of the lines mentioning the burning of Gullveig: "Lines 5-6, one or both of them probably interpolated, seem to symbolize the refining of gold by fire" (Henry Adams Bellows, note to stanza 21, *Voluspo*).

entire 9th Book of the *Rig Veda*, 114 hymn dedicated to Soma Pavamana, or Soma the Self-Purifying. Though we cannot expect processing of the juice of local Iranic and Vedic plants to match the processing of the Germanic mead very closely, the beverages of each branch likely had a yellowish color, if for different reasons, and a general process of purification could have been a part of the ritual from the most archaic steppe period, which was then adapted to different specific drinks in different geographical regions[70]. We will see, in a later section looking at the Irish and Vedic parallels of Gullveig's myth, that the Vedic myth of the churning of the milk sea also includes a poisonous gas that has to be contained (by Shiva) and neutralized while the nectar of immortality is being extracted from this sea. Thus this general concept of a process of purification is present in a less encoded form in relation to the drink of immortality within Indo-European mythology.

Second, we have the case of Mímir. Why is Mímir, keeper of the mystical well, involved in the Aesir-Vanir hostage exchange at all, and what does this mean? The wise Vanir exchanged for him in Snorri's *Ynglingasaga*, Kvasir, who was born of the saliva of both the Aesir and Vanir and whose blood made the Mead of Poetry, can be associated with the Soma theme via the shared thematic of "drinks of the gods." Thus Mímir's presence in this myth, too, reinforces the idea that "the drinks of the gods" is one of the subjects around which the war turns. Kvasir is exchanged, in Snorri's *Ynglingasaga* version, as seems fit, for the equally or more wise Mímir, who is also associated with a drinkable liquid capable of giving intellectual powers, the water of his well. The presence of these two in explicit juxtaposition reinforces the idea that Njörðr and Freyr themselves may have a deeper connection to the drinks of the gods, as we have seen, perhaps with Njörðr as master of the waters generally, which ultimately metaphysically originate the various sacred drinks, and Freyr as the orderer and

---

70 "The original sacred drink of the PIEs was mead (*médʰu). This tradition was so ancient, widespread, and central to their culture, that descendants of the word are found in Late Old Chinese (mit) and Proto-Uralic (*mete) via Tocharian. This tradition was continued in Germanicand Celtic branches (PG and PC *meduz) as well as in Proto-Balto-Slavic (*medús), but in the epic poetry of the Greeks the term shifted to meaning "wine" (epic: μέθῠ méthu) and among the Indo-Iranians it was replaced with the cult of *sáwHmas (Skt. sóma; Avestan haoma) (Witzel, 2006: 173; Watkins, 2011: 53). Nevertheless, the mythic associations remained. Sóma provided vitality and wisdom to those who drank it (Ṛgveda 9 and 8.79.2-6). It was guarded in the otherworld/heavens by the Iranian Gandarewa and Indic Gandharvā ('heavenly-bards') (Macdonell, 1897: 8)" (Dodge, "Orpheus, Odin and the Indo-European Underworld," 16).
"[…] with passages in the ṛgveda which describe: the Soma potsherds as skulls, the Soma cup as a head, and the drinking of Soma as 'the restoration of the head' (Heesterman, 1985: 46. *Taittirīya Saṃhitā* 6.4.9.1. *Kāṭhaka Saṃhitā* 27.4 and 29.4)" (Dodge, "Orpheus, Odin and the Indo-European Underworld," 18).

administer of the connected sacrifice. By their association in the hostage exchange then, we should look also at Mímir, to see if he too may have originated as in some way related to the moon.

Soma, seen by the Vedics as both the plant, the moon and the liquid that grants immortality simultaneously, forms a symbolic match to Mímir if we picture the moon as simultaneously a severed head and a round well where a divine liquid is held. Wisdom would then reside in this well that is Mímir's head, just as immortality is contained in the liquid of the moon which is also the god Soma. Commentator Timothy Stephany sees a similar connection, pointing out that the phases of the moon mimic the shining of sunlight into a well. Stephany suggests that the moon could then be considered the well, while the face on the moon could be seen as the head of Mímir. Alternately, Mímir's Well could be one location on the moon which is Mímir's head. This theory would also fit very well with the idea that Óðinn carries Mímir's head around with him, while it wisely advises him. If we accept Óðinn as – in one part – an analog of the Vedic Varuna, this would make him the god of the night sky. In this speculative line, his carrying around of Mímir's head would simply be an image of the moon floating in the night sky.

Even the pledging of Óðinn's eye to this well could speculatively be seen as another layer of this same lunar hierophany. If, as Dumezil and many others have suggested, Óðinn is a sky god parallel to Vedic Varuna, and if one of his eyes is the sun, and he is also a god of night sky, then the other eye could be considered to be the moon. (The sun is frequently referred to as the eye of Vedic Varuna and Iranic Ahura Mazda, and of the case of Varuna, Hartmut Scharfe says: "in VIII 41,9ab **Varuṇa's "two white eyes"** (śvetá vicakṣaṇā) almost certainly refer to the sun and the moon" (Scharfe, "Rgveda, Avesta, and Beyond")). However, if the moon is also considered to be this sacred well, then the moon would simultaneously be the well and Óðinn's eye, one within the other, the eye in the well. This kind of metaphysical symbolic layering, multiplying of hierophanies around a supposedly singular phenomena, is typical of religious and mythological symbolism. The myths are not simply a symbolic game, however, so this highly speculative line of thought should be balanced by an account of the other metaphysical dimensions present in the given myth, and whether this lunar connection is really valid in the case of Mímir should be looked at more closely.

The mythologist Victor Rydberg was perhaps the first to suggest the equation of Mímir and Soma, saying, "Mímir was understood as a priest because he was the author of the sacred fimbul-songs, and Óðinn's counselor, and was originally identical to Rigveda's king Soma, who is the mythic representative of the Vedic priests" (Rydberg, "Towards the Baldur Myth," 47). However, if this is so, it would create a confusing picture of three Norse Soma gods, Njörðr, Kvasir, and Mímir, and the case for Njörðr as

Soma is actually stronger than the case for Mímir from the evidence we have presented herein. Thus we should consider this theory of Rydberg's with caution.

Etymological evidence could suggest some connection of Mímir to concepts which at least are often *related* to the moon. The etymology of Mímir is generally accepted as coming from a reduplication of a word descended from the Proto-Indo-European verb **(s)mer-*. The meaning of this verb most often cited when discussing Mímir is "memory," relating to his apparent character as a god of deep wisdom. However, the verb also has the meaning of "to allot." In Persian, Kurdish and Pashto this root developed into the word for "to count," while in Hittite it is the root of the verb "mark," meaning "to divide a sacrifice." On the other hand, the word for "moon" in Sanskrit comes from Proto-Indo-European **méh₁ṇss*, probably from **meh₁-*, meaning "to measure." Hence the fact that the archaic Indo-Europeans saw the moon as being in one of its primary aspects a measurer, so crucial as it is to marking the days as it measures them out via its even and steady phases, is apparent in the words they used to name it. The moon was preeminently "the measurer." Mímir, on the other hand, with his deep memory, was "the allotter" or "the counter." This is not quite the same thing, but some connection is within reason. If we return briefly to Irish Midir, who we have shown to be equated with Chyavana-Soma and Njörðr, we find that his name, Midir (already so similar in appearance to Mímir), meaning "judge," derives ultimately from a proposed Proto-Indo-European root, **med-*, meaning "to measure." That is, the name Midir comes from a *perfect synonym* of the root of the aforementioned word for moon, a synonym which is indeed orthographically almost the same word (*med-* vs. *meh-*). *Midir* is then much closer to the name for the moon than *Mímir* is. To compound this etymological mystery, we find that the second meaning of this root (connected to Midir but *not* to Mímir), **med-,* is "to give advice" – coincidentally this is of course just the thing said to be Mímir's main function.

There are further curious cases of etymological overlap among the figures thus far discussed. The aforementioned root **med-* yields (along with Armenian *mit*, "mind"), in Old Norse, *mjotudr*, meaning "dispenser of fate." From the root of Mímir previously stated, **(s)mer-*, is yielded in Greek *moira*, the name of the Fates. Additionally, this root can mean "to worry over," and yields Greek *merimna*, meaning "care, thought" and "anxious mind," while the meaning of the Welsh Pwyll's name (whose important role in this lunar cycle we will explore in subsequent sections, and who stands in relation to the "Soma" gods as Bragi does to Njörðr in Norse myth) is "care, deliberation" and also "discretion, wisdom, judgment, mind," and derived also from its Proto-Indo-European root **kweyt-* is also the Slavic *cisti*, "to count."

This is not a clear division of meanings between clear parallel figures, but a persistent and irreducible cross-pollination of similar, identical, and connected meanings even

167

among figures who are closely positioned but who should not be strictly equal (Mímir, Midir, Pwyll), yet who are linked by this complex cycle of lunar significances.

Can we say clearly then who any of these figures are, or at least give a sense of how they interrelate? As for the Norse cases, we could of course decide to say that the Soma mythos was merely fragmented and then overlaid here and there over gods loosely connected to the central myth as best fit the narrative expediency, and that we cannot say for sure if any of these figures were definitively lunar in origin. Or conversely, we can simply take the clues we have from the myths to understand the separate aspects of the moon and sacred waters that these deities embody. This gives us: Njörðr, the moon as it relates to the wedding with "Suryā" (aka Skaði), as well as the moon as governor of the tides of the sea, perhaps of the waters in a generalized sense and indeed as the source of the sacred waters, but even more, the moon as that which brings forth fecundity from both sea and land, the fecundator moon, hence his being called wealthy. Gullveig is the golden-yellow sometimes seen in the full moon, the moon at its most dangerous full power, who must be ritually murdered for three nights to return her to placidity. She is the sometimes dangerous feminine power inherent in the moon, who is only purified when a second bride, a solar maiden (Skaði), arrives to purify the lunar waters, as we will see.

Njörðr does indeed become one of the priests of the Aesir's sacrifice in Snorri's version, while Mímir keeps his seemingly separate well, each then retaining an important possible connection to the sacred waters, whether or not Mímir is truly a lunar god himself. Njörðr would be that aspect of "Soma" which aligned with and fought for the lower gods, that aspect associated with the moon's "Third Function" powers of fecundation and wealth, who it would not be natural at first to call Aesir. Kvasir would be the embodiment of the *soma* liquid itself, which seems the most incontrovertible identification of all.

To complete this equation, then, we must bring in the Vedic figure Dadhyanc, who bears a certain outward resemblance to Mímir. We have discussed two versions of the story of the Asvins' accession to the *soma* sacrifice, but there is a third. In this version, the Asvins gain access to the sacrifice by inquiring it of the sage Dadhyanc[71]. He refuses, saying that Indra will cut his head off if he tells the secret of the sacrifice. The Asvins reassure him by saying that they will first give him a horse's head, and will store his human head safely away, so that when Indra beheads him, they will have his original

---

71 Dadhyanc, after having lost his human head, "'magically acquired wisdom, [and] fell into a lake on the mountain Saryanavat' [...] Saryanavat was connected to Soma (Parmeshwaranand, 2000: 599)" (Erick Dodge, "Orpheus, Odin, and the Indo-European Underworld," 52; quoting and commenting on Kazanas, 2013).

head ready to be put on again. The *Rig Veda* alludes to this story saying, "Upon Dadhyanc a horse head is placed by the Asvins, who wish to learn his knowledge" (RV 1.117.22), and the *Satapatha Brahmana* narrates it in more detail: "Now, Dadhyanc Atharvana knew this essence, this sacrifice – how this head of the sacrifice is put on again, how this sacrifice becomes complete" (SB 14.1.18-24). Timothy Stephany suggests once again that the horse head of Dadhyanc is another image that can be seen on the face of the moon, making the beheaded Dadhyanc, keeper of the secret of the *soma*, another possible lunar god, just like the beheaded Mímir, keeper of the secret of his well. As Stephany puts it, "The Horse Head came from Dadhyanc who was the possessor of the secret of the soma, the intoxicating drink known as the 'well of immortality'" (Stephany, *Lunar Illusions*). If this is accurate, then we would have in the Indian version Dadhyanc and Chyavana in the same contrasting positions as Mímir and Njörðr, perhaps preserving the more ancient contrast of these somehow lunar-related figures.

In this context we should also consider the myth of Svarbhanu, who drinks the *amrita*, or nectar of immortality, an analog of the *soma,* churned from the ocean of milk, and then has his head cut off by Mohini, his still animated severed head thereafter being named Rahu. Incidentally, this head, Rahu, was then seen as the being responsible for causing lunar eclipses and as representing the ascending moon. A similar theme repeats in the Vedic myth of Namuci, who steals away and drinks the *soma*, causing it to be mixed with his malignant nature. Indra and the gods must then extract the good *soma* from his body, effectively purifying it of his negative, Asuric influence. In this process, *Rig Veda* 8.14.13 says that Namuci's head is torn off by Indra.

However, though the comparison of Mímir with Soma here has demonstrated possible connections, we must bracket it and set it aside. Rydberg argues that Mímir overlaps with both Soma and the Vedic god of the Underworld, Yama. We take seriously the possibility that these Vedic gods could be closely aligned or even overlap in some sense, as we will explore further along in relation to the Greek Lunar Cycle, considering the common role of the Moon God also as a lord of the underworld in ancient societies (see Eliade, *Patterns in Comparative Religion*, "The Moon and Its Mystique"). Yet, as Rydberg's arguments demonstrate, Mímir may align even more with the figure of Yama than with the figure of Soma, and we cannot exclude the possibility that Mímir's seeming connections to Soma could be due to some incidental overlap of these archetypes or another kind of coincidence. Lastly, modern scholarship has connected Mímir to a motif of heads in wells seen commonly, for example, in Celtic folklore and hagiography (John Carey, "Irish Parallels to the Myth of Odin's Eye" and "Nodons in Britain and Ireland"; Matthias Egeler, *Celtic Influences in Germanic Religion*). As such, the possibility must be examined that Mímir's mythos comes from such a folklore motif or even from a local water spirit of some kind. This perspective remains shallow, however, as it fails to look for the deity underlying such folkloric or water spirit motifs. Under a seemingly narrow deity of wells may lie a greater divinity of waters or even of the subterranean realm, from which such wells spring, this greater deity reaching back with its roots into the pantheon of archaic gods. Irish Nechtan is one of many examples of this principle, seemingly merely a god of a well, but shown by comparative analysis to be the parallel of Vedic Apam Napat (Dumezil, "Le Puits de Nechtan"; "La saison des rivières" from the third volume of *Mythe et épopée*). Mímir as a Lord of the Underworld could then naturally be the deity who rules the waters bubbling up from the depths into his well.

Finally, as we will see in the following parts, Bragi, whose wife is a key figure in this cycle of tales and who himself narrates it, will also be associated to the moon, being the same figure as the Indian Gandharva, chief singer of the court of the gods and guardian of the Soma.

* * *

Myth Grouping 2: Freyr = Oengus

Secondly in our groupings of parallel myths, we have two figures who we have proposed to be the Northwestern European manifestations of (and this is crucial) *one* of the Horse Twins. Each of these figures sees a maiden, wastes away with love for her, and this is followed by the maiden being wooed for the first figure by an intermediary. This parallel compares the Norse poem *Skirnismal* with the Irish prose tale "Dream of Oengus," and equates Scandinavian Freyr with Irish Oengus.

Freyr = Oengus

1.Sees Maiden From High Seat or Dream

- Freyr sees the beautiful Gerðr from the High Seat Hliðskjalf which he has sneaked onto. (*Skirnismal*)

170

- Oengus sees the beautiful Caer in a dream. (*Dream of Oengus*)

2.Wasting Away From Lovesickness

- Freyr wastes away from grief and claims he will soon die if he cannot have Gerðr. (*S*)

- Oengus becomes ill after his dream and stops eating; a doctor is called. (*DoO*)

3.Father Intervenes to Send Assistance

- Freyr's father Njörðr tells Skirnir to go and speak to the ailing Freyr. (Intro to *Skirnismal*)

- Oengus' father the Dagda asks Bodb Derg to search for Caer for Aengus. (*DoO*)

4.Sends Intermediary Wooer

- Skirnir attempts to woo Gerðr for Freyr. (*S*)

- Bodb attempts to find Caer for Oengus. (*DoO*)

5.The Maiden is in Potentially Hostile Territory

- Gerðr is in Jotunn territory. (*S*)

- Caer is in a sidhe mound which has to be attacked to bring her out. (*DoO*)

6.Gift of Magic Sword

- Freyr gives his servant Skirnir his famous sword. (*S*)

- Oengus, in a subsequent story, gives his protege Diarmuid his famous sword. (*The Pursuit of Diarmuid and Grainne*)

It will be quickly noticed that for many of the cases we are analyzing, only one Horse Twin is identifiable. This holds true for the Irish (Aengus), Scandinavian (Freyr) and Welsh (Pryderi) cases. The Vedic Asvins themselves had become so unitary that they were referred to by only this single name, and they did most everything together, acting

171

essentially as one. In the Iranic version, this god also appears in singular form rather than as a set of twins. It also appears possible that this singular form is actually *more archaic* than the twin form, though the question remains open. As Hartmut Scharfe observes,

> only in India do we find two Nāsatyas, whereas the Avesta mentions just a single Nåŋhaiθya. It seems, though, that in the latter case the Avesta is more archaic. ṚV IV 3,6 once has the name in the singular (nā́ satyāya) and once (ṚV VIII 26,8) in a dual form índra-nāsatyā "O Indra and Nāsatya," implying a single Nāsatya. In the Bṛhaddevatā VII 6cd (similar Mahābhārata XII 201,17ab) we find a tradition that Nāsatya and Dasra are known as the two Aśvins. The dual nā́ satyā (ṚV I 173,4) refers to Nāsatya and his twin. ("Ṛgveda, Avesta, and Beyond," 61)

Scharfe concludes that, originally, the primary Horse God "Nasatya" may have been a chariot warrior, while his charioteer may have been seen as his twin, hence one of the two could have gained much more prominence than the other in certain branches. In these other branches, the charioteer could have not been recognized or could have been pushed aside. In the Greek case, only one of the two Dioskouroi is fully divine, and thus one is again more important than the other. They too are called by a unifying moniker, the Dioskouroi. In the Roman legend that Dumezil shows to be equivalent to the Aesir-Vanir War, that is the Rape of the Sabine Women, a single figure, Titus Tatius, stands in for the Horse Twins. We can theorize that in the Celtic and Germanic cases, either the second Horse Twin never was recognized, became seen as unimportant and was pushed aside, or that he became absorbed into the dominant Horse Twin in the myths, or again that the second Twin simply hasn't been clearly identified as of yet, possibly even being demoted to a secondary character in the mythology. We cannot even rule out the possibility that the prominent single Horse God is the more archaic form, as the singular Avestan version appears more archaic than the twinned Vedic version to Scharfe, though this is likely impossible to know with certainty. It even seems possible that in the Welsh case the second twin may have become, or been seen as, the first twin's horse: Pryderi is born the same night as a horse, is raised alongside this horse, and the horse becomes his own when they are grown. In general we should remember, of course, that a twin is no less a twin when the other twin is not present, so we will continue to use this well-recognized name of "Horse Twin," for the sake of convenience. Ultimately, it seems that, whereas the Vedic twins are primarily known by the title "the Sons of God," *divo napata*[72], and as ever youthful, the Northwestern European cases are instead

---

72 The Baltic and Greek cases are of the same type as the Vedic *divo napata: Dieva dēli* (Sons of Dievs) in Latvian; *Dievo sūneliai* (sons of Dievo) in Lithuanian; *Dios kouroi* (Zeus' boys) in Greek. All emphasize that these gods are sons or young boys (Greek *kouroi*).

characterized by the epithet "The Young Son" (Mabon, Mac Occ) – the Divine Sons simply became the Divine Son, but their status as ever-youthful divine sons remained absolutely central to their nomenclature and identity. The Greek name *Dioskouroi* also emphasizes that these sons of Zeus, aka *Dios,* are *kouroi,* young boys.

Stig Wikander, in his previously mentioned work, argues that, since there is only one Iranic Horse Twin, the second and more "domestic" Indo-Iranian Horse Twin could have become or been merged with Atar, the fire deity in the Iranic tradition (Donald Ward, *The Divine Twins An Indo-European Myth in Germanic Tradition,* 22). This is significant considering that Aengus' brother is the fire deity Aed, and, as we will discuss further on, Freyr has a myth that could parallel the Vedic fire god, as if this fire aspect were merged or originally united in him. Donald Ward also notes that the Romans generally focused only on one Horse Twin as well, specifically Castor, the more warlike and less "passive" of the two. Castor is said to be the patron of the cavalry and appears as a name or a nickname among the Roman soldiers, while Pollux does not. Ward notes that "only one brother was worshipped, instead of both Dioscuri" and concludes that "Pollux, who was unquestionably a more passive figure, and who was more involved with domestic functions, gradually faded into the background" (Ward, 23).

Having increased our understanding of the web of Horse Twin tales we have examined thus far, we must further assess the parallels which bring Oengus and Freyr into this Soma cycle, as the Northwestern European representatives of the Horse Twins.

Horse Twins: Oengus and Freyr

Based on his study of the Horse Twins motif throughout Europe, the scholar Michael Shapiro ("Neglected Evidence of Dioscurism (Divine Twinning) in the Old Slavic Pantheon") enumerates a series of characteristics common to the Horse Twins.

1. They are sons of the Sky god
2. They are brothers of the sun maiden and somehow related to the Sun god
3. Association with horses
4. Dual paternity
5. Saviors at sea
6. Astral nature
7. Magic healers
8. Warriors and providers of divine aid in battle

9.   Divinities of fertility

10.   Association with swans

11.   Divinities of dance

12.   Closeness to human beings

13.   Protectors of the oath

14.   Assisting at birth

15.   Founders of cities

To which we add other important traits based on the Vedic Asvins:

16. Swordsmen

17. Great intelligence

18. Always portrayed as youthful

19. Vanity over their own beauty, which they may even "die" from

20. May be denied the drink of immortality only to earn it later

21. Counselors

The Irish deity Oengus Og checks nearly every one of these boxes. His foster father Midir seems to fulfill a few himself; however, this is most likely only due to coincidence or overlap of motifs, as Midir's true identity is much more clearly the Moon god.

1.   Oengus is the **son of the Dagda**, who is either the primordial **sky god** or a god who has inherited that role, Dagda's daughter being the Dawn Goddess Brigid and son being the Fire God Aed. The Asvins are sons of Dyaus (RV 1.182.1; 1.184.1; 10.61.4) or one of them alone is (RV 1.184.4), while the Dioskouroi are sons of Zeus and the Baltic Dievas Deli are sons of Dievs.

2.   Brigid, the Dawn Goddess, is another one of Dagda's children, making Oengus not brother of a sun maiden, but **brothers of the Dawn Goddess**, who is frequently conflated with the sun maiden. However, Shapiro plainly oversimplifies this aspect, and Mircea Eliade points out that the Asvins are actually "always represented at the side of a feminine divinity, either Usa, goddess of Dawn, or Surya," and thus the variability between sun maiden and Dawn Goddess is insignificant. Ceisiwr Serith has pointed out how Dawn Goddess and Daughter of the Sun were frequently conflated or confused as well. Interestingly, Aengus marries Brigid in a Scottish folk tradition (Donald A. MacKenzie, *Wonder Tales From Scottish Myth and Legend*), similar to the incestuous relationship hinted between Freyr and Freyja, while he marries a Sun Maiden in the Irish tradition.

3.   Oengus is referred to as "**horseman**" in *The Fosterage of the House of the Two
      Pails* – "Aengus Og, son of the Dagda/is a horseman, is a sailor" (*Fosterage*). In
      addition, one of the best known myths in which he appears involves him helping in
      the wooing of the Horse Goddess Etain. Etain is known sometimes by the epithet
      "horse rider." In the *Dindshenchas*, a poem called "Tuag Inber" is related in which
      Oengus provides Eochu and Ablend a swift horse while they are encamped with
      their cattle. He tells them to unbridle the horse in a meadow before it "sheds its
      water" and causes their deaths. Oengus' foster father is sometimes said to be
      Elcmar, who in the *Dindshenchas* is also called "lord of horses." Horses connect
      with Oengus' genealogy at every turn. In *The Colloquy with the Ancients* he is also
      said to abide in Rath Mongaig, meaning the fort of "strong hair" or "a horse's
      mane" according to Robert Maclagan (Maclagan, *The Perth Incident*, 184). He
      rides a white steed in a Scottish folk tradition (MacKenzie, *Wonder Tales From
      Scottish Myth and Legend*).

4.   **Dual or unclear paternity** cannot be linked to Oengus on his own, but may have
      become attached to Oengus and Midir. In some versions both are made the sons of
      Dagda, thus closely linking them and making them brothers. Yet in other versions
      Midir is said to be the son of Indui, and Oengus to be his foster son.

5.   As the Horse Twins are known as **saviors at sea,** so Oengus may be interpreted as
      a protector at sea. As previously mentioned, he is called a "sailor," and it is further
      stated that "if thou repeatest the 'Nourishing' [the poem about Oengus and Eithne]
      going on a ship or vessel thou shalt go safe and sound, wave or billows"
      (*Fosterage*). This is a tentative identification, as several other blessings besides
      that of sea voyages are mentioned in succession, and the poem is referred also to
      Eithne. Success in children, in family, in judgments and hunting, in spouse and
      children, in peace at a banquet, in pleasing kings, and the gift of the sense of liberty
      from bonds are also granted by the poem, but these could also be interpreted as
      domains fittingly belonging to Oengus.

6.   The **astral nature** of Oengus is less clear on a surface reading, but comes into
      view only after understanding his divine identity via parallels in other branches. He
      brings "the promise of spring" in the morning in a Scottish folk tradition
      (MacKenzie, *Wonder Tales From Scottish Myth and Legend*), possibly associating
      him with a celestial phenomenon of the morning.

7.   In some legends Oengus is depicted as **a magic healer** who can repair injured
      bodies and return life to dead ones. When his foster son Diarmuid died, he would
      breathe life into his body whenever he wanted to speak to him. (The Vedic Asvins
      raise up the dead man Rebha in RV 10.39.9, and do similarly for Bhujyu in
      1.119.4)

8. Oengus was indeed known as **a warrior**, called by a name meaning "of the battle squadrons" (*Dindshenchas*), and another meaning "expert in arms" – "the host of Aengus were distressed. I and Aengus, expert in arms, a pair whose hidden mystery had not its like" (*Fosterage*). Oengus is also called by names meaning "mighty and stern" and "red armed" (*Dindshenchas*), seeming to describe the appearance of a bloody warrior.

9. With regard to **fertility**, Oengus is colloquially known as a god of love and beauty. His primary legends concern tales of love and wooing, and he is the one who arranges for Etain to marry Midir (before she is transformed by Fuamnach). His portrayal as ever-youthful and his name meaning "young" strengthen his connection to love tales and fertility. In *The Fosterage of the House of the Two Pails* it is said of him that "Aengus enjoined noble marriage on all in general," suggesting that his role of arranging Midir's marriage was no fluke, but that encouraging or arranging marriages was a stable trait of the god.[73] In addition, a later colloquial tradition developed in which it was said that "His kisses became birds that hovered invisibly over young men and women, whispering thoughts of love in their ears" (*Celtic Myth and Legend*, Charles Squire 1905).

10. Association with **Swans**[74] – Oengus is said to have four swans that circle over his head when he travels. When he finds Caer at the lake of the Dragon's mouth, he discovers that she and the other girls there would turn into swans for one year every second Samhain. He has to identify Caer in her swan form from among the other swan maidens, and when he does he turns himself into a swan as well and flies away with her. In the end of "Wooing of Etain" in which Oengus heavily features, when Midir wins his final wager with Eochu and is allowed to embrace Etain, Midir turns himself and Etain into swans and they fly away together.

11. If Oengus had any particular **association with dance** it is not clear; however, Oengus is a famous harper and plays the people to sleep with his harp at the end of *Dream of Oengus*.

12. Being associated primarily with the very human activity of love, while also being foster father of the *possibly* human figure Diarmuid, could demonstrate Oengus' particular **closeness to human beings**.

---

73 As for the Asvins: "Owing to their connexion with Surya the Asvins are invoked to conduct the bride home on their chariot (10.85.26). They are also besought along with several other deities to bestow fertility on the bride (10.184.2). They give the wife of the eunuch a child and make the barren cow yield milk (1.112.3). They give a husband to the old maid (10.39.3) and bestowed a wife on one of their favorites (1.116.1 &c.). In the AV (2.30.2 &c.) they are said to bring lovers together" (Macdonell, 51).

74 Their car is most commonly drawn by birds (6.63 &c. or patatrin, 10.143.5), swans (4.45.4), eagles (1.118.4), bird steeds (6.63.7) or eagle steeds (8.5.7).

13. A tenuous and certainly questionable connection to **oaths** may be that Oengus is sometimes said to be the foster son of Elcmar, who some claim to be Nuada by another name, and who was associated with justice. Elcmar is said to be a "judge" in the *Dindshenchas*. Oengus' other foster father Midir's name likewise is said to possibly come from the Old Irish word for a judge, *midithir*. The repeated association of judges with Oengus, both of his suggested foster fathers bearing the association, may suggest a role relating to the upholding of justice. Even when Oengus craftily tricks his father out of Bru na Boinne it is by forcing him to hold to the technical letter of the agreement, a bit like telling him he should have read the fine print.

14. Oengus does have an **association with birth**, found again in "The Fosterage." This text states: "Aengus said to him… 'your wife is pregnant and whatever child is born I receive to bring up and educate…Manannan went away to his fort and the time came and the wife bore the fruit of her womb, a shapely lovely daughter with a tip of curly yellow-coloured hair on her head…She was given to Aengus to bring up and educate and daughters of other rulers of her own age along with her" (*Fosterage*).

15. Oengus' role in **founding cities** is unclear.

16. Oengus was certainly a **swordsman**, and owned a famous sword named "Mortallach," meaning The Great Fury, gifted to him by Manannan and passed along to Diarmuid along with another named Little Fury.

17. **Intelligence** is no less a common theme in his legends than love. Oengus famously used cunning to trick either Elcmar or the Dagda out of their burial mounds. He is called "prodigious" and *ilchlesach*, "of the many accomplishments/tricks" in *The Colloquy With the Ancients* (73).

18. As mentioned previously, Oengus Og's name includes the title "Og," meaning "**young**," and another of his names is the Mac(can) Oc, or the "young son." His association with youth is ever-present and is a part of his identity. This could hint that he is eternally youthful.

19. While the incarnations of the Horse Twins in the *Mahabharata*, Nakula and Sahadeva, die of vanity over their own **beauty** and the Asvins are called "beautiful," as we have noted, Oengus too is associated strongly with beauty. Oengus is known colloquially as a god of beauty and it is his foster son Diarmuid who has the "love spot" on his face making anyone fall in love with him upon sight.

20. As the Asvins do not start as true immortal gods, but only later **attain the drink of immortality**, it is similarly said in a 12th Century text that Aengus Og drank a drink of immortality at Goibniu's feast *(Colloquy of the Ancients)*. Macdonell notes

that the Asvins are "guardians of immortality who ward off death from the worshipper (AV 7.53.1; TB 3.1.2.11)" (Macdonell, 51).

21.   As Sahadeva is the **counselor** of the Pandavas, so Oengus cleverly counsels Dagda on how to get rid of the satirist Cridenbel during the reign of Bres. Oengus then advises Dagda to select a dark, trained, spirited heifer as payment for his work, which ends up calling all the cattle of Ireland to it.

Freyr's Horse Twin Characteristics

Does Freyr then match any of these common Horse Twin elements? He is **brother to the centrally important (possibly Dawn) goddess** Freyja, just as Aengus is brother of the centrally important Dawn goddess Brigid. A full explication of the theory that Freyja could be the Dawn goddess is beyond our scope and was first suggested by Angriff along with Redbeard, to be elaborated in the future[75]. Our framework does not rely on Freyja necessarily being the Dawn goddess, as it is perfectly possible for a different goddess to be in this same role in the Norse myths without disrupting the overall structure. We suspect, however, that Freyja will be shown on a deeper level to have a connection to the mythos usually attached to the Dawn goddess. Among other things, Angriff points to the shining necklace *brisingamen* which is stolen from Freyja, and which would occupy the same position as the "golden glow of Dawn and Sovereignty" or "Khvarenah" that we discuss elsewhere, which in other branches is embodied by the stolen, adulterous goddess who must be retrieved by the Mitraic god or hero. Other evidence brought forward by Angriff includes the fact that the tears of Greek Dawn Goddess Eos form the morning dew, Irish Dawn Goddess Brigid first invents keening when she weeps for her dead son, and that Freyja is said to cry tears of red-gold, the color of the sunrise. Freyja is said to have two daughters, Hnoss and Gersemi, whose names are variations on the meaning "treasure," and also has the aforementioned famous necklace, while Vedic Ushas is said to be she who is "rich in spoil," "wondrously opulent," and who "rules all wealth and treasures" (RV 7.75.5-6). It is also interesting that, in the same verse, Ushas is called "consumer of our youth," while Freyja is known as "possessor of the slain" (*Skaldskaparmal*, 20). Ushas is "a skilled huntress who

---

75 "Jive Talk: Is Freya the Same Goddess as Ostara?"
  https://www.youtube.com/watch?v=6foZ_RvNfRU. Web. Accessed December 2021.

wastes away the lives of people" in RV 1.92, and is "a constant reminder of people's limited time on earth" (RV 7.77) (David Kinsley, *Hindu Goddesses*, 6-8). We see the theme of adultery and promiscuity in the figure of Helen, while it also is present in Freyja's mythos. One must wonder where the Norse cognate of this central Indo-European goddess, the Dawn goddess, would otherwise have gone if she is not Freyja, as certainly no better candidate presents herself.

Freyr is **close to everyday human concerns** like weddings, the generation of fecundity, the harvest, and general prosperity, suggesting a Third Function nature in line with that of the Horse Twins. He is a god of fertility, as can be seen from his famous ithyphallic idol from Broddenbjerg, Jutland (535-520 BCE), and Adam of Bremen's description of "Frikko," another name for Freyr. As is typical for Horse Twins, he is **associated with sailing**, being the owner of the famous ship Skíðblaðnir, which always has a favorable wind and is known as the best of all ships. This ship was made for him by the *alfar* smiths known as The Sons of Ivaldi (*Grimnismal 43)*, while the Asvins' vehicle was made for them by the semi-divine smiths known as the Rbhus (*RV*.1.20.3; 1.161.6;10.39.12). The Sons of Ivaldi and the Rbhus can be confidently identified with one another as they have been shown to share a parallel myth designated "The Contest of the Artists," wherein they must compete with other craftsmen (Rydberg, *Investigations Into Germanic Mythology*, Vol. II.15, "The Primeval Smiths"). In the *Anglo-Saxon Rune Poem,* Ing, a version of the original name of Freyr, is said to go "over the wave," with his "wagon" following after. As the Asvins' vehicle is a sort of carriage, we can picture this wagon which goes over the wave possibly becoming a ship as time passed. However, the Asvins also have a ship or ships: "they rescued him with animated, water-tight ships, which traversed the air, with four ships, with an animated winged boat" (Macdonell, 52). Freyr was also **connected with a horse cult**, and kept sacred horses at Trondheim (Hilda Ellis Davidson, *Gods and Myths of Northern Europe*, 96-97). His own horse is named Blóðughófi, meaning "bloody hoof," and he is referred to as Atriði, meaning "rider." In *Lokasenna* verse 37 he is called best of all "ball-riði," an unclear term often translated as "brave riders." In the *Rig Veda*, one of the Asvins is even addressed with the title *surih*, which can translate to several things including "lord" (*Rig Veda*, I.181), while Freyr's very name is simply a title meaning "lord."

Freyr is **a warrior**, known to do battle with Surtr at Ragnarok. In *Skirnismal* he is called *folkvaldi goda*, meaning essentially "commander of the gods in battle." These epithets remind us of Aengus, "of the battle squadrons," who is "expert in arms" as Freyr is "battle-skilled," and who is "red armed" while Freyr's horse is bloody-hoofed. As we have said in another chapter, the Horse Twins maintained a consistent connection to warrior skill, this association being brought to perhaps its highest point in Greece and Rome, with the Spartan army carrying the dókana, symbol of the Twins, before them during war. The Dioscuri were beloved by the Roman cavalry, and were said to have lead the legions of the commonwealth in the battle of Lake Regillus as their commanders. While Freyr has the golden-bristled **boar** Gullinbursti, which is said to be his *fylgja* and which is fashioned for him by the dwarves, the proposed Greek Horse Twin incarnation Diomedes' golden armor (blessed by Athena) and sword are both said to have on them the image of a boar. So close is the boar associated with Freyr, that sacrifices to him during the harvest festival took this form. Thus Diomedes is the horse-breaker who wears the boar symbol. The Asvins, though known as horsemen, are also centrally depicted as riding "humped cattle," as Eliade points out, referencing R. Otto (Eliade, *Patterns*, 97; R. Otto, *Gottheit d. Arier*, 76). In *Aitareya Brahmana* 4.7-9 (cf. RV 1.116.7) they win a race in a car drawn by asses, possibly at the marriage of Soma and Surya.

While the scholar Shapiro calls the Horse Twins founders of cities, and while the pseudo-historical Horse Twins Hengist and Horsa, for instance, actually do not found Kent but take it over and become the root of its royal lineage, Freyr or Ingvi-Freyr is known as the **founder of various tribes and royal lines**: the Ingvaeones, the Ynglings, etc. Even Freyr being given the gift of Alfheimr has a vague similarity to Aengus' inheritance (by trickery) of the great burial mound and otherworld locale Brugh na Boinne. And of course, originating as a Vanir and outsider to the society of the Aesir but eventually joining the Aesir and becoming one of the most revered gods parallels the Asvins' ascent to godhood via the attaining of the *soma* and the joining of the society of the higher gods with Chyavana's help. Just as the Horse Twins commonly begin as a lower rank of divinity, but gain equality with the higher gods and gain access to the sacrifice, so Freyr (with Njörðr) becomes a part of the community of the Aesir after the Aesir-Vanir war, and likewise becomes priest of the sacrifice. As we have demonstrated, this myth is perhaps the central myth of the Horse Twins generally, and the fact of Freyr's central role in it is a strong argument in itself for Freyr's identification as a Horse Twin. This structural argument combined with the many Horse Twin characteristics enumerated above makes the identification difficult to deny.

The Fathers of the Horse Twins

Both of the proposed Scandinavian and Irish Horse Twin gods, Aengus and Freyr, are similar in the particular nature of their close relationships with their fathers as well. We know that Freyr is the son of Njörðr, a god who, like the Dagda, father of the Irish Horse Twin Aengus, is associated with wind and with the fertility of the land. While Njörðr and the Dagda are not the same gods, we can see the similarities between them that caused them to be given the same roles in the wooing tales in relation to their respective sons. In the wooing tales, the Dagda and Njörðr each have the very same role of setting things in motion like a presiding paternal force. From the very beginning of *Skirnismal* we read, "Skirnir was the name of Freyr's servant; Njörðr bade him ask speech of Freyr" (*Skirnismal*, Introduction). It is Njörðr who initiates the main action of the poem, in the prose introduction, involving the crucial servant Skirnir in the story and giving him the task of speaking to Freyr in his lovesickness. After that, this father figure steps out of the poem. *Dream of Oengus* likewise begins with the intervention of the father, the Dagda. After relating how Oengus saw Caer in a dream, fell lovesick and was tended to by a doctor, the tale next describes how they brought the Dagda in for help. "'No help has been found for him,' said Boand. 'Then send for the Dagdae, and let him come and speak with his son'" (*Dream of Oengus*). Whereas Njörðr sends the servant Skirnir to speak with and aid Freyr, the Dagda is sent by Boand to speak to and aid Oengus. Then Dagda in his turn sends Bodb Dearg to search for the girl. In each tale, Njörðr or the Dagda acts as the ruling fatherly presence, setting things in motion and helping Freyr or Aengus, usually by sending an intermediary helper. As the paternalistic "old man" figure in his myth, Indian Chyavana also stands in a similar position to the Asvins as Njörðr does to Freyr. Chyavana is an aged man and the final transformation in the water renews his youth and beauty. For Njörðr, the water (of his ocean home) has only made his feet appear young and beautiful. He has not truly become like to the god Baldr, but nonetheless has been imparted a youthful appearance by the waters.

The central key to the comparison of these father-son relationships, however, is the realization that it is Aengus' *foster father* who is the true direct cognate of Freyr's stated father. As has been demonstrated, Midir, foster father of Aengus, has the parallel mythos to Njörðr, that mythos we have designated by its Rig Vedic name "Surya's Bridal," the marriage of the "Soma" Moon God and the Daughter of the Sun. Thus, although the Dagda himself overlaps with Midir and Njörðr, it is Aengus' role as foster son of Midir that shows most clearly his parallel with Freyr, son of Njörðr. Both the Norse and Irish branches have the same Moon God as either father or foster father of the Horse Twin, and this fact needs to be seen clearly.

What this shows is that there was somewhat of a controversy in Northwestern Europe about who the true father of the 'Divine Son' Horse Twin was, whether Moon God or Father Sky. From an astrological perspective this may come down to the fact that, as the morning star or sunrise god, the 'Divine Son' Horse Twin could be viewed as the son of the moon (due to succeeding it in the sky or due to rising out of the sea that is its domain) or as the son of Father Sky, first appearing, as it does, lighting up the vault of heaven in early morning. Perhaps the comparison of the Irish and Norse cases can be taken as evidence that these two fathers may have been seen as sharing this parentage in a metaphysical sense, one as the Horse Twin's foster father, one as his true father, and that the Celtic and Germanic branches ultimately came to slightly different conclusions as to which father was believed to have primacy. Aengus does not even know his true parentage until he eventually forces Midir to tell him. This means that, until he is a young man, Aengus, cognate of Freyr, believes or lives as if he is the son of Midir, cognate of Njörðr.

We must also note that Yngvi-Freyr is called a son of Oðinn in section V of Snorri's *Prologue* to the *Prose Edda*, and that this parentage of Yngvi-Freyr occurs again in more than one manuscript of the *Skaldskaparmal* (Faulkes, *Skaldskaparmal, xxxix;* 113). This parentage is usually simply ignored as incorrect, simply because it is assumed to be in contradiction with the many other descriptions of Freyr as son of Njörðr. However, if the Norse case were to mirror or even come from the same root as the Irish, the possibility would have to remain open that these mentions, though dubious for multiple reasons, could preserve a remnant of a tradition regarding Freyr that had been mostly forgotten: that he was son of *both* Oðinn and Njorðr, that his true father was originally Oðinn, but that, like Aengus, he was raised without this knowledge, considered officially as the son of Njorðr. This could explain why Freyr, a Horse Twin God, is not depicted as son of a Sky Father while the other instances of this god are, and why his "father" Njorðr very clearly parallels Aengus' foster father, Midir. It is not necessary that this be true, however, for these deities to be considered parallels, as the two traditions could have simply diverged in the consideration of this parentage.

* * *

Myth Grouping 3: Samvarana = Pwyll

Thus far we have demonstrated how two sets of myths have parallels across the Celtic, Norse and Vedic branches, and how these two sets of myths, the myths of the Moon God and the myths of his son or foster son(s) the Horse Twin(s), intertwine and essentially form a connected set of tales that follow one another in a greater Lunar Cycle, as we see, for example, in the way Freyr's wooing of Gerðr follows his father Njorðr's marriage to Skaði.

To fully complete the puzzle of the greater cycle, and in particular its relationship to the Welsh branch and from there its later form in the Grail legend, however, we must

182

bring in a third grouping of mythic parallels, this time stretching uncannily from Wales to India. One reason this third set must be brought into the equation is that, for the Welsh Horse Twin (Pryderi), for whatever reason, this portion of the cycle has become the more central myth, and we must ask why this is and how it connects to the Horse Twin myths from the other branches. What we uncover as we proceed is the fact that the Indian version of this tale, though it does not feature the Horse Twins, does indirectly connect back to them: the main princess of the myth, Tapati (paralleling Welsh Rhiannon), is a daughter of the Sun God, just as the princesses of the previous sets of parallels were also theoretically sun princesses (Sukanya/Skaði/Etain and possibly Gerðr/Caer). Hence the princess of this new set of parallels may have originally been seen as a sort of sister of the previously analyzed princesses, and their myths may have been seen as connected or parallel.

The final connection we find, as we proceed, is the fact that the protagonist of the Indian version of this new set of parallels (Samvarana) may be, in disguise, a chief of the heavenly beings known as gandharvas, who were the court singers of the gods. Because of this, we may be able to draw a connection between this myth set and the court poet of the Norse gods, Bragi, who narrates the myth of his wife Iðunn in *Skaldskaparmal* which has been key to the sequence of myths discussed up to this point. The main figures of this third set, then, seem intimately connected to the previous sets of parallels, and it may be that originally this third myth was seen as one more chapter of the Lunar Cycle, perhaps an early chapter, just as Bragi's wife Iðunn sets in motion the events leading to Njorðr and Skaði's marriage in the Norse version, and Pwyll and Rhiannon begin the cycle in the Welsh version.

In the Welsh version, then, it may be that a reduction (or at least a shift) of the overall cycle has occurred, combining the Horse Twin myth with the myth of the chief "Gandharva" or court singer, as if we combined the myth of Freyr and Njorðr with that of Bragi and compressed them into one continuous story. There has to be a reason why the Horse Twin Pryderi appears in this myth (though only in the second half of it), a myth in which he does not appear in any other branch, and a myth in which a different figure takes his role in the Indian version. There are as many mysteries as revelations that attend this line of questioning, but the many connections and parallels force us to address this enigmatic link in the cycle. In any case, due to the fact that it is the central Horse Twin myth in the Welsh literature, it must thus essentially stand as the Welsh Lunar Cycle, and ultimately, among other things, evidences at least one of the key features of the Grail myth: the "wasteland."

The basic plot of this third grouping of mythic parallels is as follows: a king who visits a divine mountain or mound sees an otherworldly maiden, subsequently marrying her, leading to the improper occupation of the sacred mountain or mound, which causes a wasteland that has to be put right by a return to society. This parallel equates Welsh Pwyll (as found in *The Mabinogion: Pwyll, Prince of Dyfed*) with Indian Samvarana (as found in *The Mahabharata*) but the issue is complicated by the fact that in the Welsh version, though the events seem to be the same, the myth is divided down the middle between the father and son pair of Pwyll and Pryderi (the Welsh Horse Twin, found in *The Mabinogion: Manawydan, Son of Llyr*).

Samvarana = Pwyll/Pryderi

1. Sees a Golden Princess From Sacred Mound After Hunting

- Samvarana sees Tapati when he goes hunting on the mountain frequented by celestials. She appears "like a bright statue of gold" and "the beauty and attire of that damsel" makes the mountain itself seem to be turned to gold. He regards her as "the embodiment of the rays emanating from Surya." (*Mahabharata, Adi Parva, Chaitraratha Parva, CLXXIII*)

- Pwyll sees Rhiannon after sitting on the sacred mound Gorsedd Arberth, immediately following a hunting episode. She is described as riding a pure white horse and wearing a "golden garment." (*Mabinogion: Pwyll, Prince of Dyfed*)

2. Otherworldly Princess Magically Evades Being Caught At First but Then Stops for her Pursuer

- Tapati vanishes into thin air, then reappears to him after Samvarana has searched the forest for her. (*M)*

- Rhiannon's ambling horse cannot be caught up to no matter how fast she is pursued. Finally she stops for Pwyll when he asks her a question. (*M:PPoD)*

3. Princess Says Her Father is in Charge of Marrying Her But That She Is Already In Love With The Wooer and Then They Go Their Separate Ways for 12 Days or Months

- Tapati says she is not her own master but only her father Vivasvat-Surya (the Sun god) can give her to a husband, but that she already is in love with Samvarana, then disappears. Samvarana worships Surya for 12 days unbroken. (*M)*

- Rhiannon says her father has been trying to marry her to another, but that she already is in love with Pwyll, then they go their separate ways and agree to meet in 12 months for their wedding feast. (*M:PPoD*)

4. Occupying the Sacred Mountain Improperly Triggers a Wasteland

- Samvarana and Tapati stay on the sacred mountain frequented by celestials and gandharvas, their absence causing drought and famine and for the kingdom to become a wasteland. They remain on the mountain, sporting and playing. The wasteland is described thus:

> [...] that season of drought broke out, the people of that kingdom, as also the trees and lower animals began to die fast. And during the continuance of that dreadful drought, not even a drop of dew fell from the skies and no corn grew. And the inhabitants in despair, and afflicted with the fear of hunger, left their homes and fled away in all directions. And the famished people of the capital and the country began to abandon their wives and children and grew reckless of one another. The people being afflicted with hunger, without a morsel of food and reduced to skeletons, the capital looked very much like the city of the king of the dead, full of only ghostly beings. *(M)*

- Pwyll's son Pryderi sits on the sacred mound Gorsedd Arberth, and suddenly the people and animals of the kingdom vanish, the crops which are sowed get repeatedly eaten. The wasteland is described thus:

> they looked where before they would have once seen flocks and herds and dwellings, they could see nothing at all: neither house, nor animal, nor smoke, nor fire, nor man, nor dwellings – [nothing] except the empty buildings of the court, deserted, uninhabited, without man or beast within them, their own companions lost, without them knowing anything about them; [no-one left] except the four of them.

It has ben a commonplace in Celtic Studies that this is one possible origin of the "wasteland" motif found in the later Grail legend. Pryderi and Rhiannon then get trapped in a mystical fort which vanishes, presumably imprisoning them in the otherworld. (*Mabinogion: Manawydan, Son of Llyr*)

5. The King's Magico-Priestly Companion Must Retrieve Him in Order to Revive the Land

- Samvarana's advisor, the rishi Vasistha, must bring Samvarana and Tapati back from the holy mountain, which causes the rain to return and the kingdom to return to normal.

- Pryderi's step-father Manawydan (whose Irish cognate Manannan is a much clearer magician god) must find the secret to the enchantment, eventually rescuing Pryderi and Rhiannon from the otherworld, simultaneously, though with unclear causality, returning the kingdom to normal. (*M: MSoL*)

Beyond these three primary groupings, there are numerous "remainder" parallels that do not in themselves contribute to any one strong identification. They are generally singular parallels without other support which may indicate that they are simply the evidence of small changes made to the tales over time, rather than telling us much about who the figures are in themselves. However, if we look closely, some of them add supporting parallels to the identification of both Oengus and Freyr with the Asvins. In general, such stray parallels only strengthen the sense that this set of tales was treated by the poets as strongly interlinked, a body of myths whose proximity led to partial overlapping, and over time, a degree of confusion.

Test of Choosing (Oengus/Caer, Njörðr/Skaði and Eochu/Etain)

- Oengus must pick Caer out in her swan form from among a group of swans. He chooses correctly and they live happily. (*Dream of Oengus*)

- As already discussed: Skaði must choose her husband by looking solely at the feet of her suitors. She mistakes Njörðr for Baldr. (*Skaldskaparmal*)

- These of course also parallel the previously mentioned test of choosing Midir submits Eochu to, which he fails. (*Wooing of Etain*)

Magic Spell of Madness or Transformation (Chyavana, Fuamnach and Skirnir)

- Chyavana makes the king's men unable to respond to the "call of nature." (*M*)

- Fuamnach puts a spell on Etain, transforming her shape and causing her to forget who she is. (*WoE*)

- Skirnir threatens to put a spell on Gerðr causing madness and suffering. (*S*)

A Female Goes Through a Triple Transformation and Rebirth as a New Version of Herself (Fuamnach, Gullveig)

- The sorceress Fuamnach, who is later burned, transforms the *other* wife of her husband, Etain, into three successive forms: water, a worm, and a kind of purple fly. After the final transformation she is swallowed in a cup and reborn as a lady, but she does not remember her old life or her old self. (*WoE*)

- The sorceress Gullveig, who is also burned, is killed and reborn three times, the final time gaining the new name, Heiðr. (*Voluspa*)

A Sorceress Associated With the Soma God is Burned to Death (Fuamnach, Gullveig)

- Fuamnach, wife of Midir, is burned to death by Manannan (whose parallel to Oðinn we describe later). (*WoE)*

- Gullveig, associated with the Vanir, is speared and burned to death three times by the Aesir in Oðin's Hall. (*Voluspa*)

Attaining the Drink of Immortality (Asvins, Oengus and Freyr)

- After renewing Chyavana's youth, the Asvins are helped by Chyavana to attain access to the *soma*, becoming priests of the rite and gaining immortality. (*M*)

- In a 12th Century tale, Oengus is said to drink a drink of immortality at Goibniu's Feast. (*Pursuit of Diarmuid and Grainne; Colloquy of the Ancients)*

- Freyr and the Vanir join the society of the Aesir and gain access to their tribute/sacrifice, becoming priests of their rite. (*V; Heimskringla*)

Tricked Out of Kingdom (Hengist and Aengus)

In a separate story from *The History of the Britons* and *the History of the Kings of Britain* we find further parallels to the more obvious reflexes of the Horse Twins (pseudo-historical versions of these gods), Hengist and Horsa:

- Hengist tricks Vortigern out of a kingdom, Kent. (*The History of the Britains*)

- This parallels the aforementioned Irish tale in which Aengus tricks Elcmar or the Dagda out of their lands. (*WoE, Taking of the Sid*)

Tricked Into Sleeping With and Having a Child by His Own Daughter (Vortigern and Eochu)

- In the same tale in *The History of the Britons* and *the History of the Kings of Britain,* Vortigern is shamed for taking his own daughter as wife and having a son by her. (*THotB*)

- Midir tricks Eochu into sleeping with and having a daughter by his own daughter. (*WoE*)

Initial Rejections (Sukanya/Asvins, Etain/Midir, Gerðr/Freyr)

- Sukanya says she would not give up what she has with Chyavana for the Asvins. (*M*)

- Etain says she would never give up what she has with Ailil to be with Midir who has unknown ancestry. (*WoE*)

- Gerðr says she and Freyr will never be together as long as they live. (*S*)

A few observations can be made to further elucidate the relationships of all of the groupings to one another.

The Oengus/Freyr/Asvins grouping stands in a mysterious relationship to the Midir/Njorðr/Chyavana grouping, due to the fact that in the Chyavana tale, the Horse Twins (Asvins) are central to the narrative, trying to woo the wife of the Moon god, but failing in their wooing. A follow-up myth of the Asvins successfully wooing another Daughter of the Sun is indeed known. She is called Savitri and they win her in a race contest. This Sun Princess Savitri is also called Surya Savitri in the passage that describes the race for her hand (*Aitareya Brahmana*, 4.7). *Rig Veda* 1.116.17 says the Asvins won the Daughter of the Sun in a race and she mounted their car.[76] It is also suggested in the "Surya's Bridal" hymn that the Ghandarva (and the Asvins may be

---

76 See also: The Asvins "are Surya's two husbands (4.43.6; cp 1.119.5), whom she chose (7.69). Surya (5.73.5) or the maiden (8.8.10) ascended their car. The daughter of the sun mounts their car (1.34.5; 1.116.17; 1.118.5; 6.63.5) or chose it (1.117.13; 4.43.2). They possess Surya as their own (7.68.3) and the fact that Surya accompanies them in their car is characteristic (8.29.8)" (Macdonell, 51).

suggestively implied as well) should leave Surya to Soma and "seek in her father's home another fair one" (*Rig Veda*, 10.85), that is, seek another Daughter of the Sun for your own bride. The Oengus and Freyr myth may simply be a "sequel"[77] to the myth of the Moon god's marriage, then, where they seek such a Sun Princess for themselves. This would make sense in astrological terms at least, with the union of the moon and ray of sun being succeeded by the rising of the morning star to be united in turn with another of the sun's rays.

The two sets of tales do show certain overlaps, emphasizing the fact that they are interconnected myths. Oengus, for one, undergoes a test of choosing in his pursuit of Caer, in which his beloved appears in an unrecognizable shape, just as Sukanya and Chyavana undergo a similar choosing at the end of their tale, as also does Eochu in *Wooing of Etain*. Oengus turns himself into a swan and flies away with Caer at the end of "The Dream of Oengus," as if in imitation of the end of *Etain*, when his foster father Midir changes himself and Etain into swans to make their own escape. The intermediary wooer theme, however, is a bit different in each branch. Indeed, the final parallel mentioned in the lists above demonstrates how the Moon God's wooing and the Horse Twins' wooing motifs became somewhat confused with one another across the branches: a similar formulaic rejection is given to the Indian Horse Twins by the Moon God's wife, to the Scandinavian Horse Twin by his own future wife, and to the Irish Moon God by his own previous *and* future wife. This emphasizes how complex of a puzzle we have before us, but also how certainly these are interlinked tales.

Something quite remarkable might be going on here with the role of the Horse Twins, which could explain some of the ambiguity surrounding the relationship between their wooing myth and the wooing myth of the Moon God. There remains a controversy *to this day* in interpreting the role of the Vedic Horse Twins, the Asvins, in the wedding of Soma and Surya, as found in the "Surya's Bridal" hymn of the *Rig Veda*. The controversy centers around the issue of whether descriptions of the Asvins as wooers in this hymn are intended to imply that they are fulfilling the traditional role of intermediary wooers *for* the god Soma, or whether they are being described as rival wooers competing *against* Soma for the hand of the daughter of the Sun. In even the latest translations of the *Rig Veda* by some of the most prominent of Vedic scholars we see division on this issue, with Wendy Doniger saying confidently, "The Asvins are elsewhere said to be the brothers and/or the husbands of Surya, but here they are the unsuccessful suitors," and asserting that the hymn depicts "The Asvins, who choose

---

77 Occurring "before" or "after" is not important. Mentions of the Asvins wooing The Daughter of the Sun occur in earlier books of the *Rig Veda* and it is possible hymn 10.85 shows an awareness of the intertwined wooing tales involving the different husbands of "Surya."

Surya for themselves instead of acting as intermediaries" (Doniger, 2005). Joel Brereton and Stephanie Jamison, however, heavily favoring an argument from general cultural practice recorded in later times, which may or may not be applicable to this specific line of this hymn, just as confidently state that, "Judging from later practice, the bridegroom's party sends several males to the potential bride's home, to ask her father and other male members of the family for her as bride for the man they represent. This part of the ceremony begins with the wooers identifying themselves by name and lineage—the "pointing out" of verse 15. In this hymn the Aśvins are the wooers" (Brereton and Jamison, 2014). Cheryl Steets, meanwhile, argues that in verse 14 the Asvins, going as proxies, yet ask for Surya for *themselves*, and are granted this thanks to an *allusion to* the myth in which the Asvins had been wooers and had won Surya mentioned in earlier hymns of the *Rig Veda*. According to Steets, the hymn tells a story of the Asvins "apparently sent as proxy wooers on behalf of Soma, and asking the gods for Surya for themselves, and says that the gods granted this, in reference to another version (as mentioned above) in which they become her husbands. Though this might seem an unexplainable feature in a hymn purporting, on the surface, to celebrate Surya's wedding to their competitor, Soma, their continued presence becomes clear in light of the ritual nature of this text and the Indo-European background of the myth" (Steets, "The Sun-Maiden's Wedding," 157-158). In this interpretation, the hymn would then acknowledge the existence of the different wooing tales focused on this "one" goddess who is, however, multiplied in her manifestations. Though our interpretation of the underlying ritual in question differs slightly from that of Steets, we are in full agreement that it is the ritual subtext which explains the multiple, seemingly contradictory, husbands of Surya.

Considering this apparent deep ambiguity, is it possible that the various branches themselves told their myths slightly differently precisely along these lines? Is this why the Indian Asvins appear at first as rival wooers of Chyavana, but then concede and help Chyavana regain his youth and perfect his marriage with Sukanya, while Irish Aengus woos Etain for Midir, but then becomes a temporary caretaker (a pseudo-husband) of Etain once she is transformed by Fuamnach, and in another tale is rival wooer of Midir, while Norse Freyr does not compete for the hand of Skaði at all and seeks "another fair one" for himself (as the Vedic hymn commands) in another myth, but himself uses the same kind of intermediary wooer mentioned in the hymn and modeled elsewhere by his own cognate Aengus? Enigmatic is the fact that the man who marries Etain after Midir, and who Midir ultimately steals Etain back from, is himself given the title Eochu, meaning "horseman." Indeed, a separate and eerily similar tale involving Aengus and Midir is known, in which Midir abducts the princess Engelc, daughter of Elcmar, with whom Aengus was in love, Midir thus causing distress to this rival, failed wooer, Aengus. If we have analyzed correctly thus far, then we can essentially see before our

190

eyes the slightly different permutations to which the Horse Twins' ambiguous role of wooer may have given rise in the analogous myths of the various branches.

It has been argued by the scholar Matthias Egeler (*Celtic Influences in Germanic Religion*) that, despite their close similarities, the Oengus and Freyr stories are not to be identified with one another because, among other things, Freyr first sees Gerðr from the High Seat of the gods, while Oengus sees Caer only in a dream. However, it also seems possible that the High Seat and Dream motifs have grown out of the same original, or are modifications, one of the other, in some way. In the Indian Samvarana-Tapati tale, Samvarana first sees Tapati on the sacred mountain frequented by celestials, and his experience of seeing her is akin to a dream. He sees her, but before he can stay her she vanishes like lightning, and he wanders in the wood, lost and forlorn, until she magically appears again. Similarly, in the parallel story, Welsh Pwyll sees Rhiannon riding her horse when he sits on the sacred mound Gorsedd Arberth. She rides as though she is a being in a dream, at an ambling pace, yet no matter how fast Pwyll's riders chase her, they can never overtake her. If indeed these various closely connected sets of tales increasingly overlapped as time went on, then it would not be hard to imagine visitation of the sacred mound becoming confused or equated with seeing the maiden in a dream or dreamlike state, considering that that is what happens on the mound. We see that the proposed Welsh Horse Twin, Pryderi, also sneaks onto the earthly stand-in for the divine High Seat, Gorsedd Arberth, apparently when he is not supposed to judging by the ill consequences, just as Freyr does with Hliðskjalf. Hence we can postulate that the same High Seat theme existed in connection to one case of the Celtic Horse Twins, despite the fact that the analogous Irish Horse Twin, Oengus, only sees the maiden in his dream. There is thus less need to explain this small difference as long as we are confident in identifying Pryderi and Oengus as the same deity by other evidences. Ultimately, whether this explanation is satisfying or not, a difference between dream and high seat should not be enough to throw out an entire series of other parallels between analogous gods, and could easily be explained by normal and expected changes to the tales. On its own the comparison of *Skirnismal* and *Dream of Oengus* might not be definitive. However, with all of the other parallels pointing to the identification of Freyr with Oengus and Njorðr with Midir, it would be irrational to leave out the comparison of these similar wooing tales, which merely adds supporting evidence to the larger picture.

Indeed, seeing the maiden from the sacred mountain which he has snuck onto out of turn, or in a dreamlike state, in addition to the motif of morbid lovesickness, as well as the sending of an intermediary to woo, shows that the Freyr and Oengus myths also themselves have a good deal of overlap with the Samvarana/Pwyll tales and the Pryderi tale in certain details. You can almost track certain motifs being shuffled around, shifted slightly, between the various figures. This overlapping perhaps prepares the way for the combination of these myths into the reduced composite form we find in the Welsh version. With this overlapping, it seems like a line is repeatedly being drawn connecting Aengus, Freyr, and Pryderi, who within these tales are the young sons of the powerful father figures who incite the action of the plot: the Dagda, Njörðr, and Pwyll.

Bragi and the Gandharva Archetype

Now, the whole of the Norse Lunar Cycle matter that ends in the marriage of Njorðr and Skaði begins, perhaps surprisingly, with Bragi, the god of Skaldship, and his wife Iðunn. This brings us back to the sequence of husbands found in the "Surya's Bridal" hymn: **Soma, the Gandharva, Agni.** As we will detail later, a strong parallel between Agni and the Celtic Manawydan/Manannan leads to the conclusion that Pwyll/Samvarana may then be the Gandharva mentioned in this sequence of husbands, since Rhiannon marries Manawydan directly after Pwyll (who parallels Samvarana), just as Surya marries Agni directly after the Gandharva. To restate this complex equation another way: **if Manawydan = Agni, then Pwyll = Gandharva, because Rhiannon (who is in the place of Surya) marries Pwyll then Manawydan, as Surya also is said to marry the Gandharva then Agni**. This cryptic portion of the Vedic hymn will prove a key to speculatively interpreting portions of our puzzle, and in the following sections we will test the hypothetical equation we have laid out here, for which a surprising amount of supports can be found.

Supporting the notion that Samvarana, and so Pwyll, are each manifestations of the Gandharva, are details from the story of Samvarana found in the *Mahabharata*. Firstly, he hunts and woos on the mountainside frequented by "celestials and Gandharvas." Secondly, he asks Tapati to marry him "in the manner of the Gandharvas," and it is clear that Tapati herself is a celestial goddess rather than a Gandharva, being daughter of the Sun. It is true that this is merely one form of possible marriage open to more than just gandharvas, but it is a detail to be noted nonetheless. Thirdly, there is a single named Gandharva in the "Surya's Bridal" hymn, addressed there as "Visvavasu." Visvavasu is known for one tale in which he sees the beautiful maiden Devahuti from his "airplane" as she plays on her father's roof (*Bhāgavata-purāna* III. 20. 39; 22. 17). He is so struck that he falls from the sky. If we consider the "airplane" as just one more poetic convention which has taken the place of the very High Seat in this later Purana, similar to Pwyll's Gorsedd Arberth or Samvarana's celestial mountain breast, then it is possible we have here only another version of this same myth, but this time with the central figure identified as a Gandharva explicitly. Lastly, and perhaps most illustratively, it is said of Samvarana that "king Samvarana excelled Soma in soothing the hearts of friends and Surya in scorching the hearts of foes," which, while definitively differentiating him from Soma, sounds just like the description of a skilled poet or singer, such as the Gandharvas preeminently were, having the power both to soothe and scorch hearts with their beautiful, skilled songs and cutting, satirical verses. All of these points can be challenged individually and judged inconclusive, but together they begin to paint a picture that will be supported by further comparative evidence.

The Gandharva of the Vedic hymn is one important husband of the Sun Princess and so is likely an important link in the chain of the lunar cycle myth, and there is enough here to suggest that Samvarana and Pwyll may fit this role. Now, Gandharvas are celestial singers, the court singers of the gods. However, they have also an additional role, that of guardians of the *soma* drink.[78] This fact provides another link between these sets of tales, with Samvarana, Pwyll, and lastly Bragi as possible agents of the "Soma" god in their various branches. Soma is also said to have taught the aforementioned Gandharva Visvavasu his art of seeing and discerning everything in the three worlds, making the Ghandarva a successor to and almost stand-in for Soma as a result. For these reasons it would be perfectly fitting for the chief Ghandarva to play a key role in the Soma myth cycle.

As we have said, the sequence leading to the marriage of Njorðr and Skaði, one portion of the events of the Vanir cycle of myths, a cycle that also includes the wooing of Gerðr and the Aesir-Vanir War, is begun by an incident involving the goddess Iðunn, the wife of Bragi. Hence, at a key inflection point of the Lunar Cycle we have the singer of the gods (skalds were specifically known as poets, but it has been suggested they may have used instrumental accompaniment as well. Regardless, the comparison, within Germanic culture, of the Gandharvas as court musician of the gods, to the court poet and possible musician Bragi, seems apt). Bragi narrates Iðunn's tale just as "the proud king of the Gandharvas" narrates the tale of Samvarana (within the frame narrative in which it is found). The marriage tale of Bragi and Iðunn is not preserved, yet neither is there a different clear parallel of the Samvarana/Pwyll tale to be found in Norse myth. Hence, considering the possible identity of Bragi with the Gandharva of the *Rig Veda*, we must entertain the idea that the root myth of Bragi's marriage may have fit the model of the Samvarana/Pwyll tale, if such a narrative once existed, Iðunn's golden apples possibly relating her to a solar symbolism as Tapati is daughter of the Sun God. *Hrafnagaldr Odins* 6 states that she is descended from the *alfar*, a race of beings with solar qualities, the Sun Goddess or her chariot also being called "splendor of an Alfr" (*álfröðull*), and a

---

78 RV 9.83.4 cp. 1.22.14; 9.113.3; AV. 7.73.3; MS 3.8.10. See Macdonell, *Vedic Mythology,* p. 136. The Gandharva is also "connected with the 27 stars of the moon's orbit (VS. 9, 7) and in particular with Rohini (AV. 13, 1.23)" (Macdonell, 136).

portion of the *alfar* being known as *Ljósálfar,* light-elves, *ljós* being commonly related to sunlight and firelight. Bragi is indeed seen acting in the role of guardian as well, not specifically of the *soma*, but of the court of the gods when Loki comes to it. He is the first to speak to Loki on entering the hall, telling him he is unwelcome there: "A place and a seat will the gods prepare/No more in their midst for thee;/For the gods know well what men they wish/To find at their mighty feasts" (*Lokasenna,* 8). This role of guardian thus may have been a stable and important role of the Gandharva, just as he and his wife consistently form a key link in the Soma Cycle.

Etain and the Triple Transformation

Regarding the curious triple transformation of Etain by Fuamnach a few things must be said. Just as a sorceress associated with the Vanir, Gullveig, is burned in relation to the Norse Lunar Cycle, so the sorceress Fuamnach, wife of Midir and foster mother of Aengus, is said to be burned in relation to the parallel Irish Cycle. While Gullveig is stabbed along with being burned, Fuamnach in one account is said to be burned, but in another (both accounts being recorded in *The Wooing of Etain*) is said to be beheaded. Instead of herself undergoing three deaths and rebirths, however, Fuamnach instead causes Etain, the other wife of her husband, to undergo three successive transformations: into a pool of water, a worm, and a large purple or crimson fly, perhaps a dragonfly or butterfly. In the form of this fly, Etain is then drunk in a lady's golden cup and reborn as a girl, seemingly without a great recollection of her old life. If this triple transformation is a parallel to the triple rebirth of Gullveig, it is a strange variation indeed and can be said to be exceedingly different. It would be understandable if one denied the parallel at this point. Yet the various other connections pulling these two myth cycles together force us to investigate whether the meaning of the Irish triple transformation connected to the wicked sorceress can have anything in common with that of the Norse.

While we have argued that Gullveig's triple rebirth may have a meaning connected to the moon and indeed to the production of the mead itself (as if Gullveig is the malefic lunar influence that must be purified to process and perfect the mead that comes from the moon or the lunar waters, or as if she is even the catalyst of the mead production in some way), so also Etain's transformations clearly can be read in terms of lunar significance. An in-depth comparison of Etain's changes and journeys with the cycles of the moon has been done by Ronald Hicks in his "Cosmography of Tochmarc Etain." In the same vein, Anthony Murphy has also noted:

There is evidence at Knowth and Dowth [Brugh na Boinne locations] of calculations relating to the moon, knowledge of complex lunar movements possibly including the prediction of lunar eclipses. At Knowth, the aptly named 'Calendar Stone', one of its many giant kerb stones, contains markings including crescent and full moons in a counting pattern that appears to enumerate a five-year lunar interval, part of what is known as the Metonic Cycle of the moon, which is 19 years long. There are words for this 19-year cycle in the Irish language. It was supposed to have been discovered by a Greek called Meton in the fifth century BC, and yet there are markings on Knowth's kerbstones that would indicate it was studied and recorded around 2,800 years before Meton ever existed. The number of kerb stones at the big monuments could be significant too. At Knowth there are 127 kerb stones, which is half the number of sidereal lunar months in a 19-year Metonic Cycle. In other words, if you count each kerb as a sidereal lunar month, and go once around the whole perimeter, and then back again to where you started, you'd have counted a Metonic Cycle [...] Remarkably, the legend about Dowth tells about a sudden darkness, as if from a total eclipse, falling upon the men of Erin (Ireland) as they built the cairn so that the king, *Bresail Bó-Dibad,* could reach heaven. The darkness caused them to abandon their task, and the legend said that the place would ever more be known as *Dúbhadh* (Dowth), which means 'darkness'.

Murphy then asks:

> was Newgrange designed as a chamber 'of many lights', as the mythology might imply? Was it an observation chamber not just for the sun, but for the moon, the Morning Star and perhaps also the Dog Star as well? (Anthony Murphy, "Newgrange and the Boyne Valley monuments – advanced lunar calculations and observation of the effects of precession of equinoxes in Neolithic Ireland")

We will point simply to the fact that Etain's three forms can have clear lunar meanings. The pool of water relates her to the element that the moon rules: "The moon is in the waters" says *Rig Veda* 1.105; while Eliade says "All the lunar divinities preserve more or less obvious water attributes or functions" (*Patterns in Comparative Religion,* 159). The moon itself is considered a great pool of sacred liquid in the Vedic conception. The worm is lunar in a similar manner as the snake is, and especially in its capacity for transformation, which Etain's worm has indeed. The worm that transforms itself into a fly or butterfly is one of many possible perfect lunar symbols. As Eliade explains, everything that goes through a cycle of rebirth, transformation, or periodic regeneration has the potential to be seen as a lunar symbol, whether they be snails, bears, serpents, spirals, etc. He states that the lunar influence has in particular the "magic power of 'change'" (Eliade, *Patterns*, 168), and summarizes the lunar cycle of symbols by saying: "the whole pattern is moon-rain-fertility-woman-serpent-death-periodic-regeneration" (170), a sequence that is not far at all from what we see in the case of Etain. The fact that this fly is a purplish color could also relate it to the nocturnal sky, and it is noteworthy that later in the tale both Midir and Etain are said to wear purple, possibly making it a lunar color. The fact that this purple color may have been closer to a crimson rather than a night's sky suggests other meanings, such as that of royalty. Etain seeming to forget who she is and to go and live a new life after her last transformation could parallel Gullveig becoming "Heithr" after her final rebirth and seemingly being made into a new and placid form under this new name. Finally, while we have argued that Gullveig-Heithr may be related as well to the sacred mead, it is interesting indeed that Etain is at last swallowed in a golden cup when in her final transformation. Etain is in fact connected to drinks at three points: she herself is drunk in the golden cup, she is serving drinks when Midir comes to take her from Eochu, and finally Eochu says that the thing that will most distinguish her when she is among the other identical women is her skill and grace in pouring drinks. Among many other things, Etain is a goddess of drinks.

The fly that Etain transforms into deserves yet further examination. This is a wondrous and enchanted fly with rare qualities. We read that:

> It was as big as a man's head, the comeliest in the land. Sweeter than pipes and harps and horns was the sound of her voice and the hum of her wings. Her eyes would shine like precious stones in the dark. **The fragrance and the bloom of her would turn away hunger and thirst from any one around whom she would go. The spray of the drops she shed from her wings would cure all sickness and disease and plague in any one round whom she would go.** She used to attend Midir and go round about his land with him, as he went. **To listen to her and gaze upon her would nourish hosts in gatherings and assemblies in camps. Midir knew that it was Etain that was in that shape, and so long as that fly was attended upon him, he never took to himself a wife, and the sight of her would nourish him.** (*The Wooing of Etain*, Part I)

This fly spreads a liquid spray that cures all illnesses and simply looking upon it removes hunger and gives nourishment. Though the water-worm-fly sequence is perhaps strange to our modern sensibilities, and quite different in form from what we find in the case of Gullveig, it seems far from outlandish to suggest that this fly can be read as an esoteric symbol related to the moon and especially to the sacred lunar liquid derived

196

therefrom, which gives immortality and a transcendent kind of nourishment. Indeed, *soma* is "The **food** to which all Deities and mortals, calling it meath, gather themselves together" (RV 8.48.2). Not only this, but the *soma* also is said to preserve from disease and to heal sickness and other debilities: "These glorious drops that give me freedom have I drunk. Let the drops I drink preserve me from disease. Make me shine bright like fire produced by friction, give us clearer sight and make us better" (RV 8.48.5-6); "This Soma flows like gladdening oil for him who wears the braided locks. It covers the naked and heals all who are sick. The blind man sees, the lame man steps forth" (RV 8.68.2).

Hicks goes so far as to claim that Etain is a moon goddess and not a sun goddess. He points to the fact that she is depicted with a silver basin, and that she is called *Be Find*, or "white (or bright) lady" in the later portion of the tale, which name, we would add, even though it is given to Etain, may echo the change of name of Gullveig to Heithr, the clarified one. We agree that Etain becomes a part of the moon and can be said to be a Moon Goddess from the point of her union with Midir. But we believe, as we have shown, that she does originate as a Sun Goddess, whose light then unites with the moon in a great union of the solar and the lunar (this being a prototype of human marriage in the Vedic case, the marriage of Soma and the goddess Surya), and triggering as a result of this union the transformations of the sacred liquid, which may themselves correspond to lunar cycles, as well as to the steps with which the sacred liquid is processed for sacrifice and consumption. She becomes the goddess of the moonlight and source of the immortalizing drink.

We note that in the Vedic story of the churning of the sea of milk to extract the *amrita*[79], nectar of immortality (an analog of the *soma*), Shiva has to imbibe a great poisonous gas that is emitted from the serpent that the gods churn the sea with, in order to protect the gods and other beings from it. Shiva does so, is saved from the torture of the poison by Parvati, his throat turns a bluish bruised color, and eventually the *amrita* is successfully gathered. This myth has once again a liquid (milk) which has to be processed (churned) and a destructive element (poison gas) that has to be neutralized at the same time to finally produce the purified drink of immortality. The snake divinity that emits the poison, as we have argued for Gullveig/Fuamnach, is both a necessary tool and catalyst for the processing of the liquid and the source of a destructive power which must be purified and protected against. As mentioned previously, some of these elements repeat in the Vedic myth of Namuci. Namuci steals away and drinks the *soma*, causing it to be mixed with his malignant nature. Indra and the gods must then extract the good *soma* from his body, purifying it of his negative influence. *Rig Veda* 8.14.13 says that

---

79 *Srimad Bhagavatam; Vishnu Purana 1.9; Mahabharata, Udyoga Parva* 102.

Namuci's head is torn off by Indra in the process, whereas, as noted, Fuamnach is also beheaded.

* * *

The Welsh "Aesir-Vanir War"

In the last branch of the *Mabinogi*, Pryderi also fights a war very reminiscent of the Norse Aesir-Vanir War. Gwydion desires a pretext to cause Math to go to war, and also desires the otherworldly swine belonging to Pryderi. So Gwydion offers in exchange for the swine a great deal of enchanted fungus that he has temporarily turned into dogs, war horses, and shields. Pryderi accepts the deceptive trade, and we should be reminded of the deceptive deal made in the similar circumstance by the Irish Horse Twin Aengus to win Brugh na Boinne, only the Horse Twin Pryderi has here become the dupe. "And they consulted together, and determined to give the swine to Gwydion, and to take his horses and his dogs and his shields," we read, and the third function quality of the swine is here placed in clear contrast to the war horses, dogs and shields – symbols of the higher, warrior function – exchanged for them. Gwydion is, at least in part, one of the higher function gods himself, an Oðinnic magician god of the Welsh pantheon, and father of the chief god of sovereignty and justice Lleu, and so the war that ensues, of the forces of the Horse Twin Pryderi with the forces of Gwydion and his magician uncle Math, who rules the region as high lord, is perfectly in line with the war of Freyr's tribe with Oðinn's and the ultimate integration of the third function qualities of the Vanir into the society of the higher gods. There is even a hostage exchange at the conclusion of the war between Pryderi and Gwydion's forces, just as there is a hostage exchange at the conclusion of the Aesir-Vanir war. We read, "And that he might have peace, Pryderi gave hostages, Gwrgi Gwastra gave he and three-and-twenty others, sons of nobles." In this Welsh version, the peace falls apart, however, and Pryderi is subsequently killed in a duel with Gwydion. Nonetheless, the swine of Pryderi, symbols of the third function power, even said to have come from the underworld Annwn itself (the underworld being an important source of fecundating powers), have already been taken and integrated by Gwydion into the society of higher gods, thereby perfecting the divine social order.

In fact, it is quite incredible how closely this form of the myth matches that found in the Roman pseudo-historical account given by Livy (*Ab Urbe Condita*, 1.9), that is "The Rape of the Sabine Women." The Romans, led by Romulus (First Function, parallel of

Oðinn and Math or Gwydion), desire wives, so they trick their neighboring tribes, including the Sabines, and steal their women to marry. This incites a war, which results in a stalemate and a truce, the outcome of which is that the Sabines, who possess the women and wealth symbolic of fertility and production (Third Function) are integrated into the Roman society, which is characterized by its warrior-priestly quality (Second and First Functions). Romulus and the king of the Sabines, Titus Tatius (parallel of Freyr/Pryderi), agree to share the rulership. However, after a short period, Titus is killed by Romulus' men. But the Sabines and their women have already been integrated into Roman society, the Third Function has already been integrated into the society of the higher functions. The most interesting and humorous realization while comparing the Roman and Welsh versions, along with how strikingly similar they are, is the fact that, in the Welsh version, the Swine of the Underworld take the identical position taken by the Sabine Women in the Roman version.

The Horse Goddess and the Daughters of the Sun

One important issue must be addressed regarding the various fair maidens before proceeding with a further explication of the details of the Welsh case. Most of these maidens or princesses, as we have noted, have at least a possible solar significance: Tapati meaning "hot," and being the daughter of the Sun god Vivasvat; Skaði being called "shining"; Iðunn having the possibly solar golden apples; it being said of Gerðr that "Her arms glittered, and from their gleam/Shone all the sea and sky"; Cigfa being daughter of "fair shining one." Caer Ibormeith means "yew berry," and, considering what we have seen, it seems prudent to interpret this in terms of the solar symbolism of the Yew tree: the Yew tree was the primary source of wood for archers' bows in Northwestern Europe, archery being a prime symbol of solar activity. Thus, as we have seen, Norse Ullr is the archery god who lives at the Yew Dales, *Ydalir*, among the trees that are his symbol. Yew being a symbol for the power of the sun, a yew berry then could be a poetic symbol, a kenning, essentially, of a ray or drop of sun, a berry dropped from the solar tree. The red color of the yew berry can reinforce its solar quality.

   Now, our larger argument does not necessarily rely on these princesses being Sun Princesses in every case, as it is absolutely possible for a god to marry a Sun Princess in one branch and a different goddess in a separate branch, but some strong remnants of the Sun Princess motif should appear with consistency, and we believe we have pointed to enough to make it plausible that these could be mostly solar goddesses. However, figures

199

such as Etain and Rhiannon seem perhaps even more closely tied to horse motifs, either in their myths, in their names, or both – Etain being called Etain Echraide, or Etain of the Horses, Rhiannon appearing first on her magical horse, having a son the same night that a horse is born, being condemned to carry visitors on her back like a horse, and being forced to wear a donkey's collar when she is imprisoned in the other world. This seems to present a slight difficulty to some of our proposed equations on first glance; however, these equations can be justified.

As Proto-Indo-European reconstructionist Ceisiwr Serith points out, the Horse Goddess ʔékwonā and the Daughter(s) of the Sun (reconstructed as Sawelyosyo Dhugətḗr) frequently overlapped and were even identified (Serith, "Proto-Indo-European Deities: ʔékwonā"). Though they may originally have been distinct goddesses in the Proto-Indo-European era, by the time of the written myths they were almost wholly conflated. Indeed, the image of Rhiannon riding the modestly ambling horse that cannot be caught up to should be enough of an image of the sun in the sky to demonstrate how these two symbols came to be equated, and in many other cases the horse was used as a solar symbol. As Serith puts it, "ʔékwonā overlaps the sun goddess Sawelyosyo Dhugətḗr somewhat to the point that in some of the later descendant traditions they have become identified with each other. Sawelyosyo Dhugətḗr is connected with horses (especially through the Diwós Sūnú [Divine Twins]), and ʔékwonā is described with solar imagery. Remember Saraṇyū. ʔékwonā is particularly solar in her power and the danger of approaching her. In Proto-Indo-European times, they seem to have been different goddesses, though" (CeisiwrSerith.com).

The connection of the Samvarana/Tapati or Pwyll/Rhiannon myth to the Horse Twin myth can then be explained by the fact that Tapati and Sukanya (whose true name is Suryā) are sisters (presented as being of different generations descended from the sun god, which we take to indicate that Sukanya is an incarnation of the previously mentioned Daughter of the Sun, Suryā), both, at their root, daughters of the Sun God, who, furthermore, could easily have been identified or confused with one another, or simply have been considered as figures linked by their sisterhood and whose wooing tales as a result were seen as parallel and connected. And thus, Rhiannon/Iðunn, Etain/Skaði, and Cigfa/Caer/Gerðr, though having different mythic origins and infrequently depicted as sisters, can be considered in this same sense as sisters on a hypothetical more archaic and metaphysical level, participating in parallel and meaningfully linked myths. This also explains how these seemingly separate myths can have come together around the Celtic Holy Grail legend, blended together, as we will see.

This general understanding can perhaps be strengthened by a recent article of William Reaves', who, based on the work of Viktor Rydberg, has demonstrated that Olvaldi, father of Thjazi, and Ivaldi, father of Iðunn, are likely the same figure, making Thjazi and Iðunn potentially half-siblings. "Idun and her sisters are Alfar," says Reaves, and exactly like Aengus' bride Caer, "They appear as swan maidens...accustomed to warmth and light" (Reaves, "Idunn and the Elves," The Epicist 3, 44). Hence Iðunn, Skaði, and – as we argue – Thjazi are all solar figures who are of one semi-nuclear family, all are either jotnar or are kin of jotnar, and Gerðr is another jotunn whose arms make sea and sky shine. It seems "jotunn" was a designation often given to beings associated with the sometimes asocial powers of the astral bodies such as sun and moon, among other things. While Iðunn would here be presented as the aunt of Skaði (as Tapati is the great-aunt of Sukanya, an extra generation likely added to indicate that Sukanya is a mortal incarnation), and these two as having no clear link to the other solar giantess Gerðr, we must remember that on a deeper metaphysical level they appear to come from a shared mythos of solar "sisters" (or *doubles*), due to each being Sun Princesses, goddesses of the sunbeams.[80]

It is clear that, perhaps due to this relatively interchangeable nature of the Daughters of the Sun, the Horse Twin myth and the Gandharva myth somehow became entwined into one tale in the branches of the Welsh *Mabinogion,* with the proposed Gandharva, Pwyll, and the Horse Twin, Pryderi, appearing now as father and son in one shared narrative, whereas their myths are somewhat separated in the other branches. The entwining of these tales reaches its peak in the Grail legend, where the wasteland of the Samvarana/Pwyll "Gandharva" myth is a prominent feature of the larger legend that centers around the Horse Twin-derived hero Perceval.

To complete the set of Sun Princesses, we note that the Irish god of Eloquence, Ogma, who in a later chapter we will demonstrate is the cognate of the Gandharva, Hermes, Pwyll, and Bragi, marries a woman named Etan. If the mythic structure we are laying out holds, this Etan is none other than Etain, transferred from one husband to another, just as one of the Sun Princesses almost always is (Skaði, Rhiannon, Surya).

---

80 Note that the Baltic Daughters of the Sun, the Latvian *saules meita* and Lithuanian *saules dukterys*, are also explicitly plural.

Manannan and Agni

There is nothing in particular in all of this to suggest that Njörðr, Pwyll, or Manawydan are themselves Horse Twins, which has sometimes been suggested by commentators seeking to understand this deity type, and these theories, which lack the fuller context, must be put aside. Instead, we can draw an interesting connection between the advisor of Samvarana, Vasistha, and the friend and helper of Pryderi, Manawydan. In the portion of the myth where Samvarana/Pryderi occupies the sacred mountain improperly, leading to a wasteland, it is Vasistha in the one tale, and Manawydan in the other, who must then bring Samvarana or Pryderi back to their kingdoms to break the enchantment and revive the land. Interestingly, at this time Manawydan has become husband to the previously wooed wife of the now dead Pwyll – that is, Rhiannon. If we consider again the hymn to "Suryā's Bridal," a possible link between Manawydan/Vasistha and the god Agni then comes into view. For, at the end of the hymn, we read that Suryā, the Daughter of the Sun, had a series of husbands, just as Rhiannon has now had two husbands in succession. The hymn states:

> Soma obtained her first of all; next the Gandharva was her lord. Agni was thy
> third husband: now one born of woman is thy fourth. ***Soma to the***
> ***Gandharva, and to Agni the Gandharva gave.*** (*Rig Veda*, 10.85.40-41)

Though it is possible the hymn is merely conflating various sun princesses here into one figure, and while some may believe that this cryptic passage should not be extended too far or taken too literally, it must be said that Manawydan, and his Irish form, Manannan, do have characteristics that can be interpreted in line with the fire-priest god Agni, as does Vasistha. Indeed, the application of this passage as a lens to our further comparisons proves exceedingly fruitful, and the success of this application further supports its validity, as we will see. By the end of our further investigations, it will be seen that this brief hymnal passage is one of the most important Master Keys of comparative mythology generally speaking, either codifying a mythic structure that we find repeated in nearly all the various branches, or rather giving us a glimpse of the theological essence that is enacted far and wide in the Soma marriage myths of several of the Indo-European branches.

Manawydan and Manannan are each said to be the son of the sea (Llyr/Lir), while Agni is called "child of the waters." Vasistha is said to be reborn from Varuna, who himself is a god identified with all water. Additionally, Vasistha goes as emissary to Vivasvat-Surya to request the Sun God's daughter for Samvarana, while Samvarana worships the Sun God for 12 days straight, similar to how Agni is the emissary to the gods, carrying the sacrifice to them by burning it and rising into the sky with its essence. Again, when Samvarana has stayed too long on the sacred mountain and has neglected his sacrifices, it is Vasistha's task to go as emissary to retrieve him and remind him of these sacrificial duties.

There also exists a pattern of Agni being sent, like Vasistha, as an emissary or messenger to retrieve a god and avert disaster. In Chapter 6 of the *Lāvāṇakalambaka of Kathāsaritsāgara*, when Siva and Parvati are engaged in a one-hundred year long sexual ritual to return Kama to the world, the universe comes to the edge of destruction due to their long absence. It is Agni that the Devas decide to send to interrupt Siva and Parvati in their lovemaking, as Vasistha is sent to interrupt Samvarana in he and Tapati's romantic dalliance on the mountain breast. In this case, Agni is afraid of Siva and hides in the waters, but eventually he uses his heat to stimulate and interrupt Siva, bringing a happy end to the crisis with the end of the sexual marathon and the return of Siva and Parvati. Similarly, in the *Mahabharata* (*Udyoga Parva*, 14), when Indra goes to hide in a lotus in repentance for killing the Brahmin Vrtra, the king who takes Indra's place, Nahusa, tries to make Indra's wife Indrani his queen. She asks Brihaspati for help, who sends Agni to retrieve Indra, which he does, bringing about his return and a happy conclusion. Arthur A. Macdonell asserts that Agni is "constantly and characteristically called a messenger (*duta*)" (Macdonell, *Vedic Mythology*, 96).

It seems clear that Vasistha in this myth is a stand-in for some god or other, for he takes the role directly comparable to that which the god Manawydan does in the parallel Welsh myth. And not only does Agni follow Soma and the Gandharva in wedding the Sun Princess in the hymn, just as Manawydan follows Pwyll in marrying Rhiannon, but it is also said that at Soma and Suryā's wedding, "Agni was leader of the train." Besides the Horse Twins, the wooers Chyavana and Samvarana, the princesses, and their fathers, there are almost no other figures that appear in the Indian forms of these wooing tales besides Vasistha. And he appears in an assisting capacity perfectly fitting one who would lead the train at the wedding, the primary priest and advisor of Samvarana as he is, just as Agni is priest of the sacrificial fire.[81]

Why exactly should the name of the legendary *Rig Vedic* poet and seer "Vasistha" then be used here as a stand-in for Agni? A note in Macdonell's work may shed some light on this. He explains that, in fact, "Vasistha" is a name known to have been identified with Agni in the Vedas: "The names of ancestors sometimes identified with Agni are in part those of families to which composers of the RV belonged. Some of

---

81 "[Agni] combines in himself the functions, in a higher sense, of the various human priests called by the above and other specific names (1.94.6; 2.1.2; &c.)." "Agni's priesthood is the most salient feature of his character. He is in fact the great priest" (Macdonell, 97).

these, like Vasistha, seem to have had a historical origin while others, like Angiras and Bhrgu, are probably mythical" (Macdonnell, 96). Furthermore, "the Vasisthas [clan descending from the legendary poet] claim to have first wakened her (Ushas [the Dawn]) with their hymns (7.80.1)" (Macdonell, 47). Thus Vasistha as a stand-in for Agni going as a priestly messenger to help reignite the sacrifice in order to bring about the return of the proper ritual cycle and the healing of the wasteland would be perfectly fitting. Regarding the magical influence of the sacrifice upon the rising of the sun, and thus on the cycle that holds the cosmos together, a theme central to the Samvarana-wasteland myth in question, Macdonell explains, "The notion the kindling of Agni exercised a magical influence on sunrise seems not to be entirely absent in the RV. Such appears to be the meaning of the poet when he exclaims: 'Let us light Agni, that thy wondrous brand may shine in heaven' (5.6.4). This notion is clearly stated in a Brahmana passage: 'By sacrificing before sunset he produces him (the sun), else he would not rise (SB 2.3.1.5, cp. TS 4.7.13.3)" (Macdonell, 98). Agni indeed also gives rain from heaven (RV 2.6.5) (as Indra gives rain to the land after Vasistha brings Samvarana back from his absence) among other abundant gifts.

So: beginning with the potential correspondence of Vasistha to Agni as described in the "Suryā's Bridal" hymn, and then the correspondence of Vasistha to Manawydan based on their occupying the same role in parallel tales, then of Manawydan to his cognate Manannan, we can begin to investigate the possibility that Manawydan/Manannan is also the same figure as Vedic Agni. When this comparison is opened, a staggering list of supports appear.

There are indeed numerous similarities that can carry this further comparison connecting Agni-Vasistha to Manawydan-Manannan. First, Manannan and Manawydan are commonly called Manannan mac y Leir and Manawydan fab Llyr – that is, this god's status as son of the sea god Lir/Llyr is generally so important that it is made a part of his very name, this part of his name effectively translating as "son of the sea." As for Agni, he is frequently associated with waters, so much so that the epithet *Apam Napat*, meaning descendant or nephew of waters, is numerically most often attached to him in the *Rig Veda*. This could then imply the same relationship that "mac Lir" does for Manannan. Agni is said to playfully hide in the waters (*Mahābhārata*, Anuśāsana Parva, Chapter 85; *Satapatha Brahmana* Part 1 (SBE12); RV 3.1; RV 7.49.4; RV 10.51-53. 10.124) and the fish are said to report news of his presence to the gods (O'Flaherty, Wendy Doniger, *Hindu Myths,* 97–101). Agni is said to be twice (RV 1.149.4) or thrice (RV 10.45.1) born (Gregory Nagy, *Greek Mythology and Poetics*, 99; Herman Oldenberg, *The Religion of the Vedas*, 63): from water, in the air, and on Earth, signifying the different forms fire may take. The idea that he was first born from water was the result of a complex understanding of the nature of fire, a belief that fire was contained (lived) in water and arose from it (was born of it), entering back into it when doused (Oldenberg, 65-66). Oldenberg explains that

> The water comes down from the 'highest father', the heaven; the plants suck
> their food from the rain and from the water of the earth…The plants are
> indeed the 'first-born essence of waters', 'water is their nature'. Therefore,
> the power must have remained latent in water, and it breaks forth as fire from
> the wood of the plants. If the fire then returns to the heaven as smoke, i.e. as
> cloud, the circle is completed…'The same water goes up and down in the
> course of the day: the downpour (of rains) swells the earth; the flames of
> Agni swell the heaven' (I, 164, 51). (Oldenberg, *Religion of the Vedas*, 65)

Agni is the offspring of Tvastr and the Waters or simply of the Waters (10.2.7; 10.91.6; AV 1.33.1). As Arthur A. Macdonell further lists: he is "the 'embryo' (*garbha*) of the waters (3.1.12-13); he is kindled in the waters (10.45; AV, 13.1.50); he is a bull who has grown in the lap of the waters (10.8.1) he is ocean-girt (8.91)," concluding that "the notion of Agni in the waters is prominent throughout the Vedas. Water is Agni's home, as heaven is that of the sun (5.85.2; cp AV 13.1.50; 19.33.1)." (Macdonell, *Vedic Mythology*, 92).[82] Macdonell sums this up, declaring that, "**In fact the abode of the celestial Agni in the waters is one of the best established points in Vedic mythology**" (Macdonell, 70). As such, he is described with certain other water-related imagery that may remind of Manannan. Agni is said to rescue from calamity as if in a ship going over the sea (RV 3.20.4; 5.4; 7.12), and his flames are like the resounding billows of the ocean (RV 1.44.12). Manannan has a ship that rides by the power of thought over the waves, called Wave-Sweeper (which, if it is not a remnant of the fire god paraphernalia, could also simply derive from his connection to the sea). As Manannan rides a chariot over the sea to meet Bran in *The Voyage of Bran*, Agni too is called a charioteer (RV 1.25.3). Manannan's boat, drawn by his horse Enbarr, could travel faster than the wind (Monaghan, *The Encyclopedia of Celtic Mythology and Folklore*, 311), which speed may also be compared to the speed of thought. Greek Fire God Hephaestus, meanwhile,

---

82 "Agni rests in all streams (8.39, cp Ap.SS 5.2.1). In the later ritual texts Agni in the waters is invoked in connexion with ponds and water-vessels. Thus even in the oldest Vedic period, the waters in which Agni is latent, though not those from which he is produced, may in various passages have been regarded as terrestrial. Oldenberg thinks that the terrestrial waters are chiefly meant in this connexion and doubts whether the lightning Agni is intended even in the first hymn of the third book. In any case, the notion of Agni in the waters is prominent throughout the Vedas. **Water is Agni's home, as heaven is that of the sun** (5.85.2; cp AV 13.1.50; 19.33.1). The waters are also often mentioned along with the plants or wood as his abode (2.1.1 &c.)" (Macdonell, 92).

shows more of the "Arch-Smith" side of the Fire God's nature, yet even he is said to be raised by sea nymphs after being born on Olympus and falling to earth. This detail once again positions the Fire God as a child of the sea (here a foster child), while also conveying that he has multiple parentages, both sky and sea, and is certainly a remnant of the same water-association that is much more focused on in the case of Manannan.

Second, as we have noted and supported above, Agni is primarily known as a priest and emissary between the sacrifice and the gods, as the flames and smoke rise to the sky, but he just as much is said to be a psychopomp, conveying the souls of the dead to the afterlife or to rebirth, as the flames and smoke rise from the funeral pyre. Manannan is centrally seen as a psychopomp as well, carrying the souls of the dead to the Land of Promise. This is perhaps why he was associated with the easterly isle of Man, the land of the dead seen as over the waves and to the east of Ireland. Agni himself is worshipped in the southeast corner of temples, and known as the guardian of this direction, due to this same psychopomp concept. East is the direction of Agni (*SB* 3.2.3.16; 6.3.3.2) and is under his protection (*SB* 8.6.1.5). Connected with this role of fire priest and psychopomp, Agni is said to be a wise sage (RV 10.124; *Kanvasatpathabrahmanam* (SB.IV.i.iv.11)), with the "mind swiftest among (all) those that fly" (RV VI.9.5), as Manannan always outsmarts those around him and is versed in magic.

Third, Agni remains extremely central to Hindu marriage rites to this day, with the *Panigrahana* "hand-holding" ritual taking place in front of a sacred fire, and the *Saptapadi* "seven steps" ritual of vows taking place in front of, and often including the walking around of, the fire, which is the presence of Agni. The Fire God was seen as the witness of the sacred marriage ceremony, and the ritual employment of fire in the marriage ceremony can be traced precisely to the very line of the Vedic hymn we have referenced, in which the Daughter of the Sun is temporarily given to Agni, as this line formed the basis of the marriage rites, as we can clearly see in the *Grihya Sutras*. Furthermore, as Macdonell notes, "The boons which Agni bestows are rather domestic welfare, offspring, and prosperity," and he is asked to deliver parents from childlessness (Macdonell, 98). Meanwhile, in "The Fosterage of the House of Two Pails," Manannan is directly connected with marriage as well as birth and fosterage, and is in this text said to take over the responsibility for all marriages. In "The Conception of Mongan," Manannan also takes on an active role in conceiving the child Mongan upon a mortal couple.

This son Mongan is described in riddling terms that could easily be a description of fire: "He will be in the shape of every beast both on the azure sea and on land, he will be a dragon before hosts, he will be a wolf of every great forest" (*The Voyage of Bran, Son of Febal, to the Land of the Living*). "In the shape of every beast" describes fire's general shape-changing nature; "a dragon before hosts" describes fire being carried before armies, appearing like the sometimes fire-breathing creature the dragon or simply like a fierce serpentine monster of flame (Agni is called a raging serpent in *RV* 1.79.1); "a wolf of every great forest" most obviously describes how fire devours forests like a wolf. In a prominent myth, Agni "eats" the forest of Khandava to appease his hunger (*Mahabharata, Adi Parva*, CCXXX). Agni is described eating forests up with his sharp tooth or his tongue in the *Rig Veda* (1.143.5; 6.60.10; 10.79.2), which is only to be expected.

Fourth, the Vedas describe Agni as a lord of three spheres and three corresponding forms. These were the forms of fire, lightning, and the Sun, and the corresponding spheres of earth, air, and the Sun, or earth, air and heaven, alternately (Charles Russell Coulter; Patricia Turner, *Encyclopedia of Ancient Deities,* p. 26). Having these three forms, Agni correspondingly has three legs, and is frequently depicted thus. Manannán sometimes takes the form of a wheel rolling across the ground, as in *Pursuit of the Gilla Decair* recorded in the 16th-century, in which his movement is also compared to wind, a hawk, and a swallow. Lore of the Isle of Man and some eastern Counties of Leinster (according to John O'Donovan) says that Manannán rolled about on three legs. Alternately, in some late folktales he is followed by a mysterious three-legged, rolling creature. The depiction of him as a three-legged being is seemingly connected to the hazy origin of the three-legged triskele symbol that is the flag of the Isle of Man, Manannan's eponymous island. This would imply that the triskele could symbolize fire in its three births: earthly fire, lightning, and the sun[83] — the vital, fiery essence of the cosmos in its three manifestations.

Fifth, Agni is in more than one place shown to shape-shift in order to test humans. Once, he tests King Shibi in the form of a pigeon, the king passing the test and proving his selfless virtue (*Mahābhārata, Vana Parva,* Chapter 131). He also oversees the *Agniparishka* fire test, which Sita is subjected to, also a test of virtue (*Mahābhārata,* V*ana Parva,* Chapter 201, Śloka 28). Examples of trial by fire abound particularly in the Iranic tradition. In Avestan it is called *garmo-varah*, heat ordeal (*cf.* Boyce, *History of Zoroastrianism*, Vol. 1, 1996:ch. 6), and in the text of the *Avesta*, blazing fire is the instrument through which justice is decided (*Yasna* 31.3, 34.4, 36.2, 47.2, 31.19, 51.9). Boyce points out that, "there are said to have been some 30 kinds of fiery tests in all"

---

83 "Owing to the diverse births above described, Agni is often regarded as having a triple character, which in many passages is expressly referred to as with some form of the numeral 'three.'" "The gods made him threefold (10.88.10)." "Thus one poet says: 'From heaven first Agni was born, the second time from us (= men), thirdly from the waters (10.45.1, cp. vv. 2-3). The order of Agni's abodes is also heaven, earth, waters in other passages (8.44.16; 10.2.7; 10.46.9) while one verse (1.95.3) has the variation: ocean, heaven, waters" (Macdonell, 93).

(Boyce, 2002:1). In the *Vendidad,* violating truth is tested and detected by drinking a kind of "blazing" water (fire in water), which may have had brimstone or sulphur in it. Trial by fire was used in ancient Persia as a judicial tool, either requiring the accused to pass through fire or to have molten metal poured on their chest. In the comparable Hindu *agniparishka* fire test, the accused would have to sit on a burning pyre and survive. A similar test survives in the Indian Sansi tribe, where women's purity is tested by having to carry burning embers in their hands for a hundred yards. Manannan too is a shapeshifter and a tester with perhaps the same hidden underlying meaning, appearing as a beggar or cleric (*Manannan at Play*; *The Conception of Mongan*, where he also teaches Mongan shapeshifting) or some other unassuming being to beguile or aid humans. This trait became central to his depiction in late tales, which focused on his wily and trickster-like exploits, such as his bringing Cormac mac Airt to the otherworld and tempting and testing him with otherworldly gifts, including a cup that judges truth and falsity (*His Three Calls to Cormac*) as Agni judges virtue. As such, this cup of truth is likely to be from a shared root with the aforementioned Iranic cup of brimstone or sulphur from the *Vendidad* which tests truth in a ritual context. In the Irish tale, Manannan says that he comes "from a country where there is nothing but truth." Manannan then gives Cormac his silver branch[84] in return for three unnamed wishes. These wishes end up being the taking away of his daughter, son, and wife in succession. However, in the end Mannanan returns these to Cormac in a spirit of friendship along with other gifts, Cormac's lesson seemingly learned. This could be of interest in relation to Agni's role in forgiving sin, for he is not a cruel god but a benefactor and close domestic friend of mankind, as well as a purifier: "Agni also forgives sin committed through folly, makes guiltless before Aditi (4.12.4; 7.93.7)" (Macdonell, 98). When he reveals his true identity to Cormac at the end of the tale, Manannan says, "I brought you here by enchantments that you might be with me to-night in friendship." Agni is called "the nearest kinsman of man" (RV 7.15.1; 8.49.10) and "friend" (RV 1.75.4), no doubt connected to the domesticity of the hearth fire and the many blessings connected to fire in ritual as well as domestic contexts.

Sixth, Manannan is also closely associated with the three gods of crafts, Goibniu and his two brothers, but is not one of them. Yet he does himself produce or distribute many of the famous treasures and weapons of the Tuatha de Danann. He presides over Goibniu's feast and commissions a shield from the craft god Lucra, and also crafts the magical crane bag. He is said to have the belt and smith's hook of Goibniu. This close association with crafts and weapon making, despite not being the blacksmith god or one

---

84 cf. RV 6.13.1: All blessings come from Agni as if from branches of a tree. "From thee, as branches from a tree, O Agni, from thee, Auspicious God! spring all our blessings." The red gold apples could combine this concept of blessings with a fire symbolism.

of the main craft gods himself, only seems logical when Manannan is seen as the God of Fire, fire being the necessary companion of craft work and blacksmithing. He is said to have a red spear and a yellow spear, perhaps repeating the colors of fire. His javelins are even described as scorched in both "O'Donnell's Kern" and "Manannan at Play." Agni, on the other hand, has a flaming spear (*Agni Purāṇa*, Chapter 51; Daniélou, Alain, *The Myths and Gods of India,* pp.88–89).[85] His apples, with which he tempts Cormac, are also of red gold and hang from a shining silver branch.

Seventh, Manannan is also depicted as overseeing the great Feast of Age, which keeps the gods immortal, and this association may be due either to the necessity of fire for cooking food, or, more likely, simply from the fact that fire conveys the food of the gods up to them from the burnt sacrifice. In the conception of the Vedic sacrifice, the God of Fire directly serves the life-bringing offerings to the gods (Brereton and Jamison, *The Rigveda: A Guide,* 73-74).

Eighth, Agni is also connected to the dispelling of evil spirits and, specifically, sorcerers, a function directly pertinent to Welsh Manawydan's role in his branch of the *Mabinogion.* When Rhiannon and Pryderi are taken captive in the mysterious vanishing fort, Manawydan finds himself in a battle of wits with a malicious sorcerer. This is Llwyd ap Kilcoed, who captures Rhiannon and Pryderi, enchants the land, bringing about the wasteland, and changes members of his own household into mice in order to despoil Manawydan's crops. Manawydan must outsmart this sorcerer in order to bring Rhiannon and Pryderi back and restore life and order to the land. Macdonell says of Agni that "probably the oldest function of fire in regard to its cult" is "that of burning and dispelling evil spirits and hostile magic." He notes that, when kindled, Agni "consumes with iron teeth and scorches with heat the sorcerers as well as the goblins (10.87.2-5-14) protecting the sacrifice with keen glance (ib. v. 9). He knows the races of the sorcerers and destroys them (AV 1.8.4)" (Macdonell, 95).[86] Thus we can see that,

---

85 Certain secondary sources (*World Heritage Encyclopedia, "Manannan mac Lir,"* Article Id: WHEBN0000085878; Harry Mountain, *The Celtic Encyclopedia,* 840) mention that he has a "flaming helmet", which would be significant, but we have not been able learn of a primary source for this claim as of this writing. If it is inaccurate, it could be based on the attested helmet of Manannan's, *Cathbarr,* which, in Manx folklore (*The Boyhood of Lugh*), is set with gems that flash as its wearer moves, or which, in *The Fate of the Children of Tuireann,* gives Lugh's face the radiance of the sun by its reflection.

86 "What is probably the oldest function of fire in regard to its cult, that of burning and dispelling evil spirits and hostile magic, still survives in the Veda. Agni drives away the goblins with his light (3.15.1 &c.) and receives the epithet raksohan, 'goblin slayer' (10.87.1). When kindled he consumes with iron teeth and scorches with heat the sorcerers as well as the goblins (10.87.2-5-14) protecting the sacrifice with keen glance (ib. v. 9). He knows the races of the sorcerers and destroys them (AV 1.8.4). Though this function of dispelling terrestrial demons is shared with Agni by Indra (as well as by Brhaspati, the

although this feature of dispelling the sorcerer and his magic is not present in the Indian parallel involving Samvarana and Vasistha, it is the other crucial and connected cultic function of the fire in relation to the proper sacrifice. The fire makes sacrifice possible, which brings the rains or causes the sun to shine, but first it also dispels the hostile magic that may be present and contributing to the state of affairs. One of these features is more apparent in the Welsh tale, and the other is more apparent in the Indian, but together the two versions of this myth dramatize the full scope of the fire's role in relation to bringing life, order, and purity back to the land as the sacrifice is reestablished.

It likely will be objected that, despite all these possible connections, Manannan seems not to have been depicted with fire itself. However, this is not true. During the narrative of *The Wooing of Etain*, it is said that Manannan was known, in one tradition, to have killed Midir and Fuamnach by burning (which would then symbolize the fiery purification of her malignant influence, or the setting of the moon at the same time as the dawn fires, Midir being a Moon God). It is in fact relatively rare to find fire used as an offensive weapon in Celtic myth, and so this instance stands out. Not only that, but even the other aspect of the fire god, Aed, whose name literally means "Fire," does not use fire himself in the myths but instead enacts the mythic role of fire through his mythic actions, just as Manannan and Manawydan do in their own ways. Another significant instance of Manannan being explicitly linked with fire occurs at the beginning of *The Adventures of Art, son of Conn*, wherein the Tuatha de Danann are in council deciding what to do with the wife of Labraid Luathlam-ar-Claideb, who has committed a sexual "transgression" with Manannan's son. The punishments debated are for the woman: "to be driven forth from the Land of Promise" or "to be burned according to the counsel of Manannan." In the end, Manannan says not to burn her, "lest her guilt should cleave to the land or to themselves" (*The Adventures of Art, son of Conn*). It is certainly noteworthy that Manannan is seen here as the decider of whether to execute a criminal by fire, just as he also kills Fuamnach (and Midir, seemingly) with fire himself. The fear that the woman's guilt will "cleave" to the land seems to be a fascinating glimpse into an ancient understanding of how guilt may be spread via an execution by flame. In "O'Donnell's Kern," wherein "the kern" is Manannan, it is said that "each blow they make on the kern inflicts the same wound on themselves," which sounds like what would happen if a person attacked fire.

Manannan is colloquially believed to be a god of the sea primarily. This is the image that has been passed down to us and how he appears in the most common depictions. However, the scholar David Spaan in his essay "The Place of Manannan in Irish

---

Asvins, and especially Soma), it must primarily have belonged to Agni alone [...] This is borne out by the fact that Agni is undoubtedly more prominent as a goblin slayer than Indra, both in the hymns and in the ritual" (Macdonell, 95).

Mythology" claims that this sea association is secondary to his true nature, an association likely to be derived from his abode on the Isle of Man and his connection to the land of the dead found thereabouts. Due to the fact that he lives out at sea and has to cross the ocean to carry souls back and forth, he has naturally become associated with the sea as its lord as well. Hence both his sea association and his magical wave-sweeping ship can be explained by his role as psychopomp, and can be supported further by the aforementioned epithet of Agni – Descendant of Waters – part of Agni's general association with water, to the point that Agni was seen as living in that element and being born from it. Manannan's habitual cloak of mist can then be simply explained by this sea association, or even, more fancifully perhaps, as the natural result of fire touching water. Agni, on the other hand, is "smoke-bannered" (*dhumaketu*).

Spaan further comments on the many similarities between Manannan and the Norse Óðinn, pointing particularly to Manannan as "supreme provider, accomplished magician and sorcerer, as well as custodian of the well of truth and patron of the arts and crafts. Prophet and shape-shifter," "ruler of the Otherworld," who leads chosen warriors "to his Land of Promise…to be educated there at his own hand" (Spaan, 179), likening this last facet to Óðinn's role in Valhalla. Manannan also feeds warriors in this place with pigs that are ever renewed, as Óðinn feeds the slain *einherjar* with the ever-regenerating pig Saehrimnir. This connection of Manannan/Manawydan with Óðinn is important and is crucially supported by the passing of Skaði in marriage from Njörðr to Óðinn, which we have suggested matches the passage of Suryā from Soma to Agni or of Rhiannon from Pwyll to Manawydan. However, while keeping Spaan's important comparisons in mind, we should note here that Agni/Manannan seems only to correspond to one part of the larger makeup of Óðinn, as if the Agni deity is an "aspect" of Óðinn, so to speak. This complex problem will be discussed in another chapter.

Further, more tentative comparisons can be made between Manannan and Agni. Agni is said to be a giver of weapons on more than one occasion. In one portion of the *Mahabharata* he gives a magical arrow case, four white horses, and a chariot, to Arjuna, along with the powerful Gandiva bow, which becomes Arjuna's signature weapon. He furthermore gives Krishna the *cakrayudha* weapon. Manannan, for his part, gives Lugh a self-navigating boat, a horse that could cross both sea and land, a magically fatal sword called "The Answerer," a helm, body armor, and neck-piece. He also gives Finn the shield of wood commissioned from Lucra. The story of Manannan's wife may also bear a distant similarity to that of Agni's wife. Manannan's wife Fand falls in love with the central hero Cuchulainn, son of Lugh. The two become lovers, until Cuchulainn's wife musters a force to attack Fand. Fand returns to Manannan, and Mannanan then shakes his magical cloak, causing Fand and Cuchulainn never again to meet. Agni's wife Svāhā, on the other hand, falls in love with and desires Krishna. Krishna tells her that she will become his wife, but that she has first to be the wife of Agni. Agni and Svāhā have a daughter named Agneya. Manannan and Fand have a daughter coincidentally named Áine. Meanwhile, even more strikingly, other texts call Áine the wife of Manannan. Áine is well-known as a Goddess of the Sun and of summer, which makes for a perfect match to the pattern of sun princesses we have been tracing.[87] Aine is seen by the king Aillil Aulom in a waking dream in a manner reminiscent of that in which Aengus sees Caer, after which Aillil goes mad from infatuation and rapes Aine, Aine biting his ear off in return and making him unfit to be king. Another form of the name of Áine is thought to be Aynia, even more mysteriously similar to Agneya. However, Áine is a sun goddess while Agneya's name does not indicate her as one, thus we may consider this overlap as a kind of coincidence bolstered by the deeper framework of naming surrounding the Fire God's female consorts and children. We should properly draw a line between the Sun Goddess Áine as Manannan's wife and the Sun Princess Surya as Agni's, and between Fand as Manannan's other wife and Svaha as Agni's other wife. Aynia as daughter of Manannan and Agneya as daughter of Agni could then parallel one another, and this could explain the confusion between Aine/Aynia as either the daughter or wife of Manannan. Considering the comparative cases, it seems most important to insist that Aine must have been Manannan's wife at the very least, and that Áine as his daughter is more to be suspected as a confusion. This is no perfect solution to the problem presented by this set of names, but the similarities evident here should be enough to further support the connection between Agni and Manannan.

In the *Brahmanas* and *Upanishads*, Agni is said to be the heat, light, and energy of life, as well as the swiftness of mind (see: section 5.2.3 of *Satapatha Brahmana*, Agni is all the gods and the spiritual energy pervading the universe). Agni stands somewhat

---

87 "Aine is apparently a sun deity, known as wife either of Echdae, a sun-god in horse-form (ech 'horse'), or of Mannanan, the Irish sea god (sometimes she is instead his daughter). Her name apparently means 'brightness' or 'radiance'; she is worshipped on John's night (a midsummer ritual) at Knockainey, Co. Limerick, where men circle her mound (sid) at Cnoc Aine carrying poles with flaming bunches of straw and hay tied to them. In the district of Lissan, Co. Derry, she is regarded as a lady who was taken away from her husband's side at night by the 'wee folk' and never returned; a vanishing maiden motif" ("The Sun Maiden's Wedding," Cheryl Steets, 24). This disappearance from her husband's side incidentally resembles the plight of Welsh Rhiannon, who also becomes Manawydan's Sun Princess wife. This myth then also retains the fact that Aine is passed from one husband to another. Perhaps, then, Echdae is a local variant (associated with the Eóghanacta) paralleling the first husband of Rhiannon, Pwyll, and of his Greek parallel (as we will see later), who also takes a horse form in the parallel myth, Poseidon Hippios. Aine is raped by King Ailill Aulom and bites his ear off in response, as Demeter is raped by Poseidon Hippios (originally *Wanax*, "chief/king") and reacts by becoming the violently furious Demeter *Erinys*.

outside and above the other gods, and is often identified with a great number of them in the Vedas, again pointing to his shapeshifting nature and his status as the element of divine vitality found even within other gods (especially solar gods, who can be seen as forms of fire), the life-spark. At times, because of this role as the vitality within the other gods, Agni is even seen as the true highest god and as the creator himself. As Arthur A. Macdonell notes, he is called "the germ (garbha) of what is stationary or moves and of all that exists (1.70.3; AV 5.25.7)" (Macdonell, *Vedic Mythology*, 95). This is akin to Heraclitus' view of fire as the prime element, which manifests the unfolding of Logos in the world, and the Zoroastrian understanding of the holy fire, *Atar*, as the visible manifestation of Ahura Mazda (just as "Agni" would be one aspect of the high Rudraic and Varunian god Óðinn, as will be discussed). The Zoroastrian tradition also preserves the idea that fire is a tester of virtue (trial by fire), a shapeshifter, and the vital force required by the other gods for creation. Manannan too seems to be of the gods, yet separate, a powerful magician living over the sea in his far island, yet occasionally called the chief god of all the Tuatha de Danann. For instance, in *The Fosterage of the House of the Two Pails*, Manannan claims that he is the over-king over all of the kings of the Tuatha De Danann and their true ancestor as well.[88] Even Manannan's cloak, which causes those on either side of it to never meet again, can speculatively be explained using the lens of Agni. When we hear of "never meeting again," induced forgetfulness, etc., in relation to a psychopomp god, we should immediately suspect a reference to death, the cloak of never-again-meeting being the veil between this world and the Otherworld. When death occurs, the soul experiences forgetfulness and goes to an unreachable land, as Manannan shakes his cloak, which is perhaps a cloak once again visualized as the smoke rising from the funeral pyre.

Breaking his name crudely into three parts: Irish *mana-* may mean "portent, sign" but comes from the root *men-* meaning "to think" or indicating spiritual activity. Alternately, it may more simply derive from the name of the Isle of Man. The suffix *-an* can mean "bright" or "brilliant," and, using the Old Irish spelling "Manandan" or the Welsh "Manawydan," the final portion of the name, *dan,* can mean "gift," "offering," "skill," or "fate." While deferring the topic to the experts, we can briefly point toward various potential meanings of the name as it appears to us, such as "bright portent of thought," "brilliant gift of thought," "skill of mind," etc. The general thrust of these may suggest the bright gift and portent that is fire, which is also a symbol for and the metaphysical origin of mental illumination. Even Manannan's epithet *Gilla Decair*, meaning "troublesome boyservant," begins to sound like a comic description of fire when all the

---

88 Agni is "a divine (asura) monarch (samraj), strong as Indra (7.6.1). His greatness surpasses that of mighty heaven (1.59.5)." "He is superior to all the other gods in greatness (1.68.2)" (Macdonell, 98).

other evidence is considered. This name *Gilla* appears elsewhere connected to the smith Guillean, who is from Manannan's island of Man, again associating Manannan and smith figures. In this connection, *Giolla Guilleann,* "Guillean's Servant," is said to be synonymous with an imp of the devil.[89] Clearly this reference has been Christianized, but what would be the impish servant of a smith except fire?

Coincidentally, the eldest son of Manannan's father Lir is said to be named *Aodh*, "Fire," in the Christianized romance *The Children of Lir.* All considered, this seems to us a significantly late (possibly 14th century) and highly romanticized doublet of Manannan, and at the very least is an acknowledgement that Lir has a son, his eldest, who bears the God of Fire's name, while Manannan mac Lir is the only god to carry the patronymic marking him as Lir's son. This all begins to seem so very obvious now. Manannan's most characteristic festival, when the people of the Isle of Man traditionally "paid rents" to Manannan in the form of bundles of rushes, was the festival of Midsummer, which was also the festival of his wife, Aine. Midsummer across Europe is centered on the great bonfires and the various rites that surround them. In Celtic lands it is called "Bonfire Night" or *Oiche na Teine Chnaimh* ("Sacred Night of Fire"). Most Celtic festivals prominently involve fire; however, this name in particular is indeed fitting for a festival of the Fire God.

Considering all of this, it seems that what we have in the case of Manannan is actually a form of the Fire God that has, ironically, *not* been syncretized with the "descendant of the waters" deity named Apam Napat by the Vedics, but merely has traits that make clear to us why these two gods would easily become syncretized, as they are in the Vedic case. If, instead, Irish Nechtan's etymology connects him to Apam Napat (and perhaps Neptune), the true "Descendant of the Waters," as seems likely (see: Dumezil, "Les Puits de Nechtan"; "La saison des rivières" from the third volume of *Mythe et épopée*[90]), then we would see that Nechtan (Apam Napat) and Manannan (Agni) are preserved separately in the Irish tradition, while they have become syncretized into one god only in

---

89 Nicholas O'Kearney, *Transactions of the Kilkenny Archaeological Society* Vol. 2, No. 1 (1852), p. 33.

90 In addition to Dumezil's strong arguments, a brief word on Nechtan = Apam Napat: Apam Napat in the *Avesta* is the guardian of the "Glory that cannot be forcibly seized" (*Zam Yasht,* 51), while Nechtan guards a well of wisdom called *Segais*, of which it is said "There was none that would look to its bottom but his two bright eyes would burst" (*Dindshenchas, Boand I*). Only Nechtan and his cup-bearers are permitted to approach this well. Despite being forbidden to do so, Boann approaches the well one day and does so in an improper fashion, walking around it counter-clockwise. The waters rush out of the well, blasting her arm, leg and one eye off of her and killing her or making her become one with the river that forms, the Boyne. The essence of this well then could be compared to the Avestan "Glory that cannot be forcibly seized."

the Vedic branch. What we see with Manannan, then, is as clear a picture as we can wish for of *why* the fire god, Agni, became syncretized with the Descendant of Waters, Apam Napat: because the fire god is *also* a child of waters, but in a different context. Manannan's appellation *mac Lir*, "son of the sea," has a specific esoteric meaning relating to fire's birth from water or the sea, but does not make him precisely the same as the water deity known as Apam Napat, Nechtan, etc. who is also primarily known to be descended from the waters, but has his own specific and separate function, not necessarily related to fire, as we will see. Thus the Irish "Sea God" is likely to actually be the God of Fire. Specifically he is the god of fire-in-water, a highly important Indo-European concept.

See also: Brereton and Jamison: "That fire is fueled by plants, especially wood, contributes to the belief that Agni lives concealed within the plants and ultimately within the waters that nurture the plants until he is finally born from them. The connection between fire and waters is also evident in the identification of Agni with a minor divinity going back to Indo-Iranian times, Apāṃ Napāt, the "Child of the Waters." Originally he was probably a separate deity, a glowing fiery being concealed and nurtured in the waters, perhaps configured in part as lightning. But the single Rgvedic hymn dedicated to Apāṃ Napāt, II.35, gradually merges Apāṃ Napāt with Agni by attributing Agni's functions and form to him, until in the final verse Agni emerges fully in the poet's address to him" (Brereton and Jamison, *The Rigveda: A Guide*, 75).

Agni and Óðinn

In this interpretation we would also be able to theorize the placement of "Agni" in the Norse pantheon. After the Sun Princess Suryā, in the "Suryā's Bridal" hymn, is said to be married to Soma, she is said to marry the Gandharva and then Agni. While we can say this might indicate the passing of the sun's rays from the moon at night, to the birds of dawn or the singers of the dawn sacrifice (manifestations of the Gandharvas), to the sacrificial dawn fires (Agni), we can also say that Skaði's leaving of Njörðr for Óðinn also seems to match the "Suryā's Bridal" pattern. As we can surmise that Bragi is a much more likely match for the Gandharva than Óðinn is (as Óðinn is not likely to be the lower-level court musician of the gods no matter how full of Mead of Poetry he is), it seems logical that Óðinn here may be taking the role of Agni, or more exactly, that Agni is one of the aspects of Óðinn, and that in this marriage to Skaði, Óðinn is specifically enacting a myth of the Fire God. We note that, as Curwen Rolinson has pointed out in his "Soma-Kvasir, The Eddic-Vedic Myth of the Meath of Poetry," Óðinn turning into

215

the eagle to escape from the mountain fortress with the Mead of Poetry also parallels the hawk Shyena, a form of Agni, who steals the sacred liquid from the mountain.[91]

This would also fit with the pattern of Óðinn's seeming monopoly on the great majority of magico-priestly deities as compared with the Vedic branch, whether these be Brihaspati, Varuna, Agni, etc. Each of these Vedic divine names can be shown to be connected to myths belonging to Óðinn. It would also partially explain the sometimes remarked upon similarities of Óðinn and Manannan as we have mentioned regarding Spaan's "The Place of Manannan in Irish Mythology," and would perhaps account for Óðinn's psychopomp-related roles as well, perhaps even his penchant for going about in disguise, similar to the habit of Manannan. Vedic Agni and Brihaspati are the two central priests of the sacrifice, the priest of fire and of the spoken word, respectively. As such, interpreting both Brihaspati and Agni as aspects of Óðinn would only be reuniting the otherwise divided priestly aspects in one figure (see our chapter "The High Priest of the Word" for further discussion of Brihaspati and Óðinn).

* * *

One thing has to be added as a postscript to this issue, as a possibility for further contemplation. The incarnation of Agni from the *Mahabharata*, Dhrishtadyumna, seems possibly to share a myth with Freyr as well. Dhrishtadyumna is bested by Ashwatthama in the Kurukshetra War because he is missing his sword. This fact is underlined when Ashwatthama refuses to let him die with his sword in his hand. Freyr famously gives his sword away to Skirnir, and misses it later in the battle of Ragnarok. He confronts Surtr (a demonic fire entity) in this battle, and is killed. Now, the Irish Aengus, who we have seen is cognate to Freyr, has a brother named Aed, meaning simply "fire." Both he and Manannan are likely manifestations of the Fire God in different forms as will be seen, and just because Aed's name means "fire," this should not make us set Mannanan aside as a form of "Agni" as well. Additionally, in Vedic scripture, the Dawn Goddess and the Horse Twins are sometimes called siblings (compare here Freyr and Freyja as siblings and Aengus and Brigid as siblings), and Agni is said also to be their brother (RV IV.17.4): "In about three-fourths of these instances Usas is [Dyaus'] daughter, while in the remainder the Asvins are his offspring (*napata*), Agni is his son (*sunu*) or child (*sisu*)" (Arthur A. Macdonell, *Vedic Mythology*, 21). In the *Mahabharata*, Dhrishtadyumna, incarnation of Agni, is born as a twin with Draupadi (who may or may not be connected to Ushas, as we have noted), each emerging in succession from the holy flame of the *yagna* rite. If Draupadi is related to the Dawn goddess, as we have speculated, this twin birth could be an allegory for the birth of the holy flame and the

---

91 See also Rolinson's "On Odin as Agni," which demonstrates many more correspondences between Odinn and Agni than I am able to at present.

dawn at the same moment during the dawn sacrifice. The coinciding of their appearance with the dawn sacrifice could be another reason the Horse Twins, as gods of the transition of morning or morning star, are seen as brothers of the Dawn Goddess. Horse Twins, Dawn, and Fire gods are then siblings. However, seeing that Freyr, unlike Aengus, is not said to have any brothers, could we speculate a partial combination of the mythos of this Fire God (i.e. Aed, an aspect of Agni) and the Horse Twin in the figure of Freyr, as suggested by the shared motif of dying due to missing his sword? Or reversing the causation, perhaps, could we leave open the possibility that Agni's *Mahabharata* incarnation took this myth from the Horse Twins due to their close association as brothers? As we have noted previously, Stig Wikander argues that the evidence suggests that the second and more "domestic" Indo-Iranian Horse Twin could have become or been merged with Atar, the fire deity in the Iranic tradition (Donald Ward, *The Divine Twins An Indo-European Myth in Germanic Tradition,* 22). This matches the fact that Aengus' brother is the fire deity Aed, and that Freyr has a myth that could parallel the Vedic Fire God, as if this fire aspect were merged in him or even more directly connected to him from the start.

Ultimately, what the separate existences of Irish Aed and Manannan suggest is that the fire deity must have been seen to have at least two separate aspects: one a more earthly fire, Aed, the other the high priest and psychopomp, the cosmic magician Manannan. This accords exceedingly well with the Vedic case, in which celestial and terrestrial fires were separately designated, the celestial Ahavaniya Agni and the terrestrial Garhapatya Agni (Gregory Nagy, *Greek Mythology and Poetics,* 107). Dumezil points out that a precisely corresponding division of fires appears in Roman tradition with the ordinary templum vs. the aedes Vesta (Dumezil, *Rituels indo-européens à Rome,* 1954, 27-43). The Latin word for this latter temple, *aedes,* as might be obvious, comes from the same root word that gives the Irish Aed his name, and this etymology suggests that the word came to designate temples due to the fact that these buildings housed sacred flames. Thus, if Aed can be seen as this same terrestrial, domestic fire, he would have direct cognates in the flame of the Vestals and the Garhapatya Agni of the Vedics.[92] The Dagda

---

92 There are other possible ways of dividing the Agnis that could be relevant, however. Macdonell says: "The TS. (2.5.8.6) also distinguishes three, the Agni that bears the oblation (havyavahana) as belonging to the gods, the Agni that bears the funeral offering (kavyavahana), as belonging to the Fathers, and the Agni associated with goblins (saharaksas) as belonging to the Asuras" (Macdonell, 97). It seems clear that Aed is closer associated with the hearth fire that is established on earth, while Manannan is the funeral fire. It is unclear, however, if Manannan would be connected to the oblation bearing fire as well, and this distinction may not hold in the exact same fashion as the Taittiriya Samhita is later than the *Rig Veda.* The division of the fires into three may itself be a later Vedic development, but it is also likely that there was always a negative fire aspect known, which is reflected here as the goblin fire; see Brereton and Jamison, *The*

is Aed's father, he bears the epithet *Aed* himself, and is the wind and sky god as we have seen. This could reflect an understanding also seen in the *Rig Veda* that the wind is continuous with fire, carrying the germ of the spark: "as Matarisvan, [Agni] was fashioned in his mother, he became the swift flight of wind" (*RV* 3.29.11). Perhaps more likely, it could go back to the idea, also found in the Vedas, that Agni is the son of Father Sky: "Agni's father is Dyaus, who generated him (10.45.8). He is the child (*sisu*) of Dyaus (4.15.6; 6.49.2) and is said to have been born from the belly of the Asura (3.29.4). He is often called the son of Dyaus and Prthvi (3.2.2; 3.3.11; 3.25.1; 10.1.2; 10.2.7; 10.140.7)" (Macdonell, 90). While the terrestrial aspect of the Irish Agni, Aed, is the son of the Dagda, Meanwhile, in *Altram Tige Dá Medar* (*The Fosterage*) Manannán says he is the foster son of the Dagda, which seems then to be a way of reconciling the celestial Fire God being a child of the waters and son of Father Sky at the same time.

This postscript must be marked as speculative, but it also must be noted: it may be that we find these two aspects or roles of the Fire God taken on board separately by Freyr and Óðinn respectively, as the lower and higher Fire priest gods.

Heimdallr and Apam Napat

In his *Investigations,* Viktor Rydberg contends that Agni is in fact a parallel of Heimdallr. However, it is not difficult to contest this claim. Rydberg in fact assumes that the deity Apam Napat, The Descendant of Waters, who has become combined with Agni in the Vedas, but not elsewhere, is simply an aspect of Agni. Thus he uses for his comparison the composite Agni-Apam Napat found in the Vedas under the name "Agni," then brings in the Apam Napat of the *Avesta* for further support of the Agni comparison. This of course does not work if Agni and Apam Napat are distinct deities only combined in the *Rig Veda*, as it appears. An original distinction between Agni and Apam Napat is supported by the fact that Apam Napat and the Fire God are separate in the Iranic *Avesta;* by the clear distinction we have uncovered in Irish myth between Manannan/Aed (Agni) and Nechtan (Apam Napat); by the fact that no other branches demonstrate a combination of these aspects; and lastly by the opinion of Herman Oldenberg and other scholars upon the Rig Vedic evidence. Macdonell summarizes:

Rigveda: A Guide.

"Oldenberg is of opinion that Apam Napat was originally a water genius pure and simple, who became confused with the water-born Agni, a totally different being. His grounds are that one of the two hymns in which he is celebrated (10.30) is connected in the ritual with ceremonies exclusively concerned with water, while even in 2.35 [the only Vedic hymn dedicated solely to him] his aqueous nature predominates" (Macdonell, 70). Brereton and Jamison concur with this being likely, as we have noted above, and Agni and Apam Napat are sometimes distinguished even in the *Rig Veda*, including in the one hymn dedicated solely to Apam Napat. Brereton and Jamison assert in summary that "in the Rₑgveda it [the name Apam Napat] is in the course of becoming an epithet of Agni. In this hymn we see aspects both of the identification with and assimilation to Agni and of the original independent divinity" (Brereton and Jamison, *Rig Veda*, 452). The question remains somewhat open-ended among scholars; however, the weight of comparative evidence we have surveyed points toward a very likely original separation of the two gods. Thus evidence drawn from Iranic Apam Napat or from a Vedic Agni that has been blended with Apam Napat cannot support a parallel of Heimdallr with the true archaic "Agni," that is, the Fire god. Much of what Rydberg uses as evidence of Vedic Agni's character demonstrably has its origin in this Apam Napat (as we will see below), or otherwise its origin is muddied by the uncertainty caused by the mixture of the two gods, and could originate in either.

Such evidence can, however, support a parallel of Heimdallr with Apam Napat, the deity that Rydberg was sometimes comparing Heimdallr with while supposing that it pointed toward Agni. A brief summary of details relating to Apam Napat should make this sufficiently clear for the present. Vedic Apam Napat "shines forth without fuel in the waters (2.35.4). Clothed in lightning," whereas Heimdallr is the whitest or brightest god (*Þrymskviða* 15), thus the color of lightning; "the swift (waters) golden in colour go around him (2.35.9). The Son of waters, Apam Napat, is golden in form, appearance and colour; coming from a golden womb," while Heimdallr has golden teeth (or is at least called *gullinntani*) and a golden-maned horse; "Standing in the highest place he [Apam Napat] always shines with undimmed splendour" (RV 2.35.14) and similarly Avestan Apam Napat's most characteristic title is *bərəzant-*, the "High One," (Zam Yasht, 52) or *Borz ī Ābānnāf* "The High One who is Son of the Waters"" (*Zātspram* 3.18)), as Heimdallr is the gods' watchmen from on high, near to the rainbow bridge Bifrost, and lives at *Himinbjorg*, "Heaven's Castle" or "Heaven's Mountain"; in the Veda "the swift waters carry ghee as food to their son," that is, Apam Napat curiously has multiple mothers (the waters), while Heimdallr is said also to have multiple mothers, nine of them. In fact, the common interpretation of these mothers of Heimdallr is the waves of the sea, making them identical with the Nine Daughters of the sea gods Aegir and Ran. This theory has been commonplace at least since Dumezil, as found in his *Gods of the Ancient Northmen*. Supporting this supposition is a stanza from the *Voluspa hin skamma*, which reads: "Nine giant women, at the world's edge,/ Once bore the man so mighty in arms," implying a birth at sea, which is where the world's edge is, and a few lines later, "Strong was he made with the strength of the earth,/With the ice-cold sea, and the blood of swine" (*Voluspa hin skamma,* 7, 9), further connecting his origin to the sea, his mothers having made him strong by its cold waters (among other things) upon his birth. Of Apam Napat: "The youth [Apam Napat] do the youthful waters, (though) unsmiling, circle around while they groom him" (RV 2.35.4).

Vedic Apam Napat also "has engendered all beings, who are merely branches of him (2.35.2-8)," and of Avestan Apam Napat "(It is) he who created men, he who shaped men (*yō nərōuš da'a, yō nərōuš tataša*)" (*Zam Yasht*, 52), while in *Rigsthula,* under the name Rig, Heimdallr directly engenders the classes of human society, making them his descendants. Agni is spoken of in similar terms in the Veda, in fact; however, Macdonell is at pains to emphasize that this attribution, only in the case of Agni, cannot be taken to mean he is believed to be the father of the human race in a proper interpretation: "Agni is once spoken of as having generated these children of men (1.96.2); but this is a mere incidental extension of the notion expressed in the same stanza, that he created heaven, earth, and the waters, and cannot be interpreted as a general belief in Agni as father of the human race" (Macdonell, 99). Thus when Agni and Apam Napat are seen in their separate contexts via the distinct Avestan case, it is Apam Napat who has the stronger claim to engendering humans (though engendering the *castes* is not specifically mentioned in relation to either god). Macdonell concludes that, "In the *Avesta* Apam napat is a spirit of the waters, who lives in their depths, is surrounded by females and is often invoked with them, drives with swift steeds."

Perhaps most crucially, this Iranic Apam Napat "is said to have seized the brightness in the depths of the ocean," which is one of the key pieces of evidence Rydberg uses to link Heimdallr with Apam Napat and thus with Agni by association. But this is a myth solely belonging to Apam Napat in the *Avesta*, and not to Agni at all. In fact, the Avestan Fire God, Atar, appears as a completely separate figure in the same section of the hymn attempting also to seize the "glory" or "brightness," but he is unable to do so and it swells up and goes into the sea. It is at that point that Apam Napat appears and successfully seizes the "brightness." He is its proper guardian. Thus, as Heimdallr fights Loki, on a rock in the sea according to Snorri, in the form of a seal, for the famous shining necklace *Brisingamen*, and finally returns it safely to Freyja, so also Apam Napat seizes the "brightness" or the shining "glory"[93], the *khvarenah*, from the ocean

---

93 "51. That Glory swells up and goes to the sea Vouru-Kasha. The swift-horsed Son of the Waters [Apam Napat] seizes it at once: this is the wish of the Son of the Waters, the swift-horsed: 'I want to seize that Glory that cannot be forcibly seized, down to the bottom of the sea Vouru-Kasha, in the bottom of the deep rivers.'

during a confrontation with Azhi Dahaka "of the evil law." Apam Napat watches always over this shining glory (also spelled *Xwarrah*) in the *Bundahišn (*26.91). Heimdallr's seal form then finally makes sense in this interpretation, considering that he is a proper god of the waters. In the *Avesta,* Apam Napat is also "the god amid the waters, who being prayed to is swiftest of all to hear," while Heimdallr is the great watchman of the gods who is known above all for his eyesight and hearing, being able to hear grass as it grows and wool as it grows on sheep (*Gylfaginning* 25). In the Avesta, Apam Napat is also called "kingly" (*Zam Yasht*, 52), while Heimdallr goes to the houses of Men in *Rigsthula* under the name *Rig*, from a word for "king."

One interpretation that could bring the Agni and Apam Napat parallels closer together in relation to the Heimdallr question is the idea that Apam Napat could be partially combustible himself, that despite being a god of the waters he could have his own semi-fiery or at least electric nature – for example, that he embodies a form of lightning. Macdonell himself states that, at least in the *Rig Veda* which already has conflated the two, Apam Napat "appears to represent the lightning form of Agni which is concealed in the cloud," and this overlap with Agni (along with the contemporary idea that water held fire within it in general) may have been what caused the two gods to be conflated in the first place. The loud note of Heimdallr's screaming *Gjallarhorn* could then relate to something like thunder and his location in heaven near the rainbow bridge could indicate his dwelling among clouds as lightning does. James Darmesteter agrees with Macdonell in regarding Apam Napat as a lightning-in-clouds deity, though Oldenberg and others see him as purely aqueous. It would of course be possible to picture a deity related to the lightning or electrical power residing within all water and clouds generally, distinguished from but easily confused with the Agni which lives also in water, but this could also be too reductive. The *Encyclopaedia Iranica* states: "In Indian rituals, as in Iranian ones, Apām Napāt's connection remained solely with water. Oldenberg's interpretation was accepted by L. H. Gray ("The Indo-Iranian deity Apām Napāt," *ARW* 3, 1900, pp. 18-51)."[94] The sole hymn dedicated to Apam Napat in the *Rig Veda* (2.35) at certain points does describe him in terms that metaphorically suggest a fiery nature, but this may or may not simply be the mark of the influence of Agni on Apam Napat, who is here in the process of becoming seen as only an epithet of the Fire God.

Our primary contention with this analysis at present is that Manannan and Agni (the true Fire Gods), and particularly Agni in his specifically fire-related passages, have far

---

52. We sacrifice unto the Son of the Waters, the swift-horsed, the tall [high] and shining lord, the lord of females; the male god, who helps one at his appeal; who made man, who shaped man, a god who lives beneath waters, and whose ear is the quickest to hear when he is worshipped" (Avesta, *Zam Yasht*, 51-52).

94 *Encyclopaedia Iranica.* Iranicaonline.org, "Apam Napat". Accessed May 2021.

more in common with Odinn, including actual *myths,* than Agni has with Heimdallr when the Apam Napat element is set aside and seen clearly for itself. We have not even mentioned yet that Rydberg also is required to bring in a *third* unconnected deity to make his Agni parallel function. This is the Avestan Sraosha of the "fine hearing," an embodiment of the divine word or of divine hearing, who Rydberg requires because only Avestan Apam Napat is said to have quick hearing while Vedic Agni is not. Suffice it to say that Sraosha is not a fire deity, is less connected to Agni than Apam Napat is, and indeed does not have a connection to him.[95]

* * *

The Welsh Horse Twin(s) and the Grail

As we have seen, the Welsh mythological corpus takes the central myth of the Horse Twins and the Gandharva-Wasteland myth, likely two parts of one cycle to begin with, and emphasizes their continuity, compressing them into a more unified narrative of a father and son, thus ultimately laying the groundwork for the legends surrounding the great object of mystique, the Holy Grail.

Pwyll and Rhiannon's son – Pryderi – has often been put forward as both a Horse Twin (Patrick K. Ford, *The Mabinogi and Other Medieval Welsh Tales*, 1977, 50-4) and the prototype of the grail quester (Gantz, *Mabinogion, Introduction*). So far we have seen how he takes the same role in the Welsh version of the "Aesir-Vanir War" that is taken by Irish Aengus, Norse Freyr, Roman Titus Tatius, and the Vedic Asvins. Pryderi is born on the same night as a horse, which is raised up with him as his own, and indeed almost as his twin. After being kidnapped on the night of his birth, he is fostered by Teyrnon, who is known as a great raiser of horses, and the boy is noted as well to have an affinity for horses. Pryderi is one of only two "young sons" around which the *Mabinogion* centers. The title of the main four branches of this collection, the "*Mabinogi,*" itself is believed to refer to Mabon ap Modron, Mabon meaning "young son" and being a direct cognate of Macc Oc, the title by which Aengus is called. This Mabon has certain traits that align him with the Horse Twin type as well. As M.L. West explains, citing Koch and Carey:

---

95 The conclusions we have reached in this chapter identifying Apam Napat with Heimdallr are supported by a recent article "Heimdallr and Apām Nápat: A Comparison" by Signe Cohen, *Nouvelle Mythologie Comparee 6*, 2021.

The Indo-European divine Twins, the youthful sons of *Dyeus, were especially noted for appearing in battle on their white horses and bringing assistance or deliverance [...] It may be added that in a poem in the Book of Taliesin ["Tidings Have Come to Me From Kalchvynyd"], celebrating the wars and cattle-raiding of Owein of Rheged, the young god Mabon is represented as appearing in battle on a white steed and killing all of the enemy within reach. (West 483, Koch–Carey, *Celtic Heroic Age*, 356–8)

Aengus also appears in a Scottish folktale riding a white steed and wearing a raiment of shining gold (see: Mackenzie, Donald Alexander, *Wonder Tales from Scottish Myth and Legend*). Furthermore, the Mabon is kidnapped and imprisoned at birth (*Culhwch and Olwen*) as Pryderi is also kidnapped at birth (*Pwyll, Prince of Dyfed*).

Garrett Olmsted outlines the etymological details thus:

Now the term *in Macc Óc* is only a reformation of an earlier *Mac in Óc*, which is preserved in the genitive in LU 2942 (*Bruig Meic ind Oc*) and LU 4117 (*maig Meic ind Óc*). Thus O'Rahilly (1946: 516-7) suggests that the name developed from an earlier *Maccan Óc "The Young Son". Here then the name *Maccan is cognate with Welsh Mabon. In this connection it is significant that *Maccan Óc spends the first part of his life in the *síd* with Midir and not with his mother Boand. In the Welsh *Trioedd Ynys Prydein*, Mabon ap Modron is one of the Three Exalted Prisoners of Britain (*Tri Goruchel Garchravr Ynys Brydein*) (Bromwich 1961: 140 '52). Similarly in *Culhwch ac Olwen* the motif of the prisoner is continued, where Mabon is again cruelly imprisoned.

Mabon uab Modron yssys yma ygcarch(ar) ac ny charcharvyt neb kyn dosted yn llvrv carchur a mil. (Evans 1907: 492). (Olmsted, 91)

He concludes:

The implication is that Boand may be equated with Modron. Modron in turn derives from the earlier Gaulish Matrona "the Mother", eponymous goddess of the river Marne. The fact that Modron derives from a river and source goddess Matrona confirms the identification with Boand, herself the eponymous goddess of the Boind. (Olmsted, 91)

Hence the Four Branches of the *Mabinogi* theoretically make up the book of Mabon, the book of the Young Son. The only other "young son" of the *Mabinogion* that this epithet could refer to is Lleu Llaw Gyffes, who we can confidently say is not a Horse Twin, as we have shown him to be the Mitraic god in previous chapters. Instead, Lleu appears only in the final branch of the four, and provides a thematic mirror for Pryderi, completes the cycle that he begins, in precisely the same way that Baldr is a mirror of

Freyr and he along with the mysterious Lord of the Endtimes completes the cycle that Freyr and the Vanir in a certain sense begin, the war with the Vanir being called the first in the world. In fact, Pryderi is a central figure of two out of the four "branches" of the *Mabinogion*, and appears in all four, more than can be said for any other figure. The idea that the *Mabinogion* is "Pryderi's book" then, revolving around his birth, life and death narrative, and that he is thus "the Mabon," is by no means far-fetched. Ifor Williams, for one, has argued that the *Mabinogion* as a whole may have originally centered even more obviously around Pryderi. In other medieval texts such as the poem "Preiddeu Annwn," the mysterious Mabon is said to be imprisoned somewhere in the otherworld, and figures such as King Arthur and Cei seek to free him. In Pryderi's story in the *Mabinogion*, he and his mother are lured into a mysterious fort and place their hands on a golden bowl found inside. They are frozen in place and then vanish from sight along with the fort. It is only after significant time passes that Manawydan, Rhiannon's then husband, is able to rescue them by outwitting their captors. This all occurs after Pryderi has caused the region to become an enchanted "wasteland" by ill-advisedly sitting on the mystical mound Gorsedd Arberth (from which Pwyll had first seen Rhiannon), and the land is only restored to normalcy and vitality when Manawydan rescues him from the Otherworld fort by means of his cunning. This theme of the restoration of the wasteland is one of several elements from this story that seems to have been carried through into the Grail legends, and we have seen how it exists also in the parallel Indian tale of Samvarana.

Crucially, Pryderi is also the theorized inspiration for the Welsh version of the grail quester, Peredur, whose story, exceedingly similar to other versions of the Grail legend, is collected in the Mabinogion under the name *Peredur, son of Efrawc*. This Peredur was either influenced by or himself influenced, in an unclear way, or came from the same shared source as, the better known grail quester Perceval, of Chretien de Troye's *Perceval, the Story of the Grail*. While the name *Peredur* is theorized to have its own etymology meaning "hard spear," we cannot ignore the similarity of the names Peredur and Pryderi. Whereas the Asvins in the Vedic tale end by being given the secret to attain the *soma* and are admitted among the gods, and as Aengus in his Irish tale drinks a drink of immortality at Goibniu's feast, the Welsh Pryderi in his myth places his hand on a golden bowl found in a mysterious fort and is taken to the Otherworld. The general structure of Pryderi's myth, as we have seen, is more similar to Samvarana's dalliance on the celestial mountain breast as his kingdom turns to a waste, yet the detail of accessing such a golden bowl does not appear in Samvarana's tale and is instead reminiscent of the Asvins' accessing of the *soma*, thus suggesting a colliding of these two overlapping tale types, which were probably originally seen as succeeding one another in the greater Lunar Cycle. Pryderi and Rhiannon, trapped by this golden bowl, must then be rescued by Manawydan. In the Arthurian lore, which seems a later elaboration of the theme, both the Mabon and a magical cauldron become objects of quest for King Arthur and Cei, and are said to reside in the "Otherworld" of Annwn.

Peredurus as Horse Twin

One significant clue to the identity of Peredur lies in an account by Geoffrey of Monmouth found in his pseudo-historical work *Historia Regum Britanniae*. This account contains the name of a certain King Peredurus, who appears among a sequence of brothers. Four brothers to Peredurus and one father are mentioned here, succeeding one another in kingship, and, based on our acquaintanceship with the oft-repeated pattern of the six incarnations of the gods of society, showing up as the Pandava brothers and their father in the *Mahabharata* and the primary heroes of the *Iliad* (Terrible Sovereign, Lawful Sovereign, Thunder and Wind gods, Horse Twins; see chapter: *The Heroes of the Iliad as Indo-European Gods*), as well as slightly more dispersed in the other mythologies, our suspicions should be alerted. For the Pandavas too were made up of five brothers and one father, and in descending order by age were: the incarnations of Varuna, Mitra, Vayu, Indra, and the two Horse Twins. Upon analysis this sequence of kings of the Britons appears more and more alike to the Pandava (and *Iliad*, etc.) template.

First is the father, Morvidus, who is ill-tempered but generous. His reign, like that of all the Terrible Sovereigns, is notable for its series of invasions or conquests, and Morvidus is said to have defeated invaders of his country, while Nuada defeated the Fir Bolg (who were not invaders). He was so bloody and terrible in his wrath that he personally killed every enemy captive after the battle, skinning and burning many, behavior consonant with the Varunian name "Terrible Sovereign." Eventually, Morvidus faced off against a dragon that appeared from the sea and began devouring his subjects. In single combat Morvidus fell and was eaten by this dragon, while Nuada was beheaded in the war with the Fomorians who may also have come from the under the sea. Morvidus' reign was succeeded by his son Gorbonianus, who is said to have ruled with justice and fair laws, and to have been frugal, upholding equity in his kingdom. This already seems almost a caricature of the Lawful Sovereign, Mitra, who we would expect to follow immediately after the Terrible Sovereign. But even more, Gorbonianus is said to have been very pious and to have frequently paid respects to the gods, even restoring many temples in his time. He reduced violence by giving gifts of gold and protection to soldiers and farmers. Again this seems to explicitly reflect the pious and Brahmin-like nature of the Mitra archetype – Yudhishthira, for one, depicted as an ascetic Brahmin who also brings justice and peace via victory in war. Perhaps even more similar is the Roman Mitraic incarnation Numa Pompilius (see: Dumezil, *Mitra-Varuna*), who lived a life of piety and to whom many religious institutions and reforms are attributed.

We would expect the following two brothers to then be alike to the two warrior gods, Indra and Vayu; however, at least one of the two is somewhat difficult to identify based on their exceedingly brief descriptions in this account. First is Archgallo, who is said to have been a cruel king desirous of demolishing the nobles. His focus is directly described as having been to reverse what his brother Gorbonianus had accomplished, and, in particular, to steal the wealth of the nobles. This sounds most like a description of the repeated conflict of the Indra archetype with the Mitra-Varuna archetype (whichever one takes the position of the Sovereign of Justice in a given version), that is, the Second Function's tension with the First Function. This would be the perennial theme of the warrior caste in conflict with the priestly and kingly class, chafing under the dictates of sovereign law, subject to their own warrior ethical codes that put them at odds with or outside of the norms of society, yet still remaining, uncomfortably, subject to the rule of the Sovereign and of the high Law. This conflict appears famously in the *Iliad* as that between Achilles and Agamemnon, and repeats in the *Mahabharata* with Arjuna being dishonored by Yudhishthira when the latter tells the former to give away his signature bow, symbolic of his warrior honor, prowess, and autonomy, because he has not up to that point succeeded in killing Karna. It repeats as well in the Irish conflict between the thunder god Tuireann's sons and Lugh. Compare also Roman Tullus Hostilius, who Dumezil saw as a stand-in for the warrior function gods, and who succeeds Numa Pompilius, but is a war king and believes his predecessor's pacifism had weakened the kingdom. Despite Archgallo's cruel agenda, his brother Elidurus supported him loyally and even forced dissenters to swear loyalty to Archgallo after they installed Elidurus as a replacement. Eventually Archgallo improved as a ruler and ruled peacefully, perhaps reflecting the positive light in which the Thunderer was still seen despite his perpetual conflict with the sovereign and priestly caste. On Archgallo's death, Elidurus succeeded him and ruled justly. Though it is hard to place any very specific parallel with regard to Elidurus, it can in fact be said that the second function god Vayu, seems to have been known for loyalty (evidenced in his incarnation Bhima and son Hanuman, exemplars of this virtue), which Elidurus more than anything embodies.

During Elidurus' reign, however, his two younger brothers, Ingenius[96] and the aforementioned Peredurus, are said to have teamed up and attacked him, winning the kingdom from him and trapping him in a tower. The two brothers then decide to split the kingdom of Britain in half, each one ruling simultaneously in their respective halves.

---

96 Ingenius is the name as found in certain manuscripts and used by translators Michael A. Faletra (2008), Lewis Thorpe (1977), and others. See below for a full discussion.

They are described as "his twain other brothers" who "shared the kingdom in twain" (Monmouth, *History of the Kings of Britain*, 3.13). The seeming close unity of these two youngest brothers, acting almost as one and then dividing the kingdom into two even halves, sharing "in twain," of course seems to be a reflection of the unity, to the point of identification, which we often see with regard to the Horse Twins. These gods are twins in both name and action, referred to simply by the unifying moniker "the Asvins" in Vedic myth, and frequently seem to be connected at the hip in their exploits.

To reiterate, we have first a terrible and bloodthirsty father king, followed by an eldest son who is a just and pious king who loves fair laws, followed by a king who is in conflict with the nobles who had aligned with the previous just sovereign, followed by one king whose main attribute is loyalty, followed by two fully united brother kings whose actions and division of the kingdom can be said to be twin-like, and who even team up to make war against their older brother in an action again reminiscent of the Aesir-Vanir War motif, when we consider that the older brothers and father would be stand-ins for the higher gods. Thus, if this sketchy but highly suggestive sequence of kings can be said to follow what we have seen elsewhere to be a widespread and ubiquitous pattern, a pattern deeply ingrained in ancient European myth and central to ancient European religion, then we can feel confident in identifying King Peredurus as a pseudo-historical stand-in for one of the Horse Twin gods. Already we have seen that Pryderi has been plausibly identified as one of these Twins without this added evidence, and more tentatively has been called an early form of the grail quester, whose name became Peredur in one tradition. The structural analysis of this passage of Monmouth suggests that this can be, if not verified, then strongly supported from a second angle. Here we have excavated the fact that Peredurus was likely to have been seen as one name of one of the Horse Twins. Thus we have strengthened the crucial supposition that Peredur, the grail quester, was, in his true identity, originally one of these Twins. And if Pryderi too can be confidently identified as a Horse Twin by the evidence we have previously laid out, then his identity with Peredur the grail quester is strengthened as well.

We must at the same time wonder at the name of the brother of Peredurus in this pseudo-historical account – Ingenius – so mysteriously reminiscent of Freyr's other name, Ing or Yngvi; reminiscent as well of the other coincidentally named Horse Twins from Ireland and Britain, Aengus and Hengist. It is very important to note that *Ingenius* itself is only one possible rendering of this figure's name. Due to the many different manuscripts of Monmouth's work, the name of this brother of Peredurus appears in several different forms. Of modern translators, two that reproduce the form *Ingenius* include Michael A. Faletra (2008) and Lewis Thorpe (1977). Faletra explains his manuscript source as follows:

Bern Burgerbibliothek MS 568, a manuscript of Norman provenance from the late twelfth, or perhaps very early thirteenth century, now thought to represent the best single text of Geoffrey of Monmouth's *Historia regum Britannie*. The Latin text has been edited by Neil Wright (Cambridge: D.S. Brewer, 1984). I have also consulted Acton Griscom's edition of the Cambridge MS (London: Longmans, 1929), as well as *The First Variant Version*, ed. Neil Wright (Cambridge: D.S. Brewer, 1988) and the printed Middle Welsh translation, *Brut Dingestow*, ed. Henry Lewis (Cardiff: U of Wales P, 1974). The present translation is the first to render the Bern MS in its entirety and thus the first to benefit from the monumental textual, archival, and bibliographical work done by Neil Wright and Julia Crick in the 1980s. (Faletra, 37)

Thorpe names his source as the aforementioned "Camb. Univ. Libr. MS 1706, as printed by Acton Griscom in 1929," and his translation, a Penguin edition, was the standard classroom version for a lengthy period. The Middle Welsh translation called the *Brut Tysilio* (14th or 15th C.) from the *Red Book of Hergest* translates the Latin name of its source version as *Owain*, while the manuscript of Brut Gruffyd ab Arthur gives *Iugeyn* (whose pronunciation is said to be indistinguishable from *Owain*), and the version which Rev. Peter Roberts in the introduction to his edition of the Brut Tysilio calls "from a manuscript belonging to Mr. Jones of Havod" has *Ywein*, and still other renderings exist. *Eugenius* is the Latin name that would usually be overlaid onto *Owain* to Latinize it[97], but this fact that can only partially explain the form *Ingenius*, if at all, as it is an imperfect fit. Just as possibly, *Ingenius* could have been the result of an attempt to assimilate a pre-existing name similar to *Ing* to a Latinized form reminiscent of *Eugenius*.

While this "Ingenius etc." is rendered into Middle Welsh as *Owain* in the medieval *Brut Tysilio* translation of the work, an Owain is himself identified with Mabon in the poem "A Rumor Has Come to Me From Calchvynyd" from the *Book of Taliesin* (see a similar case in Peniarth 147). In "The Three Blessed Womb-Fuls of the Island of Britain" from the *Welsh Triads*, Owein is again identified with the Mabon when his mother is said to be named Modron, who is usually the mother of "Mabon son of Modron": "Owein, son of Urien, and Morvyd his sister, who were in a single womb-load

---

97 "Eugenius stands forth again and again in the early roll of Scottish kings, but whether these sovereigns ever lived or not, their appellation was certainly not Eugenius, nor any corruption from it; but the Keltic Eoghan, Ewan, or Evan, still extremely common in the Highlands, and meaning a young warrior, though after the favourite custom of the Gael, Anglicised and Latinized by names of similar sound. The Welsh Owain or Ywain appears to have had the same fate" (Charlotte Yonge, *History of Christian Names,* 87) though she notes the latter case is less certain. Yonge also mentions the common etymology of Owain as "lamb" here, while elsewhere she calls this etymology erroneous (see footnote below).

in the womb of Modron daughter of Avallach" (Koch and Carey, *Celtic Heroic Age*, 356). Considering the above, along with the meaning of the name Owein, it seems highly likely that Owein was consciously used as a cover name for one of the Horse Twins in legendary or pseudo-historical material. In her *History of Christian Names* (1863), Charlotte Yonge explains that Owain and Owen likely come from the Irish name *Eoghan*, from *éoghunn*, meaning "a youth," or "young warrior," from *og*, "young," and *duine*, "man"[98]. If so, then Owain/Owen means "the young man," "the youth," and has in it the same word, *og,* that forms the nickname of Aengus *Og*, Aengus the Young. We have seen that this Aengus Og or *Macc Oc* is directly cognate to *Mabon*, thus there can be no accident when Owein is equated with the Mabon, the Young Son, in the instances listed above, just as there can be no accident when Owein is given as the Welsh form of name of Ingenius, brother of Peredurus, one of two closely paired brothers who function in their narrative like the Horse Twins of other branches. It is difficult at this point to claim that the seemingly singular gods, Irish Aengus and Welsh Pryderi, do not have corollaries who appear in their narrative as two twin-like brothers.

As the name of Ingenius aka Owein is so mysteriously reminiscent of Freyr's other name, Ing or Yngvi, as well as of Aengus Og, and even of Hengist, consider also the equally startling coincidence of the proposed Proto-Germanic form of Ingvi-Freyr's name, *Inguz*, with *Aengus*, despite divergent proposed etymologies of each. However, if we begin with the mythic parallel between Freyr and Aengus, then these gods would have descended from a shared root deity. If so, then they should come at one point from a shared name as well. If we then reject the admittedly speculative but popular etymology of Aengus/Oengus as "one strength"[99] (from *óen* and *gus*), which is seemingly meaningless in relation to Aengus' mythos, we can propose instead that Aengus originally derived from the Proto-Celtic descendant of the same root from which *Inguz* derives. The root of *Inguz* ("mortal, man") is PIE *nek* ("dead, mortal"), and this descends into the Proto-Celtic form: *Ankus*. *Ankus*, incidentally, also becomes, in Middle Welsh, *angheu*, demonstrating that the *nk* of the Proto-Celtic form can indeed soften to *ng,* as the *k* of the PIE root also softened to *ng* in the Proto-Germanic *Inguz*. The question remains whether this could have happened in Irish as well. The answer is yes, with a serious caveat. We can see that *Ankus* descended into both Irish *éag* and

---

98 "Owain is so like the word *oen* that in Welsh stands for a sheep or lamb, that it is generally so translated; but it is most likely that this is a case of an adaptation of a derivative from an obsolete word to a familiar one, and that Owen ought to be carried much further back to the same source as the Erse Eoghan which comes from *éoghunn*, youth, from *og*, young, and *duine*, man, and is translated, young warrior" (Yonge, 140-141).

99 eDil is tentative about this etymology, proposing "compd. of **óen**? for second syll. *cf.* Fergus". Electronic Dictionary of the Irish Language. http://dil.ie/33532.

Scottish Gaelic *eug*. However, the Old Irish form from which these derive is *éc* which apparently retained the hard *c*. On the other hand, we have already seen how Aengus' nickname *Og* can also appear as *Occ*, indicating a relatively fluid variability between *g* and *c* in certain instances. This interchange between *g* and *c* is facilitated even more by the digraph *nk* which has a greater tendency on its own to soften to *ng*.

If we speculate *Ankus* to have a range of meanings similar to the PIE and Germanic forms, then it would mean something like "dead, mortal, or man." The meaning of *Aengus Og* would then be "the young man," with his mortality being a possible underlying layer of meaning as well. This would be somewhat fitting, as Aengus, like the Asvins, must drink the drink of immortality at the feast of the gods in order to overcome his apparently mortal condition. In the Scottish version we have mentioned, Aengus is trapped in rocks as a punishment for attempting to take over the universe, perhaps echoing the death of Pryderi after his war against the high gods, or the death of Castor, who is known as the mortal of the two Dioskouroi. The meaning of "young man" incidentally would make *Aengus Og* an exact cognate of the Welsh Horse Twin cover name, *Owein*, which we have seen means "the young man/warrior," from a different root word. We would have Ankus Og vs Og duine (Owein), *ankus* and *duine* simply being two different words meaning the same thing, "a man (or mortal)," and *og* being the same word in each, meaning "young." The names would be precise cognates, synonyms. As such we would be able to understand more clearly why Ingenius is translated as Owein in the Welsh version of Monmouth's text. Ingenius would have been a latinization of a previous version of a name something like Ing/Ang, deriving from *Nekus*, via an intermediate form between *Ankus* and Middle Welsh *angheu* if not as a borrowing from Germanic *Inguz*. Of course, the name beneath *Ingenius* could have originally been the name *Owein* itself, which was then put into a bizarre latin form. However, the uniqueness of the latin form *Ingenius* forces us to put this possibility aside for now. Thus this pre-latinized form of Ingenius would have meant "the man," with the idea that he was also *og*, "young," either being attached to him as a surname or nickname, as with Aengus, or being so well known that it was left unspoken. We do see that Ingenius is one of the two youngest, twin-like sons of Morvidus. This *Ingenius* is then properly translated by the cognate name *Owein*, as we find in the *Brut Tysilio*, this *Owein* also meaning "Young Man," just as *Owein* is a precise cognate of *Aengus Og* on the other side. Taking *Ankus* as the Proto-Celtic form of *Aengus*, the Proto-Celtic form of *Aengus Og* would then be *Ankus Yowankos* – sonorous indeed. And in *Yowankos* we also see a pre-echo of *Eoghan*. The same pattern could have more speculatively once attached to the Germanic form, giving something like *Ingvi Ungr* ("The Young Man"), Old Norse *Ungr* coming from the same root as Irish *Og*, with the nickname *Ungr* dropping away over time. Such a nickname could also have been a Celtic innovation, and the youth of *Ingvi* could have simply been so well known that it was always left unsaid by the

Germanics. Notably, when Tacitus describes one instance of the Germanic Horse Twins that he comes across, who he calls the Alcis[100], worshipped by the Naharvali tribe, the specific phrase he chooses to describe them is "young men" or "youths" (Tacitus, *Germania*, Ch. 43).[101]

The close mythic parallels of Aengus and Ingvi Freyr make a derivation of Aengus from *Ankus* appear tantalizingly necessary. However, such a derivation is by no means a simple problem. Even if a softening of *k* to *g* exists as a possibility, it is not directly traceable in relation to this specific shift from *Ankus* to *Aengus*. Even more troubling, the most common form in the oldest attestations for the Irish god's name is *Oingus*, usually becoming *Oengus* in Middle Irish, and *Aengus* appearing in, for instance, the Middle Irish and Early Modern Irish manuscript Laud 610.[102] This form, *Oingus* or *Oengus,* is then what suggests to many linguists a derivation from *óen,* though an accent over the *o* is generally absent in the early attestations of *Oingus/Oengus*, and the etymology remains uncertain. Though it seems to us that a change from *An* to *Oin* is plausible based on the difficulties of Irish vowel orthography alone, as J.R.R. Tolkien similarly remarked in relation to vowels in the name of *Nodens* appearing variously as *Noudont, Nudenti, Nodenti,* and *Nuada,* among other forms,[103] if this vowel difference seems insurmountable for the present derivation then one other possibility may be proposed. As Yonge, in our footnote above, explains that erroneously deriving *Owein* from *oen* is "a case of an adaptation of a derivative from an obsolete word to a familiar one," something very similar could have happened in the case of *Ankus*, if another speculation is allowed us. In this hypothesis, the sacred name *Ankus,* or some derivative form of it, would have been kept relatively unchanged for many centuries, out of respect

---

100   Though Gemanic rather than Celtic, *Alcis* almost seems an echo of *Ankus* with a shift from *n* to *l*.

101   "[...] they are certainly worshipped as young men and as brothers" (Tacitus, *Germania*, Ch. 43).

102   Bodleian Laud Misc. MS 610 or The Book of the White Earl in the Book of Pottlerath. Introduction to "The Martyrology of Oengus". Also in the 9th-12th c. *Tripartite Life of Saint Patrick (112.6)* and the *Annals of Ulster*, among others.

103   "The variation o/u is probably due to divergent attempts at representing in Latin letters a non-Latin sound; the variation ont/ent is probably due to (correct) equation of Keltic -ont with Latin participial -ent [...] Native Keltic words had no ö. Already in the very distant period common to all branches of that group of languages ö had become ä in stem-syllables, and ü at the end of words. The three older diphthongs, au (Latin au), eu, and ou (both old Latin ou, later ü), had, however, coalesced in some common sound which may be represented ou. This sound in British approached ö, and was equated with Latin ö in the British pronunciation of Latin and vice versa; so that o would be a natural early choice of symbol (Tolkien, "The Name 'Nodens'", 177). The case of vowels referred to by Tolkien is obviously very different from the present case. However, a general cautionary lesson may be taken from the example.

for the sanctity of the name. In the intervening centuries, perhaps a millennia, the original root word, and indeed the whole language, would have changed to be unrecognizable in respect to the earlier form. We know that a direct descendant of *Ankus* became Old Irish *éc,* and this, so different from *Ankus*, would have rendered *Ankus* unintelligible in meaning. Therefore, having forgotten the original meaning of the name *Ankus* by the medieval period or before, *Ankus,* whether the *nk* had softened to *ng* yet on its own or not, would at some point have been etymologically reinterpreted in terms of the contemporary language and names, or gradually assimilated to a word or name more familiar to the people of the time, ending up in the form *Oingus* or *Aengus*. This may be asking for a special case, but Yonge demonstrates that a very similar "adaptation of a derivative from an obsolete word to a familiar one" does in fact occur, while all of the mythic connections between the gods Aengus and Ingvi warrant such speculative net-casting. Divine names *are* special cases after all, and a pattern of great conservativeness toward their archaic form, followed by forgetting, and then adaptation to the familiar language, would be suitable given the religious context of how such names are treated. This is only one hypothetical way in which *Aengus* could have come from *Ankus* by an irregular path, of which others are imaginable. A borrowing from an Old Welsh form might also be considered. The surname *Ankus* actually exists in Scotland, apparently as a derivative of *Aengus/Angus*, demonstrating that passage between these forms is possible, if here in the reverse. While we are opening the question to speculation we should also note the possibility that *Oingus* could also have been a holy name for this god retained from the pre-Celtic Bell Beaker language of archaic Ireland, a name which then had to be adapted to the Celtic language which appears to have arrived to Ireland via some sort of influence rather than via population replacement. If *Oingus* is a remnant of a pre-Celtic name for what would be essentially the same god, it could explain it being close yet dissimilar to the forms of the Germanic and Celtic root words, considering that the pre-Celtic Bell Beaker language is likely to have been somehow related to Proto-Germanic. So much for poking and prodding. These hypotheticals prove unnecessary if a direct derivation of *Oingus* from *Ankus* can be explained, and ultimately the weight of mythic evidence leaves the observer in awe at the great coincidence of names, at how Aengus and Ingvi could be mythically the same gods, but that, despite Middle Welsh even having the attested *angheu*, deriving from *Ankus*, *Aengus* would somehow not derive from *Ankus,* coming from the same root as *Ingvi*, which derivation would give his name the mythically appropriate meaning of "Young Man(/Mortal)," thereby also perfectly matching his Welsh parallel Owein/Ingenius.

For the question of why the quintessential Third Function gods, Aengus, Pryderi and Ingvi, are prominently the "Young Men" or "Young Sons," we note that English and Irish specifically link the lower class or third station to terms meaning "young man": "In

Irish too, *óc,* 'young man' could also mean 'a warrior'[…] and *óc-aire* 'the lowest grade of freeman of full age and status'[…] among the various meanings of the English word *yeoman* ('young man') one finds 'a servant', 'an attendant in a royal or noble household', 'a freeholder under the rank of gentleman', 'a freeholder […] serving as a foot-soldier', and (in the plural) 'pawns at chess' (Alwyn and Brinley Rees, 62-63). As we will shortly see, these terms perfectly describe the Grail Quester, who, though he begins as a young boy from the country with armor made of grass and rags, rises to become the exemplar of Arthur's knights. As Rees and Rees explain apropos of this, "[…] the earliest meanings of the English word *knight* are 'boy' 'youth' 'military servant'—and that the knight of the shire is the traditional representative of the Commons, the third estate" (Rees, 72). We can also see that the Irish name *Eoghan,* which, as we have said, is the same as the *Owein* of the Welsh legends, also appears in the Irish legends as a stand-in for the Third Function. In the legendary division of Ireland we are told that Conn (meaning "head" or "chief") takes the northern half of Ireland, while Mug takes the southern. Mug is also known as Eoghan and is the ancestor of the Eoghanacta clan.[104] Mug/Eoghan is known for specific Third Function traits, specifically being connected with peace and the storing of abundant food, in contrast with the First and Second Function traits of Conn the Chief: "Eoghan transcended Conn, not in number of battles and conflicts—More plenteous the food of adventurous Eoghan was being distributed according to the laws of peace" (Keating, Dinneen, *History of Ireland, II., 265*). *Mug,* meanwhile, means "servant," thus once again indicating his Third Function role and repeating the association of his alternate name Eoghan/"Young Man" with the Third Estate or Third Function. Mug/Eoghan also fights a war against the First Function king Conn, repeating the pattern of all the Third Function representatives we have seen. Mug is killed as a result, matching the fates of Pryderi, Titus Tatius, and coming close to that of the Scottish Aengus, who is trapped in rocks as punishment for his attempt at ruling the universe. Mug/Eoghan is a king of the South challenging the king of the North, just as Pryderi, a king of the Southwestern kingdom Dyfed, challenges Gwydion and Math, kings of the Northern kingdom Gwynedd, and Rees and Rees emphasize the importance of this geographic positioning in relation to the Functions.

The identity of the name *Eoghan* as the Third Function stand-in is further confirmed by Mug's grandson, who is a nominal double of Mug, named Eoghan Mor. While Welsh Pryderi is son of Rhiannon and Pwyll, born after Pwyll chases Rhiannon on his horse and finally catches her, Eoghan Mor is son of Ailill Aulom and Aine (Patricia Monaghan, *The Encyclopedia of Celtic Mythology and Folklore*, "Aine", 11), parallel of Rhiannon. Eoghan's father parallels Pwyll in the role of "he who *catches* (but in this

---

104   O'Rahilly, *Eearly Irish History and Mythology* chapter 10 and p. 282, E. MacNeill, *Celtic Ireland,* 61.

case *rapes*[105]) and mates with the sun-horse goddess," which also parallels Poseidon Hippios raping Demeter in horse form and perhaps Idunn being abducted by Thjazi. We will discuss the Greek form further along. Thus an Eoghan once again has a significant parallel with Pryderi, reinforcing the idea that Eoghan was a name connected to the same mythos, able to be used as a stand in for the Third Function Young Son Horse Twin god (especially in pseudo-historical or seemingly late material).

A further example connecting Owain and Pryderi may be found in the *Mabinogion* romance titled *Owain, or the Lady of the Fountain*.[106] In this tale, Owain goes to a mystical fountain with a bowl on a marble slab beside it, the bowl being attached by a chain of silver, as Pryderi in his tale similarly goes to a mystical fort in which, beside a fountain, he finds a bowl on a marble slab hung by chains. Filling the bowl and pouring the water onto the slab triggers a peal of thunder and a violent hailstorm in Owain's case, after which the tree nearby becomes bare and the sky then becomes clear. He then has to fight the Black Knight of the Fountain, which he does, defeating him and eventually taking his place and his wife, becoming himself the Knight of the Fountain. In Pryderi's case, the land is already an enchanted wasteland, caused when he and his companions had sat on Gorsedd Arberth and following a similar sequence: a peal of thunder, a mist with the violence of a thunderstorm, and then light all around, after which the region was in an enchanted desolation. This state then leads on to Pryderi's encounter with the bowl and the fountain in that tale. Manawydan must then outwit a hostile sorcerer to break the enchantment. The remaining portions of the two tales are generally dissimilar and we cannot say anything certain with regard to this parallel, but it seems like what we are seeing here is that the names of both of the twin-like brothers, Owain and Peredurus, appear in tales that parallel specific details of Pryderi's myth, elaborated into medieval romances, with Pryderi in his version appearing singly. It is almost as if Pryderi represents in himself both of the divinities that underly Owain and Peredurus, as if they have been simplified to the single figure Pryderi in that tradition, while being simplified to Owain in the aforesaid romance. This would be explicable if we consider that the original mythos of the brothers may have been like that of other Horse Twins, a more or less single narrative, the two brothers more or less connected at the hip. Then we can see Pryderi and Owain as two versions splitting from that original form, one version using the name of one brother as a unitary stand-in for the twins, the other version using the name of the other, both names being acceptable stand-ins for the original pair.

---

105 However, according to O'Hogain, 2006, earlier versions of the story may have excluded the hostility of their partnership, thus bringing the tale closer to the form of the Welsh and Indian myths, in which Pwyll/Samvarana catches up to and is welcomed by Rhiannon/Tapati. We discuss the possible reason for the rape motif as a variant of this tale later on.

106 As Gwilym Morus-Baird has previously pointed out.

A second proposed Proto-Germanic form of Ingvi is *Unguz*, while we find the names Ungust/Ungus in the lineages of Pictish Kings (Ungus, King of the Picts, 735?-834), and "the founder of St Andrews (Kilriemont) is called Hungus" (Robert Maclagan, *The Perth Incident*, 182) which compares closely with Hengist. However, we must stress that *Hengist* comes from a different root than **Inguz/*Ankus. Hengist* ("stallion") comes from Proto-Germanic **hangistaz,* from PIE **kankest.* Each of these forms does contain in it a curious echo of the **Inguz/*Ankus* root, however: **hangistaz* containing *angis,* **kankest* containing *ankes.* Unless Aengus derived very anciently from a malformation of *kankest,* which of course is not our claim, what this suggests is that the parallelism of these words meaning "man" and "horse" were present to the minds of ancient people and held their parallelism through the centuries, with linked and rhyming forms that remained ripe for wordplay, and this potential for interplay may have gone back to the formation of these divine names, as an acknowledged layer of their meanings. Within Old English, *Hengist* still echoes Irish *Aengus*, and vice versa, even if the root words are not at all the same and they come from different linguistic branches. Aengus mythically *is* Hengist, as man has an esoteric mirror in the horse he rides. A famous Old Norse formula found in the sagas says "the horse is man's fylgja [*Marr er manns fylgja*]."[107]

Having described this web of connections linking Peredurus and his parallels to the Horse Twins, we must examine how this Peredurus points the way toward the hero of the Grail Quest. Now Peredur (as opposed to Peredurus) is the central character of a late 12th century romance, *Peredur son of Efrawg*, telling the same story as Chretien de Troye's *Perceval*, but with a few notable differences. One of these differences is the absence of the grail itself, in its place a salver with a severed head on it. Due to the closeness of the romances of *Peredur* and *Perceval* in terms of their narrative details, scholars have sought to understand the relationship of the names of the respective heroes, Peredur and Perceval. Perceval, meaning "pierce the vale" is a difficult one to connect to Peredur "hard spear," though each name does denote something relating to piercing, in one fashion or another. Some scholars have suggested, due to the supposed dates of composition, that Peredur was an approximation of the name Percival in the Welsh language, though it is quite possible that the direction of influence could have been reversed – in any case, they could both come from other earlier shared sources. Jeffrey Gantz believed in such a general reversal of priority if not influence, saying, "inasmuch as Crestiens admits that Perceval is a Welshman, and inasmuch as the name Perceval means little, it seems likely that the name Peredur is the more original form of the hero's name. Peredur moreover looks suspiciously like Pryderi" (Gantz, *Mabinogion*, *Introduction*). He further points out two key connections, one between Pryderi and Peredur and one between Pryderi and Perceval. Pryderi is said to be accompanied by a

---

107   *Vatnsdaela Saga*, 42.

companion named Gwgri in the *Mabinogion* tale "Math fab Mathonwy." The Peredur found in Welsh history, cited as living in the fifth century, had a companion of the same name, Gwgri. Of the same opinion, Roger Sherman Loomis explains that

> The Annales Cambriae record the death of Peredur and Gwgri in the same year, 580. Of this tradition the Mabinogi of Math seems to afford a vague reminiscence. Gwydion overcoming Pryderi in battle, then Pryderi giving hostages Gwgri Gwastra and 23 others, sons and nobles. The hostages were set free to follow the men of the South. It cannot be without significance that a Gwgri should be closely associated with the deaths of both Peredur and Pryderi. (Loomis, *Celtic Myth and Arthurian Romance*)

Gantz then compares the parallel personalities of Pryderi and Perceval as both being "naive" and "freewheeling...prone to serious errors in judgment," concluding boldly that "Perhaps at an earlier stage Pryderi-Peredurus was both the focal point of the Four Branches and the central figure in the first Grail narratives" (Gantz, *Mabinogion*, 1976). Clearly, there is a well-established case for the continuity of the figures Pryderi, Peredurus, Peredur, and Perceval, and hence a strong foundation for a case that the original grail quester was based on the Horse Twin god.

* * *

Welsh Myth and The Story of the Grail

The encounter of Pryderi with the golden bowl in the mysterious fort is itself reminiscent of the grail encounter in several ways. The fort seemed to appear where there had previously been no fort, a feature common to the mystical castles of the grail legends. Pryderi finds in the fort a marble fountain and a golden bowl suspended by chains in the air. When he touches the bowl, his speech and movement are frozen. This episode follows the "wasteland" enchantment of the land in which all the people and domestic animals vanish, and during which the fields which Manawydan and Cigfa sow are repeatedly destroyed, and after Pryderi has married his shining bride and Manawydan has married Pryderi's now widowed mother Rhiannon. This enchantment comes as a result of Pryderi occupying the sacred mound Gorsedd Arberth, but apparently being found unworthy by it. As commentator Mike Ashley tallies the correspondences of this

236

narrative to that of the grail legend: the enchanted land where crops are destroyed matches the Fisher King's wasteland; the mysterious fort matches the mysterious grail castle; the golden bowl of course is like the grail, which in its earliest form is a serving dish rather than a cup; and the sacred mound Gorsedd Arberth, which judges you and finds you worthy or unworthy, is like the seat known in the grail legends as the Siege Perilous, which has the same power of judgment (Ashley, *The Mammoth Book of King Arthur*, 414).

The Grail King

The true, divine identity of the Grail King or Fisher King himself, then, is perhaps the most contentious detail of the comparison. A popular theory forwarded by John Rhys states that just as Peredur is the similarly named Pryderi, so the Grail King Pelles/Pellam is the similarly named Pwyll, father of Pryderi. This is quite an attractive theory considering the closeness of the names, the fact that Pwyll has the paternal role in the narrative in relation to Pryderi, that we have seen taken elsewhere by Chyavana and Njörðr, and most importantly the fact that Pwyll becomes the stand-in lord of Annwn, the Welsh Otherworld, at the beginning of the tale Pwyll, prince of Dyfed, and as such would be lord over the cauldron that is later said to be kept there, that cauldron which Arthur quests for in the *Preiddeu Annwn* and which is associated with the Mabon. However, as we have seen, the myth of Pwyll corresponds extremely closely to that of Samvarana rather than to that of Chyavana, and thus mythically we have connected him to the Gandharva of the *Rig Veda* rather than to Soma. Furthermore, Pwyll is already dead by the time of Pryderi and Rhiannon's otherworld abduction (not that this would need to affect a chief of the Otherworld). But due to the evidence of a weaving of the Pryderi-Horse Twin myth and the Pwyll-Gandharva myth into one continuous narrative (which appears as the two branches of the *Mabinogi, Pwyll, prince of Dyfed*, and *Manawydan, son of Llyr*), Pwyll and Pryderi each taking half of the same myth which in the Indian version is carried solely by Samvarana, we can deduce that certain elements of the Lunar Cycle were already being compressed into one tale within the Welsh tradition. It is possible, then, that as a gandharva, who were known as guardians of the *soma*, and having acquired a shared lordship of the Otherworld realm where the cauldron is kept (these perhaps being the same thing), Pwyll could have, in the Welsh tradition, taken on a more central role in relation to the liquid of immortality.

On the other hand, Robert de Boron's later version of the Fisher King is named Bron, generally equated by commentators to the similarly named Bran the Blessed. Bran takes a mortal wound to the leg just as Bron has an incapacitating wound to the thigh. However, the earliest grail legend, as found in Chretien's *Perceval*, features a head presented on a silver platter at the mysterious grail castle. The procession which presents this platter is overseen by the ailing Grail King/Fisher King. But it is Bran himself who in Welsh myth is beheaded and has his sacred head magically preserved, the head having the power to stop the aging of those who accompany it and the power to oversee and defend Britain from invasion. This then would suggest that the original Grail King was not this Bran, but instead was the keeper of his head as a relic or ritual object. Perhaps we can say Bran is present along with the other Grail King. This confusion seems to come from the fact that there were so many different lords of the underworld in Indo-European myth, each with distinct roles in that realm. Over time these distinct gods became more and more conflated and confused as the religion was forgotten. Many of the gods would have been present at the high sacrifice in leading roles, if we take the Vedic case as evidence. As we will see, Bran likely occupies an underworld role paralleling either the mythos of the Vedic Yama, whereas the "Soma" and "Gandharva"-type gods are the more central figures in the Grail mythos, with the severed head marking a notable third divine presence.

If we take instead Soma, seen to be identical to the Norse Njörðr, as either the Grail King or the higher deity who is master of that king (with the king being only the grail's guardian, just as the Gandharva is guardian of the *soma*) then we perhaps find a better explanation for why the king is portrayed as a fisher. The name "Fisher King" comes from the fact that Perceval stumbles upon the mysterious king while he is fishing and is then invited to stay at his castle. We find out later that this king's father is sustained by a single wafer of communion contained in the Grail, but also that the Fisher King himself is wounded and unable to leave his bed except to fish. Thus there are in fact *two* kings in fragile state in this castle, perhaps the younger having the role of guardian of the Grail corresponding to the role of the Gandharva and the other being a higher ruling divinity in line with the god Soma. But the act of fishing itself also connects directly to the examples of the Soma archetype we have encountered thus far. Njörðr, for instance, is explicitly lord over the wealth of the sea – that is, fish. Midir has a 5-pronged fork, which were very common eeling and fishing implements in Ireland. There are only a few other things a medieval Fisher King could wield in that activity to mark him as a fisher. Additionally, Chyavana, when first encountered in the *Mahabharata* version, is said to have begun "to practice austerities by the side of yonder lake" (*Mahabharata, Vana Parva* p. 259), while the Fisher King is encountered fishing in a lake. The Gandharva, in addition, is the *soma* when poured into the waters. Finally, we could consider the moon itself, pictured hanging above its ocean domain, as taking the part of a fisher there, both of the fish in the waters of this domain and crucially of souls, as the moon was believed to draw the souls of the dead to it for reincarnation in Vedic cosmogony. On the common understanding of the moon as a primary afterlife destination, Mircea Eliade says,

> This journey to the moon after death was also preserved in highly developed cultures (India, Greece, Iran), but some thing else was added. To the Indians, it is the 'path of the manes' (pitryāna), and souls reposed in the moon while awaiting reincarnation, whereas the sun road or 'path of the gods' (devayāna) was taken by the initiated, or those set free from the illusions of ignorance [...] the Elysian Fields, where heroes and Caesars went after death, were in the moon [...] Everywhere in Europe the half-moon is to be found as a funeral symbol [...] in Gaul for instance, the moon was a local symbol in use long before any contact with the Romans. (Eliade, *Patterns in Comparative Religion*, 172, 174)

A large amount of the confusion regarding the identity of the Grail and Fisher Kings comes from the fact that we have not yet been able to identify the Welsh Moon God "Soma" himself within the Welsh myths. However, due to the fact that we have been able to fit so many of the other Welsh gods into their parallels within the Lunar Cycle, we should look to the one possibly relevant portion of the Welsh cycle that we have so far ignored. This is the opening section of the main Four Branches of the *Mabinogi,* the very first episode of *Pwyll, prince of Dyfed*, which immediately precedes Pwyll seeing Rhiannon for the first time on her magical horse. In this episode, Pwyll, while hunting, encounters a pack of hounds chasing and then killing a stag. He then drives the hounds away from the dead stag to let his own hounds eat. Arawn arrives at the scene and declares that he has been affronted by the driving away of his hounds, and says that the only recompense he will take for it is that Pwyll must exchange places with him and become lord of Arawn's underworld kingdom, Annwn, for a year and a day, and must slay Arawn's hostile neighbor Hafgan at the end of the term. During this time, Pwyll will have the semblance of Arawn and will sleep in bed next to Arawn's wife. During the whole year and a day, Pwyll does not make love to the wife of Arawn. We read that every night, "The moment they got into the bed, he turned his face to the side, with his back towards her. From then until the next day, he did not say a single word to her" (*Pwyll, prince of Dyfed*).

If there have been any doubts about the identification of Pwyll with the Gandharva, perhaps due to his lacking clear musical associations in the existing myths, this scene should help dispel those doubts. For, as Grassman puts it, the Gandharva is known as "the guardian of virginity," and this is the specific role he plays in the crucial sequence of husbands listed in the "Surya's Bridal" hymn. Ralph Griffith cites Grassman on this score in his famous Veda translation:

> As the typical bride Surya was first married to Soma, so the young maid originally belongs to him, then to the Gandharva, as the guardian of virginity, then to Agni as the sacred fire round which she walks in the marriage ceremony, and fourthly to her human husband. (Grassman, Griffith, *The Rig Veda*)

This, as we have seen, is likely the key to the meaning of the entire series of husbands found in the Lunar Cycle myths of the various branches, but its details are even more specifically illustrated in the case of Welsh Pwyll. There is a passage in the ancient *Grihya Sutra of Apastamba* that lays out exactly the rites and actions a newly-wed couple is supposed to take, which are drawn specifically from the "Surya's Bridal" hymn, which is seen as the prototype of all human marriages.[108] Upon coming home from their wedding to their home for the first time, the couple are expected to observe a period of chastity, during which they are to place a staff between them while they sleep. And, as Narayan Aiyangar explains, this staff is called a Gandharva-samit, and is believed to have within it the spirit of the Gandharva Visvavasu, the very same chief Gandharva we have spoken of previously, who is named in the "Surya's Bridal" hymn. This period of chastity can last anywhere from three nights to a maximum of a full year, just as Pwyll's tenure is one year long, plus a day. Thus it appears that Pwyll, in this myth, is enacting this exact ancient role of the Gandharva as preserver of virginity, lying chastely in bed with the bride for one year just as the Gandharva-samit staff does in the ancient marriage rite. When removing the Gandharva-samit, the couple must even recite a verse taken directly from the "Surya's Bridal" hymn, verse 21-22, telling the Gandharva Visvavasu to leave the bride and "seek in her father's home another fair one" (which Pwyll essentially does himself by subsequently wedding Rhiannon), one of the key verses we have discussed in relation to the myths in an earlier part. At the

---

108   Cheryl Steets notes that "'v. 14 [of RV 10.85] mentions the story of them arriving at the wedding, apparently sent as proxy wooers on behalf of Soma, and asking the gods for Surya for themselves, and says that the gods granted this, in reference to another version (as mentioned above) in which they become her husbands. Though this might seem an unexplainable feature in a hymn purporting, on the surface, to celebrate Surya's wedding to their competitor, Soma, their continued presence becomes clear in light of the ritual nature of this text and the Indo-European background of the myth" (Steets, "The Sun Maiden's Wedding," 158). She further explains the Indian use of the hymn as a prototype of marriage rites: "the Indic use of the myth of Surya's wedding as a prototype for the Indic wedding ceremony may explain the large collection of Latvian songs celebrating the mythic wedding of the "Daughter of the Sun"; Mannhardt and Schroeder speculated, probably correctly, that the songs served as the basis for Latvian wedding ritual, much like their Indian counterpart; there is also Slavic evidence for similar practices and some conjecture regarding a Greek parallel" (Steets, 153; Piprek, Slawische Brautwerbungs- und Hochzeitsgebrauche (Stuttgart: Strecker & Schroder. 1914).66; Krauss. Sine und Brauch der Sudslaven, Vienna (1885) 351).

conclusion of the year in Annwn, Pwyll slays Hafgan. For these deeds, Arawn and Pwyll declare their friendship, unite their kingdoms, and Pwyll is thenceforth known as Chief of Annwn.

Although this form of the "Marriage of Soma" story seems in certain ways to be the furthest of all from the other examples we have thus far analyzed, the role of Pwyll detailed above gives us very good reason to speculate that Arawn would be the moon god "Soma." Most obviously, Soma is the one main missing deity from the larger Welsh cycle we have analyzed, and thus if Arawn were Soma it would complete the set of parallels. Arawn is also already married at the start of the series of Welsh myths, making his marriage the first in the sequence chronologically as Soma's is in the Vedic Hymn. We also see from the Vedic case that Soma is known as the teacher of the chief Gandharva, who becomes a stand-in and guardian for Soma (the *soma* poured in the waters *becomes* the Gandharva of the Waters, as in RV 9.86.36), just as Pwyll becomes a stand-in for Arawn and shares his title and kingdom. The fact that the moon was often seen as one of the primary afterlife destinations, where souls go to be renewed before reincarnating, could then explain why Arawn is the lord of the "underworld"/Otherworld of Annwn (which in the Welsh conception was not necessarily spatially "under" at all). This very Otherworld domain of Arawn's also is where the great magical cauldron, sought by Arthur, is said to be stored, which cooks food though only for the brave. The swine that Pryderi trades to Gwydion, which are explicitly symbols of fertility and general third function powers (swineherds as a symbol of the activity of the pastoralist class, swine as a form of wealth, and seen as promoting fertility of the fields due to their rooting and fertilizing activity) originate in Annwn, as gifts from Arawn. It is said of Arawn's court that "of all the Courts upon the earth, behold this was the best supplied with food and drink, and vessels of gold and royal jewels" (*Pwyll, prince of Dyfed*). Thus, these details would match, for instance, Njörðr seen as the origin of fecundating powers of land and sea that bring wealth, and his common description as "wealthy." Finally, the physical description of Arawn could also imply a lunar role. He is said to appear at first "upon a large light-grey steed, with a hunting horn round his neck, and clad in garments of grey woolen in the fashion of a hunting garb," the light grey color of steed and horse, as well as the hunting horn (a crescent shape), possibly being lunar symbolism, and his hounds also being the lunar color white, with red ears (*Pwyll, prince of Dyfed*). Recall, the animals wagered by Irish Soma god Midir: grey horses with red heads and cows with red ears. Of the fight between Hafgan and Pwyll (disguised as Arawn) it is said, "Each claimeth of the other his land and territory," which, while a broad and general statement, would accord with the idea that this is a fight between a Moon God and a hostile aspect of the Sun God – Hafgan indeed means "summer-bright" and in his structural role equates to the hostile and solar Thjazi – just as moon and sun seem to battle for lordship of the sky at the borders of night and day, or the waters of the moon (rain) with the drought of summer on another level. While Hafgan desires Arawn's lands rather than a golden object of regeneration as Thjazi does, it is true that he too is in possession of some kind of magical regenerating ability, perhaps similar to the power of the Norse golden apples, and the power of which Pwyll finally nullifies by striking him once with his sword and not more.

If we need more proof that Irish Midir and Welsh Arawn are the same god, Midir himself is frequently interpreted as an underworld lord due in part to his depiction with three cranes, likely symbols of death, who guard his castle and can steal the will to fight from any warrior. Midir's interpretation as an Irish Lord of the Underworld has been popular at least since John Rhys' *Hibbert Lectures* (p. 333 &c.) of 1886. Midir is also known to have a cauldron, which is one of the treasures of the Tuatha De Danann, and it is stolen by Cuchulainn. The Welsh underworld (or Otherworld) Annwn, whose lord is Arawn, is also said to be guarded specifically by three cranes, and the cauldron of Annwn that is sought by Arthur would then align with the cauldron of Midir taken by Cuchulainn.

Thus, if, despite its altered form, we are satisfied with the identification of Arawn with the Soma Moon God, then we have completed the picture of the Welsh Lunar Cycle. The simple explanation of Arawn's sparse depiction in the *Mabinogi* is that his marriage myth is simply not extant in the Welsh corpus and has already occurred when The Four Branches begin, whereas it would have been alike to the myth of Midir's wooing of Etain, for instance. Furthermore, Arawn and Pwyll as co-chiefs of Annwn would nicely match the fact that there are two ailing kings of the Grail castle. If the parallel is accepted, then the younger king, who is known to go fishing, and who is called Pelles, would indeed be Pwyll, the Gandharva, the guardian of the *soma*, who is also united in his essence with Arawn, as a stand-in and protege. The elder grail king would be this Arawn, or "Soma," the actual master and overseer of the grail/*soma* and the castle in which it is found, though the two, as we see in the myth of Pwyll and Arawn, have combined kingdoms and become essentially interchangeable. The presence of Bran as another central lord of the otherworld would be felt in the severed head and in the name attached, by later writers, to the grail king. The separate otherworld lords gradually are becoming confused when this occurs, but Bran's presence was certainly there from the start, and it is unlikely that the legendary grail cycles are making perfectly clear the full array of underworld gods that would originally have been present at the ritual of the sacred liquid.

The detail of the virginity-preserving Gandharva staff, in particular, makes it seem that the episode between Pwyll and Arawn, rather than being a late malformation of the Lunar Cycle, appearing in a relatively late manuscript (12th-14th Century) as it does, actually has claim to the preservation of some of the most archaic details of all the

242

versions we have examined. Indeed, if the series of husbands found in the myths are supposed to mirror those found in the ideal marriage rites of the "Surya's Bridal" hymn of the ancient *Rig Veda,* then we would expect Soma to marry first, then the Gandharva to appear as a temporary pseudo-husband, guarding the chastity of the bride, which is what seems to happen with Pwyll and Arawn's episode. The marriage of Manawydan as Agni should then come after Pwyll's marriage to Rhiannon, but Pryderi the Horse Twin's instead comes just before it. However, these two marriages happen in such close succession that apparently it was not seen as necessary to stress their strict order at this point. The Horse Twin's marriage, which, as we have seen, co-occurs in a complex way with the other marriages to the Sun Princess, had to be fit in somewhere narratively and makes a natural sequel to his father Pwyll's marriage. It is remarkable to contemplate the fact that here, in the latest of the mythic versions of the Lunar Cycle in terms of the age of manuscripts, we may have an example of something close to the proper order of myths as they appeared in the earliest times, not absolutely complete by any means, and showing some serious alterations, which we have touched on, but at least linked together into one relatively unified narrative.

Furthermore, within this narrative, in a very altered form, we can see the key elements of the "Soma" narrative as found in the other branches. First is the affront that needs recompense, Pwyll offending Arawn by driving away his hounds. This would parallel the poking of Midir and Chyavana's eye, or the killing of Skaði's father Thjazi. In the Welsh case, the recompense is significantly different, but the structural element of an offense requiring recompense is the same at its core. Next is the motif of the outsider getting in the middle of the marriage of the older god and his wife, which is of two types and corresponds to two separate portions of the Vedic Hymn: the Gandharva as second "husband" and preserver of virginity and the Horse Twins as intervening wooers. That is: Pwyll sleeps next to Arawn's wife during the whole of the year and a day, but in the end he does not make love to her, and Arawn's marriage simply continues happily. In the case of Chyavana, the Asvins first attempt to woo his wife Sukanya before ultimately helping to renew his youth and, in the Rig Vedic hymn, "leading the train" of their wedding. Aengus, too, temporarily becomes a pseudo-husband to Midir's wife Etain while she is in the form of a fly, but only acts as a noble custodian to her, perhaps even more reminiscent of the case of Pwyll in its outward character. We see the same theme of getting in the middle of a marriage repeat, as we will see, with Perceval and the Knight of the Tent. Next, the hostile neighbor of Arawn who Pwyll has to defeat seems to be in the position of the hostile Norse figure Thjazi, thief of the golden apples, who is killed to return the magical rejuvenating fruit to the gods. This appears even more likely given the fact that (as we will see in more detail) a similar figure occurs in the Grail legend as the Red Knight, the hostile, warring neighbor of Arthur who steals a golden cup (not the grail) from Arthur, and who is finally killed for Arthur by the interloping Perceval, while Hafgan is killed for Arawn by the interloping Pwyll.

The Grail Quester Perceval and The Lunar Cycle

Many additional parallels can be adduced between the stories of Perceval and Pryderi, but also between Perceval and the Horse Twin mythos in a broader sense. Perceval, like Pryderi, is deeply shaped by separation from his mother. Perceval initially is raised in the forest by his protective mother, but leaves her to pursue a career of knighthood. It is only later that he thinks of her condition and begins a journey back to her. It is on this journey that he encounters the Grail Castle and several other adventures. Pryderi is also raised away from civilization, though this is due to his abduction as an infant, which separates him from his mother. Thus when he grows to adulthood he must be reunited with his mother. A theme of a general romantic dalliance is perhaps not a rare or surprising thing for any tale, but Perceval meets and falls in love with Blanchefleur at the midpoint of his journey and just before going to the Grail castle, while, in the same way, Pryderi is said to marry Cigfa at the midpoint between the tales that revolve around him, just before he goes on the adventure that leads him to the mysterious fort of the golden bowl. As the Asvins attempt to woo another man's wife when they encounter Chyavana's wife Sukanya, but fail, so Perceval also has this very character trait, as at the beginning of Chretien's poem he naively forces kisses and a ring from a damsel whose husband (the Knight of the Tent) then returns, accuses her of unfaithfulness, and punishes her. She is only later vindicated to her husband, even though she tells him all immediately and honestly professes her innocence. In the Chyavana version, Sukanya immediately informs Chyavana of the Asvins' attempts to woo her, and he trusts her fidelity right away. In the *Wooing of Etain*, Aengus temporarily becomes the caretaker and pseudo-husband of Midir's wife, Etain, before she is again blown off course by Fuamnach. And in general, it is a recurring theme that the maidens wooed in several of the lunar cycle tales have a prior marriage or engagement that they tell the wooing stranger they would not like to give up for anything (Gerðr, Etain, Sukanya).

When Perceval arrives at court, another maiden sees him and laughs. It is then revealed that a prophecy had been pronounced that this maiden would not laugh until she laid eyes on the next supreme lord of the knights. The knight Kay strikes her for this prophetic outburst, and this abuse is the reason Perceval then desires revenge upon Kay later. If their eventual confrontation, as we will see, could be another version of the Aesir-Vanir War motif, then this prophetic woman, whose striking helps lead to the

244

conflict, would occupy the same role here that we have seen elsewhere in the sorceress or seeress Gullveig, whose triple murder is considered one of the inciting incidents of the Aesir-Vanir War. Following this episode, Perceval pierces the Red Knight through the eye with his lance. We can say then that the all-important eye-piercing motif is by no means absent from the Perceval tale, and that Perceval's spear then stands in place of the "spit" or thorny twig which pierces the eyes of Midir and Chyavana. Though no other Horse Twin figures are directly responsible for the eye-poking in the other branches, at least in the Irish case Aengus is held responsible for it by the wounded Midir as it is done by youths under Aengus' watch, leading Aengus to need to seek Etain to recompense Midir.

Not only this, but in fact we can recognize here just how similar Chretien de Troyes' version is to the Norse mythic version of events. For the Red Knight who has his eye pierced has just stolen a golden cup from King Arthur and has threatened to steal his lands as well (like Hafgan), leaving Arthur despondently musing while his wife, the queen, is said to be "well-nigh dead," it being said that it is believed she will not escape that fate, due to the shame and distress brought on by the theft of the cup. The loss of a simple cup should not have such a dramatic effect, unless of course it has a deeper significance or a magical power, and the fact that this cup fits the exact position that the golden apples do in the myth of Thjazi explains this mystery. The Red Knight, like Thjazi, steals the golden-colored food or drink related treasure from the king, and, as a result leaves the king and his family in a paralyzed, near-death state. The Red Knight, like Thjazi, is then both killed and pierced in the eye. Perceval picks apart and takes his armor after killing the Red Knight, perhaps similar to how Thjazi has his eyes picked out and placed in the sky after being killed. If the reader accepts the theory we have put forward, that Thjazi is related to a destructive aspect of the sun, then the red color of the Red Knight's armor may even be explicable, red being a common solar color.[109]

Next, after the first Grail episode, Perceval goes again to Arthur's court, after defeating more of his knights, and there does battle with Arthur's knights Sagremor and Kay, impressively defeating both. Due to the fact that Perceval is then invited to join Arthur's court as a result of this episode (Arthur and his court considered as stand-ins for the high gods and their society), and does so, we can quite confidently say that this episode stands in the exact position of the Aesir-Vanir War within the grail poem. The

---

109   Grail scholar R.S. Loomis takes red armor or coloring to be a sign of a sun god, for instance Esclados the Red, host of Ovain, and the adversary in red from *Erec* who weakens in the afternoon. See Loomis, *Celtic Myth*, p. 70. The Irish Sun Princess Caer Ibormeith, as we have seen, is also named for the red yew berry, among other instances of this color symbolism. The Vedic tradition has a name for the sun, *bradhna*, meaning "red shining one."

Horse Twin hero Perceval fights the high knights (high gods) and then is accepted into their society/court. In the final portion of Chretien's poem about Perceval, he learns who the grail serves (the Fisher King's father who he also learns is his own uncle), learns that the grail contains a single wafer of communion which is able to sustain this uncle, and then receives holy communion (which is now associated with the grail as its main contents) for the first time. The communion of course being the spiritual, life-sustaining, highest rite of Catholicism, it corresponds to the *soma* of the Vedics, Eleusinian Mysteries (or Dionysian wine) of the Greeks, and the Aesir's sacrifice of the Norse, which the Horse Twins of each of the other branches are said to take part in for the first time at the end of their myths. In other versions of the Grail legend, such as Wolfram von Eschenbach's *Parzifal*, written shortly after Chretien's poem, Parzifal the grail quester is said to become the new keeper of the grail in the end, just as the Norse and Vedic Horse Twins crucially are said by Snorri to become priests of the high rite in the outcome of the conflict.

* * *

The Grail Question

A mysterious question famously becomes central to the success of Perceval's quest in Chretien's poem. This question is of course, "whom does the Grail serve?", which Perceval at first fails to ask, but which is said (by the weeping maiden he encounters holding her dead lover) to bring the Fisher King great succor if asked. Much confusion has surrounded this question in the scholarship, and perhaps it will remain mysterious for awhile longer. However, in the Indian version we have discussed, specifically the version of the tale found in the *Satapatha Brahmana*, there in fact is a magical, riddling question associated with allowing the Asvins' to accede to the *soma* rite. Indeed, there are two such questions which come in succession. Despite this seemingly miraculous correspondence of there being key questions in these vastly distant branches, these two questions in the Indian version are difficult to fit to the question we find in the Grail version. As such, it could be that the questions in the two branches are not the same at their root and that similarities in the two sets of questions are mere coincidences. However, the evidence still has to be examined.

First, Sukanya says to the Asvins, after rejecting their advances, "But surely ye are neither quite complete nor quite perfect, and yet deride my husband!" The Asvins respond then with the first question: "In what respect are we incomplete, in what respect imperfect?" Only after they have rejuvenated Sukanya's husband does Chyavana tell them the answer to the question, which is, "yonder the gods perform a sacrifice and exclude you from it" (*Satapatha Brahmana*, IV.1.5.13). They then set off to the place of the sacrifice and demand an invitation. When they are denied, they formulate their own special riddle. "But surely you worship a headless sacrifice" they say, to which is responded the second query, "How with a headless sacrifice?" The Twins demand inclusion in the rite in exchange for the answer to their riddle. This is agreed to and so they are included, and as a result explain that they, the Asvins, are the heads because the leaders of the sacrifice, and this because they are the "Adhvaryus," a term for a kind of Vedic priest who assisted the reciter of the litanies and who took care of the physical aspects of the sacrifice, one of whose duties was to press and pour the *soma* juice into the receptacles (RV 8.4.11). This could also be interpreted as pointing to the Asvins' position as leading the way, astrologically and metaphysically speaking, for the new morning and thus for the sacrifice, as they are said to do in the *Rig Veda* with their possible identification with the morning star. Thus the riddling question and its answer reveal that the inherent divine nature of the Asvins in itself indicates their proper place in the rite, that it is in their nature and destiny to take their place in the rite and indeed that they are needed by it for its completion.

Though the match across so much time and space to the Grail question is hazy, we can see that the Grail question too reveals Perceval's proper inborn role in its keeping. For with the response to this question it is revealed that Perceval is the nephew of the elder Grail King (just as Aengus is foster son of Midir or Freyr is son/foster son of Njörðr, and similar also to Aengus finding out that his true father is the Dagda) and thus a member of the family destined to be its keepers. It is also a question directly about the functionality of the rite, just as was the Asvins' riddle. The question in the Vedic case regards the "headless" sacrifice, while the question in the Grail poem reveals who the severed head from the procession belonged to, along with other secrets related to the working of the Grail. Finally, its asking and answering allows the perfection, or the healing, of both the imperfect seekers and the wounded or headless rite. By asking whom the Grail serves, Perceval also shows his understanding of his own role to be one of serving, and accepts that role. In the same way, the Asvins proclaiming themselves "heads" or "leaders" of the sacrifice only implies that they go before the others to make the sacrifice ready, and that while now on equal footing with the other gods, they still function as one part (a head) within a body of functions that make up the rite and the divine society as a whole.

247

In essence, the questions of both branches are the question of *self-identity*, and lead to a rediscovery of who the quester has been all along. The process of this recognition has several steps: 1. The recognition of one's incompleteness (Sukanya tells the Asvins they are incomplete) 2. Learning the right question to ask (The Asvins and Perceval are prompted to raise the question) 3. Recognizing that there is a higher sacred sphere to aspire to (the Asvins learn of the higher rite; Perceval witnesses the Grail procession) 4. Asking the question of identity 5. Learning one's own deeper connection to the whole and to the sacred, discovering who one always has been despite being cut off from this identity. The quester has forgotten who he is, his true history, and his innate connection to the whole. Aengus has been raised as a foster-son of Midir and has never known his true father until he confronts Dagda. Pryderi was kidnapped as an infant and has been raised by a foster father, Teyrnon. The Asvins have been excluded from the society of high gods, but come to recognize their inborn role of Adhvaryu. Perceval, raised in the country without a father, comes to discover that he is actually the nephew of the Grail King himself and tied to the Grail by destiny. At the end of von Eschenbach's version, Parzival's name appears on the Grail itself. This element of the myth is partially obscured in the Norse version, yet Freyr still begins separate from the Aesir before ending up as one of the most beloved among them and an important officiant of the sacrifice in the end. This process of the recognition of one's identity and inborn role within the whole is Nietzsche's "become who you are," and relies on the question that each of us must first *recognize*, and then *ask*, before understanding our own role and destiny.

That which can heal either the land or the headless sacrifice in either the Samvarana or the Asvins' tale is either returning to the neglected sacrifice (via the Fire God Vasistha/Manawydan) or the rejuvenating power of the Horse Twins, their recognition, and their taking their place as the head of the sacrifice. Thus what finally heals the ailing Fisher King is Perceval asking the question which allows him to take his rightful place in, heal, and complete the rite; and likewise it is only the completed rite, the completed divine society, that can bring life back to the land which has turned waste without the rite's nourishment. While most interpreters have argued that the land has become waste simply because it is connected to the health of the king, we can see that there is much more importance placed on the "health" of the rite itself as the cure for the wasteland. While the Soma King does need specific healing in other branches (consider Chyavana and Midir needing their eyes healed; Chyavana and Njörðr needing to have their youth renewed by the herbal paste or golden apples), as accords with the ancient view of the rite perceptible in the Vedas as both bringing the rains and allowing the new day itself to be born, it is first and foremost the healed and properly observed rite which is the source of the health of both the king *and* the land: Samvarana finally returning to performing the rite heals the land; the sacrificial fire god Manawydan heals the land and retrieves

248

Pryderi; the Asvins heal the sacrifice itself by completing it and causing it to function properly, which coincides also with the completion of the divine society, the unification of the divine castes into an organic whole.

Conclusion

Thus in the Grail legend we have nearly all of the recognizable elements of this wider Lunar Cycle that we have identified elsewhere: 1.Separation of the Horse Twin hero from his mother, while also not knowing his true father 2.His involvement in an attempt to woo a married woman 3.A prophetic woman is attacked violently, leading directly to the later conflict in which the hero seeks vengeance for this violence 4.A golden consumable treasure is stolen from the king, leaving him and his family in a near-death paralysis, and it is then retrieved after a one-on-one battle 5.The eye-piercing 6.Meeting his beloved at the midpoint 7.A mysterious castle appears in which is kept a golden dish/bowl 8.An old man needing healing and rejuvenation 9.The land has become an enchanted wasteland which must be healed 10.A riddle or riddling question, relating to the functioning of the sacred object and the deeper identity of the hero, that a woman makes the hero aware of 11.The hero is excluded from the court of the "high gods" (knights of Arthur) 12.He confronts and defeats the "high gods" (knights of Arthur)13.He is accepted into the court of "high gods" as a result 14.He gains the high rite for the first time 15.He learns the identity of his true father (and of himself), which links him to the rite 16.He may become keeper of the vessel of the high rite (the Grail).

Now, if we simply understand the role of keeper of the Grail as a natural cognate to priest of the high sacrifice, we see that a Horse Twin has renewed the vitality of a wounded old man and has then gained access to the holy sacrificial relic and become its priest, also joining the society of the high gods/knights after defeating them, along with all the other connected motifs we have become accustomed to seeing in this cycle. Thus the concordance of the Vedic myth with the Holy Grail legend is uncannily close. And as we have seen that the core of this suggested myth was widespread all across Europe, it stands to reason that it could easily have been known in other Welsh or French sources, oral or written, no longer available to us, which could have served as a common basis drawn from by the texts that remain to us in this tradition. Indeed, we even see a strong connection with the Norse version of the myth in elements such as the Red Knight who steals the golden treasure and the prophetic woman who is struck, which leads to the later confrontation of Perceval and Arthur's knights. These "Nordic" elements suggest either that the French Chretien knew how to blend material from both the extant

Germanic and Celtic versions in order to craft his poem, that he very much knew what he was doing as he worked with Lunar Cycle material both from Wales and the continent, or that he was working from a version of the cycle which already retained the mythos in a wondrously unified form. Indeed, Chretien's Grail poem seems an incredible synthesis of nearly all of the associated myths we have thus far called parts of the Lunar Cycle, either representing a masterwork of synthetic genius, or simply a more ancient, unified tradition that has here been miraculously preserved. The unavoidable conclusion that we are left with is that the Holy Grail legend and the Aesir-Vanir war cycle are one and the same myth, split up and changed over time, yet holding the same esoteric truth at their core.

The Grail quest then has an undeniable "lunar" character to it. But this does not sum up its meaning or the spiritual possibilities inherent in it. After all, all the high gods, even the most solar among them, partake of the lunar *soma* in order to maintain immortality. The Horse Twins themselves have a distinctly solar association as well, riding in the sun chariot and marrying solar princesses. The Asvins were also sacrificed to at noon, and not only at dawn. Freyr riding the boar Gullinbursti, whose golden mane glows in the dark, may be another symbol of the morning star shining in the darkness and crossing the boundary between day and night or a similar phenomena of sunrise. As harbingers of the dawn, the Horse Twins more accurately form the link between the moon and sun, retrieving the lunar light from the darkness and passing it along to the high gods of the daytime. They are seemingly morning star at sunrise, bridging the gap between dark and light, between Soma and Ushas, bringing to the high gods the immortalizing nectar of the moon rescued from out of the darkness.

This combined lunar and solar character may even be hinted at in the sacred items brought before Perceval in succession at the Grail castle in Chretien's poem. After the lance there is the Grail (a dish said to be of gold) followed by a silver carving platter. A gold dish or bowl followed by a silver platter immediately strikes one as solar and lunar imagery, the two symbols united in procession. The fact that the silver platter is said to be for carving, while the moon, as we have noted, is known as a divider (of time or fates) is a further interesting coincidence. In the Pryderi tale, of course, there is only a golden bowl with no mention of a silver platter, though there is a fountain beneath it, perhaps similar to the moon seen as the source of sacred waters, or even to Mimir's Well. We may say that the Grail itself is generally gold, with possible (though not necessarily) solar significance, while the liquid held within, the *soma*, would, in its essence, be of the moon.

Ultimately the Grail legend tells of a path of elevation by submission or cooperation, and tells of the use of a lunar liquid. But this is a submission in order to be integrated into a divine hierarchy that unites both the lunar and solar. The Grail quester accepts that service is central to the functioning of the Grail, to the working of the complex system of the *soma* sacrifice, becoming thus an instrument of something higher rather than making domination and control his spiritual goal. The path of the Grail quester is a path of devotion, to the Grail and to its governing deity, the stalwart but somewhat passive character found in the concept of a "keeper" of the Grail underlining this fact. Yet, as a Horse Twin, the Grail quester is also a bringer of the necessary lunar element into the solar spiritual economy, and thus a perfecter of the solar realm by the unification of these two spheres.

The understanding of the deeper substructure of the Grail legend, with its roots going back at least 5000 years (the time of unity of these branches being around 2900 BCE), obviously makes relatively superfluous the endless speculations on where this or that individual surface-level element originated. It is perfectly possible that certain names or physical characteristics of objects or motifs may have been brought in from the mediterranean, from the middle east, from the Scythian steppe, etc. – if such importation was even necessary, given what we now can see for ourselves – without significantly altering the core of the legend, sometimes enhancing or elaborating, sometimes weakening, the existing meaning. Most obviously, the entire legend did after all undergo a transformation into the Christian symbol-language, and was reinterpreted through that religious lens to reach the form in which we have received it. Yet beneath these layers the specific elements of the original structure still show through and preserve their original significance.

The Lunar Cycle as a whole has in fact several layers of significance that we can still appreciate today in our own religious understandings. As we have pointed out, the marriage of Soma and Surya, which forms the starting point of the cycle, was seen by the Vedics as providing the divine model of all earthly marriages, and from its example we have the whole series of customary marriage rites: the "Gandharva"-aided period of celibacy after the wedding, the going around the sacred fire or "Agni," among many other elaborate procedures.

Additionally, the idea that the cycle, particularly the "Aesir-Vanir War" episode, depicts the process of coming together of the various castes of the divine society, which is reflected as well in the castes of the human society (as we see in the pseudo-historical version involving Romulus), that is, the perfection of the organic society. With this is also the acceptance of the lower caste or class, the third or "producer" caste, into the society of the higher castes. This is reflected in the Vedic society by the fact that the Vaishya caste is considered one of the "twice-born" castes, along with the higher Kshatriyas and Brahmins, and are allowed to participate in the rites of the Vedic religion and to be afforded access to the sacrifices, initiations, and reincarnation. It is a point of curiosity whether the Proto-Indo-Europeans ever experienced a period before the elevation of the producer caste to full participation in the elite religion, whether the Aesir-Vanir War motif depicts any historical material or instead narrates a primordial event that brought about a unity that has always been, in both divine and human society.

Along with this elevation of the third caste, divine and human, is the granting of the Horse Twin gods access to the immortalizing rituals. Whether this newly granted immortality consists in reincarnation, eternal afterlife, some higher transcendence, or the possibility of all of these, is a question beyond the scope of this study. Once the immortalizing rite is put in play, it is difficult to limit its spiritual possibilities from intersecting even with the "regal path," hence we see the elevation, intensification and universalization of the symbol of the Grail in the Middle Ages, which process began to conflate the Grail with the "cup of sovereignty." A three day long *soma* sacrifice was after all also an important part of the Vedic *asvamedha* "Horse Sacrifice," which scholar Nick Allen says is "the highest of the royal rituals and establishes the cosmic supremacy of a king" (Allen, "Why Did Odysseus Become a Horse?", 4). But what must be recognized is that this granted immortality of the Third Function gods was also the opening of the possibility of immortality to members of the third caste of the human society. As the divine representatives of their caste are seen to do, so the humans of that caste ought to do. Thus the quest of the Grail continues, and remains open, even to those not of the elitest status, a path toward the waters of immortality, for those who are prepared to ask the question of self-identity, to serve the king, to retrieve light from darkness, to re-unify, to re-integrate, and to lead.

* * *

Charts and Glossary

Aesir-Vanir War Motif in Various Branches (with Norse parallel names as reference):

Vedic:

The Asvins (Freyr) desire to be allowed access to the *soma* sacrifice of the high gods. The incarnation of the Moon God Soma, Chyavana (Njörðr), helps them by confronting king of the gods Indra in single combat, summoning a demon of intoxication to fight him, and making him submit with his magic. The Asvins join the society of the high gods, gain access to the *soma* sacrifice, and become its priests. In one version, Dadhyanc, the keeper of the secret of the *soma*, is beheaded by Indra but has his head preserved and reattached. The Asvins subsequently marry Savitri.

Welsh:

Welsh Pryderi (Freyr) marries Cigfa and then touches a magical golden bowl that takes him to the otherworld. Once Pryderi returns, the high god Gwydion (Oðinn) wants the Swine of the Underworld (symbol of power of fertility) so he trades the Third Function god Pryderi a bunch of warrior-related items (war horses, shields and dogs), but it is a trick, the horses etc. are an illusion. This results in a war between Pryderi's and Gwydion's forces, which ends in a truce where hostages are exchanged. Then the peace falls apart and Pryderi is killed by Gwydion in a duel, but the swine now belong to Gwydion, integrating the power of fertility into the society of higher gods.

Roman:

The legendary incarnation of the high god, Romulus (Oðinn), and his Romans want wives so they trick the Sabines and take their women. This results in a war which ends in a truce where Romulus and the Sabine king Titus (Freyr) share rulership. Then the peace falls apart and Titus is killed by Romulus' men, but the women and other Sabines have already become part of Rome, integrating the power of fertility into the higher society.

Irish:

Irish Aengus (Freyr), is foster son of Moon God Midir (Njörðr) and does not know his true parentage. When he is a young man he discovers he is actually son of Father Sky, the Dagda. He goes to Dagda to be acknowledged as his son and get his inheritance. Dagda acknowledges him, but tells him the land he is to inherit is occupied by Elcmar aka Nuada (Varunian aspect of Oðinn). Aengus goes armed to Elcmar's fort with Midir. Aengus threatens Elcmar's life with a "feint," and as a result they agree to a deal as a compromise: Aengus will get to spend a day and night as king of the land. This is a trick however, and since "all the world is spent in day and night" the deal means that Aengus gets to keep the kingship of the land forever. In another version, the method of removing Elcmar is called a magical lay or chant, both cases then depicting a kind of verbal magic. Aengus subsequently marries Caer Ibormeith and drinks the drink of immortality.

Norse:

A sorceress is burned and speared to death three times by the Norse high gods the Aesir, triggering a conflict between the Vanir, led by the Moon God Njörðr and Horse Twin/Young Son Freyr, and the Aesir, led by Oðinn. The Vanir besiege the halls of the Aesir, forcing a truce in which hostages are exchanged, and Njörðr and Freyr are integrated into the Aesir society and become priests of their sacrifice. Mimir, keeper of the Well of Wisdom/Memory, is beheaded, but his head is preserved by Oðinn and it speaks to him. Freyr marries Gerðr.

Grail Legend:

A prophetic woman is struck by Arthur's (in Oðinn's role here) knight Kay for predicting that the Grail quester Perceval (Freyr) will become the greatest of the knights. For this abuse, Perceval seeks revenge, confronting and defeating Kay and Sagremor in single combat. As a result, Arthur accepts Perceval into his retinue of knights, and subsequently Perceval takes the high rite of communion for the first time and becomes keeper of the Grail in which communion is kept. In the middle of this sequence, Perceval woos Blanchefleur.

Renewing the Youth of the Gods and The Marriage of Soma and Suryā in Various Branches (with Norse parallel names as reference):

Vedic:

The eye of Chyavana (Njörðr) is poked out by a clod of dirt thrown by playing youths. In recompense, the king gives his daughter Sukanya (Skaði) to Chyavana to wed. After meddling in their marriage by trying to woo the princess, the Asvins (Freyr) administer the magical herbal paste to the aged Chyavana, renewing his youth. Chyavana and the princess undergo a "choosing" test in which the princess must pick Chyavana out in his newly youthful form while he stands next to the Asvins. She chooses correctly and they live happily.

Irish:

The eye of Midir (Njörðr) is knocked out by a sprig of holly thrown by playing youths. In recompense, Midir must be given Etain (Skaði) to marry. After many twists and turns, Midir's rival, Eochaidh Airem, must undergo a choosing scene in which he has to choose Etain in swan form from among many other swan maidens. He chooses incorrectly and Midir and Etain live happily. Fuamnach, the sorceress wife of Midir, causes Etain to go through a triple transformation, and is later burned to death.

Norse:

The golden apples which renew the youth of the gods are stolen by Thjazi. Thjazi is killed and the apples are regained. In recompense for his death, Thjazi's eyes are removed and placed in the night sky as stars, and Thjazi's daughter Skaði is given Njörðr as husband. They undergo a choosing scene in which Skaði chooses Njörðr out from the other gods, though not entirely happily. The seeress Gullveig, associated with the Vanir, is killed and reborn three times.

Grail Legend:

The golden cup of Arthur (Oðinn) is stolen by Arthur's hostile neighbor the Red Knight, leaving Arthur and his wife in a paralytic state. Perceval (Freyr) kills the Red Knight (Thjazi) in single combat by driving his lance through his eye, and retrieves the golden cup. After meddling in their marriage at first by kissing his wife and taking her ring, Perceval helps reunite the Knight of the Tent and his wife, and they live happily.

Welsh:

Pwyll (Bragi) drives the hounds of Arawn (Njörðr) away from a dead stag and lets his own hounds eat instead. In recompense to Arawn, Pwyll agrees to be lord of Annwn for a year. During that year Pwyll sleeps next to the wife of Annwn without making love to her and defeats Arawn's hostile neighbor Hafgan (Thjazi) in single combat. Arawn and his wife continue to live happily and Pwyll is granted shared lordship of Annwn as a reward.

* * *

Key Motifs in Each Branch:

Magical Item that Renews the Youth of the Gods:

Golden apples (Norse)

Magical herbs (Vedic)

—— Irish n/a (Irish)

Regeneration ability of Hafgan? (Welsh)

Golden cup (Grail legend)

Aesir-Vanir War motif:

Aesir-Vanir War (Norse)

Chyavana battles Indra (Vedic)

Taking of the Sid Brugh na Boinne (Irish)

War of the Swine of Annwn (Welsh)

Perceval duels Kay and Sagremor (Grail legend)

Rape of the Sabine Women (Roman)

The Eye Poking:

Killing Thjazi and Removal of his eyes (Norse)

Poking of Chyavana's eye (Vedic)

Poking out of Midir's eye (Irish)

Driving the lance through the Red Knight's eye (Grail legend)

— — Welsh n/a (the single blow to Hafgan's head?) (Welsh)

The Offense that Requires Recompense:

Killing of Thjazi (Norse)

Poking of Chyavana's Eye (Vedic)

Poking out of Midir's Eye (Irish)

Driving off of hounds (Welsh)

—— Grail legend n/a (Grail legend)

Occupying Seat/Mound Out of Turn:

Freyr sneaking onto Hlidskjalf (Norse)

Samvarana occupying the sacred mountain out of turn (Vedic)

—— Irish n/a (Irish)

Pryderi occupying Gorsedd Arberth out of turn (Welsh)

Siege Perilous (Grail legend)

Attack on the Sorceress:

Burning of Gullveig (Norse)

—— n/a (purification of the nectar/soma/killing of Namuci?) (Vedic)

Burning of Fuamnach (Irish)

—— Welsh n/a (Welsh)

Striking of prophetic woman at Arthur's court (Grail legend)

Tarpeia thrown from the cliff (Roman Livy)

Transference of Sun Princess to Another Husband:

Skaði switches to Oðinn (Norse)

Suryā switches to Gandharva and Agni (Vedic)

Etain becomes temporary ward of Aengus and wife of Eochu (Irish)

Rhiannon switches to Manawydan (Welsh)

Grail n/a (Grail legend)

Interference in and then helping the Marriage of Soma and Suryā:

Norse n/a (Norse)

Asvins interfere in and then help marriage of Chyavana and Sukanya (Vedic)

Aengus helps woo Etain for Midir then becomes temporary keeper of Etain as a fly (Irish)

Pwyll becomes temporary husband of Arawn's wife (Welsh)

Perceval interferes in and then helps marriage of the Knight of the Tent and his wife (Grail legend)

* * *

Chart of Relevant Deities (some empty spaces will be filled in later chapters):

Title	Vedic	V. Epic	Norse	Irish	Welsh	W. Pseud.	Grail	
Priest of Fire	Agni	Dhrishtadyumna	Odinn	Manannan	Manawydan		The Hermit?	
Terrible Sovereign	Varuna	Pandu	Odinn	Nuada-Elcmar	Lludd/Nudd	Morvidus	Uther	
Lawful Sovereign	Mitra	Yudhishthira	Tyr	Lugh	Lleu	Gorbonianus	Arthur	
Lord of Wind	Vayu	Bhima	Thor	Dagda		Elidurus		
Thunderer	Indra	Arjuna	Thor	Tuireann	Taran	Archgallo	Kay	

Horse Twin 1	Nasatya	Nakula	Freyr	Aengus	Pryderi	Perederus	Perceval /Peredur	
Horse Twin 2	Dasra	Sahadeva			Owein	Ingenius /Owain		
Destructive Sun God	Vivasvat	Sharyati	Thjazi or Orvandil				The Red Knight	
Soma Moon God	Soma	Chyavana	Njordr	Midir			Elder Grail King/The Knight of the Tent	
Gandharva	Visvavasu	Samvarana	Bragi		Pwyll		The Fisher King "Pelles"	
Moon	Chandra		Mani					
Dawn	Ushas	Draupadi?	Freyja	Brigid	Blodeuwedd		Guinevere	
Daughter of the Sun	Surya	Tapati/Sukanya	Idunn/Skadi/Gerdr	Caer/Etain	Rhiannon/Cigda		Mother of Perceval /Lady of the Tent/Grail Maiden/ Blanchefleur	
Lunar Sorceress			Gullveig	Fuamnach			Prophetic Woman	

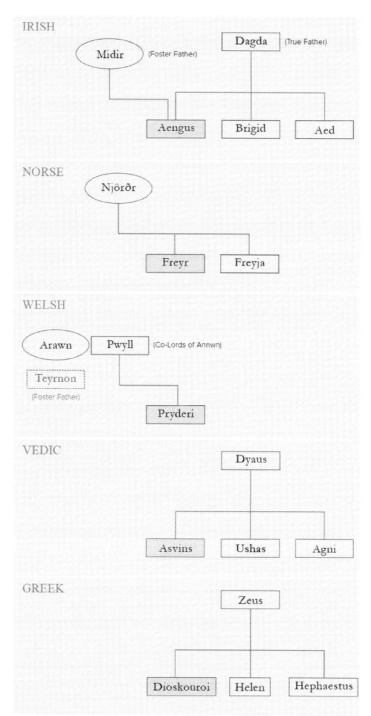

(HT Parentage Comparison Chart: Oval = Moon God; Grey Rectangle = Horse Twin)

The Welsh case is the clear outlier here, although, like the Irish and Norse cases, it again establishes the pseudo-paternal role for the Soma God (Arawn) in relation to the Horse Twin (Pryderi). As we will explore in the next part, this seems to be due to the fact that the Horse Twins have two different parentage myths in the *Rig Veda*, and furthermore reflects the fact that two separate myth types appear to be conflated around the figures Pwyll and Rhiannon.

Glossary of Names:

Aed – Son of the Dagda and brother of Aengus, name means "fire"

Aengus Og – Irish Horse Twin, foster son of Midir, son of Dagda, husband of Caer

Agni – Vedic god of fire, priestly god embodied in the sacred flame, third husband of Suryā

Arawn – Welsh lord of the underworld of Annwn, "Soma" Moon God, model of the elder Grail King and probably of the Knight of the Tent

Asvins – Vedic Horse Twins, sons of Dyaus, husbands of Savitri

Blanchefleur – Beloved of Perceval

Bragi – Court poet of the Norse gods, husband of Iðunn, narrator of the first portion of the Norse Lunar Cycle

Bran – Welsh parallel of Vedic Yama, lord of the dead. Is beheaded and his still sentient head is taken to the Otherworld

Caer Ibormeith – Irish sun princess, consort of Aengus who Aengus first sees in a dream

Chyavana – Legendary stand-in for one of the deities who were combined to make the later Vedic god Soma; sage and husband of Sukanya

Cigfa – Welsh sun princess, wife of Pryderi

Dagda – Irish chief god of sky and wind, true father of Aengus, and father of Brigid and Aed among others

Elcmar – Irish king who is occupying the land that is to be Aengus' inheritance, Aengus tricks him out of it. Believed to be another name for the god Nuada

Elder Grail King – Lives in the Grail castle and is sustained by a single wafer of communion from the Grail each day. One of the stand-ins for the "Soma" god

Eochu Airem – A husband of Etain after Midir, Midir steals Etain back by tricking him, name means "Horseman Ploughman"

Etain – Irish horse and sun princess, wife of Midir

Fuamnach – Lunar sorceress and wife of Midir, burned to death by Manannan

Freyr – Norse Horse Twin, son of Njorðr and husband of Gerðr

Gandharva Visvavasu – Chief Gandharva, court singer of the gods, protege of Soma and guardian of the *soma* and of virginity, second husband of Suryā

Gerðr – Norse sun princess and wife of Freyr

Gullveig – Sorceress burned and stabbed to death by the Aesir in Oðinn's hall, the violence against her may trigger the Aesir-Vanir War, name connects her to the mead

Hafgan – Hostile neighbor of Arawn, name meaning "summer-bright," can be killed only by being given no more than one blow, is killed by Pwyll

Hengist and Horsa – Pseudo-historical versions of the Horse Twins, names meaning "Stallion" and "Horse." Compare the Horse Twin names Hengist, Aengus, Ing, Ingenius

Kay – Arrogant knight of Arthur's court, strikes the prophetic woman and is later defeated by Perceval in a duel in retribution. Apparently an incarnation of the Thunderer.

Knight of the Tent – Husband of the Lady of the Tent, forsakes his wife for assumed infidelity, but is reconciled to her later by Perceval. One of the probable stand-ins for the "Soma" god

Iðunn – Norse sun princess and wife of Bragi, whose golden apples, which renew the youth of the gods, are stolen by Thjazi

Lady of the Tent – Lady who Perceval kisses and then takes a ring from, is forsaken by her husband for assumed infidelity but is reconciled to him later by Perceval

Mabon – Welsh "young son" who is imprisoned in the Underworld and must be rescued by Arthur. Possibly identifiable with Pryderi

Manannan – Irish fire-priest god, lord of the ocean and psychopomp

Manawydan – Welsh fire-priest god, second husband of Rhiannon

Midir – Irish "Soma" Moon God, husband of Fuamnach and Etain, foster father of Freyr

Mímir – Norse god, parallel of Yama, underworld god, keeper of the well of illumination who is beheaded after the Aesir-Vanir war

Mother of Perceval – Grail legend stand-in for Rhiannon

Njörðr – Norse god associated with the sea, one aspect of the "Soma" Moon God

Oðinn – Chief of the Norse high gods the Aesir, also Norse fire-priest, second husband of Skaði

Pelles/Fisher King – younger wounded king of the Grail castle, keeper of the Grail, Perceval first meets him fishing in a lake. Is given the name Pelles in later versions

Perceval – The Grail quester, lover of Blanchefleur, nephew of the Elder Grail king

Peredur – Welsh quester, from a common root with Perceval, his tale tells nearly the same narrative as Chretien's poem about Perceval

Peredurus – A king appearing in Geoffrey of Monmouth's Historiae Regum Brittania, unites with his brother Ingenius to take the kingdom from their older brother, divides the island between them. Probable pseudo-historical version of the Horse Twin god

Prophetic Woman – Woman at Arthur's court who prophetically laughs or smiles when she sees Perceval, and is then struck by the knight Kay

Pryderi – Welsh Horse Twin, son of Pwyll and Rhiannon, husband of Cigfa

Pwyll – Welsh Gandharva, first husband of Rhiannon, father of Pryderi

Red Knight – Hostile neighbor of Arthur who is at war with him, steals the golden cup of Guinevere and then is pierced through the eye with a lance by Perceval

Rhiannon – Welsh Horse/Sun Princess, wife of Pwyll and Manawydan, mother of Pryderi

Samvarana – Legendary stand-in for the Gandharva Visvavasu, husband of Tapati

Savitri – Vedic sun princess, daughter of Sun god Savitr, wife of the Asvins

Sharyati – Father of Sukanya. Possible legendary Vedic stand-in for an aspect of the Sun god, Vivasvat-Surya, depicted as grandson of Vivasvat-Surya

Skaði – Norse sun princess, daughter of Thjazi, wife of Njorðr and Oðinn

Soma – Vedic god of the moon, of the waters, of wealth, and of the liquid of immortality and illumination. First husband of Suryā

Sukanya – Legendary Vedic stand-in for Surya, sun princess, wife of Chyavana-Soma, daughter of Sharyati and great-grand-daughter of Vivasvat-Surya

Suryā – Vedic bride of Soma, daughter of the Sun god Surya, sun princess goddess of the sunbeam or the radiance of the sun

Thjazi – Norse sun deity, father of Skaði, possible half-brother of Iðunn

Tapati – Vedic sun princess, daughter of Vivasvat, wife of Samvarana

Vasistha – Legendary Vedic stand-in for Agni, rishi and advisor of Samvarana

Wife of Arawn – Welsh queen of the Underworld of Annwn, sun princess

Wife of Knight of the Tent – Legendary stand-in for the wife of Arawn-Soma

8

Dionysus, Hades, and Soma: The Greek Lunar Cycle

Dionysus and Soma

With a clarified understanding of this "Lunar Cycle," as it appears in the Celtic and Germanic mythologies, we can begin to look toward Greece to see if some of these same motifs and deities may be identifiable there. The prime candidate for the Greek "Soma" god becomes apparent at once by way of a near-exact myth once again involving the central Soma incarnation, Chyavana. It ought to come as no surprise that this Greek "Soma" candidate is the lord of divine intoxicating liquid, vegetation and mystical experience, Dionysus. The nexus between Dionysus and Chyavana-Soma is the close similarity of the stories of their births.

In the Indian case (*Mahabharata, Adi Parva*, 5-6), Chyavana's mother-to-be, Puloma, is pregnant with Chyavana. A conspiring *raksasa* demon, who desires to marry Puloma, turns into a pig and steals her away. This frightens Puloma into giving birth right then and there. The child's name, "Chyavana," means "born-prematurely." The bright

265

splendor of Chyavana causes the demon to turn to ash immediately. In the Greek case (Euripides, *Bacchae* 90, 245, and others), Dionysus' mother-to-be, Semele, is pregnant with Dionysus. Tricked by the conspiring goddess Hera, Semele compels Zeus to appear to her in his full glory as the form of lightning. He does so and Semele is burnt to ash immediately, causing Dionysus to fall from the ashes. Dionysus is thus considered prematurely born (and has to be temporarily sewn into Zeus' leg for further incubation). Perhaps his most characteristic epithet, "Dithyrambos," may be related to this trait of premature or double birth. This premature birth is clearly important to the essence of the god, and, as we have previously put forward, it may correspond to the moon rising in the sky before the sky has yet grown dark. The moon is born prematurely each evening, before its proper time, which is night. The sudden "burning up" that follows this first birth may correlate to the sunset which fills the sky after the first rise of the moon. The moon then appears a second time in the darkened sky after the sunrise fades, as if born a second time (as Dionysus is born a second time, from Zeus, God of Sky).

Thus, in these two cases, we have a premature birth induced by mischief, wherein one of the primary figures is burnt to ash at the moment of the birth due to the bright splendor of a gods' sudden appearing (which god is the cause of this combustion is simply switched from the father to the infant), and the fact of this premature birth is seemingly made part of the newborn god's name. It seems, of course, that the roles have slightly shifted between the two versions. A demon has either been added to the Vedic version to cause the initial mischief and to be killed, or has potentially been removed in the Greek case. The idea that the death of a goddess (Semele) might be ameliorated by the inclusion of a dispensable demon, who is killed instead, has a plausibility to it, yet it is generally difficult to speculate on such details. Then again, the Orphic version of the Greek myth involves the Titans who have consumed Dionysus being struck by Zeus's lightning, with Dionysus being "reborn" from the smoke and soot rising from their bodies.[110] Thus the Titans form a clearer match to the demon of the Vedic branch.

---

110   *The Arts of Orpheus*, Ivan M. Linforth, 307-364. Linforth notes that the limbs of Dionysus are cooked over a fire in Euphorion's version, that Arnobius and Diodorus say they were boiled, while Clement of Alexander says they were roasted over a fire as well. He states that Plutarch says they tasted the blood and that Olympiodorus, quoting an Orphic poem, says they ate of the flesh, while Firmicus Maternus says they devoured the dismembered body completely (Linforth, 313). Diodorus says the boiling of the limbs was an allegory for the boiling of the wine to improve its flavor, which nicely parallels the idea of the filtering and preparing of the sacred liquid to remove impurities as well as cut its bitterness, a process we have noted previously in relation to the *soma/haoma*. See also: *The Orphic Hymns*; Gantz, Timothy, *Early Greek Myth: A Guide to Literary and Artistic Sources*, Johns Hopkins University Press, 1996, p. 118; *The Routledge Handbook of Greek Mythology*: Based on H.J. Rose's *Handbook of Greek Mythology*, Robin Hard, H. J. Rose, p. 35.

While paralleling the Chyavana birth myth, the Orphic variant also seems to combine other elements of the *"soma"* mythos. Specifically, certain details we find in the Orphic variant parallel those myths regarding the purification of the *soma* that we have analyzed so far: specifically Namuci drinking the *soma* and the *soma* having to be extracted from him and purified (he being beheaded in the *Rig Veda* version), but also Shiva extracting the noxious gases at the milk sea, Gullveig being thrice burned and changed to Heithr, Fuamnach being burned and beheaded. When he is consumed by the Titans, Dionysus and the element he embodies, the sacred liquid, becomes mingled with the Titanic element. This mixture must then be purified by Zeus, who does away with the Titans, turning them to ash, and leading to the rebirth of the purified Dionysus. The Orphics seemingly took this mingling event as a paradigm of their religion. For them, humans derive from this mingled double source, the Titanic and the Dionysian. The Titans represent the material body, deemed to be lower, and Dionysus represents the soul, the higher aspect. To simplify the case drawn from sometimes contradictory and fragmentary sources: humans then must seek to rid themselves of the Titanic, material element in order to purify their souls, following the path of the purified and reborn Dionysus. We can now see that this whole paradigm could have derived from the same origin as the purification of the ancient *soma,* the sacred liquid, as Dionysus is the very god who embodies the sacred liquid in the Greek branch.

The entire 9th book of the *Rig Veda* is dedicated to the purification of this liquid, and as such the process must have had a profound and even esoteric significance from very early. In that book, the god Soma repeatedly goes as a bull to the sieve, the filter, the purifying cloth, or the bruising press stones (RV 9.67.19-20), symbolically dying in order to be purified. "Soma, flow on, inviting Gods, speed to the purifying cloth: Pass into Indra, as a Bull," says the fist verse of the second hymn of the 9th book. As Soma passes into Indra, recall that Zeus consumes or incubates Dionysus after he has been killed in some versions of the myth. The final animal into which Dionysus transforms just before being killed is also a bull in the Orphic myth. From this paradigmatic purification ritual, focused originally on the sacred liquid as a symbol for the soul, and as expanded and developed into a more emphatic dualism by the Orphics and other philosophers, various philosophical strains occasionally hostile to the "impure" material world may have perceived their mythical basis, if we consider the influence of Orphism on Pythagoreanism, Platonism, Gnosticism, and Christianity. As we explore in a later chapter, Soma as a bull going to the sieve is also one possible parallel of Roman Mithras slaying the bull.

Again, it should come as no surprise that the lord of the *soma* (Chyavana-Soma) and the Greek god of sacred wine would be the same god. Mead is of course the Germanic version of the *soma, ale* is possibly the Irish, and the Greek liquid intoxicant is also referred to as *methu,* it being considered possible by scholars that some kind of *mead* may have been used by the proto-cult of Dionysus before the popularization of wine in Greece: "Porphyry from 3rd century AD claimed on the authority of 'Orpheus' (a mythic poet) that Zeus intoxicated Cronus with honey (that is, mead) since there was no wine at the time" (Max Nelson, *The Barbarian's Beverage: A History of Beer in Ancient Europe*, 15).

> These authorities may in fact be right that mead was known to Greeks before wine. The most telling clue is the fact that the Greek word for 'intoxicant' is *methu,* which likely meant mead; not only is the English word 'mead' related to *methu,* but in Sanskrit *madhu* means mead, leading back to a probably Indo-European root *medhu.* Already in Homer *methu* is equated with *oinos* (presumably wine). (Nelson, 15-16)

> The name of Dionysus, the Greek god of intoxication, has also been found on two Linear B tablets (as di-wo-nu-so), in one case possibly connected to wine, and in the other to honey. This may show that Dionysus was connected to both wine and mead at this early time [...] as an ancient commentator rightly realized, Dionysus is not said by Homer to be the 'discoverer of wine'. Some scholars [See especially Harrison 1903: 323–324 and 1922: 413–425, whom Graves (1960: 108), among others, accepts.] have even argued that Dionysus was a beer (or mead) god before being a wine god, but the evidence is too sparse on this point. He may just as well have been a god of indiscriminate intoxication from various ingredients. (Nelson, 14-15)

Indeed, the identification of Dionysus as Soma ought to have been in some degree anticipated, and the close similarity of Dionysus and Chyavana's births ought to confirm the parallel in large part. However, there are yet more lines we can draw between Dionysus and the various "Soma" gods we have found in the other branches, and these ought to put the equivalency beyond doubt.

At the forefront of the relevant points is the fact that, while Soma is a god of the moon (or a "lunar" god that was eventually assimilated to the moon itself), Dionysus is absolutely covered with "lunar" symbols. This is so much the case that Eliade says flatly of Dionysus, "Dionysus is both moon god and god of vegetation" (*Patterns in Comparative Religion*, 162). The specific set of symbols that makes this statement valid (and it is important that they are a set) are the bull, the serpent, the vine, and of course the waters or divine liquid. Dionysus is often portrayed with bull horns, and even in the form of a bull as at Kyzikos. He is invoked as "bull-footed" and his epithet *bromios,* "roarer," is believed to pertain to his bull aspect, to his wind association, or both (the *soma* stalk is said to "roar" in RV 9.72.6). In the Orphic version of his myth, Dionysus

268

was said to transform into several animals, and lastly into a bull (called "bull faced" in *Orphic Hymn XXIX to Dionysos*). Bulls were sacrificed to him during his festival, the Dionysia, and he is sometimes called *Dionysus Tauros*. The image of the cow, full with white milk, makes the bovine a natural lunar symbol, which may be reinforced by the coloration (black and white together can be seen as lunar, mirroring the illuminated and darkened or spotted portions of the moon, or a pure white bull or cow can be perhaps even more obvious in its symbolism) and by the general rotundity of the animal. More pertinently, the shape of the bull's horns was "long ago compared to a crescent and likened to the moon," as Eliade says, while, "Lunar divinities of the Mediterranean and the East were represented under the form of a bull," concluding, furthermore, that in Egypt the moon god was known as "the bull of the stars" (*Patterns in Comparative Religion*, 93). (See our chapter on the Mithraic Path for more examples of Vedic Soma as a bull). The bull is the repeated symbol for the fecundating power of the sky, the waters of heaven impregnating the earth as bull impregnates cow, which applies also to the powers of the moon. Thus there are multiple celestial gods who sometimes take the bull form: Father Sky, Moon god, and later Indra, among others, each seen as masculine fecundators who bring the fertilizing waters via rain to the feminine Earth.

Dionysus' bull form and prominent horns are thus his most compelling connections to the lunar sphere, but they are reinforced by his other lunar symbolism. Dionysus is often depicted as having a crown of serpents or even as serpent-bodied. The serpent is another primary lunar symbol, according to Eliade, due to the fact that it sheds its skin and regenerates itself just as the moon is seen to renew itself each month. The serpent is thus an earthly stand-in and repetition of the power of the moon. The fact that it burrows into the earth which is connected to the underworld and to vegetative powers reinforces the connection. Eliade explains that the serpent is connected to the moon

> because it appears and disappears, and because it has as many coils as the moon has days (this legend is also preserved in Greek tradition); or because it is 'the husband of all women' [...] all the symbols are directed to the same central idea: it is immortal because it is continually reborn, and therefore it is a moon 'force'. (Eliade, 163)

The vine, which Dionysus wears and the power of which Dionysus is seen to embody, also mirrors the serpent and connects to both the serpent and the vegetative power more generally, both seen as connected forces ruled by the moon – consider Soma as lord of plants. "The plant world comes from the same source of universal fertility, and is subject to the same recurring cycles governed by the moon's movements," Eliade says. As god of wine, Dionysus was often depicted with either a bowl or chalice (as well as sometimes a drinking horn), both of course vessels used in various versions of the Holy Grail legend as the vessel of the sacred liquid. His skin is said to be white by Euripides in his

269

Bacchae, due to being "not exposed to strokes of the sun, but beneath the shade" (455 ff).

Finally, Dionysus' well-known dismemberment and rebirth is another lunar symbol. Just as the snake does, the moon sheds its old form, "dies," and is reborn each month. So Dionysus is torn to pieces (these pieces may mirror the idea that the moon, as the "measurer," is divided into phases which themselves divide the days, Dionysus thereby embodying the *month*) and then is born again whole. Consider also that Chyavana's myth centers around him being aged, having his eye violently poked out, then being renewed in youth; or that the associated Dadhyanc has his head cut off then replaced; or that the embodiment of the Norse sacred mead, Kvasir, is killed and his blood is used as the sacred liquid, whereas Dionysus is torn apart and consumed, and Mimir is beheaded but then lives again as a preserved head with the power of speech. These all seem to be connected lunar motifs, which supposition may be supported by the Slavic case, in which Jarilo (who is foster son of an underworld god Veles, and is kidnapped the night of his birth, which ought to be a recognizable motif by now) is killed, dismembered, and then reborn. Jarilo thus in several ways parallels Freyr, etc., but the fact that this motif of dismemberment has shifted merely one position, from the lunar underworld god to his foster son, only argues for its intimate connection to the lunar myth in which they both are involved. The complex problem of the Slavic material and the precise place of Jarilo remains open.[111]

---

[111] Though a case for Veles as Varunian is common, there is also one that must be made for him as a Soma God: this Soma, who becomes a chief underworld deity in some branches, and whose main associations are waters, wealth and fertility.

Njordr being the true parallel of this Soma god and not Odinn, who some have seen as paralleled with Veles, Veles would instead be parallel of Njordr. Chyavana, like Veles, fights a battle against the Thunderer king of the gods, here Indra. In the Slavic case this is the Thunderer high king Perun. Like Veles, Njordr does not have much of an *explicit* moon connection. The argument that Njordr has a lunar character is based on the comparative deductions we have laid out. Obviously, the water connection is one central detail connecting Veles, Njordr, and the Lunar mythos. The myth of Veles fighting Perun could then be the same theme we have seen in so many branches, the Soma God fighting against the high god, the battle of the low and high divine Functions or Castes.

The other thing to be said is this: Jarilo is stolen at birth and taken to be raised by Veles. As said previously, Freyr may actually have originally been foster son of Njordr. For one thing, in the Irish case, Freyr's parallel Aengus is taken at birth to be fostered by the underworld Soma god Midir and does not find his true parentage til much later. And Snorri mysteriously calls Freyr a son of Odinn twice. Freyr's Welsh Parallel Pryderi is stolen at birth and raised by another god as well.

This Pryderi is also the same figure as Peredur/Perceval, as we have seen, who is hidden in the countryside from birth so he will not know his true father, and as we will explore shortly, a parallel of Osiris' son Younger Horus, who is taken and hidden at birth to protect him from Set. Jarilo of course has the dismemberment motif also seen with Osiris and Dionysus even though those gods are the father figures and Jarilo is seemingly the young son, so there is variability in the motifs — but we are still talking about a dismemberment motif, which should tip us off that we are likely talking about the same general mythos.

It is also interesting that The Devil (usually a cover name for Veles in slavic folklore) causes God (usually a cover name for Perun) to have to drink bee's dung in one Slavic folktale, and then God/Perun changes it into honey, which becomes the source of the mead. This seems like it could be a remnant of Veles' role in making the mead, considering that he does help it come about in this tale. The Soma God is metaphysically at the origin of the mead of course, and also Chyavana, his incarnation, makes a monster called Mada ("intoxication", relating to "mead", honey etc.) to fight Indra. Dumezil has argued that this Mada parallels Norse Kvasir, a being created by the gods who embodies the intoxicating liquid (*Gods of the Ancient Northmen*).

Like Veles, Chyavana is known to be able to cast damaging magic on those who offend him, as when he makes those who have offended him not be able to heed "the call of nature" when his eye has been poked. But in this branch Chyavana essentially wins the battle and makes Indra allow the Horse Twins to join the sacrifice. In Slavic folklore there is one belief connected to moon phases. The Moon is said to disappear because it is cut by Saint Elijah, which is a cover name for Perun in Slavic folklore. So we have a direct example of moon and high thunder god antagonism. A similar antagonism is present in Lithuanian mythology, but with Perkunas mentioned directly.

While Chyavana is victorious in the Vedic instance, it seems that in the end of the Slavic version Perun is finally victorious rather than Veles. This could just be a difference in the branches. When Perun fights Zmij (the dragon conflated with Veles), Perun is victorious, but in the struggle of the moon and thunderer the moon wins more of a victory, considering that he is able to resurrect himself over and over again. Perhaps Zmij or Veles losing to Perun reflects the Christianization of the tale and demonization of Veles. The case of Zmij-Veles may even show signs of a conflation of the Lunar God with the serpent that the Thunderer fights in what is usually a separate myth (Vrtra or Vala, etc). Dionysus is also commonly shown covered in serpents and with bull horns or in bull form, while serpents and bull horns are two of Veles' main symbols as well.

The enmity of Veles and Perun is often attributed to Veles' theft of Perun's cattle, or to Perun's theft of Veles's cattle. In the Welsh case, the parallel battle is started when the high caste god Gwydion steals the Swine of the Underworld which belonged to the welsh Soma God (but had been transferred to Pryderi, the proposed parallel of Jarilo/Freyr, at this point). So this welsh Soma God, Arawn, the Lord of the Underworld, has specific domestic animals he keeps, a lord of swine instead of sheep/cows. This theft of swine/cattle parallels the theft of the Sabine women in Roman legend which starts the Sabine War.

Thus this Chyavana-Soma, an underworld god, specifically connected to waters and wealth, with dangerous magic, who fights the high thunderer god, and who is connected to the honey mead, and whose parallels also act as foster fathers to the Young Son god who is stolen at birth, is very reminiscent of Veles.

271

Dionysus and Osiris

To find the origin of the exact *form* of the motif of Dionysus' dismemberment, we have to look to the non-Indo-European god who is known to have strongly influenced the Greek depiction of Dionysus. This foreign god is the Egyptian underworld god Osiris. Though we mostly avoid non-Indo-European parallels in the present study, the equivalency of Osiris and Dionysus, which the Greeks drew, and which they perceived clearly, is about as good of an extra-Indo-European parallel as you can possibly hope to find, a fact which will hopefully become apparent. Herodotus, for one, explicitly equated the two gods, saying,

> In other ways the Egyptian method of celebrating the festival of Dionysus [meaning Osiris] is much the same as the Greek [...] they have puppets about 18 inches high; the genitals of these figures [...] are pulled up and down by strings [...] Flutes lead the procession, and the women [...] sing a hymn to Dionysus. (Herodotus, *Histories*, Book 2, 49, 2)

Furthermore, the central myth of Osiris involves his death and dismemberment in a conflict with Set (who, as we will see, is in the position comparable to Thjazi, Hafgan etc.). In the conclusion of the myth, Osiris is reconstituted and reborn, becoming by this action the god of the Underworld. Reminiscent of this pattern, Dionysus in the Orphic myth is dismembered by the Titans, consumed, and then made whole again and brought back to life. Herodotus continues by stating unequivocally that the Dionysus cult has been influenced by Egyptian religion, and not vice versa, saying, "I will never admit that the similar ceremonies performed in Greece and Egypt are the result of mere coincidence [...] Nor will I allow that the Egyptian ever took over from Greece either this custom or any other" (Herodotus, *Histories*, Book 2, 50, 3). Many other ancient authorities also explicitly equated Osiris with Dionysus, including Diodorus Siculus, Plutarch, Nonnos, and Mnaseas, Diodorus Siculus saying, "there is only a difference of names" between the festivals of the two gods (Diodorus Siculus, *The Library of History*, 1.13).

The equivalency of Dionysus and Osiris is further supported by numerous shared associations. Whereas Dionysus was the god of wine and of the grape vine, Osiris was called "Lord of Drunkenness" during the grape harvest (Sigfrid Hoedel-Hoenes, *Life and Death in Ancient Egypt*, 114), while wine was offered to and found on funerary monuments connected with him. In ancient papyri he is sometimes depicted with clusters of grapes (*Papyrus of Nebseni*, 1550 BCE; *Papyrus of Nakht*). Like the "Soma" gods generally, Osiris is associated with drink and food that grant immortality: "the bread and the beer of Osiris make the eater immortal," says the *Book of the Dead* (*Book of the*

Dead, 40), and these are called "thy bread of eternity, and thy beer of everlastingness" in the *Text of Pepi II* (390). Ivy is sacred to Dionysus, while Osiris is said in Egypt to be its discoverer. Worshippers of Osiris are described by Plutarch as carrying *thyrsoi* like that associated with Dionysus, and pine cones are important symbols found on monuments of each god. Beyond the liquid of the wine, Dionysus is also the lord of all moisture generally ("the lord and master not only of wine, but of the nature of every sort of moisture" (Plutarch, *On Isis and Osiris*, 35)), whereas, "all kinds of moisture are called the 'efflux of Osiris,'" as Plutarch records (Plutarch, *On Isis and Osiris*, 35). As such, the death and rebirth of Osiris was connected to the flood cycle of the Nile river. Both gods are connected with the origin of Drama in their respective societies as well (see H. Jeremiah Lewis, *Osiris and Dionysos Compared*). Above all, these shared traits should demonstrate why and in which details the Greeks accepted the influence of Osiris on their cult of Dionysus.

Hence, while the question of the origin of the precise form of Dionysus' dismemberment myth remains heavily debated, there is significant evidence to suggest that any shifts in its original form may have been caused by a syncretism via borrowing from the Egyptians. The fact that the precise form of the myth, the god dismembered and brought back to life, is seen in no other branches except the Slavic, in which branch it is connected instead to the proposed Young Son rather than to the Soma God, argues in favor of it being a non-Indo-European form of the myth, but the issue also remains quite a mystery. For the Slavic case we would then have to suppose either a Neolithic version of the myth shared between Egypt and Greece and the pre-Slavic lands, or alternately a later influence of the borrowed Egyptian form on the Slavs, perhaps via contact with Greek culture forms, or by some other path.

If the form as we find it in the Dionysus mythos was a borrowing from Egypt, it was at least a fortunate syncretism. Eliade says of Osiris that he too is a lunar god: "Osiris possesses all these [lunar] attributes: moon, water, plant life and agriculture" (*Patterns in Comparative Religion*, 162). Furthermore, as we can trace in *The Pyramid Texts* and other sources, Osiris has a son with his sister Isis, and this son, Horus the Younger, thus stands in the same position that we have previously seen the Horse Twins or Morning Star god: like Freyr the Young Son of Soma God Njörðr, or Aengus the Young Son and foster son of Soma God Midir. Because Younger Horus' father has been killed and he is born in danger of Set's violence, he is brought up in secret by his mother. Hence he is often referred to as "Son of Isis." This is paralleled closely, for instance, by Perceval, who is raised in the woods apart from his father, his mother attempting to protect him from the dangers of knighthood (Aengus is also explicitly brought up without knowledge of his true father or birthright). Welsh Pryderi, the possible model of Perceval, has also been argued to be the "Mabon ap Modron," or "Young Son of the Mother," which matches precisely Horus' titles "Horus the Young/Child, son of Isis," or *HarusaAset, Herupa Khered*, *Harseisis,* etc.

Even the central motif that we have seen repeated in the Indo-European cases, of the poked out eye, appears in the Egyptian myth of this father and son as well, but in the Egyptian case even more explicitly connected with the moon, which should make clear to us that we have been on the right track. Here the eye-poking motif, as in the case of Perceval with the Red Knight, and partially in the case of Aengus who is in charge of the rambunctious children who perpetrate the poking, is again shifted to the Young Son instead of the Moon God father – but the Egyptians were also clear that Horus is a re-manifestation of Osiris, and thus they partly identified the two. The losing of Horus' eye in his battle with Set was explicitly seen to be a symbol of the darkening of the moon during its cycle or eclipses (Geraldine Pinch, *Egyptian Mythology: A Guide to the Gods, Goddesses, and Traditions of Ancient Egypt*, 82-83, 91), just as we have previously theorized the symbolic meaning of the poking out of Chyavana and Midir's eye to be. The eye is then said to be either retrieved or healed, as it is also often healed in the Indo-European cases discussed. Osiris also marries his own sister, just as Njörðr is said to be consort of his sister. Horus the Younger's battle with Set, in which the eye is lost, would then be in the very same position as the fight against Norse Thjazi, that against Welsh Hafgan, and that against the Red Knight of the Grail legend. These oppositional figures, as we have argued, are destructive solar gods, while Set is said to be a god of the desert. Interestingly, Set is also associated with thunder, while Thjazi's home is called *Thrymheimr*, "thunder home" or "crash-home," and while the armor of the Red Knight is of course red, Set is associated with the color red in relation to the red sand of the desert. As one commentator puts it, Set "was associated with the desert (which takes its name from the Egyptian word 'dshrt' – the red place). He represented the fierce dry heat of the sun as it parched the land" (Jenny Hill, 2008)[112].

Considering these mythic and symbolic parallels, which put Dionysus (and his influencer, Osiris) in a continuity with the previously analyzed "Soma" gods, we should proceed to a closer look at Dionysus' mythology to see if any other "Soma"-associated myths can be found there in relatively recognizable form.

* * *

---

112   https://ancientegyptonline.co.uk/set/.

Dionysus, Hades and Soma

The crucial "eye-poking" motif, always present in a similar form in the Lunar Cycle, is not absent from the Greek version either. Just as it is performed by the young Perceval in Chretien's Grail poem, by the youths in the kingdom of the Young Son Aengus, and perpetrated on the son of Osiris in the Egyptian case, so the eye-poking is connected to the son of the Soma God Dionysus in the Greek case (in Vedic and Norse cases it is not directly connected to the Young Son(s)/Horse Twin(s)). Due to the apparent Egyptian influence on the Dionysus mythos, this son of the Greek god could be taken as repeating the lunar power of the father in the manner that Younger Horus does in relation to his father Osiris. Dionysus' son's name, meaning "wine drinker" or "wine-rich" relates him intimately to his father, to the vegetative power of the vine, and to the lunar liquid itself. The character of this son, then, could be impacted by a non-Indo-European influence of some kind, whether Egyptian or otherwise — however, we must remember that the Indo-European Young Son or Horse Twin god *is* also generally known for being a *soma* drinker (and distributer), thus the degree of outside influence on his character is indeterminate. If we trace back the wine of the Greeks to the honey mead of the PIEs and certain connected Vedic forms of the honey, we see that the Vedic Asvins are very much drinkers of the divine honey and are rich with it as Dionysus' son is rich with wine:

> Of all the gods the Asvins are most closely connected with honey (*madhu),* with which they are mentioned in many passages. They have a skin filled with honey, and the birds which draw them abound in it (4, 45, 3-4). They poured out 100 jars of honey (1, 117, 6). Their honey-goad (1, 122, 3; 1, 57, 4) with which they bestrew the sacrifice and the worshipper, is peculiar to them. Only the car of the Asvins is described as honey-hued (*madhu-varna*) or 'honey-bearing' (*madhu-vahand*). **They only are said to be fond of honey (*madhuyu, madhvt)* or drinkers of it (*madhupa*).** The priest to whom they are invited to come is called honey-handed (10, 413). They give honey to the bee (1, 112, 21 cp. 10, 40, 6) and are compared with bees (10, 106, 10). They are, however, like other gods, **fond of Soma** (3, 58,7-9 &c.) and are invited to drink it with Usas and Surya (8, 35, 1). (Arthur A. Macdonell, *Vedic Mythology*, 49-50)

This wine-drinking son of Dionysus is Oenopion, who just like his doubles, the Horse Twins, is one of a pair of twins, his twin brother being Staphylus. When the hunter and giant Orion comes to Oenopion's kingdom, he assaults and attempts to violate Oenopion's daughter, Merope. Compare this assault to Thjazi abducting Iðunn in the Germanic parallel case, as well as the fact that Thjazi too is a giant, and recall that we have mentioned the questionable epithet *skaut-giarn* from the Eddic poem *Hyndluljóð,*

275

with the slight possibility that it describes his being a bow hunter, while Volund, another name for Thjazi according to Rydberg, is indeed such a hunter. In response to the assault of his daughter, Oenopion stabs Orion in the eye, blinding him. Thus Oenopion, this Young Son of the lunar god Dionysus, as in the parallel cases, pierces the eye of the assailant hunter, just as Perceval stabs the eye of the thieving Red Knight, the youths under the watch of Aengus poke out Midir's eye, and as Thjazi (whose crime is both a theft and assault of a goddess) has his own eyes removed after his offense. Orion is said then to carry Cedalion, the servant of Hephaestus, around on his shoulders, whereas Thjazi carries Loki through the sky in the form of an eagle. This does not imply that Orion and the eyes of Thjazi must correspond to the same stellar constellations (though the possibility could be explored), as the systems of astronomy in ancient Scandinavia and in the Mediterranean have separate and unique histories.

As with the case of Vedic Soma, who shows some signs of the syncretism of two or more related deities, ancient commentators such as Diodorus Siculus believed there to have originally been several Dionysuses: "For some have handed down the story that there was but one Dionysus, others that there were three" (III.62). These of course could have been several gods who were similar but distinct, or several instances of the same identical god (particularly when he is reborn), who may then have been combined under the name of Dionysus to form the unitary mythos that has been left to us. In the Norse case we also named Njörðr and Kvasir in particular (and possibly Mímir) as associated gods who were connected to the mythos of the sacred waters and to the mead cycle and who could theoretically correspond to two or three of the separate gods who were combined in the Vedic and Greek cases. Njörðr as lord of waters and wealth generally and as the husband of the Sun Princess, Kvasir as an embodiment of the mead/*soma* itself, who is killed and consumed as Dionysus also is (particularly under the name *Zagreus*), and Mímir as the keeper of the specialized waters of illumination and arguably of an underworld domain, could each then correspond to different aspects of Dionysus/Soma, or, in the case of Mímir, to Yama insofar as he overlaps similar attributes of Soma.

Perusing the details of Dionysus' mythos, we tally several other connections between him and the other Soma gods. Like Njörðr, Dionysus is also connected with the sea. Once, he hides in it, while another time he punishes a ship of sailors by turning them into dolphins. He stays with the daughters of Nereus in the Erythraian Sea, under the waves, "sprawled among the seaweed in Thetis' bosom" (*Dionysiaca* 21.170). He is believed to have washed up in a chest on a beach of Brasia. Certain of his attendants were called the "sea women," or *Halia*. He arrives by ship during the Anthesteria, one of the central festivals in his honor. He was called "god of the sea" and "god of the seacoast," the former in Pasagae and the latter in Chios, Sparta, and Sicyon. His grottoes and temples were often in marshes (Pausanias 2.23.1) (Athenaios 11.465 A). And as previously mentioned, he was considered a lord of all moisture, of the liquid element generally.

As Njörðr is (*Gylfaginning* 23), Dionysus is also associated with the wind, called "roarer" in this connection. He is also well-known for having two forms: the older and the younger Dionysus. This well matches the Chyavana tale wherein he begins as an aged ascetic before being renewed in youth, and this again reflects the waning and then renewal of the moon. The previously encountered "wasteland" motif may also be present in Dionysus' mythos. When wine is banned by Lykourgos, Dionysus makes the king's land become a wasteland, and only renews it after Lykourgos is ritualistically killed (Pseudo-Apollodorus, *Bibliotheca 3. 34-35).*

While the Soma God generally weds a daughter or descendant of the Sun God, and Chyavana indeed marries the great-grand-daughter of the Sun God, Dionysus weds Ariadne, who, just so, is grand-daughter of the Sun, Helios. The marriage of Dionysus seems to have been reenacted during Dionysus' festival, Anthesteria. During the second day of Anthesteria, called Choës, Athens' ritual queen, called the *basilinna*, would be married to Dionysus in a special ceremony. Scholar Walter Burkert believed this to be a reenactment of Ariadne's marriage to Dionysus after being left to him by Theseus (Burkert, *Greek Religion*, §II.7.7, p. 109). Now the name of the festival itself, *Anthesteria*, is from *anthes-* (ἀνθεσ-), the combining form of *ánthos* (ἄνθος, 'flower')[113], and this root is cognate with the Sanskrit word for the *soma* plant, *andhas*, अन्धस्. Hugh Chisholm in his *Encyclopedia Brittanica* proposes that this refers to the bloom of the grape vine, since "The object of the festival was to celebrate the maturing of the wine stored at the previous vintage, and the beginning of spring." The name of the first day of the festival, *Pithoigia*, means "the opening of the casks," and involved the opening of the vintage along with many libations and bouts of ceremonious drinking. If we consider that the sacred liquid matures in the moon due to the marriage of the Soma Moon god to the Daughter of the Sun, we can see why this marriage was seen to coincide with the maturation of the earthly vintage. Ariadne also gives birth to twins (the aforementioned Oenopion and Staphylus), perhaps reflecting or doubling the birth of the Horse Twins which we have seen in other branches. Ariadne goes to the underworld and then returns, as Rhiannon does, and is made deathless and un-aging, just as the princess Surya is said to be made immortal by her union with Soma in the *Rig Veda* hymn "Surya's Bridal." Dionysus ultimately places Ariadne's crown in the sky as stars, as Njörðr's wife Skaði has her father's eyes placed in the heavens as stars. After his blinding and recovery, Orion is also placed in the sky as a constellation upon his death, at the request of the

---

113   Chisholm, Hugh. *Encyclopedia Brittanica*, "Anthesteria."
       https://en.wikisource.org/wiki/1911_Encyclop%C3%A6dia_Britannica/Anthesteria.

goddesses, just as the eyes of Skaði's father Thjazi are so treated upon his death, at the request of Skaði.

As with Irish Midir's and Norse Njörðr's marriages, Dionysus and Ariadne's marriage is not a purely happy one. Indeed, a similar drama develops as that found in Irish Midir's myth with his wives Fuamnach and Etain, who come into physical and magical conflict. For Ariadne and Dionysus' second wife, a princess from India, develop a rivalry and come into conflict as well. Ovid says: "Among the captive girls of surpassing beauty was a princess whom Bacchus [Dionysus] liked too much. His loving wife wept and, as she paced the curving beach, delivered words like these, disheveled: 'Come, waves, listen again to identical sobs. Come, sand, absorb again my weeping. I recall my cry" (Ovid, *Fasti* 3.459). In addition, Dionysus threatens Ariadne's previous husband Theseus and wins her from him, whereas Midir also must win Etain back from her then husband, Eochu Airem.

Dionysus is associated both with satyrs and music, while Soma is closely tied to the similar wild musical and sexual beings the Gandharvas. Interestingly, Hephaestus gives Dionysus two silver bowls, while the Grail (a salver) and a silver serving dish are both seen side by side in the Grail procession, and the silver bowls themselves may again be symbols of the moon.

When Dionysus is born, Hermes rescues him from the flame and gives him honey (common for birth rituals, but also an ingredient associated with the sacred drinks). We will see in a subsequent chapter, following Allen and Woodard, how Hermes is the "Gandharva," who, as with the case of Welsh Pwyll, is the protege of the Soma God and thus very closely associated with him as his guardian and attendant. There is even a vase painted with the image of Hermes, Dionysus, and Ariadne, in which Hermes is gesturing at Ariadne, as if giving her to Dionysus. This again reaffirms the close connection of Hermes with Dionysus (as the Gandharva is similarly connected with Soma), Hermes as his attendant, and also reminds us of the Welsh scene in which the Gandharva Pwyll sleeps next to but protects the virginity of Arawn's wife until the return of Arawn.

Hephaestus and Dionysus

Of further interest is the fact that, just as the Fire God Manawydan plays an important role in the latter portion of the Welsh Lunar Cycle, so the Greek Fire God Hephaestus also appears in an important episode of Dionysus' myth. In this episode, Hephaestus, having been thrown from Olympos by Hera, returns to Hera with a gift of a finely-wrought golden throne. The throne is a trap, however, and when Hera sits upon it she is bound to it by invisible restraints. The other gods cry out for Hephaestus to release her. Only when Dionysus steps in and gets Hephaestus drunk with wine is he able to return him to Olympus and get him to free Hera. The theme of a great queen of the gods being frozen to the spot and imprisoned when she touches a finely made, magical, golden object once again reminds us of the manner in which Welsh Rhiannon is imprisoned in the Otherworld when she touches the golden bowl and freezes in place. At the same time, Hera sitting on the chair that triggers the crisis reminds us also of Pryderi sitting on the mound Gorsedd Arberth and triggering the enchanted wasteland, which event immediately precedes him and Rhiannon being trapped in the Otherworld by the golden bowl, and so the two Welsh mythic events can be seen as linked, parts of one event. This motif of the treacherous seat is reflected in the later Grail legends as the chair Siege Perilous, which kills anyone who sits on it and is not worthy of it.

The freeing of Hera from this enchanted imprisonment, just like the freeing of Rhiannon and the disenchanting of the wasteland (or the same in the Samvarana tale) is brought about by an action that can only be performed by the Fire God. The Greek gods are in despair to get Hephaestus to come back to Olympus to free Hera, until Dionysus steps in to bring about this Fire God's return. In the Welsh and Indian versions the need for the instrumental action of the Fire God to end the crisis implies something to do with the sacrificial fire, generally pointing toward a renewal of the sacrifice, which is made explicit rather than symbolic in the Samvarana version, in which Samvarana must return to his sacrificial rites (with his bride) to cause the rain to fall once more and to heal the wasteland. Welsh Fire God Manawydan in his version must discover the captors of Rhiannon and Pryderi and then force them to release the great queen and her son, compelling them to lift the enchantment on the land at the same time. As such it would not be amiss to see Dionysus' pouring out of the sacred wine into the belly of the fire god, making him drunk, and then sending him up to the gods, as an allegory for the *soma* or wine sacrifice itself. "After making him drunk Dionysos brought him to heaven," says Pausanias (Pausanias, *Guide to Greece* 1.20.3). The sacred wine is poured into the fire (Hephaestus), the fire divinity becomes "drunk" and takes the offering up to the gods on Olympos, and only this, precisely as in the other cases, frees the Great Queen and solves the crisis that her imprisonment or absence has brought about. This scene is found in many ancient depictions, with Dionysus leading a drunken Hephaestus on a donkey toward Olympos. This image would then be an image of the sacred wine sacrifice itself, a fire sacrifice fueled by the burnt offering of the sacred liquid, which has the power to free the gods and goddesses from obstruction, allow them to operate for the benefit of the world, and heal the wasteland. This is the mythic embodiment of the ancient understanding that the sacrifice made possible existence, the new day, flourishing, etc.

If we are confident from the connections between Dionysus and Soma discussed thus far, we may attempt to further "read into" the other Dionysus myths in this fashion, required as we are to recognize that the Greek myths often have come down to us in cryptic form, elaborated by creative license of the famous greek poets and at times altered by syncretisms with the other dominant cultures in and around the Mediterranean. As such, we may be permitted to attempt to speculate and to actively try to find an instance of the "Aesir-Vanir War" in the Dionysian myths. If this motif is not instead to be found in the myths of the Greek Horse Twin gods, the Dioskouroi, then there are a couple of other possible candidates, confrontations or battles that Dionysus is known to take part in. The most interesting of these possibilities may be Dionysus' campaign into India. The Indians, known for their spiritual elevation and for their wise Brahmin priests, could in this case be given as a symbol for the (priestly) "First Function," in the Dumezilian sense, that function against which the "Aesir-Vanir War" is fought by the Third Function gods. Dionysus' fighting and overcoming of these Indians could then be the Soma God once again confronting and overcoming the first function, as Njörðr does in the Norse case. This interpretation may also be reinforced by the fact that Dionysus also fights against Poseidon in this war. Key to this connection is the fact that, in many places, Poseidon seems to take the role of the first function Vedic god Varuna, sovereign lord of water. For instance, when the Mitraic hero Theseus is born (as we will discuss later on), Poseidon seems to be made a double of his father Aegeus, while when the Mitraic hero Yudhishthira is born, his father Pandu's spiritual father is Varuna, thus drawing an equivalency between Poseidon and Varuna. Varuna is a temperamental god who is the lord of all water, while Poseidon is temperamental lord of the sea. Poseidon is eldest son of Cronus and could even have been the king of the gods before Zeus was, if such an interpretation of the archaeological records of the Mycenaean period is followed, while Varuna was the eldest and first chief of the gods along with or followed by Mitra, eventually yielding this kingship to Indra in the Vedic branch. Thus, while an expansion on this idea would require a separate explication, it is by no means out of the way to say that Poseidon could here be taking the role of the First Function sovereign, which we see Oðinn take in the Norse Aesir-Vanir War. We would then see Dionysus' fighting and overcoming of both the First Function priestly and First Function sovereign principles in this war.

A couple final notes to consider. Dionysus was closely associated with the three Charites, or Graces: "In the earliest times the Graces, or Charites, were the companions of Dionysus (Pind. *Ol.* xiii. 20; Plut. *Quaest. Gr.* 36; Apollon. Rhod. iv. 424), and at Olympia he and the Charites had an altar in common. (Schol. *ad Pind. Ol.* v. 10; Paus. v. 14 in fin.)"[114]. Chief among these three is Aglaea, meaning "shining one," who becomes

---

114   William Smith, *Dictionary of Greek and Roman Biography and Mythology, 1048.*

Hephaestus' wife. "Shining" is not a rare adjective for a deity, but it is after all a specific epithet we see frequently associated with the various Sun Princesses/Daughters of the Sun in the various branches we have examined, while the number three also matches the number of goddesses connected to this cycle in the Norse myth (Iðunn, Skaði, Gerðr) or in Irish (Etain, Caer, Aine) or Indian (Sukanya, Tapati, Savitri). Hence it is very likely the Graces too are another iteration of the same solar daughters. The mares of the sun in the *Rig Veda* are called in Sanskrit by a curiously similar name, *harits* or *haritas*, and are also multiple: seven or ten in number, which is "typical of his [the Sun's] rays," says John Downson's *A Classical Dictionary of Hindu Mythology and Religion Geography, History and Literature.* According to this entry, Max Müller asserted that these were "The prototype of the Grecian Charite." Thus we have the rays of the sun themselves pictured as female horses and called *haritas*, which are purportedly the same as the Charites, and we have the Daughters of the Sun as a larger group who also seem to be goddesses of the sun's rays and who in some cases are horse goddesses (Rhiannon, Etain). It can easily be imagined how these concepts could have been one and the same originally or could have become combined at some point.[115]

Hermes, the primary Greek Gandharvic god, as we will see in a later section, is himself said by Nonnus to be wedded to one of the Graces, Peitho, and she is specifically connected to marriage rites: "If quickshoe Hermes has made merry bridal with you, if he has forgotten his own Peitho [his wife]"(Nonnus, *Dionysiaca* 8. 220); and, "Lord Hermes […] entered the delicate bed of Peitho who brings marriage to pass" (Nonnus, *Dionysiaca* 48. 230). In an event occurring before he sleeps with his wife Peitho, Hermes offers his rod to go in *Persephone's* bedchamber as bride-price, attempting to win Persephone's hand in a contest for it. Recall that the *gandharva-samit* rod goes in the bed of the married couple to preserve their virginity for a space of time before consummation. Recall also that Pwyll sleeps chastely in the bed of Arawn's wife for one year, and in so doing reenacts the *gandharva-samit* ritual himself, just before marrying Rhiannon instead. "All that dwelt in Olympos were bewitched by this one girl [Persephone], rivals in love for the marriageable maid, and offered their dowers for an unsmirched bridal. Hermes had not yet gone to the bed of Peitho, and he offered his rod

---

115   See also: "Thus the Harits became the immortal steeds who bear the chariot of Indra across the sky and the car of Archilleus over the plains of Ilion. The Greeks carried away the name at an earlier stage; and the Charites, retaining simply the qualities of grace and brightness, became the lovely beings who, with Himeros and the Muses, charm earth and heaven with their song" (George W. Cox, *The mythology of the Aryan nations: The relation of mythology to language*). "In the Veda, as in Greek poetry, Sûrya has a chariot, drawn by one or seven horses, the seven Harits, or bright horses, in which, in spite of all differences, we have to recognize the prototype of the Greek Charites" (Wilhelm Schmidt, *The origin and growth of religion: Facts and theories*).

as gift to adorn her [Persephone's] chamber" (Nonnus, *Dionysiaca 5. 562 ff (trans. Rouse) (Greek epic C5th A.D.).* A Mycenaean seal ring shows two females, who have been interpreted as the Charites, dancing next to a male figure, who is interpreted as either Hermes or Dionysus.[116] A relief at the colony of Thasos from the beginning of the 5th century BCE shows the Charites with Hermes and a female who is believed to be Peitho or Aphrodite, and a 4th century vase from Apulia also shows Hermes and Peitho together. A relief of the Charites and Hermes decorated the entrance of the Akropolis. The fact that both the Fire God and the Gandharvic God of the Greeks are said to marry Graces would then reflect the repeated pattern we have seen, that one of the Sun Princesses is almost always shared and transferred from one of the husbands to another in the Lunar Cycle. These two goddesses are separate Graces, but they are the same insofar as they are both Graces, and this fact is all we have left of the bride transference motif in the Greek case. If the Greek case follows the others, Hephaestus and Hermes could even have originally been married to the same Grace, and over time these wives could have been made separate. Lastly, one of Dionysus' epithets is "completely hidden," one interpretation of which could be the moon at its minimum, at the transition to the New Moon, hidden in darkness. Alternately, the *Rig Veda* says that Soma is "hidden" (RV, 1.23.14).

Dionysus and Hades

Building on this understanding of Dionysus as Soma, we must make a further leap to consider if Hades too might be rooted in this same Indo-European "Soma" mythos. This connection is prompted by the aforementioned fact that the moon was often seen as an afterlife destination with the Moon God as the lord of this destination (Mircea Eliade, *Patterns in Comparative Religion, "*The Moon and its Mystique"). Dionysus, after all, with his vegetative powers rooted in the depths, is already a clearly chthonic god, who was considered to have a "subterranean" aspect, called Dionysus *Khthonion.* But in addition, both Dionysus' explicit Egyptian parallel and influence, Osiris, and the Welsh "Soma" God, Arawn, are named as the Lord of the Underworld/Otherworld in their respective mythologies, while the Irish parallel, Midir, is suggested to be an underworld lord as well by his depiction with three cranes, likely symbols of death, who guard his castle and can steal the will to fight from any warrior, along with his habitation in the

---

116   Barbara Breitenberger (2007). "Goddesses of Grace and Beauty: the Charites". *Aphrodite and Eros: The Development of Greek Erotic Mythology).*

burial mounds. The Welsh underworld, Annwn, whose lord is Arawn, is also said to be guarded by three cranes – if more evidence was needed that these are the same god.

Norse Mímir, too, has been argued by Victor Rydberg to be a lord of the afterlife, lord of an underworld "grove" or "holt," *mimisholt* (*Vafthrudnismal* 45). Most importantly, perhaps, the identity of Dionysus and Hades has been asserted several times before. In his book *Eleusis: Archetypal Image of Mother and Daughter,* Philologist Karl Kerenyi put forward the thesis that one of the primary secrets of the Greek Eleusinian Mysteries, one of the most central and revered mystery cults of Ancient Greece, was that Dionysus is Hades. He cites the fact that the two gods have many overlapping and identical epithets, that certain of their statues have identical facial features, and that ancient writers such as Heraclitus and Euripedes imply or assert this identification in their writings, among other evidences. Clement of Alexandria quotes Heraclitus as saying, "For were it not Dionysus to whom they institute a procession and sing songs in honor of the pudenda, it would be the most shameful action. But Dionysus, in whose honor they rave in bacchic frenzy, and Hades are the same" (*Fragment of Heraclitus* (5th C. BC), quoted by Clement of Alexandria).

Kerenyi's case for the identification of these two gods is fascinating and multi-faceted. He points out that Persephone is abducted by Hades on the Nysian Plain, at the foot of Mount Nysa, the birthplace of Dionysus, and that this plain was dedicated to Dionysus. The ground is said to gape open when Hades emerges, while Dionysus has the epithet "the gaping one." Kerenyi claims that Demeter's rejection of wine while she mourns for her stolen daughter is a sign that her daughter's abductor is really the god of wine. Demeter says the drinking of wine at that time would be "contrary to themis, the order of nature" (Kerenyi, 207). He also notes that the pomegranate, the fruit given by Hades to Persephone, is a fruit associated strongly with Dionysus, describing, among other instances, an image in which, "a bearded, long-robed Dionysos was represented lying in a cave, holding in his hand a golden cup; around him grow the vine and the apple and the pomegranate tree" (Kerenyi, 134). Kerenyi also describes a votive engraving of the nameless chief god of the Mysteries, called in the dedication only *Theos,* or "God":

> the recumbent god has the features rather of the bearded Dionysos than of Plouton [Hades]. In his right hand, he raises not a cornucopia, symbol of wealth, but a wine vessel with an animal's head, a rhyton; in his left, he bears the goblet for the wine. Over his head stands the dedication [...] 'To Theos,' befitting the mystery god [...] On his couch sits his wife, identified by the dedication [...] 'To Thea,' and differing from the Kore [Persephone] both in her features and in her headdress. Both female figures are assuredly Persephone, who showed her true face in the Mystery Night. (Kerenyi, 152)

283

Thus he asserts that Persephone is here shown as the bride of Dionysus, making Dionysus one with Hades in such imagery. He points also to a painting on the Xenokles Cup which depicts what seems to be a wedding between Persephone and Dionysus, the couple attended by Hermes and Demeter on their left. With these evidences, among others, Kerenyi confidently concludes, "Kore and Thea are two different duplications of Persephone; Plouton and Theos are duplications of the subterranean Dionysos" (155), solidifying his thesis that "the wine god in his quality of Lord of the Underworld was the girl's ravisher" (35).

Can this proposed understanding of the sacred Mysteries be any further verified by comparison of the Hades myths with the other "Soma" God myths? Indeed, if Kerenyi is correct and this identification was understood by the ancient initiates, they seemingly had good reasons, as comparative analysis will demonstrate. First of all, and crucially, if this were true we would have to treat the Hades myths as sometimes *doubling* some of the motifs we have traced already in the Dionysus myths. This doubling could have come about in any number of ways, including simple divergence over time after a splitting of the two gods. Such splitting could also come back to the idea that there were multiple connected gods who made up "Soma" and multiple known "Dionysuses." Different regions may have focused on different iterations or aspects of the god. It would also possible, if we accept this theory, that the Dionysus and Hades myths were simply rooted in the same original mythos, but diverged over time, becoming doubles or variants of one another. As Kerenyi himself puts it, discussing this tendency for the gods to be "doubled," "The student of Eleusinian mythology must acquire a kind of double sight if he wishes to do justice to the entire tradition – the literary and the pictorial – with all their contradictory statements which were allowed to stand side by side" (Kerenyi, 148).

In any event, we see once again in Hades' primary mythos (*Homeric Hymn 2 To Demeter*; Pseudo-Apollodorus, *Bibliotheca* 1. 29 and others) a myth centered around the abduction and trapping of a goddess in the underworld, repeating the "Rhiannon" theme once more, and also possibly doubling the Hera and Hephaestus myth previously discussed. Persephone, daughter of Demeter is taken to the underworld by Hades, who allows her to leave, but only if she consumes nothing while there. She eats a certain number of pomegranate seeds, however, and so as a compromise she is allowed to live away from Hades for part of the year and to stay with him as his wife for the remainder. Thus we have, combined into one story, the marriage of a proposed "Soma" God (Hades) to his bride, and the trapping in the underworld of the goddess. Crucial to this interpretation is the fact that, exactly as in the Welsh Rhiannon myth and the Indian Samvarana-Tapati myth, when the goddess is trapped or stays too long in the otherworld location, away from the society that needs her, the world becomes a wasteland. When

Persephone is away, crops die and nature is sapped of vitality. For this reason, her stay in the underworld is often seen as taking place during, and causing the conditions of, the harsh Summer (or Winter). It must be said that the similar trapping of Welsh Pryderi and Rhiannon in the Otherworld and their return can just as easily be connected to a concept of seasonal change[117], and Samvarana staying on the sacred mountain too long specifically causes the rains to stop. But the "wasteland" period caused by the absence of Persephone can also be seen in a more general sense as the archetypal wasteland as we find it in the other Lunar Cycles, connected to the more generalized drought or blight brought on by the forgotten sacrifice.

It is Hermes, the proposed Gandharva, who brings Persephone out of the underworld (a subject found on Attic vases), just as the Gandharva Samvarana accompanies Tapati, after the help of Vasistha, back to society to heal the wasteland. Meanwhile the "Surya's Bridal" hymn explicitly states that Surya passes from Soma to the Gandharva, for safe keeping, just as Hermes has become a temporary guide for Persephone, a situation we also see with Welsh Pwyll, who stays with Arawn's wife for a time, like a surrogate husband and guardian.

We can thus see just how much has shifted around in the various versions, though we can now also begin to track these shifts more precisely. Hermes' role in the myth (when he is considered as the Gandharva) also brings together the same set of gods once again: Soma (Hades), the Gandharva (Hermes), the Young Child (this time a daughter, Persephone), and the Great Queen (Persephone taking both the role of the mother Rhiannon and child Pryderi in a sense). The fact that there is no "Young Son" in this Greek version, as there is in the Welsh with Pryderi, but instead a "Young Daughter," may have a distinct cause and be the result of a specific documented syncretism.

As Kerenyi illustrates, Persephone took the place in this particular myth that had once been occupied by a goddess bearing the title *Despoina*. Likewise, this Despoina had a prominent mother figure in her myth. Kerenyi explains that "The older goddess who originally no doubt played the part of the mother was not entirely forgotten, even after Demeter had taken her place" (Kerenyi, *Eleusis*, 132). The religion of the pre-Greeks was thus dominated by a cult of a mother goddess and her daughter, a fact that has left its imprint on the form of the Demeter-Persephone myth. This mother goddess had both a daughter *and* a son (or a daughter and a *horse*, just as, for instance, Norse god Freyr is closely tied to his sister Freyja, or Irish Aengus to his sister Brigid, and as Pryderi is curiously born the same day as a special horse, as if it is his twin), but the son seems to have been overshadowed by the daughter, Despoina in this case. This could help explain

---

117   *"Celtic Mythology" (2009). Greenwood Encyclopedia of Folktales and Fairytales.
       Detroit: Greenwood Press. pp. 215–220.*

why, while in the Welsh version both a goddess and "Young Son" are trapped in the underworld together, in the Greek version it is only a "Young Daughter" who takes on this role, her male horse-associated counterpart pushed out of the picture in accordance with an earlier localized understanding.

Not only can we see the "Young Daughter" take the place otherwise occupied by "Young Son" and Mother Goddess together, but Despoina/Persephone's mother, the great goddess Demeter, has a myth directly paralleled in Rhiannon's myth as well. That is, Rhiannon parallels *both* the mother goddess Demeter *and* her daughter Persephone, seemingly taking both roles in the Welsh version. Kerenyi, in fact, believed that Persephone and Demeter should be seen as merely two aspects of one goddess, saying that "Demeter represented the earthly aspect. Persephone another, rather ghostly and transcendent," (33) and, "Demeter searched for her vanished daughter as though she were the lost half of herself and found her at last in the underworld" (130). He also explains that this doubling of aspects may have resulted from the overlaying of Demeter onto the pre-existing mother-daughter goddesses: "Obviously the grain goddess was a latecomer, fitted into an older genealogy, now in one way, now in another. The later conception that Demeter and not Rhea was Persephone's mother won out and became classical" (133). Therefore seeing the single Welsh goddess Rhiannon as taking the roles of both Demeter and Persephone would be perfectly natural from this perspective, accepting the possibility that Demeter and Persephone are actually *one* on some level.

Rhiannon's parallel with Demeter is this: in *Pwyll, Prince of Dyfed,* Rhiannon is initially seen by Pwyll, the Gandharvic god, who sends riders after her, but she cannot be caught up to, though her horse appears only to amble. Later, after Pwyll catches and weds her, she gives birth to her son the same night a horse is born (he is a "Horse Twin" god, Pryderi), then she is punished for seeming to have killed her son (even though he was only kidnapped) by having to give people rides on her back like a horse. Finally, she is made to wear the collars of a donkey during her imprisonment in the Otherworld. Repeatedly, she is made to take on the actions of a horse and to be identified and associated with horses (Irish Etain, "horse rider," is also closely tied to horses). In Demeter's myth, Poseidon *Hippios* ("of the horses") sees Demeter and chases after her. To escape him, Demeter then turns into a horse (compare Rhiannon evading pursuit on her magically ambling horse after Pwyll sees her) (Pausanias 8.42.1-4). Pausanias notes that the Arcadians set up a wooden image of Demeter with the head of a horse in her sacred cavern. Poseidon turns into a stallion, catches Demeter, and mates with her, whereas Rhiannon ultimately stops for Pwyll and pledges to be wed with him (much more similar in this last detail to the Indian version than to the Greek, which emphasizes this union as capture and violation, an important discrepancy we will explore further on). The offspring of Poseidon and Demeter is a horse, while, as Pausanias elucidates, in other sources Despoina/Persephone is the daughter of Demeter: "Demeter, they say, had by Poseidon a daughter, whose name they are not wont to divulge to the uninitiated, and a horse called Areion" (8.25.5). He cites a Pythian oracle regarding Demeter which states: "And soon will she make you eat each other and feed on your children, Unless you appease her anger with libations offered by all your people" (8.42.6), while the eating of her own child is what Rhiannon is accused of.

Bernard Dietrich also points out (*The Origin of Greek Religion*, 181) that the earlier mate of Demeter in this archaic form of the myth may have been a figure known simply as the *Wanax*, or "chief," or by the name *Paredros*, "companion." Ultimately he was syncretized to Poseidon Hippios due to the fact that Poseidon was the god most often given the title of *Wanax*, and due also to the fact that this *Wanax* was associated with underground streams as well as with horses – again this was a syncretism not to Poseidon proper, but *Poseidon Hippios*. Considering the close similarity of Welsh Pwyll's encounter with and pursuit of the equine Rhiannon to this Poseidon's pursuit of the equine Demeter, we should examine the possibility that this *Wanax Hippios* may originally have been something more like Pwyll the Gandharva than the sea god Poseidon. Note that the name of *Bragi*, the Norse Gandharva, god of skaldship and parallel of Pwyll, might be related to Old Norse *bragr/bragnar*, "chieftain or chieftains," or *bragningr*, "king," from PG *bragz*, "One who is first or foremost, a premier, chief, leader," essentially the same meaning as *Wanax*. A second possible etymology of *Bragi* is via Old Norse *bragr* (cf. Icelandic *bragur*), "poem, melody," while, as Allen and Woodard noted, *gandharva* is synonymous with "music." The gandharvas are heavily associated with the giving of horses, as we have seen. As a psychopomp (see Hermes) they are also associated with the underground liminal space approaching the underworld, and the rivers that flow and spring from that space (like the Styx, boundary of worlds, by which Hermes is often depicted on Greek vases). As this *Wanax* was a very archaic figure, it is not clear whether he was Indo-European in origin or not (his titles, however, suggest the likelihood that he was), but the question of why Welsh Pwyll takes the parallel role remains intriguing. As Jon D. Mikalson says, "In our examples Poseidon's three epithets, Soter, Hippios, and Asphaleios, each represented a distinct activity of Poseidon, and the Poseidon of each sanctuary would concern himself with only that one activity. To us they might appear as three separate gods [...] but the Greeks, for reasons about which we can only speculate, brought all three together under the name Poseidon and viewed the various activities as aspects of the same god" (Mikalson, *Ancient Greek Religion*, 33).

This is clearly one of the most knotted points of our whole tangle, and the core identity of this Wanax stubbornly evades clarity, and so we will only offer a few brief speculations. In Celtic terms, we have seen that Demeter's rapist parallels the

287

Gandharvic Pwyll, but have also noted a parallel to the rapist of the Irish Aine, Ailill Aulom, a possible double of King Echdae, the Horse God King and first husband of Aine, whose title and equine name remind us of the Wanax ("chief/king") who takes the form of a horse to rape Demeter.

Dumezil draws a connection between Varuna (horse-associated sovereign of waters and parallel of Poseidon) and the gandharvas, pointing to a myth in which Varuna becomes essentially King of the Gandharvas. Meanwhile, Varuna is also one of the chief exemplar gods of sovereignty generally speaking. But why is Varuna a king of the Gandharvas? Besides a shared connection to a certain spirited vitality and trait of liberality, the gandharvas are also water-associated, the *soma* when poured into water being called The Gandharva in the Waters, as we have previously noted. The Wanax who is syncretized to Poseidon could be like a Gandharva in the Waters, or like a king of the Gandharvas who becomes nearly identifiable with a Varunian sovereign. This is one possible way, among others that we will explore shortly, of explaining the overlap and slippage we witness, with a so-called "Poseidon" (Wanax/Poseidon Hippios) in one branch seemingly paralleling a gandharva in another (Pwyll). Lastly, Pryderi, son of Pwyll, is stolen at birth by a monstrous claw, and ends up being accidentally saved by Teyrnon Twryf Lliant, who then raises the boy. Teyrnon's name means "Lord of the Raging Sea," he is known for being a raiser of horses (compare *Hippios*), and he raises the son of Pwyll as a sort of second father to him. Guillaume Oudaer, in his article "Teyrnon Twryf Lliant," has demonstrated a high likelihood that Teyrnon is the name given within the Mabinogi to Lludd/Nudd Nuada, the Celtic Varuna. This overlap, Pwyll-Gandharva and Teyrnon-Varuna sharing of the role of father of Pryderi, could partly explain both of them paralleling the Wanax, Poseidon Hippios, in different ways. The name *Teyrnon* is even a nearly direct cognate of *Wanax*, "chief/lord/king," while both Teyrnon and Poseidon are Varunian gods of the sea. As Dumezil explains the line connecting Varuna and the Gandharvas, which could begin to explain the possible overlap of their deity-types in this myth:

> Let us not forget that Varuna is said elsewhere to have the Gandharva as his people, and that in his legend the Gandharva intervene at a tragic moment to restore his failed virility with a magic herb, just as the first Luperci, wielding their goatskin whips, put an end to the sterility of the women Romulus had abducted. Mitra as brahman, Varuna as king of the Gandharva: we could hardly have wished for a more suggestive formula. (Dumezil, *Mitra-Varuna*, 71-72)

Let us also here note further connections, brought by Dumezil, between gandharvas and horses:

In the Rg Veda the outward appearance of the (singular masculine) Gandharva is left vague, but in later writings the (masculine plural) Gandharva are beings with horses' heads and men's torsos who live in a special world of their own. As early as the hymns, moreover, they already stand in a precise relationship to horses and to the harnessing of chariots, those of the Sun and those of men alike, and they retain this feature throughout the epic literature. (Dumezil, *Mitra-Varuna*, 28)

He also mentions

[...] a particular form of igneous sacrifice (the accessories of which are made from the wood of the asvattha tree, which contains the word asva, 'horse,' in its name), which allows [Pururavas] to 'become one of the Gandharva.' (Dumezil, *Mitra-Varuna*, 29)

Another myth found in the Vedic corpus may also be the final piece of the puzzle. This is the Saranyu and Vivasvat myth. Saranyu is wife of the Sun God Vivasvat, as Aine is wife of Echdae "Horse God" who also seems to be a sun god. Saranyu bears one pair of twins to Vivasvat (brother and sister underworld deities Yama and Yami) and then leaves due to his oppressive brightness and heat.[118] She changes into a mare and he eventually seeks her out, also in horse form (thus he is a Horse God, like Poseidon Hippios or Echdae). The version found in the *Harivamsa Purana* (seen as a supplement to the *Mahabharata*) states that "apprehensive that he was a stranger, she twisted herself away from mating," also translated as "Taking him for another man the mare did not yield to his desire. Then from his nostril the two Aswinis, the foremost of the physicians, were born" (*Harivamsa*, 9.54). Thus there is a subtext of rape in this myth. She sniffs the semen of Vivasvat and becomes impregnated by it, conceiving a second pair of twins, who in this version are the Horse Twins (thus giving a second parentage for the Horse Twins, apparently separate from Dyaus). Her two sets of twins, one of them being an alternate birth of the Horse Twins, could help us envision why some motifs seem to overlap in a less than exact fashion between branches. Twins Yama and Yami, who have an incestuous relationship, would be more similar to Persephone and her husband Hades, while the Horse Twins, born elsewhere, would remain distinct. The underlying myth of Saranyu and Vivasvat is evidently somehow present in the material we have examined, a partially overlapping segment of the greater narrative.

---

118   "Having her body scorched by the rays of the sun she did not look beautiful" (2-4); "The rays of the sun are always very powerful, O my child, and the son of Kaçyapa oppresses the three worlds therewith [...] The rays of the sun were crooked and extended above. Gifted with such a celestial form the sun was not of a gentle look (41-42)" (*Harivamsa*, Chapter IX, 2-5, 41-42).

There also may be a similarity of structure (which we will not delve into here) between the myth of King Pururavas, who becomes a gandharva, and his wife Urvasi, and that of Samvarana and Tapati. Meanwhile, Vivasvat and this Pururavas are both treated as "first sacrificers to the gods," while the Gandharva-type deity elsewhere is connected to gathering wood (Ogma, Hermes), seemingly for the first sacrifice (as we will discuss later on), and the re-institution of the sacrifice is also the conclusion of the Samvarana tale. "First sacrificers" may then end up being the nexus around which these overlapped identities converge. Steets explains: "Oldenberg, comparing Avestan Vivanhvant [see: Vedic Vivasvat], the first mortal to prepare Haoma, considered Vivasvant to be simply the first sacrificer and ancestor of the human race, not a god of light [...] Hillebrandt suspects that there may be three uses of the name: one signifying the sun (god), another the name of a mythical sacrificer (originally the sun god, later degraded to a mythical sacrificer), and the third an honorific name for the ordinary sacrificer" (Steets, "The Sun Maiden's Wedding," 100).[119] This is one overlap in functions between Vivasvat and the Gandharva King which could help to explain some of the variability regarding who takes the role of the pursuer of the mare goddess.

Pwyll = Echdae = Wanax/Hippios = Vivasvat, and Hefeydd = Ogma = Hermes = Gandharva (see below) is obviously one partial resolution of the question, but it does not fully resolve the Gandharvic roles Pwyll takes within the myth (his lying in bed chastely for one year with Arawn's wife, and the passing of his wife to the fire god Manawydan) and so does not quite tell the whole story of what has happened in the development of these myth variants. Furthermore, we cannot at all say that Samvarana, Pwyll's parallel, is Vivasvat, because Samvarana beseeches Vivasvat to marry that Sun God's daughter. Some slippage between roles then seems irreducible in the present framework. We must then imagine that in the Welsh and perhaps Irish versions, we are witnessing, to some degree, the collision and combination of the "Vivasvat" and "Gandharva" myths in the figures of Welsh Pwyll and Irish Echdae. The general role these myths are summing up would be: the first sacrificer and ancestor king.

As such we may see why Samvarana/Pwyll catches up to but does not rape Tapati/Rhiannon, these pursuers instead being peacefully accepted by these princesses (Ghandarvic resolution type), while Demeter and Aine are both raped in the seemingly parallel myths (Vivasvat resolution type). Daithi O'Hogain (*The Lore of Ireland: An Encyclopaedia of Myth, Legend and Romance*) believes that an earlier form of Aine's

---

119   Steets: "[...] there is still much to describe Vivasvant as a mortal in the Vedas. As Manu's father he is believed to be the ancestor of the human race, and is closely connected with human sacrificial ritual, as the first sacrificer of Soma, especially in the ninth book of the Rg Veda. Avestan Vivanhvant has similar connections with Haoma, and he is likewise regarded in that tradition as a mortal" (Steets, 101).

myth did not include the hostility of a rape either. The variability between the two motifs, rape or peaceful acceptance, within variants of Aine's myth, may demonstrate the colliding and overlapping of the two archaic myth types within the Celtic tradition, an overlapping which may have occurred in a different way in the Greek corpus as well, although some of the evidence suggests that the Wanax and Demeter myth could be more simply analogous to the Vivasvat-Saranyu myth.

Fascinatingly, the Gandharva and Vivasvat are briefly confused or equated in the *Rig Veda* as well, and here we might have a clue that brings us close to the root of (part of) the issue. RV 10.10.4 calls Yama's parents the Gandharva in the Waters (mentioned above) and the Water Lady or Aqueous Nymph. Meanwhile, Yama's parent is elsewhere said to be instead Vivasvat (*Valakh*. iv. 1, IX. cxiii. 8, cxiv. 1, X. xiv. 1, xvii. 1, lviii. 1, lx. 10, clxiv. 2), and, in addition, Vivasvat is closely connected with both the fire and Soma rituals (L.D. Barnett, "Yama, Gandharva, and Glaucus," 703). Arthur Macdonell notes that "Soma poured into water is called 'the Gandharva of the waters' (9, 86, 36). Gandharva, connected with the Apsarases, is also said to dwell in the waters in the AV. (2, 2,3; 4, 37, 12). In the Avesta Gandarewa is a lord of the abyss who dwells in the waters (Yt. 15; 28)" (Macdonell, 137), – indeed this Gandarewa is the "sole lord of the depths" here (cf. Yast V.38, XV.28; Windischmann, Zor. Stud., p. 40). Macdonell further explains that the Gandharva "is brought into relation with the sun, 'the golden-winged bird, the messenger of Varuna' (10, 123, 6), with the sun-bird (10, 177, 2), with the sun-steed (1, 163, 3), with *Soma likened to the sun* [emphasis mine] (9, 85, 12)" (Macdonell, 136). Another cryptic connection noticed by Stella Kramrisch may add to the mystical picture of the Gandharva Pwyll, who has become united as-if "one" with the Soma God Arawn, then being conflated or confused with the role of a sun god Vivasvat and a sovereign of the waters, Varuna:

> The Gandharva precedes creation; he is the creative Soma-inspiration within the seer in sacred secrecy, when Soma himself is about to speak from within the seer, when 'the seer makes surge **the wave from the ocean**' (RV.10.123.2) of his heart, and on its crest, Soma, **the Gandharva, is born** (cf. RV.9.86.36), **the radiant Sun** (RV.9.86.29). (Kramrisch, *The Presence of Siva*, 70 [e-book pagination])

Finally, Kramrisch also identifies Vivasvat as "the archetypal poet," which suggests yet another point of convergence between him and the musician-poet Ghandarva-type gods, such as Bragi the skald: "[…] Vivasvat, the Radiant. He is luminous and illumined, he is the creative Fire of the mind, the archetypal poet; through his messenger he brought the fire to man. Vivasvat's brilliance comes from heaven and shines on earth. He is immortal by nature when he acts as priest on earth" (Kramrisch, "The Indian Great Goddess,"

236). These considerations should be brought to bear mainly on the question of a conflation that may have occurred in Celtic and other European branches.

The aforementioned Aine, the Sun Princess wife of Manannan, is important enough to this portion of the puzzle that she requires a bit more background. The king who rapes Aine, Ailill Aulom, is also experiencing a sort of wasteland in his kingdom when he perpetrates the rape. Seeing that he parallels Pwyll and Samvarana in their role as the king who "catches" the Sun Princess (though he does so in the unwanted "Vivasvat" manner), this wasteland motif is in the expected place. In Ailill's case, there is at this time a sort of famine and every time he goes to sleep the grass dies, leaving nothing for the grazing of the cattle and threatening starvation for his kingdom. He discovers that it is fairies that are despoiling the grass by magic: "that night the hill was stripped clean of all the grass that grew on it and when this happened three times the king knew that it was due to magic of some sort" (Lady Augusta Gregory, *Gods and Fighting Men*, "Aine"). A warrior Druid named Ferches who accompanies Ailill seems to take a similar role to that of Manawydan here by killing the king of the fairies that is leading this mischief. Ailill sees Aine among these fairies, a queen of the fairies as she is, and either in a half-sleeping trance, going mad with desire, or out of a sense of revenge for despoiling his crops, depending on the account, he rapes her. Bringing the parallel cases even closer together, we learn that Aine could take the shape of a red horse called *Lair Derg*, and that this horse could not be outrun. Rhiannon, as we have discussed, is depicted performing blatant horse-like activities and memorably rides a horse that cannot be caught up to. This red horse of the more explicit Sun Goddess Aine is clearly solar in its symbolism, further connecting the color red to the sun, as we have proposed in relation to the Red Knight (and another detail which confirms this color association is found at the conclusion of Vivasvat and Saranyu's myth, which states outright: "Since then the countenance of the deity, sun, is red" (*Harivamsa*, IX, 44)). As Aengus' sun princess bride Caer Ibormeith has a name meaning "Yew Berry," and as Norse Sun god Ullr lives at the Yew Dales, Aine's father is said to be named *Fer I*, meaning "Man of the Yew" (see: MacKillop, *A Dictionary of Celtic Mythology*). The Sun Princess Aine being the daughter of Man of the Yew reinforces the connection between the yew tree and the sun, being that it is the tree from which bows were made, and the sun is the great archer. Fer I, then, is likely to be another form of the Sun God, Aine being in this case a Daughter of the Sun as in the Vedic case.

Aine has other attested fathers, however, which could be doubles of this Sun God or variant genealogies altogether, and thus more evidence of the collision of separate tale types. In one version of her myth found in the tale "The Yew of the Disputing Sons," Aine is killed by Ailill after he rapes her, and her brother gains revenge by creating a wondrous yew tree and setting Ailill's son and foster sons to fight over it. Eogan, who will be recalled from our previous discussion, is the son of Ailill and Aine and he thus goes to battle against Lugaid Mac Con and Cian, Ailill's foster sons. Lugaid does seem to be another hypostasis of Lugh, since he is later killed by a spear-throw from behind and the name *Lugaid* is generally closely linked to the god Lugh. Thus this battle of Eogan, whose name we have seen to be a consistent parallel of Pryderi/Aengus/The Horse Twins, with Lugaid and Cian, could be another version of the battle of the Third Function against the First and Second Functions (if Lugh and Cian are not here both representing the First Function). In fact, it closely parallels the Welsh version from *Pwyll, prince of Dyfed*: Ailill parallels Pwyll, as we have seen, the king who catches the sun-horse princess who cannot be caught if she does not want to be. Ailill and Aine's son Eogan parallels the son of Pwyll and Rhiannon, Pryderi, as the Third Function/Horse Twin representative. Cian, as we see in a later chapter, is the parallel of Welsh Gwydion, against whom Pryderi fights his War of the Functions, and it is Gwydion who gives Second Function-coded items, war horses, weapons and dogs, to Pryderi in exchange for his Third Function-coded swine. And Lugaid is Lugh, here a general representative of the high king of the gods and the First Function, which role is taken by different high king gods in the different versions. Gwydion indeed becomes ally of Lugh when he is born later in that version of the myth, uniting these same gods once again. The incredibly compressed version of the myth seen in Aine's story also draws a direct link between the attacked Sun Princess and the starting of the "War of the Functions," which is interesting because in the Norse case it is the killing of the seeress Gullveig that starts the Aesir-Vanir War and not the abduction of Idunn, which would more directly parallel the attack on Aine. This compressed Irish version suggests that these two events could be seen as closely connected, both the abduction of Idunn and killing of Gullveig being successive episodes within the greater cycle which is the wedding of sunlight and moon, and as such these episodes also metaphysically reflect two closely linked events in the production of the mead that the lunisolar concatenation catalyzes. It is curious also that at the festival of Aine, on St. John's Night (Midsummer), according to one account, people would gather to view the *moon*, leading to some confusion about whether Aine is a moon or sun goddess.[120] We can theorize that this practice of looking on the moon during the Sun Goddess' celebration was due to the combination of sunlight in the moon that we have previously claimed to be a central component of the larger myth cycle. If the report of this practice is correct, then the people may have, within some greater forgotten context, been viewing the mystical union of sun and moon and contemplating the sacred blessings that flow therefrom.

---

120   "Some say that Aine's true dwelling-place is in her hill; upon which on every St. John's Night the peasantry used to gather from all the immediate neighbourhood to view the moon (for Aine seems to have been a moon goddess, like Diana)" (Wentz, *The Fairy-Faith in Celtic Countries*, 80).

While Persephone is closely tied to the Underworld, as the wife of Hades, and was treated with such fear that her name could not be spoken, Aine became seen in the folk tradition as Queen of the Banshees of Ireland (Michael J. Quinlan, *The Lough Gur & District Historical Society Journal Vol. 7*, p. 14) and was said to ride in the "Deaf Coach," which is driven by headless horses and seen at May Eve or when someone dies. In one folk tradition she has her golden comb stolen and then returned, which may be a fragmented remembrance of the same root myth as the theft and return of Idunn's golden apples (the false double of Saranyu is held by her *hair* so that Vivasvat can "imprecate a curse of destruction on her" (*Harivamsa*, IX, 35)). The thief of Aine's comb is magically made to waste away and die for what he has done, and Thjazi is also killed for his crime, though in a different manner.

Aine also is associated with two other goddesses who may be her doubles or sisters, named Finnen and Grian (see: Monaghan, Patricia, *The Encyclopedia of Celtic Mythology and Folklore*; Ellis, Peter Berresford, *A Dictionary of Irish Mythology*). Grian's name is a word for the sun itself, and the name is found in the hill *Knock Greine*, seven miles from *Knockaine*, Aine's Hill. Finnen's name is found in *Knock Fennel* at Lough Gur, by the shore of which lake Knockaine also is found.[121] If we consider that *Finnen*, meaning "white," could be a variation of *Be Find*, "White Lady," a name by which Etain is called, then we could picture the coming together of these variant traditions (from different regions as they are), with Finnen/Etain as a double or sister of Aine and Grian. The first two along with Caer make the three Sun Princesses we have come to expect, with Grian, the Sun Princess in her most direct manifestation, whose name is a literal name of the sun (comparable to Vedic Surya or Norse Sol), above her three hypostases. Meanwhile, Aine is also thought to go by the name of *Bean Fhionn*, "White Lady," an even more undeniable analogue of *Be Find*, "White Lady" (as it is essentially the very same name), when she takes victims to her realm below Lough Gur. This myth also gives her a further association with death and brings us back to Persephone in her fearful aspect, whose name in Greece was not even supposed to be uttered. As noted, Aine, or in some tales a euhemerized version of her, is even thought to

---

121   "The Fairy Goddesses, Aine and Fennel (or Finnen).—'There are two hills near Lough Gur upon whose summits sacrifices and sacred rites used to be celebrated according to living tradition. One, about three miles south-west of the lake, is called Knock Aine, Aine or Ane being the name of an ancient Irish goddess, derived from *an*, 'bright.' The other, the highest hill on the lake-shores, is called Knock Fennel or Hill of the Goddess Fennel, from Finnen or Finnine or Fininne, a form of *fin*, 'white.' The peasantry of the region call Aine one of the Good People; and they say that Fennel (apparently her sister goddess or a variant of herself) lived on the top of Knock Fennel' (termed Finnen in a State Paper dated 1200)" (Wentz, *Fairy-Faith in Celtic Countries*, 70-80).

die on Midsummer, which can perhaps be related to Rhiannon or Persephone going to the underworld/Otherworld during the summer period of destructive heat and barrenness.

Another figure, Macha, from the legendary layer found in the Ulster Cycle, who gives birth to twins after being made to race against horses as if she were one herself (thus reminiscent of Rhiannon who is made to carry people like a horse and to wear the collar of a horse, or of Aine who becomes a red horse that cannot be outrun), is in one place said to be the same as this Grian. *The Metrical Dindshenchas* of *Ard Macha* say: "her two names, not seldom heard in the west, were bright Grian and pure Macha […] in her roofless dwelling in the west she was Grian, the sun of womankind." When this Macha bears the twins it is said that "Fir and Fial were the names of the twins that Grian bore." Here we have a parallel of Rhiannon bearing not a single son but twins, while explicitly acting out the role of a horse. For this reason these twins have commonly been identified as either legendary/euhemerized versions of the Irish Horse Twins, or simply the directly hippomorphic manifestation of the same, and this further aligns Pryderi, son of Rhiannon, with a parallel set of horse-related twins, considering the significant similarities of Rhiannon and Macha.

The first Sunday in August, roughly aligned with the time of Lughnasa, was *Domnach Aine Chroim Duibh* (the Sunday of Aine and Crom Dubh) (Dames, 1992, 101). The folklore has it that Aine becomes the consort of the frightening and adversarial *Cromm Crúaich* aka *Crom Dubh* (a god of agriculture and possible solar god known for his golden statue surrounded by 12 stones) for three days shortly after Lughnasadh and so the pair may be associated with the oppressive heat around the beginning of August, according to MacNeill (MacNeill, 1962; O hOgain, 2006). Aine also takes on a more frightening aspect at this time, as the heat of the sun tends to do. Crom was seemingly given offerings so that he would not harm the harvest with excessive heat or miserliness, and confusing reports that this frightening god was the chief of the Irish gods (see Michael J. O'Kelly, *Early Ireland: An Introduction to Irish Prehistory*, 288; O'Donovan, John (ed. and tr.), *Annala rioghachta Eireann: Annals of the Kingdom of Ireland, by the Four Masters, from the earliest period to the year 1616, Vol. I*) may make sense if we see him as another parallel of the great but scorching Vedic Sun god Vivasvat, who we have called the parallel of various other destructive solar figures. Note that Crom Cruaich means "the crooked or sloping one of the hill," while of Vivasvat it is said "The rays of the sun were crooked and extended above. Gifted with such a celestial form the sun was not of a gentle look" (*Harivamsa*. IX, 42).

Crom's cult center and famous golden idol was at Magh Slécht, "The Plain of Genuflections," but this name has also been interpreted as Magh Slecht, "The Plain of the Cutting," while Vivasvat has his crooked and excessive rays cut shorter at the smithy of Tvastr-Vishvakarman. The name has also been proposed to be a corruption of Magh

Lecht, "The Plain of the Tombs" (Tom Smith, "The Irish God 'Crom Crúaich of Magh Slécht': a review of the sources," 15) and the proper translation remains unsettled. As such, Crom could parallel Thjazi (if not Ivaldi)/the Red Knight/Hafgan etc., the oppressive solar god who plays a key role in this cycle. St. Patrick (likely taking the place of an earlier deity) is said to defeat Crom on this first Sunday of August. However, Aine undergoes her rape by Ailill on Samhain and becomes consort of Crom near Lughnasadh, thus the actions of Ailill and Crom seem to be reflected in opposing events in the sun's yearly cycle, if the accounts are correct, and so these figures cannot necessarily be seen as doubles who *both* parallel Thjazi. The two could still have split from one original mythos, but as we will see this is not a necessary assumption. Vivasvat and Saranyu are married before he rapes her, and the reason that Saranyu flees from Vivasvat is the oppressive scorching quality of his rays, which thus seem to be present from the time of their marriage, possibly correlating with high summer. By the time he rapes her, his rays have been reduced to a more pleasing size, which could correlate to a time period after summer such as a time near Samhain. However, the idea that he is killed in August does not fit with this. Knowledge of what time of year Thjazi's abduction of Idunn was connected to, for example, could help clarify whether Ailill or Crom, or both, could be Thjazi's proper parallel. The same can be said for her possibly solar and/or Gandharvic husband Echdae, her father Fer I, and her other attested fathers, the smith Cuillean who the peasants "remembered with horror," and the fire god Manannan (who was sometimes conflated with Cuillean, which makes sense considering that fire and smith gods are nearly conflated in the Greek tradition at least, in the god Hephaestus, and Cuillean is associated with Manannan's isle).

Some of this could come down simply to separate regional traditions. It seems to us, if we are to guess, that the Gandharvic, peaceful pursuit of the Sun Princess (ie. Tapati-Surya) myth and the Vivasvat, rape of the Horse Goddess (ie. Saranyu) myth have collided in these Celtic tales, considering that Aine is both the Sun and Horse Goddess seen as one, as also is Rhiannon. In the end, Aine has multiple doubles, multiple attested fathers, multiple husbands or consort-attackers, and she or her doubles undergo multiple mythically important hardships: she is raped, killed, has her golden comb stolen, is briefly married to the adversarial Crom and gives birth to a sheaf of corn, goes mad from lovesick grief while sitting on her stone chair, and her double, Macha, is forced to run a race against horses and to give birth to twins.

Although we cannot fully untangle the contrary attestations regarding all of her consorts and fathers and their exact divine identities, some of whom may go back to the same Sun God mythos while others could connect to the Gandharvic theme (is Echdae Gandharvic, Varunian, or solar? Is Aine's harper brother Fer Fi Gandharvic?) or to other irregular traditions, what we can say is that Aine's career taken in total makes clear her parallel with Demeter as well as with the other horse and sun princesses we have considered thus far. Ultimately, it may be most correct to say that while Aine/Rhiannon parallel both Saranynu and the Sun Princess Surya, perhaps by conflation of myths, Demeter most directly parallels Saranyu and her daughter Persephone has most in common with other Sun Princesses such as Surya. This would partly go against the idea of Karl Kerenyi that Demeter and Persephone are actually parts of one goddess. However, the possible conflation of the myths of these two goddess types in figures such as Aine and Rhiannon would argue for such a close similarity between them that they are indeed almost like two parts of one.

We have previously investigated a link between Thjazi as Volundr and the Vedic smiths the Rbhus. However, in the myth of Vivasvat and Saranyu, Vivasvat is Saranyu's husband while a *different* smith god, Tvastr-Vishvakarman, is her father. Thus, Tapati-Surya's father is Vivasvat and his wife is Saranyu. If the deities cognate to Saranyu and her (step-?)daughter Tapati-Surya have become conflated in the mythos of Aine, this could explain why she has a potentially solar "Horse God" husband (Echdae), as well as a Sun God for a father (Fer I), while simultaneously having a smith father (Cuilleann), and being either peacefully wed or raped by her consorts. A similar conflation in the Norse case may shed light on why Thazi and Volundr seem to overlap or be identified, *if* we accept Rydberg, while Thjazi more so parallels the Sun God Vivasvat at least in his violence toward Idunn and his being the father of the Sun Princess Skadi, but Volundr more so parallels the smith god who was one of three brothers, the god known as the Ribhus. The smith Tvastr, father of Saranyu, meanwhile, is brother of Vivasvat (and is once described in the characteristic terms of the sun god Savitr, the "impeller," in the *Rig Veda* (*RV*, 3.55.19)), thus this would seem to be a relatively unified family cluster in both Vedic and Norse myth, and perhaps in Celtic as well.

In sum, the pattern of Aine's career that we will suggest is this: her rape on Samhain mirrors the weakening of the power of the sunlight at this time and also accounts for one variant and myth of the birth of the Horse Twin deity, here Eoghan, this variant seemingly appearing in the legendary-euhemerized rather than fully mythic-divine layer of tales. The significance of her rape is also doubtless the idea that this goddess of sovereignty must be *seized by the king*, and this would most likely be the myth that corresponds to the king's ritual copulation with the horse in the Celtic and IE Horse Sacrifice (the Irish instance of which was described by Gerald of Wales). Aine's loss of the golden comb, like the theft of Idunn's apples, may more specifically connect with the waning of light from the moon in its cycle, the temporary loss of the sunbeam's power to grant a specific renewal which perhaps returns when the moon begins to wax again or something similar. Her "death" on Midsummer is when this goddess of springtime flowering and fertility goes to the underworld for the barren summer months, a theme made explicit in Persephone's myth.

Anthony Murphy also notes "the fact that the chamber of Newgrange [see: Brugh na Boinne] accepts sunlight at dawn on winter solstice […] local folklore held that the sun shone into Newgrange on the shortest day of the year" (Murphy, "Newgrange and the Boyne Valley monuments – advanced lunar calculations and observation of the effects of precession of equinoxes in Neolithic Ireland"). If Aine is identified with the sunbeam, the entrance of the sunlight into Newgrange could correspond to one of the key episodes of her career. Her marriage to Crom during the hottest period, near Lughnasadh, may further show that two contradictory myths are being conflated here (should she not still be in the underworld, or does her destructive aspect appear precisely when she is there? Could Crom be in a role similar to Hades, who is wed to Persephone in the Underworld during the hot period?), and ultimately Crom and Ailill seem like two names for the Sun God consort (Vivasvat) of the Horse Goddess (Saranyu), seen at different points in their yearly cycle, just as Vivasvat marries and then later rapes Saranyu. Ailill in any case is a euhemerized legendary king while Crom is a purported deity name, thus they could be from the same root despite different names.

Aine's father being the smith Cuillean seems at first like it is from the same root as Saranyu being daughter of the smith Tvastr; however, when we lay out the family tree this does not work. As we have detailed previously, another smith called the Rhibus seems to be the *son* of Vivasvat, rather than his brother, as the smith Tvastr is, and it is the Rhibus who would properly parallel Volund if we follow Rydberg. Indeed, there are two kinds of smith god in the family of Vivasvat and this plainly causes confusion. Aine's father being instead Fer I ("Man of the Yew") seems to relate him to Vivasvat as father of Tapati-Surya. However, Fer I's daughter Aine is the Aine who is raped, as Tvastr's daughter Saranyu is. Therefore Fer I parallels Tvastr in that detail. But the form of the myth parallels the wasteland theme of Tapati's tale, as well as including the love despair of the one who sees the goddess, and the despoiling of the grass/crops by hostile fairies that we see in Rhiannon and Manawydan's parallel myth, and thus Fer I's version of the myth shows the greatest colliding of the two myth types. The myth form here seems to be that paralleling Vivasvat and his daughter Surya, but it includes the detail of the rape which belongs to the myth of Tvastr's daughter in the Vedic case at least. This colliding makes Fer I's myth almost nonsensical: the rapist of his daughter, Ailill, ought to be the Sun God, if it were to match the Vedic, but her father Fer I would also be the same Sun God according to other elements of the myth form. This can be partially resolved if we simply say that this is an unknown violent version of the Samvarana-Tapati myth type, a different rape from that committed by Vivasvat on Saranyu, though this lacks basis and somewhat stretches plausibility due to a certain suspicious redundancy that it introduces. In that context, the rapist would have to be either a violent variant of the Gandharva type or the Rhibus type (as Thjazi abducting Idunn or Volund raping the daughter of Nidad). These things considered, Fer I appears to be either a parallel of Vivasvat or Tvastr depending on which elements of the myth is looked at. Aine's husband Echdae seems to be the peaceful suitor, who is at least partly in the role of the Gandharva (Samvarana), as he passes her (as Surya) to the Fire God Manannan in marriage, but here it again seems possible that Echdae, as Horse God, overlaps the role of Vivasvat as god who is or becomes a horse and as first sacrificer, and/or overlaps Varuna as the king of Gandharvas, these gods all overlapping each other as the archetypal king who *seizes* sovereignty and as the first sacrificer. Instead of being the Gandharva, Echdae could simply be a peaceful variant of Ailill or Crom, considering that Vivasvat and Saranyu are married peacefully before he rapes her, and Echdae does mean "horse god." There may have been good reason that the two goddess types (Surya and Saranyu) became conflated – both are connected to horses and the sun, both are seized or caught up to by their consort, both are close family of the same Sun God and of the Horse Twins.

Finally, Etain is the daughter of another Ailill, which could be explained if the name Ailill is seen to parallel Vivasvat, as we have suggested, making Etain the Daughter of this Sun God, who also rapes Aine in the other tale. Yet another figure who falls in love with Etain, but is duped and set aside by Midir, is named Ailill. Ailill means "elf," and we must compare him then to Volund, Thjazi, and Volund-Thjazi's potential father Olvaldi "very rich in gold," who we have noted are related in some way to the Norse Elves (*Alfar*) or are among them, and to the Vedic Rbhus as an overlapping smith deity group, leading us back into the overlap between the Elves, Rbhus and the solar domain as whole which we discussed previously, the Rbhus evidently being sun deities early on. The smith Volundr, who Rydberg argues is Thjazi and is the son of Olvaldi, is called "a king of the *álfar* (elves)" and "countryman of the *álfar*"[122]. Manannan sometimes being called father of Aine can be explained as a result of his noted conflation with Cuillean, which itself comes from the same sort of thinking that resulted in the near confusion of the Smith and the Fire God in Greek myth as well as from the fact that Cuillean and Manannan are both from the Isle of Man. Considering Volund-Thjazi and Cuillean as the solar Rhibus-type smith deity, then, the idea that one of the Sun Princesses is daughter of this Rhibus-type smith deity only exists in Germanic and Celtic myth. It thus could be a shift influenced by the recollection that the Saranyu-type goddess was daughter of a different smith (the Tvastr-type smith), if not some other indeterminate development or a genuine and more archaic part of the genealogy that only these branches preserved.

---

122   John Lindow, *Handbook of Norse Mythology*, 110.

The ultimate impression that is hoped for from such a labyrinthian discussion is that we are doubtlessly dealing with the same family of gods at this point in each branch, with a parallel set of intertwining myths, accounting for often impossible-to-trace shifts and conflations in each branch.

Returning then to Demeter, another curious myth otherwise associated with the bride – Skaði – of one of the "Soma" gods – Njorðr – also occurs in Demeter's tale. This is the scene in which the goddess, having lost a family member, her daughter, is made to laugh by the attending deities, specifically in order to quell the goddess' wrath and make peace. This happens when Demeter loses Persephone to the underworld god, and is then consoled, in early versions (*Homeric Hymn to Demeter*) by the goddess Iambe, and in Orphic versions (Asclepiades of Tragilus, *FgrH* 12. 4; Orph. Frs. 49–52) by the goddess Baubo. To pacify Demeter in her grief and anger (Demeter being known for the furious form she can take, Demeter *Erinys*), Iambe or Baubo jest, dance, and perform "obscene gestures," for example exposing their genitals to Demeter. Baubo even "throws herself on her back" in this obscene dance or gesture, and the result is that, though Demeter is not consoled, she is pacified, she "grows mild and tender" (Kerenyi, 40). This is strikingly similar to the performance that is given to the Norse goddess Skaði in the *Prose Edda* text *Skaldskaparmal* when her father has been killed. She too must be pacified, as well as repaid, in order for the gods to make peace with her. She comes angered and armed with weapons of war to Asgard. To appease her, among other things, the gods must attempt to make her laugh. So Loki ties a cord around the beard of a goat and connects the other end to his own testicles. As Baubo ends her obscene dance, her genitals exposed, by falling on her back, so Loki similarly ends, his testicles humorously pulled about, by falling in Skaði's lap. Until now it has been difficult to see how the contexts of these two scenes could connect them. Only with an understanding of both of these myths as important parts of the Lunar Cycle, the husbands of Skaði (Njörðr) and Persephone (Hades) being partial parallels (or at least existing in one cycle, perhaps filling adjacent roles), Demeter and Persephone being aspects of one another and partial parallels of Skaði, indeed the abduction of Iðunn which had immediately preceded this scene also being a parallel of the abduction of Persephone, can we see that these myths are after all in their right places. Only by understanding both Hades and Njörðr either as "Soma" gods, or in another similar way intimately interrelated (as we will examine further along), can this parallel make complete sense.

Looking to the case of Iberia, we may even see a deity who forms an illuminating bridge between the Celtic underworld/Soma gods and Dionysus. This is Endovelicus, Iberian (Lusitanian) lord of the Underworld, associated with vegetation, grapes, the vine, crowns, pine cones, mountains, dreams, pigs, fertility, swans, dogs, and equated with Serapis, a Roman form of Osiris who also has a bull aspect (José d'Encarnação, 2015,

Divindades indígenas sob o domínio romano em Portugal). Each of these symbols can be seen connected with either Dionysus, Hades, or one of the other Celtic "Soma" cognates, Midir or Arawn. Grapes, vines, crowns and pine cones are all central symbols of Dionysus in his role as god of wine, fertility and vegetation. His origin on or association with a mountain is a part of his very name: *Dio nysus*, meaning "god of Mount Nysa." As Endovelicus is connected with dreams, dreams are the purview of Hades, and he is known as "Plouton, master of the black-winged Oneiroi (dreams)" in an anonymous Greek lyric (Anonymous, *Fragments* 963, from Demetrius, *On Style*). Irish Midir is closely associated with swans, turning into a pair with his wife to escape Eochu Airem. Hades famously keeps the three-headed dog Cerberus who guards his realm. Arawn gives "the Swine of Arawn" to Pwyll as a token of friendship.

Just as Norse Njörðr is known as the god of wealth, and indeed Vedic Soma is repeatedly associated with wealth, while Welsh Arawn's underworld palace is said to be "the best supplied with food and drink, and vessels of gold and royal jewels" of all courts in *Pwyll, prince of Dyfed*, so Hades too is seen as the lord of all the mineral and vegetative wealth held within the earth, and his quality of richness is emphasized in his byname, Plouton, which was also the name of his Roman analog, meaning "the rich one." Thus Hades naturally fills the role of "god of wealth" repeatedly connected with the "Soma" god in his chthonic aspect. And while Hades is known for his two-pronged bident (or a trident, in Seneca's *Hercules Furens, 559),* Irish Midir, at least, is said to carry a 5-pronged spear.

Further curiosities include the fact that Demeter goes to Helios, the Sun god, to find out who has stolen her daughter. He is the only one who can answer this question. In the Indian Samvarana tale, the (fire) priest Vasistha must go to the Sun God Vivasvat right *before* Samvarana and Tapati have their wasteland-causing dalliance on the otherworldly mountain, but this visit to the Sun God is in order to procure the Sun Princess' hand in marriage for Samvarana. Also during Demeter's mourning period, she is known to have sat on a simple chair, or, in an older version, on a particular rock, and stayed there without laughing (Apollodorus, *The Library*, 1.5; Kerényi, *Eleusis: Archetypal Image of Mother and Daughter*, 38). Due to the fact that Theseus sits on this same "laughless rock" or *agelastos petra* right before descending to the underworld, it may be said that the rock and the underworld have a close connection. In the essay on the Eleusinian Mysteries, "Mixing the Kykeon," Peter Webster describes it as "the 'Laughless Rock,' which none would dare sit upon for fear of becoming stuck, like Theseus when he visited Persephone" (22). Thus this chair/rock of Demeter may parallel the sacred mound that Pryderi and the others sit on to trigger the wasteland, and perhaps also the chair of Hephaestus that Hera sits on and becomes stuck to, causing the crisis in that variant. Meanwhile, Irish Aine is known for her stone chair on Dunany Point (Dun Aine, the Fort of Aine), called the Mad Chair of Dunany or *Cathaoir Ana*. As local folk beliefs run, when her lover left her, Aine is said to have sat on that rock seat in grief, slowly going mad. Sitting on the rock is said to trigger madness, to worsen madness, to return sanity, or perhaps to give inspiration. Another rock seat is also attributed to her on Knockadoon Hill called *Suideachan Bean-tige*, the Housekeeper's Chair. This is known as her birthing chair, on which she sat to give birth (seemingly to a golden sheaf of corn), demonstrating her motherly and harvest-related aspects, aligning her further with Demeter. Finally, Kerenyi says of the marriage of Hades and Persephone that it was "the prototype of all marriages" (174), which is precisely the role given to the marriage of Soma and Surya in the *Rig Veda* and in the Indian marriage rites that take that marriage as blueprint.

If the claims of Kerenyi and Heraclitus and the suggestion of Euripides are correct, and Hades is to be identified with Dionysus, then both the Eleusinian Mysteries and the cults of Dionysus and his unmixed wine could stem, at least in part (taking into account considerable layers of syncretism), from the myths of the Indo-European "Soma" cycle, whatever its original name would have been. In the case of Dionysus, there is significant documented Egyptian influence, while in the case of Hades we see significant influence from an earlier Greek (if not pre-Greek) substrate of myths, and these separate influences may have gone a long way to giving the two gods the seemingly separate characters they came to possess.

We have thus explored as far as we can at present the deep affinity between Dionysus and Hades. However, despite all the important connections we have arrayed in the foregoing, a more moderate possibility has to be put forward and ultimately pursued. We have seen from the Celtic case just how many underworld gods there may have been in the Proto-Indo-European society: the "Soma" God, the God of the Dead (Yama, Donn, perhaps Bran, etc.), the "Gandharva," the Fire God (Manannan), the God of the Wild Hunt (Gwyn, Rudra) not to mention underworld roles that may have belonged to the Horse Twins, Wind God, as well as to other major deities not here discussed. Hence we would be remiss if we did not consider the clear possibility that Hades and Dionysus were simply two distinct lords of the underworld who overlapped in certain ways and who shared certain traits and roles. From this perspective, it may be more proper to see the Dionysus cycle of myths that we have investigated as forming the first portion of the Lunar Cycle: Dionysus marrying Ariadne paralleling, for instance, the marriage of Arawn and his wife, that of Midir and Etain, Skaði and Njorðr, Soma and Surya, and Chyavana and Sukanya. This would also include the possible Aesir-Vanir War motif of Dionysus battling Poseidon and the Indian Brahmins, as well as the Dioskouroi winning their wives, Hilaeria and Phoibe. The Hades and Persephone cycle would follow this myth cycle just as the abduction of Rhiannon and Pryderi follows the aforementioned myths in the Welsh case.

This brings up an unanswered question from the Welsh myth: while the Soma god Arawn appears as the lord of the Underworld of Annwn in the very beginning of the Welsh Lunar Cycle, when Rhiannon and Pryderi are whisked away to the Otherworld upon touching the golden bowl it is not at all clear who has taken them. We find out in the end that it was a friend of Gwawl, the rival wooer from whom Pwyll had taken Rhiannon, and this friend is named Llwyd ap Cil Coed. This name is mysterious, however, meaning "grey-blue, son of the depths of the woods," and it is unclear if beneath this name lies some major Otherworld god, as the pair are kidnapped and taken to some mystical region, or if it is merely a hostile wizard or demon who has to be driven off. One might guess that it has been Arawn by another name, as he is a primary lord of the Otherworld, but Arawn had been so close and so fully allied to Pryderi's father Pwyll that they were nearly identified. It seems unlikely that he would perpetrate such a hostility on his ally's wife and son. The abductor of Rhiannon and Pryderi, who in a sense parallels Hades in this act of abduction, seems likely to have been a completely separate Otherworld deity from the Soma God, if he is not merely some hostile demon. His name seems almost Rudraic, but this could be misleading, as he capitulates rather meekly in the end, and there is not enough evidence to say more than that he is a hostile demonic force that has to be driven off.

If the Hades abduction myth *follows after* Dionysus' myths instead of fully paralleling or doubling them, and thus makes one long cycle of tales with them, this could still involve a certain amount of doubling, interchange of motifs, and even overlap between the sets of myths, and this could explain some of the parallels we have seen in the preceding. There is a kind of doubling redundancy to the three pairs of youths – the Dioskouroi, Dionysus' wine-drinking twin sons Oenopion and Staphylus, Persephone and her forgotten brother – that becomes visible when lining all these traditions up, and this seeming redundancy is puzzling.

This puzzle may be resolved if we recall that the Horse Twins have two sets of parents, two births, in the Vedic case: the first birth being from Father Sky (and in this birth, according to the Western traditions, as we have understood them, the twins were simultaneously son or foster son of the Moon God, hence Dionysus being father of Oenopion and Staphylus while Zeus is father of their doubles, Castor and Pollux), the second birth being from Vivasvat (but the Vedic tradition also mentions the Gandharva of The Waters as in the position of Vivasvat, and this is Poseidon Hippios, father of Persephone and the horse Arion). The Vedic branch gives us the example of the twins Yama and Manu, or alternately the incestuous twins who are the lord and lady of the dead, Yama and Yami (compare Hades and Persephone or Arion and Persephone), being one set of twins while The Horse Twins are their younger siblings, a second set of twins from the same parents, Vivasvat and Saranyu. From this perspective, the myths of Dionysus and Hades would be distinct, but would still form one long cycle of connected myths: the totality of the Great Lunar Cycle. Furthermore, the naturally overlapping nature of Hades and Dionysus as underworld gods would explain many motifs that became shared or even interchanged between them. If this conclusion is the proper one to take from what we have seen, then Kerenyi and Heraclitus' theory of the identity of Hades and Dionysus could only be true from an unattested esoteric perspective, seeing their essences as united on a deeper level despite their root deities seeming to be distinct in all other branches. Whether this is the proper conclusion or whether Hades and Dionysus are indeed one, I leave an open question. To pursue it further would require looking at, for instance, a fuller comparison of Vedic Yama and Greek Hades, and investigating whether there was seen to be any overlap of Soma and Yama, either in an esoteric sense, or if at their roots they could have ever come from a shared origin. As it stands, it appears to us most prudent to consider Yama and Soma separately and thus to consider Hades and Dionysus likewise.

However, we will add one final line of speculation to this prospect. We have discussed how both Norse Mimir and Njorðr could at least potentially be seen as aspects of the Norse "Soma" mythos, Njorðr much more securely. Reflected upon with the Hades and Dionysus example in mind, the question of Njorðr and Mimir could face a similar problem as the Greek case, and we should be sure not to lump together what ought to be kept separate. In fact, it was Viktor Rydberg who first suggested, in his *Investigations Into Germanic Mythology,* that Mimir could be read as a parallel of *both* Vedic Soma *and* Vedic Yama. This could make some sense if Soma and Yama had any overlap in the Vedic sources, which again is beyond our scope, though Hillebrandt makes an argument that Yama is the moon.[123] At present we will only state that Rydberg's argument for Mimir as Yama appears perhaps stronger than his argument for Mimir as Soma. He points out that Lif and Lifthrasir are protected in something named after Mimir – *Hoddmimis holt*, which can be translated to "Hoard-Mimir's holt or grove" – during the great Fimbulwinter, to emerge when Ragnarok has ended in order to repopulate the world. Yima, the Iranic parallel of Vedic Yama, himself has an enclosure wherein he is instructed to keep men and women to wait out the "evil winters" of "deadly frost" that Ahura Mazda will send to destroy the earth. Even if *Hoddmimis holt* is merely a kenning for Yggdrasil, which scholars such as Simek (*Dictionary of Northern Mythology*, 154) and Lindow (*Norse Mythology: A Guide to the Gods, Heroes, Rituals, and Beliefs, 179*) maintain on admittedly scanty evidence, this does not change the fact that the grove bears the name of Mimir. Lindow himself posits the case loosely by claiming that the

---

123   For Yama as the moon see: Hillebrandt, *Vedische Mythologie*, 2: 362.

grove of trees could even be in a location in the vicinity of Yggdrasil rather than Yggdrasil itself, and this would not at all disrupt the possible thread between Mimir and Yama. Even if we grant what is far from established, that *Hoddmimis holt* names Yggdrasil itself, it is not clear who else would be the overseer of the humans stored there if not Mimir, the namesake of the holt and the tree. After all, Mimir is the caretaker of the well that bears his name, the holt that bears his name should be considered by the same measure. The *Rig Veda* says that where Yama dwells, he drinks with the gods in [Griffith tr.] or under the well-leafed tree (RV 10.135.1). As such, if we could establish that Mimir parallels Yama and that Hades could as well, we could see why Mimir has his own sacred-water role similar but distinct to the Soma God, just as Hades sometimes overlaps Dionysus.

If we follow this speculative train a bit further, we can see that Bran, another likely Welsh underworld god, could fit into this larger pattern. We have said already how Bron becomes a name of the Grail King in later versions, and how the severed head at the Grail castle is reminiscent of the severed head of the god Bran that is central to Welsh myth. Thus Bran's looming but pacified presence is certainly felt in the Grail version of the Lunar Cycle. If the abductor of Rhiannon and Pryderi is unclear, Bran as such an underworld god is one possible candidate, as he is also the apparent Welsh parallel of Vedic Yama, although as noted he is the brother of Manawydan, and Manawydan is the one who fights the hostile sorcerer without any sense of recognizing his brother in this figure. Now, in the Welsh myth the severed head of the god Bran is taken back to Britain where it continues to speak and to guard the land. The island of Gwales, off the Southwest coast of Dyfed, where the survivors of the war take Bran's head, may be the match of the Irish otherworld island belonging to the Irish underworld god Donn, The House of Donn (*Tech Duinn*), likewise off the Southwest coast of Ireland, where the dead must go, as Alwyn and Brinley Rees note (Rees and Rees, *Celtic Heritage*, 179). Meanwhile, in the tale *Cath Almaine*, a legendary 8th Century Irish figure named Donn Bó has his head severed, and this severed head then sings at a feast in honor of another severed head, that of his king, Fergal of Tara, who was killed in battle. Norse Mimir himself is beheaded, his head preserved, and it continues to dispense advice to Oðinn. Yama's Iranic cognate Yama and his Iranic epic incarnation Jamshid are said to be dismembered or cut in half, while Mimir, Bran, and Donn Bó have their heads cut off, a very specific sort of cutting in twain. While Bran's name means "crow," Yama's emmisaries are said to be crows, and offerings are left to crows to please Yama. It would indeed be completely logical for the god of the dead to be named "Crow," as Bran is. The similarity between the myth of Mimir and that of Bran has remained puzzling, as in other points their myths do not seem to coincide, but if they both could be seen as versions of the same "Yama" underworld god, then the mystery might begin to be explained.

Irish Donn may indeed come from the same root as this Yama, as scholars have long noted, seeing that Eber Donn is the first of the Sons of Mil (the humans, i.e. the Gaels) to die on reaching Ireland in the *Lebor Gabala Erenn*, and Donn becomes known as an underworld god, with the rocky island Tech Duinn known as his domain, while Vedic Yama is the first human to die, and becomes the lord of the underworld as a result.[124] In fact, there is a Donn called "mac Midir," the son of Midir, in *The Colloquy of the Ancients,* demonstrating that the close connection between these two underworld deities has been no illusion and no accident. Next we have Dagda, who, while he has a much larger identity, also seems to have an underworld role, gives and takes life, and presides at the burial mount Brugh na Boinne. He is sometimes called Dagda *Donn*, which could refer to many things including simply to a dark color or an adjective meaning "noble,"[125] but could also indicate his underworld role, as if he sometimes absorbed or overlapped the role of Donn.[126] Meanwhile, we have previously suggested, and are not the first to do so, that Bran, the giant king with his cauldron of reviving could parallel the giant king Dagda with his cauldron of plenty and staff of reviving. We then would draw a line speculatively between Dagda Donn and Bran in their underworld aspects, which could overlap the role of Donn aka Yama. As such, through this long and narrow line of connections, the talking head of Bran could be an actual match to the talking head of Mimir, and these could be seen in relation to the archetype of this "Yama," whose Iranic manifestation is cut in half. Against the argument that Mimir is merely a local water spirit of some kind an objection would have to be offered: who then is the deity who governs the waters springing up from the underground in such a well and is overlord of the spirits that manifest therein? We must leave open the possibility of a deeper divinity underlying surface-level folkloric elements.

"Surya" and Her Husbands

As the "Surya's Bridal" hymn of RV 10.85 says: **First Soma weds her, then to the Gandharva, then to Agni the goddess Surya is given**. Meanwhile, the Asvins woo her, but are sent away, and in another myth wed their own Daughter of the Sun. This passage from Vedic hymn 10.85 is a Master Key that shows in the form of a mantra a mythic pattern that repeats across several of the branches. Assessing this hymnal passage brings light for perhaps the first time in centuries to the meaning of this repeating mythic

---

124   Arthur Anthony Macdonell, *Vedic Mythology,* 172.

125   eDIL (n.d.) Donn

126   O'hOgain, D., *The Lore of Ireland.*

pattern. In most every mythic branch, the "Daughter of the Sun" manifests as at least three different goddesses, while one of her manifestations transfers as a shared wife between two of the gods, a remnant of the double transference noted in the hymn above. However, it is almost always between a different two of these male gods that the goddess is shared, indicating to us that the main concept embodied here by the myths is the general idea of the transference of the Sun Princess, but that the myths reduce the double transference seen in *Rig Veda* to a single transference, a different portion of the double transference being mythically remembered in each case. It could be that over time the manifestations of this goddess, despite being "doubles" in essence, became seen as more and more distinct from one another with distinct roles, and only the general motif of a transference of the goddess was remembered, but a different transference was retained in each branch. Or three originally distinct sisters (sometimes grand/aunt and grand/niece, as in the Vedic and possibly Norse) could be depicted as doubles or as unique individuals depending on context, and this led to a different division of roles over time.

In the Irish case, we see that Midir marries Etain, while the Gandharvic Lord of Eloquence, Ogma, marries Etan, apparently an alternate spelling of the same name. However, we also have Aine who is transferred as a wife from King Echdae to Manannan, just as Rhiannon is transferred from Pwyll to Manawydan. This Echdae seems to be a Horse God by his name, which means literally "Horse God," and Aine is also raped by Ailil Aulom (possibly a double of Echdae, unless Ailil is the Elf, that is the Ribhu), while a parallel of these in the Greek case is Demeter being raped by Poseidon Hippios in horse form. As such, Aine is a closer parallel of Rhiannon in most ways than Etain is. Yet, due to these various Sun Princesses being differentiated doubles at root, there are parallels among all of them. The Irish case thus has preserved two variants of the Sun Princess' transference myth, which partially overlap and help to complete the picture (see chart on the next page).

307

Bolded names indicate the goddess who is shared between two of these gods in each branch. The transference of Aine from Echdae to Manannan is inserted in the Irish sequence, demonstrating the conflation of the Gandharva and Horse/Sun God, discussed above, but also preserving another instance of the transference of the Sun Princess.

	Irish		Norse		Vedic		Greek		Welsh	
Lunar Lord and Wife	Midir	**Etain**	Njordr	**Skadi**	Soma-Chyavana	**Surya-Sukanya**	Dionysus	Ariadne	Arawn	Wife of Arawn
Lord of Eloquence and Wife	Ogma/Echdae	**Etain/Aine**	Bragi	Idunn	Gandharva-Samvarana	Tapati	Hermes	**Peitho (Charite)**	Pwyll	**Rhiannon**
Lord of Fire and Wife	Manannan	**Aine**	Odinn	**Skadi**	Vasistha-Agni	**Surya**	Hephaestus	**Aglaea (Charite)**	Manawydan	**Rhiannon**
Horse Twin and Wife	Aengus	Caer	Freyr	Gerdr	Asvins	Savitri	Dioskouroi	Leukippides	Pryderi	Cigfa

9

Apollo, Óðinn, Dian Cecht, and Brihaspati: The High Priest of the Word

It has been argued in a post by Thomas Rowsell[127] that the Norse god Óðinn has the mythos associated with the Vedic god Brihaspati. He points to the power of resurrecting the dead, which in the *Voluspa* Óðinn has (stanza 158), and which he says is utilized by performing a chant and carving a rune, which runes he receives from hanging on the windy tree. Meanwhile, the reviving of the dead is a power which the son of Brihaspati, Kacha, also learns from Shukracharya by way of the Mriti Sanjeevni mantra (*Vamana Purana*, 62).

This appears to be on the right track, though there is a complication in it that should be expanded upon. It is Shukracharya who himself first gains this mantra from a great show of devotional asceticism to Shiva, and Brihaspati's son, in this version of the myth, only gains it from him afterward. Shukracharya also has one eye poked out by lord Vishnu,

---

127   Thomas Rowsell, "Odin as Brihaspati."

leaving him with a missing eye similar to Óðinn (though the context is very dissimilar to Óðinn's myth). Thus the question is raised, whether Óðinn matches more closely sage Brihaspati, or sage Shukra – or both. Óðinn and Shukra both seem to be the first to seek out this knowledge, in order to gain an advantage in the Great War. While Brihaspati becomes the sage and preceptor of the Devas in the Deva-Asura war, Shukra becomes the same for the Asuras, or "Demons." But Shukra's position is complex, and due to the ambivalent status accorded to sages, and due to a complicated circumstance, Brihaspati's son is able to learn from Shukra the power of resurrecting the dead for the side of the Devas. Shukra/Usana is a mysterious figure. We will first explore his hypothetical connections to Brihaspati, then look at his possible connections to Rudra, and see how the Brihaspatian and Rudraic threads intertwine on this and related levels.

One resolution of this difficulty may be to see Brihaspati and Shukra merely as doubles of one another, coming perhaps from the same original root, two versions of one deity, one for each side of the conflict. This is warranted by a few observations. First, Shukracharya has no hymns addressed to him in the *Rig Veda*, while Brihaspati is a prominent Rig Vedic god. The recognized predecessor of Shukracharya, Kavya Usana, on whom Dumezil wrote the book *The Plight of a Sorcerer,* does appear in the *Rig Veda,* but only in hymns to other gods, and is often associated with Indra, as a helper of that god. Brihaspati is also closely tied to Indra, sometimes as almost his sidekick in the *Rig Veda*, an exemplar of a warrior sage who is depicted as the liberator of the solar cattle from the cave of Vala. Brihaspati in the Veda is the high priest god of the spoken word, the god whose earthly representative is the chanter at the sacrifice. Meanwhile, Kavya Usana has the title "Kavya" or "poet, seer," clearly indicating his status as a type of a sage of the sacred word as well. Brihaspati and Shukracharya are even taught by the same teacher, the sage Angirasa. They each have the identical role with respect to their "side," each one the teacher and sage, and in the end they each are associated with gaining the power of reviving the dead, Shukracharya doing so for himself, and Brihaspati indirectly via his son. While Brihaspati is said to be born of the light, with his seven rays, who "blew and dispersed the darkness"(*Rig Veda*, 4.50.8), Shukra's name means "brightness, clearness, light." Thus Usana/Shukra (who are continuations of one figure), despite being on the side of the "demons," is still the poet-sage of brightness. As Brihaspati is the high priest of the spoken or sung hymn, so in *Rig Veda* it says also of Usana: "Like Usana, the priest a laud shall utter, a hymn to thee, the Lord Divine" (RV 4.16.2).

Roshen Dalal in *Hinduism: An Alphabetical Guide* makes an interesting remark when he states that "According to one passage in the *Mahabharata,* Shukra divided himself into two, and became the guru of the Devas and the Asuras,"[128] and notes that *Vishnu*

310

Purana 1.12.17 also calls Ushanas the preceptor of both the devas and asuras. But we have already noted that Brihaspati is known as the guru of the Devas. Hence this passage seems to be conflating the two, while also referring to the god dividing himself in two in order to fulfill the same function for both sides, just as we have proposed. As it turns out, other potential iterations of the Brihaspati deity also are ambivalent with respect to what side they are on. Brihaspati has a grandson who is said to incarnate his role in the Kurukshetra war, that is, Drona. Drona, however, fights on the side of the Kauravas, the side that opposes the incarnations of the gods of society and order. Yet, at the same time, he is the teacher of the warriors of both sides, and various warriors from both sides have affection for him as such. Like Shukra/Usanas, Drona is on the side of the "demons," but is still in a somewhat ambivalent role as the teacher of the youths regardless of their side, and is even the grandson and partial incarnation of Brihaspati himself.

Based on this evidence, it could be the case that in the earliest Indo-Iranic form of this mythos the god was seen as aligned with the forces that oppose the gods of society, and this may have had an esoteric meaning, indicating his status as one of the "indifferent" primal forces, just as we see the incarnations of the gods of the Sun, the Sky, and Destiny aligned on the side of these indifferent, oppositional forces in the archaic alignment found in the Kurukshetra War god-incarnations. In possibly the same way, Apollo, who we will compare with this grouping of sages, fights on the side opposing the protagonist Greeks. He fights on the Trojan side, which, as we have shown, is the side cognate to the Kauravas, on which side Drona fights. It may be that over time the theological meaning of the alignment of this god with the forces of fate was understood less and less, and it came to be seen as undesirable for the great sage god to fight on the side of "darkness," and so he was doubled and given to the other side as well. Or it may also be that Usana/Shukra was simply a specialized version of this god type, emphasizing certain more ambivalent and potentially dangerous traits contained within the high priest god, such traits as are indicated in Dumezil's use of the word "sorcerer" for him, and the fact that his story concludes with a tale of almost proto-Faustian hubris. Dark and light sides or versions of this god could always have been present, and it is difficult to speculate on. The Irish parallel god, as we will see, fights on the side of the gods of society, while we also will posit the theory that the *Iliad*'s Nestor may be another iteration of this deity, an iteration who also fights *for* the protagonist heroes.

Furthermore, we do not know if the separate figure Kavya Usana/Shukracharya may have been an Indo-Iranic development, and this possibility is supported by the fact that in the other branches we do not tend to find clear cognates of him that are distinct from the "Brihaspati" mythos. There seems to be only one god in these branches that covers

---

128   Roshen Dalal in *Hinduism: An Alphabetical Guide,* "Shukracharya".

this deity archetype as a whole (or a god and his son, as with Brihaspati and son Kacha or Bharadwaja, but no "demonic double"). Thus, we will hypothesize that the "Brihaspati" mythos may extend in some fashion to Brihaspati, Kavya Usana/Shukracharya, Brihaspati's sons, and his grandson Drona as well. With a hypothetical circle drawn around this grouping of archetypal sages of the word, possibly branches of one original sage god mythos, we will proceed to a closer comparison with the Greek, Norse, and Irish cognates.

The starting point for this set of comparisons is, as we have mentioned, Brihaspati as high priest of the invocation, the spoken liturgical word, the hymn, etc. If Usanas' title *Kavya* means "poet," it is not in a low, common sense, but in the highest sense. Whereas the Gandharva is divinity of bards and myth-tellers, Brihaspati is god of the higher *purohitas* (priests) who channel the most sacred hymns. This god is the sacred seer-poet, rishi, invoker of the sacrifice. As Encyclopedia Britannica says, the name *Brihaspati* is Sanskrit for "Lord of the Sacred Speech," and he is "the master of sacred wisdom, charms, hymns and rites," the "preceptor" and "sage counselor." In the same role Óðinn also has the name *Haptasnytrir*, meaning "teacher of gods," while Brihaspati is the preeminent teacher of the gods. In addition, he is said to be the "prototype of the class of Brahmans [the priestly class]" (Britannica.com, "Brihaspati"), all of which supports the idea that Usana/Shukra are simply split from this original prototype.

As such, Brihaspati forms a pair and a contrast with the other main high priest god, Agni. Agni, as opposed to Brihaspati, is the fire priest, the God of Fire seen as priest of the sacrificial fire, the governing divinity of that fire and of the priests who are its officiants. There are times when Agni and Brihaspati may seem to have overlapping traits, as when the *Rig Veda* states, "Usana Kavya stablished thee, oh Agni, as invoking Priest" (RV 8.23.17); however, in general there is a sharp and meaningful distinction between the two central priest gods. They are two sides of the high-priestly office, and perform their own roles, generally working in conjunction (curiously, Drona is killed by the incarnation of Agni, Dhrishtadyumna, hinting at the possibility of rivalry). These two priestly gods may also be seen theoretically as sub-aspects of another god such as Varuna or Rudra in his role as the primordial priest-king, which may explain why, as we have suggested, both the Agni and Brihaspati[129] deities may be aspects of Óðinn (considered in his Varunian/Rudraic aspect).

---

129   Arthur A. Macdonell describes how Brihaspati and Agni are intertwined and identified in the Vedas to an almost unprecedented degree. "There are several passages in which Brhaspati appears identified with Agni. Thus 'the lord of prayer, Agni, handsome like Mitra' is invoked (1.38.13). In another passage (2.1.3) Agni, though identified with other gods as well, is clearly more intimately connected with Brahmanaspati [Brihaspati], as only these two names are in the vocative. In one verse (3.26.2) both Matarisvan and

Thus Brihaspati connects to all forms of spoken charm as well as the arcane knowledge of the high priest sage generally. In iconography his body is often made golden, and he is said to wield a bow. For, as aforesaid, he is also a powerful warrior associated closely to Indra, sometimes almost being assimilated to an aspect of Indra as a warrior-priest (Indra-Brihaspati of the *Rig Veda*). Importantly, Brihaspati also has sons who share aspects with him. We have mentioned his son Kacha, who goes to Shukra to learn the mantra of reviving the dead. In addition, there is his son Bharadwaja, also known as Brhaspatya, the father of Drona. This Brhaspatya, son of Brihaspati, is strongly associated with the medical function, and this will become key in our later comparisons. He is known as a great physician and is even referred to in Ayurvedic treatises such as the *Charaka Samhita*, in which it is said he was taught the medical sciences by Indra in order to aid humans on their spiritual journey, and his name means "bringing about nourishment."

'Brhaspati the wise priest, the guest, the swiftly-moving' seem to be epithets of Agni, while in another (1.190.2) Matarisvan seems to be an epithet of Brhaspati. Again, by Brhaspati, who is blue-backed, takes up his abode in the house, shines brightly, is golden coloured and ruddy (5.43.12), Agni must be meant. In two other verses (I.18.19; 10.182.2) Brhaspati seems to be the same as Narasamsa, a form of Agni (p. 100). Like Agni, Brhaspati is a priest, is called 'Son of Strength' (1.40.2) and Angiras (2.23.18) as well (the epithet angiras belonging to him exclusively), and burns the goblins (2.23.14) or slays them (10.103.4). Brhaspati is also spoken of as ascending to heaven, to the upper abodes (10.67.10). Like Agni, Brhaspati has three abodes (4.50.1); he is the adorable one of houses (7.97.5), and 'lord of the dwelling', sadasas pati (1.18.6; Indra-Agni are once called sadaspati, 1.21.5). On the other hand, Agni is called brahmanas kavi, 'sage of prayer' (6.16.30) and is besought (2.2.7) to make heaven and earth favourable by prayer (brahmana). But Brihaspati is much more commonly distinguished from Agni (2.25.3' 7.10.4; 10.68.9), chiefly by being invoked or named along with him in enumerations (3.20.8 &c.)" (Macdonell, *Vedic Mythology*, 102).
"The evidence adduced above seems to favour the view that Brhaspati was originally an aspect of Agni as a divine priest presiding over devotion, an aspect which (unlike other epithets of Agni formed with pati, such as visam pati, grhapati, sadaspati) had attained an independent character by the beginning of the Rigvedic period, though the connexion with Agni was not entirely severed. Lanlois, H.H. Wilson, Max Muller agree in regarding Brhaspati as a variety of Agni" (Macdonell, *Vedic Mythology,* 103-104). Clearly, we do not agree that Brihaspati was ever a mere aspect of Agni, as his incarnation exists among the archaic Kurukshetra hero-incarnations and he has parallels in other branches, but the intertwining of the two gods to the point of identification should be taken very seriously and must have had a deeply rooted cause.

Magical Chants: Galdr and Paean

As we will see, such medical knowledge is generally connected to the gods who parallel Brihaspati in each branch (Óðinn, Apollo, and Dian Cecht) and is often specially embodied in a son of those gods as well. This medical role would connect to the general role of sage as knower of arcane knowledge, such as medical science, but more specifically to the healing charms and chants that are the special provision of the priest of invocation. Óðinn, for instance, is called "Fadr Galdr" or Galdr Father, the god of the *galdrs*. *Galdrs* are invocations or spells that were sung or chanted for specific effects. Some galdrs are clearly used for healing purposes, as to heal women during childbirth in the Eddic poem *Oddrunargratr*, verse 6. Or as Óðinn says in stanza 146 of the *Havamal*, discussing the galdrs he knows, "A second I know, which the son of men,/must sing who would heal the sick" (*Poetic Edda, Havamal*, 146). The mantra for reviving the dead that Óðinn learns, and which Shukra and Kacha alternately gain, might even be said to fall under the category of this type of healing chant as well, as the most extreme form of healing, unless prophetic necromancy is given its own category.

Proceeding from this understanding of the connection between Óðinn and the Brihaspati mythos, we move to the examples from the Greek and Irish branches. Apollo is one of the most mysterious and complicated gods in all mythology in terms of his origins and development over time. It often seems as though, by the Classical era, he has magnetized into his charismatic circle a vast array of associations and roles, becoming a kind of all-in-all god that could by no means reflect his original conception. What this original conception was, then, must be dug for in the mythological threads that can be connected to the Indo-European mosaic.

In this connection, we will examine Apollo via his byname "Paeon." This name is very archaic and is attested from Mycenaean fragments, as *Pa-ja-wo-ne* (John Chadwick, *The Mycenaean World*, 89). R.S.P. Beekes claims that the name Paeon, coming from *παιάϝων, may mean "he who heals illness through magic" (*Etymological Dictionary of Greek*, Brill, 2009, p. 1142 (see also pp. 1144 and 1159)). Paeon is the healer god in literature of the Homeric period, but is believed to have been a byname of Apollo based on the Mycenaean inscriptions. Despite Paeon sometimes being depicted separately from Apollo, Apollo is still often called by this epithet. This byname reflects Apollo's general association with healing, with protecting the people or city from disease, and connects to his several other epithets associated with the healing function:

314

Acesius, meaning "healing," *Acestor*, meaning "healer," *Iatrus*, "physician," *Medicus*, "physician." Additionally, the word *paean* came to signify any of a specific type of solemnly chanted song, perhaps originally a kind of healing song based on the meaning of the word, and eventually coming to describe songs flattering victors. Just as several of Óðinn's galdrs are said to give courage and victory in battle, so paeans are known to have been sung during battle to grant warriors courage and to ensure success. Aeschylus describes how "The Greeks were singing the stately paean at that time not for flight, but because they were hastening into battle and were stout of heart," while other instances show that paeans were often sung at the beginning of battles. Óðinn, meanwhile, states, "An eleventh I know: if haply I lead/my old comrades out to war,/I sing 'neath the shields, and they fare forth mightily/safe into battle,/safe out of battle,/and safe return from the strife" (*Havamal*, 155). We then have galdrs and paeans each as magical chants associated with both healing and granting strength or courage for battle, and we have Óðinn as the father of galdrs in Norse myth, and Apollo as Paeon/Paean in Greek, or Paeon as originally his own separate deity and later identified with Apollo. Some galdrs are also intended to avert various kinds of injury, one even driving away witches, while Apollo was viewed as a god of protection and the averting of evil or harm, his epithet *Alexikakos* meaning "warding off evil," as well as *Averruncus* meaning "averter." Other galdrs were directed toward making people go mad, creating storms, sinking ships, and bringing battle victory itself (recall the paean as a victory song), while Apollo was famous for his far-reaching arrows which could bring plague (the flipside of his healing power) and all manner of destruction. This general power of fearful destruction and the power of destruction of evil were also two sides of one coin.

As we have mentioned, Apollo has a son who himself is considered, in a more specialized manner, the god of healing. This is Asclepius, who carries a rod entwined by a snake, the snake being symbolic of healing knowledge, though its exact meaning is disputed. Asclepius and his rod were so fully identified with the healing art that even today medical facilities commonly bear this snake-entwined rod as their symbol (but often substituted by the similar *caduceus* of Hermes). As Apollo has the byname *Paean*, so Asclepius too has this epithet attached to him. Thus the specialized healing god Asclepius as son of Apollo forms a very neat parallel to the specialized healing god Bharadwaja as son of Brihaspati.

Apollo and Brihaspati have several other shared attributes that deepen this comparison, and these connect to the meaning of Apollo's name. While Brihaspati is the teacher of the gods, particularly during their youths, Apollo is also known for his role as the teacher of youths in general. He is the patron of the education of youths and the overseer of their coming of age, as well as the protector of youths, *kourotrophos*. The coming of age festival was known as the *Apellai*, and at this festival Apellon/Apollo was known as the Great Kouros (male youth) (Jane Ellen Harrison, *Themis: A study to the Social origins of Greek Religion,* 441). As scholar Gregory Nagy relates, a classic article by Walter Burkert "proposes that the Doric form of the name, Apéllōn, be connected with the noun apéllai, designating a seasonally recurring festival—an assembly or thing, in Germanic terms—of Dorian kinship groups," and that a later study by Alfred Heubeck "shows that the earliest recoverable form of the name is *apeliōn, built on a noun shaped *apeli̯a: thus the meaning would be something like 'he of the assembly'" (Nagy, *Homer's Text and Language,* "The Name of Apollo"). Just as Brihaspati is the god of the spoken word, in *Apollo, Origins and Influences,* Nagy argues that "the name 'Apollon' was connected to the verb 'apeileo' and indicated that its bearer was 'the god of authoritative speech, the one who presides over all manner of speech-acts'" (Konaris, 295). As he explains,

> The point of departure for my presentation is a Cypriote by-form of Apollo's name, Apeílōn (to-i-a-pe-lo-ni = τῶι Ἀπείλωνι), showing the earlier e-vocalism as opposed to the innovative o-vocalism of Apóllōn. […] I propose to connect the name of Apollo, with recourse to this Cypriote by-form, to the Homeric noun apeilḗ, meaning 'promise, boastful promise, threat', and to the corresponding verb, apeiléō 'make a promise, boastful promise, threat.' […] this concept dovetails with the meaning of apéllai, based on an actual context of speech-acts. Such dovetailing helps explain the essence of Apollo, 'he of the *apeli̯a', as the god of authoritative speech, the one who presides over all manner of speech-acts, including the realms of songmaking in general and poetry in particular. (Nagy, *Homer's Text and Language,* "The Name of Apollo").

Apollo is generally depicted with a bow, and as "bow-carrying" and "far-shooting." Brihaspati is said to have a bow whose string is *Rta,* or cosmic order. As Apollo is, so Brihaspati also is associated with the light of the sun, specifically with bringing light, as when he releases the solar cattle. Apollo is known as *Phanaeus,* meaning "bringing light," while Brihaspati is one who drives away darkness when he retrieves the wondrous cattle, commonly interpreted as symbolic of the illuminating light of the sun (Brereton and Jamison, *The Rigveda: A Guide,* 81-82). Apollo is known as a pastoral herdsman god as well (*Homeric hymn to Hermes*, 22, 70), which could also connect to this myth of Brihaspati freeing and returning the divine cattle.

The Irish Case

Much of this pattern repeats in the Irish case. Dian Cecht is the god of healing, the primary god who heals the other injured gods in the myths. He heals the eye of Midir and replaces Nuada's severed arm with the famous silver one. In the *Second Battle of Magh Tuireadh*, which is cognate with the other great battles of the gods, he is in charge of the healing well "Slainge's Well," in which he soaks the injured warriors to heal them (note that Apollo and his priests are also commonly associated with sacred healing springs). He is said to "chant" spells over this well along with his two sons and daughter. Even more striking, this well can seemingly heal anyone who has not been decapitated, implying a power of reviving even the dead in many cases. This power is made clear when the Formorians realize that their slain warriors do not come back the next day, but that this "was not the case with the Tuatha de Danann." The Tuatha de Danann would "cast their mortally-wounded men into it as they were struck down; and they were alive when they came out [...] Their mortally wounded were healed through the power of incantation made by the four physicians [Dian Cecht and his children] who were around the well" (*Cath Maige Tuired*). This well becomes such a destabilizing advantage in the war with the Fomorians that they send a special envoy to fill it up with boulders, finally rendering it neutralized. A later medieval incantation says, "I save the dead-alive [...] Whole be that whereon Diancecht's salve goes" (*St. Gall Incantations*), thus associating verbal incantation to revive the dead, or make whole those near death, with Dian Cecht, seeming to make him the patron of such incantations. Dian Cecht is also associated with the poetic art generally as the father of a line of poets, beginning with his poetess daughter Etan, who marries the Gandharvic god of eloquence Ogma, who together have a son, the satirical poet Cairbre. Dumezil also points to Dian Cecht's myth as the Irish cognate of the Usana/Shukra myth regarding the contentious power to revive the dead which unbalances the great war and must be neutralized, either by the other side gaining it as well, as in the Vedic case, or by its destruction, as in the Irish and Welsh cases. As Dumezil sums up the recurring motif, "one of the two parties possesses a technique, material or formulaic, either to revive the dead or to assure the invulnerability and immortality of its combatants, and the other side seeks to get hold of this technique or to destroy it" (Dumezil, *The Plight of A Sorcerer*, 56).

Just as importantly, Dian Cecht has a son who himself is a powerful healing god. This is Miach, and so specialized a healing god is he that in the myths he outdoes his own father in that art. After Dian Cecht replaces Nuada's arm with a silver one, Miach makes for Nuada a fully flesh and blood arm, thus improving on his father's work, and almost as though against the law of nature itself. Because of this, Dian Cecht kills his son,

317

seemingly for practicing a forbidden art or possibly out of a kind of jealousy, and from his body grow the 365 arcane healing herbs. Dian Cecht scatters these herbs to protect the secret knowledge they represent.

Thus Apollo and his healer son Asclepius, who parallel Brihaspati and his physician son Bharadwaj, are also paralleled again by Dian Cecht and his healer son Miach. The pattern is strikingly consistent, Dian Cecht even having a second physician son named Octriuil or Oirmiach as Brihaspati also has Kacha. As a side-note, it is interesting that Asclepius has a son named Machaon, somewhat reminiscent of Miach. But the parallelism between these father-son pairs goes much deeper. For Asclepius too is killed precisely for knowing too much of the medical art, for being too potent a healer (Apollod. iii. 10. § 4). Not only that, but his specific crime is that he is able to bring the dead back to life, exactly the contentious power we have seen used by Óðinn, Dian Cecht, Shukra, and the other son of Brihaspati, Kacha. For thus being too skilled in the arcane healing art, in a manner that threatens the law of nature itself (and causing Pluto to complain that his kingdom of the dead is being depopulated according to Diodorus Siculus, iv. 71; comp. Schol. *ad Pind. Pyth.* iii. 102.), Zeus takes it upon himself to kill Asclepius. Thus this killing of Asclepius by Zeus is the same as Dian Cecht killing his son Miach for having too great of healing power, but it also parallels the revivifying well of Dian Cecht being neutralized by the Fomorians, as it is the motif of the neutralization of the great reviving power which has unbalanced nature. It is as though the Irish case splits into two related myths what is combined in the Asclepius myth. The neutralizing of the well is in turn the same as Kacha getting Shukra to teach him the mantra of revivification, as this knowledge neutralizes Shukra's advantage and levels the playing field in the war.

Interestingly, as Nick Allen states, "Hecataeus of Miletus, as well as Pindar (FGrH 1 371), are reported to have identified Pan as the offspring of Apollo and Penelope," while Cian, who we identify as the Irish Pan (see our chapter "The Celtic Pushan"), is the son of Dian Cecht. If accurate, this would mean that at least two Greek authorities preserve the same relation between these two gods that appears also with regard to their parallels in the Irish case (though other versions of Pan and Apollo's descents also exist). Lastly and perhaps most definitively, while Brihaspati is called *vacaspati* (MS. 2, 6.6, cp. SB. 14.4.1.23), meaning "lord of speech," Dian Cecht has a second name: *Cainte*[130], which means "Speech." He is manifestly the god of the spoken word just as Brihaspati and Apollo are, and is named as such. But not just that, as this name, *Cainte,* meaning "speech," comes from the Proto-Celtic **kaneti*, meaning "to sing," from the Proto-Indo-European **kéh₂neti,* "to sing," cognate with Latin *canere,* meaning "to sing, chant,

---

130   In the romance *Oidheadh Chlainne Tuireann,* Cu, Cethen and Cian, otherwise known to be the sons of Dian Cecht, are called "the sons of Cainté."

sound, or play an instrument." The name of this god then connects him to speech, singing, and chanting, aptly reinforcing his role as god of the sacred chants and related vocalizations.

This understanding of Apollo and Dian Cecht as parallels of one another who themselves parallel Brihaspati may also explain why Apollo is seen as a slayer of a great serpent. Generally we would assume this myth type to belong to the Thunderer god, as when Indra kills Vrtra, Zeus kills Typhon, and Thor kills the Midgard Serpent, etc. This seems to come back to the central Vedic myth complex of Vrtra and Vala, which pair of monsters can be over-simplified as the "obstructing monster" and the "concealing monster." In simple terms, the slaying of Vrtra by Indra releases the waters which he has obstructed. The slaying of Vala releases the divine cattle, symbolic of the rays of light themselves, from the dark cave where he has concealed them. The Vrtra and Vala myths are closely linked, and the identity of the god who performs the slaying changes numerous times in Vedic texts. That being said, Brihaspati (or Indra with Brihaspati) is one of the gods most frequently said to be the slayer of Vala, and in this role is depicted as the one who frees the light from the cave. Thus, when Apollo slays the serpent Python (*Homeric Hymns 3 to Apollo 300;* Apollodorus i. § 1; Strabo ix., 422) this would be perfectly in line with Brihaspati slaying Vala. Scholar George Edwin Rines, for one, has seen in the slaying of Python an allegory of the sun dispersing the fogs of the marshes.[131] The fact that Apollo must slay Python before he establishes his oracle on that precise spot may also carry the meaning that the spiritual or mental darkness and fog had to be driven away before the prophetic light of Apollonian truth could emanate through (this is the same meaning given to the Brihaspati-Vala myth by commentator Sri Aurobindo in his *The Secret of the Veda,* in the chapter "Brihaspati, Power of the Soul"). As Vala is depicted as a concealing cave-monster, Apollo slays Python in a cave – the cave of the Delphic Oracle – and as Brihaspati is said to shatter Vala with his shout, the Delphic priestesses are said also to shout, while Apollo fights Python, "Hie Paean!", thus emphatically highlighting the exact aspect of Apollo (Paean) that we have seen parallels Brihaspati most precisely. This slaying of Python, then, appears to have been a Paean-Brihaspati myth at root.

Meanwhile, Dian Cecht is also given his own serpent-slaying myth and it is prominent in his narrative. He finds either one or three serpents[132] (in one version they are in the

---

131   Rines, George Edwin, ed. (1920). "Python". *Encyclopedia Americana.*

132   One in the Metrical *Dindshenchas,* three in the Prose *Dindshenchas* from the Book of Leinster, paraphrased in *Manners and Customs of the Ancient Irish,* Vol. II, p. 143, by Eugene O'Curry. John Shaw explains the likelihood that the metrical version, with only one serpent, is more archaic in its details ("Indo-European Dragon Slayers and Healers and the Irish Account of Dian Cécht and Méiche," p. 161-164).

heart of an infant) and burns them to ash in response to a prophecy that says they will destroy Ireland if they are allowed to grow. The *Dindshenchas* state: "Three turns the serpent made;/It sought the soldier to consume him;/It would have wasted by its doing the kine;/The fell filth of the old serpent," continuing, "Therefore Diancecht slew it;/There rude reason for clean destroying it,/For preventing it from wasting/Worse than any wolf pack, from consuming utterly" (*Metrical Dindshenchas*, "Berba"). Other than the serpent-slaying motif itself being associated once again with a god paralleling Brihaspati, what is interesting is the mention of "kine" (or *ell*, approximately "flock"; *anmanna*, 'animals', in the prose variant). This serpent specifically would have wasted, and "consum[ed] utterly," the cattle, which are the symbol of the light that Vala conceals in the Vedic mythos. While Vala conceals these cattle, Dian Cecht's serpent, Meichi[133], threatens to consume them. The burning of the serpent to ash would then be another image of the obliteration of the concealing monster by the deity who brings illumination via his destructive force. It may also be in this action that we find a meaning for Dian Cecht's name, which translates as "swift power" (though this likely relates to his swift healing well). The ashes of the serpent are thrown in to a river, causing the river to boil, and thus giving it the name *Berbo*, or *Bearu/Barrow*. *Berbo* comes from the same root (Proto-Celtic *beru-/*boru-*, 'boil', 'bubble') as a Gaulish theonym, *Borvo*, who was equated with Apollo due to the healing power of his spring waters. Therefore, when Dian Cecht kills the serpent and turns the river into the "bubbling" river with its ashes, this may have been another aspect of his healer function, using the once deadly serpent medicinally to create a source of potentially healing waters.

---

133   The serpent is said (in a triple form) to be concealed in the heart of the Morrigan's child Meiche (in a prose *Dindshenchas* account: LL 159b 40, Book of Ballymote 358a, II. 17b, Rennes 95a.2 and Bodleian = Rawl. B 506), or the serpent *is* the child (as a singular serpent. See: *Metrical Dindshenchas*, "Berba"). The heart of the child then takes the place of the cave of Vala as the place of concealment of the serpent. In the Vedic myth, Vala is both the cave and the serpent within it, as Meichi is alternately the child or within the concealment of the child's heart.

As mother of the serpent, Morrigan parallels the Vedic figure named Danu, the mother of Vala's paired serpent, Vrtra, along with numerous other monsters and minor demons. Thus, John Shaw, in his "Indo-European Dragon-Slayers and Healers, and the Irish Account of Dian Cécht and Méiche," argues, based on Irish texts that arguably link the Morrigan and the Irish Danu, that the Morrigan is actually an aspect of, or from a shared root with, this Irish goddess sharing the name with the Vedic one, Danu. Irish Danu = Morrigan = Anu = Vedic Danu, according to Shaw. Shaw demonstrates that Meichi's myth corresponds to many elements of the archaic serpent-slaying myth, and also argues that the various serpent slaying myths could go back to a shared original, which could explain some interchange of motifs.

Even Óðinn has a likely variant of this cattle-liberating myth, as Curwen Rolinson has demonstrates in the article "On Odin Brihaspati As Song-Smith – The Sung Seizing Of The Wealth Of Cows." He points out a passage from the *Ynglinga Saga* stanza 7 that states: "Odin knew finely where all missing cattle were concealed under the earth, and understood the songs by which the earth, the hills, the stones, and mounds were opened to him; and he bound those who dwell in them by the power of his word, and went in and took what he pleased." The cattle are once again "concealed," as Vala is the concealing monster, *Vala* meaning "enclosure" from a root meaning "to cover or enclose." They are concealed under the earth and in the mounds rather than in a cave or a child's heart, and once again it is specifically songs and the power of the word that opens the concealment and liberates the cattle. It is evidently the same myth through and through. Furthermore, Rolinson highlights chapter 6, which asserts that "He and His temple priests were called song-smiths, for from them came that art of song into the northern countries," which reminds us of Apollo and his chanting priestesses as well as Apollo's own famed art of song. In the same stanza, Óðinn is said to be a master of conversation and to speak everything in rhyme, fully in accord with his role as god of speech.

Returning to Apollo and Óðinn, we briefly note that both gods are emphatically wolf-associated gods (Apollo *Lykeios;* Óðinn's pet wolves), and also are each associated with ravens. Apollo as the leader of the coming of age of the Greek youths at the *Apellai* festival, and as their representative (which we have mentioned), was the god to whom the cut off hair of the youths who had come of age was dedicated. As scholar Kris Kershaw has shown, a similar ritual of the youths cutting and dedicating the hair to a god was associated with the bands of warrior youths who saw Óðinn as their leader and representative in Germanic society. Kershaw also shows that both prophecy and poetry were associated with these bands, as requisite skills of the warrior youth. She demonstrates, furthermore, that the root of Óðinn/Wodan's very name (*woþ-*) is also from the same root as the Italo-Celtic *vates/ovate/fáith*, the terms for "the inspired, the ecstatic, soothsayer. He was also a poet, inasmuch as he delivered his oracles in verse" (Kershaw, *Odin: The One-Eyed God*, 114).

The Intertwining of "Brihaspati" and "Rudra" Myths

This brings us to an important and complex juncture, which points to a close intertwining of the "Brihaspati" and "Rudra" mythoi in certain instances. On the basis of the network of reinforcing comparisons we have laid out, it seems more than warranted to make an even bolder comparison between the myths of Apollo and Óðinn, potentially drawing them more closely together than has heretofore been done. As has been central to our analysis, Óðinn hangs on the windy tree, wounded by a spear and enduring nine "long nights," in order to gain the runes and the powers they can give access to, these runes then being one of the central elements of the spell that revives the dead. The runes themselves are sometimes speculated to have been instruments of divination and prophecy as well. *Havamal* 79 refers to "asking" runes, and that which is asked coming true: "All will prove true that thou askest of runes – those that are come from the gods, which the high Powers wrought, and which Odin painted: then silence is surely best." Although such use is not directly attested otherwise, other divinatory objects or signs are attested during the period predating the use of the known runes (Tacitus, *Germania*, 10). Furthermore, the word *rune* means "secret, hidden," arguably pointing to the concealed and esoteric nature of their knowledge.

We purposely eschew the argument that the *myth* of Óðinn's gaining of the runes has no mystical meaning other than the gaining of a simple writing system.[134] Our argument

---

134   See also: MacLeod, Mindy; Mees, Bernard (2006), *Runic Amulets and Magic Objects*. Erick Dodge also supports the argument that the runes cannot be reduced to mere mundane letters and nothing more: "Germanic words for writing like PG *stað-, *wrîan, and *rêðan were relatively straight forward terms referring to letters. The runes (ON rúnar) that Odin learned, however, were very different. Most people when they her the word 'rune' think of carved letters, but the runes were not used for purposes of every-day communication as was the alphabetic script by the Romans, for they were employed in magic and divination, and were therefore tied up with the Germanic religion, they were largely confined to short, terse inscriptions and knowledge of them was restricted to a small, closed circle of rune-masters' (Green, 1998: 254). This can be seen the Hávamál 144 where Odin asks the initiate if he knows how to paint, test, ask, bless, send, and offer them. Green, in his massive work on Germanic historical linguistics, summarizes the word's semantic history by saying that in their maturity (i.e. in medieval christianized Iceland) they were 'mysterious sign[s], character[s] used in magic practice', prior to that during the pagan period they had connotations of being 'secret[s], secret knowledge, magic', and originally they were 'low-voiced, secretive speech' (Green, 1998: 255). Grundy notes that 'magical chants pre-dated the dissemination of the runes among the Germanic peoples' (Grundy, 2014a: 155). The original notion was borrowed into Finnish with the word runo ('poem, poetry'). The PG term was *rūnō 'secret, mystery' and the Proto-Celtic was *rūnā 'secret, mystery'. Both terms descended from late PIE *rū-no- 'secret, mystery' which came from the root *reuh$_x$- 'to intone, mumble, whisper' (Watkins 2011: 75). A similar idea can be seen in the ON blót ('sacrifice, offering') as well as the Latin flāmen and Sanskrit bráhman (PIE *bhlagh-men- 'priest, wizard'). They all descend from a close net web of root including: *bhel-[4] ('bellow'), *bhlād ('to worship') and *bhlē-[1] ('howl'), and *bhlē-[2] ('blow').
    The Germanic Rune Poems clearly show that each individual rune was a secret, full of etymological and sacred meaning, which needed to be taught and transmitted via kenning filled riddles" (Dodge, "Orpheus, Odin, and the Indo-European Underworld," 61-62).

is as follows: 1. The structure and tone of the myth of Oðinn's hanging from the tree strongly indicates a specifically mystical rather than mundane outcome. This is an initiatic self-sacrifice of the highest god of all, specifically in quest of said runes, and in no way simply relates to the finding of the mundane alphabet in other myths, such as Hermes passively noticing the flight of cranes. Even if the runes themselves were used as a mundane alphabet, as is apparent, *this particular myth* focuses its lens rather on their mystical potential. The very manner in which the speaker of the poem treats the runes is incongruent with how individual mundane letters are spoken of in relation to other scripts. Substituting "letters" for "runes" in the relevant *Havamal* verses makes this humorously apparent: from the "Sages' Seat," "Of *letters* they spoke, and the reading of *letters* was little withheld from their lips" (*Havamal* 110). "Crying aloud I lifted the *letters*" (138). "Hidden *letters* shalt thou seek and interpreted signs" (this instance also closely connecting runes with the interpretation of potentially fateful "signs"). If we continue to substitute "letters" in this stanza for further mentions of these connected "signs," we get: "Full strong the *letters* full mighty the *letters* that the ruler of gods doth write" (142). This is not how mere letters are spoken of. This would be melodramatic, and there is a palpable and obvious incongruity felt here when trying to claim the runes were treated the same as purely mundane letters within this mythological poem specifically. The author of the poem could have said *spells* if the spell was the only important unit, but said *runes* instead. 2. Certain instances of vertically stacked runes ("bind runes" using stacked *Tiwaz* runes, for instance) as well as numerous yet undeciphered runic series, appearing outwardly as nonsense, may be explicable as magical in themselves. 3. If this myth has parallels in other branches then it is quite ancient, and so, in an earlier form, before the advent of the known runes, it would have involved not the *Futhark* runes that we know today, but some other "secret" items (possibly not even any form of script, though this can only be speculated), with perhaps a more specialized esoteric purpose, as the mystical form of the myth suggests. If the myth has valid parallels in other branches then we are required to approach the question as though the myth is ancient and not tied to a single late writing system. 4. It is the following parallel with the Greek case (and the Irish parallel with Fionn mentioned later) that strengthens the likelihood that the runes, or whatever "secrets" preceded them in an earlier form of this myth, were connected to prophetic practices. At this point this is a quibble over the specific application of the runes and over semantics. It is the mythic parallel that is most important, and it is this that in turn gives validity to the above mentioned hypothesis of the prophetic power of the runes, whether that power rests in the runes considered *in themselves* or not. Oðinn is in any case known to have the power of prophecy, whether via the dead seers he raises up and speaks to with the help of the runes, or by the magical means mentioned elsewhere:

Odin understood also the art in which the greatest power is lodged, and which he himself practiced; namely, what is called magic. By means of this he could know beforehand the predestined fate of men, or their not yet completed lot; and also bring on the death, ill-luck, or bad health of people, and take the strength or wit from one person and give it to another. (*Heimskringla*, 7)

Daphne and the Windy Tree

Though on the surface it will surely seem an absurd comparison – at first – we find a similar pattern and meaning in the myth of Apollo's pursuit of the maiden Daphne. Apollo is struck by Cupid's arrow (Ovid, *Metamorphoses*, 1.452), falls in love with the naiad Daphne, and pursues her. She flees, leading to a chase. During this pursuit, Apollo suffers the torment of love, and mentions his knowledge of the healing herbs and how this knowledge has not done anything for his painful love-wound. Finally, when Apollo catches her, Daphne prays to her father Peneus, or to Zeus (Parthenius, *Love Romances*, 15), and is changed into a laurel tree. She is described as being swallowed up and concealed in the bark of the tree. In another version (Nonnus, *Dionysiaca*, 33.210), Daphne is swallowed by Gaia, the earth, but is also said to become a tree (42.386). This does not halt Apollo's love, however, for he embraces the tree and makes the iconic laurel crown from her branches, claiming the laurel for his tree – "you shall be my tree" (Ovid, *Metamorphoses*, 1.452).

Nonnus, however, says more, spelling out the fact that "she crowned his head with prophetic clusters" (Nonnus, *Dionysiaca*, 42.386), and that hers was a tree with "inspired whispers." This points us toward the answer to the central questions: *why does Apollo pursue a maiden who becomes a tree, and why is this tree the laurel?* We see from Nonnus that this tree was believed to bear "prophetic clusters," which is confirmed from the practice of Apollo's priestesses themselves, such as the Delphic Oracle, the Pythia, who chewed none other than laurel leaves in order to induce their prophetic visions. Furthermore, the laurel crown which Apollo makes has the dual symbolism of the athletic/martial victor and the poetic victor. From this we retain the title *laureate* today for our official chief poet, the one who has won the poetic contest and gained the laurel crown. Poets going back to antiquity, including Ovid himself, were depicted wearing laurels. Hence the laurel leaves had, among their chief symbolisms, both a prophetic and a poetic meaning, connecting them to the poetic chants and prophetic powers we have thus far examined. Indeed, it hardly need even be said that Apollo is known as god both

324

of prophecy (with epithets *Manticus, Iatromantis, Pythius*) and the poetic art generally, *mousike* (companion and lover of all the muses), as well as music, the laurel combining these meanings in one. Laurel leaves also have limited medicinal powers (used for upset stomach, rashes, as an anti-inflammatory for rheumatism, and as aromatherapy), thus potentially uniting all of Apollo's central aspects.

Thus, in the Daphne myth, Apollo, having been pierced by the sharp point of a weapon (Cupid's arrow), has an extended pursuit of a tree-maiden, during which he suffers anguish (and thinks on his healing knowledge), and finally he catches her (is said to embrace the tree while Óðinn hangs from his) and gains from this tree-form an item granting the power of prophecy (while also being related to poetry). The match to the Óðinnic pattern is striking when considered from this angle: Óðinn "pursues" knowledge *on* a tree (instead of pursuing the tree-maiden herself), is pierced by the sharp point of a weapon (a spear), suffers for an extended period ("long nights") while "pursuing" this knowledge, and finally receives items (runes) which are related both to prophecy and the poetic *galdr*, these connecting again to the healing art. The fact that Green, in a footnote above, argues that the runes were originally "low-voiced, secretive speech," ties together well with the fact that the secrets the Oracle of Apollo trafficked in were also spoken words, prophetic utterances induced by the leaves that Apollo receives from the tree-maiden in his trial. It would be just like the Greeks to turn a myth about the pursuit of esoteric knowledge into a lustful, one-sided love-and-chase story (and esoteric allegory). In fact, though the tone of the two myths seems so strikingly dissimilar, if one accepts that both gods come from a shared mythos, but reject the identification of these two myths, then one would have to say that two cognate gods, after a "pursuit" of some kind, gain the main symbol of their prophetic and poetic power from a tree, but that they are somehow different myths in essence.

Daphne is sealed up in the tree or transported away, leaving the tree leaves as her intermediary, just as the runes themselves are "secret" symbols that point toward a greater concealed mystery, and just as language (or symbolic signs like runes and letters) itself points toward an inaccessible referent which it represents. That is, Daphne herself vanishes from Apollo's grasp, is concealed by the bark and leaves, just as Truth itself (or knowledge of Fate specifically in a prophetic context) is always concealed and kept at a remove from mortals. Only by the intermediary means of the prophetic tools, whether the runes or the laurel leaves, can this concealed greater Truth, this knowledge of Fate, be partially glimpsed. In Ovid's version, Daphne even prays to Diana, goddess of virginity, to preserve her from Apollo. Though this could simply be a late dramatic elaboration in the manner we come to expect from the Roman Ovid, it could also point toward the idea of the inviolability of Truth. The highest Truth remains unviolated, pure, and perfect despite attempts to possess it fully, and despite the mediated visions we are granted of it. Thus the meaning of this myth of Apollo's is the passionate pursuit of Truth, its perpetual evasiveness, and its final mediation via the prophetic power of the priest of the spoken word. The emphasis is on the concealed and secret nature of this truth and the pain involved in its pursuit, as the emphasis is also on the secret nature of the runes ("secrets") in the Óðinn myth, and the same again in the myth of Dian Cecht's son, when after killing him Dian Cecht scatters the herbs that spring up so that the dangerous knowledge that they represent will remain hidden.

Supporting this reading even further is the curious portion found at the beginning of the Daphne myth in which we meet another pursuer of Daphne, Leucippus. Parthenius (*Love Romances*, 15) and Pausanius (*Description of Greece*, 8.20.2) describe how Leucippus falls in love with Daphne and dresses like a woman to get close to her. He hunts with her in this guise, but when it comes time to bathe, he is discovered, and is killed for his offense by her nymphs. Apollo pursues Daphne immediately after Leucippus' death. Read in terms of our above interpretation, this sequence of events falls in line with another Óðinnic myth. If Daphne is Truth mediated by prophecy (i.e. knowledge of Fate), then Leucippus' attempt to get close to her by wearing women's clothes would be exactly the same as Óðinn's well-known practice of the female-associated prophetic art, *seiðr*. Óðinn is mocked by Loki, for instance, for dressing as a woman and performing this female form of prophecy, and in other texts (*Gisla saga* of Surssonar and the Kings' saga *Olaf's saga Tryggvasonar* of Oddr Snorrason) it is shown that the punishment for a man performing *seiðr* could be death, just as Leucippus is promptly killed when he is discovered by the nymphs. Leucippus wearing women's clothes and attempting to get close to Daphne, then, is a depiction of a *seiðr*-like prophetic practice, a man dressing as a woman in order to possess the prophetic Truth that Daphne signifies. Thus Leucippus' myth, though it seems like an odd anomaly in relation to Apollo's pursuit, is the important other half of the Apollo and Daphne narrative, and connects the overall myth even more closely to Óðinn. Furthermore, this interpretation suggests that some kind of female prophetic practice, which was taboo for men to perform, could have been a feature of Indo-European religion going back to the time of unity of the pre-Greek and pre-Germanic peoples, or at least became common on a North-South axis in Europe at a very early date. This also potentially brings the female practitioners of seiðr (the Volvas) and the Apollonian priestesses, such as the Oracle of Delphi, into direct juxtaposition.

Apollo and Rudra

In this connection, Apollo's comparison with Vedic Rudra becomes crucial. Rudra as the "destroyer" god, wielding the bow of destruction, has been compared to Apollo, especially in Apollo's function as plague-inflicting god. This is the aspect in which he appears even in Homer's *Iliad*. This Rudra comparison is often seen to be supported by the Greek word *apollymi*, meaning "to destroy," or by a possible analogue of the god in the Hittite plague god Aplu, who both brought and ended plagues. Rudra too is connected with disease (as R.G. Bhandarkar p. 146 shows and as M.L. West mentions in the passage quoted below), and Gregoire and Goosens have connected him to Apollo *Smintheus* (Gregoire and Goosens 1949). While Apollo is associated with the land to the far north beyond the Riphean Mountains, Hyperborea, while in the *Yajur Veda* Rudra is said to have a mountain abode beyond the North, sometimes identified with Mount Kailash. Mallory and Adams note that Rudra's animal is the rat mole, while Apollo is a god of rats (Mallory, J.P. and Adams, Douglas, *The Oxford Introduction to Proto-Indo-European and the Proto-Indo-European World*, 434).

It is possible that Apollo then combines "Brihaspati" and "Rudra" aspects in one deity (an original division between Paean-Brihaspati and Apollo-Rudra is plausible), just as Óðinn seems to have among his aspects both "Brihaspati" and "Rudra," as we are not the first to have argued. It is even possible the two deities were closely linked or united from very early if they are united in the cases of both Óðinn and Apollo. We have mentioned, however, that these deities are separate in Vedic and likely in Celtic myth as well, with Fionn/Gwyn as the Celtic Rudraic reflex. There are numerous similarities between Rudra and Brihaspati to begin with. Brihaspati too blows away with his shattering shout, and his mighty arrows, and his power of soul, all that conceals and all that brings chaos and disharmony. His magical songs seem to have the power both to heal and to bring various forms of destruction as well, if we take the examples of the various Óðinnic *galdrs* for evidence.

Perhaps these shared traits were ultimately the cause of the occasional combination of these two divinities, or a sign of an underlying archaic connection. As Kris Kershaw shows in her *Odin: The One-Eyed God*, Rudra, furthermore, is the *exemplar and leader* of the ecstatic war band of youths (who were also required to be poets) and of the Wild Hunt. Brihaspati, on the other hand, is the *teacher* of the warrior youths, especially in his incarnation Drona. Perhaps with one being the leader and the other the teacher of the warrior youths, the two came to be seen as unified in some branches, as the original teacher-leader of the warrior band. Other overlaps make the Rudra-Brihaspati combination understandable: Brihaspati's incarnation, Drona, is father to (a) Rudra's incarnation, Ashvatthama. Brihaspati and Rudra are both connected to healing, and, considering the Celtic Rudra parallels Fionn/Gwyn/Gwion, to mental illumination (especially spoken poetry) and to waters of mental illumination or healing (Dian Cecht's healing well vs. the waters where the Salmon of Knowledge swims).

As such, while the Windy Tree myth may be connected to the Brihaspati mythos in the detail of the power of resurrecting the dead and in the indirect connection of the runes to the galdrs, which appear sometimes to have been used in conjunction, this particular myth may be even more connected to the Rudraic mythos in some of its other details. This also raises the possibility that the previously discussed Shukra/Usana, the "demonic double" of Brihaspati, who plays the same role for the Asuras that Brihaspati plays for the Devas, could be Rudraic rather than an aspect of Brihaspati as we have hypothetically explored up to now. Shukra's name means "bright," while this is also one of the meanings of the names of the Celtic Rudraic figures, Fionn/Gwyn, etc.; he is a poet; he has an eye poked out like Balor and becomes one-eyed like Goll; he is the one to first gain the boon of asceticism from Siva, the mantra of life and death; and while it is difficult to disentangle him from the Brihaspati-type mythos we have seen the same issue with other Rudraic gods Apollo and Óðinn. Stella Kramrisch (*The Presence of Siva*) supports the assumption that Shukra/Usana is Rudra-associated. She points out that Usana, under the name Bhargava, is reborn from Siva in the form of his semen (*sukra*) (*VmP*.43.26-44), and in this way becomes Siva's son and a mediator between Siva and a great goat demon born from Bhargava's sweat. Sukra is said to have arisen in the sign of the star Tisya (*Vap*.53.106), while Tisya is Rudra (PS.2.2.10.1-2), and thus Shukra enters Rudra's domain at least astrologically, though remaining distinct from him as well (Kramrisch, 156-7). Meanwhile, Shukra performs his extensive devotional meditation to Rudra in order to first gain the Mriti Sanjeevni mantra that revives the dead. If this is reminiscent of Odinn sacrificing himself to himself, it aligns Shukra somewhat with the Rudra to whom he is devoted in meditation. Still, Kramrisch does not directly equate Shukra to Rudra-Siva, but only highlights how they are brought into relation.

A "Rudraic" origin also seems more likely for the Windy Tree myth when we realize that it does in fact have a possible analogue in the story of the Rudraic figure Fionn mac Cumhaill called *The Hunt of Slieve Cuilinn*. In this Irish parallel tale, Fionn comes across a sorrowful girl sitting by a lake (as Greek Daphne is a naiad, nymphs who are associated with all types of bodies of freshwater) while chasing a grey faun during a hunt (Daphne is hunting at the beginning of her myth in both Parthenius and Pausanias' versions). She is the most beautiful girl Fionn has ever seen and is called "woman of the white hands." Her skin is as white as lime and eyes are like stars in the time of frost (Daphne is an archetype of virginity and also becomes "deathly pale" at the end of Ovid's account). The girl demands Fionn retrieve a ring of red gold that she has lost in the lake. He strips himself down and leaps into the lake at her command. He swims around the lake three times and searches every inch of it until finally finding the ring and bringing it back to the girl. When he does, the girl instantly leaps into the water and vanishes (Daphne's father is a river god and she ends her chase by his shore, the site where she vanishes into the tree or is swallowed by the earth). Fionn realizes that his swim in the lake has turned him into a withered old man with grey hair, weak and unrecognizable to those who knew him. When he finally deduces who this girl was – Miluchradh, daughter of Cuilinn – he goes to Cuilinn, who gives him a special drink from a vessel of red gold which returns his youth, but cannot return the color of his hair. He keeps his grey hair for the rest of his life, a mark of this trial. When he finishes drinking from this vessel, it drops into the earth, and from it springs a tree. A specifically *prophetic* tree. It is said that "any one that would look at the branches of the tree in the morning, fasting, would have knowledge of all that was to happen on that day" (*The Hunt of Slieve Cuilinn*).[135]

We can see the main features once again of the Óðinnic and Apollonian Trial of the Tree. Fionn performs a pursuit (of a grey faun), he encounters a white-skinned, virginal girl who demands a great sacrifice of him. He endures a severe trial trying to appease her (swimming the lake three times vs. Óðinn hanging for nine nights is noteworthy, both numbers being multiples of three), and grows old and unrecognizable as a result, a kind of symbolic death or ascetic transformation. As interpreters of Óðinn's myth have long recognized, this is an *initiation*. The gray hair that Fionn keeps ever after is then a mark of this initiation and a symbol of a certain kind of maturity, considering that the initiation ritual may have been a rite of passage from youth to full adulthood, or perhaps from a novitiate status to becoming a seer. The girl, Miluchradh, vanishes instantly with her treasure, just as Daphne is suddenly transported away when she is caught up to or is enclosed in the tree to preserve her virginity. Possibly of interest, Miluchradh is believed by some (Tomas O'Cathasaigh, "Knowth – The Eponym of Cnogba") to be another name of the same figure as the Druidess Birog, who makes Cian, another Óðinnic aspect, dress as a woman to perform a kind of visionary magic. If Birog and Miluchradh are the same figure, this would bring us full circle and Birog and Cian's female-clothed magic could then parallel Leucippus' attempt to get close to Daphne while wearing women's clothes, which we interpreted as an allegory of a *seiðr*-like practice, as Óðinn himself dresses as a woman to perform this feminine seer-magic. Fionn eventually drinks from a magic vessel given to him by Cuilinn as Óðinn also drinks from the mead vessel *Odrerir* given to him by a brother of Bestla just after hanging on the tree, and this revives Fionn.

---

135   Other instances also repeat Fionn's prophetic ability, for instance when he claims that the fates of individuals in battle are "showed to" him: "'Do not go my son,' said Finn, 'for it is not showed to me that you will have good luck in the battle, and I never sent out any man to fight without I knew he would come back safe to me'" (Gregory, *Gods and Fighting Men*, "The First Fighters").

Finally, the tree appears which yields prophetic rewards, telling what will happen. Not only that, but this tree will only give its prophecies to someone who is "fasting" – an ascetic practice reminiscent of Óðinn's hanging on the tree. An ascetic act is explicitly required to gain the prophetic wisdom of Fionn's tree. Moreover, Óðinn says that he is given no bread and no drink while he hangs from the tree, thus he too is explicitly fasting (*Havamal* 138). Fionn must swim the lake and then fast to gain prophecy from his tree, while Óðinn must hang from his tree and fast to gain the runes. Local beliefs hold that Fionn gained the name Fionn, meaning "white," from the grey-white hair he acquired swimming the lake (gaining a name being another mark of initiation), and that anyone who swims in the lake at Slieve Gullion to this day will also have their hair turned white like Fionn. This may then be a folk remembrance of the ritual initiations that seem to have been connected to this lake.

Though the wording is left vague, Óðinn *may* reach into Urdr's Well, as it *may* lie at the base of the tree Yggdrasil where he *may* be hanging, to receive the runes, when he reaches downward for them. In response to an early draft of this chapter, a certain Grandson of Finn pointed out to me that, in Snorri's *Gylfaginning,* Snorri states that Urdr's Well also specifically turns things white that go into its waters: "for that water is so holy that all things which come there into the well become as white as the film which lies within the egg-shell" (*Prose Edda, Gylfaginning).* Grandson of Finn further noted that the Norns, of which Urdr is one, are called "maidens" in *Voluspa 20* ("thence come the maidens"), according thus with Miluchradh's representation as a maiden, and Daphne's. If the aforementioned identification of Miluchradh with the crone called The Cailleach is correct, then this forms a strong parallel between the Norn Urdr and The Cailleach/Miluchradh, potentially answering the question of "who are the Celtic Fates or Norns?"[136] It would after all be natural for prophetic power to be catalyzed by waters belonging to the divinities of Fate.

The mountain of Slieve Cuilinn/Gullion is furthermore a sacred location and a high place. It is home to the highest passage tomb in all of Ireland, called Calliagh Birra's (aka Miluchradh's) House. The lake featured in the myth, Calliagh Birra's Lough, is near the summit of the mountain. The region called the Ring of Gullion, in which Slieve Gullion is found, was known as the District of Poets or the District of Songs in the 18th Century, which, if it represents an ancient association, could connect back to the central

---

136   In addition, *seiðr,* the Germanic cognate of the female-clothed magic of Birog, appears to come from a Proto-Germanic root word *saiðaz,* cognate with Lithuanian *saitas,* 'tie, tether' and Proto-Celtic *soito-* 'sorcery'. These words derive from Proto-Indo-European *soi-to-* 'string, rope', ultimately from the Proto-Indo-European root *seH2i-* 'to bind.'As such, the word for *seiðr* comes from a concept that can be directly connected to the fate goddesses, relating to threads and strings.

poetic theme present in the Apollo and Óðinn myths, and the fact that Fionn and his band are poets as well, suggesting that the initiatic myth associated with the locale may have referred specifically to the initiation of poet-prophets, ie. seers or *vates/faith*.

Interestingly, in Fionn's myth it is the female, Miluchradh, who bears an unrequited love for Fionn, and is acting out of jealousy of her sister who has had Fionn's affections. Meanwhile in Apollo's myth, Apollo is the one fueled by unrequited love for the nymph, Daphne, along with a noted jealousy of Leucippus. It seems that the theme of unrequited love as the motive of the trial has remained a key feature in both cases, its subject and object merely being swapped between the two figures around whom the theme centers. It is only by first aligning the myth of Óðinn and the myth of Apollo that we can finally properly see the meaning and origin of this tale of Fionn's, as it contains some elements that are paralleled in one and other elements that are paralleled in the other of these analogues. Seen together the underlying pattern becomes clear. Óðinn's separate myth of drinking from Mimir's Well would then be the more direct parallel of the "waters of illumination" myth we find in separate tales of Fionn and his parallels Gwion/Taliesin, and in the Óðinnic version these Rudraic waters and the Rudraic motif of the loss of an eye (a characteristic of Goll/Balor/Fintan) combine. Fionn has a tale specifically matching this Mimir's Well myth, in which he too drinks the waters of a well of wisdom directly, when he has the waters of Beag's "Well of the moon," which grant wisdom and prophecy, thrown at him and some of it goes into his mouth ("The Boyhod Deeds of Fionn"). As the Salmon of Knowledge, which Fionn tastes, also originates at a well of wisdom, the Well of Segais, these two Irish tales obviously overlap in their motifs and are thematically connected.

To summarize the most important points of this triple comparison:

- First, though it is a debated topic, the runes are prophetic tools in some sense, directly or indirectly connected to prophetic power ("asking" the runes in *Havamal* 80, etc.).

- Óðinn is pierced by a spear, hangs from the tree, enduring nine long nights, while being given no bread or drink (fasting), undergoes a symbolic death or ascetic transformation (an initiation), receives the runes connected to prophecy and magic, and is then given a drink from the mead vessel Oðrerir right afterward.

- Apollo is pierced by an arrow of Cupid's, pursues the virginal naiad Daphne (naiads being connected to bodies of freshwater) who is hunting. He suffers torments of love, then Daphne turns pale and then is turned into a laurel tree by a god or is swallowed by Gaia/vanishes, with the laurel tree left behind. Apollo receives the "prophetic clusters" of leaves and "inspired whispers" of the laurel tree, whose leaves were chewed by the priestess of Apollo, the Pythia, to induce prophecy.

- While hunting, Fionn sees a beautiful, pale white girl at the edge of a lake. She demands he find her ring that she has lost in the water. Fionn swims around the lake three times and searches every inch and finally finds it and brings it to her. She takes the ring, leaps into the water and vanishes. Fionn realizes he has become aged to an old man by the trial, a kind of symbolic death or ascetic transformation. He is given a magical drinking vessel by the girl's father. He drinks from it and becomes young again, but his grey hair remains as a mark of his trial. A tree springs up from the spot where he drops the vessel, and the tree gives prophetic knowledge of what will happen that day to those who come to it in the morning while fasting (as Óðinn is given no bread or drink), an ascetic act leading to gaining the prophetic knowledge given by the tree.

- Lastly, Fionn, Apollo, and Óðinn can each be shown to be connected to the "Rudraic" deity type.

***

We have previously added support to the idea that not only does Odinn parallel Vedic Rudra, but the evil-eyed foe of the Irish gods, Balor, parallels one of the rudras, the members of the destructive and ghoulish troop that Rudra leads and keeps partially in line as they go forth on the Wild Hunt.

Thus, Odinn offering himself to himself on the Windy Tree is a specifically Rudra-connected myth. Now in the Vedic branch, Ashwatthama, who we have seen is an incarnation of one of the rudras and parallel of the more destructive side of the Irish Rudraic coin, Balor, also sacrifices himself to Rudra in order to gain power for the fight. As Rudra is, in a sense, Ashwatthama's own higher divine self, this self-sacrifice is a close match to Odinn's initiatic act. Although it gives Ashwatthama war prowess rather than runic knowledge, both powers can be seen as weapons in the Great War that the Rudraic figure seeks in service of his greater role in the divine war. This scene appears in the *Mahabharata*, just before his final onslaught on the Pandava camp.

> Drona's son [Ashvatthama], armed with bow, and with fingers cased in fences made of iguana skins, himself offered up his own self as a victim unto Mahadeva [Rudra]. Bows were the fuel, and sharp shafts were the ladles, and his own soul possessed of great might was the libation, O Bharata, in that act of sacrifice. The valiant and wrathful son of Drona then, with propitiating mantras, offered up his own soul as the victim. Having with fierce rites adored Rudra of fierce deeds, Ashvatthama with joined hands, said these words unto that high-souled god.

> Ashvatthama said, 'Sprung from Angirasa's line, I am about to pour my soul, O god, as a libation on this fire! Accept, O lord, this victim! In this hour of

distress, O Soul of the universe, I offer up my own self as the sacrificial victim, from devotion to thee and with heart concentrated in meditation! All creatures are in thee and thou art in all creatures! Assemblage of all high attributes occur in thee! O lord, O thou art the refuge of all creatures. I wait as a libation for thee, since I am unable to vanquish my foes. Accept me, O god.' Having said these words, Drona's son, ascending that sacrificial altar on which a fire blazed brightly, offered himself up as the victim and entered that blazing fire.

Beholding him stand immovable and with uplifted hands and as an offering up to himself, the divine Mahadeva appeared in person [...] the divine Mahadeva entered Ashvatthama's body after giving him an excellent and polished sword. Filled by that divine being, Drona's son blazed up with energy. In consequence of that energy derived from godhead, he became all-powerful in battle. (*Mahabharata, Sauptika Parva*, 8)

One of the great paradoxes of Indo-European religion is this Rudraic god who encompasses both destruction and benevolence, and this paradox is reflected in the shifting of parts of the core mythos of the deity from his benevolent to his destructive aspect depending on the branch.

In the Irish case, Fionn, rather than Balor (parallel of Ashvatthama), parallels Odinn's hanging from the tree, even though a sacrifice of self to self is not made explicit in Fionn's myth. Ashvatthama, an incarnation of one of the rudras and so an extension of one side of Rudra's power, is the destructive opponent of the divine heroes of society rather than their leader. And yet his self-sacrifice is a clear mirror of Odinn's.

The shifting of this "self-sacrifice to higher self" myth can occur because the destructive and benevolent aspects, though divided in narrative, are unified theologically, are from one divine root. Ashvatthama, being one extension of the divinity of Rudra, must enact or even reenact this central Rudraic myth, and sacrifice himself to the Rudra who is above the divided manifestation.

Bringing this back to Apollo, M.L. West argues, just as we have, that Apollo is a match to Irish Dian Cecht as well as Vedic Rudra. He proposes, just as we have, that Apollo has "taken over" Paean, and then summarizes his comparison also with Rudra thus:

The Greek Apollo, a rather complex figure, has probably taken over the characteristics of more than one older divinity, including the healer Paiawon (Paieon, Paion, Paian). He has points of contact on the one hand with the Indian Rudra, on the other with Celtic and Germanic deities. His power over sickness and health is dramatically portrayed in the first book of the Iliad, where he first shoots his arrows to bring plague upon cattle and men, and then relieves it in response to prayer. The image has striking parallels in Ugaritic and the Old Testament. But Rudra too is pictured in the Veda as an archer whose missiles send disease and death upon humans, cattle, and horses. Prayers are directed to him imploring him to spare his worshippers and their animals. He is said to have a thousand remedies at his disposal, and a healing hand. (West, *Indo-European Poetry and Myth*, 148)

He points out that "Caesar (Bell. Gall. 6. 17. 2) reports that the Gauls had an 'Apollo' who dispelled diseases" and that "The Celtic divine healer who shows the strongest point of contact with him is Dían Cécht, who appears in Irish legend as the healer of the Tuatha Dé Danann, that is, of the gods." He furthermore makes the connection again of Apollo to Oðinn, saying,

Odin/Woden has other links with Apollo, not so much qua healer—though it is he who cures Baldr's lamed horse in the Merseburg spell (pp. 336 f.)—but rather as a kind of shamanic figure. He presides over the poetic art, and he is associated with the wolf and the raven. Just as Apollo's raven reports to him the lovemaking of Ischys and Coronis, so Oðinn's two ravens fly about the world all day and then return to perch on his shoulders and speak into his ears of all they have seen or heard. (West, *Indo-European Poetry and Myth*, 148-149)

What we can add to this question is one additional mythical comparison between Rudra and Apollo. Rudra is known to have a violent confrontation with the god Pushan at a sacrifice from which he is being excluded (*Taittariya Samhita,* ii.6.8; *Satapatha Brahmana*, 1.7.4). He causes Pushan to break his teeth on the sacrifice he has shot with an arrow (or knocks them out in versions found in the epics) and so Pushan has to eat gruel ever after. Pan is considered to be the Greek Pushan, as we will see in his own chapter, and Apollo and Pan do in fact have a face-off. Theirs is a music competition. Apollo wins, and King Midas' ears are turned to donkey ears as a punishment for his preference for Pan's music. And in a related tale, Apollo has a music competition against the satyr Marsyas. When Apollo wins, he flays Marsyas. These myths could be related to the same motif of Pushan and Rudra having a confrontation which results in a disfigurement. The Pushan and Rudra confrontation centers around the sacrifice, but sacrifice was also associated with displays and even competitions of sacred words-and-music – poetic and musical performance was central to the sacrificial rite – and the form of the myth in the Greek version could have shifted more narrowly toward the musical art that became so closely identified with Apollo, its ritual origin forgotten. It is interesting that King Midas the onlooker has something on his head disfigured (ears), while Pushan has his teeth knocked out (in the version found in *Mahabharata*, Rudra-

334

Shiva also cuts off another god Savitr's hands and puts out Bhaga's eyes). This remains far from a definitive comparison, but allows us to consider other possible layers of the mysterious god Apollo, who over time became identified with the sun itself and magnetized to himself by charismatic force an array of wide-ranging powers and associations.

Esoteric Resonances

Esoterically, Brihaspati and Apollo also have resonances, and these serve to support the exoteric identifications of these gods. Sri Aurobindo calls Brihaspati, based on his mythos of the slaying of Vala, the god of the "Power of the Soul" (compare *Dian Cecht* as meaning "swift power"), and quotes the *Rig Veda* saying, "Brihaspati, coming first into birth from the great Light in the supreme ether dispelled the darknesses; he with his host that possess the *stubh* and the *Rik* broke Vala into pieces by his cry. Shouting Brihaspati drove upwards the bright herds" (*Rig Veda*, 4.50), pointing out that he is specifically called "the first-born" (RV, 6.73.1). He says furthermore that "Brihaspati slays the Foe by the hymns of illumination (arkaiḥ)," and calls him, in this role of illuminator, "father of the Word" (Aurobindo, *The Secret of the Veda*, *Brihaspati*). Thus he is (in some sense) born first, out of the great Light, and is the bringer of illumination by way of his powerful Word, dispelling darkness with his aggressive shout, shattering Vala into pieces as Dian Cecht burns the serpent to ashes or Apollo obliterates Python with his arrows and the shouts of his priestesses. Óðinn is also the first born of the Aesir and performs the cosmogonical killing of Ymir, also rescuing the cows from their concealment in the earth. Aurobindo explains the cosmogonical sense of this, saying, "The Divine, the Deva, manifests itself as conscious Power of the soul, creates the worlds by the Word out of the waters of the subconscient," pointing to Brihaspati's key role in this, as the illuminating Word that shapes the waters, and the Power of Soul that is the power of manifesting out of the subconscient. With a similar sense, Nietzsche famously compared Apollo to the *principium individuationis*, or individuating principle, that which gives shape and unity to Being, that principle which individuates things in an orderly way from out of the chaotic element.

Meanwhile, Thomas Taylor, extracting from Proclus, says of Apollo, in his introduction to Julian's *Two Orations of the Emperor Julian*, that, "according to the first and most natural conception, his name signifies the cause of union, and that power which collects multitude into one," which strikes us as very similar to the Nietzschean formulation. The healing power, Proclus argues, is a manifestation of this same power of unification, that a diseased condition is one that requires to be restored "from incommensuration and manifold division, into symmetry and union," and that "health is symmetry." He singles out also Apollo's "enunciative power" which he says "shines forth, unfolding intelligible goods to celestial natures, and on this account he revolves together with the sun, with whom he participates the same intellect in common; since the sun also illuminates whatever heaven contains, and extends a unifying power to all its parts," and further describes how his "arrow-darting" power "extirpates every thing inordinate." He triumphantly states that "it is this divinity who harmonizing the universe, establishes about himself according to one union the choir of the Muses, and produces by this means, as a certain Theurgist says, 'the harmony of exulting light.'" Just as Brihaspati is the first-born who brings the light of illumination, so Apollo can be esoterically (Platonically) considered as the first solar monad emanated by the Demiurge, which brings things into being via "intellectual light." To this effect, Taylor quotes Proclus as saying "the first monad unfolds intellectual light, enunciates it to all secondary natures, fills all things with universal truth, and converts them to the intellect of the gods; which employment is ascribed to the prophetic power of Apollo, who produces into light the truth contained in divine natures." Taylor further explains how this proceeds from the first creative act of the Demiurge: "the Demiurgus generates solar powers in the principles of the universe, and a triad of solar gods, through which all things are unfolded into light, and are perfected and replenished with intellectual goods," and argues that this light of Apollo issues directly from the Platonic Good, as its manifestation specifically on the intellectual level: "as the splendour proceeding from the good is the light of intelligible natures; so that proceeding from Apollo is the light of the intellectual world" (Taylor, *Two Orations of the Emperor Julian, Introduction*).

Sri Aurobindo also asserts that Brihaspati, who is evidently one with Brahmanaspati in the *Rig Veda*, is also, by this linkage, one with Brahman in its original sense as the Word of power. Brihaspati-Brahmanaspati-Brahman. As he puts it, "*Brahman* in the Veda signifies ordinarily the Vedic Word or mantra in its profoundest aspect as the expression of the intuition arising out of the depths of the soul or being. It is a voice of the rhythm which has created the worlds and creates perpetually." "*Brahman* in the Veda," as he puts it, then can be argued to have a different, though connected meaning from what it would develop into in later Vedic culture. As Nagy emphasized the connection of Apollo to the power of speech, Dumezil himself took the angle of comparing Apollo to the Vedic deity Vac (*Apollon Sonore*), the goddess of divine speech, who is closely connected to Brihaspati and to the concept of the "Vedic Brahman" as the Word, as Aurobindo puts it.

If Brihaspati-Óðinn-Paeon Apollo-Dian Cecht stands for a particular social caste or subcaste, it is of course that of the High Priest. If this god offers any exemplary path intended for emulation by humans, it a path for the High Priest type specifically. Though the position of Óðinn and Apollo as patrons and leaders of the coming of age youths reveals an additional dimension to the question, Kershaw emphasizes the fact that the consecrated bands of warrior youths were after all of the ruling class, and were trained in both warrior and poetic skills: "The Vratyas, like the Männerbünde everywhere, were of the ruling classes" (216-217) and were known as "dog priests," while Óðinn and Apollo stand in the priestly role of preceptor in relation to them.

This priestly character is further reflected by the descent of Greek idealist philosophical traditions at least partly from the Apollonian milieu. We can see that the poet Orpheus was originally derived from the Apollonian mythos – he is given his first lyre by Apollo, for instance. One reference by the sophist Alcidamas even credits him with the invention of writing.[137] He is possibly then a parallel of the Rudraic national poets Oisin and Taliesin, prophets and healers like them as well. He founds cults to both Apollo and Dionysus. It is commonly suggested, and was an orthodoxy among Neoplatonists such as Iamblichus, that the philosopher Pythagoras was either a member of the Orphic cult or influenced by the Orphic milieu.[138] On the other hand, Abaris the Hyperborean, a priest of Apollo, upon meeting Pythagoras, apparently claimed Pythagoras was the reincarnation of Apollo. Plato then drew strongly from his Pythagorean predecessors[139], thus making Pythagorean and Platonic philosophy, *in part*, late, partially demythologized continuations of the Apollonian priestly cult: these were philosophies of High Priests focused on the purification of the sacred lunar liquid embodied by Dionysus (soul) from the Titanic material element (body), if we here add the notes on Orphism from our Greek Lunar Cycle chapter.

Everything in the myths we have examined repeats over and over again the same emphasis on the secret and concealed nature of the knowledge that the god pursues and becomes privy to, as well as the extreme danger it can portend, in that its potency has the ability to threaten the very order of Nature. This knowledge must be kept concealed, as Daphne conceals herself in the tree, as Miluchradh vanishes into the lake. It can only be reached by great pains and sacrifice, only by the select priestly figure, and must be kept from those who are unworthy of it, as Dian Cecht scatters the 365 healing herbs after killing his too-powerful son. The meaning of the Apollo and Daphne myth seems even to be well-hidden beneath the allegorical veneer of a love story, and the specific myths of

---

137   Ivan Mortimer Linforth, "Two Notes on the Legend of Orpheus", *Transactions and Proceedings of the American Philological Association* 62, (1931):5–17).

138   Algis Uzdavinys, *Orpheus and the Roots of Platonism.*

139   Alban Dewes Winspear, *The Genesis of Plato's Thought.*

Óðinn hanging on the tree, or Fionn retrieving the ring from the lake, may have been divine examples intended only to be ritually reenacted in their full initiatic sense by those belonging to the ecstatic warrior-poet bands. It may have been from these mannerbunde that the High Priests and Seers were then selected, which possibility could help explain the intertwining of the Rudraic (mannerbund seers) and Brihaspatian (high priests of the word) deities and myths. Though there is by definition an exclusivity to the full enactment of such an initiation, there are infinite degrees of inspiration that can be drawn, by whomever looks to it, from the associated mythos.

Nestor and The High Priest of the Word

Now that we have a strong sense of this High Priest of the Word, we can proceed to addressing the question of the *Iliad* hero Nestor. Scholar Douglas Frame has in recent years forwarded a thesis that connects Nestor, known as *Hippota Nestor*, or Horseman Nestor, to the Vedic Asvins, also known as Nasatyas. *Hippota Nestor* would then linguistically parallel *Asvin Nasatya*, both meaning loosely "Horseman Saviour." Frame shows how the name *Nestor* comes from a shared root with the Sanskrit *Nasatya*, while *Hippota* means the same thing as *Asvin*. The shared root connecting Nestor and Nasatya is *nes-*, denoting "bringing back to light and life," as Frame puts it. In his earlier work, *The Myth of Return in Early Greek Epic* (1978), Frame's original thesis had been that this similarity was merely a linguistic remnant showing a general shared Indo-European concept which had been associated with the root *nes-*, rather than necessarily making Nestor and the Asvins equivalents. However, in his more recent work, the book *Hippota Nestor* (2009), Frame has advanced a framework in which Nestor can be seen as indeed an embodiment of the Indo-European Horse Twin mythos, a full parallel of the Asvins.

Although Frame demonstrates a complex pattern of similarities between Nestor and the Horse Twins, he himself admits some issues with the comparison. For example, Nestor is never depicted as a twin, and indeed in the competing traditions that Frame cites Nestor is either said to be one of 12 brothers or one of 3 brothers. One (or more) of Nestor's brothers dies, which Frame takes to parallel the death of one of the Greek Dioskouroi, and Nestor is purportedly left to carry forward the Horse Twin mythos himself. We admit, from the foregoing, that the idea that the Horse Twins could have been reduced to, or even began as, one single Horse God, is absolutely possible, as we ourselves have argued for a single Horse Twin in Celtic, Norse, and Iranic cases. Still, being the brother of 11 or 2 other sons has not been seen in any other cases of the Horse Twins and this fraternity does not argue in favor of Nestor as such a Horse Twin. Nestor "brings back to life and light," embodying the verb *nes-*, when he heals the physician

Machaon with his famous cup of healing, and when he aids some of the Greeks in their return voyage home. Nestor is one of two main counselors among the Greeks, while the role of counselor is common among the Horse Twins, as with Sahadeva or Aengus. Beyond this, the parallels become quite arcane. We will not be able to begin to do justice in this short study to what is a masterful and learned argument on the part of Frame. But other issues arise that are pertinent to our investigation of the High Priest deity type.

For instance, in every mythos we have investigated so far, the Horse Twins (or Horse Twin) are the exemplars of youth. They are eternally youthful, embodying fertility and vitality and often having some variation of "Young Son" as part of their very name. Nestor on the other hand is the reverse of this: he is by far the oldest Greek, so old that it is incredible he is still alive and standing with the war party. He has been blessed by Apollo to live an extended period of time as recompense for Apollo's murder of his siblings. It is actually Nestor who likens Diomedes to his own "youngest born" son, and it is Diomedes, rather than Nestor, who we have argued is indeed the Young Son incarnation. Everything about Nestor is inflected by this character of great agedness, and he in no way can embody the youth of the Horse Twins, which is so central to their character. Getting around this issue requires Frame to posit that Nestor's mythos had been preserved by one particular family separate from the rest of the epic, and that inserting him into the *Iliad* narrative after also having been a key figure in narratives that had taken place many decades earlier necessitated the agedness of Nestor. This explanation, however, is asking for a special case for Nestor beyond what we have needed to grant the other heroes of the epic, and it remains only a speculative historical theory that cannot be proven or disproven. What cannot be escaped is the fact that Nestor of the *Iliad* is the exemplar of old age while the Horse Twins are the eternally young gods.

Furthermore, while several traits of the Horse Twins do seem to overlap the figure of Nestor, namely: counselor, horseman, healer, most of these traits can again be said to belong to the figure we have just analyzed, the High Priest of the Word. Not only this, but if Nestor is analyzed in relation to this High Priest divinity, *more* of his character can be explained. Like the Horse Twins, the High Priest of the Word, as we have seen, is repeatedly associated with the power of healing the wounded and reviving the dead – which is, as Frame puts it, "bringing back to light and life" – and seeing Nestor as this High Priest would also explain his name coming from the root *nes-* just as well as seeing him as a Horse Twin would. The Horse Twins are healers, but it is the High Priest Dian Cecht who has the well that revives the dead that is specifically used during the Great War. Dian Cecht oversees the well of Slainge, which during the Great Battle of Magh Tuireadh brings Tuatha De Danann soldiers back from death or near-death each day. The Horse Twins are not depicted as active healers during any of the other Great Wars, and their healing exploits always come in separate rescue stories. Meanwhile, Nestor has a great cup, with which he actively heals warriors during the Trojan War, as when the wounded Machaon is brought to him. This is not a simple cup either, but is big enough that it requires two feet to stand on and four handles, and when full is so heavy that no one but Nestor could lift it. This cup, though difficult to picture in any precise dimensions, begins to sound more like a kind of bowl or vat, closer to a well than to a goblet. While the Horse Twin does, of course, become the caretaker of the Holy Grail, in the person of Perceval, the Grail is itself not primarily a cup of healing in the early versions of the legend, though the *soma* can heal certain debilities and illnesses, and at the very least the Grail is never shown healing wounded warriors during battle. It is not a field kit healing unit for battle, while the healing well of *Slainge* is essentially used as just such a thing. The Grail primarily gives sustenance, perhaps illumination and immortality, and is generally kept in a mysterious castle. It is also the center of a specific ritual which Nestor's cup shows no signs of.

While Nestor is one of two main counselors for the Greeks, the other of the two is Odysseus, who we see paired in a (Horse)twin-like fashion with Diomedes, and who more closely parallels the attributes of the Horse Twin incarnation Sahadeva, as we have discussed previously. The High Priest of the Word is the archetypal teacher of the other gods, and as such giving counsel would fit his role perfectly. Encyclopedia Britannica calls Brihaspati the "sage counselor."[140] As the name of Dian Cecht, *Cainte*, or "speech," as well as the name *Apollo,* and the title of Brihaspati, *Vacaspati*, "Lord of speech," tells us, this is the god of authoritative speech acts generally. He may give the advice and teachings of a wise sage while in various other ways embodying the power and functions of the spoken word. This again fits Nestor perfectly, for Nestor is the hero who is known for his long-winded stories of past adventures, boasts, encouragements and all manner of long speeches. In fact, the types of speeches that Nestor gives match the types of speech-acts that the High Priest of the Word is specially known for: boast, which particularly characterizes Nestor, and as we have seen is a part of the etymology of Apollo's name (Nagy demonstrating its meaning as "promise, boastful promise, threat"); motivation to fight, as the *galdrs* and *paeans* were often said to be sung at the beginning of battles to give strength to the warriors; and finally counsel, which we have covered as an aspect of the High Priest's role as teacher. Seeing Nestor as this High Priest of the Word then makes clear why he is depicted as so fully embodying *speech* – longwinded digressions, etc. – and why these exact forms of speech. We now can see why Nestor boasts, reminisces, counsels, and why he goads, for instance, Patroclus to battle. The sometimes questionable quality of Nestor's counsels have made him appear a kind of fool to some critics, as his goading sends Patroclus to his death, but if we understand that his

---

140   Britannica.com, "Brihaspati".

incitements come from a specific theological role of goading to battle, the cause for this is explained.

The Horse Twins, in fact, are not prominently known as gods of speech. One or both of them are good counselors, but this trait does not extend to a general lordship of the power of speech. This fact fits much better with the idea that Odysseus is the counselor Horse Twin: none of Odysseus' epithets relate to his power of speech, but many relate to his craftiness, a key trait of the Horse Twins, and yet another trait that Nestor seems to lack in comparison with Odysseus or even Diomedes, he of the Diomedian Swap. When Odysseus does unleash his well-tuned speaking ability in key moments, it catches observers off guard as something unexpected in relation to his "churl"-ish and ignoble bearing, as the craftier and thus lowlier Vedic Horse Twin incarnation, Sahadeva, also is shown, in disguise, as a relatively lowly keeper of cows. Overall, Odysseus and Sahadeva's ability to speak and counsel has a more narrow application than does Nestor's. Nestor, on the other hand, is introduced as a "clear-voiced orator," of "sweet words," whose voice at all times "flows sweeter than honey." While Odysseus is a hero of counsel and craftiness, which the Horse Twins are as well, Nestor is far more the preeminent hero of *speech* itself, which the Horse Twins are not.

Frame points out that, in its Greek development, the root of Nestor, *nes-*, has another associated meaning as well: "mind," that is, *noos*. It is true, as Frame argues, that the Nasatyas are "intelligent," and that this could be one layer of the meaning of their name. However, we must look in particular at the sense of the word *noos* as it developed in Greek, and consider who it applies more to, a High Priest god or a god of worldly intelligence, a Horse Twin. Indeed, the word *noos* came to mean "mind" in the highest philosophical sense, while Frame himself argues that "if return was the basic notion of the root of noos the noun most likely designated 'consciousness' in the first place." We have already shown how the High Priest of the Word is he who returns the light of consciousness by freeing the cattle of illumination from their dark covering. Apollo, for his part, is described by Thomas Taylor as the emanation of the solar monad on the intellectual level, connecting both illumination and mind as closely as can be done, and is above perhaps any other god in this. Aligning perfectly with the meaning of the root *nes-*, The High Priest of the Word both returns consciousness to light, and returns to life with his power of reviving. We see just how much these notions overlap in the cases of the Horse Twins and High Priest of the Word, and can imagine how the root *nes-* could have been used interchangeably for both in the most archaic times and remained accurate in its meaning, and how confusion could even have developed in its application with regard to which god was most associated with it.

Furthermore, Frame discusses how Nestor is a skilled reader of *sema*, or "signs," as when he interprets events on the sea journey back home in a manner that allows he and his companions to have a safe return. Who is more a reader of signs than the High Priest of the Word, Apollo, the exemplar oracular god? What of the secret "signs" or symbols that the High Priest Oðinn receives from the tree, the runes? Indeed, there is nothing in the mythos of the Horse Twins that explains this *sema*-reading feature of Nestor's skillset, other than a general idea of aiding safe returns, which is a Horse Twin trait but more often has to do with rescues. Of oracles, such as Apollo's, it is a commonplace that they read "signs," and this also does Nestor.

Finally, in what appears an archaic genealogy that we have seen backed up in Greek terms by the Greeks Pindar and Hecataeus of Miletus (Apollo being the father of Pan, who is companion of Zeus' mother and provides his goat as Zeus' nurse, see also chapter "The Celtic Pushan"), Irish Dian Cecht is the grandfather of Lugh. This means that by the time Lugh is raised and the Great Battle that he wins with his victorious spear begins, Dian Cecht is at least three "generations old," if such a concept of age can be applied simply to a god. Nestor himself is said to be three generations old during the Great War of Troy. Perhaps this alone accounts for his great age: he is the incarnation of one of the first gods, the gods three generations back from the main gods of the Great War. From this perspective, no speculative historical argument about Nestor's mythos being separately preserved and awkwardly inserted into the epic with him now turned old is required. Furthermore, it is Apollo himself who is closest associated with Nestor's family history and childhood. Apollo kills the siblings of Nestor to punish his mother, and gives Nestor unnaturally long life to balance the bloody affair. This makes Apollo himself the divine source of Nestor's extended vitality, perhaps as if Nestor is infused with the spirit of the god. Nestor's grandson is sometimes also said to have been Homer. We must ask ourselves, who would be the more likely grandfather of this greatest of all Greek poets, an incarnation of one of the Horse Twins, or an incarnation of Apollo, god of poetry and the Word?[141]

One detail that this interpretation cannot well account for is the fact that Nestor is named "Horseman." He is Hippota Nestor. However, we have seen in our investigation how widely the title of Horseman has been applied in the various branches, and for how many different reasons. It is not at all an uncommon title. In fact, Horseman is a common solar title in particular, with the Irish Sun God Bres being called "Horseman Bres" to reinforce his solar quality, not to mention Irish Father Sky, the Dagda, being

---

141   Particularly considering that the Rudraic and Brihaspti elements seem to be intertwined in Apollo himself, as we have explored, and we have seen that the legendary national poets of the Celtic tradition, Oisin and Taliesin, are of the Rudraic type. This Rudraic-Brihaspati nexus should represent the Prime High Poet type par excellence (Apollo, Odinn) above or in a different capacity to the Gandharvic deity who is usually the god of a slightly less elevated eloquence (Hermes, Bragi).

called "Horseman Great Father." Apollo likely had a solar role from the beginning, if the esoteric interpretation is correct, and eventually became conflated with the sun itself. It is not impossible that Nestor's title could reinforce the solar aspect of his character then, or could simply derive from his own local legend as a particularly skilled charioteer. Ultimately, the concept of a Horseman who is also a reviver, a savior, could again have been an overlapping theological idea shared between the High Priest and Horse Twin deities in early times. We admit, however, that the simple linguistic comparison is striking. The present analysis, however, has been an attempt to eschew the linguistic level and instead confront the actual attributes of Nestor's character to see who is being presented to us under this name.

10

Ogma-Hermes-Gandharva

Prominent theories regarding Hermes (Oldenberg 1916, Oberlies 2000) have tended to connect him with Vedic Pushan, pastoral god of travelers and meetings who as such was also associated with commerce and wealth. However, in recent years the well-known comparativist Nick Allen, along with collaborator Roger Woodard, published an article on Hermes that proves revelatory when considering Hermes and his Vedic analog. This article, "Hermes and Gandharvas," demonstrates painstakingly that Hermes' mythos resembles in numerous very specific details the myths attached to the class of beings known in Vedic texts as the gandharvas.

Some of this article's points: A chief representative among the gandharvas (Narada) is known to have first brought the lyre, a strung tortoise shell, to humanity, as Hermes also is said to have invented the lyre by stringing a tortoise shell; gandharvas are the chief embodiments of the musical power, court singers and musical teachers of the gods ("*gandharva* means 'music,'" as Allen and Woodard say) as Hermes teaches even the master musician Apollo the lyre; they are known for their eloquence and often narrate myths, as Hermes also is a god of eloquence who narrates myths; they are often divine messengers and go-betweens as is Hermes; they are associated with raw sexuality, while the boundary marker statues of Hermes known as *hermae* were known for their prominent phalluses; they have the power of flight or even wings, as Hermes has winged sandals and flies about; a god who is distinct from but "typologically close [...] and

344

linked" to the Gandharvas (Kubera), as Allen and Woodard say, has a staff or wand with power of inducing sleep, as Hermes has the magical rod (*rabdos* or *caduceus*) with the same power. These are perhaps the most crucial among a host of other connections and similarities described by Allen and Woodard. This article is required reading for anyone who wishes to properly differentiate Hermes from other gods such as Pan and to fully understand him via comparativism. We build on this article's conclusion, regarding Hermes as the Gandharva, in our present framework. We may add that the gandharvas are the stand-ins for and proteges of the "Soma" God, intermediary spirits who can pass between worlds, with possible psychopomp roles, while Hermes is closely associated with both the "Soma" God Dionysus and underworld god Hades and is their psychopomp, passing between all worlds in this office.

As we will see, accepting this theory as an accurate clarification of Hermes' role opens also the possibility of clarifying the identity of the Irish god Ogma. To remind the reader of our framework thus far, we take the "Gandharva" of the various branches to be: Norse Bragi, Welsh Pwyll, Vedic Visvavasu (among other names), and Greek Hermes. The Irish god Ogma has remained a relatively mysterious figure, due mostly to the small quantity of details extant which pertain to him. Ogma (or his Gaulish counterpart Ogmios) has, indeed, occasionally been compared with Hermes, yet if Hermes is seen as a Pushanic god, as is often the case, then the link of Ogma also to Pushan would have very little specific support. Ogma does not form a good parallel with Pushan. Thus the Hermes-Ogma similarities have remained curious but confusing when Hermes is viewed as one with Pushan/Pan. But if we see both Hermes and Ogma as the chief "Gandharva," rather than as "Pushan," the picture makes a new kind of sense.

Key to understanding the essence of Hermes and his connection to the Gandharva is recognizing that Hermes' eloquence is his core feature. Hermes is the herald, *Kyrux*, a title coming from a word meaning "to sing," while the Gandharva's name is connected to music and he is lord of eloquence and song. As god of eloquence, Hermes is often represented with chains of gold hanging from his lips and the tongues of animals were sacrificed to him. Nearly as foundational is Hermes' position as a liminal being who moves between realms. From this liminality, traveling between the boundaries of realms, derives his psychopomp role. From the skill of persuasive eloquence derives the aforementioned role of herald, messenger, contract negotiator, and from these the well-known connection with trade and wealth. Meanwhile this persuasive eloquence also connects with his traits of trickery, deception, even thievery. His ability of moving between realms also reinforces his connection to roads, travelers, and once again messengership and trade.

Considering persuasive eloquence as one of the core traits of Hermes then connects with the most salient and well-known trait of Ogma. Ogma is known as primarily a god

345

of language and his Gaulish parallel as a god of persuasive eloquence. Ogma's name is believed to come from a root meaning "to cut," referring to the way the writing known as Oghams were cut into wood and stone.[142] He is thus the god of Ogham and its inventor. He is said in the "Ogam Tract" to be skilled in speech and poetry. He is called *Grianeces,* "sun poet," and "a man well skilled in speech and in poetry" in *The Scholar's Primer* (*Auraicept na n-Éces*). His assumed Gaulish version, Ogmios, is described by the 2nd century Roman Lucian of Samosata as being depicted with human figures following after him, with chains binding them, chains which issue from Ogmios' mouth, just as Hermes is represented with golden chains emitting from his mouth. The human figures in the account of Ogmios are said to seem happy to be chained by such chains and are eagerly following the god. He may even be leading the chained mortals on to the Underworld, if we consider a theoretical psychopomp role. Could their seeming happiness then be due to the sweetness of the "Gandharva" eloquence, which in the Vedic and Greek cases is also of the essence of music?

Connected with this shared trait of eloquence, another central parallel between Ogma and Hermes involves the invention of writing and patronage of language skill. As mentioned, Ogma is known as the inventor of the form of writing known as Ogham, and the god and writing system share a name. Meanwhile, Hermes' Roman cognate Mercury is known for a myth in which he is said to have invented the alphabet by watching the flight of cranes (Pseudo-Hyginus, *Fabulae* 277), and to have brought the letters to Egypt. He is also said to have explained or created "the languages of men" generally speaking (Pseudo-Hyginus, *Fabulae* 143). In an Orphic hymn we find him closely tied to discourse and speech: "Hermes […] prophet of discourse […] Of various speech, whose aid in works we find […] give graceful speech, and memory's increase" (*Orphic Hymn 28 to Hermes*). Hermes is also described by Hesiod to have first given mortals speech when he planted this capacity in Pandora, the first woman (*Works and Days*, 80). As god of language skill generally, it is logical that the Gandharva would be connected with the origin of writing and speech. As Allen and Woodard note, in Vedic myth, the Gandharva Visvavasu is said to exchange *soma* for *Vac*, the divine embodiment of the spoken word, thus he is here being depicted as receiving divine language or speech. As divinity of liminal boundaries, the Gandharva is said also to know the "innermost name[s]" of things (*RV* 10.123.4), "which he reveals to Indra," and they "boast of their knowledge of the Vedas" (SB 3.2.4.5) (Allen and Woodard, "Gandharvas and Hermes").

The other important invention of Hermes is that of fire, which he produces in order to sacrifice two of the stolen cattle of Apollo (*Homeric Hymn to Hermes*, 108-111).

---

142   *Jones' Celtic Encyclopedia*, "Oghma Grianainech". For a more in-depth analysis of Ogma's name and its relation to Ogmios and Ogham, see also John Carey "*Ogmios* and the eternal word" (2014).

Specifically he gathers the "firesticks" and then kindles the fire. "Hermes first brought forth firesticks and fire" the hymn reads. Thus he also invents the common mode of generating fire for sacrifice, and the fire invention and sacrifice are intimately linked. As for Ogma, he also is interestingly associated with fire and firewood. When Bres rules Ireland and subjects the Tuatha De Danann to labor, while Dagda is made to dig trenches, Ogma is made to carry firewood (*The Second Battle of Maige Tuired*). If this role of firewood carrier indicates the remnant of a once important function, it could go back to an understanding of the "Gandharva" as having an important role in preparing the sacrificial fire or being the first to do so, as we have also related to the overlapping Gandharva/Visvavasu figures in the Lunar Cycle. The Vedic figure known as Pururavas, who *becomes* a gandharva, brings to earth three kinds of sacrificial fire, "effectively introducing sacrificial fire among humankind" (Allen and Woodard, "Gandharvas and Hermes").

Hermes is known as a psychopomp, leading the dead to Hades and associated closely with both Dionysus and the god Hades (who overlap or cooperate in their subterranean aspects), and this may be yet another traceable link between him and Ogma. Specifically it is Ogma's supposed Gaulish cognate Ogmios who is clearly associated with the underworld and perhaps with the psychopomp role. Two curse inscriptions are known from Bregenz, Austria, in which Ogmios is mentioned in relation to the underworld. In one, the suppliant asks that the target of the curse be "given to (O)gmios, to be co(n)sumed (by) death" (Mees, 2489, CIL III: 11882), while the other seems to associate or identify Ogmios with the lord of the underworld, Dis Pater, saying, "Thi(s) thin(g) D(is) P(at)er with Eracura wi(l)l fix. Ogmios, ('er) 'eal(th), 'heart [etc.]… give 'em over to the spirits" (Mees, Loc. 2456, OeAI-1943-114). While Ogma may be identified obliquely here with the Roman Lord of the Underworld himself, Dis Pater, the curses specifically are invoking Ogmios to deliver the curse victim into the hands of death or the spirits of the underworld, precisely as a psychopomp would be expected to do, and this has been the conclusion of scholars such as Bernard Mees as well (Mees, *Curse Tablets*). And if the second curse actually is identifying Ogmios with Dis Pater, which is certainly not clear, then recall that in the myth of the Welsh, who were probably the closest culture to the Gauls and Austrian Celts for whom we retain a written mythology, the proposed Gandharva Pwyll becomes the double of and stand-in for Arawn, the lord of the underworld, becoming essentially identified with him, sharing his title "Lord of Annwn," and combining kingdoms with him. Thus in a Celtic conception, Ogmios could indeed be both the Gandharva-psychopomp and a co-Lord of the Underworld. These are not mutually exclusive. Mercury, the Roman Hermes, was himself a frequently named god in Roman curse inscriptions, due to his psychopomp role. Lucian also compares Ogmios with Charon, a psychopomp whom Hermes is sometimes shown bringing souls to. Ogmios' depiction as sunburned and Ogma's epithet "sun-face" have also been argued to indicate that he is an underworld deity, as the sunburned face of Ogmios is what caused Lucian to compare Ogmios to the underworld gods Charon and Iapetus (*Jones' Celtic Encyclopedia*, "Ogmios"), and the path of the sun is associated with the path of psychopomps in Vedic tradition (Savitr, Pushan, etc., see RV 10.17.4-6; 2.40.4-5[143]) , potentially explaining this sunburned face of Ogmios.

Ogmios is noted for the description of him wearing a lion skin, a feature which has been one of the main evidences in his supposed connection with Hercules, who also wears a lion skin. This skin has also been one argument against Ogmios/Ogma's identification with Hermes, who is not known for any such apparel. However, this detail can perhaps be seen more clearly when the full gandharva context is understood. The Vedic gandharvas are beings connected with wildness, sometimes depicted as half-bird and exhibiting exuberant sexuality. Welsh Pwyll and Indian Samvarana both are hunters. As such, the lion skin could be read as a symbol of this wild nature, or perhaps simply as a symbol that Ogmios was seen as a hunter, and in any case does not have any absolute connection with Hercules alone.

Connected with this skin is the purported great strength of Ogmios, which, on the surface, does not seem central to Hermes. As we have said, Ogmios was identified with Hercules by Lucian, though he specifically emphasized the fact that Ogmios' "strength" came from his eloquence. But this parallel seems to us quite a stretch on the part of Lucian and his informant, and actually emphasizes the difference between Hercules and Ogmios rather than their similarity. Irish Ogma for his part was depicted as the champion of Nuada and Lugh, and defeats one third of the Fomorian army himself. He is also the strongman guard of Nuada's hall upon the arrival of Lugh, and when Lugh shows himself equal in strength to Ogma by a stone-throwing duel of sorts, Ogma welcomes him and eventually fights for him. As Kevin Maclean has suggested, the names of the sidhe dwellings of the gods seem to be related to their functions, the dwelling of Ogma is called *Aircheltrai*, with a meaning relating to guarding or saving. But Hermes, though not always thought of in terms of strength, is yet frequently called simply by the epithet *Argeïphóntēs* meaning "killer of Argus," referring to the myth in which Hermes slays the giant with the hundred eyes, Argus. Hermes slays Argus by hitting him with a stone and then decapitating him, as Ogma also throws the heavy flagstone in his competition with Lugh. Thus, built into his most common title is Hermes' role as champion warrior and slayer of a great monster. Numerous other details emphasize Hermes' strength and warrior prowess. He is given the epithet *Areias*, "Warlike," in Mycenaean inscriptions. He is called Agônios and *Agônes*, indicating that he presides over all sorts of *agôn*: struggles, contests, and competitions (Pausanias v.

---

143   See also Gregory Nagy, *Greek Mythology and Poetics*, 114.

14.7; Pindar *Olympian* vi. 133). He is a patron god of athletics and of racing and wrestling and all gymnasiums and wrestling schools in Greece were dedicated to him. He is often depicted as an armed warrior in scenes of combat. He is called *Kratus* and *Krateros*, names that mean "mighty," and Apollo comments on his physical strength in the Homeric hymn. He was called *Promachos*, "the champion" or "the Warrior on the front lines" at Tanagra (Pausanias ix. 22.2). This is connected to the story in which he defended the town of Tanagra and defeated Ares himself in a boxing match for the hand of the nymph Tanagra.

As for the Vedic Gandharva, as previously discussed, he generally is called a guardian of the *soma*, and would implicitly require great strength for this role. And just as Ogma is the guardian of Nuada's hall when Lugh arrives, Norse Bragi enacts the role of guardian of Óðinn's hall (Óðinn seen as a parallel of Nuada in his Varuna aspect), particularly when Loki first arrives in *Lokasenna*, as we have noted. Bragi, the court skald of the gods, is also no weakling, offering to rip Loki's head off in one passage (*Lokasenna*, 14). Like Ogma and Bragi, who first greet questionable outsiders at the palace hall, Hermes is closely tied to the role of guardian and watchman. *Homeric Hymn 4 To Hermes* line 15 calls him "night guardian" or "watcher by night," and he also is called *Propylaios*, "Of the gateway." Carvings of him were traditionally present at the doors of homes in the role of guardian. He is called *Ktêsios*, "the protector of property" (Pausanias. i. 31. 2). He is the guardian of roads, crossroads and boundaries, the *hermae* pillars standing in this role. Thus the role of guardian runs as a through-line connecting all the iterations of the Gandharva, and this in itself implies strength. Besides the animal skin, Ogmios also carries a club as Hercules sometimes does: however, as Allen and Woodard say, citing Banerjea, "Gandharvas may be shown holding clubs as well as lyres (Allen and Woodard, "Gandharvas and Hermes"; Banerjea 1956: 352).

Next, it is Hermes who, closely associated with Hades as his attendant psychopomp, brings Persephone out of Hades. This mirrors the previously explored role of the Gandharva, who is the second possessor and caretaker of Surya, wife of Soma. We recall Pwyll in this role sleeping in the bed with the wife of Arawn as the protector of the bride's virginity. Just as Hades and Dionysus are overlapping underworld gods, Hermes is associated with conveying the wife of each one. As we thoroughly explored in our Lunar Cycle section, the Gandharva marries the Sun Princess, the same one that the Soma God marries or sometimes her double. Thus as Midir marries Etain, we see, just as we should expect, that Ogma marries a woman named Etan. We are far from the first to suggest that this is simply a variant spelling of Etain and that this is the same goddess once again. The coincidence is far too strong to ignore at this point. Ogma's marriage to Etan indeed completes the series of marriages of gods to the Sun Princesses that we have seen repeat in the Lunar Cycle: Soma, Gandharva, Agni. In Irish, then, this is Midir

349

(Soma) married to Etain, Ogma (Gandharva) married to Etan, and Manannan married to Aine, with Aengus (Asvin) married to the other Sun Princess, Caer. While one of the Sun Princesses always is transferred between two of these male gods, it is variable which two gods this is. In the Welsh, Rhiannon is married to the Gandharva Pwyll and the Fire god Manawydan in succession. In the Norse, Skaði is married to the Soma god Njorðr and Oðinn, in his fire aspect, in succession. In the Irish, it is the Soma God Midir and Gandharva Ogma who successively marry the same Sun Princess bride, but then Echdae (who, due to an evident conflation of roles, may take a combined Vivasvat-Gandharva role as previously discussed) and the Fire God Manannan also wed the other Sun Princess Aine in succession. Hermes indeed acquires many wives for various heroes and gods, frequently appearing on pottery in this typical role, while the Gandharva is a bringer of fertility who is one of the central gods of the marriage rite, passing along the archetypal bride to her ultimate husband.

The gandharvas are sometimes described as wind deities (RV 3.38.6; Mayrhofer 1989, p. 461-2), Hermes is described as an autumn breeze in *Homeric Hymn 4 To Hermes*, line 145, and Ogma is closely tied to the proposed chief wind god, the Dagda, generally named as his brother. While the Welsh Horse Twin Pryderi's father is the proposed Gandharva, Pwyll, we argue that this is an outlier parentage for the Horse Twin and that it does not match the Irish Horse Twin Aengus' parentage by Dagda. It may instead be the result of Pwyll combining the Gandharva and Vivasvat roles in one figure, like with Irish Echdae, or may be the result of Pwyll becoming one with the Soma god Arawn, who parallels Njordr and Midir, father and foster father of the Norse and Irish Horse Twin gods. Yet Ogma is Aengus' uncle as well, and so remains closely connected to Aengus and in a near-fatherly position, shifted only one remove laterally compared to the Welsh case. Ogma being the brother of Dagda could be due to Dagda's role as the underworld god Dagda *Donn*, or due to his connection to underworld location Brugh na Boinne. Thus the fraternal relationship of Ogma and Dagda would be similar in some ways to the relationship of Pwyll and Arawn as co-lords of the underworld. We could then see the brothers Ogma and Dagda, along with Aengus, son of Dagda, as a closely connected trio of "underworld gods" (several other gods having underworld roles as well), who are also closely connected to the highly important burial mound Brugh na Boinne.

Ogmios is known for the bearded images of his face and this is often seen to contradict the youthful depiction generally given to Hermes. However, in depictions of Hermes prior to the Classical period in Greece he was depicted as bearded too, a feature preserved in surviving *hermae* statues. Norse Bragi is called the "Long-bearded God" as well as the "First maker of poetry" (*Skaldskaparmal*, 10). Hermes also is often depicted with a money bag, while Pwyll, in the episode with Gwawl, uses a bag with a seemingly limitless capacity, which is given to him by Rhiannon. Hermes goes to pay the bride price of Herse with his bag of money, while Pwyll uses his bag to win back his bride Rhiannon by tricking his rival suitor with it, and thus these bags appear in analogous moments in their respective myths.

This wooing tale of Hermes is worth noting here more fully, as it seems to parallel the Gandharva and Pwyll wooing tales in other elements. According to Ovid, Hermes sees Herse among a group of maidens while he is flying over Athens and is powerfully struck by her beauty. The chief Gandharva from the crucial Vedic hymn, Visvavasu, as we have mentioned before, sees the beautiful maiden Devahuti from his "airplane" as he is flying over her rooftop and is so struck with her beauty that he falls from the sky. Pwyll sees Rhiannon as he sits on top of the sacred mound Gorsedd Arberth and is likewise struck with her beauty. Hermes has to present a large sum of money to Herse's sister Agraulos to favor his suit. Nonetheless, possessed by envy as a punishment for her avariciousness, Agraulos blocks Hermes' way through the door and refuses to move. Eventually, Hermes turns her to stone and then weds Herse. Pwyll, in his myth, becomes engaged to Rhiannon after seeing her from the sacred mound, but at their marriage feast he accidentally promises to grant a rival suitor anything he asks, and the suitor claims Rhiannon for his own. Pwyll must then return with the magical bag and trick his rival into stepping inside it and then ransom the trapped rival's freedom for the return of Rhiannon. Thus the pattern of both stories are: sees beautiful maiden from high location, is struck by beauty and secures an agreement to marry, a dishonest second figure steps in to block the marriage, a bag (of money or of magical capacity) is used at one point to secure the bride, the impeding figure is done away with and the marriage is completed. Clearly the Hermes myth is closer to the Visvavasu myth than to the Samvarana variant considering both Hermes and Visvavasu are specifically flying when they see the princess. However, the Hermes and Pwyll versions are more similar in the segment involving the overcoming the impeding secondary figure using the bag. Considering, in turn, how close the Pwyll and Samvarana versions are in other aspects, this circuit once again supports the idea that the Visvavasu and Samvarana tales are simply variants of one Gandharva mythos, different elements of which appear in the western versions found in the Pwyll and Hermes myths, and that any discrepancies can be explained by a conflation with the Vivasvat-type goddess-pursuit myth.

Allen also notes a repeating pattern among the Gandharvas of an initial confrontation and enmity between themselves and a second party, followed by reconciliation and friendship. This is the pattern found in the story of Hermes' theft of Apollo's cattle, followed by their reconciliation and friendship. We see this pattern also in Pwyll's first meeting with Arawn when his dogs have eaten Arawn's stag, and in the end the two parties avoid conflict and even combine kingdoms due to their great mutual amity. The

351

general shape of this pattern also repeats in the case of Ogma. When Ogma and Lugh at first confront one another as if to duel, Ogma throws a massive flagstone at Lugh. Lugh throws it back, and then they join in friendship and Ogma fights as Lugh's champion in battle. Ogma is often found in lists of the three main chiefs of the Tuatha De Danann (his name sometimes substituted by another) and this would match the importance given to Pwyll in the *Mabinogion*, as one of the book's most prominent kings who begins the mythical cycle. This importance and the fact that Ogma is said to slay such a large proportion of the opposing army in battle may be due to the importance placed on the power of eloquence by the Celts. As J.A. MacCulloch argues, this role of champion may come "from the primitive custom of rousing the warriors' emotions by eloquent speeches before battle" (MacCulloch, *The Religion of the Ancient Celts*). Ogma is strong because eloquence both is a mystical strength on its own and gives strength to all in battle, thus having a wide-ranging and powerful effect. This also accords with Lucian's aforementioned claim about how the Celts saw eloquence as strength, but avoids the mistake of trying to make Ogma and Hercules out to be the same god for this reason, as Lucian does.

Interestingly, Ogma is thought (based on etymological evidence and similarities in their descriptions) to possibly share a name with a Welsh figure, Eufydd fab Don, and possibly also with the similarly named Hefeydd Hen. Hefeydd is said to be father of Rhiannon. A possible variant of the name is found in the poem *Y Gododdin*, which says that "Hyveidd Hir shall be celebrated as long as there will be a minstrel" (*Y Gododdin*, stanza 5), which fits the gandharvic pattern perfectly as the Gandharva is of course a god of bards, poets, and musicians.

This connection no doubt seems to cast some amount of doubt on our understanding of Ogma and Pwyll *both* as versions of the Gandharva, since this Hefeydd is father of Rhiannon and our proposed Gandharva Pwyll is her husband. However, there are several possible solutions to this difficulty. Most obviously, the Welsh genealogy may be slightly jumbled at this point. Thus it would be possible the Gandharva has simply been "doubled" in the husband and father of Rhiannon. We have already seen how, in comparison with the Greek version, the Welsh seems to "compress" a couple of generations of goddesses into one, or that the Greek version presents two goddesses who are really one on a deeper level: there are mother and daughter goddesses in the Greek version of the abduction myth (Demeter and Persephone), but only one main Welsh goddess (Rhiannon) in the parallel myth, taking both of these roles herself. Could Rhiannon being daughter to a gandharva (Hefeydd) even reflect the idea that Poseidon Hippios, who ravishes the mother goddess Demeter and becomes Persephone's father, is also a Gandharva in disguise, The Gandharva in the Waters, as we have previously theorized, since Hefeydd is in the comparable position genealogically, as father of the goddess who gets trapped in the Otherworld and who parallels Persephone? This is quite complex, but we can picture Pwyll being this Gandharva in his role as the mate of the Horse Goddess (Rhiannon), and Heyfeydd being this same Gandharva in his role as father of the daughter who is abducted to the underworld (also Rhiannon). We would argue: Because the Welsh tradition has compressed two generations into one, this has necessitated splitting the husband and father into two separate figures. In fact, in no other instances is the father of the Sun Princess or Saranyu-type goddess a gandharva, unless we consider Poseidon Hippios as gandharvic and Persephone as one of these goddesses. Thus Rhiannon having a gandharvic father instead of a Sun God or Tvastr-type father would stick out like a sore thumb unless we resolve these gandharvic roles by suggesting that both Hefeydd and Pwyll take parts of the Gandharva mythos in this way, and either that Rhiannon is reflecting the role of a double goddess, mother and daughter, Demeter and Persephone, or that Demeter and Persephone reflect this single goddess who has gandharvic deities for both father and consort. We have already seen a very similar deep confusion about who the father and consorts of Irish Aine (parallel of Rhiannon, Demeter, and Persephone) are, with multiple flatly contradictory accounts given in that case. In the case of Pwyll, we have also seen that he somehow combines Vivasvat and Gandharva-type mythic elements, which may have also affected this genealogical confusion.

Finally, in Vedic myth, there are in fact numerous gandharvas. Indeed they are considered an entire class of being, with certain prominent chiefs, thus the presence in the Welsh case of two gandharvas in itself would make no specific problem whatsoever. It is possible that other divine court singers in the Irish myths could be representatives, at their roots, of this same class of beings as well, just as it is possible the Norse grouping of gandharvic deities could theoretically extend beyond Bragi, but this has not been shown at present.

In all, if we move past some of the aesthetic choices found in the common depictions of the gods Hermes and Ogma/Ogmios, which appear to imply a contrast between the physical strength of the Celtic god and the wispy swiftness of the Greek one, we can see several much stronger through-lines between them: eloquence, inventing writing, carrying firewood or firesticks, being a guardian, being connected to the underworld possibly as psychopomps, etc. As often happens, this god is both things, swift and strong, with one culture emphasizing one trait, and one emphasizing the other. The comparison between Ogma/Ogmios and Hermes has actually been a popular one in the past (consider the painting by Albrecht Durer, *Allegory of Eloquence,* uniting Hermes and Ogmios as a single god in a striking image, from the year 1514), going back to Roman times as seen in Lucian's account of Ogmios, wherein he is specifically attempting to counter this standard equivalency of Ogmios and Hermes by bringing in the figure of Hercules. However, with a clearer understanding of the Gandharva, Ogma-Hermes becomes a much stronger comparison and much less easy to dislodge on aesthetic grounds.

11

The Celtic Pushan: Gwydion, Cian, Oðinn, Pan

With Hermes and Ogma's parallel with the Gandharva much more clearly seen, and specifically with Hermes now distinguished from the Vedic Pushan who he has commonly been compared with, we are much better able to proceed to an analysis of the "Pushan" deity as he may appear in both Greek and Celtic myth. As much as Hermes has been compared to Pushan, so also has his son, Pan, been said to be the Pushanic god, and he on much firmer linguistic grounds. The name Pan is thus suggested to derive from a shared root with Pushan, the Proto-Indo-European *Péh2usōn, which is thought to have developed into the Greek form as *peh2- > Παων > Pan (Skutsch 1987, 190). Furthermore, as god of the wilds, and particularly mountain wilds, where Pushan goes to protect flocks and travelers, Pushan makes a strikingly good match to the well-known image of Pan the wild, goat-footed lord of flocks and nature. We will not go into an extensive comparison proving Pan's parallel with Pushan, as this has been done elsewhere. M.L. West summarizes:

Both are pastoral gods, with a special affinity with the goat. Pusan has goats
to pull his car (RV 1. 138. 4; 6. 55. 3–4, cf. 6; 58. 2; 9. 67. 10; 10. 26. 8), and
goats were sacrificed to him on occasion; Pan has goat's legs (Hymn. Hom.
19. 2, 37; Anon. mel. P. Oxy. 2624 fr. 1. 4 = SLG 387). Both have bushy
beards (RV 10. 26. 7; Hymn. Hom. 19. 39, PMG 936. 11) and keen sight:
Pusan goes about surveying everything (RV 2. 40. 5; 3. 62. 9; 6. 58. 2); Pan
roams the mountains and climbs the peaks to view the flocks.7 Pusan follows
and protects the cattle (RV 6. 54. 5–10, 58. 2, 53. 9; a producer of cattle, TS
2. 1. 1. 6; 2. 4. 4. 3). He is a guardian of roads who protects the wayfarer
from wolves and brigands (RV 1. 42. 1–3, 7; 6. 49. 8, 53. 1, 54. 9). Pan's
province includes 'the rocky tracks' (Hymn. Hom. 19. 7), and in Hellenistic
Egypt he was worshipped as [...] 'of good journeying' (OGIS 38, 70–2, al.).
(West, 282)

Building on this established parallel we are able to begin to investigate the elusive Celtic
Pushan.

There is one Celtic god who has not been specifically identified in our schema, who
was explicitly identified via the Interpretatio Romana with Mercury (the Roman cognate
of Hermes). Of course, there were numerous Celtic deities identified with Mercury by
the Romans and Gauls in different contexts. This particular god, however, bore the name
Mercury *Uiducus*, meaning Mercury "of the woods" (CIL XIII 576)[144]. Presumably,
Uiducus was the latinization of the name of the Gaulish deity who was here rechristened
as a Mercury. Uiducus, this "Mercury" of the Woods, does not have any extant written
mythology, but seems to have a clear linguistic cognate in one of the most important
Welsh gods: Gwydion. Gwydion and Uiducus are linguistically very close, and are both
considered to come from the root *uidu-*, meaning "woods," or *uid-/wyd-* concerning
knowledge (trees and knowledge already being connected concepts in Celtic cultures, as
we see with the word *druid*, proto-Celtic *dru-wid-s*, "oak-knower," and so a sort of pun
between the two meanings may be implied in Uiducus' name). Jones' Celtic
Encyclopedia says, "Gwydion himself would derive from *Uidugenos, which would be
similar to Uiducos, which according to Chris Gwyn contains the early patryonimic -ako-,
here -uco-, making Uiducus and Gwydion essentially the same name." Thus
Gwydion/Uiducus is the wise "Mercury" of the Woods. Would it be possible that the
ancients then confused what is actually a "Pushan" deity (Uiducus) for a "Gandharva"
one (Mercury) in this case, just as scholars have habitually done in our time, naming this
Celtic god a "Mercury" when he is really a "Pan"? Are external similarities between the
two god archetypes so close, the Greeks even making them father and son, that they will

---

144   *Jones' Celtic Encyclopedia*, "Uiducus".

always be seen as near equivalents? Would "Mercury of the Woods" not be a more fitting title for Pan himself?

This association with the tree-associated *uid-* or knowledge plays out in Gwydion's mythology. He is both a teacher, teaching Lleu all he knows, and a knower of magical means, helping create Lleu's bride Blodeuwedd out of flowers, transforming her into an owl, enchanting fungus to appear as horses and dogs in the trade with Pryderi, magically disguising he and Lleu when they go to Arianrhod, etc. Furthermore, the association of Uiducus with the woods fits well with Pushan's association with the mountain wilds generally, and this aspect may also be reinforced by the episode in which Gwydion is successively transformed into three different beasts of the wild, and seemingly made to live in the wild, as punishment along with his brother: a stag, a sow, and a wolf. Thus also, while Pan himself is half-goat, Gwydion takes the forms of certain animals for a portion of his life. In the Vedic case, Pushan is associated with pastures, liminal spaces and mountainous heights, which his goat chariot allows him to traverse (compare to Pan's goat feet) and it is said of him, "he shares with Soma the guardianship of living creatures." Specifically he watches over the herds and is especially prayed to for their protection and in the case that cattle are lost. He is the god who both protects cattle and crucially retrieves them when lost.

Gwydion's Irish cognate Cian must be mentioned here as well. Indeed, this investigation must start from the assumption, which we will reinforce as we go, that Irish Cian and Welsh Gwydion are the same god. This, at first, seems to rest on only a couple similarities; however, as the investigation continues, the full pattern will become much clearer. Irish Cian is father of Lugh as Welsh Gwydion is ambiguously father or foster father of Lleu. Just before Cian's death, he transforms himself into a pig (or dog, depending on the interpretation of the manuscript) to try to escape the sons of Tuireann. Thus both he and Gwydion transform into animals, and these animals overlap, as the pig is one of those which Gwydion is transformed into as well (the wolf being another).

Pushan's central pastoral association connects with perhaps the most important piece of evidence marking Cian and Gwydion as the Celtic "Pushans." Prayers were directed to Pushan when cows strayed and he is said in the *Rig Veda* to have found a lost "king" who had been hidden away. This king is understood from context to be the god Soma himself. Not only this, but the finding of Soma and the trait of the retrieving of cattle seem to be combined in this myth, for a mantra found in hymn 1.23.13 of the *Rig Veda* reads, "Bring him [Soma] […] O Luminous Pushan, like a lost animal." Soma must be found by Pushan as if he is a lost animal. In the next verse, verse 14, we read, "Pushan found in the cave the most hidden Soma." Of this pair of mantras, Vedic translators Brereton and Jamison say, "most commentators identify this king as Soma," while stating that context implies that it is likely Soma or Agni.[145] See also: "Pusan chose a drop of Soma" (*Yajur Veda, Taittiriya Samhita*, iii. 3. 9.). Stella Kramrisch describes Pushan's journey thus: "In the darkness of the night, where he extinguishes the futile fire brand of the two-faced enemy, he finds the Treasure. It is King Soma, the elixir of life [...] Born in the depth of midnight, Pusan is found by Agni, and Soma is found by Pusan [...] There, in the night of the year, glowing Pusan found the hidden King, on his shining carpet as he finds a lost animal or hidden treasure (8.29.6)" (Kramrisch, "Pusan," 110). Kramrisch further explains that Pushan and Agni are united as if one in this quest, exactly as we argue Odinn is both Pushan and Agni in one in his quest for the mead, and also as Cian joins Manannan in his extraction from Balor's island: "Pusan, born in the pit, is the Liberator and Illuminer, the guide who leads to Light. He is creative Fire kindled, when, **having been found by Agni, they are one (2.1.6). Agni-Pusan, the creative Fire, finds Soma**, the 'offering,' the luminous, formative principle, the Treasure" (Kramrisch, "Pusan," 110)[146]. Brereton and Jamison also call Pushan's ability to locate lost cows "proverbial" (Brereton and Jamison, *Rig Veda*, 117). [147] Gwydion, too, is one of the main shepherds of his mythic branch, called one of the three great shepherds of Britain in the Welsh Triads: "The three shepherd retinues of the Isle of

---

145   They prefer the Agni interpretation based on the fact that Agni hides himself away in other myths: "particularly the notion of finding and returning a hidden deity" is "much more characteristic of Agni." This guess, however, relies on the present verse referring the same Agni myth, which can only be an unsupported assumption. We assert that the comparative cases we present in the following pages make it much more likely that this is an entirely different myth to the Agni myth, and that the hidden king is Soma, as most other commentators have concluded. It is clear the sacred liquid in Vedic and Norse myths, and the cow in Irish myth, are all hidden away just as much as Agni is, and in the Irish case we specifically deal with an animal that stands in for the sacred liquid, just as the hymn implies.

146   She continues: "Images of kine, horses, wealth, riches and substance (vasu, rai) are symbolical synonyms (cf. pecunia-pecus) of the treasure which Pusan finds and disperses. His 'substance' is illumination" (Kramrisch, 110). "Pusan, having found the Hidden King, drives him hither (1.23.14) in their chariot (2.40.3) and while they ascend on the way of the gods, the Vipra prays: 'And may he with the Soma-drops driving forward for me [...] plough as it were a grain-field with oxen' (1.23.15). In the chariot are Pusan and Soma, the Treasure found, the elixir of life, sparkling with its drops, ready for work, arising to fertilize the field of the Vipra. The chariot is drawn by the 'six yoked together,' by the pairs of draught-animal which are the months of the year when viewed as positions of the Sun [...] He sprinkles[the *soma* drops] on the yielding ground. Pusan sows, as it were, the seed of the field while his draught-animals, which are the months, are ploughing like oxen [...] The herdsman of creation is the ploughman of the field of the mind which he illumines and inseminates with the scintillating drops of Soma, the Treasure and Elixir of Life" (Kramrisch, "Pusan," 111).

147   Cf: "Pushan is the only god who receives the epithet *pasupa*, 'protector of cattle' (6.58.2) directly (and not in comparisons)" (Arthur A. Macdonell, *Vedic Mythology*, 37).

Britain […] Second, Gwydion son of Dôn, who kept the cattle of the tribe of North Wales above the Conway, and in that herd were 21,000" (*Trioedd Ynys Prydain*).

Now Cian, the Irish parallel of Gwydion (because these two are the father figures of Lugh/Lleu who transform into specific animals), has a myth closely matching that just outlined. Cian is the shepherd god who loses the mystical cow and then goes to retrieve it. While this myth is gathered from several variant folktales, such traditions have deep roots, and these variants agree on most of the core elements of the story, implying an ancient tradition, which is well vindicated if verified by comparative analysis. In Lady Gregory's version as found in *Gods and Fighting Men,* "The Coming of Lugh," we have: First, Cian is tasked with watching the wondrous cow Glas Gaibhnenn as its shepherd. The cow, however, is taken captive by Balar. Cian then must go to Balar's fortress to attempt to retrieve it. As we can see in various versions, at the fortress he seeks work as a gardener and finally sneaks into the chamber of the daughter of Balar. He woos her and lies with her. Soon she helps him obtain the cow and also gives birth to his sons, all of whom are drowned but one. Cian returns with the cow and in some versions with the infant.

This tale is closely paralleled in many precise details by a myth belonging to the Norse god Óðinn. In this myth (*Havamal,* 101-108; *Skaldskaparmal*, I), Óðinn goes to retrieve the Mead of Poetry (paralleling the retrieval of the lost cow) at the fortress of Suttungr, infiltrates the fortress, romances and sleeps with the giant's daughter, and makes off successfully with the mead, the giant's daughter being the one who helps him obtain the mead. We have noted elsewhere ("The Case for Tyr = Mitra") Thor Ewing's essay "Óðinn and Loki Among the Celts," in which he explains the features shared between the myths of Óðinn and Cian and Gwydion. Beyond those parallels just mentioned, Ewing mentions that wages that are promised are not paid by Baugi as wages that are promised are not paid by Balar, and while Cian follows a wandering cow, Gwydion in the Welsh myth, at one point, follows a wandering sow.

As we have seen that the mead is the Norse name for the *soma*, and if we accept this myth as a match of the Irish one, then it lends great support to both the general scholarly supposition that the king who Pushan finds, like a lost animal, is Soma, and that in the same way the cow Glas Gaibhnenn, lost by Cian and then sought after, *is* also Soma (like Norse Kvasir, the god who embodies the liquid). The Greek Soma God Dionysus is often found in bull form, and it would be understandable for the god to also manifest as a cow given the milk-producing power of that animal, sacred milk being an easy analog for the sacred liquid. The god Soma is throughout the *Rig Veda* frequently depicted as a bull, and the extraction of the *soma* juice is sometimes described with the verb *duh*, "to milk" (RV 3.36.7), while the shoots are described as giving milk like the udders of cows (RV

8.1.17; 2.36.1; 6.40.2; 9.86.2). A spring of *soma* is said to be set within the heavenly cows in RV 6.44.24, and *soma* is the milk of heaven in RV 9.51.2 and other verses.

Additionally, and crucially, in the *Havamal*, Óðinn uses an auger drill in this mission to drill his way into Suttungr's mountain fortress to steal the mead. True, in the version of the tale found in Snorri's prose *Skaldskaparmal* a second figure, Baugi, appears and does the drilling. However, scholars such as John Lindow (Lindow, John, *Norse Mythology: A Guide to Gods, Heroes, Rituals, and Beliefs,* 72) believe that this figure was likely an invention of Snorri based either on wordplay or, less likely, misreading of the *Havamal*, and that Óðinn was alone in the drilling in the original form of the myth, as we see in the earlier *Havamal* version[148]. As the *Havamal* passage states, describing the auger named Rati:

> Rati had gnawed a narrow passage,
>
> Chewed a channel through stone,
>
> A path around the roads of giants:
>
> I was like to lose my head
>
> Gunnlod sat me in the golden seat,
>
> Poured me precious mead. (*Havamal*, 103)

But even in Snorri's version, the auger that Baugi uses to drill belongs to Óðinn, and Óðinn hands it to Baugi and instructs him to drill. Thus we can say that this auger is Óðinn's. Now, Pushan in the *Rig Veda* is well-known to have his own "awl," a similar implement with which he drills penetrating holes. He is the only Vedic god described as having such a drilling tool, and it is one of his primary tools or weapons in the Vedas.

> Penetrate with an awl, O Sage, the hearts of avaricious churls,
>
> And make them subject to our will.
>
> Thrust with thine awl, O Pūṣan: seek that which the niggard's heart holds dear,
>
> And make him subject to our will.

---

148   "The major problem with Baugi is his absence outside Snorri, especially from Havamal, which Snorri seems to be paraphrasing in most of the story of the acquisition of the mead of poetry. A. G. van Hamel argued that Snorri found Baugi in another source (indeed, that Odin obtained the mead from Baugi) and that the version we have in Skáldskaparmál is thus an artful blending of the two sources. Others have argued that Snorri invented Baugi, and Aage Kabell thought he knew why: because he misunderstood stanza 110 of Hávamál" (John Lindow, *Norse Mythology: A Guide to Gods, Heroes, Rituals, and Beliefs*, 72-73).

Thou, glowing Pūṣan, carriest an awl that urges men to prayer;

Therewith do thou tear up and rend to shreds the heart of every one. (RV 6.53)

By this series of connections we can strongly support the proposition that Cian and Óðinn's myth is the Pushan myth just as it is mentioned in the *Rig Veda,* and that the lost cow and lost king Soma are simply being used interchangeably here in the two versions, while the auger *Rati* and the awl of Pushan are one and the same, an archaic clue left to us confirming from one direction what the Irish myth suggests from the other. Perhaps coincidentally, *Rati* may have the meaning of "traveler," while Pushan is himself the tutelary god of travelers, protecting and guiding them on dangerous journeys.

Interestingly, a version of Cian's myth ("The Gloss Gavlen," told by John McGinty, William Larminie, *West Irish Folk Tales and Romances,* 1) relates how the Irish Fire God Manannan conveys Cian to and from the island of Balar to retrieve the cow, either by magical boat or by plain magic[149]. Meanwhile, Óðinn transforming into eagle form upon retrieving the Mead of Poetry has been argued to be a myth belonging to the god Agni, or the Vedic fire god, as Agni in the form of the falcon Shyena retrieves the sacred liquid in one Vedic version of the myth ("Soma-Kvasir, The Eddic-Vedic Myth of the Meath of Poetry," Curwen Rolinson). "The Falcon rent [Soma] from the mountain," says the *Rig Veda* (RV 1.93.6). Agni is also called the eagle of the sky (RV 7.15.1) and a divine bird (RV 1.164.52). In *Culhwch and Olwen,* seen as a Welsh legendary parallel of this myth, a figure named Menw appears to be the legendary version of Manawydan/Manannan. He has the power of invisibility and shapeshifting, directly reminiscent of Manannan, and is the advisor of Culhwch (Gwydion/Cian). While Manannan helps convey Cian from and possibly to Balor's island, Menw is Culhwch's

---

149   In another version, "Balor on Tory Island," the man who helps Cian (here called Fin mac Kinealy) to sail to Tory Island and infiltrate the fortress is named *Gial Duv,* "Black Jaw." This name is too vague to draw any real conclusions from. However, the Fire God could be pictured as having a black jaw from the soot and the burning material he consumes. Agni is said to have "sharp" (RV 8.49.3) and "burning" jaws (RV1.58) or iron grinders (RV 10.87.2), and the rims of his wheels and the track of he and his steeds are described as black (1.141.7; 2.4.6-7; 6.6.1; 7.8.2; 8.23.19; 1.140.4). Manannan is also said to be black of limb and to have a black shield in *The Pursuit of Gilla Decair.*
In the variant utilized by Lady Gregory, the figure who helps Cian transport to Balor's Island is the female druid Birog. Cian consults Birog, she has him dress as a woman, and then magically transports them both to the island, where they gain entry and access to Eithne's chamber in this disguise. As we possibly see in the case of Odinn and Rindr, where Odinn disguises himself as a medicine woman and uses magical runes to enchant and rape Rindr, the Pushanic type may be connected to such "female" types of magic.

magical assistant who spies on the Twrch Trwyth, the boar they must hunt in order to win Olwen. Menw spies on the boar specifically in the form of a bird, and thus this bird-transformation is in an analogous place in the quest myth to the bird-transformation of the Norse and Vedic branches. Although its function is significantly different here, the bird-transformation still is a key event that helps the quester retrieve the boar (as opposed to the cow of the Irish form) which leads to access to the princess. Menw is poisoned in his espionage mission when he tries to steal one of the needed items from the boar, and is said to be never without injury thereafter, which detail has a curious echo of the permanent lameness of Greek Fire God Hephaestus. Thus, although Óðinn combines both the Pushanic and Agni aspects in himself and they are divided into separate gods in Irish myth, this may yet be another remnant of a shared archaic pattern, both Agni and Pushan involved in the retrieval of the sacred liquid, Agni specifically in charge of the conveyance to and from, fitting his character as the conveyor *par excellence* – of the sacrifice (indeed of the offered *soma*) to the gods and of the gods' blessings to the sacrificer, among other things, and Pushan as the one who drills into hidden places and finds what has been kept there.[150]

Furthermore, it is the Vedic craftsman god Tvastr who is the keeper of the *soma* in the Vedic version of this myth, it being called "the mead of Tvastr" in Macdonell's translation of *RV* 1.117.22[151], and he having fashioned its cup. Not only is the Irish smith Goibniu the giver of the feast at which the ale of immortality is served, "the Feast of Goibniu," but he is also the original owner of the cow Glas Gaibhnenn, which is debatably named for him, and is the one who asks Cian to tend it. Thus the milk of Goibniu's cow seems to transform somehow into Goibniu's immortalizing drink, the milk of the cow and the ale being two versions of essentially the same sacred liquid (Not impossible even that some mixture was used in earliest times: as P.B. Chakrabarty says of the admittedly distant Iranic *haoma,* "The juice was frequently mixed with water, milk or sour milk and then poured back and forth into different barrels to cause fermentation to prepare an alcoholic drink"; the milk used in preparation of the *soma* is also frequently mentioned in the Vedic hymns, and it may be that milk was an important ingredient for these pastoral people going back to the time of unity. This is not necessary either, as the milk of the wondrous cow could simply be a symbol for the sacred liquid). And just as this liquid is kept by the craftsman god in Vedic myth, so it is in Irish. Other specific details identify Goibniu with Tvastr, such as the fact that Tvastr and Goibniu both make the great weapons of the highest gods, and Tvastr sharpens the weapons of

---

150   See also: "The theft of the gods' food (in the Germanic case, Mead; in the Indic case, Soma), especially by a bird, is its own PIE, even international, motif. See Sterken (2018) and Horrell (2003: ch. 3)" (Dodge, "Orpheus, Odin, and the Indo-European Underworld," 23)

151   Arthur A. Macdonell, *Vedic Mythology*, 116.

the gods while Goibniu repairs and remakes them during the Second Battle of Maige Tuired. Thus again we have the same set of gods in the Irish myth as in the Vedic: the Pushanic God, the Fire God, the Craftsman/Smith, and the god manifested by the sacred liquid, the Irish cow or Norse Kvasir producing that liquid from within their bodies (Dionysus-Zagreus, who is dismembered in bull form, being the Greek analogue of these). The daughter of Balar and consort of Cian, Ethniu, must then be understood as a cognate of the Vedic Saraswati-Vac, who plays a comparable role in the Vedic myth. This idea gains great support from the fact that, in a variant version of the "birth of Aengus" episode in *Wooing of Etain,* Ethniu/Eithne plays the same role usually taken by the goddess of the Boyne river, Boann, that is, as the wife of Elcmar who is seduced by the Dagda. As the text states outright: "Elcmar of the Brug had a wife whose name was Eithne and another name for her was Boand" (*The Wooing of Etain*, I). Ethniu/Eithne is simply a doublet name of this great river goddess, and this is further supported by the comparative parallel.

The identification of Eithne/Ethniu as Boann/Saraswati is supported by the Welsh legendary parallel of the Cian-Ethniu myth: *Culhwch and Olwen.* Culhwch is the wooer of Olwen, the daughter of the one-eyed giant Ysbaddaden. We have previously noted that Welsh Cerridwen is the likely parallel of Irish Boann, *Cerridwen* meaning something like "crooked white," and *Boann* meaning "white cow," while her river, the Boyne, is understood as identical with the great white celestial stream, the Milky Way. Meanwhile, *Olwen* has the same ending as Cerridwen: -*wen,* meaning "white." *Olwen* means something like "white track," a perfect name for a white river and for the Milky Way in particular. The Milky Way in Welsh myth and folk tradition is given the name the Castle of Gwydion, *Caer Wydion*[152], and so it only makes sense that Gwydion's legendary incarnation, Culhwhch, would wed the Milky Way goddess. *Culhwch* on the other hand, means something like "slim swine," and is connected to an Irish name relating to humanoid pigs. Will Parker says that *Culhwch* is "a parallel formation to the Irish *Caelchéis* (lit. 'slim swine'), who appears as one of a group of humanoid pigs to appear the Irish *Dindsenchas* (MD vol.3 pp.386-395, 404-407, 552; see also Ní Catháin, 1979/80, p.202). Alternatively, the name may have derived from a gloss on the North European substrate form form *keulV-* (c.f. Lithuanean *kiaule* 'pig' etc.), as suggested by E P Hamp ('Culhwch, the Swine' *Zeitschrift für Celtische Philologie* 41 (1986) pp. 257-258)" (Will Parker, *Culhwch and Olwen, A Translation of the Oldest Arthurian Tale. http://www.culhwch.info/*). Gwydion steals the swine of Annwn from Pryderi and victoriously brings them back to his lands and is turned into a swine as part of his

---

152   *Caer Wydion,* The Milky Way, is seen as one of the paths taken by the dead journeying to the Otherworld, which matches the idea of Pushan as a psychopomp who leads souls of the dead up the far path. See: Rhŷs 1901: 645.

punishment from Math, and Cian himself turns into a pig just before being killed. As we will see, another Welsh legendary derivative of this mythos, Merlin, talks to pigs. Thus a name relating to swine marks Culhwch as associated with one of the signature animals of the Celtic "Pushanic" mythos.

A second key item in our comparison is found in the relationship between Gwydion and his sister Arianrhod[153]. In the myth of Lleu's birth found in the *Mabinogion*, it is left unspoken who Lleu's father is. Yet Gwydion takes Lleu and raises him, and when Gwydion returns to Arianrhod later, she is angry to see him. Scholars have proposed that Gwydion is the father of Lleu, and that he is thus the incestuous lover of his sister, but that the tale is vague regarding the details of their taboo relationship. The suggestion has even been made that in an earlier version of the myth, Gwydion was explicitly Lleu's father and his sister Arianrhod's lover (MacKillop, *Oxford Dictionary of Celtic Mythology*, 24)[154]. When we look at Vedic Pushan we see that he is known as the god who is the lover of his own sister. Indeed, this attribute sticks to him and is commonly referenced in his Rig Vedic hymns. In hymn 55 of book 6, for example, he is called both "he who loves his sister" and "his sister's lover" (RV, 6.55), this sister being the Sun Princess, Surya, as hymn 10.85 on "Surya's Bridal" also mentions Pushan in this capacity. Thus Pushan, like Gwydion seems to be, is the god who is famous as the lover of his sister (though not the only god with this trait, of course), while on the other side his Irish parallel Cian is the retriever of the sacred (*soma*)-cow, as Pushan is.

Pushan is a nourisher[155] and protector[156], and it is after all Gwydion who raises and nourishes the sovereign god Lleu, depicted at length in this role of teacher and provider,

---

153   As Gwydion is Pushan, Arianrhod may be the parallel of Pushan's sister-bride, who is again the many-husbanded Sun Princess, Surya, in RV 10.85. If Arianrhod is not the female Surya, then she would likely be a parallel of Cian's consort, Ethniu-Boand, who in Welsh myth is also named Cerridwen. Being a member of the "sun"-associated House of Don, however, Arianrhod seems more likely to be the solar goddess, and her father Beli Mawr appears to be a Sun God like Vedic Vivasvat or Aditya, making Arianrhod another possible Daughter of the Sun.

154   Gael Hily supports this position, pointing, among other things, to one tradition that describes a "Huan," who bears the same death story as Lleu, as the son of Gwydion [translated]: "another version of the history of Math, copied around 1600 by J. Jones of Gellilyfdy and kept in MS Peniarth 112: 'Huan ap Dôn's wife (= ap Gwydion) took part in the plot to kill her husband, and she claimed that he had gone hunting. And his father, Gwydion, the king of Gwynedd, traveled all the countries to find him, and in the end he built Caer Gwydion, that is, the Milky Way, which is in the sky, in order to find him.' We can certainly criticize the value of this text, which gives Gwydion as Lord of Gwynedd, when he never will be. Huan seems in any case to be another appellation of Lleu, who is specifically the son of Gwydion" (Hily, *Le Dieu Celtique Lugus*, 162)

155   "May Pusan further our every prayer./By the lord of the field/As by a friend may

also bringing Lleu back from symbolic death on the tree. While Gwydion is shown as a wise and very wily magician, Pushan is said to be a "seer," "all-seeing," "wise," as well as "wonder-working" (RV 1.42.5; RV 6.56.4) in the *Rig Veda* and was worshipped by magicians and conjurers (Danielou, 124). "All magic powers thou aidest," says RV 6.58.1, addressing Pushan. Pushan is also a psychopomp due to his association with the steep solar path of the fathers, on which he climbs and guides souls to the divine realm, which adds to his general mystic character. In this connection, Pushan is said to be born on the distant path (RV 10.17.6), while Cian's name is believed to mean "distant" or "enduring/ancient one." It is Pushan's frequenting of the steep far path that necessitates the feet of the goat for his cart, which seem to become Pan's own goat feet in the Greek case. Pushan is furthermore said to be "born of old" (RV 10.26.8), possibly matching the second suggested meaning of Cian's name, "ancient/enduring."

Incidentally, Thor, son of Óðinn, has this Pushanic cart, that cart which is memorably pulled by goats. As Thor shows little else to connect him to Pushan, we can see that this cart was a gift from his father. Perhaps Óðinn deemed that the goat-driven cart was not dignified enough for the Allfather and would suit his son better.

Gwydion, like Pan and Pushan, is associated with music and bardic skill. Pan is known for his rustic pipes and for being a lord of music, being called "melodious Pan" (Nonnus, *Dionysiaca*, 45.174), "adornment of golden choruses" who "pours forth the god-inspired song" (*Greek Lyric V Anonymous Fragment* 936), and Pushan is said to be "quickening poetic vision" (RV 6.58.1-2). Gwydion is also both a singer and poet: he sings the famous *engelyn* that coaxes Lleu down from the mystical tree when he has been wounded in the climactic moment of "Math fab Mathonwy," and he goes in the guise of a bard to get the Swine of Annwn from Pryderi, calling himself "the chief of song," and the narrator stating that "Gwydion was the best teller of tales in the world" (*Math fab Mathonwy*).

Even Pan's lecherous pursuit of the extremely chaste nymph Echo (*Homeric Hym 19 to Pan*) has a resonance with the tale of Gwydion helping his brother to rape the ritually pure virgin Goewin. Echo is not raped, but Pan causes her to be torn to pieces instead by driving the shepherds mad. Both gods are thus associated with lechery and the violation of virgins. We have to wonder if the theme of the rape of Rindr by Óðinn (in Saxo Grammaticus' *Gesta Danorum*) could be a remnant of the Pushanic myth, Óðinn even causing Rindr to go mad with runes while dressed as a medicine woman as Pan incites

---

we win/What nourishes our kine and horses;/May he be [2] favourable to such as we are./O lord of the field, the honey-bearing wave,/As a cow milk, so for us milk" (*Yajur Veda Taittiriyra Samhita*, i.1.14.f-h).

156   "Guard of the world" (RV 10.17.3).

panic and terror, and being said to "enchant" her (Kormakr Ogmundarson, *Sigurdardrapa*, 3) as the Pushanic god is specifically a seer-magician. Cian may also be connected to a female kind of sorcery, consulting a Druidess Birog and then by her guidance, and alongside her female magic, dressing as a woman to gain admittance to the fortress and Ethlinn's chamber (*Gods and Fighting Men,* "The Coming of Lugh," 20).

One final speculative parallel has to be hazarded here. We will say in passing, without a long argument, that while superficial analyses of Zeus almost always compare him to Vedic Dyaus or Indra, Father Sky and Thunderer, when we attempt to strip back the alteration and syncretism, though these aforementioned parallels still make some sense (Zeus' battle with Typhon parallels an Indraic myth in the *Rig Veda*, though it may only have been attached to Indra during the development of Indo-Iranian religion[157], and many of Zeus' familial relations, such as being father of the Horse Twins, Fire God and Dawn-incarnation Helen, do reflect those of Dyaus), Zeus actually comes to appear to have much in common with Vedic Mitra, and so with the Irish Mitra, Lugh. Zeus is not the withdrawn sky itself, as Dyaus is – that is rather Ouranos. Considering the adoption of Near Eastern myth forms in relation to Zeus by poets such as Hesiod (see the Kumarbi Cycle cited previously), and the prominence of thunder-wielding gods in the region, the centrality of Zeus' thunder attribute could even have been partially a Near Eastern influence. At the same time, the Mitraic-type deity actually possesses the lightning occasionally, especially if we look at Iranic, Roman and Celtic cases (Mithra with his *vazra*, possibly Dius Fidius with his *fulmen* if we follow Dumezil, and Lugh with his lightning spear). Meanwhile, the slaying of Typhon may instead be a "Verethregna*"* (destroyer of Vrtra) myth at its root, rather than strictly tied to Indra, as Shaw explains[158],

---

157   "Renou (116, 192) has concluded that the Vedic evidence provides no reason to doubt that Vrtrahan was originally distinct from Indra, as the Iranian evidence also suggests" (John Shaw, "Indo-European Dragon-Slayers and Healers, and the Account of Dian Cecht and Meiche," 155). As Roger Woodard comments: "Comparing the birth narrative of Vahagn, preserved by the Armenian historian Moses of Chorene, with the Brahmanic account of the rebirth of Indra following his defeat of Vṛtra, Dumézil can argue that the common linguistic antecedent of Vedic Vṛtrahan and Avestan Vərəθrayna was a denotation applied already to Proto-Indo-Iranian Indra (see especially pp. 117, 128–129). Even so, there is good reason to suspect that the monster Vṛtra has acquired his name derivatively from the epithet of his slayer (see Watkins 1995: 298, 304, with references to Benveniste and Renou 1934)" (Woodard, Indo-European Sacred Space, 194).

158   According to Kershaw, in the Iranic *Avesta*, Mithra, "'the supreme god of the brotherhoods,' is himself the dragon-killer. Indra, with the other *daevas*, became a demon in Iran, while Vrtragan, as the god Varathrayna, appears in close association with Mithra; he evolves from companion to satellite, and finally becomes an attribute of Mithra; and Mithra becomes varathragan" (Kershaw, *The One-Eyed God*, 308).

citing Dumezil and others. We can see that this Verethregna became a title of Indra in Vedic religion, but that in Iranic hymns he is tied closely instead to Mitra, and so his serpent slaying could even have been retained by the Mitraic god in some western branches. It is difficult to say if some of the specifically Mitraic mythos could even have been taken over by Indra as he rose to prominence in Vedic society, considering the seemingly diminished role of Mitra in the Vedas. Dumezil noted most of these things and himself (tentatively) pointed toward Zeus as his guess of where the Greek Mitraic god was to be found, while also stating that the Greek mythology is so overwhelmed by non-Indo-European, Aegean influence, that it is difficult to distinguish which "shreds" are genuinely Indo-European (Dumezil, *Mitra-Varuna*, 119). The power of the Zeus of the *Iliad* does not reach to the night sky, while Mitra is the sovereign of the day sky. Thus Zeus' overthrowing of Cronus could in its essential features match Lugh's slaying of Balor to bring about peace and order at last. Both Zeus and Lugh are also quintessential late-coming gods when they accomplish these feats. The late occurrence of Zeus' birth and war certainly fits more with the Mitraic archetype than with the Father Sky one, as it is hard to imagine Dyaus, Father Sky, being born after so many other gods, after even Pan. Indeed it is difficult to deny some overlap between Lugh and Zeus, though in certain aspects Zeus does also parallel Dagda, namely in their shared Father Sky roles including the identities of some of their children.

Thus, if we do take Zeus' confrontation with Cronus as similar to Lugh's with Balor, the Zeus case would be as if Balor was Lugh's father rather than grandfather, both Cronus and Balor being prophesied to be overthrown by their nearest male descendant, whether son or grandson. In the Greek case, the Pushanic god would seem to be absent from the high god's parentage. Yet Pan actually does play a very important role in relation to Zeus' birth, and this is yet another clue that supports our Celtic and Greek parallel, buried under many centuries of changes. Pan is said to be the shepherd of the goat Amaltheia that nurses Zeus when he is taken and hidden after his birth, just as Gwydion is described as finding a woman who will nurse Lleu and giving him to her after his birth, before becoming his teacher once he is nursed (both Zeus and Lugh have to be hidden away upon their birth as well). In Nonnus' account, Zeus says, "goatfoot Pan [...] once was mountain-ranging shepherd of the goat Amaltheia, my nurse" (*Dionysiaca*, 27.290); while the *Mabinogi* of *Math fab Mathonwy* says, "And [Gwydion] took up the boy in his arms, and carried him to a place where he knew there was a woman that could nurse him. And he agreed with the woman that she should take charge of the boy. And that year he was nursed" (*Math fab Mathonwy*).[159][160] In fact, several

---

159   "Fin mac Kinealy," a folktale version of Cian, helps his son "Lu" be nursed in
       "Balor on Tory Island." The tale says that he "gave the child to Balor's daughter before
       her father could come near her; she gave him to one of the women, and he was passed on

versions of the Greek myth state that Zeus' nurse was actually a nymph and not a goat at all.[161] But furthermore, Pan is known from the poetry of Pindar as the "companion" of Zeus' mother Rhea[162]. Gwydion of course, as we have said, was brother of Lleu's mother and was also likely her lover. Meanwhile, as we have also noted previously, Cian is the son of the Irish Apollo, Dian Cecht, while Pindar and Hecataeus of Miletus also claim that Pan is the son of Apollo, potentially bringing the Irish and Greek traditions well into alignment on this point.

If Cian indeed parallels Óðinn in as precise a manner as we have suggested, then another avenue for speculation opens itself to us, which we have pointed to in an earlier chapter, but will reiterate here for the sake of clarity. There remains a meaningful confusion about who the true father of the Norse Tyr is. The *Poetic Edda* poem *Hymiskviða,* stanza 5, calls him the son of the jotunn Hymir, while *Skaldskaparmal* instead names him a son of Óðinn, and even does so in the context of saying that "Son of Odin" is a skaldic kenning or paraphrase for Tyr (*Skaldskaparmal*, IX). We can see in the case of Cian that he fathers Lugh, cognate of Tyr, on the daughter of the Fomorian Balar, Fomorians being cognate to Jotnar. Lugh then is sent to be fostered by various figures, including Tailtiu, Goibniu and Manannan, depending on the source, and Welsh Lleu is also given to another woman to be nursed. One resolution to the disagreement regarding Tyr's father could be the possibility that Tyr was only a foster son of Hymir, but a true son of Óðinn. Óðinn then could have fathered Tyr on Gunnloð (who he does indeed lie with), daughter of the jotunn Suttungr, when he stole back the mead, as Cian fathered Lugh on Ethniu, daughter of the Fomorian Balar, when he stole back the wondrous cow. Óðinn could either have abandoned Gunnloð with the infant Tyr, forcing

---

till all twelve had had him. It was found that all had milk, and Balor consented to let the child be nursed" (Jeremiah Curtin, *Hero-Tales of Ireland*).

160   In the Persian *Shahnameh,* to protect the infant future-hero Feredun from Zahak, a parallel of Balor, the boy is given to a cowherd for nursing. This cowherd has a wondrous cow known for its fantastic colors, which helps to raise and nurse Feredun. Zahak is prophesied to be killed by Feredun and it is said that Zahak will have killed the beloved prized cow and the father of Feredun. Zal, the father of a later hero in the epic, Rostam, also resembles Lugh/Lleu's fathers Cian/Gwydion. Zal must first visit his lover Rudabeh by sneaking up a rope into her chamber. He is known for his great learning and is taught divination among other things. Particularly notable in relation to the Pushanic god, Zal is raised in the wild among birds and is able even to talk to the birds that raised him and to call upon them in a time of need.

161   Schol. *ad Hom. Il.* 21.194; Eratosth. *Catast.* 13; Apollod. 2.7.5; Lactant. *Instit.* 1.22; Hygin. *l.c.,* and *Fab.* 139, where he calls the nymph Adamanteia. See: *A Dictionary of Greek and Roman biography and mythology,* William Smith, Ed.

162   Pindar, *Maiden Songs Fragment 95 (trans. Sandys):* "O Pan, that rulest over Arkadia (Arcadia), and art the warder of holy shrines . . . thou companion of the Great Mother [Rhea-Kybele], thou dear delight of the holy Kharites (Charites)!"

her to have the child raised by another jotunn, Hymir, or himself could have sent Tyr to be raised by Hymir, as Lugh is given to another to be raised. Hróðr, called Tyr or Thor's mother in *Hymiskvida* 8 (much more likely Tyr's considering they are visiting Hymir in this myth), then could actually be his foster mother (if not another name for Gunnloð – this Hróðr, after all, is here depicted serving drink). This is the interpretation that would bring the Irish and Norse cases into the closest alignment while also explaining the discrepancy within the Norse texts. However, there is of course no reason why the Norse would have to match the Irish pattern here, these exact details are not attested, and we mark this only as a suggestive possibility.

Gwydion: Prototype of Merlin

All of this points to a very interesting upshot in the legendary figure of Merlin, the Arthurian archetypal magician. Gwydion is the most obvious Welsh divine forerunner of the Welsh Merlin. Gwydion is a wily magician who raises, teaches, advises, helps and rescues Lleu, as Merlin advises and aids Arthur. Merlin even helps Uther conceive Arthur via his magical illusions, while Gwydion seems to have been more directly involved in the conception of Lleu. Gwydion, as we have said, is probably Lleu's true father but acts like a foster father since the details are left ambiguous (perhaps the incest subtext had become too taboo to state outright), while Merlin's advisory role positions him like a second father to Arthur in the absence of Uther. Gregory Wright points to the fact that Gwydion resembles Merlin when he uses "trickery to allow his brother to lay with a woman" as Merlin does for Uther Pendragon with Igraine, "and in being able to change forms, albeit sometimes against his will."[163] Lleu is the forerunner and divine model of Arthur in many specific ways, as will be discussed in a subsequent chapter, and Gwydion has the same kind of relationship to Lleu that Merlin has to Arthur. In all, Merlin/Arthur is a clear repetition of Gwydion/Lleu on the legendary plane.

Gwydion, as we have mentioned, has all kinds of magical abilities, and uses magic the most of any figure in the *Mabinogion*. Commentators have often compared him to Óðinn and he is the most obvious "Welsh Óðinn" to be found in the myths. Even his name (G)wydion (the hard *g* only being a late addition to Welsh[164]) has a resemblance to the

---

163   Gregory Wright, *Mythopedia*, "Gwydion", Mythopedia.com.
164   "Brythonic speakers appear to have commonly rendered Germanic 'w-' as 'g-'; the *Historia Brittonum* for example (which is found in the same manuscript as the genealogy – Harleian MS 3859) records 'Giulgis' for 'Uilgils,' and 'Gechbrond' for 'Wegbrand' (Thor Ewing, "The Birth of Lugh – Óðinn and Loki Among the Celts," Introduction).

name Wodan and some have attempted to connect the two names. While it is hard to directly tie them, it is possible there is some resonance there. *Wyd-/Uid-* comes from a root meaning "to see" (*weyd-*) while Wodan comes from a seemingly separate but similar PIE root meaning "excited" and "seer" (*wéh₂t-i-s* ("seer")) which is the root of the name for seers in certain linguistic branches: Latin *vates*, Irish *faith*, and as such Odinn's name is linguistically connected to the name of Fionn/Gwyn rather than to that of Gwydion. Thor Ewing adds that close contact between the Welsh and Germanic peoples could have reinforced the parallel between Gwydion and Óðinn, stating, "It is highly unlikely that the names Guidgen and Óðinn are etymologically related in a conventional sense, though it remains possible that their similarity is a result of continued cultural contact. Brythonic speakers appear to have commonly rendered Germanic 'w-' as 'g-'" (Ewing, "The Birth of Lugh – Óðinn and Loki among the Celts," Preface).

Now, as we have said, Pushan is called "wise," "wonder-working," and "a seer" in the *Rig Veda* and was prayed to by magicians and conjurers. These epithets may seem relatively common on their own, but the direct association with magicians and conjurers is not something you often read in Vedic commentaries. One hymn of the *Veda* addresses him saying, "you give aid to all magical powers" and describes him as "quickening poetic vision" (RV 6.58.1-2). Greek Pan was also seen as a major prophetic god, so closely tied to this art that he is said to have been the one who taught it to Apollo, who then became its Greek exemplar: "Apollon learnt the mantic art from Pan" (Pseudo-Apollodorus, *Bibliotheca* 1.22). Once again, Gwydion, too, is an exemplar of this power in his branch, listed as one of the three great prognosticators of Britain in the Triads: "The three renowned astronomers of the Isle of Britain: Idris the giant; Gwydion son of Dôn; and Gwyn son of Nudd. Such was their knowledge of the stars, their natures and qualities, that they could prognosticate whatever was wished to be known until the day of doom" (*Trioedd Ynys Prydein*). The Gwyn who is also mentioned here is of course the parallel of Apollo in his Rudraic aspect, and thus we have again the same two exemplars of prophecy in Welsh and Greek myth when we align them properly.

Meanwhile, the earliest stories and poems of Merlin, depict him as more emphatically a prophet than even a magician (see Paul Zumthor, "Merlin: Prophet and Magician"). In such stories and poems he is called "Myrddin Wyllt," that is, Merlin the Wild, and "Merlin Sylvestris," or Merlin of the Woods. These accounts paint him as a man who "goes wild" and goes off to live in the woods. In Geoffrey of Monmouth's version, he has a sort of mental break when his allies are killed in battle, and he goes to the woods to become a wild man. "He became a Man of the Woods, as if dedicated to the woods. So for a whole summer he stayed hidden in the woods, discovered by none, forgetful of himself and of his own, lurking like a wild thing" reads Monmouth's *Vita Merlini.* In the woods he learns how to speak to wild pigs and sings to apple trees and acquires the power of prophecy (remember that Pushan is specifically a "seer" and Pan a *mantic* expert). That is, he gains magical powers relating to communicating with plants and animals and seeing into the very web of nature after becoming a wild man. He returns to society as the specifically prophetic magician Merlin who delivers his prophecies to the king, a "seer" of the wilds just like Pushan, a wizard of the woods just like Uiducus/Gwydion, a mantic lord of nature like Pan.

Throughout the early Merlin literature he is associated with pigs or boars, stags and wolves, which are precisely the three animals Gwydion is transformed into when he is punished by Math. As Jean Markale summarizes in his essay "Master and Mediator of the Natural World": "In the Vita Merlini, he appears mounted on a stag, suggesting that he is a stag, and he is accompanied by a wolf, suggesting that he is a wolf" (also commenting that Óðinn similarly is seen to transform into "a wild beast, a fish or a dragon, and travels in the blink of an eye to far-away lands" in *Ynglinga Saga* VII). He further notes that in Chretien de Troye's *Chevalier au Lion*, and in the Welsh text *Owein*, a figure called The Wild Man appears, who takes the recurring role of Lord of the Beasts and who Markale claims is one of the "manifestations of Merlin." We are not as certain that The Wild Man is *always* Merlin or Pushanic generally, though it is possible, but Markale's examples are worth weighing nonetheless. Indeed, Markale points out that in the *Vulgate*, we are told that the Wild Man is Merlin himself, and he too leads wild animals and first appears as a hind. In Chretien's poem, the Wild Man states of these wild beasts: "But no one except me can go among them without being killed. I am lord of my beasts." In the version found in *Owein*, as Markale explains:

> Kynon, the person in question, asks the Wild Man 'what power he had over those animals.' The Wild Man takes his stick and strikes a hind. 'The hind bellows, and immediately animals as numerous as the stars in the sky come in response to his voice, to the extent that I had trouble keeping my footing amid them in the clearing. Also there were snakes, vipers, all sorts of animals. He glanced over them and ordered them to go graze. They lowered their heads and treated him with the same respect as humans show their lord.' The Welsh tale is more explicit in its roughness: the Wild Man, by his voice, and by the hind's voice, exercises total control over all the animals of the forest. (Peter Goodrich, Jean Markale, *Merlin A Casebook*, 407)

Markale also compares Merlin's magic to that of Gwydion, stating that "as Gwyddyon changed mushrooms into golden shields, Merlin transforms bushes and pebbles into a marvelous castle" (Markale, *Merlin A Casebook*, 406). And while Cian makes apple trees cover Balar's island grove, Merlin speaks and prophesies to apple trees in the wild in the stanzas known as "Yr Afallennau." Cian calls himself "the best gardener in the world" in the variant of the tale titled "Balor of the Evil Eye and Lui Lavada his Grandson," (Jeremiah Curtin, *Hero-Tales of Ireland,* 308) a possible remnant of a Pan-like power over the cultivation of nature. Pan is addressed as "O all-producing power, much famed, divine, the world's great ruler, rich increase is thine" and "All-fertile Paian," "in fruits rejoicing" (*Orphic Hymn 11 to Pan*).

Cian himself has a brother named Cu, meaning hound or wolf. Pan is known as "breeder of hounds" (Nonnus, *Dionysiaca*, 16.185) and "beast-tending Pan" (Castorion of Soli, *Fragment* 310). As Kevin Maclean points out, the brothers of Cian die of fright, and he suggests that this may be part of a larger pattern of deities dying of that with which they themselves are associated. We have to wonder if this could make Cian's brothers lords of "panic" as Pan is, connected to their wild natures, but the traces here are far too thin to say for certain. Pan accosts travelers with a "sudden awe or terror" (Euripides, *Rhes.* 36), and also uses this power to cause terror in the battles against the Titans (Eratosthenes, *Catast.* 27) and again against the Persians (Herodotus, vi. 105). "Causeless terrors" are attributed to Pan (Pausanius, *Description of Greece* 10.23.7). It is certainly interesting, then, that Cian's brothers die of fright in battle and that Merlin himself is stricken by a kind of "panic" when his allies are defeated in battle.

It is true that the figure of Merlin seems to have been assembled from various, not necessarily harmonious sources, pertaining to both legendary and historical figures, and thus he may contain in him elements from more than one original type. Stories of various unconnected prophets and sorcerers may have stuck to his name over time. However, the question we are asking must be asked in earnest: what was the organizing principle around which these various sources were assembled, what was the germ of and the guiding divine principle within the figure of Merlin? Was there not one main deeply-set track, with a greater gravity than the others, already existing in the folk-consciousness and literary tradition of the people of Britain, one mythic slot into which these elements were gathered by their learned compilers, as if magnetized into a unity? And despite his spontaneous and partially composite development is it not clear who the most significant divine contributor to, the ruling principle of, the character of Merlin is?

Essentially, what seems to have happened is that the Greeks turned the Pushanic god, in the form of Pan, into the goat-footed god of nature, while the Celts instead turned him into a specifically prophetic wizard who can communicate with and magically manipulate nature and can turn into animals as well, but the Wild Man element remained, if it is still less known to today's audience. Paul Zumthor, in his "Merlin: Prophet and Magician," better explains the unity of these ideas:

> This knowledge of which Merlin is a master [...] is an ideal of which the late
> Middle Ages dreamed, a perfect union and an image of the Absolute in the

knowledge and mastery of nature […] Merlin is thus the model of the perfect alchemist and astrologer, a model which Comparetti calls "il mago" (the magician). (Merlin, 143)

We have here followed a winding trail of clues as Cian followed the lost cow; at last we must draw a line that links: Pan, Uiducus, Gwydion, Cian, (aspect of) Óðinn, Merlin, Pushan.

12

Math fab Mathonwy, the Celtic Savitr-Prajapati, and Goewin, Goddess of Night

Despite Welsh Blodeuwedd being a striking parallel of Helen of Troy, her "Dawn"-related role is somewhat unclear in the existing texts, though she is, suggestively, made of flowers and turned into an owl, while Homer says that Dawn Goddess Eos' robes are woven with flowers and that she has the white wings of a bird. A larger theoretical framework of the tale *Math fab Mathonwy* must be developed, then, in order to see Blodeuwedd in her auroral position. Other than in her parallel with Helen, Blodeuwedd's auroral role can perhaps only be seen in relation to her creator, Math fab Mathonwy[165].

---

165   An Irish version of this name appears as Mathu in *O'Mulconry's Glossary*: The pagans had three "prophets": Mathu, Núada and Goibne. *Faithi fis la geinti.i. Mathu, Nuada, Goibnend."* Gael Hily points out two other Welsh instances outside of the *Mabinogi*: "The famous poet Dafydd ap Gwilym (14th century) gives in one of his compositions three names of magicians: Math, Menw and Eiddilig the Dwarf. The Book of Taliesin provides us with another testimony: Taliesin himself claims to have been

As such, a Vedic parallel myth will be given for the myth of Math and his cohort, which will then suggest his role as the creator of a goddess who must be closely related to, or identified with, the Dawn.

The parallel is sketched out as follows: Math "could not exist" without resting his feet upon the lap of the virgin goddess Goewin, as Vedic Savitr, god of the solar power at night and during sunrise and sunset, rests before rising with his virgin "household maiden" Ratri, or Night. It is said that Math cannot make the circuit of his lands while resting in the lap of Goewin, as the sun makes such a circuit during the day, but seems to leave off doing so at night. Math is the equivalent of Savitr and Goewin of Ratri.

While Goewin's virginity and close physical connection to Math are central, Ratri is "The lively woman, household maiden [ie. virgin], night, of god Savitar"[166] in the *Atharvaveda*. As Goewin's beauty inspires an overwhelming desire in Gilfaethwy that leads to his rape of her, Ratri is "desirable, welcome, well-portioned" and is asked, perhaps suggestively, "mayest thou be well-willing here"[167]. Savitr and Ratri are even placed side by side in the *Rig Veda,* balancing one another within the line of one hymn: "I call on Night, who gives rest to all moving life; I call on Savitr the God to lend us help"[168], and are habitually linked in other hymns: "Night closely followed Savitr's dominion"[169], "Around, on both sides thou encompassest the night"[170]. According to Arthur A. Macdonell, "Savitr is twice (1, 1233; 6, 714) even spoken of as 'domestic' (*damfinas),* an epithet otherwise almost entirely limited to Agni," which detail paints Savitr in a domestic existence with his domestic maiden Ratri who gives rest. Math rests while physically linked to his maiden Goewin in a manner similar to how the names of Savitr and Ratri are linked in the line of the hymn, and Goewin gives him this rest as Ratri gives all moving life rest. Math's rest then, is the same as the rest of Savitr, the Vedic sun deity at night, who also enacts the sunrise and sunset.

Practically everything that Math does in his narrative can be closely identified with descriptions of Vedic Savitr, to the point that the gods of the Welsh story seem almost to be acting out passages from the Vedas at times. It is said that Math can only remove his feet from the lap of his virgin footholder in order to go to war, and this time of war is

---

conceived by the magic of Math or by the magic wand of Mathonwy" (Hily, *Le Dieu Celtique Lugus,* 155) Remember that dwarves, one of whom is mentioned in the Welsh list, are smiths, as is Goibniu in Irish list. A wizard named Mathgen (son of Math?) also fights for the Tuatha De Danann in *Cath Maige Tuired* 78.

166   *Atharva Veda*, XIX.49
167   AV XIX.49.3
168   RV 1. XXXV.1.
169   RV XXXVIII, 3.
170   RV LXXXI.4.

then a metaphor for sunrise and daytime, a metaphor the Vedic hymns also use in the case of Savitr: "he putteth on his golden-coloured mail"[171]. After "Uprisen is Savitr, this God, to quicken"[172] we read "Savitr hath sped to meet his summons. He comes again, unfolded, fain for conquest"[173]. He is called "the Warrior"[174]. This analogy of day with war is further supported by the fact that the war which eventually calls Math away from Goewin is that with Pryderi, a "Horse Twin" god. Via parallels with the other Horse Twin gods, Pryderi can be classed as a deity of the morning star or first light of day, and thus the war that Math goes to, which action itself is the metaphysical enactment of the rising of the sun, is a war with another god appearing (from out of the lunar darkness in which his tale originates) at the break of day.

Savitr, like Math, is both a lord and a priestly-magical figure. Indeed Math's name is said in *O'Mulconry's Glossary* to have a meaning connected to "learn"[175]. Savitr is called a "Priest" who dutifully rises to "quicken" life[176], "the sapient Lord"[177], "the Sage"[178], "He only knowing"[179], "the sapient one"[180], "the thoughtful God"[181], "Full of effectual wisdom"[182]. Math is "lord" of Gwynedd, rather than king, and Savitr is "lord"[183] and also "asura"[184], another term for a divine lord, but is likewise not called king or sovereign in the *Rig Veda*.

---

171   RV LIII, 2.
172   RV XXXVIII.1.
173   RV XXXVIII.5.
174   RV LXXI.1.
175   *O'Mulconry* §665: "*Matha enim graece .i. disce interpretatur, unde dicitur.*" However, according to scholar Gael Hily, the most common hypothesis for the etymology derives Math from **matu-*, "bear" (Gael Hily, 153). Hily posits that this meaning could also connect with another etymology which relates *math* to a sense of "good, favorable": "Elle peut venir de **mati-* « bon, favorable », issu d'un radical **mā-*, qui désigne l'idée de ce qui est favorable, d'abord dans un sens mystique et religieux. Karl-Horst Schmidt a suggéré que **matu* a pu être traité comme un adjectif au sens de « bon, fortuné, propice, favorable ». Cette extension sémantique peut être due à une équivalence entre l'ours, un animal symbolisant la royauté (**matu-*), et le principe d'une application correcte de la royauté qui qu'exprime **mati-*" (Hily, 154).
176   RV. XXXV.11.
177   RV LIII.1.
178   RV LIII.2.
179   RV LXXXI.1.
180   RV LXXXI.2.
181   RV LXXXII.8.
182   RV LXXI, 1.
183   RV LIII.2; RV LXXXII.7.
184   RV XXXV.7, 10; RV LIII.1.

Math is a judge who passes unswerving judgements on Gwydion and Gilfaethwy for their violation of his law, sits as judge of Arianrhod's virginity, attempts to give compensation to Goewin for her rape, and advises Lleu on the matter of executing his own justice upon Gronw later on. Savitr is "ne'er to be deceived, Savitr, God," who "protects each holy ordinance," and "with his laws observed, rules his own mighty course"[185]. He "willingly protects us with his triple law"[186] and he is "like a God whose Law is constant"[187].

Of the irresistible justice of Savitr's it is said: "However they may fly and draw themselves apart, still, Savitr, they stand obeying thy behest"[188], while Gwydion and Gilfaethwy seem to act this very thing out, first attempting to flee Math's court after they have raped Goewin and then returning to accept their punishment from him when this becomes unsustainable:

> And Gwydion and Gilvaethwy came not near the Court, but stayed in the confines of the land until it was forbidden to give them meat and drink. At first they came not near unto Math, but at the last they came. 'Lord,' said they, 'Good day to thee.'
>
> 'Well,' said he, 'is it to make me compensation that ye are come?'
>
> 'Lord,' they said, 'we are at thy will.'[189]

Indeed, Savitr "hast domination over all this world"[190], and "None may impede that power of Savitr the God whereby he will maintain the universal world"[191]. As Gwydion and Gilfaethwy cannot resist Math's law, neither can the other great Vedic gods resist Savitr's law generally speaking: "These statutes of the God Savitr none disobeyeth. With utmost speed, in restless haste at sunset Varuna seeks his watery habitation./ Then seeks each bird his nest, each beast his lodging. In due place Savitr hath set each creature./ Him whose high law not Varuna nor Indra, not Mitra, Aryaman, nor Rudra breaketh,/ Nor evil-hearted fiends"[192]. Though Savitr exacts justice, this justice is fair and it absolves of sin: "If we, men as we are, have sinned against the Gods through want of thought, in weakness, or through insolence, Absolve us from the guilt and make us free from sin, O Savitr, alike among both Gods and men"[193]; "Sinless in sight of Aditi

---

185   RV LIII.4.
186   RV LIII.1.5.
187   RV CXXXIX.3.
188   RV LIV.5.
189   *Math fab Mathonwy.*
190   RV LXXXI.5.
191   RV LIV.4.
192   RV XXXVIII.5-9.
193   RV LIV.3.

through the God Savitr's influence"[194], which may comport with Math's seeming to absolve Gwydion after his punishment and then collaborating with him to create Blodeuwedd. Like Gwydion perhaps has after Math's commandment, "Each man hath come leaving his evil doings, after the Godlike Savitr's commandment"[195].

Connected with this power of judgment, Math is said to have the special property "that if men whisper together, in a tone how low soever, if the wind meet it, it becomes known unto him"[196]. Nothing so exactly specific can be ascribed to Savitr; however, various features of Savitr may, together, express the same general idea. As mentioned above, Savitr is "ne'er to be deceived" and called "he only knowing." Additionally it is said that "Even the waters bend them to his service: even the wind rests in the circling region"[197]. These powers are not perfectly identical, but it does not take much to see how one original concept could have developed into these two separate yet very similar expressions in descriptions of Savitr and Math over time. This god cannot be deceived and the wind and waters follow his bidding.

Math is a magician whose just magic gives rise to the life of three lineages of animals, via the enforced mating of Gwydion and his brother as punishment for the rape of Goewin – a deer, a wolf and a swine – and it is Math's magic that quickens the life also of the maiden Blodeuwedd, with Gwydion again acting in an assisting capacity. Savitr too is repeatedly connected to the role of giving life and place to animal life as well as to other kinds of beings. "The wild beasts spread through desert places seeking their watery share which thou hast set in waters […] Then seeks each bird his nest, each beast his lodging. In due place Savitr hath set each creature"[198]; "Lord of the whole world's life"[199]; "Savitr hath stretched out his arms to cherish life"[200]; "who brings to life and lulls to rest, he who controls the world"[201]; "thou openest existence, life succeeding life"[202]; "for quadruped and biped he hath brought forth good"[203]; "Full of effectual wisdom Savitr the God hath stretched out golden arms that he may bring forth life"[204]; "For thou art mighty to produce and lull to rest the world of life that moves on two feet and on four"[205];

---

194   RV LXXXII.6.
195   RV XXXVIII.5-9.
196   *Math fab Mathonwy.*
197   RV XXXVIII.2.
198   RV XXXVIII.5-9.
199   RV LIII.2.
200   RV LIII.3.
201   RV LIII.6.
202   RV LIV.2.
203   RV LXXXI.2.
204   RV LXXI.1.
205   RV LXXI.2.

"Like a Director, lulling to slumber and arousing creatures"[206]; "He who gives glory unto all these living creatures with the song, And brings them forth, is Savitr"[207].

The rape of Goewin, which is then the violation of Night by light, is facilitated by another god of the first light of morning, Gwydion, who is related to the first light by virtue of being the Welsh parallel of Vedic Pushan, as we have seen. Pushan, in a similar but distinct fashion to Savitr, is a god of the sun also instrumental in its rising. In her article "Pusan," Stella Kramrisch explains that Pushan is related to Savitr as material cause is related to efficient cause, but that they are both connected gods of the solar power, "sun gods"[208]. This relation is borne out by the relationship between Savitr and Gwydion and will be returned to. Math teaches Gwydion his charms and spells, according to the Welsh Triads: "Three Great Enchantments of the Island of Britain: The Enchantment of Math son of Mathonwy which he taught to Gwydion son of Dôn"; "The three illusive and half-apparent men of the Isle of Britain: Math son of Mathonwy, who showed his illusion to Gwydion son of Dôn" (Triad 90). On the other hand, Bromwich cautions that "it is possible that item (a) is no more than a deduction from the Mabinogi itself"[209]. Math also goes to war in alliance with Gwydion, while Savitr is said to speed to meet his summons, hungry for conquest, and that in all his goings forth he *is* Pushan, which is reflected in the combined power of Math and Gwydion in the war:

> And when they saw the day on the morrow, they went back unto the place where Math the son of Mathonwy was with his host; and when they came there, the warriors were taking counsel in what district they should await the coming of Pryderi, and the men of the South. So they went in to the council. And it was resolved to wait in the strongholds of Gwynedd, in Arvon. So within the two Maenors they took their stand, Maenor Penardd and Maenor Coed Alun. And there Pryderi attacked them, and there the combat took place[210].

As we have quoted already: "Savitr hath sped to meet his summons. He comes again, unfolded, fain for conquest"[211]; Savitr is "the Warrior"[212]; "Pusan art thou, O God [Savitr], in all thy goings-forth"[213]. Gwydion thus acts as an extension of Math's power in a similar fashion to the manner in which Pushan is an extension of Savitr's. As Math justly punishes Gwydion and Gilfaethwy, Savitr is said to have a law that none of the

---

206   RV LXXI.5.
207   RV LXXXII.9.
208   Kramrisch, 105.
209   Bromwich 439
    210 *Math fab Mathonwy*; trans. Gray 1982.
211   RV XXXVIII.5.
212   RV LXXI.1.
213   RV LXXXI.5.

other gods can escape and to "become Mitra" when he exercises his justice. Indeed, Savitr is said to "become" Pushan and Mitra in different senses, and as Gwydion and Lleu are the nephew and grand-nephew of Math and are his heirs, each one carries on roles similar to that of Math and can even be said to have been taught by or to inherit certain qualities from Math, who has prefigured these qualities in them. Gwydion mainly inherits the magical and vivifying qualities of Math, while Lleu mainly inherits the qualities pertaining to justice. "Over all generation thou art Lord alone: Pusan art thou, O God, in all thy goings-forth," says a hymn to Savitr[214], which implies that Pushan is the extension of Savitr's power of impelling life in its direct application (goings forth) within the realm of generation, within the growth of the living material world. Hence Gwydion helps Math generate the goddess Blodeuwedd with magic, and also even in his punishment he is the generator of three lineages of animals, executing Math's proclamation in a direct act of generation paired with his brother. In these scenes, and indeed seemingly every time Math is said to go forth to do anything, Gwydion is with him and they are combining their powers. In the scene of punishment, by his command Math gives the first impetus resulting in the life of these newly generated animals, while Gwydion acts out and generates what Math has put in motion by mating with his brother and siring these animal offspring. Along with this act of generation which strikingly transgresses taboo, Gwydion is also implicated in two other sexual acts that rupture the boundaries of taboo and can be considered as sordid violations: the rape of Goewin and the fathering (generation again) of Lleu with Gwydion's own sister, Arianrhod. As the connection between Savitr and Pushan is both a prefiguring of Pushan in Savitr and extension of Savitr into Pushan, similarly with Savitr-Mitra: "Thou, O God [Savitr], art Mitra through thy righteous laws" says the Veda[215]. This implies that Savitr enacts Mitra-like justice and has strict laws, which can indeed be seen in Math's unswerving punishment of Gwydion and Gilfaethwy and his attempt to compensate Goewin for her rape by making her queen, as well as in his strict testing of the virtue of Arianrhod. Later, Math directly tells Lleu to pursue justice against Gronw because what Gronw has taken is rightfully Lleu's. As with Savitr becoming Pushan, the Vedic verse describing Savitr "becoming" Mitra also implies the passing on of Savitr's power of justice, which has been prefigured in Savitr, to Mitra, who he also "becomes" in the sense of his essence passing to Mitra in a form of metaphysical inheritance, one divinity of the morning solar power passing chronologically to the next. This is well-illustrated by Lleu's following of Math's advice and fully embodying the Mitraic justice in the climactic reckoning against Gronw, killing him with his spear for his crime. We can then see a parallel of this divine trio expressed in the three generations found in *Math fab Mathonwy*: Math, his nephew Gwydion, and great-nephew Lleu = Savitr, Pushan, Mitra.

---

214   RV LXXXI.5.
215   RV LXXXI.4.

To restate once more: Goewin, the virgin footholder of Math, then, is Night (Ratri), and Math is comparable to Savitr. Savitr is the sun during the night and is known as the impeller of the life of the world. Thus each night Math, as the cognate of Savitr, would be resting his feet in the virgin lap of Night, unable to go about his lands until war (morning) calls him. Math has to have his feet always in the lap of the virgin Goewin, which is the main activity in which he is depicted, except when he is called to "war," which would be when day begins. This maiden happens to be raped at the exact moment that Math is roused to go to war against another god of the first light of morning or morning star (the horse twin Pryderi). Thus this rape is the end of night, her violation, and her rapist or rapists would then be divinities of light or of the transition between night and day. What is interesting is that the rape is entirely facilitated by the Welsh Pushan, Gwydion, the primary rapist being Gwydion's brother, although due to the lack of description the possibility of Gwydion also participating in the rape is potentially implied by certain portions of the text. Pushan is the luminousness of the sun and directly succeeds Savitr metaphysically, according to Stella Kramrisch. Kramrisch describes Pushan as the material cause of the same power of which Savitr is the efficient cause:

> Savitr, the Impeller, the causa efficiens 'becomes Pusan' (5.81.5; yamabhih), the primordial stress that was ante principium is beheld in Pusan, concreted in his ardour, the glowing essence of the Sun, its 'substane ante principium.' Savitr is the efficient cause and Pusan the material cause of the Sun that glows and shining moves. Savitr, Pusan and Surya refer to the same symbol in the cosmos, the Sun. It is validated as cause and effect. The cause is beheld in the effect and is named differently in the salient stages of its transition[216].

Gwydion is Math's nephew and is taught his magic by him and they collaborate in the war and later in the creation of the seemingly auroral maiden Blodeuwedd (in this sense generating and impelling her life). Whose rape would a Pushanic god be likely to be aiding in? As a Sun God it would be the rape of Night. Likewise, what goddess would the two primary solar gods of the sunrise be generating to wed their own heir apparent? Though it cannot be narrowed down to perfect certainty, it would clearly be some goddess connected to the time of Dawn, the time which comes along immediately generated as a result of the rising sun. Even if Blodeuwedd, made of flowers, can not be identified with Dawn herself with certitude, she would still have to be a goddess so closely connected to the time of Dawn, the time when Math and Gwydion apparently create her, that she would be nearly indistinguishable from that high and glowing goddess. Greek Hemera, goddess of Day and daughter of Nyx (Night) and Erebus would be one other possible parallel. The son of Norse Dellingr and Nott (Night) is Day, and so

---

216   Stella Kramrisch, "Pusan," 105.

the maiden Math creates could be a female form of the same divinity of Day, who, for the Greeks at least, was female. The placement of Imbolc, festival of Irish Dawn Goddess Brigid, before Beltane, around which time Welsh Blodeuwedd would be created, suggests that Blodeuwedd could be distinct from the Dawn Goddess. This also could be a difference between Irish and Welsh branches. It is true that if Blodeuwedd is not the Dawn Goddess, the Welsh branch has no other clear Dawn Goddess in our interpretation. Thus there seems a strong possibility that the Dawn Goddess and Day/Flower Goddess are being conflated in the figure of Welsh Blodeuwedd as they are often confused or equated in Greek sources. Blodeuwedd as Dawn following Gowein as Night would, nonetheless, present the most direct parallel to the frequently paired goddesses of Night and Dawn in the *Rig Veda*, the former disappearing just when the latter arises.

***

One further level of comparison must be brought to bear on this picture by examining an esoteric analogy of the Savitr-Ratri myth. This Night goddess, Ratri/Goewin, can also be seen as a repetition of the cosmic "Uncreate" (that is, the dark, unmanifest state underlying existence), but within the material cycle. In the Vedic interpretation of scholar Stella Kramrisch, this "pre-cosmic" darkness is analogous, though on a different level, to the darkness of the cycle, which is Night. Night's rape would be a reflection on the level of the individual day of the violation of the Uncreate by Prajapati ("Lord of Creatures," Vedic creator god), who, according to Kramrisch, in some sense creates the cosmos out of a violation of the Uncreate in the Brahmanas[217]:"Creation is an act of

---

217   "The Father [Prajapati] had broken the state of wholeness that existed before the fall of the seed. This state is beyond words. It is indescribable and inaccessible to the senses. It is 'neither nonbeing nor being' (RV.10.129.1). But if that much can be said about it, it has also been said that it is 'nonbeing and being' (RV.10.5.7), and that out of nonbeing came being in the first age of the gods (RV.10.72.2). It is then that the indefinable wholeness of the total absence or the total presence of both nonbeing and being appears to recede and to set up the screen on which are seen the large figures of gods and their actions. This state of 'neither nonbeing nor being,' or simultaneously 'nonbeing and being,' is not within the range of thought. It is a plenum that defies definition, for it has no limits. **Yet it is not chaos, the 'darkness covered by darkness,' said to have existed before the beginning of the ordered universe (RV.10.129.3). In its precosmic, preconscious totality, everything is contained,** including consciousness and nothingness. Metaphysically, it did not cease when the cosmos came into existence, for it is not subject to time. Mythically, its wholeness had been injured. Mystically, its nameless plenum is inaccessible except in the state of samādhi, the final stage of yoga

violence that infringes upon the Uncreate, the undifferentiated wholeness that is before the beginning of things" (Kramrisch, *The Presence of Siva*, 20 [e-book pagination]).

The only use of the title Prajapati within the most archaic "Family Books" of the *Rig Veda* is attached to Savitr and he is thus the Prajapati within the cycle, as several other details suggest. This archaic use of the title Prajapati occurs when Savitr is called the "Prajapati of the world" in RV 4.53.2. Prajapati is not depicted as his own distinct deity until the 10th and final mandala, usually considered a less archaic section of the *Rig Veda*. Arthur A. Macdonell also notes that "In the SB [*Satapatha Brahmana*] (12, 3, 5, 1) people are said to identify Savitr with Prajapati; and in the TB [*Taittiriya Brahmana*] (1, 6, 4, 1) it is stated that Prajapati becoming Savitr created living beings. Savitr is alone lord of vivifying power and by his movements *(yamabhih)* becomes Pusan (5, 82, 5)"[218]. Jan Gonda notes that

> at JB. 1, 6 with a motivation which reminds the reader of the connexion with the god's creative activity: the appearance of light at the moment of offering is Savitar, who is Prajapati, who generated the creatures at daybreak [...] the light at these moments (daybreak and sunset) is Savitar and Savitar is Prajapati [...] That is why the agnihotra is sacred to Prajapati. When here at daybreak the light appears, in this very appearance of light Prajapati created the creatures.[219]

He states that "in Sb. 11,5,4,2 ff, Prajapati and Savitar are named together as the two most important (varisthe) deities. Prajapati has generated the bhutas or living beings, of which he is said to be the self, see SB 10,4,2,2; 10,4,2,3; 10,4,2,27."

He explains that Savitr is the same as Prajapati in: SB 10,2,2,4; 12,3,5,1 and that Savitr functions as an intermediate (madhyatah) progenitor in SB 2,5,1,10; however, in SB 11,5,4,3 they are two distinct deities[220]. Savitr is also compared to a "linch-pin, firm" on which rest "things immortal"[221]. This "Prajapati of the world" quality ought to be

---

leading to mokṣa, the total release from all contingencies. Words like plenum, totality, and wholeness are used here merely as symbols of the Uncreate" (Kramrisch, *The Presence of Siva*, 53 [e-book pagination]).

218   Macdonell, *Vedic Mythology*, 33.
219   Gonda, *Prajapati's Rise to Higher Rank*, 13.
220   SB. (12, 3, 5, 1).
221   RV 1. XXXV.6. RV 1. XXXV.6. See also Savitr described as in a role at the beginning of creation in Mandala 10: "Well knoweth Savitr, O Child of Waters, where ocean, firmly fixt, o'erflowed its limit.
Thence sprang the world, from that uprose the region: thence heaven spread out and the wide earth expanded" 10.CXLIX.2. "Then, with a full crowd of Immortal Beings, this other realm came later, high and holy.
First, verily, Savitr's strong-pinioned Eagle was born: and he obeys his law for ever"

clear in the actions of Math from the foregoing discussion, in his role of creating various beings and setting the cycle of the day in motion.

As Arthur A. Macdonell explains, regarding the myth of Prajapati's rape of his daughter which begins creation:

> A myth is told in the MS. (4, 2, 12) of Prajapati being enamoured of his daughter Usas. She transformed herself into a gazelle; whereupon he transformed himself into the corresponding male. Rudra incensed at this aimed his arrow at him, when Prajapati promised to make him lord of beasts if he did not shoot (cp. RV. 10,61, 7). The story is several times referred to in the Brahmanas (AB. 3, 33; SB. 1, 7, 4, 1; PB. 8, 2, 10). The basis of this myth seem to be two passages of the RV. (1, 71, 5; 10, 61, 5-7) in which the incest of a father (who seems to be Dyaus) with his daughter (here apparently the Earth) is referred to and an archer is mentioned[222].

Although the original protagonist of this myth seems to be Dyaus in the two *Rig Veda* hymns cited, and the identity of the daughter is not stated (Macdonell interpreting her as Earth), the Brahmanas versions seem to indicate a merging of the two myths: the Dyaus motif of the rape of his daughter from the Vedas, and the "Prajapati" motif that we have seen with regard to Math as Savitr-Prajapati. This conflation found in the Brahmanas version draws from Savitr's archaic role of "Prajapati" and Dyaus' "Prajapati-like" role in the myth of the rape of his daughter.

We can see that a conflation may have happened here because, when compared to the myth of Math, we see some overlap of elements in the Brahmana tale: the creative heavenly lord at the time of origin, rape of a primordial goddess (here Dawn or perhaps Earth, here performed by the creator rather than by a second deity as in Math's tale), a punishment for the violation, and finally a transformation of two deities into deer and an incestuous mating in this form, though the order of these elements is not exactly the same, and the animal-form mating may have been an original element of the Dyaus myth as well. This Prajapati of the Brahmanas also creates reptiles, fish, birds, then animals with teats, milk and food[223] and creates the castes[224]. Compared to Math, who, via Gwydion and Gilfaethwy, creates three lineages of animals, this makes it seem as though the deer, wolf and swine that the brothers sire could reflect the ordering of the human castes: deer as First Function (sovereign-priest), wolf as Second (warrior), swine as Third (producer). As Dawn is Prajapati's daughter in some Brahmanas, in the *Kausitaki*

10.CXLIX.3.
222   Macdonell, 119.
223   JB. 2, 228 f.
224   SB 2, 1, 4, 11.

Brahmana Prajapati also is said to create the goddess Dawn, while Math creates Blodeuwedd. In all, the Prajapati of the Brahmanas has more in common with the Vedic Dyaus, with some possible bleed-over with motifs found in the myth of Math-Savitr, which suggests that Dyaus was also seen as a cosmic Prajapati, elements of whose myth are being echoed in Math-Savitr's, the god who repeats part of his role within the cycle.

Drawing Math-Savitr and Dyaus into alignment as two successive Prajapatis helps us to see Math-Savitr's relationship to the goddess Night as echoing Dyaus' relation to the dark state of the Uncreate, however we choose to conceptualize it, the state which Dyaus breaches by his rape. As Math rests in a goddess' lap, there is also a theme of laps in the *Rig Veda* connected to Savitr and the primordial cosmic goddess Nirrti, whose "lap" is the dark abyss of the Uncreate, a sort of chaotic cosmic or pre-cosmic darkness. As Kramrisch quotes and explains:

> 'Three are the heavens of Savitr, two are his lap, one in the world of Yama.' The lap of Savitr, the Impeller, which is on high, is at the very end of the axis, opposite to the 'lap of Nirrti' (note 15) at the lower end of the axis. Below, in the lap of Nirrti, yawns the chasm, into which have fallen beyond release those who have gone against the rta, the cosmic order. Above, in the lap of Savitr, at the height, is the opposite place of 'no return' where the Liberated dwell. (Kramrisch, "Pusan," 120)

> Below the pit of danger and treasure lies the Lap of Nirrti (7.104.9), the lap of destruction with its endless pit (7.104.17) below all creation (7.104.6). This deep dark place is the Asat, the Non-existent, 'The Rg Vedic Equivalent for Hell,' as shown by W. Norman Brown, JAOS, vol. 61, pp. 76-80. This deep substratum of the ordered cosmos, of the Existent (sat), the abyss that yawns at the bottom of the pit, in the lap of Destruction (nirrti) is the necessary opposite in the first pair of contraries. There they are from the beginning of things prior to which neither of them existed. The Asat, the Non-existent below the pit, is the remainder 'apud principium' of the all engulfing darkness, ante principium. The Cosmic Darkness ante principium is distinguished from the darkness of the 'night of the cycle.' (Kramrisch, "Pusan," 108)

We see Nirrti here identified with the Cosmic Darkness and the "remainder." This important concept of the remainder will be returned to as we will see it develop in an interesting direction in later texts. Nirrti is not identical to Ratri then, but is goddess of disordered non-existence and absolute darkness, the Uncreate, and so an analogy between Nirrti and Ratri must be imagined, just as an analogy is drawn explicitly between Prajapati and Savitr within the Vedic corpus. As Savitr is the Prajapati of the world and Prajapati has the same role as Savitr, but on the scale of the cosmos rather than of the day, Ratri is the Nirrti of the world, and Nirrti is the mirror of Ratri on the cosmic scale. To put it in directly applicable terms relating to the cycle of the day: the cosmos begins out of the dark Uncreate which is Nirrti, the pre-cosmic "night," while the day begins out of the dark night which is Ratri.

Rātri (रात्रि) is thought to have a literal meaning of 'bestower', from the root √rā, from PIE *Hréh₁trih. What appears to be a secondary etymology of Ratri's name is "rest," thus, "season of rest," *viz*, "night," deriving from √*ram,* रम्, (see Monier-Williams p. 867, Whitney p. 137). This root is also found in the name *rātrau śayanam*, a festival on the 11th day of the month Āṣāḍha, which is regarded as the "night of the gods," and is said to be when Viṣṇu reposes for four months on the serpent Śeṣa. This Śeṣa is depicted as forming the bed of Visnu upon the cosmic ocean, while Visnu is attended by his consort Laksmi.

Śeṣa is called Ananta, "endless," and his own name means "remainder," as he is what remains when the cosmos has been destroyed at the end of the *kalpa*. As the great *naga* or serpent, he is conceived in the *Bhagavata Purana* as the *tamasic* or dark energy of the supreme being Narayana, and has lived in the dark realm of the nagas since before the creation of the universe. Under the name of Sankarshana, Śeṣa is said in this text to expand himself as Garbhodakshayi-Vishnu in the beginning of the universe to create Brahma, a creator god who takes over the role of Prajapati in Puranic and other later texts. Śeṣa also incarnated during the Satya Yuga to form a similar seat for Lord Narasimha and additionally is once[225] tasked by Brahma to go under the earth to become its support. As such, the Brahmanical and Puranic mythos of Śeṣa may be an elaboration of the earlier Rig Vedic concept of the dark element (which is Ratri or Nirrti) forming the seat of rest for the creative solar deity during the cosmic night before the creation.

With this we must also consider the Greek case in which the goddess of Night (Nyx) is born directly from primordial Chaos according to Hesiod[226], sister of primordial darkness Erebus and mother of day (Hemera) among many other beings. In Orphic fragments[227], not Chaos but Nyx is the first being who gives birth to the rest of the primordial beings and the rest of the cosmos, and in Aristophanes' *The Birds*[228], Nyx is presented as the first principle and the mother of Eros. Many other sources record similar descriptions of Night at or just after the origin of all things: even Aristotle three times in

---

225   *Mahabharata, Adi Parva.*
226   *Theogony,* 115.
227   *The Orphic Fragments of Otto Kern.*
228   Aristophanes, *693.*

the *Metaphysics* mentions theogonies that begin with Night as the first being: "The theologians who generate everything from Night" (*Met.* 1071b); "Chaos and Night did not endure for an unlimited time" (*Met.* 1072a); and he names "Night and Ouranos or Chaos or Ocean" (*Met.* 1072a7) as deities who appeared as the first in certain ancient poets. Night appears as the first deity in both the Derveni and Eudemeian theogonies, but Aristophanes also mentions Chaos, Erebus (a male god of cosmic darkness), and Tartarus along with Nyx. See also *Orphic Hymn 3 to Nyx*: "parent goddess, source of sweet repose from whom at first both Gods and men arose"; and *Nonnus, Dionysiaca 31*: "Do not provoke Gaia (Earth), my [Nyx's] father's [Khaos'] agemate, from whom alone we are all sprung, we who dwell in Olympos."

Phanes, the bringer of light, is then paired with Nyx, either as her husband (consider the light-bringing Math as husband of Goewin), child or father, and from him Day is created, the world is brightened and begun. *Orphic Fragment 97* has Orpheus saying, "In the cave (of Nyx) the Father (Phanes) made (all things)," which brings Phanes and Nyx into a juxtaposition similar to that of Math and Goewin. *Fragment 104* says that Night "produces all life in conjunction with Phanes from unapparent causes." Phanes also invents the method of creation by means of mingling, which brings to mind the mingling of Gwydion and Gilfaethwy to sire the animals or castes. Phanes even gives his scepter to Nyx (*Orphica, Argonautica 12)*, while Savitr promotes Goewin to queen after her rape, and Phanes' scepter is eventually passed to Zeus, as Lleu also finally inherits part of Math's rulership.

Phanes is also known as Protogonos, which has been linked linguistically with Prajapati (see Kate Alsobrook, "The Beginning of Time: Vedic and Orphic Theogonies and Poetics"). He is said at first to rise from the watery abyss to give birth to the cosmos, and this compares well with what we know of both Savitr and Prajapati in the *Rig Veda*. In the *Rig Veda,* Savitr is said to know where the ocean overflowed to bring forth the world, and in a different hymn Prajapati is described as the golden germ (which is described as an egg in the Brahmanas[229]), *hiranyagarbha*, arisen from the waters, from which the cosmos has sprung:

> Well knoweth Savitr, O Child of Waters, where ocean, firmly fixt,
> o'erflowed its limit. Thence sprang the world, from that uprose the region:
> thence heaven spread out and the wide earth expanded/ Then, with a full
> crowd of Immortal Beings, this other realm came later, high and holy. (RV
> CXLIX.2)

---

229   In *Atharvaveda,* Kala, God of Time, makes Prajapati from an egg, as Greek
       Chronos (Time) coils around the cosmic egg. The Iranic *Bundahisn* also speaks of a
       cosmic egg at the time of creation, which contains everything.

In the beginning rose Hiranyagarbha, born Only Lord of all created beings (RV CXXI.1)

What time the mighty waters came, containing the universal germ, producing Agni, Thence sprang the Gods' one spirit into being. What God shall we adore with our oblation?/ He in his might surveyed the floods containing productive force and generating Worship (CXXI.7-8)

Neer may he harm us who is earth's Begetter, nor he whose laws are sure, the heavens' Creator, He who brought forth the great and lucid waters. What God shall we adore with our oblation?/Prajāpati! (CXXI.9-10)

In Ovid, Chaos is at the beginning and the Earth is bare. Eros, god of love, pierces the bosom of the Earth with his arrows, causing verdure and animal life to spring forth. This again has several of the elements seen in the Vedic and Brahmanical tradition: the "piercing," if not exactly rape, of a fundamental, supporting goddess, here Earth; an archer; and the resultant springing of life and growth. In the aforementioned play of Aristophanes, *The Birds*, it is Eros with shining wings who is born from an egg which is generated by Nyx and which is then placed in the "boundless lap" or "bosom" of Erebus, which image brings us, once again, back to the theme of the "lap" of darkness on which a bringer of life rests: "First there was Chaos and Night, black Erebus and wide Tartarus, but neither earth nor air nor sky existed. In Erebus' boundless bosom first of all black-winged Night produced an egg"[230]. Eros then mates with Chaos and (with satirical intent on Aristophanes' part) brings forth the birds first of all things, while Math brings forth other kinds of creatures, as does Savitr. *Orphic hymn 6 To Protogonos* states: "You scattered the dark mist that lay before your eyes and, flapping your wings, you whirled about, and throughout this world you brought pure light. For this I call you Phanes, I call you Lord Priapos, I call you sparkling with bright eyes."

Zeus is even said, according to *Orphic Fragment 129*, to swallow Phanes, his forefather, and thereby to take into his bosom all of Phanes' powers. This seems to us a clear analogy of what Lugh/Mitra does in relation to Math/Savitr: Math/Savtir *becomes* Lugh/Mitra; that is, Lugh/Mitra succeeds Math/Savitr chronologically and specifically absorbs his powers, as though Lugh/Mitra is swallowing his predecessor and taking over his functions going forward. Not only that, but this Phanes is also identified with just one other god, Pan, just as Savitr becomes both Mitra and Pushan, or Math passes his powers to Lleu and Gwydion: "And the third god of the third triad this theology too celebrates as Protogonos (First-Born) [Phanes], and it calls him Zeus [Mitra/Lleu] the order of all and

---

230   Aristophanes, 693.

of the whole world, wherefore he is also called Pan [Pushan/Gwydion]" (Orphica, Theogonies Fragment 54 (from Damascius)).Understanding this makes other Orphic Fragments intelligible, which we here quote at length[231]:

> Jupiter (*Ζεύς*) [*we must consider this role of Zeus to be the point of conjunction of Math/Savitr and Lugh/Mitra, when the former 'becomes' the latter, when Zeus has swallowed Phanes and taken his powers and roles*] therefore, comprehending in himself wholes, produces in conjunction with Night (*Νύξ*) all things monadically and intellectually, according to her oracles, and likewise all mundane natures, Gods, and the parts of the universe. **165. (122)** *σχόλιον Πρόκλου επὶ Τιμαίου Πλάτωνος* **I 28c (I 313, 31 Diehl):**

> And this is the strong bond, as the theologist says, which is extended through all things, and is connected by the golden chain. For Jupiter (*Ζεύς*) after this, constitutes the golden chain, according to the admonitions of Night (*Νύξ*).

> 'But when your pow'r around the whole has spread a strong coercive bond,

> a golden chain suspend from æther.'

> **166. (122)** *σχόλιον Πρόκλου επὶ Τιμαίου Πλάτωνος* **I 28c (II 24, 23 Diehl):**

> Orpheus also indicating these things says, that the intelligible God [Phanes] was absorbed by the Demiurgus of wholes [Zeus]. And Plato asserts that the Demiurgus looks to the paradigm, indicating through sight intellectual perception. According to the theologist, however, the Demiurgus [Zeus] leaps as it were to the intelligible God [Phanes], and as the fable says, absorbs him. For if it be requisite clearly to unfold the doctrine of our preceptor, the God who is called Protogonus by Orpheus, and who is established at the end of intelligibles, is animal itself, with Plato. Hence it is eternal, and the most beautiful of intelligibles, and **is in intelligibles that which Jupiter (*Ζεύς*) is in intellectuals**. Each however is the boundary of these orders. And the former indeed, is **the first of paradigmatic causes**; but the latter is **the most monadic of demiurgic causes**. Hence Jupiter is united to the paradigm through Night as the medium, and being filled from thence, becomes an intelligible world, as in intellectuals.

> Then of Protogonus (*Ἡρικεπαῖος*) the mighty strength

> Was seen; for in his belly he contain'd

---

231   These translations are cited with gratitude from https://www.hellenicgods.org/the-orphic-fragments-of-otto-kern.

The whole of things, and mingled where 'twas fit,

The force and powerful vigour of the God.

Hence, with the universe great Jove (Ζεύς) contains, &c

(trans. Thomas Taylor, 1820)

Alternate translation:

Thus then taking hold of the power of first-born Irikæpaios (Ἠρικεπαῖος)

He carried the form of all things in the hollow of his own belly,

He mingled his own limbs with the power and strength of the God,

for that reason with him all things within Zeus were made new.

But Orpheus gives a name to the Demiurgus, in consequence of being moved [*i.e.* inspired] from thence; whom Plato himself likewise elsewhere follows. For the Jupiter (Ζεύς) with him, who is prior to the three sons of Saturn, is the Demiurgus of wholes. After the absorption therefore of Phanes, the ideas of all things shone forth in him, as the theologist says:

'Hence with the universe great Jove contains,

Extended æther, heav'n's exalted plains;

The barren restless deep, and earth renown'd,

Ocean immense, and Tartarus profound;

Fountains and rivers, and the boundless main,

With all that nature's ample realms contain;

And Gods and Goddesses of each degree;

All that is past, and all that e'er shall be,

Occultly, and in fair connection lies, (v. fragment 169)

In Jove's (Ζεύς') wide belly, ruler of the skies.'

(trans. Thomas Taylor, 1820)

In fact, Orphéfs (Ὀρφεύς) says that after the swallowing of Phánîs (Φάνης), all things were born (new) in Zeus (Ζεύς), inasmuch as first and in unity, the causes of all of the mundane things were brought to light in him, and second and separately in the Dîmiourgós (Δημιουργός); for there the sun, the moon, the sky

390

itself, the elements, unifying Ǽrôs (Ἔρως), and all things he had produced, simply become one in the belly of Zeus.

σχόλιον Ἑρμείου ἐπὶ Φαίδρου Πλάτωνος **247 c p. 148, 10 Couvr.:**

πρὸς δὴ τοῦτο εἴρηται, ὅτι δεῖ ἄχρι τινὸς εἶναι τὴν συναφήν. διὰ τί δὲ ἄχρι τούτου; ὅτι δὴ οὐδὲ οἱ ὑπὸ τὸν Δία θεοὶ λέγονται ἐνοῦσθαι τῶι Φάνητι, ἀλλὰ μόνος ὁ Ζεὺς καὶ αὐτὸς διὰ μέσης τῆς Νυκτός. Vs. 6 v. also fragment 169 p. 208.

In addition to this it is said, that up to some point there is union. But why up to this point? Because that **not even the Gods under Zeus (Ζεύς) are said to unite with Phánîs (Φάνης), but only Zeus, and him in the middle of Night**.

Once again, Zeus falls in line with what is a Mitraic mythos in other branches. Likewise, the fragments connect Zeus intimately to justice, a power we have seen pass directly from Math/Savitr to Lugh/Mitra:

Wherefore also, from Justice, Zeus (Ζεύς) follows, who (Ζεύς) is making ready to distribute the mundane allotments to the Titans, as Orphéfs (Ὀρφεύς) says:

'And therefore punitive Justice followed him, propitious to all.'

For whenever she is propitious to all (and) punitive, that she sets in order all things with the Dîmiourgós of the whole, who rules over the Gods, presides together (with him) over the daimonæs (δαίμονες), judges souls and, altogether, judgement passes completely through all the souls." **158. (125)** *σχόλιον Πρόκλου ἐπὶ Πολιτείας Πλάτωνος* **II 144, 29 Kr**

For Justice is, as Orpheus says, the companion of Jupiter (Ζεύς); since, according to him,

'Laborious Justice follows Jove (Ζεύς) . . . . '

(trans. Thomas Taylor, 1820)

160. (126) *σχόλιον Πρόκλου ἐπὶ Ἀλκιβιάδου α' Πλάτωνος* **p. 499, 2 Cous.**

Once more, since before the world, Justice (Δίκη) follows Zeus (Ζεύς) (for Law is the companion of Zeus, as Orphéus [Ὀρφεύς] says).

Epiphanius states that the cosmic egg was surrounded by Time and Inevitability like two serpents. Recall here the endless and *tamasic* or dark serpent Sesa again, who is the seat of Visnu when nothing else remains. Together Time and Inevitability constricted the egg until it divided in two, and thus Protogonos is called "two-natured." Interestingly, before the 10th mandala, Prajapati is used only as a title of Savitr (the sun at night) and Soma (the moon), which could theoretically correspond to the two halves or natures of the creative germ of light as they first appear and then divide in the cosmic night. This also brings us back to the *Mabinogi*; for the tale *Math fab Mathonwy* is the final, climactic part of a four-part cycle, and as we have previously shown at length, the parts or branches which precede *Math fab Mathonwy* constitute a "Lunar Cycle," centering around and concerning the events that are set in motion by the lunar king of the underworld, Arawn, the parallel of Soma (who is also called Prajapati along with Savitr). If *Math fab Mathonwy* is the myth of the rising of the sun, the Lunar Cycle portion that precedes it could then be interpreted, on a cosmogonic level, as occurring during the cosmic night, ruled by the lunar half of the original divine germ of light, the Moon God Arawn/Soma.

The tale of Math and Goewin is followed by the birth of Lleu, Mitraic sovereign of early morning sky, son of Gwydion. Lleu is then cuckolded by his Dawn-connected wife with another Sun God, Gronw (Surya), the daytime sun taking away the glow of dawn/sovereignty, which Lleu has to retrieve by overcoming the sun god, completing the cycle. Thus this series of myths which is collected as *Math fab Mathonwy* would be the series of precise divine events, starting in the dead of night, considered the time of cyclic beginning, that were seen as beginning the day and the greater cycle by analogy. Math marries the no-longer virgin Goewin after her rape, but he still needs a new virgin footholder, as this is his trait — this footholder would be the next Night, and the cycle repeats. Math does not succeed in finding a new footholder in the story as we have it (though he does attempt to), but we must assume that at the next turn of the daily cycle essentially the same story begins once again, a new Night appears who is virgin once more. Savitr being succeeded by Pushan — this then would be what we are seeing with Math and his nephew Gwydion, who he teaches his magic to and with whom he collaborates but whom he also rules over.

We may see another, more obscure version of this myth in the Norse material: Dellingr's name has been glossed as "the Dayspring" or "Shining One," and his son with the goddess Nott (Night) is Dagr, the god of Day. Dellingr's people are called "bright and beautiful" in *Gylfaginning*. Even more striking, Dellingr is said to be the third husband of the goddess Nott, Night. If we consider that Gwydion and Gilfaethwy both had a hand in the rape of Goewin and as such are punished equally for the crime, then Gwydion and Gilfaethwy may be considered Goewin's first two husbands before Math marries her as a result of her loss of virginity. Goewin's rape is alluded to in two passages as follows:

And at night Gwydion the son of Don, and Gilvaethwy his brother, returned to Caerdathyl; and Gilvaethwy took Math the son of Mathonwy's couch. And while he turned out the other damsels from the room discourteously, he made Goewin unwillingly remain.

And afterward:

> 'Now the attack was made by thy nephews, lord, the sons of thy sister, Gwydion the son of Don, and Gilvaethwy the son of Don; unto me they did wrong, and unto thee dishonour.'[232]

The fact that, after the rape occurs, Goewin names both Gwydion and Gilfaethwy as her attackers, and they both do indeed return to Caerdathyl together before the crime is committed, makes it plausible that Gwydion was directly involved in some part of the rape. His punishment matching Gilfaethwy's supports this possibility, and in a metaphysical sense Gwydion is certainly present at the divine conjunction that this rape marks. In this sense, Gwydion and Gilfaethwy can reasonably be said to match the first two husbands of Nott. Dellingr is the "dayspring" or "shining one," and with him Nott then gives birth to Dagr, the god of the Day.

After the rape of Goewin, which is the violation of Night by a transition into day, and after the war of Math with Pryderi, who in another respect is deity ruling over a precise phenomena related to the morning star or early morning transition, Math and Gwydion, who in this capacity (as equivalent to Savitr and Pushan) are two divine aspects of the sunrise, then collaborate to create the woman Blodeuwedd for Lleu, the son of Gwydion and Arianrhod who was born in the interim and is now reaching maturity. As such, the creation of Blodeuwedd out of flowers commemorates the creation of Dawn for the Mitraic lord of the morning sky by the Savitrian and Pushanic deities, sunrise deities who though distinct are as though extensions of one another, one the Impeller of life and the other the lord of glowing luminosity who extends the Savitrian power in a direct manner into the sphere of generation.

---

232   *Math fab Mathonwy.*

13

The Irish Prometheus Myth: Corrgend and Aed

An interesting dissertation was published in 2011 reappraising the theories surrounding the Indo-European origin of the Greek Prometheus myth. *Gifts of Fire: An Historical Analysis of the Promethean Myth* by Marty James John Sulek argues that linguistic evidence newly validates an age-old etymological connection between Prometheus and Vedic fire priest Matarisvan[233] which had fallen out of favor during the 20th century. He argues particularly that Prometheus' original crime for which he was punished must not have been theft of fire (or only that) but instead must have had to do with a prohibited lust or even rape directed toward Athena. He argues that Prometheus, seen as a Fire God, and the other Greek Fire God, Hephaestus, are actually doubles (who he theorizes arrived to Greece via separate migrations), just as Vedic Agni and Matarisvan are split from one root Fire Priest divinity, and thus Prometheus' crime is actually a variant of the

---

233   Sulek concludes his linguistic and mythic reassessment thus: "Given this evidence, plus the endorsement of West (Ibid.) and Watkins (1995, p. 256), two of the pre-eminent living authorities in the respective fields of classics and Indo-European linguistics, the existence of a genetic relationship between Mātariśvan and Prometheus becomes about as certain as any conclusion can possibly be within the field of comparative linguistics" (Sulek, 27).

episode in which Hephaestus attempts to take Athena in passion, but is rebuffed and his seed is spilled on the ground, impregnating the Earth, Gaia. In this context the Fire God Hephaestus' seed would have to be seen as fire dropping down to earth, whether as lightning or by other means. The myth of Hephaestus' near-rape of Athena, along with variant of Prometheus' punishment which claims "passion" for Athena was the crime, form the basis of Sulek's claim. The variant I refer to comes from Duris of Samos, who passes on the claim that Prometheus was punished 'because of his passion [*èrasthênai*] for Athena.' For this reason those dwelling in the region of the Caucasus refuse to sacrifice to Zeus and Athena alone, because they were the cause of the punishment of Prometheus, but extravagantly worship Heracles on account of his shooting the eagle with his bow" (L. Okin, *Studies on Duris of Samos*, 1974, p. 152). Though we should note that this comment does not negate the possibility of a punishment for the theft of fire *in addition to* the stated passion, Sulek nonetheless reads the sentence to be making a claim "that Prometheus was punished, not for his theft of fire, but rather for his passion for Athena" (Sulek, 50). Sulek notes further that a punishment of a bird eating the liver exists also in Homer, and in that case it is specifically a punishment for rape, that of Leto by Tityos (Sulek, 44). He summarizes: "As Pease observes: 'Most scholars agree that the punishment of Tityos is made poetically appropriate to his offense' (1925, p. 277). In other words, Zeus moulds Tityos' punishment to fit his crime, as the liver was considered the seat of lust or passion among the ancient Greeks" (Sulek, 41). Finally, as Sulek argues, the etymology of Prometheus can potentially be interpreted to mean "to rob" but also "one who loves to rape" (Sulek, 33) and this, according to Sulek, supports the conclusion that lust was the original crime for which he was punished. Thus Sulek pictures an original form of the myth in which the proto-Prometheus was "a stone-age fire-priest who lusted and sought after the beautiful red light of the crack of Dawn, and brought down upon himself the punishment of her Father, the Day-lit Sky" (Sulek, 47).

In summary, Sulek claims that Prometheus was originally punished for his lust or passion rather than the fire theft and that the well-known moralized punishment of Prometheus for aiding mankind with the theft of fire rather than for the rape must have been a later Greek innovation, considering that the Vedic case shows no sign of punishment for the fire gift. However, if we take this theory and test it against the Irish case, we find surprising results.

If the Prometheus(/Hephaestus?)/Matarisvan myth is a myth of the Fire God, or Vedic Agni, as Sulek suggests, formed by a splitting of that Fire Priest into two aspects, then we will have to look at the Irish fire gods as we have indicated them previously. It is not Manannan, who we have suggested to be the *celestial* fire god, but Dagda's son Aed, whose name means "Fire," who has a myth curiously similar to the Prometheus myth as reconstructed by Sulek. First, we can clarify the etymological relationship between the names Aed, Prometheus, and Matarisvan, according to Sulek's argument. As Sulek claims, these latter two names both seem to contain derivations of *math-*, "rubbing," "stealing," etc., which in the name *Matarisvan* may theoretically be combined with the Sanskrit *mātari*, meaning "mother" and this last may have within it the term for fire, **atar,* as well as the Sanskrit root 'mā-', "to make, produce, create" (Burrow, 1980). As Sulek puts it, "In this conception, Mātariśvan may be interpreted as a composite word formed from the locative Sanskrit word for 'mother' (mātari), itself derived from the Indo-European word *ma- ('to create'), perhaps also combined with the Indo-European word for 'fire' (*atar), and the addition of the root śvi, meaning 'to grow or swell.' Given these considerations, it is reasonable to assume that Mātariśvan and math are, in fact, cognate terms derived from a common Indo-European root *ma" (Sulek, 24). He further explains that, "*Math is also likely cognate with earlier Indo-European words *mā (to make) and *atar (fire), both of which were likely employed to construct Mātariśvan as an epithet," and concludes with the equation, "Mātariśvan: as the maker (mā) / mother (mātari) in whom the fire (*atar) grows or swells (śvi)" (Sulek, 29). Irish *Aed* does not come from the same root as this reconstructed Indo-European root word for fire, **atar,* but comes from PIE **h₂eydʰ*, and the two words for fire have an unclear relationship, **h₂eydʰ* yielding in Ancient Greek, *aîthos*, "heat, fire."

Laura Massetti clarifies one important point here, long recognized, that *Prometheus* does not come from the word for the fire-drill: "it is impossible to derive a basis **pro-math-* [...] from a root **menth₂-*. The coincidence between Prometheus and pramantha- 'fire drill' can therefore be classified as a Scheingleichung, that is to say, as an 'apparent/superficial coincidence' which can be proved false through the analysis of the linguistic details." Furthermore: "The name of Prometheus can actually be traced back to an Indo-European verbal root **math₂-* 'to rob', which underlies Vedic *mathⁱ* 'to rob'. The past participle *mathitá-* happens to be identical to the one of Vedic *manthⁱ* 'to rub', which opens to a palette of different interpretations in the passage involving the fire-theft episode: take, for instance, the final phrase of *Rigveda* 3.9: *devébhyo mathitám pári*, which, as noticed by Jamison – Brereton (2014:481), 'is translated 'stolen from among the gods,' could also mean 'churned from among the gods.'"[234]

The Irish myth is found in the *Dindshenchas of Ailech* and is as follows: Aed (name meaning "Fire") sleeps with Tethra, the wife of one Corrgend. In response, Corrgend kills Aed. Aed's grieving father, Dagda, ie. Father Sky, then takes revenge on his son's killer by forcing him to carry Aed's body across the earth until he finds a proper stone

---

234   Laura Massetti, *Προμηθεύς and Ἐπιμηθεύς (Promētheús and Epimētheús).* *https://archive.chs.harvard.edu/CHS/article/display/6686.* 2020.03.31.

for his grave. The carrying of Aed and heavy lifting of the large stone causes Corrgend's heart to burst, killing him.

Thus, if we begin with Sulek's theory, then both the Greek Prometheus myth and this Irish myth would center around a crime of prohibited lust enacted by the fire god: Prometheus/Hephaestus' lust for or rape/near-rape of Athena in the Greek and Aed's adultery with Tethra in the Irish. Not only is Tethra married, but this adultery is also said to violate an oath. Both myths involve a subsequent punishment carried out by the sky sovereigns (Zeus and Dagda), though the Irish version also includes a second crime, a murder, performed by a second figure. In the Irish case this second crime is the crime punished by torture. At the beginning of both myths, there is a mention of either the feast of, or a sacrifice to, Father Sky — Dagda or Zeus. That is, the Irish tale opens with a mention of Dagda, who is said to be "a just-dealing lord over the feast till even; his mound remains, long may it remain!" (*Dindshenchas 22, Ailech I*). In the Prometheus myth, Prometheus initially tricks Zeus into accepting an inferior part of the ox sacrificed to him at Mecone. In each case, the woman lusted after has a name relating her to a kind of seabird. Tethra means sea or scald crow, while Athena transforms into an eagle, and has the epithet "Aethyia," a title related to the greek word for the seabird known as the shearwater. She appears as an eagle accompanying Odysseus on his *Odyssey* sea voyage and is called "gleaming-eyed," or "gray-eyed," epithets believed to relate her to birds[235]. The owl eventually became her common symbol. In both the Irish and Greek cases there is also honor in the crime that is to be punished: Prometheus' theft of fire is intended to aid humans, while Corrgend's killing of Aed is justified as revenge for the crime against him. The text states of Corrgend: "he gained him honor through jealousy" (*Dindshenchas, Ailech I*).

The revenge of Father Sky in both cases involves torture of the body, suffering, and the giving of the criminal no peace. As the Irish tale states, "in wood nor fields nor sea found he never refuge under the white sun, nor riddance from the man's body on his back," and, "There was no peace for him nor healing of the harm to be had from the Dagda for the loss of his son, save by torture of his body strong in fight, and a grave-stone laid on the tomb," and finally, "Corrgend died with travail of body" (*Dindshenchas, Ailech I*). Both criminals are known for a trait of swiftness of hand. Corrgend is described as "swift of hand," while Prometheus' name contains the verb *math* which, as discussed, is theorized to have had the connected meanings of "to rub," "to rape," and "to snatch away," and his crime is that of pickpocket-like theft, stealing back fire right under Zeus and Helios' noses, so to speak. Both criminals are also "degraded by love" in their crime. This is the specific description of Corrgend, when he

---

235   Henry George Liddell. Robert Scott. *A Greek-English Lexicon.* "γλαύξ".

kills Aed, while Duris of Samosata claims Prometheus is punished for "passion," and, if we include Hephaestus, that god is clearly degraded in the act, being rebuffed by Athena and ejaculating onto the earth. Sulek points out that "The word the scholiast attributes to Douris' description of the passion of Prometheus – *èrasthênai* – is cognate to *ëros* and based on the root word *ëramai"(32-33)*. Both *ëramai and ëros* refer to a passionate form of love, *ëramai* being glossed as "I love," usually in a romantic or sexual context. Thus when Corrgend is said to be "degraded by love" and when Prometheus is said to be punished for "*èrasthênai,"* the phrases are nearly the same in meaning.

Interestingly, Prometheus' brother Atlas is punished alongside Prometheus by being made to hold up the heavens in perpetuity. Meanwhile, Corrgend is punished by having to carry the body of Aed on his back and to lift a stone so heavy it kills him. Both the punishments of Prometheus and Aed refer to the torturing of a specific organ which was seen as the seat of passion, thus the punishment fits the crime. Crucially, as Sulek mentions, the liver was seen as the seat of passion for the Greeks of Hesiod's time (Sulek, 41), and it is eaten over and over as Prometheus is tied to the rock. Corrgend is said to bear the stone "over road after road" and to say all the while "Ach! Ach! The stone! 'tis by it my heart is bursting!" (*Dindshenchas, Ailech II*). Hence his heart, often considered the seat of passion in medieval Europe, is tortured by a repeated action, resulting in bursting, just as Prometheus's liver, also the seat of passion, is tortured by a repeated action, being repeatedly consumed, resulting in its destruction and regeneration. Prometheus and Aed are thus also associated with a stone by the attachment to which they are tortured: Prometheus is tied to such a stone while Corrgend has to carry one on his back. Connected to this stone, Corrgend of the swift hands is also implied to be a skilled craftsman, whereas Prometheus is often taken as a progenitor of the power of technology among men. Referring to the erection of this stone, the *Dindshenchas* reads, "who was he by whom was wrought thereafter the shining work?" and, "Round his son's seemly grave he raised the tomb nobly-bright" (*Dindshenchas, Ailech II*). Finally, as mentioned, Hephaestus' presumably fiery semen goes into the earth and impregnates it. Meanwhile, Aed, who is fire itself, is said to be buried in the earth. Could these conclusions have the same mythical meaning, perhaps telling the origin of how fire came to be a property that can be born out of the earth, that is, why the earth-born fire is indeed in the earth to begin with? Aed is said to be covered with a round tomb, around which the ringfort the Ailech of Imchell was built. We recall again, from a previous chapter, the round temple of the Roman earthly, domestic fire, which is an etymological match to the Irish god buried in the round house: the Roman *Aedes Vesta*.

Based on which elements we can see have remained consistent between the Irish case and the Greek, we deduce that Sulek may be correct in stating that the original "Prometheus" myth was more closely centered around the crime of passion committed by the Fire God. However, we can also see that another crime against "fire" does also occur in the Irish version and not only in the Greek version, and that the action of Corrgend is moralized in a fashion somewhat similar (though also distinct) to that of Prometheus, this action of Corrgend's being painted both as honorable and as a moral crime at the same time, the criminal then being tortured by the sky sovereign. We can also deduce that the "killing" of the Fire God, Aed, by Corrgend, may then be an alternate form of the taking of the fire from the heavens by Prometheus. When Aed is killed he is cut off from the heavenly realm and ends up buried in the earth. The burying of the body of "Fire" in the ground is then the same as Prometheus giving the fire to humans or Hephaestus impregnating the earth with his seed, because we can theorize that the round house and ring fort built around Aed's grave was in all likelihood a fire temple similar to the Roman Aedes Vesta. Thus the burying of the Fire God in the ground was really the establishing of the flame at this sacred shrine, first of the hearth fires, on and within the earth. The *Dindshenchas* say that this ring fort where Aed was buried, the Ailech of Imchell, "that bright home of horses, would not be strong in fame" without Corrgend's shining work (*Ailech I*).

* * *

Thus, while Sulek prefers one variant of the existing myths over the other and argues that Prometheus was punished for sexual passion rather than for the theft of fire, Corrgend's myth actually gives an example of what he Sulek did not consider: a neat combination of the claims found in both of these Greek Promethean variants in one narrative. After all, Duris of Samos does not actually state that Prometheus was *not* punished for the theft of fire, only that he *was* punished for passion. Corrgend is punished for the passion which causes him to "kill" Fire, that is, he is explicitly being punished for his passion and his violence (which amounts to the theft of fire) at once, as they each form a part of the murder which he commits, as motive and act. His heart, the seat of passion, is therefore duly tortured, but he has committed no rape or prohibited lust as Sulek infers from the mention of "passion." Instead, the crime of romantic passion that Corrgend commits is a crime of a passion inspired by the passion for his own lawful wife who has been adulterously enjoyed by Aed. His love is so overpowering that it causes him to commit a grievous crime and leads to his punishment.

If we were to dare project this Irish form onto the Greek myth it would resolve the supposed contradiction between the variants that Sulek perceives, and we would then envision a similar three-way drama between Hephaestus, Athena, and Prometheus, two aspects of the Fire God, or Fire God and Fire Priest, fighting over the Seabird Goddess

399

of Wisdom. In this projected narrative, which would theoretically be an earlier form of the Greek myth, Hephaestus would attempt to rape Athena (or would do more than attempt, as in the Irish), and Prometheus (either her husband or at least desirous of being so) would be so wracked with fury and passion that he would be driven to his crime of the violent theft of fire (Hephaestus' essence) from Heaven, or violence toward Hephaestus, as these are interchangeable, being punished for both the passion and the theft in the end, as the Greek variants confusingly imply. This is only one way to view the parts coming together, however, and the fact that loose ends still abound in this projection signals the importance of variant traditions, as there could have been one tradition closer to the Irish form and one that focused entirely on the fire theft rather than the element of passion. Furthermore, the myth form of both the Irish and Greek branches likely underwent numerous changes from any shared original form, causing various features to no longer fit together in a single narrative. However, Sulek is right to point out that the fact that Prometheus is tortured in the liver, the seat of passion, requires an explanation and implies an earlier form of the myth where this passion was in some way or another a central part of the crime as in the Irish form.

This myth then explains the origin specifically of the earthly, as opposed to the celestial fire –why fire exists in the earthly realm at all. More specifically perhaps, it tells us how fire came to be established in earthly shrines and hearths dedicated to the gods.

The etymology of the name of Prometheus' Vedic parallel, Matarisvan, shows that the name refers to the process of the fire "growing in the mother," which scholars have theorized to relate both to the rubbing of the fire sticks[236] and/or to the generation of the lightning in the cloud, which then strikes down on earth and brings fire to the earthly realm in that way. We can see also how the ejaculation of the fire god Hephaestus, which impregnates Earth, may in the same manner be an image of the lightning falling to earth from out of the tumultuous clouds. The storm cloud and the rubbing sticks are then two levels of the same concept. They are "the mother" in which the flame grows, and each one can be said to be the site of the attempted rape or adultery of the sea-bird goddess which is followed by the crime of violently bringing the fire to earth, by theft, murder, or ejaculation. If the Irish form is correct the order is: first the act of prohibited lust originating from the Fire God, which perhaps generates the fire in the cloud where the Seabird Goddess is, then the passionate violence in reaction to this sexual transgression which brings the fire to earth, unless these aspects of fire generation occur

---

[236]   Though a direct etymological link of Prometheus to the fire-drill has been shown to be specious, the verb *math-* that links Prometheus and Matarisvan, according to Sulek, implies a "rubbing" that could still theoretically refer to the action of the fire-drill, as he argues (Sulek, 22).

simultaneously in a sense. As such, these versions are all interrelated, and, if we accept Sulek's arguments, may have essentially the same meaning on different levels.[237]

We also can see that the relationship of the Fire Priest God who brings the fire to earth is consistently related to the idea of artifice. Prometheus has been built up since Hesiod's time as a model of technological ingenuity, the father of the development of new and often forbidden powers stolen from the heavens, while Corrgend, for his part, is known for the swiftness of his hands and is an artificer who sets up a "nobly-bright" monument for Aed's tomb, and it is said of this tomb that he has "wrought [...] the shining work." This tomb's brightness is interesting both in relation to its status as a fire temple and in relation to the image of the shining stone, which calls to mind metal works and the specter of later technology. Pliny the Elder also writes of a famous stone known as the Hephaestus Stone. As Corrgend's stone is "bright" and "shining," the Hephaestus Stone is said to be as reflective as a mirror. It had the color of red and could set fires or cool hot water. Hephaestus, of course, is the Fire God with his Smith aspect empasized, thus the artificing and metalworking, proto-technological principle is part of him as his active function already.

As Sulek implies when he claims that the punishment for the fire-theft is a later addition, but as the Irish and Vedic cases also reinforce, none of the crimes of the parallels of Prometheus that we have examined (Corrgend and Matarisvan) are moralized in precisely the same way that we find in the Greek case (at least as it is later reinterpreted), as a heroic rebellion. In these branches the crime instead is depicted either as a more morally neutral (Vedic), if perhaps violent action (rubbing, snatching away), and a necessary prerequisite to the earthly sacrifice which honors the gods, or as a half-noble crime of passion (Irish). Neither of these parallels involve an intentional heroic rebellion against the high god. The fire-bringing action, as we can see in the etymology of the names of these figures, inherently involves friction and a concept of quick-handedness (possibly connected to the fire-drill) and these concepts of friction and quick-handedness were metaphysically reflected, it seems, in the myths of the Greeks and Celts, as the violence of theft or murder.

In the Greek case, this violent action tended to put the Earthly (Fire Priest) principle in hostile opposition to the Heavenly (Zeus), which in turn triggered a general realization:

---

237   More speculatively, perhaps what occurs in the storm cloud also occurs in the stormy mind of the earthly fire priest: the female Divine Wisdom, which is secretively guarded, is transgressed by the male Fire Within the Mind, leading to the seminal knowledge of how to generate fire by rubbing, and in consequence of this knowledge the fire priest violently rubs the sticks to draw the fire from the celestial realm and into the earthly, reproducing the original theft once performed by the divinity each time he ritually generates fire.

that once the divinity of creative development (Prometheus) was divided from and set against the Sky God, the Sky God was now at risk of being seen as an overbearing tyrant in opposition to this principle of dynamism. The Greeks, that is, must have felt that a tension within the myth was forcing itself into consciousness. The Dagda does not come off as a tyrant in the same way that Zeus does, as he is justly (and emotionally) avenging his son's murder when he punishes Corrgend. He does embody a harsh retributive justice even to the point of torture, but overall the potential for Corrgend to be seen as a heroic martyr against the tyrant sovereign god is much more buried. The way the Irish myth is presented, cryptically encoded in metaphors of the "killing" and the "tomb" of the Fire God, completely obscures the potential heroic nature of Corrgend's deed – the bringing of fire to humanity – and without close analysis and interpretation his heroic potential would remain fully submerged. At one point Corrgend is even called "every man's foe" for his crime, and overall he is treated as little more than a tragic and half-honorable murderer.

If we accept the Irish parallel as a third version of this Prometheus/Matarisvan myth, then we can critique Sulek's conclusions with this additional information and see if his hypotheses about the original form and moralization of this myth were correct. It is true that in the Irish version a heavy emphasis is placed on an initial sexual crime (as Sulek also claims of the Greek original), the adultery with Tethra which is in place of the rape of Athena, as well as on the passion of Corrgend. Yet it is neither a crime of lust nor of adultery that is the reason for the Irish Sky Sovereign's punishment, and the Irish version still has the second crime, the violence done to "Fire" itself (standing in place of Prometheus' theft of the fire). The Irish Sky Sovereign still engages in harsh retributive justice involving repetitive physical torture for the crime done to the god named "Fire," thus remaining relatively close to the Greek version. However, in line with Sulek's claim that the original form of the myth did not include the same moralization with regard to this crime and its punishment, the Dagda's motivation for this torture is at least more sympathetic than Zeus', an emotionally driven action of a grieving father and a sovereign prosecution of a murder. In this sense, the Dagda is much less prone to being read as a tyrant than Zeus in the parallel situation, and for this reason it is much less likely that the moralization of "humanity against the tyrannical high god" would be able to arise from the Irish version in later reinterpretations. It is true that Zeus has ample justification for the punishment of Prometheus within the dictates of Divine Law in his myth. However, considering the myths only on the level of appearance and emotional impact, it is important to contrast the fact that the Dagda does not explicitly punish Corrgend for allowing humanity to have fire and its techno-cultural upshots. He does not seem to be trying to keep fire from humans at any point, at least *on the face of it,* while Zeus does. In fact, Dagda is the one who forces Corrgend to bury Aed, to bury "Fire," in the earth, and to set up a tomb-temple over him, effectively giving fire to the earthly realm.

Yet despite this it is still possible that the latent meaning of these variants is the same at the core. If the killing of Aed is the bringing of Fire down from the upper realm to the terrestrial, then Dagda still is reacting to the same action that Zeus is, only in an almost romanticized form, depicted here in the context of an emotionally grieving father, this personal drama concealing the core meaning that still mostly matches that of the Prometheus myth: in both cases the criminal is punished for cutting "fire" off from the celestial sphere. Thus we cannot say that the Irish form of the myth can truly shed light on whether the Sky Sovereign's motive for the torture we see in the Greek form was merely a Greek innovation absent form the proto-form of the myth. From the evidence presented, it instead appears possible that something close to the same meaning has merely become more latent in the Irish form or less latent in the Greek. The transgressive heroic meaning that accrues to the figure of Prometheus over time, though not nearly as present in the figure of Corrgend, can yet be said to be present there in latent form as well, as Corrgend is still the half-justified criminal who ultimately brings humanity Fire and pays the price of torture for this action. True, in the Irish telling it is not Corrgend's conscious intent to altruistically give the gift of fire to humanity, he merely is following passion and avenging a wrong done to him. But his action still is the source of what comes after, of all future "shining works," and he still gains honor through his passionate action. All this being said, we can see that, in particular, the specific way the Greek myth presents the opposition of the criminal to the high god, particularly with a more blunt, even theologically decontextualized depiction of Zeus, which leaves him open to being misconstrued as more of a paper tyrant with a seemingly anti-human motive (not wanting humans to have fire, wanting revenge for being outwitted), only appears in the Greek version. As a result of such details of the depiction, we end up over time with the moralization we are familiar with. We can say that while the core of the myth seems to have remained relatively stable between the Irish and Greek cases, these particular Greek narrative *colorings* do not exactly accord with the *colorings* of any other versions of the myth that we have examined here[238], and it should be obvious that different philosophical fallout in each case would be explained well enough by such different colorings.

---

238   However, compare Parallels of Prometheus' torture in the myths of Pkharmat of the Vainakh people, Amirani of the Georgians, and Batraz of the Narts. The forms of the myths in legends such as these suggest that the colorings found in the Greek myth form may have been generally consistent with others in the region between Greece and Western Asia.

What are we seeing in the Greek form of this important myth, then? The aspect of the Fire God which is the principle of dynamic unfolding *separates* himself from and contrasts himself against the Sky Sovereign in the figure of Prometheus. What is a specifically religious allegory about gaining fire to sacrifice to the gods in the projected archaic form, in the Greek version becomes *also* a psychological (as opposed to strictly theological) allegory about the existential danger inherent in this separation of the principle of dynamic unfolding from the Sky Sovereign. When this dynamic principle is exteriorized from the order given by the Sky Sovereign, it becomes chaotic and volatile, potentially even more dynamic and also more destructive at the same time. It poses itself against the Sky Sovereign in this form, but this is a sovereign who in this moment is set on negating and punishing. However, as we have suggested, the particular psychological emphasis given in the Greek form of this myth says more about how the Greeks saw themselves in their relation to the religious forms of their time than it does about the theological status of Zeus and the Fire Priest God. A Titanic energy within the Greeks, developing after Hesiod's time with the Athenians almost exclusively at first, led them to reinterpret this opposition more and more as heroic and paradigmatic. A mythic self-deconstruction, initiated by the Athenian reception of Hesiod's depiction of Prometheus, has continued over the succeeding centuries and continues to influence the historical process we find ourselves within today.

14

Neit/Neto: A Celtic Vishnu?

Is there a Celtic god who we can say resembles Vishnu in a meaningful way? Though we search through the most prominent Celtic deities, we find parallels to other Vedic gods, but, thus far, nothing believable pointing to Vishnu.

However, one god, not one of the most well-known, a god named only in a handful of sparse fragments, offers a suggestive possibility, and so we can offer this speculation. Macrobius mentions a god of the Iberian Celts named Mars Neto/Neton (elsewhere also spelled Neithi) who wears a radiant crown like the sun, and according to him this is because the passion or fervor to act with valor is a kind of solar heat.

> In Accitana, too, the Spanish nation, an image of Mars ornamented with beams is most religiously celebrated, they call it Neton […] the fervor with which the mind becomes incensed and arouses to anger and at other times to virtue, and sometimes to the excess of temporary fury, through which things also arise in wars, they named Mars […]

> In short, it is to be pronounced the effect of the sun, from which the heat of the soul, from which the heat of the blood is aroused, is called Mars. (Macrobius, *Saturnalia*, 19)

Thus, this solar "heat of the soul" or radiant passion that enables the warrior's valorous action is a key element of Mars Neto, even if we known little else about him.

405

Now Vishnu specifically aids Indra in battle with his *tejas*, sometimes embodied in a banner (compare the solar beams that ornament Neton), as we see below, and this word *tejas* means "radiant heat" or "spirit." A line of the *Mahabharata* addressed to Indra reads: "O lord. Resorting to the foam of the waters that was strengthened by the splendor of Viṣṇu, thou hast slain Vṛtra of yore" (*Mahabharata* 5.16). Thus Vishnu, a war god, aids the other primary war god specifically with a kind of radiant heat or solar splendor.

Vishnu's solar aspect has long been obvious to interpreters (see Macdonell, *Vedic Mythology*, 38-39), but he is also an extremely important war god. This war aspect of his is often forgotten or under-emphasized, even though early recognized avatars of Vishnu were frequently known as conquering warriors, such as the heroic warrior-king Vasudeva, depicted with a battle mace, Krishna, who urges Arjuna, Indra's incarnation, to war, giving him the spirit to fight as Vishnu does for Indra himself, and Narasimha, the fierce part-lion avatar who violently destroys evil. We see in the quotations below from Roger Woodard that Vishnu is not only a war god, but that he is one of the most important Vedic war gods, and, furthermore, that being a warrior and aiding other war deities with his radiant spirit are two of his most central functions.

> The banner of Indra is described in the *Bṛhatsaṃhitā of Varāhamihira* 43 and the *Bhaviṣya Purāṇa* (summarized in Gonda 1993: 255–259; Kramrisch 1947). Fearing the demons, the gods took counsel with Brahmā, who instructed them to obtain from Viṣṇu a banner which would protect them from the demons (*VarāhBS* 43.1–2). **The banner that Viṣṇu provided was created from his own radiant energy (*tejas*), shining like the sun. With the raising of this banner, decorated with garlands, bells, and other small objects, Indra defeated the enemy** (*VarāhBS* 43.5–6).
>
> The king recites verses to the *Indradhvaja*, calling it 'unborn, imperishable, eternal, of unchanging form'; addressing it as 'Viṣṇu, the wild boar' as well as 'Indra' (Gonda 1993: 256). Invoking Agni and Indra, destroyer of the monster Vṛtra, the king prays that his warriors will achieve victory (*VarāhBS* 43.52–55). (Woodard, 76)
>
> Like the *linga* of Śiva—and the Irish stone of Fál—the Vedic *yūpa* is also possessed by a warrior deity. The *yūpa* belongs to Viṣṇu, affiliated with the warrior element of divine society, and is also associated with Indra (compare its alloform, the *Indradhvaja*, 'Indra's banner'). (Woodard, 95)
>
> The Maruts are a band of warrior deities, sons of Rudra (later Śiva), who are especially closely linked to Indra as comrades-in-arms, but are at times also associated with Viṣṇu, and also with Parjanya, god of rain and thundering

storm, or Trita Āptya, another warrior deity affiliated with and showing similarities to Indra. (Woodard, 169)

Viṣṇu (see especially §§2.6.1; 2.6.3; 2.7), the three-stepping god who is companion to Indra, assisting him in the fight against the dragon (§§4.9.2.4; 4.9.2.8.1) and at times affiliated with Indra's warrior band, the Maruts (§4.8.2). (Woodard, 259)

[…] when Viṣṇu is celebrated by himself, Indra is the only other god who is given a place; when about to perform his supreme feat of slaying Vṛtra, Indra implores Viṣṇu to step out more widely. (Woodard, 259)

Viṣṇu, in taking his three steps, transcends and **conquers** the spaces of the universe (see Gonda 1993: 55 with references). (Woodard, 260)

Indra is at times drawn into **Viṣṇu's conquering advance**, creating space for humankind. In the Soma ceremony hymn of *Rig Veda* 6.69, for example, Indra and Viṣṇu (denoted by the dvandva *Indrāviṣṇū*) are invoked to come to the Soma feast on their 'enemy-conquering horses' (stanza 4); are urged to lead the sacrificers forward on paths free from obstructions (stanza 1); are praised for stepping broadly and thereby increasing the space of the air and making broad the regions of space for humankind (stanza 5). The hymn ends (stanza 8) by addressing the two warrior deities as conquering but unconquered, as having brought about limitless threefold space when they had fought. (Woodard, 260)

Viṣṇu, is the god who conquers and creates space. (Woodard, 260)

Thus the "space" that Vishnu is often associated with can more specifically be the living space conquered through war. This conquering of space was enacted via Vishnu's role in the sacrifice as lord of sacred space:

The questing journey of the sacrificer and priests into the great sacred space of the Mahāvedi, the staking out of that space with altars and huts, and the continued progress toward the column that stands on its distal, eastern border (a boundary which is not) constitute an odyssey in which gods of war play a fundamental role. Most notable in the event is Viṣṇu, the god who transcends, conquers, and expands space. Indra, most renowned of the warrior gods, accompanies him. (Woodard, 261)

Lastly, Woodard directly analogizes Vishnu and Indra to Mars, the deity with whom Neto is syncretized in Macrobius.

Homologous to the conspicuous presence of the warrior gods Indra and Viṣṇu in the space of the Mahāvedi is the presence of Mars in the space of

407

the Ager Romanus. To phrase the matter somewhat differently: whatever it is that Indra and Viṣṇu are doing within the Mahāvedi, Mars is doing the same within the Ager Romanus. The procession of Vedic priests through the Mahāvedi and the ambarvalic movement of Roman priests through the Ager Romanus are both descended from a common ancestral rite of the questing journey from the small sacred space into the great. The journey is an invasion; the gods of war must be invoked to take the lead, to vanquish the opponent, to secure possession of the invaded space. As warrior Indra and, especially, Viṣṇu, the god who enlarges space, are bound to the Vedic *yūpa*, the marker of the unboundary, source and means of blessing, so Mars is linked to the Roman *terminus* (deified as Terminus). He is present and invoked around the distal rim of the Ager Romanus, at those terminal points of ritual salience. (Woodard, 262)

Looking to Ireland we have Neit/Net, a dangerous war god who may be the Irish variant of Neto, and whose name means "fighting" or "passion" (perhaps a solar passion similar to the *tejas*), and this Neit is one generation above even the Dagda. He is the Dagda's uncle, Nuada and Dian Cecht's grandfather, and Lugh's great-great-grandfather on *both* sides. This positions Neit as potentially more primordial, closer to the Source or Origin, than any of the better-known chiefs of the gods. The only names *of note* that are further back than Neit's in the genealogy are his mysterious father, Indui, "king of the north country, lord of horse breeding peoples," and Fintan (seemingly a primordial Rudraic manifestation). Vishnu is called an "ancient" ritual expert or ordainer in RV 1.156.2, and "the ancient one who is by birth the embryo of truth" in verse 3 of the same hymn. Verse 5 of this hymn says he "enlivened the Arya," which ties back to his role as solar enlivener.

Another of Vishnu's most important qualities is that he is identified with the sacrifice. He is said to be the sacrifice, for example in *Śatapatha Brahmana* 3.6.4.1–2, 9. He is also asked to give heat or fervor to the sacrifice in *Atharvaveda* 5.26.7. One of the few things we know about Irish Neit is that when Aed is killed by Corrgend, Aed is buried either in a fort called Ailech Neit, Neit's Stonehouse, given to the Dagda by Neit, or in Ailech Imchell, described as "in the precinct where dwelt Neit and Nemain [his wife]" (*Dindshenchas, Ailech I-II*). Both of the attested gravesites of Aed are directly and solely connected with Neit and his wife. If we recall that Aed's "grave" would actually be a site of the first fire shrine, considering that he is Fire directly comparable to the fire stolen and brought to earth by Prometheus/Matarisvan, and thus that his grave-shrine would be a potential location of sacrifice, we can see that Neit's "Stonehouse" could very well be a primordial sacred enclosure used for sacrifice and fire worship. Vishnu, on the other hand, is identified with the sacrifice itself and also is the lord of the sacred space of the sacrifice, both enlarging it and setting its boundary (which can also be an *un*boundary), as Woodard notes above. If we consider Neit to be, like Vishnu, the lord of the sacred space of sacrifice, this could explain the involvement of Neit, a supposedly narrow War God, in the burial of Aed in his Stonehouse in particular and in no one else's. We may never know who Neto and Neit are with certainty, but if the Celts had a variant of the god Vishnu he would have had to look something like this God of War, Solar Passion, and Sacred Space.

15

The Celtic Creation Myth: Branwen, Matholwch, and Efnysien, or: Earth, Sky, and Rudra

Is Efnysien Rudraic?

The Second Branch of *the Mabinogi, Branwen, daughter of Llyr*, is a tantalizing canvas on which interpreters have painted many a colorful thesis. We will add our own here, as certain considerations point to a momentous Rudraic quality in the sower of strife, Efnysien.

Marcel Meulder in his article "Nisien and Efnisien: Odinic couple or dioscuric?" has shown a strong parallel of Efnysien, known as the sower of strife, and his brother Nisien, known as the bringer of peace and accord, to Scandinavian figures Bolwis and Bilwis of Saxo's *Gesta Danorum*, two figures who are also described in very similar terms, as a bringer of strife and a bringer of peace. Meulder has then demonstrated that these are each Odinnic pairs in terms of their qualities and mythic parallels[239]. The Mabinogi of *Branwen, daughter of Llyr* describes Nisien and his brother Efnysien thus: "one of these youths was a good youth and of gentle nature, and would make peace between his kindred, and cause his family to be friends when their wrath was at the highest; and this one was Nissyen; but the other would cause strife between his two brothers when they were most at peace" (*Branwen, daughter of Llyr*). Of Bolwis and Bilwis, similarly: "The temper of these two men was so different, that one used to reconcile folk who were at feud, while the other loved to sunder in hatred those who were bound by friendship, and by estranging folk to fan pestilent quarrels." One of these brothers, like Efnysien, incites a war: "So Bolwis began by reviling the sons of Hamund to the sons of Sigar, in lying slanders, declaring that they never used to preserve the bonds of fellowship loyally, and that they must be restrained by war rather than by league. Thus the alliance of the young men was broken through; and while Hagbard was far away, the sons of Sigar, Alf and Alger, made an attack, and Helwin and Hamund were destroyed by the harbour which is called Hamund's Bay" (Saxo Grammaticus, *Gesta Danorum*, Book 7). Meulder points next to brothers Deiphobus and Helenus of the *Iliad*, who seem to repeat the pattern of strife-bringing and peace-bringing brothers and may form another direct parallel to the Welsh and Scandinavian pairs. Meulder concludes that, as these are Odinnic heroes, these pairs are Varuna-Mitra-type dual sovereigns, considering Odinn's well-known parallel to Varuna.[240]

---

239   See also Alaric Hall who connects Efnisien to Odinn from a different angle: "Efnisien's third appearance emphasizes his similarity to *Odinn*-heroes. Entering the hall which the Irish have built, he 'wnaeth … edrych golygon orwyllt antrugarawc ar hyt y ty' ('he looked about throughout the house with very wild, ruthless glances')" (Alaric Hall, "Gwŷr y Gogledd? Some Icelandic Analogues of Branwen Ferch Lŷr," 42).

240   "HE Davidson, recalls that Bilwisus and Bolwisus have been interpreted as two different aspects of Odin; this god is, according to the *Ynglinga Saga* (chap. 7), helpful with his friends and terrifying with his enemies, and, adds HE Davidson, Saxo Grammaticus would have given the two brother advisers two names that Odin bears in the *Grímnismál*, namely Báleygr (fiery eye) and Bileygr (rogue eye). But R. Simek, followed by J. Renaud, proposes by this second name a completely different interpretation, since it translates it as 'who is provided with a weak sight', allusion made to the lost eye of Odin. In this case, we could not only interpret the names of the brother advisers, one Bilwisus as meaning 'wise tending to weakness', the other Bolwisus as a 'wise man brought to ardor', but still bringing them closer to the Trojans Helenos and Deiphobe; because if the two adviser brothers of the king of Denmark represent the type of Odin in his ambivalence, then, as Odin is the Germanic counterpart of Mitra – Varuna, Bilwisus and Bolwisus would be the fraternal couple of royal advisers, as are Helenos and Deiphobe in

This is a fascinating alignment of pairings, but the ultimate conclusion seems to us misguided. Odinn is more than only Varunian, and we have demonstrated a strong alignment of Lleu, rather than the very minor character Nisien, to the Mitraic god. The Four Branches of the *Mabinogi* are a linked cycle of myths where one god should not usually appear twice under different names, unless they are a deity type prone to multiplicity, like Rudra or the Gandharva. Mitra and his parallels are not prone to such multiplicity in any branches, but instead the Mitraic god has a well-defined role that we have closely tracked. Furthermore, Efnysien and Nisien are not even sovereigns, while the Mitra-Varuna-types are nearly always sovereigns, with limited exceptions if any (Tyr), sovereignty being one of the core facets of their role. The Varunian god may also appear elsewhere in the Four Branches of the Mabinogi. According to Guillaume Oudaer, whose interpretation seems highly plausible to us, the water-associated figure named Teyrnon Twryf Lliant from *Pwyll, prince of Dyfed,* or the First Branch, whose name means "Lord of the Roaring Sea," may be the Varuna/Lludd/Nuada of the Mabinogi[241]. While there are thus figures already taking the Mitraic and Varunian roles in the *Mabinogi*, there is no other destructive Rudraic figure among the heroes of these Four Branches. This role is taken by Balor in the Irish myths, and Balor's most obvious direct analogue appears as the giant Ysbadadden in *Culwhch and Olwen,* but this tale is part of a different cycle of tales not part of the Four Branches of the *Mabinogi*, and as such Efnysien and Ysbaddaden having different names is no problem in our interpretation. Taliesin (born Gwion) makes an appearance in the particular war found in *Branwen*, alongside Efnysien, but Taliesin proper is more of a direct parallel of Irish Oisin, son of Fionn, at least in terms of the division of Rudraic roles we have previously analyzed. Efnysien and Taliesin fighting side by side then would be something like Fionn and Oisin or one of the other Fianna fighting together, and would not imply redundancy. Furthermore, as we see with the Irish Fianna, the Rudraic figures are many and appear in several different roles. The figure we will propose is the primordial Welsh Rudra (Efnysien) would not then have to share the identical name of the Welsh "Rudra of the world" (Gwyn/Gwion). Rudra is the god above all others who may appear under a multiplicity of shapes and names, as the case of Odinn, he of the many names, makes abundantly clear. As such, the Rudraic angle should be tested in the case of both Efnysien and his contrasting brother Nisien, as several points suggest its plausibility. Moreover, we have already suggested Deiphobus as a Rudraic hero in another connection, considering his death by Menelaus to end the war, his disfigured face upon death, and his name meaning "hostile panic," from δᾱῐος (*dāïos*, "hostile") + φόβος

---

some Greek literature" (Meulder, 4-5).

"*Bolwisus* has never been compared to a nickname of Odin, namely *Bolverkr* 'troublemaker'" (Meulder, 4).

241   "Teyrnon Twryf Lliant," Guillaume Oudaer, *Ollodagos* 24, p. 5-42. 2010.

(*phóbos*, "panic flight"), each element of which echoes Balor and other Rudraic figures. The name *Efnyisien* also contains the word *efnys*, meaning "hostile, wrathful,"[242] thus establishing a close linguistic connection between he and Deiphobus. Note that one perhaps similar name of Odinn, which expresses an Efnysien-like characteristic, is *Þrasarr*, "quarreler." In this interpretation, the quarrelsome and strife-bringing Efnysien would be the destructive half of the primordial form of the Rudraic deity, and the peace-bringing Nisien would be the auspicious and peaceful side of the Welsh Rudra, otherwise known as Siva by the Vedics, for indeed Rudra is a god well-known for having two sides precisely along the lines expressed by the two contrasting Welsh brothers: Rudra "has two natures or two 'names': the one, cruel and wild (rudra), the other kind (śiva) and tranquil (śānta)" (Kramrisch, 26). Indeed, Rudra is Siva at least as far back as the *Rig Veda* (RV 10.92.9).

Efnysien begins his action in the tale by mutilating the horses of the King of Ireland, Matholwch. As we have seen, the destructive killing of cows and their calves belongs to the Rudraic type. In our chapter on the Celtic Rudras, the Rudraic Fianna warrior Caoilte was seen to go on a rampage "killing the calves with the cows," while Kris Kershaw was cited summing up Rudra as "cow-man-killer = fructifier" and describing the archaic mannerbunde as storming into farmsteads and slaughtering cattle. While Efnysien mutilates horses rather than cows, the theme of the frightening and seemingly inexplicable violence done to livestock links him to Rudra.

As the rudra incarnation of the *Mahabharata*, Ashwatthama, sacrifices himself in a fire on a magical altar at the climax of the war, Efnysien also sacrifices himself at the climax of his war. Ashwatthama does not die in his sacrifice, while Efnysien does. However, both sacrifices are aimed at similar ends. Ashwatthama sacrifices himself to gain battle prowess to defeat his enemies in the desperate moment near the end of the war, when nearly all of his side's generals have been killed and things look grim. Efnysien sacrifices himself at a very similar late, desperate moment, to remove the thing that is causing his side to be defeated in the war: the cauldron of regeneration that is in the possession of his enemies.

Efnysien kills the young child of the opposing king, Matholwch, while Ashwatthama kills all the children of his opposing king, Yudhishthira, as well as the children of the other Pandavas. Efnysien performs his self-sacrifice right after killing this young child of Matholwch, Gwern, while Ashwatthama performs his self-sacrifice right before his

---

242   *efnys*: "hostile, wrathful; enemy, foe, enemies, adversaries." Geiriadur Prifysgol Cymru, A Dictionary of the Welsh Language. https://welsh-dictionary.ac.uk/gpc/gpc.html?efnys. Accessed November, 2021. See also: https://www.oxfordreference.com/view/10.1093/oi/authority.20110803095743687. Accessed November 2021.

assault on the camp of the Pandavas during which he kills their children. Thus far, each of these figures are attackers of livestock, self-sacrificers, and killers of children.

When brought into alignment with the *Iliad* pair, Deiphobus and Helenus, who themselves are portrayed as brothers in some sources which Meulder cites, more becomes apparent. As brothers, one is gentle (Helenus), while the other's name means "hostile panic" (Diephobus). Helenus, a gentle and skilled prophetic seer (seership being a well-established Rudraic role[243]), is responsible for the removal of the magical object that is keeping the Achaeans from winning the war. He is captured by the Achaeans and tells Odysseus that the only way Troy can fall is if the Palladium, the sacred wooden statue of Athena, is taken from the city. Thus Odysseus and Diomedes steal the Palladium and Troy, losing its divine protection, becomes conquerable. Though Helenus does not remove the Palladium himself, he reluctantly gives the direction which leads to its removal. While Ashwatthama has a gem in his forehead which grants him special powers in battle, and the ability to speak to ghosts (remember that Rudra's power of prophecy is connected to seeing ghosts and that Odinn's power of prophecy involves reviving dead seeresses), Helenus has had his ear (located also in his head) licked by snakes and the power of prophecy given to him by Apollo, who is the primary Greek Rudra and the Greek high god of prophecy next to Pan. Ashwatthama, with the same sort of reluctance we had seen in the parallel action of Helenus, removes the overwhelming gem of power from his own forehead after his slaughter of the Pandava camp, opening up the way for the final victory of his opponents, thus paralleling the removal of the Palladium under the direction of Helenus[244]. Welsh Efnysien is also directly responsible for the destruction of the powerful object that is keeping his side losing the war. This is the Cauldron of Regeneration and he goes to its destruction with a lamentation which emphasizes the desperation of the state of himself and his allies at this moment: "Alas! woe is me, that I should have been the cause of bringing the men of the Island of the Mighty into so great a strait. Evil betide me if I find not a deliverance therefrom" (*Branwen, daughter of Llyr*). The war is hopeless for Efnysien and his compatriots until in one act he sacrifices himself and destroys this cauldron which keeps reviving the warriors of the opposing side. In Efnysien's case, his side does not achieve true victory, but this act allows them a better chance. Matholwch and his army end up being obliterated, and a handful of Efnysien's allies escape back to Britain as a result: "In consequence of [the destruction of the cauldron] the men of the Island of the Mighty

---

243   "Rudra, the thousandeyed god, puts into the right hand of the seer an herb that makes him see everything—the three heavens, the three earths, and all existences down to the sorcerers and the ghouls (AV.4.20.1-9)" (Kramrisch, 94).

244   Credit to Zagreides for bringing this connection to my attention.

obtained such success as they had; but they were not victorious, for only seven men of them all escaped" (*Branwen, daughter of Llyr*).

As Meulder notes, citing Gl. Goetinck, it thus can be said that all of the seemingly psychopathic actions taken by Efnysien are in fact aimed at the greater good of his people:

> [Efnisien] tries first of all to prevent the marriage itself, ie the removal of the early representative of the female divinity and the source of power, then when the alliance proves to be unsatisfactory and there is a chance of restoring the old order, he tries to destroy Gwern, the fruit of alliance, so that Branwen may be brought home to begin anew with no ties to the unsuccessful venture [...] [Efnisien] is presented as a man overcome by repentance at the sight of the slaughter he has caused, but his real motivation may be despair at the destruction caused by Brân's arrangements to alter the order of succession. Efnisien gives his life in a desperate attempt to salvage something from the wreck caused, not by himself, but by someone else. (Goetinck, G., "Dioscuric and other themes in Branwen," *Ollodagos,* vol. 6, p. 219-254, 1994)

His mutilation of the horses, a result of his objection to the marriage of Branwen and Matholwch in the first place, is an attempt to avert the whole situation, and, as it turns out, he is perhaps right to mistrust Matholwch who in the end abuses Branwen and brings on the war. His killing of Matholwch and Branwen's son is another attempt to sever what he sees as the ill-fated connection between these nations, not to mention the fact that, at the moment Efnysien kills the child, Matholwch is attempting to covertly kill Bran and him, and so the alliance that the boy represents is already poisoned. This sort of "policing" role of Efnysien, taking brutal action to attempt to avert disaster, falls in line with the rest of what he is seen to do, as when he sniffs out the plot to assassinate himself and his brother and kills all of the men who are lain in wait in the sacks of grain in the house provided by Matholwch. As such, though not outright called a prophet, Efnysien has a power very similar to a prophetic figure, over and over again foreseeing the destruction that will come and attempting to head it off. How indeed does he foresee the war and destruction the marriage would bring and how indeed does he instantly find out the plot against him and his brother? Meanwhile, Helenus of Troy is called the best of all augurs, and it is specifically he who prophesies that if Paris takes Helen the Greeks will pursue and kill them all. Thus Helenus explicitly objects to the marriage of Paris and Helen, an objection resulting from his prophetic power, and does so for the reason that it will bring war and destruction. Efnysien essentially does the same thing, objecting to the marriage of Branwen and Matholwch. The prophetic element is not made explicit in his case, and the idea that he has sniffed out a specific danger in the match is also only an inference on our part from his other actions, which are consistently aimed at averting bad outcomes that others do not foresee.

The scene of the plot against Efnysien and Bran in the house given by Matholwch can also be set against the cosmological role of Rudra which we briefly touched on in our "Math fab Mathonwy" chapter. Rudra, as Stella Kramrisch describes the scene in her book *The Presence of Siva*, is a policing wanderer of the pre-cosmic wilderness. When Rudra (united in some sense with Fire God Agni[245], as Fire God Manawydan is also one of Efnysien's allies in the war) sees Dyaus obscenely copulating with his "daughter," he shoots his arrow at him, causing the seed of Dyaus/Heaven/Sky to spill onto Earth, creating the site of sacrifice there from the lake of fiery sperm and spawning the fire youths, also known as the fire priests or Angirases, who become the ancestors of humanity. Macdonell explains: "The story is several times referred to in the Brahmanas (AB. 3, 33; SB. 1, 7, 4, 1; PB. 8, 2, 10). The basis of this myth seem to be two passages of the **RV. (1, 71, 5; 10, 61, 5-7)** in which the incest of a father (who seems to be Dyaus) with his daughter (here apparently the Earth) is referred to and an archer is mentioned" (Macdonell, *Vedic Mythology*, 119).

As this creation myth is told in explicit detail in two hymns of the *Rig Veda*:

> He whose (penis,) which performs the virile work, stretched out, discharging (the semen)—(that one,) the manly one, then pulled away (his penis, which had been) 'attending on' (her).

> Again he tears out from the maiden, his daughter, what had been 'brought to bear' on her—he the unassailable.

> When what was to be done was at its middle, at the encounter when the father was making love to the young girl—

---

245   "Agni, the sacrificial fire, had in view mankind and its life in this world. Agni-Rudra, on the other hand, was outraged. He aimed his arrow of fire at the Father, not because it is his daughter with whom he has intercourse but because it is the substance itself of the Uncreate that he is spending into procreation. Rudra acted as guardian and avenger of the Uncreate and metaphysical wholeness; Agni is the guardian of ṛta, of cosmic order in creation and of human life lived in accordance with it. Though one in nature, Agni and Rudra face in opposite directions: Agni's concern is the life of man, and Rudra's concern is man's freedom from the contingencies of life, his reintegration into the absolute as it was and is from before creation" (Kramrisch, 46-47).
"Agni acts in Rudra and Rudra exceeds him in intensity. **He is Agni's incandescence.** As such, Rudra is 'king of the
sacrifice' (RV.4.3.1), 'priest of both worlds' (TS.1.3.14.1), and 'fulfiller of the sacrifice' (RV.1.114.4). Rudra, for
not playing Agni's sacerdotal role, is overcompensated and raised above Agni, the high priest" (Kramrisch, 50).

as they were going apart, the two left behind a little semen sprinkled down on the back and in the womb of the well-performed (sacrifice).

When the father [Dyaus] 'sprang on' his own daughter, he, uniting (with her), poured down his semen upon the earth.

The gods, very concerned, begat the sacred formulation [the magical *raudra brahman* poem], and they fashioned out (of it?) the Lord of the Dwelling Place [Vāstoṣpati], protector of commandments.

Like a bull in a contest he threw off foam. Heedless, she went away, hither and yon.

Twisting away, she hastened like the Gift-Cow on foot. [The father:] 'Now those caresses of mine have not grasped (her)' (RV 10.61.5-8).

When he [Agni or Rudra-Agni] made the sap [=semen] for great Father Heaven [Dyaus], noting the caresses he stealthily crept up (on him).

The archer [Rudra-Agni] boldly loosed a missile at him (when) the god placed his 'spark' in his own daughter. (RV 1.71.5)

When the (missile's) sharp point reached the lord of men (for him) to release it, Heaven [Dyaus], at the moment of contact, (released) the blazing semen poured out.

Agni engendered the faultless young troop of good intention [=Aṅgirases, who are the fire youths/ancestors of humans] and sweetened it. (RV 1.71.8)

In other seemingly later elaborations on the theme, as Kramrisch lays it out, Rudra is not invited to the sacrifice of Daksha, and so, lurking on the outskirts, he shoots his arrow at the sacrifice itself, which causes it to become filled with strangely destructive power, and when Pushan bites into it he breaks his teeth. In this myth, the fact that Rudra has not been invited to the scene of sacrifice, that he is a lurking, policing outsider, is made clear. This is characteristic of him. Efnysien, in the Welsh case, is specifically said to be angered to begin with because he has not been consulted in the marriage – he has been excluded from the marriage plan at the assembly where the arrangements are made. This can then be seen to mirror the exclusion that Rudra experiences, excluded from the sacrifice, which "outsider" quality, in the Rig Vedic myth, is also connected to a sexual conjunction, thus a kind of marriage, to which he also actively objects. Both Efnysien and Rudra similarly object to a sexual union, and do so with a direct reaction of violence aimed toward the involved male.

Thus if we interpret the marriage of Branwen and Matholwch and the later scene of the attempted assassination of Bran and Efnysien, followed by the killing of Gwern, all as symbolic events related to the scene of primordial sacrifice, then they can be made to align, with startling closeness and ease, with the Vedic myth of Rudra and the primordial sacrifice, and the full meaning of *Branwen, daughter of Llyr* gradually becomes clear. While Rudra either shoots his arrow at Dyaus, causing his fiery seed to spill while in the act of union, creating the site of sacrifice and fire youths, or shoots his arrow at the sacrifice itself, Efnysien instead takes the child who has been born to Matholwch and Branwen and throws him into the fire. Thus the fiery seed of Dyaus, which becomes the fire youths and site of sacrificial fire = the child of Matholwch, who is instead thrown *into* the fire. Seed = Child. Each one is the vital emission, the would-be offspring, cut short, of the Father. The fiery seed falls and becomes sacrificial fire = The child is thrown into fire. As Kramrisch says of the seed of the Father, Dyaus-Prajapati: "Prajāpati is the target of Rudra. When his seed falls on earth, it is surrounded by Agni [Fire]" (Kramrisch, 27), and forms a lake of seed and fire which is then the sacrificial site. Gwern too, the seed of his father, is "surrounded" by fire as a result of Efnysien's action.

Other than the fact that any fire in myth might symbolically be sacrificial, we should also be tipped off to the possibility that the fire into which Gwern is thrown is a sacrificial one by a couple of other details. It has been said at this point in the tale that a house had never contained Bran, the king of Britain and brother of Efnysien and Branwen, and so this is what Matholwch has sought to do, to give Bran a house that will contain him. We have seen in the case of Neit that "stonehouse" can mean the site of sacred fire and sacrifice. Thus the "house" that is made to contain the giant Bran should be suspected of being a similar type of building, a sacred space of ritual. The house is specially rigged to be the place where Bran is killed, which may imply that he is meant to be the sacrifice. Meanwhile, we have mentioned previously that in the *Rig Veda*, Yama, the apparent parallel of Bran, is said to be sacrificed at Brihaspati's sacrifice. In other instances, Yama or his parallels are cut apart or beheaded (Donn, Jamshid, etc.), and a different god, Daksha, is also beheaded at the sacrifice from which Rudra is excluded, while Bran too is beheaded in the battle just after the scene at the "house." The fire into which the boy Gwern is thrown appears in this house that was intended to contain and kill Bran, reinforcing the possibility that this specially made containing-house with the fire, is a sacrificial space. In sum: as Dyaus rapes his daughter and shoots his fiery seed onto Earth and is shot with the arrow of the excluded, strife-bringing, policing figure Rudra-Agni, which creates the site of the fire sacrifice (or the sacrifice itself is similarly shot by Rudra), Matholwch abuses Branwen, has a child with her, and then the child is quickly thrown by the excluded, strife-bringing, policing figure Efnysien into a fire in a specially made house.

If this were a fair comparison, we might find a parallel of both the Vedic and Welsh accounts in the Greek theogonies. Rig Vedic Dyaus (Sky) rapes a daughter who scholars have interpreted as Earth (Macdonell) or Dawn (Brereton and Jamison), though it is truly unclear who this daughter-victim is in the *Rig Veda*, and then Rudra shoots Dyaus in the act, severing their conjunction and causing the seed to spill onto the earth in a creative act. In the Greek case (particularly Hesiod's *Theogony*), we know that Ouranos (Sky) is the consort of Gaia, Earth, and they form a *hieros gamos*, a primordial union of Sky and Earth. However, Gaia grows upset because Ouranos is trapping her children, the Titans and others, in Tartarus, deep in her bosom, which causes her pain. Thus she summons Cronus and he severs his father's genitals and deposes him as Ouranos is approaching Gaia to forcefully mate with her once more: "And Heaven [Ouranos] came, bringing on night and longing for love, and he lay about Earth spreading himself full upon her. Then the son [Cronus] from his ambush stretched forth his left hand and in his right took the great long sickle with jagged teeth, and swiftly lopped off his own father's members" (Hesiod, *Theogony*, 176-180). This causes an outpouring of creative seed which spawns Aphrodite, who may be related to the core essence of the fire itself, as she is the spouse of the Fire God Hephaestus. The wife of the Vedic Fire God Agni is Svaha, who has been interpreted in the *Brahmavaivarta Purana,* as the *shakti* or power within the fire sacrifice that cannot be burned by Agni, and one of her sons is the embodiment of beauty as is Aphrodite herself[246]. The fiery seed of Dyaus spawns the fire youths and creates the site of the sacrificial fire. We thus would see in Branwen the primordial Earth Goddess and her conjunction which spawns the boy, the seed of the Father, destined for the fire, would be that *hieros gamos,* that divine union, between Sky and Earth. If so, this would make Matholwch Father Sky.

In an earlier investigation, we have noted provisionally some myths related to Father Sky that may have resonances with myths of Bran. However, these seem either to be coincidental or to have resulted from a displacement of myths onto closely connected sovereign figures, two opposing but linked kings of Celtic myth. Consider that Irish Father Sky Dagda sometimes is called Dagda *Donn*, Donn being the parallel of Bran/Yama. Additionally, as the first "mortal" king of the world, Bran aka Yama is a repetition of Father Sky within the first "mortal" king, and thus a certain amount of slippage of motifs between Father Sky and the King that is as if a repetition of his image could be expected. One etymology of *Math* is in fact "good,"[247] which would relate

---

246   Roshen Dalal, *Hinduism: An Alphabetical Guide, "Svaha, goddess".*

247   Gael Hily states that *Math* "can come from **mati-* 'good, favorable', resulting from

Matholwch directly to the Dagda, whose name means "the Good God." While Math fab Mathonwy, the separate sunrise god, is not a parallel of the Dagda, Matholwch, supported by his mythical role, would be the Welsh Dagda/Father Sky instead, and his name would be a key piece of evidence of this. For another thing, while Bran begins with the magical cauldron, it is Matholwch who is then given the magical cauldron and is its final owner before it is destroyed, and thus both Dagda and Matholwch are the last known owners of their respective cauldrons.

As for Branwen, while the pain caused to Greek Gaia by the trapping of the Titans deep in her bosom causes her to seek Cronus to depose Ouranos, the thing that causes Branwen to send for Bran and Efnysien to attack Matholwch is another kind of abuse that brings her pain. Hesiod says that when the Titans are trapped within Gaia it causes her pain: "vast Gaia groaned within, being straitened" (Hesiod, *Theogony*, 147). Branwen's ears are boxed each day while living with Matholwch and she is made to work in the kitchens by Matholwch's men. The forced kitchen work may then be a simple symbol of Earth's food-producing role, while the box on the ears would either parallel the pain experienced by Gaia having the Titans trapped in her bosom or otherwise is a euphemism for the violence and pain of the primordial rape, which is expressed more explicitly in the Vedic and Greek versions but is left unsaid in the Welsh case. We can see that the boxing of Branwen's ears is indeed a motif already in the process of euphemism, as other traces of change in the motif are clear in the records. For instance, in Welsh Triad 53, only one "unhappy blow" is said to be given to Branwen, rather than three blows or daily blows as in other versions, and this single blow is said to be given by Matholwch himself. This single "blow" is then likely to be a euphemism for the primordial rape, which became further euphemized in the tale *Branwen, daughter of Llyr*.[248] Branwen is buried in the earth, in a four-sided grave, which could symbolize her unification with the land as well as pointing to the four cardinal directions, the four sides of her earthy domain. Miranda Green notes a physical connection between Branwen and the land in the mountain Cadair Fronwen, "Bronwen's Seat" (Green, *Celtic Goddesses*, 55-57). Lastly, there is strong cause given by scholars to believe that Branwen's original name may have been instead *Bronwen*, which means "white/shining/holy breast."[249]

---

a stem *mā-*, which designates the idea of what is favorable, first in a mystical and religious sense. Karl-Horst Schmidt suggested that *matu* could have been treated as an adjective in the sense of 'good, fortunate, auspicious, favorable'" (Gael Hily, *Le Dieu Celtique Lugus*, 154).

248   "The blow given to Branwen is called in the Mabinogi one of the 'Three Unhappy Blows' (WM 61, RM 43) and in the triads (TYP no.53) the blow which Matholwch Wyddel struck upon Branwen is called one of the 'Three Harmful Blows' of Ynys Prydain. Note the discrepancy here in that only one blow is inferred, and according to Triad 53 it was struck by Matholwch" (Peter Bartrum, *A Welsh Classical Dictionary*, 61)

White "breast" (*bron*) rather than White "raven" (*bran*) makes a great difference, for the surface of the earth is often referred to as a breast or as having breasts in various figurative contexts. In particular, hills and mountains are commonly analogized to the breasts of the earth, while Bronwen/Fronwen is directly associated with a mountain as we have noted. Cybele-Agdistis, who we will discuss shortly, is also a mountain goddess and Earth Mother. Furthermore, though "white/fair" or "sacred" could be a general descriptor of the breast of the beloved Earth, it could also specifically refer to the "White Isle" of Britain, sacred to its people and also known as *Alban,* from PIE *alb^ho-* "white." As we know that the Irish Mother Earth, Eriu, shares her name with the Island of Ireland, it is possible that *Bronwen*, the White Breasted, is in like manner a figurative title referring to the "White" Island of Britain.

If this marriage of Branwen and Matholwch is indeed the primordial conjunction of Earth and Sky to which we refer, then the incest found in Vedic and Greek branches has clearly been displaced in this case, and Matholwch is not depicted as a close relative of Branwen in the existing tale. Even in the *Rig Veda* the scene seems to cause the poets some discomfort, for they speak of it in sometimes explicit and sometimes highly coded language, leaving such a vague final impression that scholars are still baffled by many of the details of the scene, including the identity of the daughter. In the Greek case, the parent-child incest theme is actually kept intact; however, the roles are reversed compared to the Vedic parallel, and Gaia is there the mother of Ouranos rather than his daughter. Such a close inversion bolsters the idea that the parallel is accurate and highlights the fact that which being is the parent and which is the child is not of utmost importance as this is a primordial unity being described, the parent and child are two aspects of one primordial conjunction, either one of which may be called the child of the other.

While there is a division among commentators regarding whether the unnamed daughter of the Vedic hymns is the Dawn Goddess or the Earth Goddess, the idea that Branwen could be the Dawn Goddess seems very unlikely here as well. This family of

---

249   "The Welsh poets nearly always refer to Branwen as Bronwen, e.g. Dafydd ap Gwilym, and it is actually spelt this way once in the White Book text of 'Branwen ferch Llyr' (WM 42). The name Branwen is probably to be explained as an adaptation of Bronwen, 'white breast', in which the vowel has been influenced by the name of her brother, Brân. Thus her name is preserved near the river Alaw in Ynys Bronwen, the site of a cromlech known traditionally as Bedd Bronwen. There is also a Tŵr Bronwen at Harlech. (TYP p.287)" (Peter Bartrum, *A Welsh Classical Dictionary,* 61). See also: "There has been some debate over this last name, some holding that it is a corruption of *bronwen* 'fair or white breast,' others holding that it is simply a feminine form of Bran plus the feminine adjective gwen 'white, holy.'" (Patrick K. Ford, *The Mabinogi and Other Medieval Welsh Tales*, 55-56).

Welsh gods are called the House of Llyr, the Sea, and they are Llyr's children. The opposite great house found in the *Mabinogi* is the house of Don. We have seen that the House of Don appears in the final branch of the *Mabinogi* and involves all solar deities who are involved in the sunrise itself, the daytime, and the "day" half of the yearly cycle. Thus the House of Llyr, in contrast, seems to refer to earthly and perhaps chthonic, primordial or underworld deities in some sense, the sea being a portal to the underworld as well as existing on a level with the earth itself. The chthonic connection matches the presence in this house of Efnysien, potentially a Rudraic figure, Rudra being one of the lords of the sacred dead. It matches also the identification of Bran, son of Llyr, as Yama, the Lord of the Dead, whose severed head is taken back to a southwestern island off the coast of Wales matching the southwestern island belonging to another severed head god, Donn, the Irish Yama. Manawydan, another sibling of this house, is Fire God Agni, a psychopomp in his own right. This is a house of very primordial gods, arising from the cosmic sea, Llyr, their father. This myth of Branwen, Bran, Efnysien, Manawydan and Matholwch should also be occurring in the "Night" portion of the greater cycle, as it is the second branch of the *Mabinogi* and thus leads up to the final branch which tells the myth of the sunrise/beginning of Summer or the "Day" of the cycle. If this Welsh myth is the cosmic conjunction of Sky (Matholwch) and Earth (Branwen), which is disrupted by the Rudraic god (Efnysien), and which dramatizes a primordial sacrifice in the fall of the Father's seed (Gwern) into the first sacrificial fire, along with the death and beheading of the great giant and first "mortal" king of the world Bran (Yama), then it must occur somehow in the "beginning," which is the cosmic darkness before the sun is made to rise and day is made to break.

As such, it seems that this Welsh myth would have its Irish analog in the war of the Milesians or Sons of Mil against the Tuatha de Danann, as found in the Irish pseudo-historical account of the *Lebor Gabala Erenn*. Yes, the Milesian arrival to Ireland, as it appears in the Irish *Lebor Gabala Erenn,* happens *after* the other great myths of the gods, *after* the Second Battle of Maige Tuired, while the myth of Branwen appears in the Second Branch of the *Mabinogi* of the Welsh tradition, thus happening *before* any final battle of the gods, before the conclusion of the cycle that is reached in the Fourth Branch. However, if we plot these events on a calendrical map, which is cyclical, we see that the conclusion of the Irish Battle of Maige Tuired is known to occur on Samhain, the last day of the year, leading into Winter. Thus whatever happens right after this battle is occurring at the beginning of the cycle again, in the Winter of the year and during the "Night" of the cycle. What happens "after" the Battle of Maige Tuired is actually happening sometime "in the beginning" of the great cycle. Let us also re-emphasize that the Irish case is a pseudo-history, the intention of whose authors was to lead from the great ancestor gods directly into human history, creating a direct link that would weave the great myths into the human lineages. Hence we have Sons of Mil, Eber Donn (Bran,

Yama) and Eber Finn (Efnysien, Rudra), arriving from the East to Ireland to fight the inhabitants, as Welsh Bran (Donn, Yama) also arrives with Efnysien (Eber Finn, Rudra) from the East to Ireland to fight the inhabitants in his tale, in each case resulting most notably in the death of Eber Donn or Bran, the Yama analogues in each branch. In both cases another great poet also accompanies these heroes, Amergin in the case of the Sons of Mil, and Taliesin in the Welsh case, and some of their most famous poems are eerily similar: see Amergin's *Song of Amergin*[250] and Taliesin's *The Battle of the Trees*[251]. It

---

250   "*I am the sea blast*
I am the tidal wave
I am the thunderous surf
I am the stag of the seven tines
I am the cliff hawk
I am the sunlit dewdrop
I am the fairest of flowers
I am the rampaging boar
I am the swift-swimming salmon
I am the placid lake
I am the summit of art
I am the vale echoing voices
I am the battle-hardened spearhead
I am the God who inflames desire
Who knows the secrets of the unhewn dolmen
Who announces the ages of the moon
Who knows where the sunset settles" (*Song of Amergin*, tr. Michael Burch).
251   "*I have been in a multitude of shapes,*
Before I assumed a consistent form.
I have been a sword, narrow, variegated,
I will believe when it is apparent.
I have been a tear in the air,
I have been the dullest of stars.
I have been a word among letters,
I have been a book in the origin.
I have been the light of lanterns,
A year and a half.
I have been a continuing bridge,
Over three score Abers.
I have been a course, I have been an eagle.
I have been a coracle in the seas:
I have been compliant in the banquet.
I have been a drop in a shower;
I have been a sword in the grasp of the hand
I have been a shield in battle.
I have been a string in a harp,
Disguised for nine years.
in water, in foam.

seems possible that either Taliesin is in this text taking on a role otherwise taken by what some scholars believe to be the "Manu"-type figure Amergin, or that Amergin is not a "Manu"-type after all, but is instead yet another Rudraic manifestation. Indeed it is also possible that these two divinity types are verging on conflation in the Celtic tradition, and the line of continuity between Amergin and the Rudraic Taliesin should be clear from the poetic excerpts we have quoted, which themselves are reminiscent of the *Satarudriya* litany to Rudra of the *Yajurveda* and *Mahabharata*. The outcomes of the war of Branwen and that of the Sons of Mil are perhaps slightly different, as the Sons of Mil win a more thorough victory than do the Welsh attackers in the tale of Branwen. However, the Irish inhabitants are fully destroyed in both cases, the main heroes of the attacking side live and rule into the future, and the significance of the death of the analogue of Yama (Bran and Eber Donn) in the primordial scene, which in both cases seems to be occurring in the cosmic night before the sun of the cycle again rises, may have a significance which cannot be displaced in its role at the "beginning" of the cycle.

Finally, we have once more in the arrival of the Sons of Mil a marriage of the Earth Mother Goddess. We know from our previous investigations of her son, the Sun God Bres, that the Irish Earth Mother is Eriu, an embodiment also of the land of Ireland itself. In the *Lebor Gabala Erenn*, just before the Sons of Mil arrive, Eriu's marriage to the grandson of the Dagda is noted: "The three sons of Cermad son of The Dagda were Mac Cuill, Mac Cecht, Mac Griene: Sethor and Tethor and Cethor were their names. Fotla and Banba and Eriu were their three wives" (*Lebor Gabala Erenn*, 62). Immediately after this, we learn that the Sons of Mil arrive and that the grandsons of the Dagda fall by them: "Twenty-nine years had the grandsons of The Dagda in the kingship of Ireland, to wit Mac Cuill, Mac Cecht, and Mac Greiene: they divided Ireland into three parts. To them came the Gaedil to Ireland, so that they fell by the hands of three sons of Mil" (*LGE*, 63). Thus this marriage of Mac Greine, grandson of Father Sky, the Dagda, to Eriu, Mother Earth, appears in the new cycle, in the pseudo-historical layer. As such, in terms of the mythical narrative, the Dagda has already died of his wound from the Second Battle of Maige Tuired and has ended his reign. Therefore, now that we are in a new cycle of the year, his grandson Mac Greine (or all three of them) must be taken as a reincarnation of the Dagda himself, at least in his marriage to Eriu. The idea of a son or grandson being the incarnation of the father or grandfather, especially in a legendary or pseudo-historical text, should be very familiar to us by now and is a well-attested convention in ancient Indo-European literatures. The "death" of the Dagda at the end of the yearly cycle has necessitated his grandson to fill his role in the start of the next cycle, due to the odd order the compilers of this particular tradition have placed the myths in,

---

I have been sponge in the fire,
I have been wood in the covert" (*The Battle of the Trees*, tr. W.F. Skene).

tacking the creation myth onto the "end" of their book in order to lead into the next phase of human history as if starting anew.

The three grandsons of the Dagda (Mac Cuill, Mac Greine, Mac Cecht), who marry the goddesses of the three names of Ireland (Fodla, Eriu, Banba), may simply be three hypostases of the one Father Sky, considering that their three brides are hypostases of the one Mother Earth/Goddess of Ireland. It can be speculated that Mac Cuill, Mac Greine, and Mac Cecht are names indicating the seasonal phases over which the Dagda (Father Sky) otherwise rules: Mac Cuill (Son of the Hazel) relating to the Winter, considering that Elcmar-Nuada, sovereign of the night sky and thus of the winter half of the cycle, carries a hazel wand, Mac Greine (Son of the Sun) relating to the spring and summer for obvious reasons and being the husband of Eriu herself at the moment of their conjunction which dramatically begins the Spring phase of the year, and Mac Cecht (Son of the Plough/Power) relating to Autumn and the time of ploughing and harvesting.

In the war that develops, we see that prophecies have alerted Eriu and her people to the coming strife, reminiscent of the foresight of both Helenus of Troy and Efnysien of Britain. Eriu addresses the Sons of Mil when they arrive to her island: "Warriors, said she, welcome to you. Long have soothsayers had [knowledge of] your coming. Yours shall be this island for ever" (*LGE*, 79). The war then breaks out, and in this war the warriors of The Sons of Mil's side are made to see the opposing army as mere sods by the magic of the invaders: "The Book of Druim Snechta says that it was in Sliab Mis that Ériu had colloquy with them, and that she formed great hosts to oppose them, so that they were fighting with them. But their druids and poets sang spells to them, and they saw that these were only sods of the mountain peat-mosses" (*LGE*, 79). Bran likewise appears like a great mountain to the Irish when he approaches from the sea to battle them.

The Irish account is brief and highly fragmentary, and much is different in the Irish and Welsh versions of this myth, but enough key elements are closely aligned that we can be confident these are recounting the same primordial scene, more or less jumbled, compressed, or historicized in form. This is once again the marriage of Mother Earth to (in this case a reincarnation of) Father Sky, and the war which brings the Rudraic and Yama-type deities to break apart this marriage and to begin the unfolding of History, which is the beginning of Time from the pre-existent state, the cosmic Winter of the cycle. Subsequent to the victory of the Sons of Mil over the grandsons of the Dagda, the upstart Eber Finn (Rudra) comes into conflict with his brother Erimon and Erimon kills Eber Finn. This then clearly matches the death of Efnysien, as well as the deposing of Cronus by Zeus, for Erimon, as a likely linguistic and functional match of Vedic Aryaman, is a stand-in for the Mitraic god-type, per the previously discussed unity of Aryaman and Mitra. Thus this case of the Mitraic Erimon overcoming the Rudraic Eber

425

Finn matches most closely to the Greek case of the Mitraic Zeus overcoming the Rudraic Cronus.

Moreover, in the climactic scene of the *Tain Bo Cuailgne* we may have another, even more compressed and encoded or jumbled form of the Irish creation myth that we will very briefly touch upon. In a climactic moment of this text, a battle between two bulls, who had been enchanted cowherds, the Donn Cuailgne and Fionnbeannach, is related. We see already in the names of these two bulls that these may be incarnations of Donn and Fionn, two primordial gods who are present at the other form of the Irish creation myth. Of course, Eber Donn and Eber Finn do not fight one another in the story of the Sons of Mil, and their parallels Bran and Efnysien do not fight one another in the Welsh case either, and so some compression and jumbling of elements must be imagined if we wish to read this battle of bulls as a coded form of the creation myth. In the end of the battle of the bulls, the Donn Cuailgne defeats Fionnbeannach and spreads his entrails across various significant locations of Ireland. He then dies himself, having been mortally wounded. Eber Donn and Eber Finn do indeed both die in the tale of the Sons of Mil, Donn first at sea and Eber Finn when he challenges his brother Erimon for the supremacy of Ireland. In the Welsh case, Efnysien bursts his own heart, while Fionnbeannach is eviscerated and has his entrails spread about the land. But this spreading of the entrails is more reminiscent, perhaps, of the dismemberment of a figure such as Ymir, and we must note that no clear Father Sky appears in this battle of the two bulls. Thus we might imagine that Fionnbeannach, by a great mystical simplification of the myth, is meant to represent both Father Sky and Rudra/Fionn in one, as if he is the primordial Father and the Pure Mind-Fire of Rudra-Agni imagined as one being. Matholwch and Mac Greine, the Welsh and Irish "Father Skys," are after all both killed by the armies of Donn/Bran, and this may be what we are seeing when the Donn Cuailnge kills Fionnbeannach, although Eber Donn himself dies before his armies gain this victory in the Sons of Mil account. Donn, as the bull Donn Cuailnge, here successfully kills his opponent as the army of Eber Donn successfully kills his, and the subsequent deaths of Father Sky and the Rudraic god are perhaps combined into one as the death of Fionnbeannach, whose entrails are spread about the land, reminiscent of the evisceration of Ymir and/or the burst heart of Efnysien. Subsequently, the Donn Cuailnge too dies, as Eber Donn and Bran also do.

Let us look a bit closer now at Efnysien with the more esoteric role in mind as elucidated by Kramrisch's reading of Rudra's myth. Rudra is attempting to stop the Father, Father Sky of the Vedas or the "Prajapati" of the Brahmanas who carries the same Dyaus myth, from the sexual effusion that will begin the life of the world, that will bring on the Spring of the cycle. Kramrisch, perhaps influenced by the philosophy of the Brahmanas, interprets the state that Rudra is protecting in the myth as a true pre-cosmic phase, when all is undifferentiated and simultaneous, when Time does not yet exist. However, Rudra cannot stop the conjunction, his arrow reaches the Father "too late," and the primal seed is made to spill, bringing forth the fire youths from the fiery seed, the ancestors of mankind. Rudra is thus the god whose power of destruction is aimed at the act of procreation. He was propitiated to spare both born and unborn children[252]. The rudra incarnation Ashwatthama kills a camp of children. Rudra is also the yogi whose ascetic path would lead the mystic back to the state of inner unity, control of the senses and the sexual energies. As Kramrisch explains, semen retention and re-uptake are important parts of this Rudraic path, which repeat Rudra's aiming at the procreative act of the Father and his threatening the lives of children:

> Rudra, the guardian of the Uncreate, an indefinable transcendental plenum, avenged the infringement of that wholeness. He became the avenger of the descent of its substance, the semen, the 'heavenly Soma,' into the cosmos. The arrow in his hand threatened the coming into existence of life, and it disturbed the procreative act of the Father, the Lord of Generation, an act of incontinence *sub specie aeternitatis*. Rudra, the avenger, is the Lord of Yoga and of self-containment. (Kramrisch, 53-54)

> The primordial discharge of Rudra's arrow against the Father marked the direction of his operation in the cosmos. The arrow aimed at the act of generation. It flew in the opposite direction of the generative emission of the father. Its countermovement is consonant with that of yogic and tantric discipline, according to which the drawing up of the seed (ūrdhvaretas; cf. Sāyaṇa on TA.10.12; MBh.13.17.45) has its mystical psychosomatic equivalent in the upward flow of the sex power. Its phases are realized as it

---

252   "(RV.4.3.6-7) Rudra's piercing arrow is directed toward the seed, toward nascent life, which lies protected within the span of Viṣṇu's three footsteps, from the earth to the empyrean (cf. RV.1.154.2-5; 1.155.3-5)" (Kramrisch, 84).

"His is the arrow (ŚB.2.6.2.3), the power of death. For this reason the tryambaka offerings belong to Rudra (1, 3). They consist of rice cakes. Tryambaka offerings were made to protect from Rudra's arrows the descendants, born and unborn, of the sacrificer, one cake for each descendant and one more for the issue not yet born. The cakes would deliver each of the descendants from Rudra's power" (Kramrisch, 84).

"The cake was buried and concealed, for an embryo is concealed. By this offering, the unborn descendants were delivered from the power of Rudra. Rudra's arrow is directed toward the seed and the embryo. For the yet unborn a special offering was made, larger by Rudra's part than the cakes offered for the welfare of the living descendants. Moreover, the cake for the embryo had to be buried in a mole hill and concealed—Rudra was given no part of it; instead, the mole became Rudra's victim. The mole was Rudra's share. Rudra would not claim the embryo, though Rudra is greedy like a jackal for embryo flesh (VāP.30.212)" (Kramrisch, 85).

ascends through the subtle centers (cakras) of the body, including the highest center of mind, which it fecundates, being itself transubstantiated into the nectar that contributes to the state of samādhi, where integration, oneness is realized. The cosmic equivalent of the realization of this state of oneness is the Uncreate that was and is before the beginning of things. The arrow of Rudra was directed into the cosmic scene of the myth, while yoga is effected within the body of the yogi. Rudra-Śiva is the lord of yogis and the Lord of Yoga. (Kramrisch, 77-78)

As the Great Yogi, he is the consciousness and conscience of the Uncreate whole (Kramrisch, 54).

In Kramrisch's reading, Rudra is trying to prevent the dissolution of the primal unity by the breech caused by the primordial coupling and the effusion of the Father. Thus he is the god who wants to maintain or reconstitute the integration of the primordial unity, and hence he is the meditating god. In calendrical terms, this primordial unity must correspond to the dead of Winter, and the act of generation perpetrated by Father Sky is the first event that begins the movement toward the new day of the cycle, the early Spring. Kramrisch connects this myth to the Vernal Equinox of March, the end of Winter and the beginning of Spring (Kramrisch, 98-100).

The tense moment in which Efnysien enters the house gifted by Matholwch, which would be the death of himself and his brother if Matholwch's plan succeeded, may encode further esoteric material associated with the roles of the Rudraic god. Efnysien is the first to enter this house, and he immediately sniffs out the plot against them, calmly and silently going to each sack of grain and crushing the skulls of the warriors hidden within with his bare hands. When he does this he sings a brief *engelyn*, a magical poem:

> *Yssit yn y boly hwnn amryw ulawt,*
>
> *Keimeit, kynniuyeit, disgynneit yn trin,*
>
> *Rac kydwyr cad barawt.*

There is in this bag a sort of flour, champions, warriors, attackers in

conflict, prepared for battle against battle-men. (*Branwen, daughter of Llyr*)

Alaric Hall notes of this poem, "That the one verse in *Branwen* (one of only five stanzas in the Four Branches, three of which occur together) should be in the mouth of a character who seems so similar to Odinn-heroes, in a story sharing much of its narrative with a fornaldarsaga, is unlikely to be pure coincidence" (Hall, "Gwŷr y Gogledd? Some Icelandic Analogues of Branwen Ferch Lŷr," 47). Indeed, this is the only piece of verse in the tale, and only one of five stanzas of verse in the Four Branches, and thus its secret importance must be great. Kramrisch describes how, in the primal scene, after shooting his arrow, Rudra is named as Vastospati, the protector of the "house." Vāstoṣpati is "Rudra" according to *Taittiriya Samhita* 3.4.10.3. This "house" that Vāstoṣpati protects, as Kramrisch explains, has the quadruple significance of the dwelling, of the sacred site of sacrifice, of the universe as the cosmic house, and finally of the poetic and artistic construction. Specifically, the form of Rudra as Vastospati emerges from a wild, sacred poem of the gods, a magical Rudraic incantation called a *raudra brahman,* and this is connected to his emergence as the lord of the poetic order as well as of the other "houses." Kramrisch states:

> [...] as Vāstoṣpati, guardian of the dwelling and guardian of sacred order (vratapā). In this shape he emerges from the poem of magic power, the *brahman.* Poetry in the sacred order of its meters is his domain. Therein the fire of the Wild Archer sustains the form. Vāstoṣpati, created by the gods, the celestial intelligence, is the guardian of his domain, the world of sacred order—a rhythmic structure that is art, a cosmos. These are *vāstu,* the house that he guards. (Kramrisch, 240)[253]

Efnysien is clearly the guardian of this dwelling that ends up as a site of sacrifice, and he enacts this role of guardian simultaneous with the singing of a rare sacred poem. Is this

---

253   "The Wild Hunter in the precosmic wilderness is Rudra. In the form of their poem, a magic creation (brahman), the gods give shape to him as Vāstoṣpati. The vāstu that he guards is the cosmos, the site that is his domain is the site of the sacrifice. The sacred order of the cosmos is enacted on the site of the sacrifice in the rhythm of rites and hymns. They are analogous to the rhythms that pervade the cosmos" (Kramrisch, 25).
"The dwelling that he guards and the sacred order that he guards are forms in which—in the poem by the gods—his presence arises out of and on the strength of his fierceness. Vāstoṣpati is the guardian of the sacred order of the cosmos; he watches over all rhythms and rites of life" (Kramrisch, 29-30).
"Here there are two forms of the unnamed god. One is the appalling Hunter who aims 'against nature,' against the primordial act of Father Heaven that he as Agni had instigated, against procreation, by which mankind was to come about.The other form is that of Vāstoṣpati, created by the gods, the celestial intelligence, the creativeness itself of mind. The two forms imply the tension between life and its negation on the one side, the wild untamed world, the wilderness in man and nature, and on the other side the world of art and cosmic order. Both are his domain. In the one he acts as the Wild Hunter. In the other he manifests as guardian of the dwelling" (Kramrisch, 29).
"In rhythms and rites, the guardian of sacred order, Vratapā, surveys his domain" (Kramrisch, 30).
"[...] the guardian of the site, the guardian of sacred rites, Vāstoṣpati" (Kramrisch, 33).
"In the Ṛg Veda myth of Rudra, the origin of mankind, beginning with the Aṅgirases, the mythic Fire-youths, is interwoven with the creation of poetry, the archetypal act of art in divinis" (Kramrisch, 31).

mere coincidence, once again? We recall also that other Rudraic gods, Fionn, Taliesin, Odinn, and Apollo, are chiefs of the poetic art in their respective branches, while Efnysien too is a poet, a rare and significant role in the Mabinogi.

Efnysien has attempted to stop the marriage of Branwen and Matholwch, but this has failed. He has only made the situation worse. His mutilation of the horses of Matholwch may be seen as an "inflammation" of *tensions* that leads directly to the violence done to Branwen, which would then be analogous to the moment when Rudra-Agni inflames the *passion* within Dyaus, leading him to rape his daughter. Efnysien has then thrown their offspring, their divine seed, the boy Gwern, into the fire, as Rudra's arrow causes Dyaus' fiery seed to fall to Earth and mark the place of the fire sacrifice. *Gwern*, the name of the boy, the product of the divine seed, means "Alder," while the blood of Ouranos spawns the Ash-Tree nymphs the Meliae, who are the ancestors of the humans of the Bronze Age. The Giants, *Gigantes,* which also come from his blood, are ancestors of other human lineages, and he is also the father of the race of Titans. Meanwhile the Norse Odinn, along with his brothers, invests qualities into the first man, *Askr*, meaning "Ash," who is also the ancestor of mankind, and Ymir is also called the father of the race of *jotnar*, the Norse "giants." In each case, the violence to the father's procreative act spawns a tree-named ancestral figure, although in the Welsh case the connection of Gwern to later generations is narratively cut. Instead, five pregnant Irish women escape the battle that follows just after the burning of Gwern, and these repopulate Ireland. Gwern is thrown in the fire, a battle happens, then the five pregnant women are found in a cave. Thus the Welsh myth too leads to the generation of the ancestral race. The destructive war/sacrifice in which the tree-named Gwern perishes is in this way also generative of the coming race of humans, the cause-effect relationship of these sequential events has merely been narratively obscured. As Gwern and the "seed" of future humanity are produced by Matholwch and Dyaus respectively, a son and daughter (whether human or jotunn is not specified) also are said to be born from under Ymir's armpit in *Vafthrudnismal* 33: "They say 'neath the arms of the giant of ice/Grew man-child and maid together." Though it remains unclear, this description of the generation of the first male and female from the body of Ymir could then amount to the same thing as saying Askr and Embla washed up on a shore, which would be the shore of the lake of Ymir's procreative fluids, these fluids being much more explicitly described in Greek and Vedic cases. Interpreters have often been confused by these seemingly contradictory narratives of the first couple, but from this perspective they might be harmonized. The avenging Furies of the Greek myth, the *Erinyes*, also sprung from Ouranos' seed, could perhaps be fragments manifesting out of the avenging nature of the Cosmic Cronus/Rudra as well, akin to the terrible hunter Pasupati or the cleanser of the house Vāstoṣpati who are given form by the gods from out of the manifest horror of the primal scene. Finally, in an act of remorse, Efnysien sacrifices himself to destroy the magical cauldron. But what does this enigmatic final act mean?

If we attempt to connect Efnysien's self-sacrifice with certain parallels in the myths we have thus far brought together, we may approach an answer to the question of its meaning. Efnysien must play dead to be first thrown into the cauldron by the Irish who have it in their possession. For one thing, the human Rudraic mannerbund warriors of the *koryos* bands were believed to *become* the dead ancestors, to be sacrally bound to them in battle, and thus Efnysien *becoming* as-though dead could be an enactment of this Rudraic activity. Furthermore, the Rudraic self-sacrificial trials of other branches also often carry a symbolic, initiatic death as part of the myth. Odinn, most famously, sacrifices himself to himself, and in so doing can be said to undergo a death or at least a symbolic death. Fionn swims what we will call the "lake of fate" three times and comes out aged to an old man, so decrepit that no one recognizes him, and thus this can also be taken as a symbolic death. He must drink a special drink to return to the society of his men and regain his youth. Ashwatthama, incarnation of a rudra, sacrifices himself to Rudra in a fire on an altar that appears to him when he prays to Rudra. He emerges alive and empowered from this action, but stepping into a sacrificial fire can also be seen as a symbolic death even if we do not see Ashwatthama physically die. Efnysien, being thrown into the cauldron, actually *does* seem to die there, but bursts the cauldron apart first. Thus he completes his self-sacrifice to aid the battle effort of his kinsmen.

More specifically, however, Efnysien bursts his *heart* in this sacrificial act. In such a compressed story, layered with esoteric symbols, every word and symbol must be considered important. We have seen one other figure whose heart bursts in a physical act of atonement, and that is Corrgend, the Irish Prometheus.[254] In that tale, the heart is the

---

254   There are indeed strange echoes shared between the fire theft myths and the Father inseminating Earth myths. Hephaestus attempts to approach Athena sexually, is rebuffed, and ejaculates onto the earth, where the fire-seed is buried and even impregnates Gaia. The Vedic Father Sky rapes Earth or an unnamed daughter, and his fiery seed, prepared for him by Agni or Rudra-Agni, falls onto the Earth, giving rise to the fire youths. Corrgend and Efnysien's hearts both burst in atonement, Corrgend after killing "Fire" and burying him in the ground and Efnysien after killing a boy, the equivalent of the Vedic fire-seed, by throwing him in a fire. The fall of the seed of Hephaestus the Fire God to earth is then of the same type as the primordial fertilization by the Father, but on a lower level of manifestation. It is an echo of the first fall of the fire seed, a specific case of a larger sacred paradigm, and the bursting of Corrgend's heart similarly repeats the bursting of the similar but more primordial Efnysien. An Orphic fragment says, "through the theft of fire, and giving it to humans, Prometheus draws down the soul from the intelligible into generation" (*Orphic Fragments,* 143), and this comment supports the idea that the bringing down of fire to earth is a specific repetition of the primordial act that begins generation and the human lineage, the fall of the first fire-seed. The Celtic Coligny

symbolic site of *passion*, and, like Prometheus' liver, its bursting is the punishment fit to the crime of passion. If we know that Rudra is the god who aims his arrow at the passionate act of procreation, and we know that other parallels of Efnysien's self-sacrifice involve acts of fasting and asceticism, we will be permitted to read the bursting of Efnysien's own heart along the same lines. Thus the bursting of Efnysien's heart, the site of passion, may be one more symbol of the extinguishment of passion in the ascetic self-sacrifice rather than simply a colorful way to narrate a death scene. We are required to imagine that this particular manner of death was told for a reason.

Furthermore, the object that Efnysien destroys with his final act is a cauldron of (re)generation. It is an item that causes a cyclical rebirth of warriors who live again and again, but can no longer speak. There is an almost inescapable gravity to the reading of this cauldron as symbolizing the cycle of rebirth under the sign of *samsara:* humans being born to live, suffer, fight, die, and be reborn again in a circle, cursed with the lack of "speech," which perhaps here is a symbol of a link to higher divinity, considering the role of Vedic *Vac*, "speech," as a primordial manifestation of the cosmic Word and the spiritual essence of the cosmos. Alternately, the cauldron could represent the metaphysical engine of a state which existed at first in the cosmos, in this early age of creation, a kind of earthly immortality that was yet lacking a bridge to the divine, a bridge that could only appear via the paradigmatic self-sacrifice, and Efnysien's destruction of the cauldron could be an annihilation of this cursed and voiceless state by creating that bridge with his act. Let us recall that the Titans, who would be on a parallel with Efnysien himself (who is the same as the Titan Cronus), are trapped in Tartarus by Ouranos, which is in fact a kind of Hell deep in the Earth, before being liberated by Cronus' actions. Thus the breaking of the cauldron could be an analogy for the freeing of *all* descendants of Father Sky from a Tartarus-like existence cut off from the divine upper region. Kramrisch in fact points to a direct connection between the "Vedic version of Hell" and the lack of "speech" in the *Rig Veda*: "the *asat* whose exiled darkness lies below, outside cosmic order (*rta*), outside creative power. Into the *asat*, the non-existent, 'the nearest equivalent of hell,' fall those defenseless whose speech is sapless and ineffectual (4.5.14)" (Kramrisch, "The Triple Structure of Creation in the Rg Veda,"

Calendar from Gaul calls the month of March *Aedrinios* or *Edrinios,* which Xavier Delmarre says can be compared to Irish *Aed*, "fire." March, when the first fall of the fire seed occurs and the primordial fire sacrifice is enacted, is thus the Celtic month of Fire, and is also the time of the Vernal Equinox, the time commemorating the fall of the primordial seed of the Father. It seems possible that the echoes of this myth, the theft of fire as with Prometheus/Corrgend/Matarisvan and the second emission of the fire seed as with Hephaestus, could also have been seen to happen in this same month of Fire, manifestations of the same primordial event on lower levels of reality. Matarisvan is also a known epithet of Siva.

147). "The darkness of Nirrti is disintegration in the deepest pit, below this earth" (Kramrisch, "The Triple Structure of Creation in the Rg Veda," 156-157).

If a more plain explanation is sought, the salient accomplishment of the destruction of this cauldron is that it brings balance to the war. Furthermore, if the power of the cauldron remained, not only would Efnysien's side be obliterated, but Matholwch's people might overrun the world with future uncontrolled profusions of human life, their numbers unbounded by death, a threat we see repeatedly in myths of other cultures regarding the early phase of the cosmos just after creation. Like in parallel myths that we have analyzed previously, one side of the war having the power to resurrect the dead unbalances the world, causes disorder in nature, in multiple ways. In fact, the cauldron's destruction, if read straightforwardly, balances life and death and instead brings about our natural manner of death by removing the useful but hellish magic of the cauldron. Rather than regeneration in the same body in a cursed state, the repairing of the process of natural death allows for humans to die fully, and for them then to either enter the celestial realms or be fully reborn in new bodies rather than being trapped in silent husks. Natural death furthermore ensures the neutralization of the profusion of numbers and the inevitable destruction of the world this would bring. Now the only paths are for humans to die and be taken to the Otherworld, or for a rebirth in a new body to take place. Either way, Efnysien brings balance to the sides of the war and brings the chance of a truer rebirth through the destruction of that which unbalances nature. Death and the regeneration of life from death, instead of eternal living-death, is made possible, by an act of the Destroyer god who destroys to heal.

Efnysien successively becoming as-if dead, extinguishing the passions by bursting his own heart, and then breaking the cauldron of regeneration which could be seen as a symbol of the cycle of regeneration, or of some other hellish living-death cut off from divinity, could point ultimately toward Efnysien being the model of a mystic state of which well-known post-Vedic and Buddhist concepts, such as the aforementioned samādhi, might offer general approximations. What state, indeed, does Odinn attain when he sacrifices himself to himself on the tree or when he becomes castrated as one of his epithets (*Jalk/Jalg*) implies? Is the state the Buddha gains in a similar meditative act under a tree different or the same as that which Odinn or Efnysien attain?[255] Kramrisch

---

255   Kramrisch's interpretation of this state points toward the concepts of samādhi and moksa: "The Father had broken the state of **wholeness** that existed before the fall of the seed. This state is beyond words. It is indescribable and inaccessible to the senses. It is 'neither nonbeing nor being' (RV.10.129.1). But if that much can be said about it, it has also been said that it is 'nonbeing and being' (RV.10.5.7), and that out of nonbeing came being in the first age of the gods (RV.10.72.2). It is then that the indefinable wholeness of the total absence or the total presence of both nonbeing and being appears to recede and to set up the screen on which are seen the large figures of gods and their actions. This

notes that Rudra is a liberator who, having entered the world of Generation, becomes

state of 'neither nonbeing nor being,' or simultaneously 'nonbeing and being,' is not within the range of thought. It is a plenum that defies definition, for it has no limits. Yet it is not chaos, the 'darkness covered by darkness,' said to have existed before the beginning of the ordered universe (RV.10.129.3). In its precosmic, preconscious totality, **everything is contained, including consciousness and nothingness.** Metaphysically, it did not cease when the cosmos came into existence, for it is not subject to time. Mythically, its wholeness had been injured. Mystically its nameless plenum is inaccessible except in the state of samādhi, the final stage of yoga leading to mokṣa, the total release from all contingencies. Words like plenum, totality, and wholeness are used here merely as symbols of the Uncreate."

"The state before creation is beyond the polarity of opposites. It is as vast as chaos, but having no qualities whatsoever, it lacks disorder. It is known in later Indian mystical realization as brahman; it is realized through samādhi (at-onement) as mokṣa (release), nirvana (extinction of the flame of life), śūnyatā (emptiness). These names apply to an inner realization of that state beyond the last frontiers of thought (cf. RV.10.5.6-7). The archer, whose arrow hits the Father at the very moment when the Father is spending himself into creation, acts as avenging consciousness and guardian of the Uncreate in defense of its integrity. The arrow and the shot of the archer are decisive symbols in the myth, though they were only partly effectual in the course of its events. Indeed, the arrow hit just a fraction of a moment too late. Meant to prevent the act, the flowing of the seed, the shot failed to prevent its consequences. The failure in timing at the dawn of the world was due to time itself, for the latter had not set in as yet; it was just about to begin. The transition from an integer without dimension of space and time into existence is a danger zone between eternity and the passing moment. It lies between metaphysics and myth. Had the timing been perfect, the flying arrow of Rudra would have prevented the coming into existence of man and the flowing down on the earth of the substance of the Uncreate" (Kramrisch, 65).

A simpler concept could be "integral wholeness," or simply that state in which a direct link to the divine is attained, the "voice," the essence of the heavenly state, is recovered, even while existing with the cycle which has been set in motion. Samādhi indeed roughly means "total self-collectedness," which expresses this idea of integral wholeness well, while also describing the paradigmatic Rudraic action, which is to draw generation back into himself, to collect himself totally and to become complete again and again. The state of samādhi has been described in terms curiously similar to those seen in the poems of the Rudraic poet Taliesin, the experience of consciousness expanding into identity with all things. Another analogy of what may be described in the myth of Efnysien, who seeks to return to the "Golden Age" before the rupture of Creation, is simply the regaining and reconstituting of the Golden Age within the self, despite existing within the cycle of Time. What this reconstituting process and final state of wholeness is precisely can be interpreted through numerous mystical terminologies.

In the language of contemporary philosophy, Gilles Deleuze calls the pre-existential state of undifferentiation "the black nothingness," and above this, "the white nothingness" of unconnected determinations: 1. "The undifferentiated abyss. The indeterminate animal in which everything is dissolved (Deleuze, *Difference and Repetition*, 28, 36); 2. "The white nothingness, the once more calm surface upon which float unconnected determinations

ferryman who then leads to the *other shore*, and this could well describe what Efnysien is doing in the scene of his self-sacrifice in the caldron of regeneration: forging a path back to the higher divine realm.

> At certain spots [Rudra's] presence is acutely felt. These are fords (*tīrtha*), and at them he is the ferryman. He ferries across to the other shore, into the far beyond of which he is the guardian. He is the liberator, but—paradoxically—he is also the ferryman from death to life. The fierce guardian of the Uncreate, at the inception of life on earth, having entered into the created world, is the ferryman who leads to the other shore. (Kramrisch, 169-170)

In myths found in various Vedic and post-Vedic texts, Rudra-Siva performs feats precisely in line with the destruction of the cauldron by Efnysien. Most importantly, Rudra-Siva is said to go into the waters when Brahma commands him to create sons subject to birth and death (Kramrisch, 260; *KuP* 1.10.36; *VrP*.21.6) and to castrate himself (*Mahabharata* 10.17.10-11, 21), as Efnysien bursts his own heart in the cauldron containing the remnant of divine liquid. Rudra refuses to create mortal sons (*VaP* 10.56-57; *LP* 1.70.316) and instead creates mind-born sons, rudras, who are not subject to death, and the power of his meditation in the waters generates vegetative life of its own

---

like scattered members" (Deleuze, *Difference and Repetition*, 28, 36). See Henry Somers-Hall, *Deleuze's Difference and Repetition*, 22: "The first of these represents a space that has not been differenciated. Without difference, we cannot have anything other than pure abstract identity. Difference as a concept is what allows us to draw distinctions within this identity ('this differs from that'). The second quotation brings out the second role of difference: difference is a relation, and therefore allows things to be related to one another." Kramrisch similarly notes the "Abyss" of Nirrti to be an aspect of the pre-cosmic state (see Kramrisch, "Pusan," p. 108: "Below the pit of danger and treasure lies the Lap of Nirrti (7.104.9), the lap of destruction with its endless pit (7.104.17) below all creation (7.104.6). This deep dark place is the Asat, the Non-existent, "The Rg Vedic Equivalent for Hell," as shown by W. Norman Brown, JAOS, vol. 61, pp. 76-80. This deep substratum of the ordered cosmos, of the Existent (*sat*), the abyss that yawns at the bottom of the pit, in the lap of Destruction (*nirrti*) is the necessary opposite in the first pair of contraries. There they are from the beginning of things prior to which neither of them existed. The Asat, the Non-existent below the pit, is the remainder '*apud principium*' of the all engulfing darkness, *ante principium*").

The Neoplatonist Plotinus describes the mythic creation in philosophical terms: "in order that Being may be brought about, the source must be no Being but Being's generator [compare the Uncreate], in what is to be thought of as the primal act of generation. Seeking nothing, possessing nothing, lacking nothing, the One is perfect and, in our metaphor, has overflowed, and its exuberance has produced the new: this product has turned again to its begetter and been filled and has become its contemplator and so an Intellectual-Principle [Cronus]" (Plotinus, *Ennead* 5.2.1).

force rather than by procreative act[256]. He refuses the procreative act, refuses assent to the cycle of death and rebirth, and instead becomes the castrated and illuminated ascetic, symbol of the attained state of integral wholeness or samadhi, an example of this state of wholeness to all thereafter. As Kramrisch says of his withdrawal to the waters:

> The motionless pillar is Śiva, the ascetic, in whom the fire of life burns upward inwardly while he stands still. This is the mystery of Sthāṇu (cf. *MBh*.17.173.92). He is motionless, like a log in which the potentiality of fire is latent (cf. *ŚUp*.1.13) and controlled. Sthāṇu is Śiva the yogi, an aeviternal, immovable presence, pillar of the world. (Kramrisch, 266)

> 'Since Rudra stands burning upward, and since he stands and exists as the origin of life, and since the *lihga* is aeviternally erect, he is known as Sthāṇu' (*MBh*.7.173.92). The *Mahābhārata* sees Sthāṇu not in his immutability as master over sexual power but as the immutability of that power itself—and as the origin of life. (Kramrisch, 266)

> Keeping the semen drawn up, Sthāṇu stood still until the great deluge. Because he said: 'Here I stand (*sthitosmi*).' (Kramrisch, 264)[257]

> Then Rudra withdrew into himself. He became Sthāṇu, motionless in aeviternal samādhi, ceaseless illumination, contained within himself, his seed withdrawn into himself (*BP*.1.2.9.88-89). In his pillar shape Rudra restores the unspent wholeness of the Uncreate. His seed and his breath are held. The fire seed of

---

256   In Plotinus, cosmic emanation proceeds naturally from the act of contemplation of the Intellectual-Principle [Cronus] as life proceeds from Shiva in meditation without his taking procreative action: "In the Intellectual-Principle, the Being is an Act and in the absence of any other object it must be self-directed; by this self-intellection it holds its Act within itself and upon itself; all that can emanate from it is produced by this self-centering and self-intention; first- self-gathered, it then gives itself or gives something in its likeness; fire must first be self-centered and be fire, true to fire's natural Act; then it may reproduce itself elsewhere" (Plotinus, Ennead 5.3.7).

257   "Rudra became Sthāṇu, a motionless pillar, a branchless stem. He stood in aeviternal illumination. Sthāṇu (from the root *sthā*, "to stand"), "a post," is Rudra's concrete symbol. Its upward direction shows his inflexible stance across the universe (cf. LP.1.86.139), as well as suggesting the upward withdrawal of his semen. The visual concept of Sthāṇu, the pillar, is the paradoxical negation of the erect phallus, which the pillar shape suggests" (Kramrisch, 265).

"Sthāṇu in the simplicity of its shape is the monument of Rudra's paradoxical truth. Its dual significance comprises the irreducible nature of Rudra, the Fire, the origin of life, and Rudra, the Great Yogi, who, counter to nature, is master of the unspent life-giving power" (Kramrisch, 267).

creation and the breath of life are held within his motionless shape. No mortals will ever be created by Rudra, but such things as knowledge, truth, asceticism, and illumination are in him, and he is in the gods, sages, and all beings; he is honored by all the gods (*BP*.1.2.9.89-92). The gods are 'this side of creation' (*RV*.10.129.6). Rudra at the beginning of things acted as the guardian of the Uncreate, and became its pillar in the myth of creation. (Kramrisch, 268)

Having refused to engender mortals and having ceased to create immortals, the Great God says of himself: 'I stand as the destroyer. Because I stand like a pillar, so I am sthāṇu' (*SkP*.7.2.9.13-14). His withdrawal from the world signals his destruction of the world. (Kramrisch, 269)

In another myth (*MP* 249.3-22), during a war of the devas and asuras in an early phase of the cosmos, Rudra-Siva is the one who swallows the poison that is released by the act of the churning of the sea of milk to gain the *amrita*, nectar of immortality. Thus he chooses to sacrifice himself, or to take on the deadly burden, to neutralize this poison in order that the gods may have immortality and escape death and rebirth. He is not killed, but is saved from the tortures of the poison, and is left with his characteristic blue throat. A clear pattern establishes itself in this Rudra-Siva body of myths of a god who desires to help open pathways around the cycle of death and rebirth rather than to participate in it, and who, like Efnysien, actively snuffs out his passion or performs some sort of self-sacrificial act to achieve this.

However, in yet another myth (*Mahabharata* 12.248.13-14), humans are increasing without dying and are overcrowding the three worlds, and it is Rudra-Siva who instantiates the cycle of death and rebirth as an alleviation of the prospect of total extinction which would be brought on if this profusion of living beings were to go on indefinitely. Thus the relation of Rudra-Siva to the cycle of birth and death is reiterated here, but we see that it is somewhat ambivalent or multifaceted even in the Vedic tradition. As Kramrisch states:

Rudra allotted to death its position in the order of cyclical time. Death would be the open gate through which the current of time would take its course [...] Rudra brought the cyclical sequence of time into the cosmos as a remedy; Brahma summoned Death from within himself to make the remedy effective, to keep intact the order of the cosmos [...] The time that Rudra brought into the world is a lived time [...] It came to be when Rudra was moved to pity by the imminence of total extinction. (Kramrisch, 278)

Perhaps then Efnysien, when he destroys the cauldron, is instantiating natural death and time in order to balance the order of the cosmos and avoid greater disaster, or perhaps he is making a path to a form of immortality possible. Possibly, though we may only speculate, he is doing both at once, rebalancing the cosmos by destroying the unnatural immortality of the cauldron that is a living hell and will bring extinction if continued, and then opening a pathway back to wholeness, the divine realm, and the overcoming of death in one action. From the destruction of the cauldron "such success as they had" follows as a consequence, as the Mabinogi tale states.

This interpretation of Efnysien's heart as symbolic of passion should not seem frivolous. Cronus himself in the end of his myth, like Rudra-Siva, is castrated (Orphic Fragment 154) repeating the severing of the member of his father Ouranos, but with a different meaning, and this castration of Cronus should again be interpreted as the snuffing out of desire or passion in the god, as further parallels will make clear: "This therefore, takes place, and Saturn [Cronus] being bound is emasculated in the same manner as Heaven (Οὐρανός))" (Orphic Fragment 154, trans. Thomas Taylor)). Robert Graves (Graves, *Hebrew Myths* 21.4) cites another tradition for Cronus' castration, from John Tzetzes, a Byzantine writer of the 12th century. Thus the castration of the Father, Ouranos, matches the disruption of the marriage of Branwen and Matholwch, the casting of their son into the fire, and the death of Matholwch in the war, while the castration of Cronus matches the bursting of Efnysien's heart. Though it often goes unnoticed, Odinn too is castrated, for he is called *Jalk/Jalg/Jalkr*, "Gelded" (*Grímnismál* (49, 54), *Óðins nöfn* (7), *Gylfaginning*)[258]. This castration of Odinn then parallels and has the same meaning as that of Cronus and of Rudra-Siva, and parallels likewise the bursting of Efnysien's heart[259].

---

[258] My thanks to Anhaga for bringing this to my awareness. Additionally, the priests who followed the Phrygian Attis and Cybele (discussed below), the *galli*, castrated themselves, following the model of the castrated Attis who parallels Cronus and Odinn in his myth. Thus we could speculate that Odinn's title *Jalk/Jalg*, "the Gelded One," could also imply that he would command certain of his priests to overcome their own passions in order to follow his example via the ascetic or yogic overcoming of the passions, by various means.

[259] Pandu of the *Mahabharata* is cursed to never again embrace his wife on pain of death after shooting a pair of mating deer in the woods who turn out to be a rishi and his wife. He ultimately forgets the injunction, embraces his wife romantically, and dies "lust-bewildered." Although Pandu is an incarnation of Varuna, this could be a form of the same Rudraic myth which has been attached to him due to the frequent overlap between Rudra and Varuna that we have noted, with the mating deer as the primordial pair in conjunction. My thanks to Zagreides for pointing out this connection.

When Cronus is castrated he is in a death-like state, lulled to sleep by divine honey. This state then matches the as-if dead state that Efnysien is depicted in when entering the cauldron. Furthermore, the Orphic poets say of this honey of Cronus that,

> Saturn [Cronus], being filled with honey, is intoxicated, his senses are darkened, as if from the effects of wine, and he sleeps [...] the theologist obscurely signifying by this that divine natures become through pleasure bound, and drawn down into the realms of generation [compare the cauldron of Efnysien as the negative image of the cycle of generation, muted and cut off from the divine] [...] the sweetness of honey signifies, with theologists, the same thing as the pleasure arising from generation, by which Saturn, being ensnared, was castrated. (*Orphic Fragments,* 154)

Thus the mutely reborn warriors could be like those bound by sensuality in the realms of generation, with no link to the divine, and Efnysien, entering this realm of generation in a sleep-like or death-like state, breaks this state of sleep asunder by the snuffing out of his own passion. The cosmic honey that Cronus is fed can make a clear parallel to the substance held in the cauldron, and these to the remainder of Dyaus' seed in the Vedic tradition, the dangerous residue of the lake of sperm left on earth left by Dyaus' procreative outburst. All three of these, honey, cauldron, and lake of sperm, can be seen as forms of the heavenly liquid substance, one form of which is the *soma* or mead, which commonly appears in cauldrons or as honey. This self-sacrifice of Efnysien then opens a path to regaining the divine "voice," *Vac,* which is elsewhere commonly identified with the waters of Saraswati/Cerridwen, and escaping the state of being "mutely" bound, the senses darkened by the honey of the senses, the residue of the sacred seed that is cut off from the divine realm. Notably, Gwion-Taliesin, a re-manifestation of the Welsh Rudra, is said in his own tale to drink of the liquid from the cauldron of Cerridwen (Saraswati), and from there to gain his divine voice and to remember that he has been in the many hosts of things that make up the cosmos (*The Tale of Taliesin*; "The Battle of the Trees"). Perhaps we may say that he rediscovers the primordial Rudra Efnysien's path and remembers who he is.

If we follow Kramrisch's suggestion that this overall myth connects to the time around the Vernal or March Equinox, we find further parallels confirming these readings. The Roman New Year is known to have taken place on the Ides of March, perhaps originally being tied to the full moon of this period, marking the end of Winter and the coming of Spring. The first inkling of the new light of the day of the year and the beginnings of fertility were for the Romans the moment the New Year would begin. A well-known myth from Phrygia connected to the festivities of the later Imperial Roman period, including the festival day *Canna intrat,* tells of Attis and Agdistis. Agdistis is a divine being having both male and female genitals and thus should be taken as an image of the primordial union of "Sky" and "Earth" or "Father/Son" and "Daughter/Mother," the *hieros gamos* contained in one being, the unity of the Uncreate not yet broken. Connecting this idea of the primordial hermaphrodite to Vedic Dyaus' rape of his daughter, Kramrisch elucidates this crucial point thus:

> The divine mating of Father and daughter is a symbol of ontic truth. Elsewhere, primal being, nearest to the wholeness of the Uncreate, is male and female in one. (Kramrisch, 59)

> The daughter with whom the Father cohabits is a hypostasis of the Father himself. She was one with him before he knew her. Ardhanārīśvara, Lord Śiva, is male on the right side and female on the left. As the Purāṇas know him, Śiva is one who divides himself into god and goddess, Śiva and Sivā. Then, for a thousand years he did not cease in his ardent love making to Sivā (cf. ŚP.2.4.1.27-28). Their love has not been considered incestuous by anyone. (Kramrisch, 60)

> Father Heaven covered this blushing maiden, part of himself, discernible and other from himself, only to be united with himself. They are not two persons but one self-begotten, begetting entity. (Kramrisch, 62)

> [...] in the beginning the Creator embraced his daughter, a hypostasis from within himself in which he asserts himself. To this act of self-love, the emission of seed is biologically a sequel and metaphorically a jolt to the unassailable and undiminished metaphysical plenum. The intercourse of the Creator with his daughter is the two-faced symbol of the rupture of pre-existential wholeness and of the descent to earth of its immortal substance, the seed of life. (Kramrisch, 64)

> the infringement of the Uncreate and pre-existential wholeness, a spurt from self-contained fullness, the loss of integrity of the absolute. (Kramrisch, 64)

The primordial Phrygian hermaphrodite Agdistis is equated with the great Earth Mother Cybele and is a mountain deity, Mount Agdistis being its namesake, and thus the underlying Earth Mother nature is apparent, a mountain also being where a union of sky and earth occurs. We recall Bronwen's association with a mountain as well. A potion puts Agdistis to sleep, and the being is self-castrated at the instigation of Dionysus, who is the god of the sacred liquid which becomes the seed of the primordial progenitor. The blood from the severed genitals gives rise to a tree, as Ouranos' genitals give rise to the Ash-Tree nymphs, and Matholwch's son is named for a tree, *Gwern*, "Alder." This tree bears an almond and the daughter of a river nymph takes an almond from the tree and is impregnated by it. Attis is born, and now Agdistis falls in love with his beauty. At Attis' wedding Agdistis appears and drives everyone mad, resulting in Attis castrating himself.

440

Agdistis repents and causes Attis' body to neither rot nor decay – he attains the state of perfection, of the unmanifest, overcoming the cycle of generation and decay (Pausanias, *Description of Greece*, 7, 19). Thus we have once more a *double* castration motif of father and son, while the motif of the sleeping draught also seen in the honey of the Cronus myth is transferred to the first castration rather than the second. The fact that the castration of Cronus and that of Attis align and these further align with the bursting of Efnysien's heart bolsters the idea that Efnysien is indeed extinguishing his own passion in his sacrificial act. The myth of Attis is generally taken as symbolic of the fertility of the land that dies in winter and returns in spring, which is the same idea as what the other myths mark generally, the return of fertility with Spring. However, in such an interpretation the full meaning of the myth has been broadened and become vague, and something of the precise theology of the original myth may be in process of being lost. The self-castrating *corybantes* and *galli* are considered to be priesthoods or brotherhoods directly connected to this myth and the worship of its gods, Attis and Cybele-Agdistis, and their ascetic practice could then be seen as in line with Efnysien's sacrifice and even with the ascetic practice of Odinn. Kris Kershaw and others have extensively commented on the *corybantes* as a type of Rudraic *koryos*.

What we have seen thus far is also the general theme of the Vernal Equinox celebrations found in Hinduism, and these too can be connected back to the Welsh myth. In Shaivite tradition, 40 days before the Vernal Equinox festival of Holi, an event is commemorated on the day called Vasant Pachami, which appears to be an elaboration of the paradigmatic myth of Rudra shooting his arrow at the sexual desire of Dyaus. In the Shaivite form of this myth, Siva, who is the all-in-all god, is of course both Rudra and Dyaus in one. He is the Father containing the procreative seed and the ascetic destroyer in one, and the cosmic drama of desire plays out within his own being. Kama, the god of Desire, approaches Siva, who is in deep meditation, in an attempt to lure him to return to his spouse Parvati. Kama shoots his arrow at Siva, but Siva shoots fire from his third eye and incinerates Kama, thus killing Desire in blazing mental fire. Kama's wife then performs asceticism for 40 days, until the Vernal Equinox, when Siva finally agrees to revive Kama, signaling the return of fertility to the world and the end of Siva's period of wintry meditation. The interpretation of this myth should be familiar and clear by now. The Father in Siva is seduced to release his fertilizing energy into the world, but the ascetic Destroyer kills Desire with a bolt of fire before this can happen. The shooting of an arrow is again a central event in this myth, as in the original Vedic form, but this time the arrow is shot by Kama and directed at Siva as Father. Siva then returns his own kind of arrow at Kama, a bolt from his third eye. An ascetic practice then appears in the myth both in relation to Siva and in relation to Kama's wife Rati, and finally Desire is allowed to return to life and fertility flows out again from the cold, unmanifest state that Siva had maintained until then in meditation, the state of cosmic Winter.

In the Vaishnava tradition, the day of Holi corresponds to the myth of Holika, a demoness who tries to burn a young boy, Prahlada, in a fire. Knowing the Welsh version, we know that the burning of the boy in the fire is a symbol of the attempt to destroy the generative seed that would bring new life and thus is a symbol of the vitality of the cosmos and of the coming Spring. However, as the attempt to stop the emission of the Father fails in the Vedic version, the attempt to burn the boy Prahlada fails also, though he is held in the fire, due to the intense devotion of the boy to Vishnu, for which he also suffers punishment from his father, and furthermore thanks to the special mantras he employs. The motif of these mantras is perhaps a remnant of the magico-ascetic practices of the various parallels, ie. the fasting, runes, and galdrs of Odinn. The demoness is instead burned and the demon father of the boy is eviscerated by Vishnu as well. The festival of Holi involves the throwing of colored powders, which symbolize the incinerated demoness Holika, and is a celebration of the undaunted life of the new Spring to follow. We can thus see that the Vedic role of Rudra-Siva and the Welsh role of Efnysien has been made into a demoness in this Vaishnava tradition, which is understandable when we consider that the Rudraic Destroyer of the procreative seed appears like a psychopath in some versions of the myth. The demoness Holika also has clear similarities to the castrated Phrygian Earth Mother Agdistis-Cybele, who causes the wedding party of Agdistis to go mad. "Rudra" is a very easy god to demonize, if a given tradition desires, for he or his troop may manifest in destructive forms and his trait of aiming his arrow at the seeds of life can make his motivation appear obscure and cause him to seem to be an excessively cruel god. The incineration of this demoness also reminds us of the parallel incineration of Kama, and the evisceration of the Father is a more tactful or conservative echo of the castration of the Father in other parallels.

In the Vedic version of the myth another element appears that could be a variation of the castration of Rudra-Siva/Cronus/Odinn/Attis motif, or the bursting of the heart of Efnysien, further bolstering the consistency of the motif overall. In the *Maitrayani Samhita* of the *Black Yajurveda*, when Rudra first aims his arrow at The Father, Dyaus-Prajapati, and interrupts his procreative act, Rudra spares his life. The Father then makes Rudra into *Pasupati*, the Lord of Animals, as a reward for his mercy. The *Aitareya Brahmana* tells the story somewhat similarly, except it is the other gods who turn Rudra into Pasupati after the horror of the primal scene, as an expression of that primal horror. As Pasupati, the Lord of Animals, Rudra's hunter aspect is focused and foregrounded, and his intimate connection to the wilds and the animal life therein gains its official title. As such, we find parallels such as Irish Fionn who is a hunter living in the wilderness, and Rudra-Siva-Pasupati himself wears the skin of an animal to signify this role. However, as Kramrisch clarifies, the "animals" that Rudra-Pasupati is lord of also signify the passions within the self: "Within man the microcosm, the animals are the passions. Rudra, the archer, aims at Father Heaven, and inasmuch as the Father

442

embracing the daughter acts according to his passionate nature, the Father is Rudra's prey. Śiva, the Great Yogi, tames and subdues the animals that are the passions" (Kramrisch, 55). Just as Rudra hunts and fires his arrow at the procreative passion of the Father in the primordial scene, he continues this tendency by hunting and mastering the passions at large, within the self. The role of Lord of Animals means the one who is at peace with and in control of the wild and vital nature within. The image of the hunter, at peace, legs folded as if in meditation or a hunter's crouch, with the wild animals crowding tamely around him, illustrates this trait. Thus the Vedic Rudra, too, becomes, by a process of formal transformation, even by a transubstantiation of his being into Pasupati, the master of the passions, just after his role in the primal scene, thereby paralleling the more vivid castration and more symbolic heart bursting in the parallel myths at the analogous points.

In this context, Cronus unfolds himself to us as the Primordial "Rudra" of Greek myth, now seen in his proper character as the parallel of Efnysien and Rudra, adding to the alignment of Cronus with the Irish rudra Balor that we have examined previously (Cronus and Balor each are prophesied to be deposed or killed by their Mitraic son or grandson, Zeus or Lugh). Like Nisien and Helenus, and like Fionn, Apollo, and Odinn, Cronus is in fact a prophet. Prophecy, as we have repeatedly noted, is a prime Rudraic power. Orphic Fragment 129 notes Cronus' power of "foreknowledge into the sensibles": "And Krónos (Κρόνος) surrenders the principles of all creation to Zeus, and of foreknowledge into the sensibles, and endowing himself with intelligence, is unified with the primary intelligibles, and is satiated with the good things from there" (*Orphic Fragments* 129). Cronus' name is said to mean "he who strikes (awakens) the mind (κρούων τον νοῦν)." From this, Thomas Taylor says: "Saturn (Κρόνος) [Cronus], therefore, according to Plato, is *pure intellect, viz.* the first intellectual intellect: for the intellects of all the Gods are pure in the most transcendent degree; and therefore purity here must be characteristic of supremacy. Hence Saturn subsists at the summit of the intellectual order of Gods, from whence he is received into all the subsequent divine orders, and into every part of the world" (Taylor, note on Κρατύλος Πλάτωνος 396b-c).[260] Cronus' is called "wily" as well as "most terrible" by Hesiod (*Theogony* 126, 147), both Rudraic descriptors, and it is for these traits that Gaia tasks him with the mission against Ouranos. He is thus no mere brute, but is aligned with the highest aspects of Intellect and even seership.

---

260   "[…] when Saturn is called κόρος [boy], it does not signify a boy, but the purity and incorruptible nature of his intellect." It has been suggested to me that the myth of Fionn sucking his thumb to trigger his mystical insight carries with it a deeper symbolical meaning: that of returning the state of boyhood, to the eternal infant within, who is the symbol of the pure and incorruptible nature of the Intellect and of the Golden Age that the Rudraic god guards and leads back to, especially in moments of inspiration.

As Rudra seeks to guard and then desires to return to the state of perfect integral wholeness before manifestation, a few of Cronus' traits may point in a similar direction. Cronus, and no other god, is made the lord of the Blessed Isles, the highest afterlife destination. Hesiod states: "And they live untouched by sorrow in the islands of the blessed along the shore of deep swirling Okeanos (Oceanus), happy heroes for whom the grain-giving earth bears honey-sweet fruit flourishing thrice a year, far from the deathless gods, and Kronos rules over them; for the father of men and gods released him from his bonds. And these last equally have honour and glory" (Hesiod, *Works and Days* 156). Indeed, only after living three faultless lives and going to Elysium after each can the perfected soul go to Cronus' Blessed Isles[261] [262]. Furthermore, in a description of the Golden Age, of which Cronus is king, which sounds just like the Uncreate that Kramrisch discusses in the Vedic case, or like the state of Rudraic samadhi that leads back to it, Plotinus says of Cronus that:

> That archetypal world is the true Golden Age, age of Kronos, who is the Intellectual-Principle as being the offspring or exuberance of God. For here is contained all that is immortal: nothing here but is Divine Mind; all is God; this is the place of every soul. **Here is rest unbroken: for how can that seek change, in which all is well; what need that reach to, which holds all within itself; what increase can that desire, which stands utterly achieved? All its content, thus, is perfect, that itself may be perfect throughout, as holding nothing that is less than the divine, nothing that is less than intellective.** Its knowing is not by search but by possession, its blessedness inherent, not acquired; for all belongs to it eternally and **it holds the authentic Eternity**

---

261   "But those who had good courage, three times on either side of death, to keep their hearts untarnished of all wrong, these travel along the road of Zeus to Kronos' (Cronus') tower. There round the Islands of the Blest, the winds of Okeanos (Oceanus) play, and golden blossoms burn, some nursed upon the waters, others on land on glorious trees; and woven on their hands are wreaths enchained and flowering crowns, under the just decrees of Rhadamanthys, who has his seat at the right hand of the great father, Rhea's husband [Kronos (Cronus)], goddess who holds the throne highest of all" (Pindar, *Olympian Odes* 2.55).

"Now in the time of Kronos there was a law concerning mankind, and it holds to this very day amongst the gods, that every man who has passed a just and holy life departs after his decease to the Isles of the Blest (*Nesoi Makaron*), and dwells in all happiness apart from ill; but whoever has lived unjustly and impiously goes to the dungeon of requital and penance which, you know, they call Tartaros (Tartarus)" (Plato, *Gorgias* 525a).

262   Apollo, the Greek Rudra within the present age, is the god of the land of Hyperborea, a place that is a sort of Golden Age on Earth, and is said to visit there each Winter, which, as we will see, is the Kronian time. Winter, as should be clear by now, is also the phase in the cycle that Rudra attempts to preserve by staving off the cosmic "Spring."

imitated by Time which, circling round the Soul, makes towards the new thing and passes by the old. Soul deals with thing after thing – now Socrates; now a horse: always some one entity from among beings – but the Intellectual-Principle is all and therefore its entire content is simultaneously present in that identity: **this is pure being in eternal actuality; nowhere is there any future, for every then is a now; nor is there any past, for nothing there has ever ceased to be; everything has taken its stand for ever, an identity well pleased, we might say, to be as it is**; and everything, in that entire content, is Intellectual-Principle and **Authentic Existence**; and the total of all is Intellectual-Principle entire and **Being entire**. (Plotinus, *Enneads* 5.1.4)

This seems to us the parallel of the state of perfection sought by the Rudraic mystic and indeed by Rudra himself, the reintegration of the Uncreate state. Cronus' well-known trait of devouring his children would then signify his desire to draw nascent life and generation back within himself, wanting to return to the state of "darkness," for Orphic Fragment 136 says, "Krónos (Κρόνος), in turn, intends to punish the Gods again, and seize his kingdom; that is to say, he intends that ancient darkness, to rule the zodiacal circles, those possessing the stars." Similarly of Vedic Rudra, Kramrisch says that "Rudra, to whom *tamas* [the guna of darkness] belongs, would annihilate the constituents of the cosmos and dissolve them in darkness, steeped in its own density" (Kramrisch, 183).[263] This ancient darkness of Cronus/Rudra is thus an analogy for the dark night of the cycle, the unmanifest wholeness which Cronus/Rudra wishes to reinstate. Cronus is indeed explicitly associated with Winter in the Orphic Fragments, the Night of the cycle, and this is directly connected to the concealment of the seeds, to which the Rudraic withholding of the seed can be compared: "And on which account, they say of the seasons that wintertime is Kronian, concealing under the earth the seeds, just as the fruits are there from himself – if you wish to speak theologically – and through chilling her, he provides naturally to their coming into being" (σχόλιον Πρόκλου επὶ Πολιτείας Πλάτωνος II 61, 22 Kr). Just the same, according to Kramrisch Rudra appears the mythology as "the possessor of the seeds and their light" (Kramrisch, 356). She states that

> Śiva is the carrier of the seed. At will, he may release or restrain it. As Lord of Yoga he restrains its movement, absorbs the seed in his total being. As the

---

263   "Tamas [the guna of Rudra] is darkness; when this guna increases its activity, the darkness becomes deeper, denser, and heavier, and by its weight tends to obstruct the other two gunas. It can be considered the first efficient cause of physical manifestation or of the five elements of which the cosmos is composed. It leads the descent from prematter into matter. The descent into matter—beyond which the cooperation of the three gunas does not extend—would end with the dissolution of matter" (Kramrisch, 183).

> Mahābhārata expresses it, he is the yogi; he holds the great (cosmic) seed; he is
> one with tapas, fire and fervent self-control; he is one with the golden seed
> (MBh.1.13.17.39). He effects and is the transition from transitive action to an
> intransitive state. (Kramrisch, 371-372)

Thus Cronus' drawing his children back into himself is a reiteration of the same
tendency to conceal the seed, to draw generation back into the state of contraction and
integral wholeness, which is also the state of ancient darkness. It seems plain that this
tendency is the esoteric parallel of the mystic Rudraic practice of semen re-uptake which
Kramrisch discusses at length, the reabsorption of the seed being the same
metaphysically as the swallowing of Cronus' "children." Cronus' swallowing of his own
children also repeats the trait of child-killing which is constantly connected to the
Rudraic gods, and this goes back to the same metaphysical theme again: destroyer,
concealer, and re-absorber of the seeds of new life, propitiated in Vedic religion to spare
the born and unborn child.

   Perfectly in line with this comparison, Plotinus exclaims regarding Cronus, who is
"The Intellectual-Principle":

> A being of this quality, like the Intellectual-Principle [Cronus], must be felt to
> be worthy of the all-pure: it could not derive from any other than from the first
> principle of all; as it comes into existence, all other beings must be
> simultaneously engendered – all the beauty of the Ideas, all the Gods of the
> Intellectual realm. And it still remains pregnant with this offspring; for it has, so
> to speak, drawn all within itself again, **holding them lest they fall away
> towards Matter to be 'brought up in the House of Rhea' [in the realm of
> flux].** (Plotinus, Ennead 5.1.7)

An Orphic fragment points out that Cronus is not only the consumer of all things, but
also their restorer, much like Rudra-Siva: "Oh clever, pure, mighty, brave Titan, you
consume all things and restore them yourself." Another comment of Plotinus sounds like
a devotion of a Shaivite when read in terms of Cronus-Siva: "The sensitive principle is
our scout; **the Intellectual-Principle [Cronus] our King. But we, too, are king when
we are moulded to the Intellectual-Principle**" (Ennead 5.3.3-4).[264] And this comment

---

264 Meanwhile, this inquiry by Plotinus regarding the breaking up of what is "self-
gathered" could be spoken by Siva himself, the self-gathered one, the vengeful guardian of
the wholeness of the Uncreate, and clearly comes from a shared theology:

> from such a unity as we have declared The One to be [compare: The Uncreate], how
> does anything at all come into substantial existence, any multiplicity, dyad, or
> number? Why has the Primal not remained self-gathered so that there be none of this
> profusion of the manifold which we observe in existence and yet are compelled to
> trace to that absolute unity? (Ennead 5.1.6)

of Plotinus on the Intellectual-Principle [Cronus] would be to a Shaivite a clear description of the state of Rudra-Siva in stillness and meditation, embodying the withdrawal or immunity from action, as the immovable yogi, the pillar or *sthāṇu*:

> [...] **self-gathered** and unalloyed, it is Intellectual-Principle through all the range of its being – for unintelligent intelligence is not possible – and thus it possesses of necessity self-knowing, as a being immanent to itself and one having for function and essence to be purely and solely Intellectual-Principle. **This is no doer; the doer, not self-intent but looking outward, will have knowledge, in some kind, of the external, but, if wholly of this practical order, need have no self-knowledge; where, on the contrary, there is no action – and of course the pure Intellectual-Principle cannot be straining after any absent good – the intention can be only towards the self; at once self-knowing becomes not merely plausible but inevitable**; what else could living signify in a being immune from action and existing in Intellect? (Ennead 5.3.6).

Internet Encyclopedia of Philosophy describes the salvific path according to Plotinus, which can be seen to directly mirror the act of liberation performed by Efnysien or Rudra in the ways we have laid out: "Plotinus, who described the Intellect [Cronus] as proceeding directly from the One, thereby placing Mind before Thought, and so making thought the process by which the Intellect becomes alienated from itself, thus requiring the salvific act in order to attain the fulfillment of Being, which is, for Plotinus, the return of Intellect to itself" (IEP, "Neoplatonism," 4).[265] A successor of Plotinus, Iamblichus, says of the practice of Theurgy, that it renders humankind, "who through generation are born subject to passion, pure and unchangeable" (*On the Mysteries* I.12.42; in Fowden 1986, p. 133). This seems to describe the precise path that Efnysien/Cronus/Rudra models, when he enters the realm (or cauldron) of generation and sensuousness, and then snuffs out his own passion and becomes pure and

---

And this description of Plotinus' practice describes the attitude of a Shaivite devotee: "'likeness to God' had meant, for Plotinus, a recollection and perfection of one's own divine nature (which is, in the last analysis, identical to nous; cf. Ennead III.4)" (*Internet Encyclopedia of Philosophy*).

265   "Proclus understands the movement of existence as a tripartite progression beginning with an abstract unity, passing into a multiplicity that is identified with Life, and returning again to a unity that is no longer merely abstract, but now actualized as an eternal manifestation of the godhead. What constituted, for Plotinus, the salvific drama of human existence is, for Proclus, simply the logical, natural order of things. However, by thus removing the yearning for salvation from human existence, as something to be accomplished, positively, Proclus is ignoring or overly intellectualizing, if you will, an existential aspect of human existence that is as real as it is powerful" (*Internet Encyclopedia of Philosophy*, "Neoplatonism," 4).

unchangeable, like the incorruptible body of Attis, or like Cronus becoming ruler of the Blessed Isles. The Intellect proceeds directly from the One, becomes alienated by plunging into the realm of Generation, requiring the salvific act, which returns it to the One as the perfected and unchanging pillar. As a dramatic model of the salvific process of the cosmos for those who come after, this is at the core of the divine drama.

Several other of the major Greek philosophers, including Plato, Aristotle, and Anaxagoras, elevated this same principle of Intellect, which is also called *Nous*/Mind, to a high position and described it in terms matching those we find in the theology of Siva. In Plato's *Philebus* 28c Socrates says: "all philosophers agree—whereby they really exalt themselves—that mind (nous) is king of heaven and earth. Perhaps they are right." He then states after discussion that "the utterances of those who declared of old that mind (nous) always rules the universe" are verified upon analysis. He further associates *nous* with the *logistikon*, the ruling portion of the human soul. For Plato, the *nous* was the only immortal part of the soul. For Anaxagoras, the Cosmic Mind, *Nous*, ordered all things, an idea echoed in other terms by Aristotle. In *Metaphysics*, Book XII, ch.7-10, Aristotle equates *nous* as an actuality, or active nous, which is when *nous* becomes what is thought about, with the "unmoved mover" of the universe, and God: "For the actuality of thought (nous) is life, and God is that actuality; and the essential actuality of God is life most good and eternal." This echoes Plotinus' description of the Intellectual-Principle being one with the contents of its contemplation, and not being a "doer," yet emanating the cosmos by his self-knowing thinking. This is of course almost exactly what Siva is described as doing when he refuses to procreate, enters the waters, becomes the immovable pillar, and yet emanates life in the waters via the inherent paradoxical overflowing power of his tapas and self-contained, self-focused meditative contemplation. Indeed, the Intellectual Principle/Nous of the Greek philosophical world seems mostly to be a narrowed down but still theologically faithful version of Cronus who is Rudra/Odinn etc.

Cronus' apparent Roman analogue, Saturn[266], is also the lord of the Winter festival of Saturnalia, which recreates and commemorates a Golden Age without the strictures of social conventions and with their notable inversion. Cronus' own festival, the Kronia, is in fact at the other end of the year, in Summer. However, it still marks the beginning of the year in the regional Attic calendar, and thus its position apart from the otherwise

---

[266]   In later Hindu texts, the planet Saturn is identified with a god named Shani. However, as Curwen Rolinson notes: "*Shani* turns up within the Thousand Name Hymn of Shiva; Shani is possessed of the terrifying glare of destruction; Shani beheads Ganesha in some myths" (Rolinson, "Saturday – Shani Dev's Day – Saturn's Day"). Shani also considered Lord Shiva as his guru and is called by the Siva-related title *Shaneeshwar*. Thus, he has been said to represent Lord Shiva's *Vairagya* principle. Furthermore, Shani is half-brother of Yama just as Efnysien is half-brother of Bran who is Yama.

"Kronian time" of Winter could speculatively be the result of a particular calendar reform, the festival moved to the Summer when the start of the year was moved there. On the other hand, the Kronia being in the Summer and marking the first harvest could simply connect to Cronus' role in the harvest, being the god of the sickle as he is, the god who draws life back to the unmanifest like cutting a gourd from its stalk[267]. The Kronia likewise enacts a memorial of the Golden Age with social strictures suspended or reversed, and is thus notably similar to the Saturnalia of Winter, though at the opposite point in the seasonal cycle. The *corybantes* are usually called the offspring of Apollo, the primary Rudra within the Greek world of the present age, and as such these *corybantes* would be a match of the Fianna/rudras/vratyas/Ulfhednar of other branches. However, the *corybantes* are in one account (Strabo, *Geographica* 10.3.19) instead said to be the children of Cronus, a curious and impenetrable attestation unless we consider Cronus as the primordial Rudraic manifestation, who re-manifests, in the created world of Becoming, as Apollo.[268]

---

267   "'Whatever destroys any existing thing, movable or stationary, at any time, is . . . Rudra' (VP.1.22.39). His power is deadly. Like a gourd from its stalk, he cuts off life or spares it (cf. RV.7.59.12). As Paśupati, he spared the life of animals. The archer has the power over life and death. He may avert or restrain his arrow. This is the grace by which he frees from death. He is the liberator" (Kramrisch, 83).

268   This understanding of Cronus/Saturn as Rudra also helps to explain the Hermetic conception of Saturn as expounded by esotericist Julius Evola:

"Saturn-Kronos is the king of the primordial age, who is asleep in the Hyperborean seat; according to some myths he was castrated at the beginning of a new cycle.[...] Moreover, in the Hermetic tradition Saturn-Kronos is the deceased who must be resuscitated; the royal art of the heroes consists in freeing lead from its 'leprosy;' namely, from its imperfections and darkness, transforming it into gold, thus actualizing the Mystery of the Stone. Moreover, Kronos, gold, and 'foundation stone' are different references to the primordial regal tradition" (Julius Evola, *The Mystery of the Grail*, 98-99).

Rudra's lingam, symbol of the high essence of the god, is a stone which contains in it paradoxically the negation and the potentiality of life, and which represents the force standing at the foundation of existence, and thus explains the meaning Evola ascribes to Saturn, the lead or stone which is the mystical origin point substance that must be turned into gold in Hermeticism.

"Saturn's Kingdom Transformed into the Golden Age. In Hermeticism the theme of a primordial state that needs to be reawakened takes the form of the production of gold through the transformation of Saturn's metal, lead, in which it is hidden. In a hieroglyphic drawn by Basil Valentine we can see crowned Saturn atop a complex symbol that represents the overall Hermetic Work. Beneath Saturn is the symbol of sulfur, which in turn contains the symbol of resurrection, the Phoenix. According to Philalethes, the wise find the missing element in Saturn's race, after adding the needed sulfur: here the key is provided by the double meaning of [...] both 'sulfur' and 'divine.' Moreover, sulfur is often the equivalent of fire [compare Rudra being

Dan Attrell's comments[269] on his translation[270] of the 11th century magical text known as *The Picatrix* seem to prove that this text somehow preserved true archaic material relating to Saturn and other gods, material that further affirms the direct identification of Saturn and Rudra. As the *Picatrix* says of Saturn:

> Saturn is the source of retentive power [recall Saturn-Rudra's connection to semen retention]. He governs an aspect toward profound knowledge; the science of law; the search for causes and effects; the origins of things; the utterance of magical words; and the knowledge of deep and occult properties [...] he governs all black cloth [...] among locations he governs black mountains [...] from the

---

> united on the primordial scene with Agni as Rudra-Agni, Odinn with Lodurr, and Efnysien with Manawydan], the active and vivifying principle of the Hermetic tradition. In the Hellenistic texts we find the theme of the sacred black stone, the power of which is stronger than any spell. This stone, in order to be truly regarded as 'our Gold;' 'namely Mithras [compare Cronus fathering the Mitraic god Zeus, who is also called the Soul by Platonists];' and to produce the 'great Mithraic mystery;' must possess the right power or the 'medicine of the right action'; this is just another way to express the mystery of awakening and of reintegration. What we have here is a further parallelism with the themes of the Grail: symbols of a primordial regality and of a stone that await a virile and divine power (sulfur = divine) in order to be manifested as 'gold' and as the 'philosopher's stone' endowed with the medicinal power to destroy every 'illness' [consider Rudra as healer and bringer of illness]" (Evola, 153).

Evola speaks further of

> [...] the divine or heavenly stone described in Hermetic texts: the latter has also been perceived as an elixir or as a principle that renews itself and bestows eternal life, health, and victory. When we read in a text by Kitab-el-Focul, 'The stone speaks but you heed it not: it calls to you and you answer not! O you sleepers! What deafness stops your ears? What vise grips your hearts and minds?" [...] When Zacharias wrote 'Our body, which is our occult stone, cannot be known nor seen without inspiration ... without this body our science is vain' [...] according to one of its most recurrent themes, the Royal Art of the Hermetists is focused on a 'stone' that is often identified with Saturn; this stone contains the phoenix, the elixir, the gold, or 'Our King' at the latent state. Moreover, I also wish to recall that the 'strange and terrible mystery that was transmitted to the disciples of king Hermes' and to the 'Heroes' who try to find their way to the 'earthly paradise' through 'fierce fighting:' consists in destroying that state of latency often referred to as 'death' or 'disease' or 'impurity' or 'imperfection:' through operations of an initiatory character" (Evola, 154).

269   Dan Attrell, Youtube Channel: The Modern Hermeticist, "Honoring the Outermost: Saturn, Ficino, and Astral Magic [1/2]".
https://www.youtube.com/watch?v=dq_fgdqRdi8. 40:00-1:00:00. Web. Accessed December 2021.

270   *Picatrix: A Medieval Treatise on Astral Magic.* Trans. Dan Attrell and David Porreca. Gratitude to Kalin for bringing this material to my attention.

stones he governs onyx and all black stones […] and all black, musty metals […] he governs black camels, pigs, monkeys, bears, dogs, and cats. From the birds, he governs all those with a long neck and a powerful cry, like cranes, ostriches, duga, and crows […] he governs every black and tawny color [recall that Rudra's is the guna of darkness]. (*Picatrix* 3.1.3)

Saturn's talismanic image is said to be "the shape of a black man wrapped in a green cloak with a dog-like head and a sickle in his hand" (3.3.4) which brings up the image of the "dog-priests" or *vratyas*, the devotees of Rudra.

A full prayer to Saturn is preserved in *The Picatrix* which is strikingly Rudraic and highlights the ambivalence of the god, his role as bringer of both good and ill:

> **Oh lord on high whose name is great and stands firm in a place above all the heavens' planets, he whom God placed sublime and lofty! You are lord Saturn, cold and dry, dark, author of good, honest in your friendship, true in your promises, enduring and persevering in your amity and hatred. Your perception is far and deep; honest in your words and promises, alone, lonely, removed from others in your works** [recall Rudra excluded from the sacrifice]**, with sadness and pain, removed from rejoicing and festivities** [again, Rudra as the excluded one at the sacrifice]**. You are old, ancient, wise, the despoiler of good intellect. You are a doer of good and of evil. Wretched and sad is he who is cursed by your misfortunes. The man who attains your fortunes is blessed indeed. In you God placed power and strength and a spirit doing both good and evil. I ask you, father and lord, by your lofty names and wondrous acts, that you should do such-and-such a thing for me.** (3.7.16)

In another translation, by Hashem Atallah, "doer of good and evil" is instead rendered as "the fixer, the destroyer," while "the destroyer" is a well-known title of Rudra. Atallah also renders "despoiler of good intellect" as "the double-crosser, the deceiver," while Rudra in the *Satarudriya* litany is called deceiver or arch-trickster (21) and lord of thieves (20), and one of Odinn's names in the skaldic poem *Odins nofn* is an exact match: *Ginnarr*, "Deceiver." *Picatrix* translator Dan Attrell highlights the fact that in the text Saturn is specifically ambivalent, dual-natured, that

> up in his lofty seat he is a liminal figure, a sign of eternity's descent into normal time, or vice-versa, a sign of the last rung in one's ascent from normal time into eternity. He is both an evil sorcerer and a holy prophet; with his old age comes both wisdom and senility; with his perseverance comes enduring good and evil; with his honesty, great hope and great fear are mixed in together […] Picatrix

highlights the hidden treasures he hides behind his somber disposition, and it was this two-fold nature of Saturn which would become so prominent in Ficino.

Saturn is in this text associated particularly with certain types of people and among them we should note in particular kings, slaves, thieves and hermits, that is, the highest, the lowest, the outcasts, and the ascetics, each of these being particularly associated with Rudra in his tradition. Attrell comments on the list of Saturn's associations as follows: "[…] the elderly, generous men, elders, kings of cities, hermits, those who work the lands, returns to cities, inheritances, exceptional men, farmers, builders of buildings, slaves, thieves, fathers, grandfathers, and great-grandfathers. If you were caught up in deep thought and grief, in melancholy or grievous illness, in all these things or affairs, seek petitions from Saturn, and request things assigned to his nature."

Precisely as we have seen Rudra called on to heal the misfortunes that he brings, Attrell notes that "Here Saturn not only signified but could also help to cure many of the negative things traditionally assigned to his nature — one simply had to invoke and petition him in a ritual." The Picatrix describes a sacrifice designed to apprehend "the dominion and motion of Saturn, which according to them is the first motion, because in him motion begins and ends" (3.7.38). According to Attrell, the sages cited in the Picatrix sought to ward off Saturn's "malefic or unfortunate effects, since every evil, every cursed thing, and every tear shed upon the earth were believed to proceed from him." "He is lord of all poverty, misery, pain, imprisonment, turpitude, and lamentation"; "He signifies these things while descending and unfortunate. When he is in a good disposition and in his exultation, however, he signifies purity, lifespan, social standing, rejoicing, honor, riches, inheritance, and the durability of inheritance in sons and grandsons" (3.7.2). Finally, the best things for which to entreat Saturn are "delaying movement, concealing purity, the destruction of cities, humbling hearts, and calming waters" (4.4.5).

***

With frightening precision, the Welsh Efnysien follows the same pattern that Kramrisch describes with respect to Rudra: he causes the "catastrophe" and then he avenges or sets right what he himself has set in motion. This arc is apparent in Efnysien's own words: "Alas! woe is me, that I should have been the cause of bringing the men of the Island of the Mighty into so great a strait. Evil betide me if I find not a deliverance therefrom" (*Branwen, daughter of Llyr*). He first mutilates the horses of Matholwch, *inflaming* tensions, which causes Bran to give the cauldron to Matholwch (Father Sky), the cauldron which will later lead to the destruction in battle of Efnysien's allies. The mutilation is also at least one of the causes of the "abuse" of Branwen by Matholwch and his men, the abuse which brings on the war and is the analogy of the

452

primordial Vedic rape. Thus Efnysien sees his own culpability in the unfolding of the events and takes it upon himself to throw the boy Gwern (the divine seed) into the fire and then to destroy the magical cauldron, the unbalancing remainder left from the breach of the divine liquid substance escaping into the realm of Generation, into the created World. In Kramrisch's words, Rudra is "the cause and also that effect on which again he acts," when he, as the incandescent essence of Fire, prepares the seed in the Father, which he then avenges with the arrow from his bow.

> Inasmuch as he is Agni, he prepares the seed. Inasmuch as he is Rudra, he is intent on the destruction of the effect that he has caused. He incites toward creation, and when it takes its course he lets fly his arrow against it. The sequence of contradictory actions is far from self-defeating. It is of the very nature of Rudra, who creates in order to destroy, for he will create again in an inexhaustible renewal of life on earth, where creation is the aeviternal answer to destruction, and both have their ground and antithesis in the Uncreate. This is the course that Rudra set. More truly than any other god he could have said of himself: 'I am not a puzzled-out book, I am a god with his contradictions.' His contradictions, his polarities operate on all levels of his ambience, radiating from his center. (Kramrisch, 28)

"Rudra caused the seed of the Father to fall down to earth. But did not the avenger also avenge his own action?" (Kramrisch, 56) she asks. Can precisely the same thing not be said of Efnysien, the avenger of his own inflammation of the tensions between Matholwch and Branwen, the avenger of the giving of the cauldron of sacred liquid to Father Sky, the avenger of the catastrophe which he set in motion?

Thus we are left with parallel sets of Rudraic groupings across several branches, generally including a primordial Rudra, and a prime Rudra-of-the-world, with a destructive, lower-case "rudra" also often appearing as an offshoot of these, sometimes interchangeable with them: The primordial Greek Rudra Cronus and Rudra-of-the-world Apollo; Irish Eber Finn(/destructive rudra Balor) and Fionn; Welsh Efnysien-Nisien(/destructive rudra Ysbaddaden) and Gwyn-Gwion. Odinn, being the Norse "Ur-Rudra," is given as the primordial Rudraic god on the scene of creation and is not given a separate name on that scene as happens to the Primordial Rudras in the Greek and Welsh branches. The jotunn Suttungr, on the other hand, parallels Balor as a destructive rudra, who also parallels Cronus in his role as the Fatherly rudra who must be overcome by the Mitraic god. In this way, Suttungr is only a particularized manifestation of the essence of this primordial divinity in a more narrow context. He is only a "rudra" of the world in the myths we have, an offshoot, a metaphysical descendant of the primordial Odinn from whom he has apparently become distinct, manifesting the sometimes *jotunn*-like nature of the frightening "rudras." It may be noteworthy that the name of Suttungr's father is *Gilling*, meaning "screamer," while Rudra is the god who "cries" or "howls," as the colloquial meaning of his name denotes. However, many *jotnar* bear similar names and this could be insignificant. In any case, Rudra and his rudras are divine beings who can manifest in any form they choose, and very often appear in destructive or frightening guises, spooking, obstructive, misshapen, near-demonic. The idea that both Suttungr and Gilling could be "rudras," even though classified as *Jotnar*, should not seem odd in the least, and is even to be expected. Suttungr's parallel Balor is called a Fomorian, the Irish grouping directly paralleling the *Jotnar*, and Balor is after all a "rudra," as we have seen, especially under his alternate name, Goll, who is a member of the Fianna. The fact that Odinn sacrifices himself to himself on the Windy Tree also implies this sort of concept of "levels" within the deity. When Odinn, in his manifestation as the "Rudra" of the world, sacrifices himself to himself, this may then be a sacrifice of the "Rudra"/Odinn of the World to the Primordial "Rudra"/Odinn from the primordial scene, who is the higher Self of "Rudra"/Odinn.

For the Vedics, all these Rudraic roles are named "Rudra," yet there are also titles such as Pasupati, Vāstoṣpati, and Siva, names which are used contextually, as names for precise manifestations of the divinity, and also interchangeably.

In the Welsh myth, the divine "seed" child of Matholwch, the tree-named boy Gwern, walks, in one curiously charged scene, from Bran to Manawydan (Fire) to Nisien (benevolent Rudra aka Siva) to Efnysien (primordial avenging Rudra) in the moment just before being cast into the flame. Setting aside the giant Bran, the king of Britain who is once mistaken for a mountain and then becomes a talking severed head, and who would parallel the jotunn Mimir and Vedic Yama in our schema, it seems to be possible to match this Welsh scene to the Norse scene involving the investing of the first tree-named humans with qualities by Odinn and his two divine colleagues. Odinn, Lodurr, and Hoenir are said in *Voluspa* 17-18 to give the first tree-humans *Askr* (Ash) and *Embla* the vital qualities of life. While Odinn in the primordial scene can be seen to parallel Efnysien, who is the primordial Welsh Rudra, this Lodurr on the other hand has sometimes been connected to heat and fire[271], especially considering that he gives "goodly hue" and blood or film of flesh to humans and his name can be connected to the German word *lodern*, "to blaze." We will accept this theory without digression for the present interpretation as it appears to us well-supported, and, furthermore, is greatly bolstered by the Welsh parallel which tends to directly confirm it. From this perspective, Lodurr would match Manawydan, the Fire God as he manifests on the primordial scene. Hoenir, next, is said to have special prophetic abilities (*Voluspa* 63: "Then Hönir wins the prophetic wand") and to give *óðr* (perhaps "understanding," "mind," "inspiration")

---

271   Credit for this connection to the work of Carla O'Harris.

as his gift to the ancestral humans. Indeed, *óðr,* the word for the gift that Hoenir gives, has long been recognized to share its root with Odinn's very name, and as such the idea that he is only nominally distinct from Odinn, a hypostasis of an Odinnic aspect, is not new, and ought even to be the default hypothesis due to the name of his gift. Hoenir (or Hone) is depicted as excessively passive or indecisive in Snorri's account in *Ynglingasaga* 4, which then appears to be an exaggerated way for Snorri to demonstrate him to be the softer, more peaceable or passive Siva to Odinn's Rudra, considering the other Rudra-Siva pairings we have identified in Efnysien-Nisien, Diephobus-Helenus, and Bolwis-Bilwis. Hoenir's passiveness is indeed simply a caricature of the famous Siva tranquility. As the passive and prophetic "Siva," Hoenir would most closely parallel Helenus of Troy, also gentle and possessed of prophetic power, and, in the primordial Welsh scene of the gods surrounding Gwern one by one before the boy is thrown into the flames, Hoenir would parallel Nisien, the peaceable brother of Efnysien. If this is an accurate comparison of primordial trios, then it may be that during the strange scene in which Gwern walks from one god to the next, seemingly for no reason, before being thrown into the "sacrificial" fire, these gods are doing more than is stated on the surface. In the original version of the myth, they may in fact have been investing the tree-child with the vital qualities of life, the divine gifts of all humans to come thereafter. In terms of the proposed Norse Primordial Fire God Lodurr, united on the primordial scene with Odinn as Agni is with Rudra, once the world was created and Time was begun he would have split into the good fire, which remained an aspect of Odinn, as we have seen, and the destructive fire, which would eventually arise in its final apocalyptic form as Surtr.

***

We leave off this analysis with a few more quotations from this very great book of Kramrisch's, which, though certain marks of influence by later Indian philosophy should be noted, is the book of a seer, and is the key to unlocking the deep meaning of this Welsh creation myth. I hope that these quotations elucidate some of the esoteric connections between the myth and the larger paradigm of the sacrifice.

> Agni [see: Manawydan] celebrates the union of the Father [Matholwch] and his daughter [Branwen]. The target of Rudra-Agni [Efnysien], the Wild Archer, is the incontinence of the Father that makes him shed into creation the substance [Gwern] of the Uncreate. Rudra [Efnysien] avenges the violation, that is the rupture of the Uncreate. Rudra—Fire and Archer—is Rudra Lord of Yoga and Guardian of the Uncreate. But the Lord of Generation's seed [Gwern] fell down on the earth. (Kramrisch, 46)

This primordial assault on Prajāpati [Dyaus/Matholwch], the Lord of Generation, who himself had violated pre-existential totality, was the bond in creation between the abiding and paradoxically inviolate pre-existential integrity, the fire of creation, and the agony of the Lord of Generation, that foaming bull, the primordial sacrificial victim. (Kramrisch, 73)

Creation was flawed from the start, yet was redeemed at the same time by the intervention of the gods, who out of the substance and rhythm of their magic words fashioned Vāstoṣpati. (Kramrisch, 76)

By rape and incontinence, powers of creation and procreation came down to earth from the Uncreate. It had never been tapped before, nor depleted. Henceforward it would be known in its fulness by a return to it in the state of samādhi or in moments of creative intuition. (Kramrisch, 79)

Rudra, in a time-caused reverse effect of his intention, brought the life itself of mankind to this earth, and with it he brought time. (Kramrisch, 96)

Rudra as the consciousness of the absolute had failed to preserve its integrity. (Kramrisch, 174)

It was Rudra alone who got ready that very substance [the cauldron of regeneration] for Father Heaven and, having given it to him and having avenged the violation, brought guilt on himself. The fierce Wild God then was given a shape of conglomerate horror [Pasupati, Yogi and master of passions/Lord of "Animals"] for his appearance in the wasteland of this earth. (Kramrisch, 179)

There is much darkness in Rudra. When he sinks low and into the abyss of his own being, he draws the world with him into the cosmic night of dissolution [as Cronus is said to wish to return all to ancient darkness]. *Tamas* [*guna* of darkness] is the heavy downward pull into disintegration. *Tamos* is the dark ground of Rudra's being, whence the flame of destruction leaps upward. It ends physical existence and liberates from ahamkāra, from individuation and the ego. When the thousands and thousands of arrows ready in the hands of Rudra (TS.4.5.10.5) have hit their targets, Rudra is seen as Sambhu, the cause of tranquillity, Saṅkara, the giver of bliss, Śiva, the liberator (TS.4.5.8.1). As liberator and giver of happiness, Śiva is in all beings, their indwelling potential of freedom and peace. (Kramrisch, 184)

The Mahāmṛtyuñjaya mantra invokes Rudra, the conqueror of death, who has the power to inflict or to withhold death (RV.7.59.12). (Kramrisch, 187-188)

Śiva, the destroyer who **leads out of the cosmos**, is the Great Yogi who **within himself annihilates the world of experience [Efnysien destroying the cauldron of regeneration]**; he is **the ferryman and the ferry leading from this world to the other shore** (TS .4.5.8.2), to a nameless beyond to which the darkness of dissolution is only an allusion. When there is no darkness, there is neither day nor night, neither being nor nonbeing, only the one (Śiva) alone. Śiva in absolute transcendency, Śiva in manifestation and its destroyer, Śiva in the darkness of dissolution is at the same time the lord of sentient beings, Paśupati, Lord of Animals, their fierce hunter of a hundred shapes. (Kramrisch, 188)

As Agni-Rudra he is the protagonist of the drama of creation, leading into it and lashing back, letting the arrow fly against it […] This arrow too will be set flying by Rudra within man, in inner realization. Then 'the syllable AUM is the bow, the ātman (self) is indeed the arrow; brahman (ultimate reality) is its target; carefully should it be pierced. Thus one becomes united with it like the arrow (with its target)' (MUp.2.2.4; RHUp.38). (Kramrisch, 82-83)

16

Ymir and the Norse "Father Sky"

Armed with this understanding, we broach a more controversial issue. If Father Sky rapes, or abuses and impregnates, Mother Earth, and then is violently separated from her in the primordial scene in all these other branches, why does this myth of the violation of Mother Earth by Father Sky not seem to appear in the Norse creation, or in Norse myth anywhere? This moment is so charged and indeed so important mythically that it leads to the creation of the life of the cosmos and it is not even absent in the Welsh and Irish traditions, though buried deep in coded narratives that have not been fully understood. In these other branches, Mother Earth and Father Sky always are depicted as consorts of one another, there is usually some violence done to Mother Earth, the divine seed or child is produced, and Mother Earth and Father Sky are always violently separated, whether Father Sky is killed in a war as in the Celtic version or simply castrated or struck with an arrow in the Greek and Vedic cases respectively.

Having seen Odinn clearly in his role as parallel of Cronus/Efnysien/Rudra and understanding the metaphysical significance of this primordial scene a bit better, an answer to the question of what has happened to the Norse myth of the division of Mother

Earth and Father Sky makes itself apparent. Odinn is indeed the god who violently divides Earth and Sky in the primordial moment, but this conjunction of Earth and Sky is given the name Ymir. This fact is very plain in the mythic sources: Ymir is divided up by Odinn and his two brothers (or aspects of Odinn), and Ymir's skull and brains are made into the sky and clouds, while his body becomes the earth, neither of which had been in existence before this event.

> Out of Ymir's flesh was fashioned the earth,
>
> And the mountains were made of his bones;
>
> The sky from the frost cold giant's skull,
>
> And the ocean out of his blood. (*Vafthrudnismal, 21*)

> Out of Ymir's flesh was fashioned the earth,
>
> And the ocean out of his blood;
>
> Of his bones the hills, of his hair the trees,
>
> Of his skull the heavens high.
>
> Mithgarth the gods from his eyebrows made,
>
> And set for the sons of men;
>
> And out of his brain the baleful clouds
>
> They made to move on high. (*Grimnismal,* 40-41)

> The sons of Borr [Odinn, Villi and Ve] slew Ymir the giant (*Gylfaginning,* VII).

> They took Ymir and bore him into the middle of the Yawning Void, and made of him the earth: of his blood the sea and the waters; the land was made of his flesh, and the crags of his bones; gravel and stones they fashioned from his teeth and his grinders and from those bones that were broken.' And Jafnhárr said: 'Of the blood, which ran and welled forth freely out of his wounds, they made the sea, when they had formed and made firm the earth together, and laid the sea in a ring round about her; and it may well seem a hard thing to most men to cross over it.' Then said Thridi: 'They took his skull also, and made of it the heaven, and set it up over the earth with four corners.' (*Gylfaginning* VIII)

In no other Norse myth, besides that of Ymir, is Earth divided from Sky. In *Orphic Fragment 57*, when the cosmic egg is divided the top of the egg becomes Ouranos (Sky) and the bottom becomes Gaia (Earth), precisely matching the division of Ymir, and directly resulting in Father Sky as the top portion of the division: "[…] a huge egg, which, being filled full, by the force of its engenderer was broken in two from friction. Its crown became Ouranos (Uranus, Heaven), and what had sunk downwards, Gaia (Gaea, Earth). There also came forth an incorporeal god [Protogonos-Phanes]." Meanwhile, as Kramrisch explains with regard to the primordial Vedic scene, the "daughter" with whom Dyaus, Father Sky, is locked in violent conjunction is in fact a hypostasis existing within himself who is the primordial being. We repeat the relevant quotations we have noted previously:

> The divine mating of Father and daughter is a symbol of ontic truth. Elsewhere, primal being, nearest to the wholeness of the Uncreate, is male and female in one. (Stella Kramrisch, *The Presence of Siva*, 59)

> The daughter with whom the Father cohabits is a hypostasis of the Father himself. She was one with him before he knew her. (Kramrisch, 60)

> Father Heaven covered this blushing maiden, part of himself, discernible and other from himself, only to be united with himself. They are not two persons but one self-begotten, begetting entity. (Kramrisch, 62)

> […] in the beginning the Creator embraced his daughter, a hypostasis from within himself in which he asserts himself. To this act of self-love, the emission of seed is biologically a sequel and metaphorically a jolt to the unassailable and undiminished metaphysical plenum. The intercourse of the Creator with his daughter is the two-faced symbol of the rupture of pre-existential wholeness and of the descent to earth of its immortal substance, the seed of life. (Kramrisch, 64)

> […] the infringement of the Uncreate and pre-existential wholeness, a spurt from self-contained fullness, the loss of integrity of the absolute. (Kramrisch, 64)

As such the primordial scene has the character of a yin-yang: two natures locked in embrace, though in another sense they are only one being at this moment. The one who divides this embrace is as-though the line curving across the yin-yang, cutting it in two. Mythically this can be narrated as Sky, as the male progenitor deity, raping Earth and emitting the seed of the first life into the realm of existence, or it can be narrated as the one hermaphroditic primordial being reproducing out of itself. These are indeed the same thing metaphysically speaking. This is why in the Vedic case we can have Dyaus (Sky) raping his *daughter* who is a hypostasis within himself, but in Greek we have Ouranos (Sky) raping his *mother*. It makes no difference which is parent and which is child: in the true meaning of the myth, these beings are locked together as one, and one can be seen as the hypostasis of the other depending on which is given priority in the narrative. When they are finally separated it is as if each is born from the other as the distinct Sky and Earth.

Kramrisch, based on her reading of the Vedic texts, explains the daughter who is raped by Dyaus as *really* a hypostasis within himself, which implies that the version of the myth in which the primordial union of earth and sky is seen only as a single, hermaphroditic being, could in some sense have a claim to greater metaphysical truth than the version where Sky rapes a goddess who is nominally separate from him. Indeed, the Phrygian form of the myth that we have noted previously also tells of a primordial hermaphrodite, Agdistis, who is castrated like Greek Father Sky, Ouranos, leaving "her" with only the Earth Mother nature thereafter, and whose son Attis is then also castrated like Ouranos' son Cronus. The "primordial hermaphrodite" form of the myth can be said to be more "philosophical" in terms of representing the full metaphysical unity of the two divine natures, and it can also be said to be, in terms of sensibility, the more conservative, less sexually shocking form of the myth. No incestuous rape has to be spoken of in this narrative form. However, the line between the two narrative forms is very fine, and we can see that the meaning is the same in either case, both forms portraying the same metaphysical reality faithfully with only slightly different emphasis in each case. Ymir produces the first human couple from out of the sweat of his armpit or legs, depending on the account, which is then the equivalent of the violent rape depicted in the other branches: the metaphysical "rape" happens only within Ymir, in the procreative combustion between his internal male and female natures that leads to the emergence of life from his armpit and/or from his legs.

In Vedic and Greek myth, a defining feature that identifies "Father Sky" is that he is in fact the Sky *itself* and not only a lord *of* the sky. Based on the Vedic and Greek branches, the clearest instances we have of the primordial scene, it might be fair to say that a god cannot be the primordial Indo-European "Father Sky" without *being* the object we call the sky. This was one reason we sought, in a previous investigation, to see if the Irish Father Sky, the Dagda, had the myths of a second deity beyond those of Father Sky alone, as if this second deity were his more active aspect, and we ultimately identified this active aspect with the Wind God. In the primordial Norse scene, there is no question who and what the sky itself is: it is the skull and brains of Ymir. Ymir himself, the controlling, "head" part of Ymir, is the sky. He is also the earth, but as this is the female hypostasis of himself in our reading, his sky nature being the male, procreative nature, the earth gains another name upon separation, becoming the domain of the goddess *Jord*, "Earth." Indeed, in no branch does the Indo-European Father Sky himself ever divide Earth from Sky from a position outside of Earth+Sky in the primordial scene, and something similar to this could only be narrated if he was dividing *himself* in two or castrating *himself*, as does occur, though by the instigation of an exterior trickster (Dionysus), with the Phrygian hermaphrodite Agdistis. Siva, who in later Shaivite texts takes the role of both Rudra and Dyaus, and is both the Desire-afflicted, procreative Father and the violent attacker of Desire in one, also comes close to combining both roles in his version of the myth, but once again the Father Sky aspect is not outside of the primordial unity looking in. When a second deity is present to divide Earth from Sky, this is always, apparently, "Rudra," who we know Odinn himself to be from numerous other parallels which we have examined previously. Cronus is the divider of Earth and Sky. Efnysien is the divider of Earth and Sky. Rudra is the divider of Earth and Sky. We see the same in Kalash myth: Mandi (Mahadeva, ie. Rudra) is the divider of Earth and Sky.[272] Odinn is the divider of Earth and Sky. Ymir, and in particular his head, which is the location of his active principle, is that Sky itself, just as he is the procreative Father

---

272   This refers to the Kalash/Nuristani god *Mahandeu* or *Mandi* (from *Mahan deva*, near-identical to Rudra-Siva's name *Mahadeva*) who changes into a boy (reverting to the nascent state) and pushes his finger into a door he is not supposed to open, causing it to turn golden (think of Fionn who smashes his finger in an otherworldly door or puts his finger on the Salmon of Knowledge and sucks his finger, first to gain and then to tap into his power of mystical sight and knowledge). Mandi then cuts the heads off of a demon who has hidden the sun and moon and brings them back to the world, in what is recognized as a creation myth. In another version of the same tale, he shoots his arrow at the rope that connects the castle of the demons suspended between Heaven and the Earth, this castle holding sun, moon, waters, fertile fields, gold and silver. Under the instruction of Mandi, seeds (consider the seed of Dyaus) are then sowed by the goddess Disni and the ripened chaff turns white on the rope causing the rope to be visible. Mandi's arrow then strikes the rope and causes the castle to crash to the ground. He then gets excited by the white skin of the goddess Disni (compare Bronwen "white breast") and uses his body to break the door of the castle, though it is not a self-sacrifice as when Efnysien breaks the cauldron. Still, he is essentially breaking into Heaven here. He survives the breaking of the door and kills the demons within the house, thus cleansing it like Vastospati or Efnysien. Thus Mandi too is the severer of Heaven from Earth with his arrow in the scene of creation and the cleanser of the "house." The fact that Mandi is excited by the goddess' skin before breaking the door of heaven could carry the same meaning as when Cronus is drunken with honey just before being castrated and becoming lord of the Blessed Isles, or when Efnysien plays dead before entering the cauldron of generation and bursting his own heart: the idea here seems to be that the Rudraic god must enter the sensuous realm of generation before bursting back into the divine realm, thus bridging the gap. This process may be mirrored in some esoteric practices such as those of Tantra. See M. Witzel, "Kalash Religion," 3-5, 9-10.

of the first life. Thus he is "Father Sky" (or what is left of Father Sky in Norse mythology), the great ancestor and primordial divine being who has emitted the first seed in conjunction with the feminine nature which in this case is within himself. It should be remembered that Ymir is never said to be definitely killed in the poetic sources when he is thus split in half. Only in Snorri's account is he said thus to be killed, and this can be taken as a further ossification of a more and more distant divine conception. Meanwhile, the Celtic Father Skys, Welsh Matholwch and Irish Mac Greine, at least in the versions of the tales we have, are indeed killed, and so whether this primordial Sky being is said to be killed or not when divided from Earth is not the most important detail of the myth. The Rudraic God is the Divider. Father Sky is the Divided. This is fundamental and in the nature of these respective divinities. This is the archaic PIE theology of the Creation.

Along with being the sky itself, Dyaus and Ouranos each are notable for being a *deus otiosus,* a more or less idle god. They are important in the primordial scene and then recede into the background, having less and less of an active role in the lives of humans thereafter. After their initial progenitive outbursts, they are characterized by inertness and distance. This once again accurately describes Ymir, who, after his moment of dramatic procreation of the first beings, and after being divided into earth and sky, seems to become only an inert thing, a skull that is the sky far overhead, bones that are the rocks underfoot. He does not actively contribute much more to the lives of humans and the rulership of society from this point on, but is remembered in kennings for parts of the sky and earth, and his brains that are the clouds still bring rain, though now under the control of Odinn and the other gods. He is now a *deus otiosus,* an aspect of the rain-bringing process and not much more, a symbol or perhaps a kind of motor of celestial rain-fecundation, just like Dyaus and Ouranos. In addition, we must note that in the archaic layer found in the *Mahabharata* and *Iliad* heroes, the incarnation of Dyaus, Bhishma, and the incarnation of the Greek Father Sky (some of whose familial and other mythic associations have been attached to the Mitraic god Zeus despite Zeus not being the primordial sky), Sarpedon, both fight on the side of the indifferent, obstructive divinities, against the incarnations of the gods of society. That is, the primordial Indo-European Father Sky seems likely to have been depicted as reluctantly opposing or obstructing the gods of society in the great war of the gods. This aligns once again with Ymir, who is a member of the Jotunn race, a race that is an active obstacle and opponent in war to the main gods of society and their efforts to forge the disordered cosmos into social and ethical order. Though it may seem strange to our sensibilities, this oppositional alignment of the Indo-European Father Sky is what the myths of Matholwch, Ouranos, Sarpedon and Bhishma all suggest. He is closer in nature to what has not yet been brought into the social order by the gods of society. He is distant and relatively indifferent, though he lends his procreative energies to the world and does not ever actively wish harm to man or god, and in the epics he is reluctant to fight the incarnated gods of society and even dispenses wise discourses of dharma to them in the end as a divine model of kingship.

The etymology of Ymir's name, which has been interpreted as deriving from a root meaning "Twin," may indeed imply that he is the sort of double, hermaphroditic being that we have suggested. This has in fact been the conclusion of the scholars Rudolf Simek and Hilda Ella Davidson, among others.

> Not only the myth recorded by Snorri but also the etymology reveal Ymir as a hermaphrodite being because the name is etymologically related to Sanskrit Yama, Avedic Yima (likewise mythical ancestors), Lat. *geminus*, Middle Irish *gemuin* 'twin' from the Indo-Germanic root **iemo-* 'twin, hermaphrodite'. Also → Tuisto who Tacitus names as being the ancestor of the Germanic tribes Ingvaones, Hermiones and Istvaones is revealed to be a hermaphrodite being according to the etymology, so that here too common concepts within Germanic cosmogony may be assumed. (Rudolf Simek, *Dictionary of Northern Mythology*, 377)

> Ymir's name has been related to Sanskrit *yama,* meaning 'hybrid' or 'hermaphrodite'. According to Tacitus, the Germans had a primeval ancestor Tuisto, whose son Mannus was the father of mankind. Attempts have been made to connect Tuisto with Tiwaz, but it seems more likely that his name is connected with Old Swedish *tvistra*, 'separate', and that, like Ymir, it means a two-fold being. An explanation of such a name is given in *Vafprudnismal*, where we are told that a man and woman were born from under the arm of Ymir, and a giant engendered from his two feet. Another example of a primeval being from which the first male and female spring is found in Indian mythology. Ymir indeed is a two-fold being in another sense, since from him both giants and men are born. (Hilda Ellis Davidson, *Gods and Myths of Northern Europe*, 199)

More or less the same that we have said for Ymir can be said for the Iranic Cosmic Man Gayomard, of whom it is said that at the moment of his death his sperm fell to the ground and was purified by the sun. Forty years later the first human couple arose therefrom, not as trees, but indeed as rhubarb plants (*Bundahisn* 4, 10-28; 6F, 9; *Zadspram* 2, 10-11, 18-22; 3, 67-76). This is a direct parallel in nearly every aspect of what happens to the seed of Dyaus in the earlier Vedic myth, which is understandable considering that no outright

"Father Sky" appears as such in Iranic myth. Furthermore, Keuymars, the legendary version of Gayomard found in the *Shahnameh,* according to Sadri's translation, is said to cry tears of blood when his beloved son Siamak is killed (*Shahnameh,* Ahmad Sadri, Chapter 1). As we have seen in previous sections, the father god crying tears of blood for his dead son is a verifiable archaic myth of Father Sky, considering that the Irish Dagda cries tears of blood at the death of his son Cermait, and the Zeus of the *Iliad*, in the inherited role of Father Sky, cries tears of blood at the death of his son Sarpedon. Keuymars is also said to begin his reign in Spring, which is when the Father Sky creation myth is generally set according to Kramrisch. Keuymars is the first lawgiver and establishes justice, whereas Father Sky incarnation Bhishma discourses on dharma to teach Yudhishthira good rulership. As Father Sky Matholwch is clearly distinct from Yama parallel Bran, and as Ymir is clearly distinct from Mimir, so Keuymars is also clearly distinct from the legendary version of Yima/Yama found in the *Shahnameh*, Jamshid. We once more have two consistently separate figures: the primordial giant and the Yama-type figure.

The Purusha

A Vedic concept that could form an objection to this analysis in the eyes of some is that of the Purusha. The Purusha appears first in the supposed least archaic of the Rig Vedic books (Book 10, hymn 90), and is conceived as the Cosmic Soul or Cosmic Man who is sacrificed and whose divided body forms the parts of the universe, the castes of humanity, and who is the paradigm of the sacrifice. This giant "man" may be seen to have obvious similarities to the jotunn Ymir whose divided body serves similar cosmogenic ends, but the connection between the Norse Ymir and the Vedic Purusha is usually poorly understood. Some might claim that if Ymir is like to the Purusha, he cannot in fact be Father Sky, Dyaus. The foregoing discussion should prime us to understand the similarity of the conjunction of Sky+Earth, which is divided, to the single primordial being who is cut apart, but it can also be shown that the concept of the Purusha is either directly derived from, or was a parallel concept connected to, the Rig Vedic Dyaus.

The progression follows thusly: Dyaus rapes his "daughter" in the version of the myth told in the *Rig Veda* and is divided from her by an arrow shot, dropping the primordial seed onto the earth. In later texts such as the Brahmanas, as Kramrisch painstakingly shows, the Father of this myth is renamed "Prajapati," the title for a Creator God, while the narrative remains essentially the same. This is not Savitr-Prajapati, or Soma-Prajapati, although those had been the named Prajapatis of the most archaic part of the

465

Rig Veda. Instead, the Brahmanas are narrating the same myth as the Dyaus myth from the *Rig Veda*, but under the name of Prajapati. As such, Dyaus has joined Savitr and Soma as the Third Prajapati, having taken over the title in the Brahmanas due to his role as a prime generator of life.

Now, Prajapati is said repeatedly to *be the sacrifice itself.* "Prajapati is the sacrifice" is the refrain (*Satapatha Brahmana* 1.7.4.4; cf. 3.2.2.4; 5.1.1.2; 5.2.1.2; 11.1.1.1; *Taittiriya Samhita* 2.6.8-4). However, when the concept of the Purusha appears in the 10th and least archaic book of the *Rig Veda* (and even then many scholars have taken it to be a later addition to the text), this Purusha too *is the sacrifice.* As Brereton and Jamison explain: "The *púruṣa* here serves as a symbol of the sacrifice itself, which especially in the middle Vedic tradition is a locus of creative power. The púruṣa is thus similar to the later divine figure Prajāpati, who in the Brāhmaṇas personifies the sacrifice" (Brereton and Jamison, *Rig Veda*, 1538). Prajapati (or really, the combination of the Three Prajapatis) is the sacrifice because he is the primordial creator who is violently divided from the female hypostasis within himself, dividing the celestial and the earthly natures, creating heaven and earth, and whose seed creates the fiery site of the sacrifice and generates the ancestors of the first humans, among other beings. Purusha is the sacrifice because he is the totalizing Cosmic "Self" who is cut apart to create the cosmos and whose division is the model of the division of the social castes among humans. The Three Prajapatis seen as a single unity is essentially the same being as Purusha, but described from a different angle, although Purusha is a broader totality than these Prajapatis as well. Dyaus-Prajapati is this being seen in his Procreative Father aspect. Purusha is this being seen as a Cosmic Soul in which all things subsist and originate. For this reason, Purusha is sometimes said to sacrifice himself, combining the Rudra and Dyaus roles in one. As he is the Cosmic Soul, there is no one beside him.

Both Prajapati and Purusha can be said to be the sacrifice itself because they are essentially describing the same being, although the concept of the Purusha evidences a development toward an even broader, more abstracted, philosophical idea of the primordial being as a more totalizing entity. It is once again a question of what aspect of the primordial scene is emphasized, what angle is privileged, whether this or that philosophical dimension is brought to the fore and elaborated. The Purusha, then, is a concept either drawn directly from, or running parallel to, the Vedic Dyaus, but made into a broader abstraction gradually divorced from any specific divine personality, being expanded to emphasize its metaphysical universality, its status as the Soul of the *whole* cosmos, and its role as model of the sacrifice, a role once again first enacted by the Dyaus of the *Rig Veda*.

In its character of soul of the cosmos, Kramrisch can say that, in fact, according to one major tradition, it is Rudra-Siva who is the Purusha: "Siva, who is the absolute reality, 'the imperishable Purusa" ([*Linga Purana*] 1.20.70)" (Kramrisch, 366). "As Purusa or Cosmic Man, the god is born at a sacrificial session and out of a golden bowl held by Prajapati" (Kramrisch, 235; *KB* 6.2). She repeats that Rudra is the Purusha many times over, as for instance in the sections "The Golden Bowl," "The Memory of the Initial Evil," "Rudra Issues From the Head of Brahma," "The Meaning of the Linga," "The Linga and the Face of Siva," and "The Severed Head: The Cause of its Fall," among others. Like Dyaus, Ymir is only one subdivision or dimension of the total Cosmic Being or Purusha. Ymir does not take in himself all things, for Odinn, Audhumbla, and other things are outsides of him. He then cannot be the Purusha alone, the soul of the whole cosmos, although he is a primary component of it. We have to draw a circle around the Prajapatis and Rudra, or around Ymir and Odinn and Audhumbla, to begin to reach the full concept of the Purusha. Thus Dyaus/Ymir both *are* Purusha and are not the *totality* of Purusha.

When Purusha (which is roughly the equivalent of the Cosmic Egg) is split apart, this is the same metaphysical event as the splitting of Sky and Earth, as the two Prajapatis of lunar and solar light (Soma and Savitr) and the Male/Celestial and Female/Earthly natures are separated in this event. We see that the splitting of the Cosmic Egg is indeed the same event as the dividing of Earth and Sky in the Orphic fragments, where we read that there was "[…] generated a huge egg, which, being filled full, by the force of its engenderer was broken in two from friction. Its crown became Ouranos (Uranus, Heaven), and what had sunk downwards, Gaia (Gaea, Earth). There also came forth an incorporeal god [Protogonos-Phanes, the cosmic Light]" (Orphica, Theogonies Fragment 57). This is plainly the splitting of Earth and Sky, Gaia and Ouranos, which event happens only once. It is a more philosophical presentation of the myth of Cronus dividing Ouranos from Gaia. Furthermore, while it is the division of the Purusha that creates the three castes in the Purusha hymn, we have noted previously that it is Prajapati's role to create the castes in the Brahmanas (*SB* 2, 1, 4, 11.), and it is Math (who is Savitr-Prajapati) who creates the three lineages of deer, wolf, and swine in the *Mabinogi*, which may likewise symbolize the three castes of priest-sovereign, warrior, and producer.

Rudra, as the Intelligence or Soul of the total Cosmic Man can then be argued, as does the tradition Kramrisch cites, to be the true essence of the Purusha which has the several main components we have described. Plotinus says this same thing in different words, describing the total pre-cosmic scene which in Vedic terms is Rudra-Shiva + the Three Prajapatis (Soma, Savitr, Dyaus), this being the total Purusha or Primal Being, the Yin Yang with line through it, or the Cosmic Egg with serpent around it:

> Thus we find that the Intellectual-Principle [Cronus], the Intellectual
> Realm and Real Being constitute one thing, which is the Primal Being

[see: Purusha]; the primal Intellectual-Principle is that which contains the realities or, rather, which is identical with them. (Plotinus, Ennead 5.3.5)

The argument over which god is the core essence of the Purusha indeed came to the forefront in the later metaphysical and sectarian speculations. However, we see that there is no giant Purusha who is divided up but who is distinct from Dyaus himself, Dyaus being the Celestial Progenitor component of the Purusha who is united with his own female aspect in the pre-cosmic moment and divided from her during the division of the Purusha. There is no way, then, that Ymir can be the whole Purusha in a simple fashion. He can only be connected to the Purusha in the same manner that Dyaus is connected to the Purusha, as a primary part of its greater totality.

There is also a popular Proto-Indo-European myth reconstruction which equates Ymir with Yama, the God of Dead (based largely on possible linguistic similarities as evidenced by Simek's comment above), who in the Vedic myth is the first or one of the first kings and first mortal man to die on earth, and who himself or whose parallel iterations or incarnations may be cut apart or have their heads severed, as we have discussed in previous investigations. Yama gains his lordship of the realm of the dead as a result of his death. However, not only does Norse Ymir not die *on* earth whatsoever, as Yama does, considering that earth is said not to exist until it is divided and created out of Ymir's own body, but our foregoing analyses allow us to draw a much clearer line from Yama instead to the Norse jotunn Mimir, whose head is severed from his body, in a similar but distinct fashion to Ymir. Thus Mimir's decapitation does echo the dismemberment of Ymir and we can see how a Mimir parallel could be confused for a parallel of Ymir, especially considering possibly overlapping, echoing etymologies. In a sense, as the first king of the world who is mortal and dies, Yama is indeed a re-instantiation of the cosmic being that was Dyaus/Purusha, and this is what allows human kings, who follow his archetype, to be themselves a bridge to the divine. As Bran, the Welsh Yama, says in his myth when he enters Matholwch's land just before battling him, and as he makes his own body into a bridge spanning a lofty ridge over a rushing river: "he who will be chief, let him be a bridge. I will be so"[273] (*Branwen, daughter of Llyr*). He is thus the model of the worldly king, just as Yama, the bridge to the celestial land of Matholwch. Just after the rape-creation myth is recited in the Rig Vedic hymn, the earthly king is lauded by the poet, and this should be taken as a direct parallel of

---

273   "'Lord,' said his chieftains, 'knowest thou the nature of this river, that nothing can go across it, and there is no bridge over it?' 'What,' said they, 'is thy counsel concerning a bridge?' 'There is none,' said he, 'except that he who will be chief, let him be a bridge. I will be so,' said he. And then was that saying first uttered, and it is still used as a proverb. And when he had lain down across the river, hurdles were placed upon him, and the host passed over thereby" (*Branwen, daughter of Llyr*).

Bran's act: "This king praised here has been extolled as a ritual adept, and as inspired poet he crosses the waters, creating his own bridge" (RV 10.61.16). In the Welsh myth, Father Sky Matholwch abuses Mother Earth Branwen, they have their child, the child is thrown into the fire, there is a battle which kills Matholwch and so ends his marriage to Branwen, and then Bran is decapitated. All of the events that parallel the dividing of Earth and Sky *precede* the decapitation of the giant Bran, aka Yama, then, at least in this branch (in the Irish case, however, Bran's parallel Eber Donn dies *before* the battle that kills Father Sky). The separation of Earth and Sky is itself divided in time from the separation of Bran's head from his body by a battle. As such, Bran's decapitation is indeed a sequel to and repetition of the more primordial division of Earth and Sky, but it is not the same event nor does it come first. In like manner, the decapitation of the jotunn Mimir, though it echoes the cutting of Ymir's head from his body, occurs in a later age from the dividing of Ymir, after the first war *in the world*. Based on the strong parallels that have been gathered between Yama and Bran/Donn/Mimir, the idea that Yama is Ymir should therefore be discarded. Yama is not the primordial being in any attestation, and is only projected backward as a primordial being via faulty comparative reconstructions and the sway of close linguistic estimations, which may then be interpreted to mean something they do not in fact mean. Yama is instead a repetition within the now-created World of the primordial being who is Dyaus/Purusha. Any etymological problems with the supposed linguistic connection of Yama to Ymir do not even need to be gone into when the mythic concepts are understood accurately.

If Ymir is then the Norse instantiation of the deity known to the Vedics as Dyaus, then no other deity can strictly speaking be the Norse "Father Sky" in the same sense that Dyaus is. Neither Odinn nor Tyr are the sky itself, nor are they divided from the earth after a procreative outburst in the primordial scene. They are each other than this primordial being that is Earth+Sky, in some sense, for in the Norse myth the Divider is not one with the Divided although they do inhabit one ontological space together somehow. However, the most common confusion that arises around this topic is regarding the colloquial title "Sky Father." The loosely applied term "The Sky Father" may not mean precisely "Dyaus" or "Father Sky," the name of a specific divinity within Indo-European myth. Odinn, however, is indeed the inheritor of Ymir's domain (the sky), acting as the great king of the sky in his "Varuna" aspect. The sun and moon are his eyes, as is said also of Varuna. It is evidently in this Varunian aspect that he is consort of the now distinct Earth goddess, Jord, just as the incarnation of the Vedic Varuna, Pandu, is consort of the incarnation of the Vedic Earth Goddess, Pritha-Kunti. From the pairing of Odinn and Jord is produced Thor, while Arjuna, incarnation of Indra, is produced from the pairing of Pandu and Pritha-Kunti, and this is the parallel we should look to with regard to the coupling of Odinn and Jord. For no violence nor separation occurs in the relationship of Odinn and Jord, as their coupling does not take place in the primordial scene. Varuna himself, however, is a bringer of rains from the clouds and the celestial ocean above, he is a fecundator and a bull who rains down upon Earth, and he is both a father and a First Sovereign of the skies in the chronology of the cycle. This Varunian role would well explain the relationship of Odinn to Jord (Earth), which is the relationship of the rain-bringing sovereign to the earth within the cycle of unfolding time rather than in the primordial moment.

Two other branches in addition to the Norse also favor the Varunian god as the great "Sky Father" above others: early Rig Vedic (Varuna), Avestan (Ahura Mazda). And thus the Varunian god as the Sky *Sovereign* or "Sky Father" should not seem in any sense to be out of sync with the larger Indo-European pattern, but is equally or more common compared to other possibilities. Meanwhile, the Celtic branches place the Mitraic (Lugh/Lleu) and the Varunian (Nuada/Lludd/Nodens) sky sovereigns on relatively equal footing, though they appear to lean toward a preference for the Mitraic sovereign. The Roman does similarly (the Varunian Jupiter Summanus and Mitraic Jupiter) and the Greek branch seems to favor a Mitraic god in Zeus who has absorbed or swallowed the roles of several other deities, possibly even certain Varunian roles, making him, similar to Jupiter, a god who could be Mitra-Varuna and more. We will look at the theology of this "swallowing" below. If we accept Ymir as the Norse Father Sky, then Norse myth has essentially every piece of the Indo-European Creation Myth as seen in other branches; if not, then the Norse Creation Myth is a curious outlier from essentially all other branches, except perhaps late Iranic, featuring a procreative giant who becomes the sky but somehow is not the Father who is the Sky.

The Greeks, as we have discussed in our analysis of Math (Savitr)→Lleu (Mitra) and Phanes→Zeus, had a clear theological concept, as recorded in the Orphic sources (*Orphic Fragments 129, &c.*), that the Mitraic King of the Gods, Zeus, absorbed the powers and roles of his predecessors, "swallowing" and becoming them for the present age, until he was considered to be the All within the world. They applied this theology to Zeus, and as such Zeus fathers the Fire God, the Horse Twins, and the possible incarnation of the Dawn Goddess, Helen, children or descendants who attach to Dyaus in Vedic myth, even though mythically Zeus falls much more in line with the Mitraic god-type. It is possible that in Norse myth Odinn and Tyr could once have shared dominion of the sky, as the duality of Vedic Mitra-Varuna might suggest, sovereign of Night sky and Day sky respectively, of the Night of the cycle and the Day of the cycle in succession. This is not necessary to assume in the Norse case, however, considering the prominence of the Varunian sky sovereign in some branches. The Celtic case is perhaps the best example of the paired Varunian and Mitraic sovereigns placed on relatively equal footing. Still, Welsh Lleu absorbs the roles and powers of his predecessors Math and Gwydion in a manner directly reminiscent of Zeus, and Irish Lugh may also be exemplifying this same theology when he arrives late to the kingdom of Tara, displaying all the powers of the other gods in himself.[274] He, like Zeus, is the late-comer who is the All within one sovereign being, and for this reason he is called *Samildanach,* "equally skilled in many arts." If Tyr and Odinn were ever closer to equals, then Tyr's role as such has certainly been obscured in existing sources, leaving the full dominion of the sky seemingly to Odinn alone. Still, the apparently Mitraic Lord of the Endtimes hints at a possible remnant of this theology.

In this sense Odinn would be an Indo-European Sky Father, a true inheritor of the domain that Ymir *is*, that primordial Father who *is* the Sky. As "Rudra," Odinn furthermore transcends above and beyond both Varuna and Mitra, and even above Dyaus in some sense, for he, as the Greeks knew of Cronus, is the great Pure Intellect that cuts through Sky and Earth and, as god of Fire, a role we have previously supported, he is also the heat that burns within Ymir and prepares the procreative seed. He is the god who manifests and re-manifests again and again under names and masks that cannot be counted. He is the wily and policing hunter in the pre-cosmic wilderness who forges existence out of what otherwise would be mere undifferentiated substance, mere Uncreate. Though he himself is not the first sacrifice, he is the first sacrificer and, like Rudra-Vāstoṣpati, the "house" that is the cosmos *is* his domain.

Thus seeing Zeus and Odinn as direct equivalents is a serious error in terms of their mythic essences, while theologically they are in somewhat comparable positions within their traditions. The one crucial thing that could speculatively harmonize these two contrasting Sky Sovereigns is the idea that we have suggested previously: that the Norse Lord of the Endtimes who appears cryptically in the *Voluspa* is in fact Tyr, the Mitraic God, who parallels Zeus in his Mitraic essence. Because we have seen some fragment of the idea that the Mitraic god absorbs the roles of his predecessors in Greek tradition (Zeus), in the *Rig Veda* (Savitr *becoming* Mitra) and in the Welsh myths (Math teaching Lleu and passing roles of justice, light, and rulership, as well as inheritance, to him), we can then say that such a concept of the Mitraic sovereign absorbing roles of predecessors, in some form, was likely to be PIE. The main question would be whether the Greeks took this concept further than the original theology implied, further than the other branches did, or not. We then are bound by logical necessity to ask whether the Norse Lord of the Endtimes, who must be Mitraic and thus some form or incarnation of Tyr as we have shown, will, in the final stage when he appears, have absorbed or combined with his predecessor(s), namely Odinn. If the Lord of the Endtimes follows the pattern of the Greek theology, which shows traces in the other branches as well, he could be a re-manifestation of Tyr-Odinn as the absolute final sovereign, or he could be

---

274   Thanks to Kalin and McAulay for pointing to this connection.

a Tyr who has absorbed and carried on the Odinnic essence (Odinn being his true father, conceived as he is with Gunnlod, as we have shown) in some sense for this final phase. This conception would also parallel the composite duad Mitra-Varuna often found in the Vedas. If this were so, it is *this* Lord of the Endtimes who could accurately parallel the Greek conception of Zeus, who himself is the late-coming Mitraic sovereign of justice and light who has become the all-in-all sovereign after the reign of Cronus. This would imply that Greek tradition, in Zeus, has merely focused its devotion on the final, Mitraic sovereign, the sovereign of the "day" half of the cycle and of the endtimes, while the Norse, in Odinn, has focused on a penultimate, Varuna-Rudra sovereign, who yet is pointing toward the one who will come after him, the Mitraic Lord of the Endtimes. We repeat that this line of thinking is speculative, but appears to us the only harmonization of the Greek and Norse sovereigns possible.

In this connection, the full chain of development of the Mitraic divine principle clarifies itself as well. Zeus (who is Mitra) is the Soul to the Platonists, just as we have described Lleu-Mitra-Menelaus as the archetypal Soul in his esoteric process from birth to rebirth to immortalization in our analysis of the *Iliad*. A chain of names known from Mithraic inscriptions[275] as Zeus-Helios-Mithras-Phanes then describes the exact process we have traced of Savitr/Phanes, the light-bringing sun at night and during sunrise, "becoming" Mitra, that is, Zeus, and this Mitraic god, the archetype of the Soul, finally overcoming and merging with the Sun, Helios, in the final achievement of immortality, at the end of the cycle or day. This is why both Jupiter and Mithra could be identified with the Unconquerable Sun, Sol Invictus, for they are one and the same. The details of the Mithraic theme are expanded upon in our discussion of the Mitraic Path of Immortality.

Furthermore, the understanding of Cronus as the Primordial Rudra vindicates the Greek theogony from many claims of foreign influence, whether Near Eastern or otherwise, and instead clarifies the Indo-European core of the sequence of sovereigns from Ouranos, to Cronus, to Zeus. Degrees of influence on this element or that are still likely to spark intense debate, but the succession myth is paralleled in its details and its meanings in essentially all of the Indo-European branches that we have examined. Only from the perspective of seeing Cronus as Rudra can this clarification and harmonization

---

275   Ulansey, David, *The Origins of the Mithraic Mysteries*, pp.120-1: "The identification between Mithras and Phanes indicated by CIMRM 860 is also explicitly attested by an inscription found in Rome dedicated to 'Zeus-Helios-Mithras-Phanes' and another inscription dedicated to 'Helios-Mithras-Phanes'." See also: Clauss, M. *The Roman cult of Mithras*, p. 70, photo p.71. My thanks to Kalin for pointing out these inscriptions and helping me to clarify this pattern.

be firmly established and only from this perspective can the underlying theology be accurately understood.

The Celtic tradition thus has essentially every element of the creation myths found in the Norse, Greek, and Vedic mythologies, with only a couple of items possibly missing. These could be enumerated as the Norse Cosmic Cow, Audhumbla, and the Norse Yawning Gap, Ginnungagap. It is possible the Cosmic Cow could have an analogy to some coded symbol or other in the Celtic myths that we have not examined, or perhaps some resonance with the Cauldron of Regeneration of Bran and Matholwch, which we may presume to be a container of a divine liquid. The Cow might also parallel the god or goddess of sacred liquid, Arawn (Soma) or goddess Cerridwen (Saraswati-Vac). Arawn appears in the First Branch of the Mabinogi, one tale before the Creation Myth of *Branwen, daughter of Llyr* within the Mabinogi myth cycle. Arawn is Soma/Dionysus/Midir, and this god also appears in Irish mythology as the cow of wondrous milk, the Glas Gaibhneann. The Glas Gaibhneann most directly parallels Kvasir, another Norse Soma analogue, in its mythical placement, but the lord of sacred liquid appearing as a cosmic cow does point to a possible connecting line also to Audhumbla here. In the *Rig Veda*, certain hymns are simply dedicated to the "Cows," and these divine cows appear here and there in other hymns throughout the Veda as well. These Cows evidently inhabit the upper regions of the cosmos and their milk is the divine substance which humanity asks of the gods. Their milk could perhaps be seen to flow in the Milky Way, called by the Irish the *Bealach/Bóthar na Bó Finne,* the Way/Road of the White Cow, and its patron goddess, the embodiment of the waters of the sacred river, is Irish Boann/Bo Finne, the White Cow, or Welsh Cerridwen, keeper of the cauldron of Inspiration. In the Iranic creation myth, the soul of the Cosmic Cow Gavaevodata, who accompanies the Cosmic Man Gayomard, is said to go to be housed in the region of the Moon, and this cow is repeatedly associated with the moon. Arawn/Midir/Soma, being the lord of the sacred liquid of the moon, would thus be the lord who oversees and overlaps with the soul of this Iranic Cosmic Cow who might be connected somehow to the cow-named goddess of the sacred river and the Milky Way. Boann is dismembered in the dramatic myth telling the creation of the Boyne river as a result of her breaking the taboo of Nechtan's Well, while in the Iranic creation myth the Cosmic Cow is killed and medicinal plants grow from its body. Boann is thus a cow goddess who is dismembered in a myth about the creation of the life-giving cosmic river with all that it brings.

It is clear that all these gods and symbols of the heavenly sacred liquid run together and overlap, and lead again to the cauldron and the seed of Father Sky. For, as Kramrisch explains, the seed of Dyaus is also the sacred *soma* liquid, the divine substance of the Uncreate or of the Divine Realm, the milk of the moon or of the celestial river that is the Milky Way, which, being first placed within him, is being spent into the realm of Creation by Dyaus' outburst. Dyaus' ejaculation forms a great lake of fiery semen, which is both the site of the sacrifice and the cause of much trouble to the gods and priests thereafter, as the Cauldron of Regeneration also causes trouble to Bran and Efnysien, and these objects seem to align at several points. Ymir feeds on the milk of the cow Audhumbla when he generates the first beings from his body, and thus it is the cow that seemingly provides the fuel for this creation of life, with her sacred liquid. Similarly, Rudra-Agni prepares the seed for Dyaus and places it within him, this seed being a sort of fiery *soma,* inflames his passion, and then avenges the procreative outburst that follows, setting things right by reestablishing order and a mystic yogic pathway back to the divine as the newly made Master of Animals. Precisely so, Efnysien causes the cauldron to be given to Matholwch (the divine seed-liquid prepared for Dyaus by Rudra-Agni or the milk of Audhumbla that Ymir drinks) when he inflames the tensions between Matholwch and Branwen by mutilating the horses of Matholwch, leading directly to Branwen's abuse (the inflaming of Dyaus' passion leading directly to his rape of his daughter). Efnysien then remorsefully avenges what he himself has set in motion, lamenting especially the fact that the cauldron has fallen into Matholwch's hands, and a war is fought against Matholwch during which Matholwch is killed and the cauldron is destroyed by Efnysien's sacrifice (as Rudra avenges the procreative outburst he himself has prepared, given to Dyaus, and inflamed, when he fires his arrow at Dyaus and separates him from his daughter, at the same moment as the fall of the seed to earth and the creation of the lake of fire-seed). The edge of this lake of fire-seed would also be the likely analogue of the ocean beach where the first humans, Askr and Embla, are said to be found by the gods in Snorri's account in *Gylfaginning,* for the lake of fire-seed creates the ancestors of the first humans in the Vedic case.

No clear Ginnungagap yet appears to us, but the Celtic myths are set in the unassuming form of medieval romances, and such cosmic void space should not necessarily be expected of them when working with such a seemingly mundane setting. Still, the mysterious man and woman who are said to be the original owners of the cauldron and who are almost burned alive in a house along with it at the beginning of the tale of *Branwen,* before the cauldron is given to Bran and then to Matholwch, may represent, once again in symbolic code, a similar cosmic moment: the meeting of the heavenly liquid and the flame in the void-time before the conjunction of Earth and Sky. This event could also simply show the preparation of the seed of the father by fire, before it is given to him. The man who first owns the cauldron is said to be "yellow-haired." Arawn is the Soma God who keeps the cauldron of Annwn in his otherworld realm. Midir, his Irish parallel, is said to be yellow-haired with blue eyes in *The Wooing of Etain,* and also keeps a cauldron that is stolen by Cuchulainn as Arawn's cauldron is also sought by adventurers like Arthur. Thus this first owner of the Cauldron of

Regeneration could be Arawn, Welsh Soma God, which might be the most logical supposition to begin with, although it should be noted that this man is also said to be "of horrid aspect." We should remember, however, that Arawn is the Lord of the Otherworld/Underworld, and that he might age and grow young again as does his parallel Chyavana or the moon itself, and so he may indeed have a frightening aspect at times. His wife is twice his size, which, though we can only speculate, could refer to the larger, dangerous, golden-yellow moon we have previously noted, or it could perhaps refer to the darkness covering the crescent moon which is larger than the crescent itself. He and his wife, along with the cauldron, are said to have escaped an "iron house" around which coals were heaped and fire ignited. This could simply be a description of the purifying of the analogue of the *soma* liquid, paralleling myths such as the burning of Gullveig or Fuamnach, wife of Midir, that we have previously analyzed. As such, it would be a depiction of the preparation of the analogue of the *soma* liquid before it is given to Father Sky, Matholwch, to be used in the creation event. This preparation of the sacred liquid in the time before Creation is, however, nearly the same thing as the fire and ice of Ginnungagap colliding and forming the creative liquid that becomes the procreative giant Ymir and the Cosmic Cow that provides the giant's vital force with its milk.

The Celtic Creation myth is heavily coded and its symbols remain a challenge to read. However, the egg has now been cracked and the secrets begin to issue out into the world again. Never again will it be permitted to say that the Celts do not have a creation myth in every essential aspect as complete and as theologically deep as those of the other Indo-European branches. The Welsh *Mabinogi*, in particular, encode a version of the Indo-European Creation Myth on par with venerated esoteric traditions such as the Orphic, and even preserve details that can fill gaps in the Creation myths of other branches.

The Three Prajapatis and the Festival Calendar

We are thus left with three "Prajapatis," or cosmic progenitors, to borrow the Vedic term. These are Soma and Savitr (the "Prajapatis" so titled in the more archaic portions of the *Rig Veda*), and Dyaus, who takes on or even takes over the title of Prajapati in the texts of the Brahmanas.

We can see that Dyaus does indeed share traits with these other two Prajapatis and can fairly be titled as a Prajapati for his central role in the procreation of the life of the cosmos. As an analogy is thus drawn between Dyaus, and the two Prajapatis Savitr and Soma, an analogy is also drawn between Matholwch (Dyaus) and Math (Savitr) in the Welsh cycle, as can be seen in the closeness of their names and in repeated themes shared between their myths. These three Prajapatis are thus the lord of the light and liquid of the moon (Soma), Father Sky (Dyaus), and the lord of the light of the sun at night and upon sunrise (Savitr). In Welsh terms, these are Arawn, Matholwch, and Math fab Mathonwy. The cosmogenic events that these three gods preside over are the advent of the light and sacred liquid of the moon, the advent of the life of the cosmos via the spending of this sacred liquid into the world, and the advent of the light of the sun which brings the full blooming of the life of the world.

These myths are thus laid out in perfect chronological sequence in the Four Mabinogi, a fact which has never been understood. The First Mabinogi begins with Arawn (Soma), the First Prajapati, already having married his bride, and he is thus the presiding god of this earliest part of the mythic cycle, the dead of night of the cycle which is naturally ruled by the first lunar light. The Second Mabinogi tells of Matholwch (Dyaus), the Second Prajapati, who begets Gwern, the divine seed of new life, and whose tale has just been told. The Third Mabinogi finishes the tale which had been begun in the First Branch, when the Fire God Manawydan (Agni) heals the wasteland and symbolically cleanses the site of sacrifice of the evil influence of a hostile sorcerer, so acting as the sacred flame itself via his actions. This flame which he *is* allows the sun to rise, which is what the Fourth Branch then depicts, with the third Prajapati, Math (Savitr), rising from his rest on the lap of the violated goddess Night and impelling the life of the Day and of the Day-half of the cycle (Summer) which now follows. It has always been a mystery why the First and Third branches, which tell two halves of one tale, were interrupted by the Second Branch, which is a different tale altogether. But with this understanding of the myths in hand, we can see that, due to this sequence and due to the insertion of the Second Branch between the First and Third, the branches are in the perfect chronological order.

When we map the Four Branches to the calendrical events they appear to correspond to, the great perfection of their order becomes clear. As Greek Anthesteria, during which was reenacted the marriage of Dionysus and Ariadne, the Greek parallel of the marriage of Arawn (Soma) and his wife, likely occurred at the full moon around what we would call January, roughly speaking, we can surmise that the First Branch of the Mabinogi, when this marriage of Arawn has already taken place and the Gandharva (Pwyll) comes on the scene, must occur sometime around mid January or just after. The events of the wooing of Pwyll's wife, which fill the rest of this First Branch, would then likely

476

correspond to the following full moon, around Valentine's Day or the Roman Lupercalia of mid-February, which Dumezil indeed believed to be a festival related to the Roman analogues of the Gandharvas: "Luperci, in a ritual practiced at the end of every year, centaurs, in fabulous narrative, and Gandharva, in legends in which we glimpse a ritual (year-end) reality, all display the same fundamental features" (Dumezil, *Mitra-Varuna*, 29-30). Next, the Second Branch, as we have stated, corresponds to the cosmic creation set in motion by the conjunction of Sky and Earth, of Matholwch, who is the Second Prajapati, and Branwen. This marks the beginning of Spring in the still raw "Dawn" period of the cycle. The Third Branch, whose central figure is Manawydan, the God of Fire who heals the wasteland by acting as the sacred ritual fire and cleanses the site of sacrifice in particular, would correspond to the events leading to the great fire of Beltane. The Fourth Branch would correspond to the events set in motion around the time of the Celtic festival of Beltane or thereafter, the fire which Manawydan *is* giving rise to the rising sun that is Math fab Mathonwy, the Third Prajapati. This event at last sets the Summer and the Day of the cycle fully in motion, and the full mythic sequence of Creation is completed in its proper order, just as the Mabinogi cycle lays it out.

These Three Prajapatis might be seen to correspond in Greek terms to both Phanes and Ouranos: Phanes, who is also called Protogonos (a title which has been linguistically and mythically compared to Prajapati: see Kate Alsobrook, "The Beginning of Time: Vedic and Orphic Theogonies and Poetics") is called "two-natured." We have also previously shown Phanes to have several alignments with Math-Savitr, who himself is an archaic Prajapati of the Veda. However, Phanes is also called Phanes-Dionysus[276] (Greek Dionysus being Vedic Soma/Welsh Arawn), which becomes an important part of Dionysus' myth and cult. This direct connection of Dionysus to the original light-seed of creation is one of the reasons that his cult brought with it the potential for experiences of ecstatic unity with the cosmos and a mystic path to a more favorable afterlife. Thus, as Phanes is the light-seed of creation, we may imagine that he appears in two forma as Dionysus (Soma/Arawn) and Phanes (Savitr/Math), the deities of the lunar and solar lights, respectively, as these lights arise in their first forms in the Night of the cycle. Phanes as Dionysus, then, is "Prajapati" in terms of the light that sparks creation, helping to mature and purify the sacred liquid in the moon in the dead early Night of the brand new cycle, which becomes the seed of the Second Prajapati, Dyaus/Matholwch/Ouranos, and then he is Prajapati again in terms of the god of the solar light that rises as the sunrise, who is swallowed and absorbed by Zeus. In either case, this Phanes is the seed of light resting on the bosom of Night which divides into lunar and solar and triggers the creation of life in the new cosmos. This also explains why the Great Lunar Cycle

---

276   Orphic Fragments 54, 68, 70, 75. Leeming, David Adams (2010). *Creation Myths of the World: An Encyclopedia*. p. 119.

precedes the Creation: the sacred liquid must first be matured and purified before being given to Dyaus as his seed, and we can see this process play out in the myth of Arawn passing on to that of Matholwch, or Phanes to Ouranos. This Phanes is Prajapati, the instigator and impeller of Creation, specifically in terms of of light and the development of the sacred liquid, while Ouranos is Prajapati in terms of the action of the celestial dimension (Sky) upon the earthly matter, this earthly matter being his essential other half or a hypostasis formed from within him. Light. Sky. Earth. The Divine Liquid. Mind and Fire. And the world is created.

17

The Two "Aesir-Vanir" Wars

When we have aligned the mythic events with the calendar we see one other important thing that must be noted. The war of Pryderi against Gwydion and Math, the gods of the sunrise, which we have called the Welsh "Aesir-Vanir War," occurs in the myth simultaneously with the sunrise (the rising of Math from Goewin's lap), or with the beginning of the Day of the cycle, that is, Summer, marking the time around the festival of Beltane. Pryderi is killed following this war. However, in the Irish case, Pryderi's parallel Aengus brings his men to take the sidhe of the Varunian sovereign of the night sky, Elcmar-Nuada. He is not killed after this confrontation. The moon god Soma-Arawn does not help Pryderi in his battle against the sunrise gods, though the swine from his otherworld domain are present. The moon god Soma-Midir does help Aengus in his taking of Elcmar's sidhe, on the other hand. Furthermore, we know that the taking of Elcmar's sidhe by Aengus was thought to have occurred on Samhain, the end of the Celtic year and beginning of Winter or the Night phase of the cycle.

Thus we must picture *two* "Aesir-Vanir War" type events happening at the opposite points of the cycle, mirrors of one another. The times when these events occur are the beginning of Night/Winter, and the beginning of Day/Summer. It should be clear, then, that they correspond to the time of the sunset and sunrise transitions and to the time

479

when the evening and morning star moves across the sky. The evening star piercing into the night sky is the taking of Elcmar-Nuada's sidhe by Aengus, while the morning star rising with the sun is the confrontation of the solar gods by Pryderi. The Asvins, after all, are said to be born "here and there," and were sacrificed to at sunrise, midday, and sunset. It seems, then, that each branch usually only retained a memory of one of these transition events and made it their main "Aesir-Vanir War"-type myth connected to the Horse Twin god. This reduction of two mirrored events to one myth could have gone along with the reduction of the twin gods to a single god that we have investigated previously. We see that the names of Pryderi and Aengus do not directly match – Aengus might linguistically be the closer match to Pryderi/Peredurus' brother and twin Owein/Ingenius, and this could be the reason their myths do not match exactly, while still showing great overlap. Indeed, the two mirrored wars, at sunrise and sunset, share so much mythically that they seem almost to be one event repeated twice, except for certain details, e.g. who their opponents are. It would be understandable if they were combined to make one narrative myth, or if only one of the two wars were remembered by a given branch, considering that either war carries the essential mythic information about the nature of the Horse Twin god, god of the transition between night and day or day and night.

The Norse case of the actual "Aesir-Vanir War" would more closely align with the war at the transition from day to night. This is the "first war in the world," as we are told, and thus should happen at the beginning of night (unless the archaic calendar began at the opposite point), the night being the starting point of the cycle. Freyr fights against Odinn and his allies, Odinn being Varunian like Elcmar-Nuada. It is true that Pryderi fights Gwydion, another Odinnic aspect, in his war at sunrise, and so this fact leaves the question open. Freyr is not killed after his war while Pryderi is killed after his war at sunrise, which, in Pryderi's case, perhaps reflects the fall of the morning star after its rise. Aengus is also trapped in rock after trying to become King of the Universe in the Scottish folkloric tradition, an event which is said to correspond to Spring and which then would be an instance of Aengus taking part in the sunrise "Aesir-Vanir War," the mirror image of his taking of the sidhe of the sovereign of the night sky upon sunset in the Irish case. Freyr sitting in Odinn's seat Hlidskjalf could be a trace remembrance of this second war at sunrise in the Norse case, as when Aengus tries to become King of the Universe. Similarly, the episode of Pryderi being fostered by Teyrnon (Elcmar-Nuada/Varuna) may be the Welsh remnant of the Horse Twin myth marking the transition from day to night, here become only a fosterage of Pryderi by Teyrnon rather than the hostile taking of this lord of the night sky's sidhe as in the Irish parallel involving Aengus and Elcmar-Nuada. Instead of taking the fort of the king of the night sky, he simply lives there with him, both versions of which can refer to the rise of the Evening Star into the night sky. However, this version of the myth would suggests that this event occurs after the marriage of Arawn-Soma and his wife, not before as other versions and indeed the calendar would suggest. This problem then could imply a simple variation that has developed to meet narrative needs or a mismatch in the comparison.

All in all, the motifs of these two mythic wars overlap and are interchanged and perfectly clear lines are difficult to establish, for these events are mirrors of one another, with each branch placing the emphasis differently.

18

The Aspects of Óðinn Compared to Irish Myth

This chapter will be a summary of our previous conclusions regarding Óðinn. It relies on our previous chapters, and these can be referenced to supply more thorough evidence for each point. As is natural with this sort of summary of a complex issue, each point will remain highly debatable and necessarily incomplete, and further refinement of the details of the question at hand should be encouraged.

When comparing the Norse myths of Óðinn to the Irish mythology as a whole, one thing is difficult to ignore, and it is an enormous key to understanding Celtic myth in its relation to the Norse: Óðinn shares myths with *several* Irish deities. While other Irish gods can often have close to a one-to-one correspondence to Norse counterparts, in the case of Óðinn it takes in the range of 5-7 Irish deities to cover all the mythic roles found in that dominant Germanic god.

We find that Óðinn seems to have, at least in part, the same root mythos as Dian Cecht, the Irish god of spoken word, magical chant and healing who is keeper of the power which allows warriors to be restored to life (his well), as Óðinn also can make the dead rise and speak again and is the master of the spoken magic of the *galdrs*.

482

Óðinn shares the mythos of Cian, son of Dian Cecht, who infiltrates Balor's fortress to retrieve the wondrous ("*soma*"-)cow and sleep with Balor's daughter, in remarkably similar fashion to the way in which Óðinn infiltrates the mountain fortress to steal the mead of poetry and sleep with its keeper's daughter.

He shares the mythos of Manannan at several points, as lord of a specific kind of elite afterlife destination (with self-regenerating pigs), as well as being a mischievous shapeshifter and magician. Fuamnach is burned by Manannan while her parallel Gullveig is burned in Óðinn's hall. This fire priest Manannan conveys Cian to and from his infiltration mission at the fortress, as Óðinn himself turns into an eagle – and parallels the Vedic Fire god Agni-Shyena in doing so – to convey the stolen mead away from the mountain fortress. Agni turns into the hawk Sheyna to steal the *soma* from the mountain and fly away with it. Furthermore, Manannan's Welsh counterpart Manawydan is the second husband of Etain, as Óðinn is the second husband to the Norse goddess in the parallel role, Skaði. One of Óðinn's names, after all, is Sviðurr, which is debatably translated "the burner," from Proto-Germanic *swīþaną, "to burn."

As Georges Dumezil has argued, Óðinn also has the mythos of the Terrible Sovereign, Varuna (that is, Irish Nuada), Varuna being associated with a motif of one-eyedness, being a god of the sovereignty of the night sky, of the magico-religious aspect of war generally, and of the creative frenzy which forges kingdoms (or worlds). Varuna's role, as Dumezil explains in his *Mitra-Varuna*, is that of the "First King." This is the sovereign associated with the creative vitality required to forge kingdoms as opposed to the regulative power of the Mitraic sovereign who comes after. Rudolf Simek summarizes the Dumezilian position connecting Varuna and Odinn:

> Theologically speaking, Odin is related [to] the god Varuna, who has sorcery, the gift of shape-changing and the directing of the fortunes of battle in common with the Germanic god. Both are the gods of rulers and poets, both receive human sacrifice. Dumezil has identified the Indian ruling pair of gods Mithra — Varuna with both the representatives of sovereignty in Germanic mythology, Tyr and Odin, whereby both these gods can be traced back to Indo-Germanic times. Tyr, however, faded more and more in status over the years so that in the literary period he was totally subordinated to Odin. (Simek, *Dictionary of Northern Mythology*, 245)

Kris Kershaw has argued admirably for Óðinn as the analog of Vedic Rudra as well (*The One-Eyed God and the (Indo-)Germanic Mannerbunde*), in his capacity as the representative and leader of the ecstatic warrior band that has its otherworldly reflection in the Wild Hunt, which Óðinn leads. This role, as we have argued, also matches perfectly the leader of the Irish warrior band, keeper of hounds, and hunter, Fionn, grandson of Nuada, who is also known for a myth about his sudden enlightenment, and matches as well Fionn's Welsh linguistic cognate Gwyn, son of Nudd, the leader of the Wild Hunt who also has his pack of hounds. Fionn's trial of retrieving the ring from the lake for Milucradh and then fasting before the mystical tree to gain prophetic knowledge is the direct parallel of Óðinn hanging from and fasting on the windy tree to gain the runes. Fionn's tasting of the salmon of knowledge and of the well of knowledge parallel Óðinn drinking from Mimir's Well of knowledge. Fionn and Gwyn's names comes from the Proto-Celtic *windos*, believed to derive from Proto-Indo-European *weyd-* "to know, to see." Óðinn's name comes from the similar but distinct PIE *wéh₂t-i-s* "seer, excited." Furthermore, as the Primordial Rudra on the scene of creation, Óðinn matches the Welsh Primordial Rudra Efnysien and Irish Primordial Rudra Eber Finn.

At least in his role of giving *Önd,* life-breath, to the first humans[277], Óðinn could have a connections to the higher, priestly aspects otherwise seen in the Vedic Vayu, Lord of Wind (who otherwise, in his brutish character traits, is paralleled by Thor, as Dumezil has argued). Thus we have suggested here that the traits seen in Vedic "Vayu" could be differently distributed between Thor and Óðinn, the "lower," brutish traits associated with this Vedic Vayu (as seen in his named incarnation Bhima) belonging to Thor, and the priestly roles usually seen as part of Vedic Vayu seemingly being taken by the priestly Óðinn who dominates the majority of priestly roles. This could reflect the differentiation in Vedic terminology between "Vata" and "Vayu," these being combined in Vedic as "Vata-Vayu," but perhaps not in the same way in Norse. As Brereton and Jamison elucidate:

> The ordinary word for the wind is vā́ta, and unlike Vāyu, the god Vāta closely reflects the character and activity of the wind. He goes shattering and thundering, raising the dust (X.168.1); he moves through the midspace and is the companion of the waters (X.168.3). The symbolic features of Vāta likewise reflect the wind. Vāta is the breath (ātmán) of the gods (X.168.4), and as the lifebreath, he is the father, brother, and companion of the man

---

277   For Odin as god of wind and breath see: de Vries 1970, p. 93. *Altgermanische Religionsgeschichte*. Grundriss der germanischen Philologie. See also Erick Dodge: "the PIE term that Óðinn derives from (*wet-¹) also meant 'blow' and was closely tied to another root meaning 'to blow' (*wē-; originally *h₂weh₁-, and later contracted as *h₂wē-) (Watkins, 2011: 98). This root eventually produced Sanskrit Vāyú (i.e. the wind god). This matches with Óðinn's giving of ON ǫnd to humans ('breath of life; soul'; it has a different PIE root from the ones we have been looking at, *h₂enh₁, but with a close meaning nevertheless 'to breathe') (De Vaan, 2008). It also matches with some of his other names: Váfǫðr ('Wind'), Viðrir ('Weather-Causer'), and Ýrungr ('Wild, Stormy')" (Dodge, "Orpheus, Odin, and the Indo-European Underworld," 23-24)

whom he makes live (X.186.1–3). (Brereton and Jamison, *The Rigveda: A Guide*, 95)

Dumezil has similarly argued that the roles attached to the Vedic Indra may likewise be distributed differently between Thor and Óðinn, Thor taking the thunder weapon and serpent-slaying mythos and Óðinn taking some of the chivalrous or aristocratic roles attached in Vedic myth to Indra, who is a great *soma* drinker among other things, like Óðinn. Dumezil is very unclear which "chivalrous" Indraic roles he means in this context, and overall it quickly becomes a very complex, even messy, picture.[278] And yet, if Óðinn was indeed seen as the Priest god *par excellence*, it would be an understandable theological difference between the Norse and the Vedics for Óðinn to be seen to monopolize the priestly offices which are seen as the domains of various different divinities in the Vedic conception. This different distribution of "Vayu" and "Indra" traits in the Norse understanding would indicate an important theological difference between these two branches, the Norse favoring a division of roles much more along the lines of higher vs. lower, priestly vs. warrior, chivalrous vs brutish, instead of simply along the lines of "Wind" vs. "Thunder," for example. This concept is reinforced by the fact that we find the Pushanic mythos connected to Óðinn, but we find that Pushan's very un-aristocratic vehicle, the goat-driven cart, which has a specific necessary function in the Pushanic mythos as he must climb the steep far paths, has been given to Thor.

However, a great note of hesitation should be mentioned here. When we have understood the Welsh Creation Myth, we see that the three gods who surround the tree-named first child of Earth and Sky are Efnysien-Rudra, Manawydan-Agni, and Nisien-Siva. In the parallel moment, Óðinn gives **önd**, "breath-soul," to the tree-named first humans, but in the Welsh case no wind god is explicitly present to give the tree-child any of the qualities of life. Instead Odinn's only Welsh parallel in this scene is Efnysien-Rudra. Rudra indeed gives life-breath to the world in Vedic tradition, as Stella Kramrisch notes:

---

[278] "This is a precious lesson; the two types of warrior god—represented in the pre-Vedic period, presumably, by Vayu and Indra, combined in the *RgVeda* under the name of Indra, but attested as distinct in their sons, the heroes Bhima and Arjuna, up to the time of the epic – have their counterparts, in Scandinavian mythology, in Thorr and Odinn. The structure of this latter pair results from a phenomenon especially characteristic of Germanic religions: the overlapping of the warrior function onto the sovereign level. Odinn, the sovereign god, while keeping his traits as a sovereign—the only ones with which he enters into the career of Starcatherus—has also annexed to himself the patronage of the brilliant, chivalrous side, or aspect, of the warrior function, illustrated by the Einherjar in the other world and by heroes such as Sigurdr and Helgi in this one" (Dumezil, *The Destiny of a Warrior*, 90).

Rudra's mind-born sons [rudras], unlike Brahmā's, did not all monotonously withdraw from the world. On the contrary, they activate the movement in creation. They are the breath (*prana*) of life (*LP*.1.22.24 ŚP.y. 1.12.25-30) beings, for Rudra is the origin of that breath. (*Mahabharata* 7.173.92-93). (Kramrisch, 263-264)

Although unpredictable and frightening, the Rudras, these uncanny vital powers, are recognized; they are to be accepted and worshiped along with the other gods. They are the movement of breath itself (*prana*), whose origin is Rudra. (Kramrisch, 267)

Rudra, the avenger, at the dawn of creation was born into creation from Brahmā's wrath, from the middle of his forehead, where the world of the senses and the intellect meet. Or he left the body of Brahmā by his mouth as his life breath, as the breath itself of life (KūP.1.10.22). (Kramrisch, 253)

Radiant, glorious Rudra, the breath itself of life (cf. BṛUp.3.9.4), light of the sun and fire of doomsday, was born of Brahmā's anger. (Kramrisch, 254)

One way to still include a wind aspect in this event, if a reader were to insist on such, would be either to presuppose that Efnysien-Rudra has a wind aspect as part of his makeup, considering considerable overlaps of Rudra and Vayu in Vedic tradition, or, perhaps more questionably, to imagine Bran, who is also present in this scene, as having such a wind aspect, considering some similarities between himself and Dagda, who is the Irish Vayu. As it stands, a clear Vayu-type wind god is difficult to identify in the Welsh mythology, and this could be the result of his erasure or conflation with another god, if not a reflection of an idea that the Wind God was one with the Rudraic god in the primordial moment and was born as a distinct individual only later. We do not take this particular position at present, but only wish for now to note that no clear Wind God appears in the Welsh "tree-child" moment. Instead, as Efnysien-Rudra parallels Óðinn in this moment, and as Rudra himself is identified with the life-breath, we may suppose that it is the Rudraic god who is seen to give the life-breath as such on the primordial scene. Likewise, the traits that Dumezil saw as Indraic could have instead been Rudraic or otherwise. Although one of Óðinn's names is in fact *Thundr*, Rudra also wields the lightning in Vedic religion. Varuna is also a fierce sky sovereign and Brihaspati also rescues the cattle like Indra and Óðinn.

The Dian Cecht "well of rejuvenation" motif, the general theme of which Dumezil wrote an entire book discussing (*The Plight of a Sorcerer*), is that associated with Vedic

486

Brihaspati, the high priest of the gods, whose son acquires the power of reviving the dead and uses it in the great war in the same way the well is used. As the god of chants, Dian Cecht, saves the kine from the serpent Meichi, so also Óðinn, god of *galdrs*, saves the cattle from beneath the earth with his chants and songs. The aforementioned Cian is Pushan, who finds the lost *soma*-cow just as Cian finds the wondrous cow Glas Gaibhnenn in a myth clearly paralleling Óðinn's theft of the mead. Manannan is Agni, based on Manawydan's role in the Lunar Cycle of marriages to the Sun/Horse Princess, and the multiple other connections we have pointed out in our "Great Lunar Cycle." As we have stated, the Dagda, the Great Father of Being, is Vedic Dyaus-Vayu. Thus we have Irish Dian Cecht, Cian, Nuada, Manannan, Nuada, Fionn, and more speculatively, certain aspects of Dagda; or Vedic Brihaspati, Pushan, Varuna, Agni, Rudra; and, with caution, we add the possibility of aspects of Vayu, and possibly of Indra as well, if we choose to follow Dumezil.

Our interpretation explicitly opposes an identification of Óðinn with Vedic Soma and so of Óðinn with Greek Dionysus. As our "Great Lunar Cycle" series has demonstrated, there is a continuity between Irish Midir, Greek Dionysus, and Vedic Soma, and this "Soma" God is paralleled in the Norse case by Kvasir, the god whose blood makes the sacred liquid, and, perhaps surprisingly, by Njorðr, lord of wealth and waters, rather than by Óðinn. While Njorðr parallels Dionysus, Kvasir parallels Dionysus-Zagreus. The Soma God is the direct producer (never the thief) of the sacred drink, which is even seen to come from his very body in some cases, or at least from his special domain, something that cannot be said of Óðinn. The liquid is generated and held in the moon/the moon god/the waters, and dispensed therefrom, and Óðinn by no means enacts this role of physical container of the liquid or guardian of its domain in any sense. The roles of thief or drinker of the liquid can much more be traced to gods such as Agni, Pushan, Indra and Rudra-Siva than to the Soma God who in one aspect *is* the drink itself, and in the myth of Óðinn stealing the mead he is paralleling Agni-Pushan. Put simply, Óðinn does not have any overlap of specific *myths* with Soma or the other parallel "Soma" gods, while both Njordr and Kvasir have been shown to have such mythic overlap to a very great extent.

Our interpretation also opposes the opinion, ubiquitous in both ancient and modern commentators, that Óðinn is a genuine cognate of Mercury/Hermes[279]. A much clearer

---

[279]   Pushing against the idea of a deep connection between Mercury and Óðinn, Rudolf Simek also comments: "The identification was based on the external attributes of the two gods. Mercury and Wodan/Odin: Mercury's broad-rimmed hat, cloak and staff (the Greek god Hermes had the same attributes; a fusion of the Roman and Greek gods had already begun at the beginning of the Christian era) corresponding to the hat, cloak and spear belonging to Wodan/Odin. Admittedly, Odin is only described in this way in the literary

case, following Allen and Woodard, not based only on vaguely similar traits, has been made that Hermes in particular shares a root with the Gandharva, who parallels Norse Bragi, the court bard of the gods. Óðinn's Mercury-like traits can be accounted for by the mystical, prophetic and psychopompic traits he has from his shared roots with Pan, Apollo and the Fire God. Furthermore, understanding that the increased emphasis on Mercury's mystical role may itself have come from a separate Egyptian influence offers further avenues for understanding the surface similarities exhibited by Óðinn and Mercury.[280] Óðinn is by no means the messenger god, court singer, and guardian of the door (a god clearly of a lower level than the high priest-sovereign), as Hermes is.

Not only are the majority of the above listed parallels the central priestly-magical deities, but in the Irish myth nearly every one of them[281] is a "paternalistic" predecessor of Lugh. Dian Cecht is Lugh's grandfather, Cian is his father, Nuada is the king who reigns immediately before him, and Manannan came to be seen as his foster father in later folktales. Not only are all of these the immediate preceding paternalistic figures to Lugh, and not only are they all thematically related in their priestly-magical character, but we find a distinct absence of most of these deities as distinct individuals in the Norse pantheon. Indeed, where specifically has Brihaspati, has Rudra, has Pushan, has Varuna gone in the Norse mythology, if they are not seen as aspects Óðinn? Other options may be suggested of course, but each must be weighed against the connections of these deities to the mythoi of Óðinn. And predictably, and impossible to ignore, Óðinn is the father of Baldr, and in Snorri's account of Tyr too, who we have shown to be, combined,

---

works of the Middle Ages, and the image of the classical god was almost certainly not without influence here" (Simek, *Dictionary of Northern Mythology,* 211). "[…] Mercury was by no means as important a god for the Romans as Odin was for the Scandinavians. Odin's main role was certainly not that of a god of trade, as Mercury was" (Simek, 211-12).

"One convincing parallel between Odin and Mercury is that both had the function of being the companion of the soul in death. Another similarity, taking into consideration the already progressed Hellenization of Mercury, was that the Greek god Hermes was also the god of speech and as such could be linked with Wodan/Odin, if Odin/Wodan was indeed thought to be a god of poetic art so early on" (Simek, 212). We have shown that Óðinn's psychopomp role is connected instead to his Fire Priest aspect, while his connections to poetry and the runes derive from Pushanic, Rudraic and Brihaspatian-type myths, while Hermes is instead Gandharvic.

280   Fowden, Garth. *The Egyptian Hermes: A Historical Approach to the Late Mind.* Cambridge and New York: Cambridge University Press, 1986. Boylan, Patrick. *Thot, the Hermes of Egypt: A Study of Some Aspects of Theological Thought in Ancient Egypt.* London: Oxford University Press, 1922.

281   With the exception of Fionn, though his Rudraic counterpart Balor is after all the maternal grandfather of Lugh, and so the one-eyed Rudraic element is certainly present among Lugh's paternal predecessors, and very prominently.

equivalent to Lugh. Hence in the Norse version the several fatherly, priestly aspects are seen as one in the god Óðinn, a possible sign of a theological centralization which occurred around him, or of an original mega-divinity that was elsewhere divided. We have demonstrated in several instances how many of these Óðinnic gods or aspects are intertwined with each other in Irish, Vedic and Greek cases, often to the point of identity or near-identity. Meanwhile, in the Irish case, a degree of parallel centralization seems to have occurred around Lugh, as he may have absorbed elements seen in Vedic as part of the Indra mythos and taken some of the preeminence within the "Mitra-Varuna" pairing for himself. Óðinn would then represent the "Varuna" half of the "Mitra-Varuna" pairing and has within him all adjacent priestly and paternalistic roles. In the end, Óðinn calls himself Fjölnir, "The One Who is Many,"[282] a fitting title for a Rudraic god, he who is everywhere and whose names are uncountable.

By looking at the Irish and other branches, we can also see roughly why the Óðinnic aspects may have been seen as intertwined in the Scandinavian case, as the numerous parts of one deity. In Irish myth, Nuada is the Varunian sovereign and his closely connected descendant (perhaps grandson) is Fionn, both being Óðinnic aspects. Fionn's Welsh counterpart is called Gwyn ap Nudd, his near descent from Nudd (Nuada) being indicated in his name, which is echoed in the Irish formulation Fionn ua Nuadat. As we noted already, John Carey ("Nodons in Britain and Ireland") considers Fionn/Gwyn and Nuada/Nudd/Nodens as so intimately overlapping that he claims they are almost to be taken as aspects of one deity, a deity who he argues is summed up best in the British Nodens. Meanwhile, Fionn is the Rudraic god, and we have seen that the Rudraic aspect is inextricably combined with the Brihaspatian aspect in both Apollo and Óðinn, and that the two are extremely closely aligned in Vedic myth, their incarnations being father and son in the *Mahabharata*. These two deities are both healers associated with magical waters, they both have the power of magical speech and poetry, they both are associated with the most high class and sacred forms of the poetic art and with the priestly caste in general. They are both connected to elite sacred knowledge that must be protected from those unworthy of it. They are both deities who are potentially connected to the training of the bands of warrior-poet youths, Fionn/Rudra as the representative and leader of the band and Brihaspati as the archetypal teacher, which can be taken as one and the same role in a sense. Hence, when these two are seen as one god, we have Apollo, the High Priest of the Word who is also an ideal of the youthful perfection of the mannerbund. The Irish Brihaspatian deity is Dian Cecht and his son is Cian, another Óðinnic aspect,

---

282   See also Joshua Rood's *Ascending the Steps to Hliðskjálf: The Cult of Óðinn in Early Scandinavian Aristocracy,* which intensively demonstrates that the aristocratic cult of Óðinn may have expanded and absorbed other gods as Scandinavian society and religion became more centralized in response to the pressures imposed by the Roman Empire and the post-imperial political landscape.

corresponding to Pushan/Pan. Cian is a magician god who parallels Gwydion and manifests as Merlin, and as such his connection to the magico-priestly role of his father Dian Cecht, god of magical chants, is ever-present. Cian carries a magical role that marks him as a bit more wily and unorthodox than his father, as seen when he takes part in a female-clothed magic akin to *seiðr* and then infiltrates and tricks Balor. His parallel Gwydion uses illusions to trick Pryderi and Arianrhod, a use of illusory magic that continues with Merlin, and he even uses his trickery to help his brother perpetrate a rape. Some of the more *questionable* traits of Óðinn may then correspond to this aspect. Thus the father, Dian Cecht, represents a more pure magical power and his son a sometimes more ambiguous one that walks the line of being almost villainous, or at least taboo, as with Óðinn's practice of *seiðr* and his use of runes and charms to rape Rindr. The division between the father, Dian Cecht, and his son Cian aka Gwydion/Merlin may be simplified as that between the priestly healer and the sorcerer, or perhaps even, quite loosely, between "white" and "black" magic. However, it is easy to see how this father and son could be seen as two sides of one greater deity of the magical arts, comprehended in the figure of Óðinn. Meanwhile, Cian is the father of Lugh, as Óðinn is the father of Baldr (and possibly of Tyr, as we have suggested), Baldr and Tyr being the parallels of Lugh. Nuada is the king who precedes Lugh while Dian Cecht and Cian are Lugh's father and grandfather, and these paternalistic predecessor roles could all be united in a conception of Óðinn as the father and predecessor on the throne to his son Baldr (and possibly Tyr). Lugh's other grandfather is Balor, who strictly speaking parallels Suttungr, but we have seen how Balor is the destructive side of the Rudraic deity-grouping embodied in its more positive side by Fionn, and in the case of Óðinn it may be that he takes some of the Rudraic traits that are attached to the destructive Balor in the Irish case: particularly the one-eyedness and the power of inflicting paralysis to enemies on the battlefield. Balor being Lugh's other grandfather, we can see how these traits could be seen as belonging to the paternal predecessor of Lugh's Norse parallel. One-eyedness is not solely Balor's trait of course and is also a feature of the beneficent Rudraic figure Fintan. Manannan is the Fire God, Vedic Agni, and we are aware of a deep overlap of the Agni and Brihaspati deities in the Vedic material, as previously delineated. These are the two archetypal high priests, the Fire Priest and the Invoking Priest, and we have noted how frequently they are conflated or described with identical terms in the Vedas, to the point that some scholars have theorized that they may have split from one original deity.

Aligning these aspects, we can first see the Varunian/Nuada aspect as the archetypal priest king, the First King, who could also be the representative of and come from out of the youthful war-band (Rudra/Fionn), and whose natural powers or sub-aspects would logically be those of the High Priest roles, the Fire Priest and Invoking Priest, and who could also be a master of the more taboo side of magic, which could be seen as a lower or more questionable aspect of his power but still an essential element of it.

The Spear of Mitra-Varuna

A significant question remains which can be answered with this context. If the spear-throwing scene is so central to the Lugh/Mitra mythos, then why is Óðinn the Spear God and not Tyr or Baldr, who we have said are Lugh's parallels? Indeed, Irish Nuada has no spear, but only a sword, just as Norse Tyr does, one reason that this sword-wielding but Varunian Nuada and sword-wielding but Mitraic Tyr have been mistakenly identified many times. We should begin by saying that while the use of a certain weapon by a deity is a key piece of evidence, it should not be given undue power to decide questions of identity, and this is perhaps most important of all to keep in mind in the case of the Mitra-Varuna pairing. This is for the reason that Mitra and Varuna, as much as any two deities, and as much as they contrast, share features, share roles, overlap and in the Vedas are often even treated as one composite deity, Mitra-Varuna. It is apparent that the spear as a weapon was the weapon of Mitra-Varuna generally, and in the case of Irish and Norse myth, ended up being wielded by the deity who rose to the leadership position, a sign of their ultimate sovereignty. More even than that, it was a sign of their role as what the Vedics called the "Dharmaraj," god of Dharma, Order, Justice, this spear being the Spear of Dharma or of Rta. Varuna, for instance, is said to wield the bow whose string is Rta, or Cosmic Law. No less is the spear of Lugh/Óðinn the spear of Cosmic Law, and it may be that the bow of Varuna was seen as a weapon that could be sometimes alternated with the spear, in their similar capacities as projectile weapons. The spear of the Mitraic Lleu Llaw Gyffes goes through stone like it was paper, just as Cosmic Law controls all and wins out no matter the opponent.

To show that the spear was associated not with only one of the Mitra-Varuna pair, but with each one depending on the context, we need only look once more at the *Iliad*. Here we find the brothers Agamemnon and Menelaus, as we have shown, incarnations of Varuna and Mitra, respectively. Menelaus performs the myth matching uncannily to Lleu Llaw Gyffes' spear throwing sequence when he duels Paris to have revenge on him for stealing his wife, and throws his spear through Paris' shield just as Lleu throws his spear through the stone slab behind which Gronw hides. He then also kills Helen's second lover Deiphobus (see: Balor) with his spear at the end of the war. Even with this clear association and even prowess with the spear shown by the Mitraic Menelaus, enacting one of its quintessential mythic displays, his Varunian brother Agamemnon, paralleling Óðinn, is still considered the great spear warrior of the epic. So overwhelming with a spear is he and so famous is he for its mastery, when the spear-throwing contest comes up during Achilles' funeral games, the match is called off before it can even begin because it is said that no one could beat Agamemnon with a spear. He has already won before the match can begin, which fits well the idea of the Spear of Cosmic Law. Thus in this case, while the spear of retributive justice is already on display in association with Menelaus-Mitra, its wielding is still also known as the terrible forte of Agamemnon-Varuna. Ultimately, we learn from all of these examples that the spear could be the signature weapon of either deity, in perhaps slightly different contexts – the Varunian Óðinn's spear *beginning* battles and the Mitraic God's spear *ending* them or inflicting retributive justice, in line with their roles as sovereign of beginnings and sovereign of endings respectively, ie. First King and Second King – whichever of the pair rose to preeminence in a given society and took the responsibility of leading the charge of Righteousness.

19

Ragnarok: The Doom of the Gods in Germanic, Vedic, Celtic and Greek Branches

Besides the Aesir-Vanir war, a second war found in Norse myth also is frequently cited as unique to the Norse, and by commentators is often considered a poor match to the wars found in the other Indo-European branches. In this war, Ragnarok, we are told (*Voluspa,* 40-58; *Gylfaginning; Vafthruthnismal*) there will be a great series of cataclysms as well as the deaths of nearly all the gods, resulting in the end of this world as we know it, with the returned Baldr and the mysterious Lord of the Endtimes leading the way into a newborn age. All bonds of kinship, duty, and morality will disintegrate, the Sun will be swallowed by the wolf, the stars will disappear, winter will last for years, mountains will crumble, and the whole world will be burned by Surtr's fire. If we look at the great wars of the gods and god-incarnations found in the Indian *Mahabharata*, the Irish *Battle of Maige Tuired*, and the Greek *Iliad*, this apocalyptic imagery is nowhere to be found. In these cases, the Great War is finished with a certain handful of gods or heroes surviving, many dying, and the victorious king ruling his people for another period of time (40 years for Lugh, 37 years for Yudhishthira, an unstated period for

493

Menelaus) in an age of righteousness and peace. Generally these kings then die (Lugh) or ascend to Elysium (Menelaus) or Paradise (Yudhishthira), and other kings inherit the kingdom from them and history continues. It is very difficult to read these other wars as in any sense world-ending. In fact, they seem merely to set the stage for history to begin unfolding up to the present, if anything.

However, we have already noted the numerous consistent parallels in these other branches to the events leading up to and following Ragnarok, from the wooing of Gerthr by Freyr, to the Lunar Cycle as a whole and the Aesir-Vanir conflict, to Tyr's cuckolding and the loss of his hand during the binding of Fenrir, to Loki's mockery of Freyja as unchaste, to the retrieval of the sacred liquid, to the death of Baldr, to Baldr's return from the underworld to lead a golden age along with the mysterious Lord of the Endtimes, and as such we are confronted with the unavoidable implication that these myth cycles are telling us the same underlying story. And indeed, these are presumably, if we take the Indo-European Perennialist perspective, the same gods whose stories must have derived originally from one source, one body of original myths. These were either a single large cycle of myths at one point or they were not, and if many of the god-heroes in the non-Norse branches are said to die in one Great War, are we to believe that they were supposed to have lived again and died again in a different cataclysmic war to end the cycle as well? Why would the deaths of some of these Celtic, Greek and Indian gods or heroes who embody the mythoi of gods not correspond to their deaths in the Ragnarok cycle, if they are at their cores the same gods with the same original myths, for which thesis we have up to now seen evidence?

This is a difficult but not impossible question for a critic to answer. It could be that the gods die in one early war, come back later, and then die again in the war of the end times. Yet this gives an unshakably redundant flavor. More likely, perhaps, the Germanic branch may have developed their own war myth completely whole-cloth and unique to them, telling only the tale of the endtimes while never developing an earlier great war besides the Aesir-Vanir conflict. But this runs into the same problem: we either believe these branches were united at one point or not. Which branch then diverged and invented a new, unconnected war story, while forgetting the story of the original primordial war, a myth presumably so important and central? How exactly do two branches split off and then develop different War of the Gods myths that can be said to be actually unconnected, while retaining numerous shared individual mythemes? It is not impossible, but it is not the simplest answer.

It is because of this difficulty that many have wished instead to see the Aesir-Vanir war as comparable to the Irish Battle of Maige Tuired, Greek Trojan War, or Indian Kurukshetra War, or at least to draw lines between these wars and other conflicts like the Deva-Asura conflict in the Vedas, and thus put them off to the side. We have shown how these equations simply do not match the identities of the combatants or reasons for war in these cases, and that, furthermore, if we take the equation for the Aesir-Vanir war (as we have previously proposed) as Horse Twin(s) + battle against the higher gods + gain acceptance into the society of higher gods + gain access to the high rite + become priests of the sacrifice, then it is clear that this structure is instead a match to the Asvins' story of Chyavana battling Indra and them joining the Soma sacrifice as priests, and, furthermore, that this myth sometimes appears as a full-blown war, but in several cases appears as a much smaller conflict or battle. Only a very superficial understanding of who and what is involved in the war myths can lead to an equation of the Aesir-Vanir war with one of the Great Wars of the Gods found in the other branches.

The greatest obstacle to the acceptance of Ragnarok as identical to the other Great Wars may be the apocalyptic imagery seemingly unique to it. However, if we look at the name of Ragnarok itself, we find that it is not semantically centered on the concept of the endtimes in itself. Instead, the word *Ragnarok* means something like "the doom or destruction of the gods," while other terms for the event also tend to refer specifically to the time when the gods die: *regin þrjóta* ("end of the gods") from *Hyndluljóð, þá er regin deyja* ("when the gods die") from *Vafþrúðnismál,* and *unz um rjúfask regin* ("when the gods will be destroyed") from *Vafþrúðnismál Lokasenna,* and *Sigrdrífumál.* Terms like *aldar rök* (*aldar* means age, "end of an age") from *Vafþrúðnismál* and *aldar rof* ("destruction of the age") from *Helgakviða Hundingsbana II* do clearly reference the end of the age, but not of the world or cosmos itself, and it could plausibly be claimed that "an age" has ended after any of the other Great Wars, especially as when the gods recede and make way for human history in the Irish case. Though there is much other specific description of endtimes occurrences in the mentions of Ragnarok, its name and the other most well-known terms for the event itself seem to emphasize that its primary significance centers instead around the deaths of the gods, with the material cataclysm being secondary to its deep meaning.

If so, then we can say that the other branches also definitively tell of the deaths of the main gods, either during the Great War of the Gods, or closely following. In the *Mahabharata*, almost the entire army of the Pandavas is wiped out in the Kurukshetra war, including their own children (Ashvatthama's final great slaughter of their camp makes sure of this), though the Pandava brothers themselves survive at least til after the war. During the war, the incarnations of Dyaus Pitr (Bhishma), of Surya (Karna), of Agni (Drishtadyumna), of Brihaspati (Drona) and of many other incredibly important deities perish. The incarnation of Varuna (Pandu) dies before the war itself. Many of the other main incarnations die in a fire in their forest retreat where they go to live ascetically after the war. The Pandava brothers themselves, incarnations of the central gods of the social classes (Mitra, Vayu, Indra, the Asvins), after Yudhishthira's reign of

495

37 years, go on a pilgrimage into the Himalayas. They are said to drop dead one by one on this pilgrimage, each due to a sin characteristic to them, until only King Yudhishthira remains. He finally reaches Paradise on the Holy Mountain, passes the tests presented him, and enters. Thus, accepting that these heroes do stand in for the gods, this war and its aftermath can indeed be called the twilight and doom of the gods, especially considering the argument we have previously forwarded, following Dumezil and Wikander, that in the epic heroes we actually find a version of the myths of the gods that is sometimes of the most archaic layer.

Similarly in the Greek epic tradition, we have the deaths of the figures we have proposed as incarnations of the Sun God and Father Sky (Paris and Sarpedon) during the war, along with incarnation of the Thunderer (Achilles) and possible incarnation of the Son of the Moon, (Patroclus). The great Hector is said to slaughter 31,000 from the Greek side, then to die himself. It is the aftermath of the Trojan war, as in the Vedic version, where many of the main heroes die, however. Ajax commits suicide after the funeral games of Achilles, while still in Troy, insulted by his comrades and shamed by his own actions. Agamemnon is killed by his wife or wife's lover immediately on returning home. Odysseus is said to reach home safely, but later to be killed inadvertently by his own son Telegonus. As for Menelaus and Diomedes, these are the only two said to be taken to Elysium and given immortality, which perfectly matches the concept that Menelaus parallels Yudhishthira reaching Paradise on pilgrimage and Baldr along with the mysterious Lord of the Endtimes overcoming death and attaining the golden age, while Diomedes is the Horse Twin who expectedly gains the gift of immortality and joins the society of the gods. Nearly every god-hero falls in the events surrounding the Trojan war, and this fact certainly must have had great significance. Finally, in the Irish version, we see that Nuada, the Varunian Terrible Sovereign, is beheaded during the war, that Bres, the Sun God, is killed right after the war comes to a close, while his double Cermait is killed by Lugh later on. The Dagda, the Sky and Wind god, is wounded in the leg with a poisoned dart during the battle and dies of it 120 years later. Ogma and Indech are said to kill one another in single combat, though the poet or scribe then confusingly depicts Ogma alive again at the end of the battle. Perhaps the most central god, Lugh, rules for 40 years after the war, but then is killed by the sons of Cermait, avenging their father's death. Once again, the great majority of main gods all are depicted as dying in the war or the aftermath, even if it is not as clean of a sweep as in the Norse case, and even there some gods survive. In what way then, is this not the war *þá er regin deyja,* "when the gods die"? How is this not literally "the doom or destruction of the gods," Ragnarok?

Furthermore, apocalyptic imagery similar to Ragnarok is by no means absent from all other Indo-European traditions, and should not be seen as pure anomaly or as necessary

496

outside influence on the Norse myth. The Vedic branch has a mysterious motif of a horse or horse's head that will emerge from under the waters in the endtime to consume the world in flame. As Wendy Doniger puts it:

> The fire of doomsday is said to have the form of a mare (vadava) at the bottom of the ocean; inextinguishable flames issue from her mouth. The destructive fire which cannot be quenched can at least be made to wait for the moment appropriate for destruction; the fire that blazes from Siva's eye to burn Kama is the fire of untimely doomsday, which yawns wide to burn up the universe until it is placed beneath the sea. Agni Vadava-vaktrya (the fire of the mare's mouth) drinks the waters of the ocean and lets them out again; eventually this fire of the underworld will destroy the universe, at the end of an aeon. (Doniger, "The Submarine Mare in the Mythology of Siva")

Compare here Fionn (Siva/Rudra) killing with a spear throw the fire deity Aillen who destroys Tara each Samhain (the end of the yearly cycle): perhaps Aillen was only temporarily suppressed and was destined to return again at the end of the larger cycle, or perhaps this is a reduced version of a myth that was once cosmological in scale. Fionn kills another destructive figure with a spear throw on Samhain called Aed, who thus is a parallel of a destructive aspect of Agni, and may then be a doublet of Aillen. Doniger demonstrates that this motif of the Submarine Mare originates from elements in the earliest Vedic layers and is elaborated throughout subsequent late Vedic literature. In the Iranic branch, as recorded in the *Bundahishn,* we also find mention of an end of days when all will be washed in a sea of fire. It is said that fire will "melt the metal in the hills and mountains, and it will be upon the earth like a river" (*Bundahishn* 34.18) burning away all that is unrighteous. *The Selections of Zātspram* (34.52) speaks of a Great Battle that brings about the endtimes and the ultimate renovation of the righteous.

Opponents of this attempt to align Ragnarok with the other wars of the gods will of course point to the many surface differences we can find between the branches. The rebuttal to this objection forces us to look to the esoteric core of the myth. Firstly, while the age certainly ends and the world undergoes great destruction, the world itself does not in fact end even in the Norse case. Time continues forward and a new age or cycle is begun without intermission. Secondly, we must take the perspective that the myths have not just a material, historical significance, but a religious one as well, central as they have been to their cultures. As such we can say that these myths are relating events from an eternal, metaphysical timeframe, from what Mircea Eliade calls *illo tempore*, "that-ideal-time," "that time before."[283] In our interpretation of the Eliadic, esoteric understanding of myth, myths depict timeless events which occurred at the beginning,

---

283   Mircea Eliade, *The Sacred and the Profane*, 70, 95.

are occurring presently, and will occur at the end of the cycle. That is, they recur eternally within the microcosm of the individual, or of the day, as they do in the time-out-of-time of eternity. They pierce through, and have relevance to, all levels. They are prisms of ultimate meaning. Hence the central myth of the end of the age and of the gods could not be merely a literal rendition of what will happen on the material plane at a certain time. Instead it is the story of the cycle generally, which occurs below as it does above on the transcendental plane. This is how it is known about by the seers and by the gods. It has happened before, will happen, and is happening.

We have shown previously that the basic framework of the War of the Gods myth involves the King who is the God of the Early Morning Sky (the Lawful Sovereign) wedded to the Dawn Goddess or another goddess who fulfills the same role, who is stolen by the Sun God, the pursuit and overcoming of the Sun God and the gods of Fate, Time and Destruction, the deaths of all the other gods, and the achieving of the Golden Age both internally and externally by the Sovereign. The union of the God of Early Morning Sky and Dawn Goddess represents the primordial unity of the Golden Age, a time of both peace and naïveté, while the adultery of the Dawn Goddess with the Sun and the wounding of the Sovereign by the Sun is the fall into matter, into *samsara*, into Time, and ultimately into the Last Age. The overcoming of the Sun God is the esoteric mastery over Time and Decay, resulting in the end of the age and the achieving of a new Golden Age both internally and externally. This cycle can be seen in the great cycle of Time, with our world historically going through the great ages and then ending in cataclysm before beginning again, but can also be seen in the microcosm of the process of the Day, with its early morning calm, burning hot midday, as the Sun tyrannically rules and leads us with each passing moment toward death, and the sunset when the forces of light and order seem to die but so does the tyrannical aspect of the day, the kingdom or even world itself seeming to burn up in the sunset, while the principle of order survives the night to initiate a new dawn. And again, this framework can apply to the even smaller microcosm of the individual esoteric seeker (the core Mitraic structure of this myth likely being the elitist esoteric path reserved only for kings and possibly High Priests in ancient times), who begins in primordial unity with the All or the Unmanifest before birth and is united with the Golden Glory or Khvarenah (the early morning golden age), who falls into matter and Time (Mithras trapped in the rock), breaks free from the rock and overcomes the Sun God, the lord of Time who guards the mystery of immortality, and finally attains the inner golden age and spiritual elevation or reintegration of the whole.

As such it should be permissible to suggest that just because the other branches do not depict a total cataclysm of the world that this does not mean that this meaning is not already present in the story of the widespread deaths of the gods in these other branches.

Simply by telling the story of the war and deaths of the gods, these other branches implicitly convey the end of a great age and the beginning of a new cycle, which the poets have then tied, clumsily or not, into human history. In fact, as scholar John Carey explains in his "Myth and Mythography in Cath Maige Tuired," there is much evidence that the Irish Second Battle of Maige Tuired narrative was not originally placed in the constructed historical narrative in which we find it today, but that it originally was seen as a battle that occurred "once upon a time" – that is, clearly, *in illo tempore.* As he puts it,

> it seems safest to presume that CMT in its original form existed independent of the historical scheme which was to evolve into LG and that the battle of Mag Tuired was portrayed as having been fought 'once upon a time' rather than at a definite point in the canonical sequence of invasions. (John Carey, "Myth and Mythography in Cath Maige Tuired," 54)

While this eschatological meaning is then present-but-effaced in these branches, it is possible that the apocalyptic imagery has likewise been further emphasized in the Norse version or lessened in the Irish. It is impossible to say for certain exactly what this myth looked like in its "original" form, whether the full extent of the material and temporal apocalypse was part of the original vision or became elaborated more as Germanic society developed its own unique perspective on the myth over time. It is not hard to imagine the apocalyptic imagery being elaborated or reduced in one version or another, one society wishing to tie the myth into known history, with another showing it as the end of (almost) all things. We should ultimately be able to reach a position where these superficial trappings do not change our understanding of this shared myth, a position where we can see the core meaning of the Great War of the Gods, the time when the gods always have and always will reach their doom, a position from which we can finally grasp the implications of this greatest of myths on every level.

20

The Mitraic Path of Immortality and the Mithraic Mysteries

Basing his interpretations on Franz Cumont's work *The Mysteries of Mithra* as well as the ancient text known as the "Mithraic Liturgy," the comments of various ancients such as Nonnus the Grammarian, and the well-known Mithraic reliefs, Julius Evola lays out a speculative reconstruction of the inner meaning of the Mithraic initiation in his essay "The Path of Enlightenment in the Mithraic Mysteries." According to Evola, the initiate, reenacting the actions of the Roman god Mithras, goes through several stages with a series of attendant trials. He begins as Mithras born in the rock by the side of a river, the rock and waters symbolism indicating the material element into which the divine spark has descended. From this rock, which is both a prison and necessary foundation, Mithras must break free, and then must traverse the waters, which symbolize the cravings of the material body. He then is chafed by strong winds which he must endure, symbolizing the passions and energies which inhabit his being and which he must overcome, but also from which he must differentiate and separate his spirit. He next approaches a tree whose fruit he eats and whose leaves he uses to clothe himself with a new garment. Eventually, he enters the presence of the Aeon, also identified here as the Sun God himself (Sol), the keeper of the Golden Glow of Sovereignty, ontological elevation, and immortality, which Evola identifies with the Iranic concept of the *Hvareno* (also conventionally spelled *Khvarenah*). "Beyond them all is the Sun, the flaming Aeon" says Evola (16). Mithras must confront the Sun God's "solar stare" with his own, which is to say he must withstand and overcome this high god. When he is able to do so, the Sun God yields and offers a pact of friendship, and Mithras is thereafter identified with the solar principle itself, being depicted with the solar "halo." As Evola puts it, "The brightness of the *hvareno*, of the glorious and radiant Mithraic halo, arises only out of a frightful tension, and it only crowns the "eagle," which was capable of "staring" at the Sun" (11). Finally, Mithras enacts the famous climactic scene from the hundreds of known reliefs that remain of him, called the *tauroctony*, the killing of the bull. Evola describes the way in which this bull represents the life-force, comparable to the tantric *kundalini*, and when Mithras rides this bull back to its cave and slays it, its blood generates spikes of wheat as it falls, which Evola calls "the food of Life." Manfred Clauss, in his book *The Roman Cult of Mithras: The god and his mysteries*, presents a slightly different summary of the Mithraic narrative as involving: birth from rock, water struck from stone by an arrow, killing the bull, Sol submitting to Mithras, Mithras and Sol eating the bull at a feast, ascent of Mithras to heaven.

However, the bull has also alternately been interpreted as a symbol of Father Sky himself, the great Bull of Heaven, as in Peter Georgiev's *The Mysteries of Mithra or the Mysteries of Sabazios*. If so, the relief would represent a slaying of the Sky Sovereign by Mithras. This highly charged possibility could then perhaps be reminiscent of the defeat and castration of Ouranos by his son Cronus, after which the genitals symbolic of fecundating virility were cast into the ocean and spawned giants, nymphs and furies; or it may even remind us of Óðinn's killing of the giant Ymir to make the world with his body, the same Ymir who is born from the ice licked by the cosmic cow Adhumbla, herself a bovine embodying the great source of cosmic fertility and life. Indeed cosmic cows and bulls were frequent symbols of general fecundity, and on this level of meaning overlapped with Father Sky seen as the great fecundator, the bringer of rain and the impregnator of the earth, massive and powerful. Mircea Eliade argues that Father Sky only became symbolized by the bull once his mythos had deteriorated from its original high and remote dignity and he had become seen as only an instrument of the Earth Mother, as her subservient impregnator, reduced only to his fecundating function as opposed to his transcendental function (see: Eliade, *Patterns*, "The Sky and Sky Gods"). Though it cannot be said for certain whether the Mithraic bull is intended to signify Father Sky, and with what exact implication, we can see how these symbolisms may run together.

A second strong option for the possible identity of the Mithraic bull, however, is the god known to the Vedics as Soma. Soma himself (RV 9.83.3) and his Greek form Dionysus both frequently appear in bull form. "Or, quite often, Soma is a bull racing to mate with a herd of cows, who represent the milk with which the juice can be mixed," say Jamison and Brereton (*The Rigveda: A Guide*, 80). The possibility of identifying Soma specifically with the Mithraic bull arises from the fact that a myth exists in the Taittiriya and Caraka-Kasha Samhitas of the *Yajur Veda,* and in the *Satapatha Brahmana*, about the killing of the god Soma, which symbolizes the pressing of the *soma* plant for the *soma* sacrifice. Herman Lommel (in Adolf Jensen, *Das religiose Weltbild einer fruhen Kultur*, Stuttgart 1948) has shown that in the *Yajur Veda*, Mitra, at first refusing to participate in the slaying of Soma, eventually does so: "(Although) he is Mitra [friend] he has done a cruel deed" (TS 6, 4, 8, 1).[284] Lommel connects this to a West-Iranian cult of Mithra wherein he slays a bull (Lommel, "Mithra und das Stieropfer"). P.B. Chakrabarty comments how the Iranic reformer Zoroaster disclaimed with "holy anger" against the popular bull sacrifice, condemning "the Haoma [analogue of Soma] sacrifice although he did not mention the name Haoma but used instead, an old unmistakeable title of Haoma" (Chakrabarty, "Parallelism Between Indo·Iranian 'Soma Haoma' Rituals & The 'Chi·Dyo' Rituals of the Lepchas of Sikkim," 4). B. Schlerath has furthermore traced the myth of the Soma slaying back from the *Yajur* to possible traces in the earlier *Rig Veda*: for example, in RV 9.67.19 violent language is used when it is said that, "Bruised [or wounded, per Schlerath] by the press-stones and extolled, Soma, thou goest to the sieve." Furthermore, he argues that the word for "kill" may be euphemistically avoided in this context throughout the *Rig Veda*, suggesting that the poets were tiptoeing around and thus tacitly acknowledging the violence of the myth, which would indirectly suggest that this violence against Soma was known to them. "If the verb *han-* [slay, kill] was intentionally avoided and given instead of it euphemistic circumscriptions, we can conclude, that the idea of killing the Soma even in Rgvedic times existed" (B. Schlerath, "The Slaying of the God Soma"). If this myth of the slaying of Soma existed in Yajurvedic and perhaps even Rigvedic times, and can be connected to the Mithraic slaying of a bull in West Iran, as Lommel claims, then Soma certainly stands as one possible identification of the bull of Roman Mithras. And if so, the myth would prove archaic indeed.

---

284   "'Soma was Vrtra; when the gods killed him they said to Mitra: 'Kill him, you also!' He would not, and said: 'I am the friend (mitra) of all things […]' 'We will exclude you from the sacrifice, then!' Then he said: 'I, too, kill him!' The animals drew away from Mitra, saying: 'He who was a friend, he has become an enemy (amitra)[…]'" (*Satapatha Brahmana*, IV, 1, 4, 8). "So Mitra is opposed, by his nature at least, to blood sacrifice" comments Dumezil in *Mitra-Varuna*, which could explain why Roman Mithras has to look away from the bull as he slays it in the Mithraic tauroctonies.

In yet another Iranic variant, found in the *Bundahishn*, the great opponent of the good gods, Ahriman, kills a primordial hermaphroditic bovine called Gavaevodata[285], producing the abundance of the world, including grains and medicinal plants that grow from the bovine's marrow, while this process is also aided by Ahura Mazda.[286] This bovine is said to be placed in the care of or to be contained in the moon and to be "white and shining" "just like the moon." Though Ahriman's role in this act could be the product of the Zoroastrian reforms (i.e. placing the onus and stigma of the now outlawed killing onto a demonic figure), the question remains unresolved. However, we have already seen the presence of demonic figures as the catalysts or killers in the mythic parallels of the slaying and purifying of the "Soma" God: the Titans in the Orphic myth who are the killers of Dionysus, the sorceress Fuamnach who transforms Etain, the dwarves Fjalar and Galar who kill Kvasir and collect his blood, and so a variability between the presence of demonic and divine beings connected to the role of killer/sacrificer of Soma may have existed in the background of the myth from an early time. Ahura Mazda places the "sperms of men and animals" inside Gavaevodata and the first man, Gayomard, before the killing of Gavaevodata, so that all beings would propagate from there. Meanwhile, the Orphic myth, in the *Orphic Hymn to the Titans* and in Proclus' version, tells us that all beings, men and animals alike, descend from the Titans who have consumed the body of Dionysus. An article from the Circle of Ancient Iranian Studies states: "Honey is the sugar of antiquity and Herodotus stresses its preservative quality. According to the ideas of the ancient Persians honey comes from the moon, where the semen of the bull slain by Mithras was also taken and purified, henceforth to produce new fruits and plants. Thus the moon is the temporary guardian of the fruits" (Circle of Ancient Iranian Studies, "Mithra & Mithraism, The Seven Grades of Initiation"). The "honey" corresponds to the honey mead or *soma*, which is directly

---

285   Note that the bovine here said to be "just like the moon" is named Gavaevodata or "The Gav," while the Irish cow of the sacred lunar liquid is named Gavlen or a variation of the same, both apparently going back to the same PIE root simply meaning "cow."

286   "Then the Evil spirit came to the 'Gav.' The 'Gav' fell towards the Southern side, on the right hand: she first folded her right leg.

Having seized the astral body of the 'Gav' and the archetype of the 'Gav', Ohrmazd entrusted them to the Moon; as this is the illuminer which the Moon reflects towards the material world.

As one says, "The Moon having the seed of the beneficent animal;" that is, the archetype of the 'gavs' and the beneficent animals is on the Moon station.

Then, when the Evil Spirit came to Gayomard, Gayomard fell towards the Southern direction, on the left side; he too first folded his left leg.

Taking hold of his astral body, Ohrmazd entrusted it to the Sun station; as this is the light wherewith the Sun shines over the material world

For the 'Gav' was just like the Moon, and Gayomard was just like the sun" (*Greater Bundahishn*, VII "As Regards the Archetypes of These Creations", 4-9).

connected to honey in the Vedas and which, in other parallels, is sometimes simply represented by honey. The "Father Sky" bull and the "Soma" bull may also be seen as repetitions of the same primordial sacrifice, Mithra being cast in the role of the primordial sacrificer.

Eliade also cites a possible Egyptian parallel to the killing of the great bull in the initiation rites of the Pharaoh which conveyed immortality and true sovereignty upon him: "It was from the Field of Reeds that the Pharaoh's soul set off to meet the sun in heaven, to be guided by it to the Field of Offerings. At first, this ascent was no easy matter. In spite of his divine character, the Pharaoh had to fight the guardian of the 'Field', the [Bull of Offerings], for the right to take up his abode in heaven. The Pyramid texts refer to this heroic testing-of an initiatory character-which the Pharaoh had to undergo" (Eliade, *Patterns*, 139-140). Mithra/s, as we will see further, is the god whose mythic path must be walked by the king in order for him to become a bridge between heaven and earth for his people, to gain the Golden Glory of Sovereignty and immortality.

Looking, then, at the pattern we have uncovered in the epics and mythologies of Europe and India, and in particular in the path of the Lawful Sovereign, the Mitra archetype, it is difficult to ignore the similarities between that narrative and the one proposed by Cumont and Evola for the path of Mithras in his mysteries. Our mythical Mitraic path seems to be remarkably similar to Evola's proposed initiatic Mithraic path. Both Cumont/Evola's narrative and our own can be called products of speculative reconstruction, yet the similarities must be recognized all the same. As we have summed up the clarified meaning of the *Iliad* narrative, for one, the Mitraic hero Menelaus begins, symbolically speaking, in a state of naivety wedded to the beautiful Helen, which we have identified as the marriage of the god of early morning sky with the goddess of Dawn (or a similar goddess), or the God of Sovereignty married to the goddess of the Regal Glory, the golden glow of Dawn being the same as the golden glow of the *Hvareno* mentioned by Evola. The Sun God figure, Paris, then steals this Dawn princess away from Menelaus, which in esoteric terms is the breaking up of the primordial unity by birth, the divine spark separating from the pleroma and entering the world which is ruled by the Sun as lord over Time and Samsara. Menelaus then marshals all his allied forces and, significantly, crosses the waters of the Aegean sea, as Mithras too crosses the waters. Menelaus is shot by Pandarus, but does not succumb, a symbolic death from which he presumably returns more determined in his mission. This "temporary or symbolic death" episode is made much more explicit in the parallel tale of Lleu Llaw Gyffes, in which Lleu is temporarily killed by Gronw, and then flies in the form of an eagle to the top of an otherworldly tree, from which his wounded or dead body drops carrion onto the ground. It is made even more explicit in the death of Norse Baldr. This is esoterically the state of death which allows the shedding of the material shell. Lleu's perching on the otherworldly tree and subsequent regeneration also seems to parallel the point at which Mithras encounters the tree from which he gains divine food and new clothing. Menelaus duels Paris and Lleu duels Gronw (though the order of the duel and the wounding are reversed in each case), in which confrontation the Mitraic hero bests his nemesis the Sun God with his Spear of Justice. For Menelaus, he must wait until later for Paris to be finished off, to kill Helen's second foreign husband, and ultimately to repossess Helen. But in the case of Lleu, his spear pierces the stone shield of Gronw, killing him on the spot. Gwydion turns Lleu's wife into a lunar bird, the owl, as punishment, perhaps signifying the glow of dawn undergoing a nightly penance before its reunion with the Mitraic King of Morning the next day/cycle. In the end, each figure, whether Yudhishthira, Menelaus, or Lleu/Lugh, confronts and overcomes the Sun God hero, and kills whoever has cuckolded him (the exception being in *Mahabharata,* where Yudhishthira has Arjuna kill his solar nemesis Karna for him just after Karna badly wounds Yudhishthira). As the Roman Sun God yields and offers Mithra a pact of friendship, remember Bres being spared by Lugh after their battle, in one version of the Irish myth, in exchange for knowledge of agriculture. Moreover, as Mitra is born in a rock, Lleu is placed into a chest immediately after birth.

Not only do these Mitraic figures confront and overcome the Sun God, they also sometimes (in the *Iliad* and *Mahabharata* at least, which represent an archaic stratum) lead the forces that overcome Father Sky, or rather his incarnation. For Father Sky, as a god too neutral and distant, perhaps even too primordial, to be seen as a god of society, is relegated in the great wars of these branches to the side of the gods of Fate and Time, the ambivalent gods who are positioned as obstacles to the gods of ordered society. In Father Sky's case, whether he is found in his incarnations Bhishma or Sarpedon, he is reluctant to fight the heroes of society and has no animosity toward them, but is forced to fight them due to his bonds of alliance with the other non-societal heroes. In Bhishma's case, he is even the societal heroes' uncle, and tries his best not to kill them in battle, until at last they have to slay him and he dispenses to them an extended outpouring of wisdom about Dharma and good rulership. Thus the societal gods' confrontation and slaying of Father Sky (particularly in *Mahabharata*) is not one of animosity, but of circumstance and of Fate itself. However, the scenes of Bhishma and Sarpedon's deaths do not appear similar in their details to the Mithraic tauroctonies, unless we say that the bull returning to his cave is reminiscent of Sarpedon and Bhishma both being returned to their native soil after death. Hence, this comparison of tauroctony to the death of the Sky Father is difficult to make. The imagistic details simply may have been changed beyond recognition between the different cases, the sky god reduced to his barest symbolic form as the great bull in the Mithraic case, or the comparison may not hold in the end. Nonetheless, we still must observe the fact that in the epic myths themselves the Mitraic

505

God-hero confronts the Sun God-hero in order to regain his *Hvareno* or sovereign glow of glory/wife, also sometimes leads the confrontation of Father Sky, known as the Bull of Heaven, and that in the end of each myth this same Mitraic figure is either the only one to attain immortality and to reach Paradise, or is accompanied by one of the Horse Twins (i.e. Diomedes in the *Iliad*) who has made his own path to immortality as well (a pair of torch-bearing twins also appear on many reliefs of Mithras, called Cautes and Cautopates).

This would only be expected if we consider the fact that Mitra is the paragon of the just ruler, the ideal king, even called by the cover name *Dharma* in the *Mahabharata*. He is the natural possessor of the *Khvarenah*, without which his kingship would not be blessed and his society would not flourish. The apparent derivation of Mithras' name from the Iranic Mithra should be indication enough, as well, that he too derives from the Mitraic archetype of the Lawful Sovereign, *somehow* (how this derivation occurred historically is what is most controversial), Mithra retaining much importance still in Avestan texts as a great sovereign and warrior, with the longest Yasht of the *Avesta* devoted to him.

There is a tendency in current scholarship to judiciously deny that direct links between the Mithraic Mysteries and the Iranic religion are demonstrable. However, this tendency seems to us based largely on a lack of information regarding the Mitraic mythos as a whole. Not enough is left of this mythos in the *Rig Veda* and Iranic *Avesta* alone, and it requires a full comparative reconstruction, as we have attempted, in order to visualize *why* this Roman god bears the name of the Iranic Mithra. Could it then be that the framework of the Mithraic mysteries was after all *not* invented whole cloth, as some believe, not simply a wild deviation or a fantastical bit of oriental fetishism, but that somehow at its core it was derived from a mythic and religious narrative framework which seems to have been widespread and deeply ingrained across Europe and Western Asia, if not always spelled out for us in the records? Could it be that the Mithraic mysteries derived their general narrative framework from the archaic Indo-European mythological narrative itself, from the clearly central and important path of the great Sovereign of Justice, the Mitraic god? If so, then we can also deduce immediately that this path was, in its original (perhaps pre-Romanized) form, a path reserved for the Sovereign, the king being the one who must follow the mythic path trod by Mitra/Lugh/Menelaus himself.

Jaan Lahe, in his "Mitra-Mithra-Mithras: The Roman Mithras And His Indo-Iranian Background," charts a prudent path between the extremes of seeing the Mithraic Mysteries as either being a direct import of a complete Iranic cult and seeing them as having no relation to the Iranic religion other than the name of the god. Evola and Cumont's reconstructions may be said to be approximations, not exact or complete, and

506

only give us a framework from which to assess possible parallels and lost esoteric meanings. Lahe puts it well when he explains that the coexistence of a set of motifs ("connection of Mitra/Mithras with friendship and a contract of friendship; certain military traits; connection with cosmogony and the cosmic order; connection with light, the Sun and the chariot of Sol; the role of the god as a giver of water and fertility; the idea of a sacrifice that stimulates fertility") "in the mythology of the Roman cult of Mithras cannot be a coincidence but testifies to the wider Indo-Iranian background of the central figure of the cult, the god Mithras, which should not be ignored even if the Roman cult of Mithras is viewed as a new cult that evolved in the Roman Empire and within the context of the Greco-Roman religion" (Lahe, "Mitra-Mithra-Mithras: The Roman Mithras And His Indo-Iranian Background"). Whether the cult of Mithras was a new creation by Romans rather than an import of actual Iranic cult *practices* is not our dispute at present. We only would add support to the idea that the existence of this set of motifs connected both to the Roman Mithras and Indo-Iranic Mitra/Mithra cannot have been coincidence, but that what was admittedly a new Roman formation must have been at minimum inspired by Iranic iconography, mythology, or theology, and more than that is possible given the cultural interchange of the Roman empire, as Lahe implies. While Cumont's optimism about Roman Mithraism being a full and direct theological borrowing from Iranian religion seems untenable to most scholars today, including Lahe, Lahe concludes fairly, saying, "we cannot prove that Mithras' mysteries grew out of the Iranian religion, as was argued by Cumont and Widengren, but nevertheless similar features of those two deities allow one to talk about the contribution of Iranian (or, more broadly, Indo-Iranian) mythology to the emergence of the new god in the era of the Roman Empire" (Lahe, 491).

The idea that this path was originally intended for the King matches what we know of ancient initiatic cults and sovereignty rituals, which in the most archaic times were elitist and reserved only for the High Priest-King, the King considered as originally also the central High Priest. Kershaw speaks of the Iranic "New Year's feast, Mithragin, when the king performs a ritual dance and becomes (ritually) intoxicated on the 'golden water' of which only the king and his eldest son may drink" (Kershaw, 309). For when we look at the Mithraic Mysteries, it is odd to consider that this religion, seemingly practiced by the general populous, bears the name of a king of the gods, and outlines a path to ontological elevation which, in the myths, even the other high gods or god-heroes, besides the Mitraic god or hero, fail to attain. It must then be that this archaic Mitraic path was gradually appropriated, following the widespread democratization of religion and initiatic cults leading up to and including the Roman Age, by the military and civic layers of society, particularly via Mithras' strong association with war and law, as a leader of soldiers and a god of justice. Eliade explains:

In fact, we have actually seen how the idea that immortality was something heroic, requiring initiation, offered to a handful of privileged persons who could win it by a struggle, turned into an idea that immortality was given to all privileged persons. Osiris [compare the Soma god as his IE parallel] developed this profound change in the notion of immortality further in the direction of 'democracy': anyone could attain immortality by emerging victorious from the trial [perhaps this Osirian event relates also to the Soma god helping the Horse Twins gain immortality]. The theology of Osiris took up and developed the notion of trial as a sine qua non of after life; but for the heroic, initiatory type of trial (the struggle with the Bull) [compare the Mithraic Mysteries], it substituted trials of an ethical and religious nature (good works and so on). The archaic theory of heroic immortality gave way to a new conception, humbler and more human. (Eliade, *Patterns*, 141)

As a god of war (like Tyr and Lugh), Mithra would have been well-known and loved by soldiers of all levels, and over time he must have been seen as their patron and ideal leader. Hence, by the time of the Roman Empire and the rise to the light of day of the Mithraic Mysteries, the path once reserved only for the King himself must have emerged, perhaps containing a germ of, or at least being inspired by, genuine Iranic sacred practices of some kind, and become a path for, if not the common man *per se*, then at least for any soldier of sovereign mind, even if not sovereign birth. If indeed the mythic pattern we find in Menelaus' story in the *Iliad*, in Yudhishthira's story in the *Mahabharata*, in Lugh/Lleu's story in Irish myth, and divided between the Tyr and Baldr's stories in Norse myth, is the underlying framework, perhaps half-forgotten but culturally ingrained on a deeper level, of the Mithraic Mysteries, and if this root framework originally was the framework of the esoteric path of the strata of society represented by the Mitraic archetype, that is, the sovereign and sometimes priestly caste, then perhaps we may say that the Mithraic Mysteries represent the survival, indirect and altered in whatever degree, of a genuine archaic path, once seen as eminently actualizable, and as absolutely necessary for the king, whose role is to center his society and to act as a bridge between this world and the realm of the divine. This then would be the Kingly Path of Immortality, the Solar Mitraic Path of Divinization.

Mitra, King Arthur and Theseus

As an expansion of this idea we must offer two further targets for comparison. First, having looked at the Mithraic Mysteries and at the mysteries of the Holy Grail, we must further investigate the resonances of this broad pattern to the other legends related to the Holy Grail, specifically those involving King Arthur and Merlin. If we take once more the pattern we have here compared to the Mithraic Mysteries, that of the ideal Sovereign of Justice, who is particularly known for being cuckolded, but also specifically for marshaling and uniting his armies and pursuing his enemies, winning peace and victory for his kingdom by making the climactic kill in battle, and at some point dying or symbolically dying, often near water, under mystical circumstances, only to rise again (or in Lugh's case, being drowned in a lake with only the vague possibility of returning one day) in order to rule in peace and justice and even attain the golden age, to reintegrate the *Khvarenah* and gain Elysium and immortality, then we begin to come strangely close to that dominant later legendary pattern of medieval Welsh and French literature, the story of Arthur.

We must clarify first that, depending on the story, the figure of Arthur may be a stand-in for different sovereign deities. We have seen that in Chretien de Troye's Grail poem Arthur more closely stands in for Odinn, and that poem seems to reflect a more Germanic mythic milieu blending with a Celtic one. Other tales of Arthur may reflect other sovereign gods, the gist being that Arthur usually stands for "The King of the Gods," whoever that may be in a given context, and in Irish myth, for instance, there are *at least* three of these: Lugh, Nuada and Dagda. However, Arthur has one central mythos that became the most well-known and fleshed-out over time, one in which he figures as the central character, rather than as a side character as in the Grail poem. In this most well-known form, elements of which occur early on but which was summed up and codified by Thomas Malory in his *Le Morte d'Arthur*, Arthur manifests clearly the Mitraic divinity.

Arthur, like Lugh and Yudhishthira, is known as a just king, destined to bring peace and victory, but is specifically depicted as a uniter, the great Round Table an explicit symbol of the ideal unification of his knights and nobles, of his allies and of his realm in general, brought into balance. It is the Mitraic *yatayati* in action, it is the great *contract* of *friendship* in a visual symbol of a perfected warrior-aristocratic order, balanced and unified by the perfect sovereign, opposites united and brought into alliance. Arthur too is conspicuously cuckolded by a young and handsome knight, one who is supposedly his ally, just as, for instance, Paris is at first the ally of Menelaus before betraying him, or as

Karna and Dhritarashtra are the ally of Yudhishthira before opposing and tricking him, or Bres the ally of the Tuatha de Danann before opposing Lugh and his people in war. And why, we must ask ourselves, why all these cuckolded kings? Why all these kings cuckolded by their exceedingly handsome young allies, kings who happen to be models of justice and social unity, and who, as Arthur does, die in a mystical manner with the idea that they will return to rule in a golden age, Arthur taken bodily to Avalon across the water as Lugh is plunged into it?

We have seen that Merlin, as the wise wizard and advisor of Arthur is reminiscent of no figure more than the wily Welsh Óðinnic magician god Gwydion, who raises Lleu as a kind of foster son (though in reality he may have been his *actual* son), tricks Lleu's mother into giving him his name and birthrights, magically revives Lleu when he is mortally wounded on the tree, and punishes Blodeuwedd by transforming her into an owl when they catch up to her. Evola even marks, in his "Mithraic Mysteries," the fact that King Arthur's sword in the stone is likely to carry the same symbolism as Mithras' birth from the stone. The divine spark or virile principle must be broken free from the prison of rock which is its foundational starting point in order to begin to progress toward spiritual perfection. If this train of thought can be pursued in earnest and with honest appraisal, then we may arrive at the conclusion that the totality of the great archaic mythological pattern which we have laid out thus far, stretching seemingly back multiple millennia even to before the time of the division of the Indo-European branches, has formed the structural spiritual basis for the Mithraic Mysteries, the Holy Grail, and the legends of King Arthur generally, not to mention once again the great epics such as the *Iliad*. If so, then this mythical foundation must have been widespread and deeply ingrained indeed, providing the very forms by which our ancestors in ancient times approached spiritual questions, and giving them, time and again, the paths which constituted their hopes for spiritual perfection.

Second, the legend regarding the Greek Athenian hero Theseus (Plutarch, *Parallel Lives,* "Theseus") comes into view as yet another story of this same type. This is interesting in particular as Dumezil points out in his *Mitra-Varuna* how Plutarch placed Theseus and Lycurgus in contrast with one another, but with Theseus as a "Varunian" hero, a founder via his brute force, contrasted with the famous lawgiver Lycurgus, supposedly "Mitraic." Dumezil straightaway points out that this is merely a surface level contrast, however, which can be instructive but should not be carried too far. When the similarities between Theseus' legend and the other Mitraic myths is analyzed, the Plutarchian opposition in fact comes to appear quite ironically misleading. This may once again be due to the paradoxical nature of the Lawful Sovereign, a warrior as much as a pious lawgiver, or may again be due to the blending of Varunian traits into the Mitraic which appears sometimes to happen.

The parallels between Theseus and the other Mitraic figures turn out to be far from negligible. Theseus is born to a father, Aegeus, who dies by leaping into the sea, thus becoming one with it and also giving the sea its name (the Aegean). Theseus is conceived, however, when his mother Aethra, who has lain with Aegeus, pours a libation to Poseidon and that god is said to impregnate her in response. Aegeus himself had previously been unable to conceive a child, and so Aethra's appeal to the god solves his problem. Thus Theseus has two sea-associated fathers, and not only that but he is conceived in much the same way that the Pandava heroes in the *Mahabharata* are conceived, when their parents, struggling with childlessness, pray to various deities and these deities thus become spiritual fathers to the children they subsequently bestow directly on their mother. As Yudhishthira's father Pandu is an incarnation of the god of sovereignty, sky and water, Varuna, so Theseus is son of the namesake of the Aegean Sea, and spiritual son of the Sea God Poseidon. In the Indian version, being the spiritual son of the Sea God would make him an incarnation of that god, and with Poseidon being a much closer match to the temperamental and water-centric Varuna this would give more weight to the idea that Theseus is a Varunian rather than Mitraic hero. But the two methods of portraying how this spiritual parentage worked, the Indian and the Greek, clearly are not a perfect match, and a much closer identity seems to be drawn between Poseidon and Aegeus in this myth. This point is supported also by the fact that Aegeus, just like the Varunian incarnation Pandu, is unable to beget children, resulting in his wife having to look to the gods for this office. If anything, Theseus' parentage shows once again the potential slippage between the Varunian and Mitraic archetypes, while most of the actual details of Theseus' life mark him as primarily Mitraic. In fact, Pittheus, who is father of Aethra, and so grandfather of Theseus, may be a stand in for the Pushanic deity and indeed stands in nearly the same relationship to Theseus that the Pushanic Gwydion does to the Mitraic Lleu. Pittheus, Theseus' grandfather while Cian/Gwydion is the father/foster-father of Lugh/Lleu, is said to be very pious, was the instructor of Theseus, and was known for his great wisdom. He is called pure and holy, is associated with the unfailing payment of pledges, and is skilled in interpreting oracles, while the Pushanic god is of the first rank in the art of prophecy, Pan having taught prophecy to Apollo and Gwydion being one of the three great prognosticators of Britain. Pittheus is also an expert in speaking, while Gwydion is "the best teller of tales in the world" (Lugh's grandfather is also the god of speech, *Cainte*, "speech," aka Dian Cecht, and there could be slippage between these archetypes in the figure of Pittheus. Still, the "Pushanic" divinity seems the more likely option due to the mentorship pattern repeating with Gwydion/Lleu and the other traits mentioned). Pittheus also is the one who causes Aegeus to sleep with Pittheus' daughter on the same night that daughter is raped by Poseidon. This trick of Pittheus ensures that Aegeus will take Theseus as his heir. We must recall that Merlin similarly uses a ruse to help Uther lay with Igraine in order to conceive Arthur, and that Gwydion tricks Math into leaving in order to allow Gilfaethwy to rape Goewin. Thus the tutelage of Theseus by Pittheus is very reminiscent of that of Lleu by Gwydion or that of Arthur by Merlin, and seems to stand here in precisely the same mytho-syntactic slot.

Aegeus leaves Theseus and his mother before Theseus is grown, and leaves behind a sword and pair of shoes under a great stone. He tells Aethra that if Theseus is able to lift this stone and receive sword and shoes when he grows to manhood that he should then be sent to Aegeus to claim his birthright as heir to the throne. When he is of age, Theseus lifts the stone and retrieves sword and shoes. This episode is a clear and obvious parallel to the Arthurian sword-in-the-stone motif, which we have pointed out falls in line also with the Mithraic motif of the breaking of the rock into which Mithras is born. When he arrives at Aegeus' palace, Theseus is opposed in the acquisition of his birthright by his father's wife and queen Medea, who even sends him to capture the great Marathonian Bull in the hope that he will die in the attempt. He succeeds however, sacrifices the bull, and is then reunited with his father (after one last unsuccessful attempt on his life by Medea), and Theseus gains his birthright and becomes heir to his father's throne.

Medea's opposition to Theseus gaining his birthright is highly reminiscent of the Welsh Arianrhod's opposition to the naming and arming of Lleu Llaw Gyffes in the *Mabinogion*. Arianrhod, mother of Lleu, places a series of magical *tyngedau* on Lleu to prevent him from being named, then from being given arms, then from marrying a woman of any earthly race. However, Lleu and Gwydion outwit her each time, eventually gaining Lleu all three of these markers of the full acquisition of manhood and maturity: proper name, arms, and wife. In both cases, the frightening maternal figures act as testers of the young heroes, guardians of manhood who must be overcome in order for the youths to gain their full identities, maturity, and places in the sovereign succession.

On his way to the palace, Theseus also encounters a series of deadly chthonian bandits, all of whom he kills in the same manner that they treated their victims, thus exercising precise justice and fitting his punishments to their crimes. The episode therefore demonstrates three things essential to the Mitraic character: that he is a carrier out of strict justice, in the form of retribution both precise and unswerving; that he is a hero of a wide array of skills; and that he is a uniter and improver of the kingdom, cleansing the criminals and forces of chaos from the region (Mithra is called "the best cleanser of these creatures" in the *Avesta, Mihr Yasht,* 92). He beats one bandit with a club, tears one in half between two trees, pushes one off a cliff, defeats one at wrestling, uses the famous bed of Procrustes to cut off the legs and head of the bandit that is its namesake, and kills a great pig. Though these feats are all relatively closely related to the skills of combat, they may connect to the concept found in the title of Irish Lugh, *Samildanach*, the concept of the many-skilled god. Theseus' entry into the palace just

512

after this display of various feats is reminiscent of Lugh's entrance into the court of the Irish gods when he is made to list his many competencies.

Theseus' entrance into court disrupts the planned succession to the throne of another court member, Pallas, as Lugh perhaps similarly takes the presumptive heir position under Nuada which Bres had held but had been forced out of. Bres' ejection from his temporary kingship incites the Great War in which Bres and the Fomorians are killed, while Pallantides and his sons' displacement from the sovereign succession leads to a fight in which Theseus and Aegeus massacre the Pallantides even as they attempt his assassination. Theseus kills both the Marathonian Bull, and sacrifices it, as mentioned, and later, the half-bull Minotaur, as Mithras in his most central depiction is shown killing the previously discussed great bull. This may be the most imagistically striking correspondence of all, and may even suggest that the Theseus legend was a possible forerunner of this particular Mithraic detail, or at least that the two myths share a common deeper origin. The fact that this Mitraic hero, Theseus, is so involved in bull killing as well as bull sacrificing, is itself a powerful argument that Roman Mithras is not at all out of place performing such a sacrifice. Theseus is also known prominently as a uniter, responsible for the synoecism that led to the growth and ascension of Athens (the cleansing of the bandits is often taken as symbolic of this process of the creation of order and unity). Mitra, of course, is prominently the god of uniting, via contracts, alliances, and friendship, as we have seen in a clear case in King Arthur, for one. The name "Theseus" comes from a word meaning "rule," "precept," or "institution," associating him closely with the law-guided nature of the Lawful Sovereign archetype, the one who establishes the ordered institutions and regulates the law. Later in his legend, Theseus comes to *believe* he has been cuckolded by his wife Phaedra (with his own son by another woman), and, as we have seen, cuckolding in one form or another is a central theme of nearly every Mitraic hero. As Lleu and Baldr die temporarily and go to the Otherworld, while Lugh and Arthur die and are hinted to return one day, so Theseus also becomes trapped in Hades for a time. He too is ultimately rescued therefrom, as again both Lleu and Baldr are brought back from their temporary deaths and Otherworld imprisonments. Worth noting, Theseus also brings the *géranos*, or "Crane" Dance to Delos (Plutarch, *Parallel Lives*, "Theseus," 21), while Lugh dances what has been referred to as a Crane Dance before the Second Battle of Maige Tuired.

We can see from this brief outline that Theseus too has been formed out of the same Mitraic elements we have seen again and again. He has a water-associated paternal figure and an oracular tutor, he rescues sword from stone, demonstrates his many skills, gains his sovereign birthright, kills the bull, defeats the pretenders who would steal his throne, in this case *thinks* he has been cuckolded and gains revenge, is temporarily imprisoned in the underworld, but is brought back to rule once more, uniting his

513

kingdom and bringing peaceful flourishing. His actions symbolize both strict justice and the uniting forces of friendship and peace at once. He is once more the ideal king, the Dharmaraj, the Lawful Sovereign.

21

Conclusion

Thus, besides the path of the warrior caste strictly speaking, there are three paths to immortality – or ontological elevation – in Indo-European mythology which we should bear forever in mind. The first two of these are the Mitraic path of the King, who wins the golden age, the path of the lower gods, the Horse Twins, who rise to immortality and join the high gods as priests of their sacrifice. The first is a purely solar path which involves the sovereign god of the daylit sky overcoming the Sun God himself as the King overcomes and reintegrates the solar principle, leading to deification, immortality, and societal regeneration. Though seemingly democratized (and many would even argue hybridized and bastardized) over time into the Roman Mithraic Mysteries, we should consider that the *original form* of this path was at one point seen reverentially, as truly fit only for the sovereign or great hero, not to be trod by the unworthy and hubristic, and above all as a spiritual ideal with the capability of turning the king into a bridge to the gods, a center around which the kingdom and its spiritual aspirations could turn. The second path is one naturally within the purview of the common folk, that is, the producer class. The gods of the Third Function, somewhat as representatives of the people with whom they mingled, paved a road upward, leading to integration with the high rite. Their path, strictly speaking, is both lunar and solar: it is at the behest of and guided by the Moon God and god of the sacred liquid, Soma, and yet the Twins themselves are fairly solar or stellar in nature. They are associated with the time of sunrise and the morning star, and at least one of them, in the Veda, is said to be the harbinger of the sun, as night transitions into day. They ride in the solar chariot with the sun himself. But as Evola says, "In the "lunar" path […] what matters is to turn oneself into an obedient instrument of higher entities," which describes the character of the Grail mysteries quite well, as the quester makes himself a helper and subservient to the lunar Grail King. The Twins come as helpers but also as suppliants, just as the Grail quester does. They confront the high gods in order to assert their right to the sacrifice, but ultimately they are assisted by the Soma God himself in gaining this place and are installed as his instruments, as priests in an undertaking larger than themselves, serving rather than ruling. Simply asking the question of "whom does the grail *serve*" indicates the Grail quester's readiness for this position, his willingness not to simply assert himself as master, but to defer to the teaching of what is higher, and to take his proper role, one of service. The Horse Twins' initial question revealed to them by Sukanya is "in what way are we imperfect?" implying that they come to the high gods from a position of lack. When they arrive to the sacrifice, their riddling argument is that they are needed in the sacrifice because they constitute the "head" of the sacrifice. Hence they herein acknowledge their instrumental role, one part in a body of deities who together officiate the important office. The third path to ontological elevation, then, is that of the Rudraic God, who leads the way to the Blessed Isles, or whatever state of ultimate perfection they represent.

The semi-lunar character of the Grail myth may have been one reason that it was so readily christianized. Christianity being characterized by a thorough submission to that which is higher, while simultaneously being shaped by a marked degree of spiritual democratization in relation to the archaic elitist cults, the Grail quester, modeled on the gods of the third social caste or common folk, was a perfect representation of the ideal everyman Christian in his seeking of God's grace, of spiritual perfection as an instrument of his will, and of mystical absorption in his perfection.

Inevitably, both the Roman Mithraic Mysteries and the legends of the Holy Grail show signs of the democratization of ancient esoteric paths, the loosening of the elite exclusivity of access to the rites of immortality. If we peer back past the latest forms in which they have come down to us, we find that these are paths which demanded the utmost of the initiate, and, no matter who they were opened to, stood always as shining ideals that would only ever be achieved in their fullest sense by the blessed few.

Maps

Celtic – Vedic Direct Comparison:

Irish	Welsh	Vedic
Dagda	Matholwch	Dyaus(/Vayu)
Dagda Donn/Donn	Bran	Yama
Lugh	Lleu	Mitra
Nuada	Nudd/Lludd/Teyrnon	Varuna
Midir	Arawn	Soma
Aengus	Pryderi	Asvins
Dian Cecht	?	Brihaspati
Ogma/(Echdae)	Hefeydd/(Pwyll)	Gandharva
Cian	Gwydion/Culhwch	Pushan
Goibniu	Gofannon	Tvastr
Manannan	Manawydan	Agni
Aed	?	Agni
Etain	Wife of Arawn	Sukanya-Surya

Aine/Macha	Rhiannon	Tapati-Surya/Saranyu
Caer	Cigfa	Savirtri-Surya
Grian	Arianrhod	Surya (goddess)
Bres	Gronw	Surya (god)
Elatha	?	Surya (god)
Eithne-Boann	Cerridwen	Saraswati
Math/Mathu	Math	Savitr
?	Goewin	Ratri
Eriu	Branwen	Prthvi
Fionn/Eber Finn/Fintan	Efnysien-Nisien/Gwion-Taliesin/Gwyn	Rudra
Balor/Goll	Ysbaddaden	A rudra
Brigid	Blodeuwedd?	Ushas
Cuilleann	?	Rhibus
Morrigan-Danu	Don	Danu
Corrgend	?	Matarisvan
Fand	?	Svaha
Neit	?	Vishnu?
Nechtan	?	Apam Napat

Branch Cross-Comparison Map:

Title	Vedic	Norse	Irish	Welsh	Greek	Greek Epic	Vedic Epic	Norse Pseu.	Theseus	Welsh Pseu.	Arthurian/Grail
Priest of Invocation	Brihaspati	Oðinn	Dian Cecht		Paean-Apollo	Nestor	Drona				
Shepherd of the Wilds	Pūṣaṇ	Oðinn	Cian	Gwydion/Culhwch	Pan				Pittheus		Merlin
Priest of Fire	Agni	Oðinn	Manannan	Manawydan	Hephaestus	Neoptolemus?	Drishtadyumna				The Hermit
The Auspicious-Destroyer	Rudra-Siva	Oðinn-Hoenir	Fionn/Oisin/Fintan	Efnysien-Nisien/Gwyn/Gwion/Taliesin	Cronus/Apollo/Orpheus?	Diephobus-Helenus					
Destroyer Troop	The Rudras	The Ulfheðnar/Suttungr	The Fianna/Balor-Goll	Ysbaddaden	Cronus	Deiphobus	Ashwatthhama				
Terrible Sovereign	Varuṇa	Oðinn	Nuada	Lludd/Nudd/Teyrnon Tyrwf Lliant	Poseidon	Agamemnon	Pandu	Othinus	Aegeus	Morvidus	Uther
Lawful Sovereign	Mitrá	Tyr	Lugh	Lleu	Zeus	Menelaus	Yudhishthira	Mithothyn	Theseus	Gorbonianus	Arthur
God of Noble Society	Aryaman	Baldr	Erimon	Dylan?			Vidura				
Father Sky	Dyáuṣ Pitṛ	Ymir	The Dagda	Matholwch	Ouranos	Sarpedon	Bhishma				
Lord of Wind	Vāyu/Vata	Thor/Oðinn?	The Dagda		Heracles	Telamonian Ajax	Bhima			Elidurus	
Thunderer	Indrā	Thor	Tuireann	Taran	Heracles	Achilles	Arjuna			Archgallo	Kay
Horse Twin 1	Nāsatyā	Freyr	Aengus	Pryderi	Kastor/Oenopion	Diomedes	Nakula			Peredurus	Perceval/Peredur

519

Horse Twin 2	Dasra				Polydeukes/Staphylus	Odysseus	Sahadeva			Ingenius	
Sun God 1	Sūrya	Ullr	Bres/Cermait?	Gronw	Helios	Paris/Pandarus?	Karna	Ollerus	Pallas/Hippolytus		Lancelot
Sun God 2	Vivásvat	Alvaldi	Crom Cruach		Orion?		Sharyati?				The Red Knight
Elder Sun God	Sūrya	Egil-Aurvandil?	Elatha								
Soma Moon God 1	Soma	Njörðr	Midir	Arawn	Dionysus		Chyavana				Elder Grail King/Knight of the Tent
Soma Moon God 2	Soma	Kvasir	Glas Gaibhnenn	Trwch Trwyth?	Dionysus-Zagreus		Mada				
Gandharva	Viśvāvasu	Bragi	Ogma	Hefeydd/Pwyll	Hermes		Samvarana				Pelles the "Fisher King"
God of Destiny	Bhaga	Hoðr	Indech?		Zeus Moiragetes?	Priam	Dhritarashtra	Hotherus			King Lot
Dawn Goddess	Uṣás	Freyja	Brigid	Blodeuwedd?	Eos	Helen	Draupadi?		Phaedra		Guinevere
Moon	Chandra	Mani			Selene						
Daughter of the Sun	Sūrya	Iðunn/Skaði/Gerðr/Sol	Etain/Aine/Caer/Grian	Wife of Arawn/Rhiannon/Cigfa/Arianrhod	Charites/Ariadne/Leucippides/Persephone?		Tapati/Sukanya/Savitri				Grail Maiden/Blanchefleur/Lady of the Tent
Demon of the Last Age	Kali	Loki				Hector	Duryodhana				Agravain/Mordred
Nephew of the Waters	Apām Napāt	Heimdallr	Nechtan								
Sea God		Aegir	Lir	Llyr	Pontus						

Lunar Sorceress		Gullveig	Fuamnach								Prophetic Woman
Lord of the Dead	Yáma	Mimir	Donn	Bran	Hades		Dadhyanc?				
Demon of Dwapara Yuga							Shakuni				
Thief of Fire	Matarisvan		Corrgend		Prometheus						
Seabird Goddess			Tethra		Athena						
Goddess of Beauty	Svaha?		Fand		Aphrodite						
River Goddess	Saraswati-Vac	Gunnloð	Enthniu-Boand	Cerridwen/Olwen	Rhea						
Earth Goddess	Prthvi	Jorð	Eriu	Branwen	Gaia	Prtha-Kunti					
Craftsman	Tvastr	The Dwarves	Goibniu, Creidhne, Luchtaine	Gofannon	The Cyclopes						
Artisans	The Rbhus	The Elves/The Sons of Ivaldi	Cuilenn		The Telchines?						
Sun God Impeller	Savitr	Dellinr	Mathu/Math	Math	Phanes						
Goddess of Night	Ratri	Nott		Goewin	Nyx						
Mother of Waters	Danu		Danu-Morrigan	Don							
The Fates		The Norns	The Cailleach/Milucradh/Birog		The Moirai/Daphne						

Appendix: Notes on Tvastr = Dwarves

The list of correspondences below points to an identification of: Vedic Cosmic Craftsman God **Tvastr** = The Irish **Tri Dee Dana** (Goibniu, Creidne, Luchra) = The Norse **Dwarves** = The Greek **Cyclopes** (Brontes, Steropes, Arges).

– Tvastr made Indra's lightning weapon the *Vajra*. Dwarves made thunder god Thor's *Mjolnir*.

– Tvastr specifically engages in a smithing contest against the Rbhus, a rival group of smiths. Dwarves compete in a smithing contest against The Sons of Ivaldi, who themselves are referred to as Dwarves but also set apart as *svartalfar*, both by Snorri in different parts of his account. The items that the two groups of smiths make have been shown to have a close parallel to the items that the Rbhus vs Tvastr make in their contest.[287]

– Tvastr is the "Omniform," implying a shape-changing power that is central to what he is. Dwarves are shapeshifters, into animals, for instance. They are also an entire race, a multiplicity, which could correspond to the idea of having all or multiple forms.

– Tvastr's attendants are the wives of the other gods, possibly due to his role in embryo creation and childbirth. Dwarves famously sleep with Freyja, a wife of one of the gods.

– Tvastr creates the cup that holds the *soma* and it is stolen from him. Odrerir, the cup that holds the mead, is a possession of the Dwarves Fjalar and Galar, and it is stolen from them. Directly analogous events occur in parallel myths about the theft of the sacred liquid in other branches. In the Irish version of this myth the *soma*/mead is

---

[287]   See: Viktor Rydberg, *Investigations into Germanic Mythology,* "The Results of the Judgment Passed on the Works of Art Produced by the Ivalde Sons. Parallel Myths in Rigveda".

represented by a wondrous cow, and it is stolen from its owner, Goibniu the Smith God (whose name simply means "smith"), who is a much more obvious parallel of Tvastr. The rest of this myth precisely parallels Odinn's retrieval of the mead, as we have seen, making the parallel of the Dwarves with Goibniu very conspicuous, as the theft occurs in the analogous position in each myth. Odrerir, the mead cup, is stolen from the Dwarves, and *then* Odin has to retrieve it. The Cow is stolen from Goibniu and Cian, and *then* Cian has to retrieve it. The cup of *soma* is stolen from Tvastr, and *then* is retrieved by Agni-Pushan, as we have noted above. A direct line is thus established between these smith divinities in this set of myths.

– Tvastr is an artificer of the material cosmos and is the creator of human and animal forms, forming the embryos in the womb. Scholars such as John Lindow suggest that the Dwarves may have had a role in creating the bodies of the first pair of humans before the gods give them soul. Dwarves may also have a role in forming the cosmos considering the fact that they appear conspicuously in the primordial scene, their skills of craftwork would fit the task of building out creation, and the placement of their list of names toward the beginning of *Voluspa* suggests a link to the cosmogenic events that are there described. As such, Viktor Rydberg considered the dwarf Sindri to be the world-artist.

– In the Greek branch, the parallel deity-type is also represented as a race rather than a single god: the Cyclopes, who also forge the lightning weapon. Specifically, there are three most central named Cyclops brothers who work in the Fire God Hephaestus' forge with him, and these then parallel directly the three smith god brothers in Irish myth, the Tri Dee Dana, Goibniu, Creidne, and Luchra. Thus we can see the range of fluctuation from "one" Omniform deity in Vedic, to three brothers in Irish, to a whole race (though almost always showing up as pairs of brothers, such as Fjalar and Galar or Sindri and Brokkr) in Norse, and in Greek appearing both as a race and as three specific brothers. In Irish, these smiths are also set aside as a group unto themselves within the larger group of gods, as they have their own classification, the *tri dee dana*, "the three gods of skill," also called the *aos dana*. The idea that Tvastr is "Omniform" could even extend to the fact that he can manifest in multiples or singly, can take multiple forms. Quantity-multiplying would be a type of shape-changing. This fluctuation is also no different than the case of the Gandharvas, who appear as a whole race in Vedic, but as only one deity in the closely related Iranic branch, despite bearing the nearly identical name, and again usually as one deity in the other branches.

– Tvastr has a strange hostility or tension with some of the gods and scholars have speculated that he was from a different group or tribe of gods, according to A. A. Macdonell in his *Vedic Mythology*. The Dwarves are of course a separate race, which matches this concept of the smith(s) being from a group of separate divinities. The Cyclopes are as well. And the setting apart of the Irish *tri dee dana* via this label may mark a similar concept.

– Essentially every time we find a specific Norse parallel of a role in a myth that Goibniu or Tvastr take in the Greek and Irish branches, the Dwarves await us there in the Norse version. In an odd coincidence, Tvastr wields an axe. Despite the fact that axes may not have a genuine connection to mythological Dwarves, it is interesting how Tvastr is the Axe God considering the ubiquitous popular image of Dwarves today as axe wielders in works of fantasy. Finally, why should the Dwarves not be the parallel of Tvastr? As Tvastr is the great smith of the Vedic religion, the Dwarves are the smiths of Norse myth, next only to Volundr, who is an elf, while we have seen a potential alignment of the Elves/Sons of Ivaldi instead with the Vedic craftsmen the Rbhus, the Irish smith Cuilleann, and possibly the Greek Telchines (in the theory of Carla O'Harris, see: "The Telchines, the Ur-tsunami, and Atlantis: An Investigation").

– In Welsh myth, the father of Efnysien (Rudra, Odinn, etc.) is Euroswydd. His name means "gold enemy," which sounds somewhat like a kenning for a dragon, and he is said to imprison Llyr, the God of the Sea. As such, and considering that his myth appears in the mists of the pre-creation phase, he may be the parallel of Vedic Vrtra, the monster or dragon who imprisons the cosmic waters, and who is surprisingly also depicted as a Brahmin in the Brahmanas. In the Norse case, Odinn's father is Borr, who would then parallel this Euroswydd, as Efnysien and Odinn are the same. Borr's father is then Búri/Buri. Buri is also the name of a dwarf in *Voluspa* 13, and so we can say that Odinn's grandfather *could* be a dwarf if we momentarily disregard the differing accent sometimes found in the orthography of the names. If Odinn's grandfather Buri is a dwarf, this would require that Snorri is speaking vaguely when he does not mention this Buri being of the race of dwarves and the tale he tells of Buri being licked out of the ice would have to be a variant account of the generation of the rest of the Dwarf race. The father of Vedic Vrtra, meanwhile, is Tvastr, who we are arguing parallels the Dwarves. Thus the Welsh and Norse genealogies would align on this interpretation. In Welsh: an unnamed figure who we would assume to be the Welsh Tvastr (presumably Gofannon) we can postulate as the father of Euroswydd, the "gold enemy" deity who imprisons the waters of the cosmic sea, and Euroswydd is father of Efnysien. In Norse: a being named

524

Buri is father of Borr, who is father of Odinn. Once again, where we might expect a Tvastr parallel in the Norse case, we have a name that mysteriously echoes that of a dwarf, Buri. This point of course strains speculation. It is also hard to know from the existing extremely sparse evidence if Borr and Euroswydd are identical, and it may not be necessary that they be so, as the grandfathers of Odinn/Efnysien (Buri and the theorized Gofannon) could be the more important element that has remained consistent here. Furthermore, this reading could prove one more piece of the Creation Myth puzzle. Gofannon (?) > Euroswydd > Efnysien. Buri > Borr > Odinn.

– Dwarves are said to live in rocks while Cyclopes live in caves.

– We note finally a mysterious similarity between the Proto-Indo-European root of *Tvastr* and the various roots of *Dwarf*. The PIE root of *dwarf* appears to be unknown, and the similarities between the etymologies below are either ignored or considered by linguists to present definite difficulties. However, the mythic similarities above suggest that a linguistic concordance between *dwarf* and *Tvastr* should be considered.

Dwarf:

Proto-Germanic: **dwergaz*, whose PIE root is unknown

Old Norse: *dvergr*

Old High German: *twerc*

Tvastr:

PIE: **twrk̑-tēr* from PIE **twerk̑-* ("to cut, trim, carve off")

The relationship of Fire God (top) to the Smiths (bottom) would then be as follows:

Agni	Manannan	Hephaestus	Odinn
Tvastr "The Omniform"	The Tri Dee Dana: Goibniu, Creidne, Luchra	The Cyclopes: Brontes, Steropes, Arges	The Dwarves: Fjalar and Galar, Brokkr and Sindri

525

Selected Works Cited

"Yr Afallennau"

Aelian, *Tactics*

Aiyangar, Narayan, *Essays on Indo-Aryan Mythology*

Allen, Nick and Roger D. Woodard, *"Hermes and Gandharvas,"* 2014

Apastamba, *Grihya Sutra*

Ashley, Mike, *The Mammoth Book of King Arthur*

Atharvaveda

Athenaios, *Deipnosophistae*

Beekes, R. S. P., *Etymological Dictionary of Greek, Brill, 2009.*

Britannica.com

Bromwich, Rachel, *Trioedd Ynys Prydein*

Carey, John and John T. Koch, *Celtic Heroic Age*

Carmody, Isolde, www.storyarchaeology.com

Castorion of Soli, *Fragment*

Cath Maige Tuired, tr. Elizabeth Gray

Clement of Alexandria, *Fragments of Heraclitus*

Collitz, Hermann, *Wodan, Hermes und Pushan,* 1924.

Curtin, Jeremiah, *Hero-Tales of Ireland, "Balor of the Evil Eye and Lui Lavada his Grandson"*

Daimler, Morgan, *Cath Maige Tuired: A Full English Translation*

Danielou, Alain, *The Myths and Gods of India*

Davidson, Hilda Ellis, *Gods and Myths of Northern Europe*

Demetrius, *On Style*

SELECTED WORKS CITED

Dietrich, Bernard, *The Origin of Greek Religion*

Doniger, Wendy, *The Rig Veda*

Dronke, Ursula, *The Poetic Edda*

Dumezil, Georges, *Archaic Roman Religion*

Dumezil, Georges, *Destiny of a Warrior*

Dumezil, Georges, *Gods of the Ancient Northmen*

Dumezil, Georges, *Mitra-Varuna*

Dumezil, Georges, *The Plight of a Sorcerer*

Egeler, Matthias, *Celtic Influences in Germanic Religion*

Egyptian Book of the Dead

Eliade, Mircea, *Patterns in Comparative Religion*

Eratosthenes, *Catasterismi*

Euripides, *Rhesus*

Evans-Wentz, Walter, *Fairy-Faith in Celtic Countries*

Ewing, Thor, *"Óðinn and Loki Among the Celts"*

Frame, Douglas, *Hippota Nestor*

Frame, Douglas, *The Myth of Return in Early Greek Epic*

Gantz, Jeffrey, *The Mabinogion*

Gonda, Jan, *Prajapati's Rise to Higher Rank*

Goodrich, Peter, *Merlin: A Casebook*

Grammaticus, Saxo, *Gesta Danorum*

Grassman, Hermann, *Wörterbuch zum Rig-Veda*

Gregory, Lady Augusta, *Gods and Fighting Men*

Griffith, Ralph T., *The Rig Veda*

Guest, Lady Charlotte, *The Mabinogion*

Hall, Alaric, "Gwŷr y Gogledd? Some Icelandic Analogues of Branwen Ferch Lŷr"

Harivamsa

Harrison, Jane Ellen, *Themis: A study to the Social origins of Greek Religion*

Heimskringla

Hermann Oldenberg, *Religion of the Vedas*

Herodotus, *Histories*

Hesiod, *Theogony*

Hesiod, *Works and Days*

Hewitt, *James Frances Katherinus*

Hill, J., *https://ancientegyptonline.co.uk/*

Hily, Gael, *Le Dieu Celtique Lugus*

His Three Calls to Cormac

Homer, *The Iliad*

Homer, *The Odyssey*

Homeric Hymn to Hermes

Jamison, Stephanie and Joel Brereton, *The Rig Veda*

Jamison, Stephanie and Joel Brereton, *The Rigveda: A Guide*

Jones and Ryan, *Encyclopedia of Hinduism*

Jones' Celtic Encyclopedia https://www.maryjones.us/jce/jce_index.html

Kausitaki Brahmana

Kerenyi, Carl, *Eleusis: Archetypal Image of Mother and Daughter*

Kershaw, Kris, *The One-Eyed God: Odin and the (Indo-)Germanic Mannerbunde*

Kramrisch, Stella, *"Pusan"*

Kramrisch, Stella, *The Presence of Siva*

Kuusela, Tommy, *"Halls, Gods, and Giants"*

Lahe, Jaan, "Mitra-Mithra-Mithras: The Roman Mithras And His Indo-Iranian Background,"

Lebor Gabala Erenn

SELECTED WORKS CITED

Lempriere, John, *Bibliotheca Classica*

Lewis, H. Jeremiah, *"Dionysos and Osiris Compared"*
http://alkman1.blogspot.com/2006/12/osiris-and-dionysos-compared.html

Lindow, John, *Norse Mythology: A Guide to Gods, Heroes, Rituals, and Beliefs*

Linforth, Ivan Mortimer, *The Arts of Orpheus*

Linforth, Ivan Mortimer, "Two Notes on the Legend of Orpheus", *Transactions and Proceedings of the American Philological Association* 62, (1931):5–17)

Livy, *Ab Urbe Condita*

Loomis, Roger Sherman, *Celtic Myth and Arthurian Romance*

Lucian of Samosata, *The Works of Lucian*

MacDonell, Arthur Anthony, *A Vedic Reader*

MacDonell, Arthur Anthony, *Vedic Mythology*

MacKillop, James, *Oxford Dictionary of Celtic Mythology*

Maclean, Kevin, *https://www.youtube.com/c/FortressofLugh/about*

MacLeod, Mindy; Mees, Bernard, *Runic Amulets and Magic Objects*

Markale, Jean, *"Master and Mediator of the Natural World"*

Matthews, John, *Sources of the Grail*

Meulder, Marcel, *"Nisien and Efnisien: Odinic couple or dioscuric?"*

Mikalson, Jon D., *Ancient Greek Religion*

Monmouth, Geoffrey of, *Historiae Regium Brittaniae*

Monmouth, Geoffrey of, *Vita Merlini*

Montinari, Franco, *"Introduction to the Homeric Question Today"*

Nagy, Gregory, *Greek Mythology and Poetics*

Nelson, Max, *The Barbarian's Beverage: A History of Beer in Ancient Europe*

Nonnus, *Dionysiaca*

O'Donovan, John *(ed. and tr.), Annala rioghachta Eireann:Annals of the Kingdom of Ireland, by the Four Masters, from the earliest period to the year 1616*

529

O'Harris, Carla, "The Telchines, the Ur-tsunami, and Atlantis: An Investigation"

O'hOgain, Daithi, *The Lore of Ireland*

O'Kelly, Michael J., *Early Ireland: An Introduction to Irish Prehistory*

O'Mulconry's Glossary

Oberlies, Thomas. 2000. *"Pūṣans Zahnlücken und Hermes Vorliebe für Backwerk: Ererbte Strukturen des Pantheons der ṛgvedischen Religion."* In Bernhard Forssman and Robert Plath (eds) Indoarisch, Iranisch und die Indogermanistik, 369-389. Wiesbaden: Reichert. Ogmundarson, Kormakr

Oldenberg, Hermann. *1993 [1916]. The Religion of the Veda. Translated by S. B. Shrotri. Delhi: Motilal Banarsidass.*

Oosten, Jarich G., *The War of the Gods*

Orphic Fragments, https://www.hellenicgods.org/the-orphic-fragments-of-otto-kern.

Orphic Hymns

Oudaer, Guillaume, *"Teyrnon Twryf Lliant," Ollodagos 24*

Ovid, *Fasti*

Owein

Papyrus of Nakht

Papyrus of Nebseni

Parthenius, *Love Romances*

Pausanius, *Description of Greece*

Pindar, *Odes*

Plutarch, *On Isis and Osiris*

Pseudo-Apollodorus, Bibliotheca

Quinlan, Michael J., *The Lough Gur & District Historical Society Journal Vol. 7*

Reaves, *William, Odin's Wife*

Reaves, *William, The Epicist no. 3, "Idunn and the Elves"*

Robert Hockert

Rolinson, Curwen, *"Soma-Kvasir, The Eddic-Vedic Myth of the Meath of Poetry"*

SELECTED WORKS CITED

Rydberg, Viktor, *"Toward the Baldur Myth"*

SanskritDictionary.com

Satapatha Brahmana

Shapiro, Michael, *"Neglected Evidence of Dioscurism (Divine Twinning) in the Old Slavic Pantheon"*

Simek, Rudolf, *Dictionary of Northern Mythology*

Stephany, Timothy J., *Lunar Illusions*

Taittiriya Brahmana

The Adventures of Art, son of Conn

The Fosterage of the House of the Two Pails

The Pursuit of Diarmuid and Grainne

The Upanishads

Scharfe, Hartmut, *"Rgveda, Avesta, and Beyond"*

Schmidt, Wilhelm, *The origin and growth of religion: Facts and theories*)

Serith, Ceisiwr, *http://www.ceisiwrserith.com*

Siculus, Diodorus, *The Library of History*

Sigrid Hoedel-Hoenes, *Life and Death in Ancient Egypt*

Smith, William, *A Classical Dictionary of Biography, Mythology, and Geography*

Spaan, David, *"The Place of Manannan in Irish Mythology"*

Squire, Charles, *Celtic Myth and Legend*

Sri Aurobindo Kapali Sastry Institute of Vedic Culture Trust

Sturluson, Snorri, *The Prose Edda*

Sulek, Marty James John, *Gifts of Fire: An Historical Analysis of the Promethean Myth*

Text of Pepi II

The Avesta

The Dindshenchas

The Dream of Oengus

The Mahabharata

The Poetic Edda

The Prose Edda

The Wooing of Etain

Theoi.com

Uzdavinys, Algis, *Orpheus and the Roots of Platonism*

Virgil, *The Aeneid*

Ward, Donald, *The Divine Twins: An Indo-European Myth in Germanic Tradition*

West, M. L, *Indo-European Poetry and Myth*

Wikander, Stig, *"The legend of the Pāṇḍava and the mythical substructure of Mahābhārata" ("Pāṇḍava-sagan och Mahābhāratas mytiska förutsättningar")*

Winspear, Alban Dewes, *The Genesis of Plato's Thought.*

Yajurveda

Zumthor, Paul, *"Merlin: Prophet and Magician"*

de Troyes, Chretien, *Chevalier au Lion*

de Troyes, Chretien, *Perceval, the Story of the Grail*

von Eschenbach, Wolfram, *Parzival*

Printed in Great Britain
by Amazon